Human Resource Management in Europe: Evidence of Convergence?

Cranfield Network on International HRM

As at end 2002: with team leaders in each country

Australia   Macquarie University, Dr Robin Kramer

Austria   Vienna University of Economics and Business Administration, Prof. Wolfgang Mayrhofer

Belgium   Vlerick Leuven Gent Management School, Prof. Dirk Buyens

Bulgaria   International Business School, Dr Elizabeth Vatchkova

Cyprus, North   Eastern Mediterranean University, Cem Tanova

Cyprus, South   Cyprus University, Eleni Stavrou-Costea/Cyprus Productivity Centre, Maria Mikellides

Czech Republic   Katedra Personalistiky, Doc.Ing. Josef Koubek CSc

Denmark   Copenhagen Business School, Prof. Henrik Holt Larsen

Estonia   Estonian Business School, Prof. Ruth Alas

Finland   Helsinki School of Economics, Dr Sinikka Vanhala

France   EM Lyon, Dr Francoise Dany

Germany   University of Paderborn, Prof. Dr Wolfgang Weber

Greece   Athens University of Economics and Business, Prof. Nancy Papalexandris

Hungary   Institute for Political Science of the Hungarian Academy of Sciences, Dr András Tóth

Iceland   Reykjavik University, Dr Asta Bjarnadóttir and Dr Finnur Oddsson

India   International Management Institute (New Delhi), Prof. Venkata Ratnam

Ireland   University of Limerick, Prof. Patrick Gunnigle and Dr Micheal Morley

Israel   Bar llan University, Amnon Caspi

Italy   Università degli Studi di Milano–Bicocca, Dr Francesco Paoletti

Japan   Osaka-Sangyo University, Prof. Toshitaka Yamanouchi

The Netherlands   Erasmus Universiteit, Dr Jacob Hoogendoorn, Dr Erik Poutsma

New Zealand   The University of Auckland, Dr Erling Rasmussen

Norway   Norwegian School of Economics and Business Administration, Prof. Odd Nordhaug

Poland   Technical University of Lódz, Prof. Dr Czeslaw Szmidt

Portugal   Universidade Nova de Lisboa, Prof. Rita Campos e Cunha

Slovenia   University of Ljubljana, Prof. Ivan Svetlik

South Africa   University of South Africa, Prof. Pieter A. Grobler

Spain   ESADE, Prof. Ceferí Soler

Sweden   The IPF Institute, Dr Bo Manson

Switzerland   University of St Gallen, Prof. Dr Martin Hilb

Taiwan   National Central University, Dr Tung-Chun Huang

Tunisia   University of Sfax, Prof. Riadh Zghal

Turkey   I.U. Isletme Fakültesi, Doç Dr Ayse Can Baysal

UK   Cranfield University, Prof. Shaun Tyson and Dr Richard Croucher

Human Resource Management in Europe: Evidence of Convergence?

Edited by

Chris Brewster, Wolfgang Mayrhofer and Michael Morley

ELSEVIER
BUTTERWORTH
HEINEMANN

AMSTERDAM • BOSTON • HEIDELBERG • LONDON • NEW YORK • OXFORD
• PARIS • SAN DIEGO • SAN FRANCISCO • SINGAPORE • SYDNEY • TOKYO

Elsevier Butterworth-Heinemann
Linacre House, Jordan Hill, Oxford OX2 8DP
200 Wheeler Road, Burlington, MA 01803

First published 2004

British Library Cataloguing in Publication Data
A catalogue record for this book is available from the British Library

ISBN 0 7506 4717 5

For information on all Elsevier publications visit our website at
http://books.elsevier.com

Typeset by Charon Tec Pvt. Ltd, Chennai, India
Printed and bound in Great Britain by
Biddles Ltd, Kings Lynn, Norfolk

Contents

Preface

The increasing number of cross-border alliances and mergers both within Europe and between Europe and other parts of the world have made it imperative for students of management to have a thorough understanding of the European context for human resource management (HRM). This is partly reflected in the increasing attention being paid by MBA programmes in Europe to cross-border management issues. Likewise, e.g. the Community of European Management Schools' (CEMs) exchange programme and joint masters' programmes are further testimony to the growing emphasis leading European business schools are placing on broadening the outlook of their students. The aim is to develop graduates who are "fluent" in the many various environments, approaches and practices that exist across Europe for managing human resources.

Our understanding of these approaches and practices is constrained by the limitations of the available knowledge. The chief of these, and the most common, relates to the lack of access to strictly comparable data encompassing a broad range of countries. However good the conceptual discussion of the issues involved in European HRM and however comprehensive the country descriptions, there is rarely any basis for making genuine cross-country comparisons. A related limitation is that, because of this, changes to HRM in Europe are often imputed to be taking place purely on the basis of anecdotal evidence. A final flaw is that many texts lack the necessary native expertise for each of the European countries they are dealing with. Ethnocentricity is the invariable result.

The text offered here aims to redress these shortcomings. First, it employs comprehensive comparable representative data collected longitudinally during the last decade (the "Cranet" surveys: see Appendix 1 for details). It is thus able to address the typical organisation rather than just the contentiously named "leading-edge" companies or through stories based on small numbers of examples. It also draws directly on the expertise of leading HRM scholars within each of the countries covered by the text. Each chapter is written by leading scholars of HRM in those countries. In addition, our text presents entirely fresh analyses of HRM in Europe, based on new and hitherto unpublished data. Such an analysis is critically important for students and researchers – and, we would argue, also for practitioners – throughout Europe and wherever else in the world people want to understand European HRM.

The approach is to explore the issues involved; to create comparisons between, mainly, pairs of countries using the same sets of tables from the same data; and to draw conclusions.

Content

The book is, consequently, divided into three parts. In Part 1 we introduce the concepts and theoretical issues associated with the convergence and divergence thesis in HRM. Are there trends in HRM which indicate that countries are moving close together in the way they manage their people? Assuming that there might be such a movement, is it towards a US model or can we see the development of a separate European model? Or is it the case that each country remains distinct in their HRM? These issues and their disparate underlying logics will be explored: they include HRM policies and practices in recruitment, the use of performance appraisals, the use of reward systems, flexibility in working patterns, training and development, employee involvement and industrial relations and the adaptations made by multinational companies in relation to different national environments. We go beyond simplistic analyses to argue that convergence may take place nationally, within regional blocs or across Europe as a whole.

In Part 2, trends in relation to these issues will be discussed on the basis of in-depth comparisons between individual countries. These chapters are authored by experts from the relevant countries: they provide an insider's view. Each comparison is prefaced by brief country descriptions outlining their respective institutional features, in order to set the discussion of HRM in those countries into context. We have encouraged our country experts in writing the chapters to develop any areas that they felt appropriate and to write in their own style. We hope this comes through in the text. However, the chapters are also written to a consistent format, drawing on the same comparative data source, and using the same major set of charts and tables, in the same order. Some authors have added in other comparative countries or included other data, but each chapter has these same major sets of data. Readers will thus be able to use the book to draw their own conclusions across topic areas (e.g. comparisons of recruitment methods in all countries): a useful teaching and learning device. Results are presented in a readily accessible manner – in the form of bar charts or tables. An additional feature is that each chapter ends with relevant practical example of "HRM in Action" (a case study, an interview or a press cutting, as the authors felt appropriate) and some learning questions aimed to enhance the value of the chapter in teaching and learning.

Part 3 starts the process of summarising the main findings and draws conclusions on the issue of convergence and divergence firstly on a regional basis and at the European level.

To address these issues this book uses a unique and powerful data source. Over more than a decade the Cranet-E survey has been collecting comparative data from many different countries. The data has been collected at roughly three yearly intervals, on organisational level policies and practices. Currently, that data set includes over 20,000 organisational responses: the 1999/2000 round of the survey, added almost 7000 further responses, making this the largest longitudinal and comparative survey of HRM in the world. Full details are provided in Appendix 1.

Using the book

Our previous work based on this data (see Appendix 2) has yielded many attempts to understand the comparative nature of HRM – an approach that we have been flattered to see inspire authors in other parts of the world too (Zanko, M. (2002) *Handbook of HRM Policies and Practices in Asia-Pacific Economies*. Cheltenham: Edward Elgar; Zanko, M. and Ngui, M., eds. (2003) *Handbook of Human Resource Management Policies\ and Practices in Asia-Pacific Economies*, Vol. 2. Cheltenham: Edward Elgar). Most of these have been explicitly and deliberately research texts. Although this book also presents, for the first time, unique information, this text has been written so that it can be used on relevant courses. We are sure that researchers and practitioners reading the text will find much of benefit here, but our focus has been on the needs of students and teachers on such programmes.

The introductory chapter (Chapter 1) introduces students to the notions of the convergence and divergence of HRM in Europe and the final chapter (Chapter 13) attempts to draw together the evidence in the chapters to come to some conclusions about this debate. These chapters can be used to explore these issues in a variety of ways, either in combination with the later chapters or as stand-alones (some of the potential learning questions are given at the end of each chapter).

The central comparative chapters are also capable of different uses. Students might be asked, or might ask themselves, whether the explanations for similarities and differences between the countries in each chapter are convincing, or whether there are others. They might want to explore how different combinations of practices fit or are in tension with the context. They might want to consider the "cultural" and "institutional" explanations for the similarities and differences in HRM.

The most obvious use of the book, however, is to take issues and explore them across the countries. Thus, students could ask themselves what can be learnt from comparing through the chapters the data on, for example, training and development. Because each chapter uses the same set of data, this not only provides a consistent framework, but allows such comparisons to be made easily. Students could ask themselves, or be asked, whether the context is more or less important than the Europe-wide pressures; and whether, how and why they would agree or disagree with the conclusions drawn in Chapter 13.

As editors, we are convinced that the material presented here lends itself to a dynamic and positive learning experience. We have used it that way in our own teaching. We are convinced that seeing the ways that policies and practices in HRM manifest themselves in their different national contexts is both a fascinating and an important opportunity. We hope that students and teachers will find the text to be as rich, as valuable and as meaningful as we have.

Chris Brewster
Wolfgang Mayrhofer
Michael Morley

Acknowledgements

A complex book such as this is never put together without the editors incurring many psychological debts. We are first of all grateful to the authors represented here and to their and our other colleagues in the Cranet network. One in particular, Prof. Paul Gooderham of the University of Bergen in Norway, was the prime mover for this book. Without his initiative and enthusiasm in the early stages the book would not exist. Sarah Atterbury, the Cranet co-ordinator at Cranfield School of Management, is responsible for many of the good things about the network and has been a tower of strength in preparing the data for use here. Malcolm Stern provided excellent professional editorial advice and Maggie Smith and her colleagues at Elsevier have been an unfailing source of encouragement and help. In the final analysis we could not have written the book without the baseline data and that has been collected by our colleagues in Cranet and supplied by the tens of thousands of senior HR specialists across all the sectors and all the countries: we thank them all.

List of Contributors

Ruth Alas (Estonian Business School)
Sarah Atterbury (Cranfield School of Management)
Batia Ben-Hador (The School of Business Administration, Bar Ilan University)
Chris Brewster (Henley Management College)
Dirk Buyens (Vlerick Leuven Gent Management School)
Amnon Caspi (The School of Business Administration, Bar Ilan University)
Christine Communal (Cranfield School of Management)
Christine Cross (University of Limerick)
Rita Campos e Cunha (Universidade Nova de Lisboa)
Françoise Dany (EM Lyon)
Koen Dewettinck (Vlerick Leuven Gent Management School)
Bart Dietz (Erasmus University)
Erik Døving (Norwegian School of Economics and Business Administration)
Gonen Dundar (Istanbul University)
Christiane Erten (Vienna University of Economics and Business Administration)
Martin Gjelsvik (Norwegian School of Economics and Business Administration)
Jean-Claude Gonzalez (University of St Gallen)
Patrick Gunnigle (University of Limerick)
Paul Gooderham (Norwegian School of Economics and Business Administration)
Martin Hilb (University of St Gallen)
Henrik Holt Larsen (Copenhagen Business School)

Job Hoogendoorn (Erasmus University)
Rüdiger Kabst (University of Paderborn)
Josef Koubek (Vysoka Skola Ekonomická)
V. Lale Tuzuner (Istanbul University)
Tina Lindeberg (IPF Institute)
Bo Månson (IPF Institute)
Michael Morley (University of Limerick)
Odd Nordhaug (Norwegian School of Economics and Business Administration)
Carlos Obeso (ESADE)
Francesco Paoletti (Universita degli Studi di Milano–Bicocca)
Nancy Papalexandris (Athens University of Economics and Business)
Anna Patrizia Rogaczewska (Aalborg University)
Miguel Pina e Cunha (Universidade Nova de Lisboa)
Bérénice Quinodon (EM Lyon)
Anja Schmelter (University of Paderborn)
Guido Strunk (Vienna University of Economics and Business Administration)
Eleni Stavrou-Costea (University of Cyprus)
Ivan Svetlik (University of Ljubljana)
Cavide Uyargil (Istanbul University)
Sinikka Vanhala (Helsinki School of Economics)
Elizabeth Vatchkova (International Business School, Transbusiness-E Ltd)
Jacob Weisberg (The School of Business Administration, Bar Ilan University)

Part 1

1

Human Resource Management: A Universal Concept?*

Paul Gooderham, Michael Morley, Chris Brewster and Wolfgang Mayrhofer

---

LEARNING OBJECTIVES

By the end of this chapter readers should be able to:

- Outline the origins of human resource management (HRM) in the US and some of the implications of that origin.
- Explain the concepts of universal and contextual HRM.
- Distinguish between hard and soft variants of HRM.

- Outline the differences between the convergence and divergence theories of HRM and the different models that have been mooted.
- Understand aspects of the European context for HRM.
- Understand the structure of the remainder of the book and how the book can be most effectively used.

INTRODUCTION

How are, and how should, people be managed? This is one of the most fundamental questions in the field of business management. After all, effective people management is an important, if not the most important, determinant of organisational success and it has been argued that it is one of the factors which distinguish the high-performing organisation. However, there is much complexity facing those responsible for people management. This complexity transcends both the strategic and the operational and includes key questions such as: What vision do we have for people management in the organisation? At what level should the specialist human resource (HR) function operate? How does HR contribute to organisational performance? How do we recruit, select, develop and reward for best fit? These issues and all their consequences for the organisation are the substance of "human resource management" (HRM) which may be interpreted in specific or general terms, referring to the professional specialist role performed by the HR manager or more generally to any individual who has responsibility for people management issues. Whatever the scope of our focus, management theorists have long argued that if one could develop people management systems that could be proved to be effective, they could be applied universally. In other words there is a belief that there is "a right way" of managing people that can be implemented by management consultants throughout the world.

---

* Many of the arguments presented here are derived from two key sources, namely: Gooderham, P. and Brewster, C. (2003) Convergence, stasis or divergence? Personnel management in Europe. *BETA Scandinavian Journal of Business Research*, 17(1): 6–18; Gooderham, P. and Nordhaug, O. (2003) Chapter 5: Transfer of US HRM to Europe. In: *International Management: Cross Boundary Challenges*. Oxford: Blackwell.

This chapter traces briefly the origins of HRM and explores some of the basic questions about the universality of HRM. It also examines the context for HRM in Europe as a prelude to exploring the rest of the book.

HRM: THE US ORIGINS OF THE FIELD

Scientific management

In the early part of the 1900s, Taylor came to the conclusion that American industry was woefully inefficient because of the absence of any systematic approach to management. He observed the lack of a clear structure of command, resulting in confusion in the assignment of tasks combined with a general lack of skills in the workforce. Based on his work at the Bethlehem Steel Company (1900–1911), Taylor encouraged employers to adopt a more systematic approach to job design, employment and payment systems (Taylor, 1947). His experience at Bethlehem led him to develop four main principles of management which became the cornerstones of his subsequent work, namely: the development of a true science of work, the scientific selection and development of workers, the co-operation of management and workers in studying the science of work, and the division of work between management and the workforce. Described as "scientific management", it was designed to enhance the efficient use of manpower. The task of management was to divide the work process into discrete tasks and, on the basis of time and motion studies, to analyse each task in terms of its skill and time requirements. The individuals being managed were to be assigned tasks and given the training required for the effective and efficient performance of those tasks and provided with a physical environment designed to maximise performance. Teamwork, or any form of co-worker consultation, was regarded by Taylor as unnecessary and even undesirable. Problems encountered by employees in the course of performing their tasks were to be immediately reported to supervisors who functioned as "troubleshooters". The supervisors were also responsible for measuring individual task performance. Task performance over and above a prescribed level would trigger individual bonus payments.

It is difficult to gauge precisely the impact of scientific management but it would appear that derivatives of it continued to exert a powerful influence on American

managers well into the 1980s – until the rise of HRM, in fact. From a HR perspective, the spread of scientific management placed greater weight on the careful selection and systematic training of employees. Associated with this trend was increased attention to job design, working conditions and payment systems. However, beyond the promotion of efficiency, scientific management has also been seen as the source of many of the problems associated with industrial work, such as high levels of labour turnover and absenteeism, and low levels of employee motivation. Indeed, the emergence and growth of alternative schools of thought can be traced to criticisms of or reactions to scientific management and to suggestions that improvements in organisational effectiveness could be achieved through greater attention to worker needs and, particularly, by providing workers with more challenging jobs and an improved work environment.

For our purposes here, HRM can trace its genesis to three major reactions to scientific management. The first of these surfaced as early as the late 1920s, forming the basis of what is popularly referred to as the human relations or behavioural perspective. The second was human capital theory and the third reaction centred on a consultancy text *In Search of Excellence*. Let us briefly examine each in turn.

The human relations perspective

In contrast to scientific management, the human relations movement focused on the human side of management and sought to provide insights into how social and psychological factors could be important in understanding and influencing workplace performance. Elton Mayo, a Harvard professor and a keen disciple of scientific management, along with his colleague, Fritz Roethlisberger, was called upon by the giant utility company General Electric (GE) to investigate the causes of chronic low productivity at its Hawthorne works. Commonly known as the Hawthorne Studies, and chronicled by Roethlisberger and Dickson (1939) in *Management and the Worker*, these investigations were to prove hugely significant in the evolution of management thought (Tiernan et al., 2001). Mayo assumed that the root problem lay in the physical context and that it needed fine-tuning. He divided the workers into two groups, an experimental and a control group. After explaining his general intentions to the experimental group in an amiable and respectful manner, he began systematically to improve their lighting, noting its effect on productivity. The resultant productivity improvement, combined with the corresponding lack of change in the control group, appeared to confirm the validity of scientific management. However, Mayo's decision to provide further verification by, after informing the experimental group, *decreasing* the strength of the lighting caused him to question the scientific management paradigm. This was because instead of the productivity of the experimental group declining, as had been confidently expected, it continued to rise.

Mayo concluded that what was happening was more complex than had been understood hitherto. Two effects in particular seemed to him significant. First, the fact that they were the subject of attention was a new experience for most of these workers. Previously, they had more or less been treated as living machines. Employees enjoyed the attention that was paid to them and worked more effectively as a result. Second, despite the intentions of the management at GE, employees had formed informal groups that exerted a powerful independent influence on individuals' performance. Mayo surmised that individuals have needs over and above the purely material, i.e. they have social needs, or a need to belong. Not only had scientific management failed to take these needs into account, it had attempted to suppress them. Moreover, it had also failed to recognise that groups that are consulted and informed can generate a commitment that can be harnessed to the aims of the firm.

It is reasonable to say, however, that America's managers largely ignored Mayo's conclusions. They continued to be wedded to the tenets of scientific management. In later years the human relations perspective enjoyed a revival, not least in works by Maslow (1943) and McGregor (1960). Maslow emphasised needs over and above the purely materialistic, arguing that work must be designed in such a way that it provides opportunities for interest and personal growth. This was seen to be important on the basis of the existence of a series of needs ranging from instinctive needs for sustenance and security to higher-order needs such as self-esteem needs and the need for self-actualisation. Lower-order or fundamental needs, according to this theory, must be satisfied before higher-order needs can be activated and dealt with.

McGregor (1960) in his seminal contribution *The Human Side of Enterprise* focused on managerial assumptions about workers and the implications for managerial behaviour. He attacked the underlying assumptions of many American managers, which he referred to as "Theory X". Core assumptions were, according to McGregor, that employees would never seek, let alone exercise, responsibility and were to be treated accordingly. McGregor argued that such assumptions were self-defeating and should be replaced by an assumption (Theory Y) that employees, given the right conditions, were more than willing to play a responsible role. However, although the ideas of this new wave of human relations theorists enjoyed some measure of academic influence, their impact on the hearts and minds of American managers was limited.

Human capital theory

During the 1970s economists began to turn their attention to the significance of HRs for productivity. Economic theory had traditionally regarded labour as a cost rather than an asset. Human capital theory challenged this view by pointing to the rapid post-war recovery of countries like Japan and Germany. Despite having had much of their physical capital stock destroyed during World War II, these countries recovered much more quickly than had been predicted by economists. Schultz (1971) argued that this could only be ascribed to the quality of these countries' human capital. Moreover, it became apparent in international comparisons that these two countries were, when one controlled for the effects of traditional assets such as technology and hours worked, out-performing their competitors. It was argued that such differences stemmed first and foremost from the quality of the human capital at these countries' disposal. Human capital economists dubbed the source of these differences "the black box" of economics because of the difficulties involved in assigning values to human capital. Indeed, even today these difficulties have not been overcome although efforts are still being made to do so, not least by leading consultancy firms in conjunction with valuing the assets of enterprises (Johanson and Larsen, 2000). In particular there is some conceptual confusion as to what constitutes human capital. The term "human capital" can be construed as an umbrella term encompassing competencies, values, attitudes, capabilities, information, knowledge and organisational processes that can be utilised to generate wealth. However, as Garrick and

Clegg (2000) suggest, human capital capacities are only of value when integrated with financial objectives.

Given the imprecision of the concept of human capital it has, so far, shared the same fate as that of the human relations movement, namely to be consigned to an academic existence whose impact on managerial thinking was marginal.

In search of excellence

It was not until the early 1980s that the scientific management approach to management was seriously questioned by US management practitioners. In the light of chronic economic difficulties in the US, especially in comparison with the success of Japan, they experienced a severe crisis of confidence. Some 10 years after the human capital critique, it became received wisdom that Japanese firms were not only out-competing their American counterparts in terms of price but, more importantly, they were also surpassing them in terms of quality. This crisis of confidence finally opened the door to alternative approaches to management, many of which drew heavily on the ideas contained in the human relations perspective and human capital theory. One of the most influential responses to this threat came from two McKinsey consultants, Peters and Waterman, who attempted to discover the sources of excellence in those American firms that remained globally competitive. In their examination of these highly successful organisations, they unearthed eight cultural values (see box) that were viewed as significant.

Their findings suggested that in order to achieve quality, the structures of scientific management were considerably less important than the presence of shared values and a shared vision among employees at all levels. It was these properties that created the foundation for a culture of employee commitment to the overarching aims of their firms which Peters and Waterman concluded was essential if quality demands were to be met consistently. Tiernan et al. (2002), among others, suggest that the limitations of the approach here are associated with it being an unscientific approach, that organisational cultures are not easily unearthed in this manner, and that several of the organisations identified and investigated in the research have subsequently performed poorly.

Human resource management

The issues crystallised around questions about how managers could establish links between the strategic aims of the organisation and the kinds of employees they had and the attitudes and activities of those employees. The outcome of this dialogue was to propel personnel administration away from its position on the outer fringes of management. Traditionally it had been "partly a file clerk's job, partly a housekeeping job, partly a social worker's job and partly fire-fighting to head off union trouble ..." (Drucker, 1989: p. 269).

CHARACTERISTICS OF THE EXCELLENT ORGANISATION

1. Bias for action: managers are expected to make decisions even if all the facts are not available.
2. Stay close to the customer: customers should be valued over everything else.
3. Encourage autonomy and entrepreneurship: the organisation is broken into small, more manageable parts and these are encouraged to be independent, creative and risk-taking.
4. Encourage productivity through people: people are the organisation's most important asset and the organisation must let them flourish.
5. Hands-on management: managers stay in touch with business activities by wandering around the organisation and not managing from behind closed doors.
6. Stick to the knitting: reluctance to engage in business activities outside of the organisation's core expertise.
7. Simple form, lean staff: few administrative and hierarchical layers and small corporate staff.
8. Simultaneously loosely and tightly organised: tightly organised in that all organisational members understand and believe in the organisation's values. At the same time, loosely organised in that the organisation has fewer administrative overheads, fewer staff members and fewer rules and procedures.

Now it was to begin to occupy a very much more central position: personnel administration was reinvented as HRM, a move which in academic circles has been characterised by many ideological debates, while in practice it has been seen as giving ongoing recognition and newfound expression to the complexity of the task that faces those who have responsibility for "people matters" (Monks, 1996).

The theoretical approaches to HRM that emerged as a consequence of the search to provide answers as to how to achieve the strategic deployment of a highly committed and capable workforce have been divided by Storey (1992) into "hard" and "soft". This is, conceptually, a useful categorisation, even if, in practice, the two approaches are not necessarily discrete. That is, firms are rarely wedded exclusively to one or the other and often use both, sometimes simultaneously. With that caveat in mind, let us briefly review these two approaches.

"Hard" HRM

In 1984, Fombrun et al. launched a model, the "Michigan" model of HRM, which emphasised that organisational effectiveness depends on achieving a tight fit between HR strategy and the business strategy of the firm. In short, this school was advocating increased strategic consideration of HRM on the basis that only when this has been achieved can appropriate HRM systems be developed. Gunnigle et al. (2002) suggest that because its focus is overtly managerial, encouraging employers to employ the HR policies that will yield the best returns in terms of organisational performance, it has tended to become associated with the concept of "hard" HRM. Figure 1.1 summarises the thinking behind the model.

Their core recommendation is that the business strategy should be employed to define and determine the types of employee performance required. Once performance has been specified, four systems that ensure its realisation must be put in place (see Figure 1.2).

The first of these is a system for personnel selection, i.e. a system that ensures the deployment of individuals with the appropriate aptitudes, knowledge and experience. Second, there should be an appraisal system that enables the firm on a regular basis to assess whether performance is satisfactory. Third, there should be a system of rewards that distinguishes between different levels of performance. Finally, they

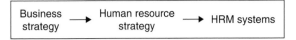

Figure 1.1   Fombrun et al.'s strategic approach to HRM

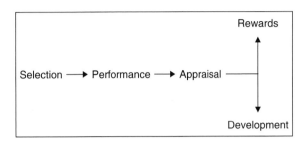

Figure 1.2   The Michigan model of HRM (Reproduced from *Strategic Human Resource Management* by Fombrun, C.J., Tichy, N. and Devanna, M.A. Copyright © 1984. Reprinted with permission of John Wiley and Sons, Inc.)

recommended that a development system should be available in those instances where the appraisal system indicates performance shortcomings. Although there are no surveys that have established how widespread the use of this system is as a whole in the US, we do know that the use of rewards differentiation is widespread with as many as 60% of US firms currently using cash-based recognition systems.[1]

On the surface the Michigan model bears a strong resemblance to scientific management. Its HRM systems, selection, performance criteria, appraisal, rewards and development systems, were all to the forefront in Taylor's thinking. Thus, Sparrow and Hiltrop (1994) have characterised the rationale of the Michigan model as managing people like any other resource: "they are to be obtained cheaply, used sparingly and developed and exploited as fully as possible". However, beyond the strategic element, the important difference lies in the much greater devolvement of responsibility and initiative to the individual employee. Rather than the detailed and precise rules of scientific management, the HRM systems of the Michigan model aim at creating a dominant, strategically based value system within which the employee performs.

---

[1] *Source*: Survey of 700 American companies in 1997 published in *The Economist*, A Survey of Pay, Supplement, p. 12, 8 May 1999.

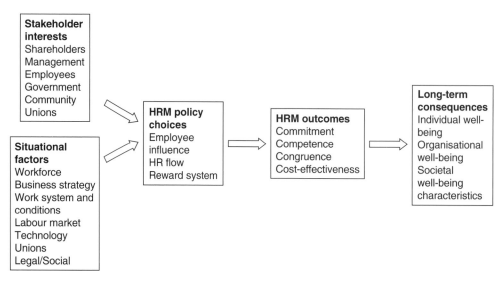

Figure 1.3 The Harvard model of HRM. *Source*: Beer et al., 1984

"Soft" HRM

The "Harvard" model developed by Beer et al. (1984) presents a map of the determinants and consequences of HRM policy choices and argues that systems designed to encourage and develop commitment are crucial to successful HRM (Figure 1.3).

They describe HRM as "involving all management decisions and actions that affect the nature of the relationship between the organisation and its employees – its human resources". Beer regards employee commitment as vitally important regardless of the type of strategy being pursued. This is because employees are not just another resource, they are a critical resource, the one that can create value from the other resources, so that personnel activities must be guided by a management philosophy which seeks to involve them. Furthermore, they are a resource with views and expertise of their own. For Beer et al. the business strategy should never be considered in isolation but always in relation to the employees.

As a consequence, Beer recommends reward systems that aim at tapping into employees' intrinsic motivation coupled to a system of employee relations which delegates authority and responsibility. Typically, to achieve this, considerable effort is expended on creating and recreating mission statements that communicate the business strategy to employees. For example in 1999 Steven A. Ballmer, after 9 months as president of Microsoft, concluded that because of the impact of the

Internet Microsoft needed to reinvent itself. One tool he and Bill Gates employed to generate a change of direction was a new mission statement. Out went "a PC on every desk and in every home" and in came the new rallying cry "giving people the power to do anything they want, anywhere they want, and on any device". For Ballmer the point of this so-called Vision Version 2 was that Microsoft needed "to give people a beacon that they could follow when they were having a tough time with prioritisation, leadership, where to go, what hills to take".[2]

Coupled to mission statements are employee communication policies and systems for conducting employee briefings at all levels.

Another typical "soft" HRM initiative has been aimed at creating environments conducive to teamwork. Weinstein and Kochan (1995) point to a transition towards the adoption of a variety of total quality management (TQM) practices including employee problem-solving groups, work teams and job rotation. Indeed, by the early 1990s 64% of US manufacturing firms reported that at least half of their core employees were covered by one or more of these workplace innovations, although relatively few were covered by all of them (Osterman, 1994).

---

[2] *Source*: *Business Week*, Making Microsoft, p. 48, 17 May 1999.

Note, though, that none of these collaborative techniques were rooted in governance systems that involved any increasing role for the employees' trade unions. On the contrary, as HRM established itself in the US, unions became even more marginalised in an institutional environment characterised by increasing management and shareholder power.

One refinement to the concept of matching the business strategy to HR systems in the Michigan model is found in the work of Schuler and Jackson (1987). Borrowing from the work of Porter, they argued that business strategy could usefully be subdivided into three generic strategies – quality enhancement, innovation and cost leadership. (Again, it is not clear that this conceptual distinction can be found in a pure form in practice.) Once it has been established which of these is to be pursued, the structuring of each of the four HRM systems can easily be specified. Thus, e.g. pursuing a strategy based on innovation as opposed to one based on cost leadership will mean using group criteria rather than individual criteria in order to encourage the exchange of ideas. Likewise, one would seek to develop a rewards system that offers internal equity rather than market-based pay in order to minimise internal competition and to maximise a sense of group membership. Although in recent years the strategic emphasis in HRM has been evident in academic writing, as Luomo (2000: p. 769) notes while it is often said that a company's HRM practices should be aligned with the strategy of the company, and while nobody denies the importance of such a connection, the deeper nature of this relationship receives amazingly scant attention. The concept of strategic HRM refers to the development of a strategic corporate approach to workforce management whereby HRM considerations become integral to strategic decision-making as organisations seek to establish a corporate HR philosophy and strategy which complements their business strategy (Mayrhofer et al., 2000). Referred to as "matching" by Boxall (1992), and often alluding to the messages advanced in the resource-based view of the firm (Barney, 1991), and human capital accumulation theory (Garavan et al., 2001), the alignment of business strategy, organisational configuration and HR policies and practices in order to achieve valuable, more rare, less imitable sources of competitive advantage becomes the core objective. Though complex, it is, as Monks (2001) notes, a literature that is now becoming more established.

It also seems likely that this strategic focus will continue since HRM considerations have been a neglected area within strategic management thinking generally (Mayrhofer et al., 2000). Part of this prediction is based on the premise that this aspect of the HRM field is, at present, marked with a serious hiatus. For example, Beattie and McDougall (1998: p. 220) note that much of the literature in the field is "either normative (written mainly by those in consultancy roles) or conceptual (written by academics)" and in their view there have been relatively few attempts to integrate the conceptual with the normative in the generalist HRM literature. Similarly, Ferris et al. (1999: p. 408) point to the gap between the science and the practice of HRM in this area. They refer to Buckley et al. (1998) who characterise the hiatus as "a disconnect".

Thus, despite an extensive and growing body of literature addressing the concepts of strategy and a strategic approach to the HRM, there remains limited consensus as to the substance, nature and implications of these concepts. Indeed, Mayrhofer et al. (2000: p. 18) note that "some of this literature [strategy in HRM] is flawed by rather simplistic notions of strategy", while more of it points to the complex, multidimensional nature of the concept of strategy. Here they quote Mintzberg (1987) who notes that strategy has been used in at least five different ways, namely as a plan, a ploy, a pattern, a position and a perspective. It would seem that diversity of meaning continues to be the order of the day with Chadwick and Cappelli (1999) recently arguing that scholars have varying goals with respect to their particular research in the strategic HRM area with the result that there is considerable variation in the use of the term "strategic". Consequently, many methodological problems arise when seeking to unearth the linkages between business strategy and HRM because of these differences in meaning associated with the concept of "Business Strategy", not to mention "HRM strategy", the nature of HRM itself and the highly problematic notion of "integration" and "measurement" (Buller and Napier, 1993; Tyson et al., 1994).

HRM IN THE EUROPEAN CONTEXT

Is the US-derived vision of HRM outlined above a universal one, one that will apply anywhere in the world, or is it a US-bounded one? This is an important question in the context of organisations being socially embedded

HRM IN AMERICAN COMPANIES

The various HRM practices American firms actually deploy can seldom be exclusively subsumed under the label of either "hard" or "soft". Variable pay is as widespread as employee communication. This deployment of a mix of hard and soft techniques is particularly apparent in, e.g. General Electric. GE went from being an old-line American industrial giant in the early 1980s to representing what Tichy, a management professor at the University of Michigan, regards as "a new, contemporary paradigm for the corporation".[3] Here is a "Business Week" special report[4] on the leadership style of its chairman, Jack Welch:

Rarely do surprises occur. Welch sets precise performance targets and monitors them throughout the year. And every one of Welch's direct reports – from his three vice-chairmen to each of the operating heads of GE's 12 businesses – also receives a handwritten, two-page evaluation of his performance at the end of every year …

As if in lockstep, each business chieftain then emulates the behaviour of his boss, and their reports in turn do the same … As Thomas E. Dunham, who runs services in GE Medical Systems, puts it, "Welch preaches it from the top, and people see it at the bottom." The result: Welch's leadership style is continually reinforced up and down the organisation.

Above all, however, Welch skillfully uses rewards to drive behaviour. Those rewards are not inconsequential … Welch demands that the rewards a leader disburses to people be highly differentiated … especially because GE is in so many different businesses. "I can't stand non-differential stuff", he says. "We live in differentiation …"

In practice differentiation at GE means that each of its 85,000 professionals and managers is graded in an annual process that divides them into five groups: the top 10%, the next 15%, the middle 50%, the next 15% and the bottom 10%. The top tier will get options, nobody in the fourth tier does, and most of the fifth tier will probably be culled. Each unit must segment its managers in this way each year, so that it cannot get away with claiming that they are all in the first tier.[5]

On the other hand we also learn that the HRM philosophy at GE encompasses considerably more than a set of hard HRM practices.

Welch's profound grasp on GE stems from knowing the company and those who work it like no other … More than half (of his time) is devoted to "people" issues. But most important, he has created something unique at a big company: informality …

If the hierarchy that Welch inherited, with its nine layers of management, hasn't been completely nuked, it has been severely damaged. Everyone, from secretaries to chauffeurs to factory workers, calls him Jack …

Making the company "informal" means violating the chain of command, communicating across layers, paying people as if they worked not for a big company but for a demanding entrepreneur where nearly everyone knows the boss …

"We're pebbles in an ocean, but he knows about us", says Brian Nailor, a forty-something marketing manager of industrial products …

---

[3] *Source*: Business Week, Special Report, Jack A Close-up Look at How America's #1 Manager Runs GE, p. 43, 8 June 1999.

[4] Business Week, Special Report, Jack A Close-up Look at How America's #1 Manager Runs GE, pp. 40–51, 8 June 1999.

[5] *Source*: The Economist (1999).

in their external environment and affected by external forces that require them to adapt their structures and behaviours to deal with these forces (Berger and Luckmann, 1967). For many years, institutional theory has directed the attention of students of management to the influences of social processes, beyond the organisation's boundaries. Summarising the institutional perspective, Hoffman (1999: p. 351) states that "a firm's action is seen not as a choice among an unlimited array of possibilities determined by purely internal arrangements, but rather as a choice among a narrowly defined set of legitimate options. ..." Obtaining legitimacy is not simply a matter of complying with legislation, it also involves abiding by the unwritten, tacit codes peculiar to the firm's setting. Thus, firms are located in settings not only of legislation but also of cultural and social norms to which they have to react. In short, culture provides meaning and purpose, rules (including legislation) and norms (ethical standards). Each nation or region constitutes a unique or idiosyncratic institutional setting that skews corporate behaviour in particular ways. From an institutional perspective, given that HRM is a product of the North American institutional setting, determining whether it is readily transferable to the European setting remains a conceptual and empirical challenge.

There are a number of critical differences between the North American institutional context and the European. Of course, such a comparison involves substantial generalisation. We must remain aware of the substantial differences within North America, even within individual states in the US; and the differences between the European countries are, after all, the basis of this book. Brewster (1995) has used the analogy of a telescope: with each turn of the screw things that seemed similar are brought into sharper focus so that we can distinguish between, say, the forest and the fields, then with another turn between one tree and another, and then between one leaf and another. Each view is accurate, each blurs some objects and clarifies others and each helps us to see some similarities and some differences. In the rest of the book we examine differences between countries in Europe: here we concentrate on the substantial differences between the North American and European personnel management regimes, because the US approach has been so dominant in our understanding of HRM. However, we shall not argue that the one regime is innately superior to the other. To underscore our viewpoint we, in

the penultimate section of this chapter, explore the issue of HRM and economic success. Finally, we argue for the need to adopt a multi-level approach to HRM which takes into account the institutional context.

Core assumptions

Brewster (1994) has pointed out that a core assumption of North American HRM is that the employing organisation has a considerable degree of latitude in regard to the management of personnel, including inter alia: freedom to operate contingent pay policies; an absence of, or at least a minimal influence from, trade unions; and an assumption that the organisation has sole responsibility for training and development.

In other words, central to the notion of North American HRM is an assumption of considerable organisational independence. This assumption is reasonable, given the weakness of the trade union movement in the US (where membership is currently probably less than one-tenth of the working population, and its activities are predominantly site based), coupled with the comparatively low levels of state subsidy, support and control. It also fits comfortably with the notion that the state should interfere in business as little as possible and that it is the right of every individual to do the best for themselves that they can without external interference (Guest, 1990). The question is: How valid are such assumptions in the context of Europe? Addressing this question is important, given the rather different employment relations context in Europe.

While Europe has witnessed similar challenges to its employment relations including intensified international competition, changes to the structure of product and service markets, and new approaches to the management of manufacturing technologies, the response to these pressures is not the same in every country. Lansbury has argued that even though "all European countries are experiencing intensified pressures to adapt their traditional industrial relations (IRs) practices in response to increased global competition and changing technologies. ... Most European countries are uncertain about the precise nature of the IRs system they should be seeking to establish and which will be appropriate in decades to come" (Lansbury, 1995: pp. 47–48). Locke et al. (1995: p. 158) suggest that the different responses can be accounted for by the fact that "employment relations are shaped in systematic and predictable ways by institutions which filter these external pressures and the strategies of the key actors. Patterns of adjustment in countries that have a history of strong centralised IRs institutions tend to follow an incremental, negotiated pattern and aim to achieve results that balance the interests of different social groups and economic interests". In other countries, they argue that the "adjustment has tended to be unilateral with unions and their traditional institutional supports and political allies put on the defensive."

Closely related to the assumption of a firm's autonomy is a second core assumption, that the close involvement of HRM with business strategy represents a radically new departure for the management of personnel. What theorists of North American HRM overlook is that the connectedness of HRM and corporate strategy does not have to be a product of "bottom line" calculations. It might equally be a consequence of laws, regulations or custom, in which case it may be an established feature of other contexts, such as the European one.

We note below some of the challenges to these core assumptions in the European context.

A culture of individualism

At the most general level, while the empirical data on national cultural differences is limited (Hofstede, 1980, 1991; Laurent, 1983; Tayeb, 1988; Adler, 1991; Trompenaars, 1993), it does point to the unusual nature of the US. The US, one of the leading researchers in this field writes, "is quite untypical of the world as a whole" (Trompenaars, 1985). US culture is significantly more individualistic and achievement-oriented than most other countries (Hofstede, 1980). Indeed, it has been argued (Guest, 1990) that the North American assumption of business freedom and autonomy is peculiarly American and is related to the American view of their country as a land of opportunity which rewards success. It is an American's birthright, if not duty, to stand on his or her own two feet and to start-up some kind of enterprise.

Certainly when we examine the proportion of adults who are active in business start-ups there is a significant gulf dividing the US from Europe. Table 1.1 indicates that, while 8% of American adults were involved in business start-ups in the winter of 1999, the average figure for European countries, despite generally higher levels of unemployment, was much lower.

Table 1.1 Percentage of adults involved in business start-ups (Winter 1999)

Country	Adults (%)
Finland	2
France	2
Denmark	2
Germany	2
UK	3
Italy	4
Canada	6
US	8

Source: Financial Times, 1999.

In Germany and France, e.g. the average was about 2%, while for the UK and Italy it was only slightly higher.

This culture of individualism, or entrepreneurialism, extends to the legal situation when individuals have not been successful. In the US they are free to start-up another business to replace their failed business with far fewer constraints than is the case in Europe. It is clearly discernible, also, in the thinking that underpins North American notions of reward systems, with their emphasis on individual performance-based rewards. That is, just as a free market differentiates between successful and unsuccessful individual enterprises, so should firms have the freedom to reward those employees who have made critical contributions to their success. Given the relative lack of a culture of entrepreneurialism in Europe, we should not assume, without evidence, any ready acceptance of individual performance-related rewards.

Legislation: the firm and the individual employee

One German authority, Pieper, pointed out that "the major difference between HRM in the US and in Western Europe is the degree to which (HRM) is influenced and determined by state regulations. Companies have a narrower scope of choice in regard to personnel management than in the US" (Pieper, 1990: p. 82). We can distinguish three aspects to this concept of management scope: the degree of employment protection, the legislative requirements on pay and hours of work, and legislation on forms of employment contract.

In regard to the first of these, Blanchard (1999) has attempted to quantify differences in employment protection, within both Europe and the US. He argues that employment protection has three main dimensions: the length of the notice period to be given to workers, the amount of severance pay to be paid according to the nature of the separation and the nature and complexity of the legal process involved in laying off workers. Blanchard finds that the US is significantly different from Europe in general and Italy, Spain and Portugal in particular. There is less protection in the US.

In relation to the legislative requirements on pay and work there are also marked differences. For example, whereas in Europe legislative developments have ensured that average hours worked have fallen over the last two decades, in the US they have risen. Thus, in the US, almost 80% of male workers and 65% of working women now work more than 40 hours in a typical week.[6] By contrast, in France the working week is by law limited to 35 hours with overtime limited to 130 hours a year. This policy even extends to making unpaid overtime by senior employees a penal offence. Indeed, in June 1999 a director of a defence company, Thompson Radars and Countermeasures, was fined after the government's jobs inspectorate had monitored executives, researchers and engineers and uncovered substantial unrecorded overtime. In the US such a case would be inconceivable.

Finally, with respect to legislation on employment contracts, although this varies within Europe, it exists everywhere and is now the subject of European-level legislation. Legislation in Europe goes beyond anything found in the US, limiting the ways people can be recruited, the documentation necessary when they start work, how much they can be paid, how management must consult with them and a host of other matters.

The "Rhineland" model

The legislation that determines the firm–employee relationship is a product of wider, normative, concepts of what role the state should play in the economic arena. In his book *Capitalisme contre Capitalisme* Albert (1991), a former director of the French planning agency, distinguished on the one hand between an Anglo-Saxon capitalism (principally the US, but also the UK) and a continental, West European type of capitalism which he labelled the "Rhineland" model. The former is a "shareholder economy" under which private enterprise is concerned with maximising short-term profits for investors rather than any broader harmony of interests. In contrast

---

[6]*Source*: International Labour Organization.

Table 1.2 Public spending as a percentage of nominal GDP (1997)

Country	GDP (%)
Sweden	62
Finland	54
France	54
Italy	51
The Netherlands	49
EU total	48
Germany	48
Spain	42
UK	40
US	32

Source: OECD Economic Outlook, 1998.

"the Rhineland model may be seen as a regulated market economy with a comprehensive system of social security. Government, employers' organisations and labour unions consult each other about economic goals [in order to] try to achieve a harmony of interests" (Bolkestein, 1999). In short the Rhineland model is a "stakeholder economy" in which competition and confrontation are avoided in the belief that they undermine sustainable economic growth. Patrolling this economy is the state, which acts variously as referee, guarantor, employer and owner.

Table 1.2 provides one indication of the role of the state in the Rhineland model. Whereas public spending as a percentage of gross domestic product (GDP) averages nearly 50% in the EU, it is only 32% in the US. These differences in attitude towards public spending as between the US and European economies are replicated in respect of the labour market.

As well as being substantial employers in their own right, Rhineland states also subsidise jobs extensively. In France between 1973 and 1997 the number of French workers in subsidised jobs grew from 100,000 to 2.2 million according to the OECD, while the total in unsubsidised jobs shrank from 21.4 to 20.3 million. Nearly a quarter of the French labour force now relies on government handouts, whether in the form of unemployment benefit or subsidised jobs (Pedder, 1999: p. 11).

On becoming unemployed, Americans initially receive a benefit of about two-thirds of their income, not far below levels in Rhineland Europe. But those benefit levels drop sharply after 6–9 months. In many Rhineland countries, in contrast, benefits are either not time limited or actually increase the longer people are out of work. In Sweden and Finland the income replacement

Table 1.3 Union density and bargaining coverage (2001)

Country	Union density (%)	Bargaining coverage (%)
Denmark	88	83
Finland	79	90
Sweden	79	90
Belgium	69	90
Austria	40	98
Italy	35	90
Portugal	30	87
Germany	30	67
UK	29	36
The Netherlands	27	88
Japan	21	21
Spain	15	81
US	14	15
France	9	90–95

Source: EIRO.

rate of 89% rises to 99%. It has been argued that this virtual absence of a margin between benefits and wages for the low-skilled unemployed represents a serious disincentive to seeking new jobs in many European countries. A recent French study reported by Pedder (1999) showed that the unemployed in France take five times as long to find a new job as in America; yet those in work are five times less likely to lose their jobs.

Another core feature of European states is the legislative status and influence accorded to unions. Table 1.3 shows that most European countries are more heavily unionised, in terms of membership, than the US. However, in reality trade union influence cannot be accurately gauged by studying union density rates. A more important issue is trade union recognition, that is whether the employer deals with a trade union in a collective bargaining relationship which sets terms and conditions for all or most of the employees (Morley et al., 1996). It is in this respect that Rhineland states diverge to a considerable degree from the US. In most European countries, there is legislation requiring employers over a certain size to recognise unions for consultative purposes. Morley et al. note that "Europe has a tradition of collectivism and consensus building and trade unions have a social legitimacy in Europe on a much grander scale than in the US" (p. 646).

Closely related to the issue of trade union recognition is the European practice of employee involvement. Typically the law requires the establishment of workers' councils with which managements must consult. Legislation in countries such as the Netherlands, Denmark

and, most famously, Germany requires organisations to have two-tier management boards, with employees having the right to be represented on the more senior Supervisory Board. These arrangements give considerable (legally backed) power to the employee representatives and, unlike consultation in the US, e.g. they tend to supplement rather than supplant the union position. In relatively highly unionised countries it is unsurprising that many of the representatives of the workforce are, in practice, trade union officials. In Germany, for instance, four-fifths of them are union representatives.

A central theme of HRM is the requirement to generate significant workforce commitment through developing channels of communication. However, in Rhineland countries it is noticeable that the provision of information to the workforce involves the use of the formal employee representation or trade union channels. And when upward communication is examined, the two most common means in Europe, by a considerable margin, are through immediate line management and through the trade union or works council channel (Mayrhofer et al., 1999; Morley et al., 2000).

Patterns of ownership

Patterns of ownership also vary from one side of the Atlantic to the other. Public ownership has decreased to some extent in many European countries in recent years; but it is still far more widespread in European countries than it is in the US. And private sector ownership may not mean the same thing. In many of the southern European countries particularly, ownership of even large companies remains in the hands of single families rather than of shareholders. On the other hand, in Germany, a tight network of a small number of substantial banks own a disproportionate number of companies. Their interlocking shareholdings and close involvement in the management of these corporations mean less pressure to produce short-term profits and a positive disincentive to drive competitors out of the market place (Randlesome, 1994).

The link between HRM and business strategy

One of the most widely discussed distinctions between HRM and old-fashioned personnel management is the closer linking of the former to business strategy. There are many who take the view that this desire to bring about the alignment of business strategy and people management policies and practices provided the springboard for both the transition from personnel management to HRM in the first instance, and the more recent evolution towards "strategic" HRM. Linking here refers to the degree to which HRM issues are considered as part of the formulation of business strategies. Though complex, it is, as Monks (2001) notes, a literature that is now well established. In particular, there is an ingrained assumption in the North American literature that HRM is the dependent variable and business strategy is the independent variable in this relationship and that there are advantages to be gained from the integration of HRM with business strategy. In this regard and drawing upon several contributions advancing difference concepts of fit in strategic HRM, Wright and Snell (1999: p. 210) note that essentially three generic conceptual variables in the form of HRM practices, employee skills and employee behaviours which should fit with the firm's strategy, are evident in the literature.

However, the degree to which this linking is or can be achieved in practice is debatable. Tyson (1999: p. 111) suggests that attempts to find fit between generic business strategies and HR strategies are based on "shaky foundations", while Luoma (2000: p. 770) notes that: "The concepts of strategy and HRM are both some-what ambiguous. What is the outcome when we put these two together? The result is a strict definition of strategic HRM or a more general idea of valuing people as key elements in a company's business – or something in between ... It all depends on the way we view these terms."

Thus, the concept of strategy needs to be treated with caution. As the business environment becomes steadily more turbulent, it is increasingly problematic for firms to create clear, coherent strategic plans. Mintzberg (1978) even argues that strategy is not actually formulated – the process is much less explicit, conscious or planned. Likewise Hamel and Prahalad (1989) signalled the end of the planning ideal by coining the term "strategic intention": strategy is no longer to be a detailed plan so much as a sense of direction that stretches the organisation. Second, there is considerable evidence from the US that insofar as business strategy does exist there are few firms that have actually integrated HRM with business strategy (Kochan and Dyer, 1992). For some time now, knowledgeable commentators on

strategy (Quinn, 1980; Joyce, 1986; Mintzberg, 1987, 1990; Gomez-Mejia, 1992) have seen it as incremental, developmental, messy and dynamic. Strategic management "inevitably involves some thinking ahead of time as well as some adaptation en route": effective strategies will encompass both (Mintzberg, 1994: p. 24).

Collins and Porras (1994) found that among their 18 high-performing "visionary" US companies there was no evidence of brilliant and complex strategic planning. Rather, their companies "make some of their best moves by experimentation, trial and error, opportunism and – quite literally – accident. What looks in retrospect like foresight and planning was often the result of 'Let's just try a lot of stuff and keep what works' (p. 9). Behn (1988) had already found similar results in the public sector. None of this would have come as a surprise to Lindblom (1959), whose prescient article pointed out much the same thing many years ago, but which fell into disuse over the years of dominance of the "command" model. Lengnick-Hall and Lengnick-Hall (1988) also challenged the assumption that strategic decisions were taken at a particular point in time such that the influence of HRM on that process could be measured.

The evidence from Europe is not only that the strategy process is more complicated than is often assumed in the textbooks, but that it may well work in different ways and through different systems involving different people. Thus, the strategic implications of a management decision in Germany or the Netherlands will be subject to the involvement or scrutiny of powerful Works Council representatives or the worker representatives on the Supervisory Board of the company. Indeed, in most of these companies the knowledge that their decisions are subject to scrutiny – and can be reversed or varied – at that level inclines managers to operate with these issues in mind. Inevitably, this means that the assumptions in the universalist paradigm that HRM strategies are "downstream" of corporate strategies cannot be made: the process is more interactive, with both sets of strategy potentially influencing each other simultaneously. And assumptions that strategies are the preserve of senior managers (or even just managers) cannot be sustained either.

Paradoxically, the evidence regarding the link between HR issues and business strategy in Europe is more persuasive, but shows that much of it is a product of legislation rather than corporate decision-making. For example in Germany the Codetermination Act of 1952, as amended in 1976, requires the executive boards of large companies to have a labour director with responsibility for staff and welfare matters. Likewise in the Scandinavian countries any changes to company strategy that have employee implications must be discussed with employee representatives. In Europe then it is generally common for personnel specialists to be involved at an early stage in the development of corporate strategy (Brewster et al., 2000; Mayrhofer et al., 2000).

All in all, despite advances, according to Ferris et al. (1999) the linking of HRM with business strategy remains "troublesome" (p. 392), principally because of the measures of strategy used in the studies to date. In their review they rightly note that: "Recent conceptual pieces have been critical of researchers in this area, suggesting that they have incorporated anti-quated notions of firm strategy. Most studies have utilised such typologies as those of Porter (1980) or Miles and Snow (1978). These generic categorisations have little in common with the realities of the modern competitive environment with which organisations are confronted. First, categorisations are exclusive, assuming that organisations pursue a certain strategic goal while ignoring other strategic concerns. Second, they depict the competitive environment, and conse-quently organisational strategy, as being static instead of dynamic."

In the light of this, they suggest that future tests of the HRM–strategy relationship must view strategy along a continuum involving a broader range of strategic factors and must regard it as a dynamic, rather than a static phenomenon. Finally they suggest that the almost exclusive focus on deliberate intended strategy, to the detriment of the emergent or realised strategy, remains problematic. It, they suggest, represents a flawed view of reality in the omnipresent unstable, dynamic environments that we have all become accustomed to.

HRM and economic success

Because the American economy has, during the end of the last century and the beginning of this, gone from strength to strength, one seemingly credible conclu-sion would be to recommend to the world, and not least to Rhineland model countries, that they create the conditions for North American HRM. That is, they should adopt the American model of shareholder capitalism and flexible labour markets. For example, Friedman et al. (1998: p. 25) of Arthur Andersen state: "Managers must be free to manage. Our experience all over the world shows that the systems used for develop-ing human capital can make a critical difference in the survival of and success of companies. Technology and markets are changing so fast that companies need to be in a state of change and readiness, and they need the freedom and flexibility to change in every area from recruitment to compliance. They must invest in their human capital – but the nature of their investment must be driven by market and company strategy, not govern-ment policy."

Of course, even if the statement is accepted at face value there are problems at both ends of the equation: the meanings of HRM, as we have already seen, and of success in organisational terms are open to much debate. Nevertheless, the views expressed in this quota-tion are widespread. The viewpoint is commonly justi-fied with reference to macro-economic data that are deemed to prove the desirable societal outcomes of granting firms autonomy. For example, Smith (1999) points to America's success in creating employment – more than 30 million net new jobs since the early 1970s and more than 12 million in the 1990s – in contrast to Europe's 4 million net new jobs since the 1970s and a net reduction in private-sector employment. Others have looked at the period from 1992 to 1998 and noted that, while America experienced an annual GDP growth of 3%, for Germany, the archetypal social-market econ-omy, it was only 2%. This debate over the perceived "economic dominance" of the US and its consequences in terms of the appropriate managerial model to be pur-sued is therefore highly significant. As Gunnigle et al. (2002: p. 261) note: "At a public policy level, American economic success and the contrasting sluggish perform-ance of many of the EU economies during the 1990s has sparked considerable debate on optimal approaches or "systems" of industrial relations and HRM. It is often argued that the EU's preferred "social market" approach, characterised by comparatively high levels of labour regulation and strong trade unions, has served to impede competitiveness and employment creation. In contrast, the American free market approach, which apparently affords organisations and managers greater autonomy, is often portrayed as a "better alternative" in this respect, most particularly in terms of its capacity for employment creation."

Table 1.4 Annual average economic performance for the period 1989–1998 (%)

	Germany*	Japan	US
GDP per head growth	2	2	2
Productivity growth	3	1	1
Unemployment rate	8	3	6

*West Germany before 1992.
Sources: Eurostat; IMF.

To older readers, however, this unequivocal approval of the American model in terms of both of its core assumptions – corporate autonomy and a strong strategy – HRM link – may seem ironic, for in the 1980s most experts believed that it was the American model that was fatally flawed. Not only was the Japanese model regularly touted as a superior model, so was the Rhineland model. From the perspective of the 1980s and early 1990s it was those nations which allow the least autonomy to their managements that appeared to be the most successful (Brewster, 1994). The argument was that this was because the American model was short-termist in its shareholder orientation and this in turn undermined employee commitment and employer commitment to training and development.

There are in fact a number of problems in determining which model is superior. The first of these is statistical and relates not only to the time frame one chooses for a comparison of economies but also to which countries one chooses as the basis for a comparison. "The Economist" (1999b) examined the three big economies, the US, Japan and the Rhineland model country, Germany, in terms of three measures: growth in output per head, productivity growth and the unemployment rate (Table 1.4). They argued that if the impact of the economic cycle is stripped out, by adopting a 10-year perspective, rather than a shorter perspective, the figures do little to support any notion of the superiority of the American model. Indeed "The Economist" (1999: p. 90) issued a note of warning by remarking that: "in their zeal to make a successful economy fit their favourite theory, economists of one persuasion or another are too quick to swallow myths about the nature of that economy".

Careful readers will realise that the bases for these figures are not directly comparable. For example, measures of unemployment vary. Thus, in Europe, where many women work, or wish to work, and in Japan, where older women are not expected to be, or be registered, in the workforce, different phenomena are being measured. Another sceptical view regarding the statistical basis for announcing the superiority of the American model has been propounded by Kay (1998), who points out that Denmark, and most other small west European states, are more than a match for the US in terms of economic performance regardless of time frame. This is despite their displaying most of the features of the supposedly defunct Rhineland model: i.e. interlocking networks of corporations, employers' and workers' organisations whose relationship is governed by both explicit and consensual regulation, and a high spending state. Kay notes wryly that if you go into a British business school library "you will look in vain for titles like *Great Entrepreneurs of Norway*, *The Coming Economic Powerhouse – Denmark, Iceland – Europe's Tiger Economy*. This is not because we have not bought the books. It is because no one has written them." In other words Kay is chiding critics of the Rhineland model for having been conveniently selective in their choice of countries.

A second problem is methodological. It is difficult, if not impossible, to find nations or companies which at some point in time were equal in all substantial areas but which then diverged in terms of HRM. In other words it is difficult to isolate the contribution a HRM system makes at either the corporate or the national level.

Third, within the same country there may be substantial differences in the use made of specific elements in any one HRM model, making it highly problematic to compare across nations. For example, Pfeffer and Veiga (1999) have found considerable variation in the use US firms make of many of those practices that are considered integral to the North American model, including selection, performance-contingent pay, training and development and information sharing. They conclude that: "… one-half of (US) organisations won't believe the connection between the way they manage their people and the profits they earn. One-half of those who do see the connection will do what many organisations have done – try to make a single change to solve their problems, not realising that the effective management of people requires a more comprehensive and systematic approach" (1999: p. 47).

Clearly the practice of HRM cannot be divorced from its institutional context. The North American model is a viable alternative or possibility for American firms because of the context within which they operate. Whether it can – or even should – be replicated in the European context is a matter of empirical evidence and opinion.

What is needed is a model of HRM that acknowledges the influence of such environmental factors as culture, legislation, the role of the state and trade union representation. At the same time the model should take into account the potential for firm-level activities. It is our contention that HRM theory needs to adopt a multi-level view of the actors in the system if it is to become a theory that can be applied internationally.

The model of HRM we propose shows, in a simplistic form, that the business strategy, HR strategy and HR practice are located in an environment of national culture, national legislation, state involvement and trade union representation (Brewster, 1995). It places HR strategies firmly within, though not entirely absorbed by, the business strategy. What is more, the dividing line between HR strategy and business strategy is blurred indicating that the potential for absorption of the former by the latter will vary according to the impact of institutional factors. In other words it is conceivable that in extreme contexts institutional factors will be a sufficient guide to understanding HR strategy and that business strategy may be more or less ignored. Equally, in contexts of extreme corporate autonomy the importance of environmental-level factors for HR strategy will be minimal in comparison with business strategy.

CONVERGENCE AND DIVERGENCE IN HRM

So far, we have located HRM within its early home in North America and compared the situation of HRM there to that found in Europe. But given that there are differences, another key question arises: are these differences increasing or decreasing? As business becomes more global, is HRM becoming more uniform? Or might different regions even be becoming more distinct?

We turn now to this question of convergence or divergence. If the policies of market de-regulation and state de-control are spreading from the US to Europe, are European firms moving towards a North American HRM approach to managing their personnel? Or is it the case that, because of the increasing economic and political integration of EU countries, a convergence towards a distinctly European practice is under way? There is, of course, a third possibility: that European firms are so locked into their respective national institutional settings that no common model is likely to emerge for the foreseeable future.

The studies presented in Part 2 of this book are uniquely equipped to explore these issues in that we have access to comparative data for most European countries collected at regular intervals. We are thus in a position to analyse developments in a range of precisely defined HRM practices across these countries and over a significant period of time.

To set Part 2 within a broad conceptual framework, we examine the convergence and divergence arguments in more detail. As part of this process we consider two distinct versions of the convergence thesis, the free market US model and the institutional European model. Although these two theses of convergence and divergence are very different from one another there is one underlying similarity: they all view firms' latitude in regard to selecting and developing personnel management strategies as being shaped, governed and given impetus by a mix of factors which may be defined as technological, economic or institutional.

The main arguments

The convergence vs. divergence debate has been a strand of the literature on management in general for decades and this has more recently been reflected in HRM theorising. Convergence theory suggests that antecedents specific to the organisation explain the existence of HR policies, while-country specific differences are less significant (Sparrow et al., 1994; Weber et al., 2000; Tregaskis et al., 2001). Thus, while differences in management systems have arisen as a result of the geographical isolation of businesses, the consequent development of differing beliefs and value orientations of national cultures are being superseded by the logic of technology and markets which requires the adoption of specific and, therefore, universally applicable policies, approaches and management techniques (Kidger, 1991). Arguably, Max Weber's theory of bureaucracy and rationalisation, first written in German (*Wirtschaft und Gesellschaft*, 1921) and subsequently translated into English, represents one of the earliest contributions to this thesis of long-term convergence. Regardless of whether the economic system is organised on a capitalistic or a socialistic basis, Weber argued that applying technical knowledge efficiently requires the adoption of the bureaucratic system with its universal characteristics. Early post-war thinking was also for the most part convergent. Galbraith contended that, given the decision to have modern industry, modern man's "area of decision is, in fact, exceedingly small" (1967: p. 336). Much of what happens is inevitable and the same so that "the imperatives of organisation, technology and planning operate similarly, and as we have seen, to a broadly similar result, on all societies" (1967: p. 336). Burnham (1941), Drucker (1950) and Harbison and Myers (1959) all contended that there was a trend toward a world-wide rise of the professional manager who would successfully impose professional, as opposed to patrimonial or political, management systems on their respective societies.

Closer to our sphere of interest, Kerr et al. (1960) believed not only that the convergence of systems of IR was inevitable, but that the convergence would be toward US practices. Kerr et al. argued that there was a logic to industrialism which would lead to greater convergence, with, in particular, technological and economic forces bringing about greater similarities in systems. They argued that management systems represented attempts to manage technology as efficiently as possible. As the United States of America was the technological leader, it followed that US management practices represented current best practice, which other nations would eventually seek to emulate as they sought to adopt US technology. Thus "patterns in other countries were viewed as derivative of, or deviations from, the US model" (Locke et al., 1995: p. xvi).

Characteristic of these various convergence perspectives is their functionalist mode of thought. The practice of management is explained exclusively by reference to its contribution to technical and economic efficiency. Thus, it is a dependent variable that evolves in response to technological and economic change, rather than with reference to the socio-political context, so that "much of what happens to management and labour is the same regardless of auspices" (Kerr, 1983).

More recently, the convergence thesis has received support from transaction cost economics, which also contends that at any one point of time there exists a best method of organising labour (Williamson, 1975, 1985). "Most transaction cost theorists argue that there is one best organisational form for firms that have similar or identical transaction costs" (Hollingsworth and Boyer,

1997: p. 34). Likewise, parts of the industrial organisation literature argue that firms tend to seek out and adopt the best solutions to organising labour in their product markets, long-term survival being dependent on their ability to implement them (Chandler, 1962, 1977; Chandler and Daems, 1980). Thus, there is a tendency for firms to converge towards similar organisational structures.

Of course, the "convergers" recognise that there are many variations in management approaches around the world. However, they argue that, in the long term, any variations in the adoption of management systems at the company level are ascribable to the industrial sector in which it operates, its strategy, its available resources and its degree of exposure to international competition. Moreover, they claim, these factors are of diminishing salience. Indeed, once they have been taken account of, a clear trend toward the adoption of common management systems should be apparent.

Proponents of the divergence thesis argue, in direct contrast, that personnel management systems, far from being economically or technologically derived, reflect national institutional contexts which do not respond readily to the imperatives of technology or the market. According to this institutionalist perspective, organisational choice is limited by institutional pressures, including the state, regulatory structures, interest groups, public opinion and norms (DiMaggio and Powell, 1983; Meyer and Scott, 1983; Oliver, 1991). Moreover, many of these pressures are so taken for granted "as to be invisible to the actors they influence" (Oliver, 1991: p. 148). One observable effect of differing institutional contexts is that "the same equipment is frequently operated quite differently in the same sectors in different countries, even when firms are competing in the same market" (Hollingsworth and Boyer, 1997: p. 20). As a consequence, Kerr (1983: p. 28), in a retrospective analysis of his work with Dunlop, Harbison and Myers (1960), concedes that they had been wrong to suggest that industrialism would "overwhelmingly impose its own cultural patterns on pre-existing cultures". Kerr now argues that "industrialism does conquer and it does impose, but less rapidly and less totally than we implied."

Divergence theorists, however, refuse to subscribe even to this thesis of partial and delayed convergence. They argue, on the contrary, that national, and in some cases regional, institutional contexts are slow to change, partly because they derive from deep-seated beliefs and value systems and partly because significant re-distributions of power are involved. More importantly, they argue that change is path-dependent. In other words, even when change does occur it can be understood only in relation to the specific social context in which it occurs (Maurice et al., 1986; Poole, 1986). Performance criteria or goals are thus, at any point in time, socially rather than economically or technologically selected so that they first and foremost reflect principles of local rationality. Convergence of management systems can therefore only take place if supranational institutions are able to impose their influence across national contexts. Increasingly, it is being argued that that is what is taking place in the EU (Brewster, 1994). That is, there is an argument for the existence of an institutionally driven convergence of HRM practices within Europe.

In summary, we may observe that in addition to the divergence thesis there are two distinct versions of the convergence thesis. On one hand there is the traditional version of the convergence thesis that contends that convergence of HRM practices is driven by market and technological forces and that changes in the US are a harbinger of trends elsewhere. On the other hand there is a newer, institutional, version that argues that institutionally driven convergence is taking place within the EU. There is a debate between these two viewpoints (Brewster, 1999). We now examine these two models in more detail, before presenting the divergence thesis as applied to the European context.

The market forces, or US convergence, model

Weinstein and Kochan (1995) divide US employment relations from the late 1930s to the present day into two phases: the New Deal industrial relations system which extended from the 1930s through the 1970s, and more recent developments, which we will refer to as US HRM.

As we have noted, in the 1970s American mass production grappled with the persistent effects of increased international competition and a more uncertain business environment. New flexible productive techniques emerged in the wake of advances in information technology, stimulating a shift in competitive strategy toward flexible specialisation aimed at producing differentiated, high-value-added products (Piore and Sabel, 1984).

As a result a new management model, less compatible with unionisation than the old, began to emerge. This new (US HRM) model has a number of distinctive features aimed at removing the rigidities intrinsic in the mass production system so as to lay the ground for the use of flexible production techniques. One set of these features is designed to increase individual flexibility and employee self-regulation of quality control. New job designs allowed employees, in co-ordination with their supervisors, to formulate their own job descriptions. Furthermore, whereas wages in the traditional system had been attached to jobs rather than individuals, in the new model there was a move to relate wages to individual performance and competency in the form of individual incentives. Job security could only be extended to the core labour force, so that another feature of the new model of employee relations was the increase in contingent, or non-core employment, i.e. part-time, temporary, and contract work.

As Weinstein and Kochan (1995: 27) observe: "Government played an important role by weakening its enforcement of labour and employment laws and by allowing (some would say encouraging) a harder line by management in its resistance to unions."

In short, the emergence of US HRM may be viewed as an attempt by US firms to cope with the disappearance of large and stable markets by moving beyond mass standardised production to flexible production by synthesising the elements required for co-operation and self-regulation. At the same time US HRM is attempting to counteract the inheritance of a lack of trust and co-operation between workers and managers, and the effects of short-term systems of cost–benefit calculation.

The institutional, or European convergence, model

Whereas the market forces model regards developments in the US as a precursor of universal developments, it has been contended that in Europe there are powerful non-market, institutional, factors. Not only do these make the central features of US HRM inappropriate to European organisations, they are arguably generating a specifically European model of convergence in HRM (Brewster, 1995). Let us briefly recall the nature of these factors.

We have pointed out that in Europe organisations are constrained at a national level by culture and legislation and at the organisational level by trade union involvement and consultative arrangements. It is clear that, in general, European countries are more heavily unionised than the US, and indeed most other countries. Trade union membership and influence varies considerably from country to country, of course, but is always significant. Indeed, in many European countries the law requires union recognition for collective bargaining. In most European countries many of the union functions in such areas as pay bargaining, e.g. are exercised at industrial or national level – outside the direct involvement of managers in individual organisations – as well as at establishment level (Hegewisch, 1991; Gunnigle et al., 1993; Traxler et al., 2001). Thus in Europe, as opposed to the US, companies are likely to be dealing with well-founded trade union structures.

It is worth noting that studies of HRM in the US have tended to take place in the non-unionised sector (Beaumont, 1991). In fact a constant assumption in research programmes in the US has been the link between HRM practices and non-unionism (see e.g. Kochan et al., 1984, 1986). "In the US a number of ... academics have argued that HRM [the concept and the practice] is anti-union and anti-collective bargaining" (Beaumont 1991a, p. 300).

We have also indicated that state involvement in HRM in Europe is not restricted to the legislative role. Compared to the US the state in Europe has a greater involvement in underlying social security provision. Equally it plays a more interventionist role in the economy, provides far more personnel and industrial relations (IR) services and is a more substantial employer in its own right by virtue of a more extensive government-owned sector.

Finally, we would also point to developments at the level of the EU or the European Economic Area which affect all organisations in Europe. In a historically unique experiment, EU countries have agreed to subordinate national legislative decision-making to European-level legislation. These developments have indirect effects upon the way people are managed and direct effects through the EU's adoption of a distinct social sphere of activity. In particular it would appear that the European Community Social Charter and its associated Social Action Programme are having an increasing legislative influence on HRM (Brewster and Teague, 1989; Brewster et al., 1993).

In these circumstances it is unsurprising that some have argued that the time is now ripe for distinguishing specifically European approaches:
"European Management

- is emerging, and cannot be said to exist except in limited circumstances;
- is broadly linked to the idea of European integration, which is continuously expanding further into different countries;
- reflects key values such as pluralism, tolerance, etc., but is not consciously developed from these values;
- is associated with a balanced stakeholder philosophy and the concept of Social Partners."

(Thurley and Wirdenius, 1991: p. 128)

Divergence in Europe

Opposed to this institutionalist thesis of convergence in European HRM are a number of approaches that emphasise the existence of broad, relatively inert, distinctions between the various national contexts of personnel management in Europe that make convergence to a European model of HRM unlikely. Here, therefore, one can argue for the critical role played by the societal context in explaining differences in the extent to which MNCs can and will pursue distinctive HRM practices. Katz and Kahn (1978) and Cheng (1989, 1994) argue that certain aspects of organisational functioning are more subject to external influences than others and that cross-national analysis should take cognisance of the range of contextually based societal variables that can determine how organisations exist within their operating environments. Within the field of HRM it is generally accepted that there are a range of societal-based institutional factors that have a significant influence on the kinds of polices that organisations adopt and the practices and postures that they enact. Such institutional arrangements and traditions have their roots in national business systems and reflect the impact of factors such as the national IR system, the historical pattern of industrialisation, the political system and traditions, the framework of corporate governance, labour, product and capital markets, education and training systems and the legal framework (Sparrow and Hiltrop, 1994; Tregaskis, 1995; Ferner, 1997; Edwards, 1998; Gooderham et al., 1999).

Due et al. (1991) identify, on the one hand, countries such as the UK, Ireland, and the Nordic countries where the state has a limited role in IR. On the other hand there are the Roman-Germanic countries, such as France, Spain, Germany, Italy, Belgium, Greece and the Netherlands where the state plays a central role in IR. A particular feature of Roman-Germanic countries is their "comprehensive labour market legislation governing various areas, such as length of the working day [and] rest periods" (Due et al., 1991: p. 90). In other words, unlike either the Anglo-Irish or the Nordic systems, the scope for corporate decision-making in Roman-Germanic countries in regard to employment issues is relatively low. Such differences, according to Gunnigle et al. (2002) give rise to difference in business and management traditions, and lead to the development of distinctive management cultures and value systems.

Hollingsworth and Boyer (1997) focus on a different dimension, the presence or absence of communitarian infrastructures that manifest themselves in the form of strong social bonds, trust, reciprocity and co-operation among economic actors and which they regard as "essential for successful flexible systems of production" (1997: p. 27). They distinguish between social contexts characterised by self-interest and those in which "obligation and compliance with social rules are the guiding principles shaping human actions" (Hollingsworth and Boyer, 1997: p. 8).[7] It is their contention that because of the pervasive market mentality that limits trust and co-operation between workers and managers within firms, as well as between firms and their suppliers, the UK (and likewise the US) does not have the social environment necessary for a successful flexible social system of production. In contrast, German and Scandinavian firms are embedded in an environment in which the market mentality is less pronounced, with trusting relationships and communitarian obligations more prevalent, thereby making flexible production systems a viable alternative. Finally, Hollingsworth and Boyer distinguish France as an environment that, while not having a market mentality, is nevertheless deficient in communitarian infrastructures. Instead, the public authorities play a *dirigiste* role in the economy, enabling France to partially mimic flexible systems of production. "But for flexible forms of production to become widespread, firms must be embedded in a social environment very different from that which exists in most of

France" (Hollingsworth and Boyer, 1997: p. 27). That is, an environment in which employer–employee conflict is endemic and there is an absence of "a spirit of generous co-operation" (Maurice et al., 1986: p. 86).

COMPETING PROPOSITIONS

We have described three broad theses in relation to Europe, the market-forces convergence model, the institutional convergence model and the divergence model. Three fundamentally different propositions may be derived, respectively, from these:

1. Market forces are generating a convergence in HRM practices among European firms towards a US model of HRM.
2. Pan-European institutional forces are generating a convergence in HRM practices among European firms towards a common European model that is distinctly different from that of the US model of HRM.
3. Deep-seated and fundamental differences between European countries mean either continuing divergence, or, no convergence in HRM practices among European firms.

The following chapters provide evidence that the thoughtful student can use to apply to these different propositions and offer a route map through which to explore these issues of convergence and divergence within Europe. To that end each chapter compares a pair, or in some cases a trio, of countries using data from a series of identical surveys carried out in those countries. The chapters have been written by HR academics from each of the respective countries. Following a brief outline of the countries' institutions and their labour markets, each chapter proceeds with a comparison of HRM in the countries involved. Here, the role and operation of the HRM department, HRM strategy formulation, employee relations and the role of the trade unions, employee resourcing, flexible working patterns, performance measurement and rewards, and training and development are all examined. In preparing their chapters the authors have, of course, applied their own local understanding and analytical skills to these issues and reflected the debates current in those countries. However, because they have all used 11 key tables from the same international survey of HRM practices, students will be able to take a topic such as training and development, for example, and "read it

---

[7] See also Maurice et al. (1986) and their analysis of work systems in France and Germany.

through" the different countries. In addition to the survey data each chapter contains case vignettes designed to illustrate selected aspects of HRM in action, as well as teaching questions.

TEACHING QUESTIONS

1. Do you believe that there is one best way to manage the HR?
2. Discuss the different schools of thought that have contributed to the development of HRM.
3. Distinguish between "hard" and "soft" HRM.
4. What do you see as the main difficulties involved in linking an organisation's HR strategy with its business strategy?
5. Outline what you consider to be the chief institutional differences between the US and Europe. What are the implications of this institutional context for the practice of HRM?
6. What are the core tenets of the Rhineland model?
7. Convergence and divergence theorists have differing views on how HRM is developing as a field. Discuss the core arguments on both sides.

REFERENCES

Adler, N.J. (1991) *International Dimensions of Organizational Behavior*, 2nd edn. Boston: PWS Kent Publishing.

Albert, M. (1991) *Capitalisme contre Capitalisme*. Paris: Seuil.

Barney, J.B. (1991) Firm resources and sustained competitive advantage. *Journal of Management*, 17(1): 99–120.

Beaumont, P. (1991) *Trade Unions and HRM. Industrial Relations Journal*, 22(4): 300–308.

Beattie, R. and McGougall, M. (1998) Inside or outside HRM? Locating lateral learning in two voluntary sector organisations. In: Mabey, C., Skinner, D. and Clark, T. (eds.), *Experiencing Human Resource Management*. London: Sage, pp. 218–235.

Beer, M., Spector, B., Lawrence, P., Quinn-Mills, D. and Walton, R. (1984) *Managing Human Assets: The Groundbreaking Harvard Business School Program*. New York: The Free Press.

Behn, R.D. (1988) Management by Groping Along, *Journal of Policy Analysis and Management*, 7(4): 643–663.

Berger, P. and Luckmann, T. (1967) *The Social Construction of Reality*. New York: Doubleday.

Blanchard, O. (1999) European unemployment: The role of shocks and institutions. Unpublished working paper. Massachusetts Institute of Technology.

Bolkestein, F. (1999) The Dutch model. *The Economist*, 351(8120): 115–116.

Boxall, P. (1992) Strategic human resource management: beginnings of a new theoretical sophistication. *Human Resource Management Journal*, 3(3): 60–79.

Brewster, C. (1994) European HRM: reflection of, or challenge to, the American concept? In: Kirkbride, P.S. (ed.), *Human Resource Managment in Europe*. London: Routledge.

Brewster, C. (1995) Towards a European model of human resource management. *Journal of International Business Studies*, 26(1): 1–21.

Brewster, C. (1999) Strategic human resource management: the value of different paradigms. *Management International Review*, 39.

Brewster, C. and Teague, P. (1989) *EC Social Policy and Britain*. London: Institute of Personnel Management.

Brewster, C., Hegewisch, A., Lockhart, T. and Holden, L. (1993) *The European Human Resource Management Guide*. London: Academic Press.

Brewster, C., Larsen, H.H. and Mayrhofer, W. (2000) Human resource management: a strategic approach. In: Brewster, C. and Larsen, H.H. (eds.), *Human Resource Management in Northern Europe: Trends, Dilemmas and Strategy*. Oxford: Blackwell.

Buckley, M., Ferris, G., Bernardine, H. and Harvey, M. (1998) The disconnect between the science and the practice of management, *Business Horizons*, 41: 31–38.

Buller, P. and Napier, N. (1993) Strategy and human resource managment integration in fast growth versus other mid-sized firms, *British Journal of Management*, 4(2): 77–90.

Burnham, J. (1941) *The Managerial Revolution*. New York: John Day.

Chadwick, C. and Cappelli, P. Alternatives to generic strategy typologies in strategic human resource management. In: Wright, P., Dyer, L., Boudreau, J. and Milkovich, G. (eds.), *Research in Personnel and Human Resource Management*. Greenwich, CT: JAI Press, Supplement 4, pp. 11–29.

Chandler, A.D. (1962) *Strategy and Structure*. Cambridge: MIT Press.

Chandler, A.D. (1977) *The Visible Hand: The Managerial Revolution in American Business*. Cambridge: Harvard University Press.

Chandler, A.D. and Daems, H. (eds.) (1980) *Managerial Hierarchies: Comparative Perspectives on the Rise of the Modern Industrial Enterprise*. Cambridge: Harvard University Press.

Cheng, J.L.C. (1989) Towards a contextual approach to cross-national organizational research: a macro perspective, *Advances in International Comparative Management*, 4: 3–18.

Cheng, J.L.C. (1994) On the concept of universal knowledge in organizational science: implications for cross-national research, *Management Science*, 40(1): 162–167.

Collins, J.C. and Porras, J.I. (1994) *Built to Last: Successful Habits of Visionary Companies*, London: Century.

DiMaggio, P.J. and Powell, W.W. (1983) The iron cage revisited: institutional isomorphism and collective rationality in organizational fields. *American Sociological Review*, 48: 147–160.

Drucker, P. (1950) *The New Society: The Anatomy of the Industrial Order*. New York: Harper.

Drucker, P.F. (1989) *The New Realities: in Government and Politics, in Economics and Business, in Society and World View*. New York: Harper & Row.

Due, J., Madsen, J.S. and Jensen, C.S. (1991) The social dimension: convergence or diversification of IR in the single European market? *Industrial Relations Journal*, 22(2): 85–102.

Economist, The (1997) Beer, sandwiches and statistics. *The Economist*, 12 July.

Economist, The (1999a) General Electric. *The Economist*, 18 September 352(8137): 23–30.

Economist, The (1999b) Desperately seeking a perfect model. *The Economist*, 10 April, 351(8114): 89–90.

Edwards, T. (1998) Multinationals, labour management and the process of reverse diffusion: a case study, *International Journal of Human Resource Management*, 9(4) 696–709.

Ferner, A. (1997) Country of origin effects and HRM in multinational companies, *Human Resource Management Journal*, 7(1): 19–36.

Ferner, A. and Edwards, P. (1995) Power and the diffusion of organizational change within multinational enterprises. *European Journal of Industrial Relations*, 1: 229–257.

Ferris, G., Hochwarter, W., Buckley, M., Harrell-Cook, G. and Frink, D. (1999) Human resources management: some new directions. *Journal of Management*, 25(3): 385–427.

Financial Times (1999) Varying states of start-up. *Financial Times*, 22 June.

Fombrun, C.J., Tichy, N. and Devanna, M.A. (1984) *Strategic Human Resource Management*. New York: John Wiley.

Friedman, B., Hatch, J. and Walker, D.M. (1998) *Delivering on the Promise*. New York: Free Press.

Galbraith, J.K. (1967) *The New Industrial State*. London: Hamish Hamilton.

Garavan, T., Morley, M., Gunnigle, P. and Collins, E. (2001) Human capital accumulation: the role of human resource development. *Journal of European Industrial Training*, 25(2/3/4): 48–68.

Garrick, J. and Clegg, S. (2000) Knowledge work and the new demands of learning. *Journal of Knowledge Management*, 4(4): 1–9.

Gooderham, P.N., Nordhaug, O. and Ringdal, K. (1999) Institutional and national determinants of organizational practice: human resource management in European firms. *Administrative Science Quarterly*, 44(3): 507–531.

Gomez Mejia, L.R. (1992) Structure and process of diversification, compensation strategy and firm performance, *Strategic Management Journal*, 13(5): 381–397.

Guest, D. (1990) Human resource management and the American dream. *Journal of Management Studies* 27(4): 377–397.

Gunnigle, P., Brewster, C. and Morley, M. (1993) Changing patterns in industrial relations. *Journal of European Foundation for the Improvement of Living and Working Conditions*, Dublin.

Gunnigle, P., Heraty, N. and Morley, M. (2002) *Human Resource Management in Ireland*. Dublin: Gill & Macmillan.

Gunnigle, P., Murphy, K., Cleveland, J., Heraty, N. and Morley, M. (2002) Localization in human resource management: comparing American and European multinational corporations. *Advances in International Management*, 14, 259–284.

Gunnigle, P., O'Sullivan, M. and Kinsella, M. (2002) Organised Labour in the New Economy: Trade Unions and Public Policy in the Republic of Ireland. In: D'Art, D. and Turner, T. (eds), *Irish Employment Relations in the New Economy*, Dublin: Blackhall Press, pp. 222–258.

Hamel, G. and Prahalad, C.K. (1989) Strategic intent. *Harvard Business Review*, May–June, 63–76.

Hegewisch, A. (1991) The decentralisation of pay bargaining: European comparisons, *Personal Review*, 20(6): 28–35.

Hoffman, A. (1999) Institutional evolution and change: environmentalism and the U.S. chemical industry. *Academy of Management Journal*, 42(4): 351–371.

Hofstede, G. (1980) *Culture's Consequences: International Differences in Work Related Values*. Beverley Hills, CA: Sage Publications.

Hofstede, G. (1991) *Culture and Organizations: Software of the Mind*. London: McGraw-Hill.

Hollingsworth, J.R. and Boyer, R. (1997) Coordination of economic actors and social systems of production. In: Hollingsworth, J.R. and Boyer, R. (eds.) *Contemporary Capitalism*. Cambridge: University Press.

Johanson, U. and Larsen, H.H. (2000) Human Resource Costing and Accounting: Putting a Price on Human Resource Investments. In: Brewster, C. and Larsen, H.H. (eds), *Human Resource Management in Northern Europe: Trends, Dilemmas and Strategy*, London, Blackwell, pp. 170–194.

Joyce, W.F. (1986) Towards a theory of incrementalism, *Advances in Strategic Management*, 4: 43–58.

Katz, D. and Kahn, R. (1978) The Social Psychology of Organizations (2nd Ed.) New York: Wiley.

Kay, J. (1998) Crisis, what crisis? *Financial Times*, 25 November.

Kerr, C. (1983) *The Future of Industrial Societies*. Cambridge: Harvard University Press.

Kerr, C., Dunlop, J.T., Harbison, F. and Myers, C. (1960) *Industrialism and Industrial Man*. Cambridge: Harvard University Press.

Kidger, P.J. (1991) The emergence of international human resource management. *International Journal of Human Resource Management*, 2(2): 149–163.

Kochan, T.A. and Dyer, L. (1992) Managing transformational change: the role of human resource professionals. Sloan Working Paper 3420-92-BPS, MIT, Mass.

Lansbury, R. (1995) Workplace Europe: new forms of bargaining and participation, *Technology, Work & Employment*, Vol. 10, No. 1.

Laurent, A. (1983) The cultural diversity of Western conceptions of Management. *International Studies of Management and Organization*, 13: 75–96.

Lengnick-Hall, C.A. and Lengnick-Hall, M.L. (1988) Strategic human resources management: a review of the literature and a proposed typology. *Academy of Management Review*, 13(3): 454–470.

Lindblom, C.E. (1959) "The Science of 'Muddling Through'" *Public Administration Review*, 19: 79–88.

Locke, R., Piore, M. and Kochan, T. (1995) Introduction. In: Locke, R., Kochan, T. and Piore, M. (eds.), *Employment Relations in a Changing World Economy*. Cambridge, MA, MIT Press.

Luoma, M. (2000) Investigating the link between strategy and HRD. *Personnel Review*, 29(6): 769–790.

McGregor, D. (1960) *The Human Side of Enterprise*. New York: McGraw-Hill.

Maslow, A. (1943) A theory of human motivation. *Psychological Review*, 50(4).

Maurice, M., Sellier, F. and Silvestre, J. (1986) *The Social Foundations of Industrial Power*. Cambridge, MA: MIT Press.

Mayrhofer, W., Brewster, C. and Morley, M. (2000) The concept of strategic European human resource management. In: Brewster, C., Mayrhofer, W. and Morley, M. (eds.), *New Challenges for European Human Resource Management*. Basingstoke: Macmillan.

Meyer, J. and Scott, W. (1983) *Organizational Environments: Ritual and Reality*, Beverly Hills, CA: Sage.

Miles, R and Snow, C. (1978) *Organizational Strategy, Structure and Process*, New York: McGraw Hill.

Mintzberg, H. (1978) Patterns in strategy formation. *Management Science*, 24(9): 934–948.

Monks, K. (1996) Ploughing the Furrow and Reaping the Harvest: Roles and Relationships in HRM. The 1996 Examiner/University College Cork Lecture in Human Resource Management, September, University College Cork.

Monks, K. (2001) The role of the corporate human resource function in Irish international firms. In: Linehan, M., Morley, M. and Walsh, J. (eds.), *International Human Resource Management and Expatriate Transfers: Irish Experiences*. Dublin: Blackhall Publishing.

Morley, M., Brewster, C., Gunnigle, P. and Mayrhofer, W. (1996) Evaluating change in European industrial relations: research evidence on trends at organizational level, *International Journal of Human Resource Management*, 7(3): 640–656.

Morley, M., Mayrhofer, W. and Brewster, C. (2000) Communication in organizations: dialogue and impact. In: Brewster, C. and Larsen, H.H. (eds.), *Human Resource Management in Northern Europe: Trends, Dilemmas and Strategy*. Oxford: Blackwell.

OECD (Organization for Economic Co-operation and Development) (1995) *Economic Outlook*. Paris: OECD.

OECD (Organization for Economic Co-operation and Development) (1998) *Economic Outlook*. Paris: OECD.

Oliver, C. (1991) Strategic responses to institutional processes. *Academy of Management Review*, 16(1): 145–179.

Osterman, P. (1994) How common is workplace transformation and how can we explain who adopts it? Results from a national survey. *Industrial and Labor Relations Review* (January): 175–188.

Pedder, S. (1999) A survey of France. *The Economist*, 5 June, 351(8122).

Peters, T. and Waterman, R. (1982) *In Search of Excellence: Lessons from America's Best-run Companies*. New York: Harper & Row.

Pieper, R. (ed.) (1990) *Human Resource Management: An International Comparison*. Berlin: Walter de Gruyter.

Pfeffer, J. and Veiga, J.F. (1999) Putting people first for organizational success. *Academy of Management Executive*, 13(2): 37–48.

Piore, M. and Sabel, C. (1984) *The Second Industrial Divide*. New York: Basic Books.

Poole, M. (1986) *Industrial Relations – Origins and Patterns of National Diversity*. London: RKP.

Quinn, R.E. (1988) *Beyond Rational Management: Mastering the Paradoxes and Competing Demands of High Performance*, Jossey-Bass, San Francisco.

Randlesome, C. (1994) *The Business Culture in Germany: Portrait of a Power House*. Oxford: Butterworth-Heinemann.

Roethlisberger, F. and Dickson, W. (1939) *Management and the Worker*. Cambridge, MA: Harvard University Press.

Schuler, R. and Jackson, S. (1987) Linking Competitive Strategies with Human Resource Management Practices. *Academy of Management Executive*, 1(3): 207–219.

Schultz, T.W. (1971) *Investment in Human Capital: The Role of Education and Research*. New York: The Free Press.

Smith, D. (1999) *Will Europe Work?* London: Profile Books.

Sparrow, P. and Hiltrop, J.M. (1994) *European Human Resource Management in Transition*. Hemel Hempstead: Prentice-Hall.

Sparrow, P., Schuler, R. and Jackson, S. (1994) Convergence or divergence: human resource practices for competitive advantage worldwide. *International Journal of Human Resource Management*, 5(2): 267–299.

Storey J. (ed) (1989) *New Perspectives on Human Resource Management*, Routledge, London.

Tayeb, M. (1988) *Organizations and National Culture: A Comparative Analysis*. London: Sage Publications.

Taylor, F.W. (1911) *Principles of Scientific Management*. New York: Harper & Row.

Thurley, K. and Wirdenius, H. (1990) *Towards European Management*, London.

Thurley, K. and Wirdenius, H. (1991) Will management become "European"? Strategic choices for organizations, *European Management Journal*, 9(2): 127–134.

Tiernan, S., Morley, M. and Foley, E. (2001) *Modern Management*. Dublin: Gill and Macmillan.

Traxler, F., Blaschke, S. and Kittel, B. (2001) *National Labour Relations in Internationalised Markets. A Comparative Study of Institutions, Change and Performance*. Oxford: Oxford University Press.

Tregaskis, O. (1995) The link between HR Strategy and Training: an examination of French and UK Organizations. In: Whitfield, K. and Poole, M. (eds.) *Organizing Employment for High Performance*, Hull: Bonnick Publications.

Tregaskis, O., Heraty, N. and Morley, M. (2001) HRD in multinationals: The global/local mix. *Human Resource Management Journal*, 11(2): 34–56.

Trompenaars, F. (1993) *Riding the Waves of Culture*. London: Economist Books.

Tyson, S. (1999) Human resource strategy: a process for managing the contribution of HRM to organizational performance. In: Schuler, R. and Jackson, S. (eds.), *Strategic Human Resource Management*. Oxford: Blackwell.

Tyson, S., Witcher, M. and Doherty, N. (1994) *Different Routes to Excellence*. Cranfield University HRM Research Centre Working Paper.

Weber, M. (1921) "Wirtschaft und Gesellschaft", translated and edited in 1968 by Guenther Roth and Claus Willich and published by Bedminster Press, New York.

Weber, W., Kabst, R. and Gramley, C. (1998) Does the Common Market Imply Common Human Resource Policies? *Conference Proceedings of Sixth Conference on International Human Resource Management*, University of Paderborn, 22–25 June.

Weber, W., Kabst, R. and Gramley, C. (2000) Human resource policy in European organizations: an analysis of country and company specific antecedents. In: Brewster, C., Mayrhofer, W. and Morley, M. (eds.), *New Challenges for European Human Resource Management*.

Weinstein, M. and Kochan, T. (1995) The limits of diffusion: recent developments in industrial relations and human resource practices in the United States. In: Locke, R., Kochan, T. and Piore, M. (eds.), *Employment Relations in a Changing World Economy*. Cambridge, MA: MIT Press.

Williamson, O. (1975) *Markets and Hierarchies: Analysis and Antitrust Implications*. New York: Free Press.

Williamson, O. (1985) *The Economic Institutions of Capitalism*. New York: Free Press.

Wright, P. and Snell, S. (1999) Towards a unifying framework for exploring fit and flexibility in strategic human resource management. In: Schuler, R. and Jackson, S. (eds.), *Strategic Human Resource Management*. Oxford: Blackwell.

Part 2

2

The UK and Ireland: Traditions and Transitions in HRM

Sarah Atterbury, Chris Brewster, Christine Communal,
Christine Cross, Patrick Gunnigle and Michael Morley

INSTITUTIONAL BACKGROUND

UNITED KINGDOM OF GREAT BRITAIN AND NORTHERN IRELAND

Area	244,590 km^2
Population	59,231,900 inhabitants
Density	244 inhabitants per km^2
Capital and population	London (7,355,000)
Other major cities and population	Birmingham (961,041) Manchester (2,936,300) Leeds (680,722) Glasgow (662,853)
Official language	English
Others include	Welsh, Scottish Gaelic
Religions	72% Christain 3% Muslim 3% Others 22% No religion

The United Kingdom of Great Britain and Northern Ireland is situated off the coast of France between the North Atlantic Ocean and the North Sea. The coastline is 12,429 km long.

Topography and climate

The United Kingdom (UK) comprises Great Britain (England, Wales and Scotland) and Northern Ireland. Physically, the country is traditionally divided into a highland and a lowland zone. The highland zone covers the majority of Scotland with Ben Nevis as the highest summit (1342 m above sea level), northern England, Wales and the South West Peninsula of England. The lowland zone largely extends throughout the rest of England.

The relation to the sea and the topography broadly determines the climate in the UK, a traditional British topic of conversation. Rain usually arrives from a westerly direction. The highest peaks in the highland zone can receive significant amounts of rainfall whereas areas such as East Anglia and the Thames Estuary receive less.

Four nations

England is by far the most populated area with 49,181,300 inhabitants compared to Scotland (5,064,200 inhabitants), Wales (2,903,200 inhabitants) and Northern Ireland (1,689,300 inhabitants). Scotland and Northern Ireland put together have a population roughly equal to that of Greater London.

Diverse cultural identity

The UK is characterised by a mixed cultural identity, more recently enhanced by a number of ethnic minorities, in particular, Indians, Pakistanis, Bangladeshis, Chinese, Africans and Arabs.

Today's diversity reflects the influence of the British Empire in the nineteenth century. Since the end of World War II, the British Empire has been dismantled, giving way to the British Commonwealth, which is a loose association of countries. In 1973, the UK joined the European Union (EU). Britain today is a prosperous and modern European nation with significant international influence.

Current economic and political issues related to national identity for the UK include the question of whether to join the single European currency, the Euro, and constitutional reform covering the House of Lords and devolution of power to Scotland, Wales and Northern Ireland.

Figure 2.1　Tower of London, England

Principal characteristics

Figure 2.2 shows the relative position of the UK in relation to other European countries on a number of standardised items.

People

The UK is one of the four most populated countries in the EU. The total UK population has been continuously growing over the last decade. This is partly due to migration and partly due to natural population increase. People are also living longer, as illustrated in Table 2.1. Women in particular have a life expectancy which is higher than men (79.3 years for women and 74.4 years for men). These figures closely mirror the European average.

In the UK, the average number of people per household is 2.4. This figure has been shrinking over recent decades as traditional family patterns are breaking down. A significant and increasing number of individuals live on their own – 29% in 2000 against 22% in 1981 – and an increasing number of couples remain without children (increasing by 3% since 1981). Single parents and one person households jointly account for 38% of households.

Economy

As elsewhere in Europe, the UK economy is a mixture of public and private sector but here, more than elsewhere, Government policy has for two decades been directed at building an environment which encourages the private sector. The election victory of the Labour Party in May 1997, which replaced 18 years of Conservative

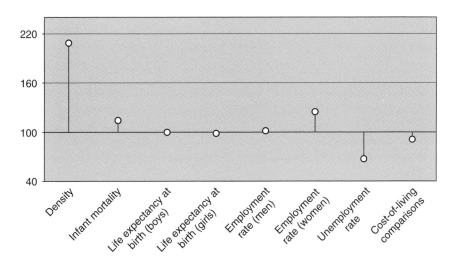

Figure 2.2   Principal characteristics in relation to EU-15 = 100

Table 2.1   Population by age and gender (% of total population)

Age (years)	UK		EU-15 2000
	1986	2000	
<15	19	19	17
15–24	16	12	12
25–49	33	36	37
50–64	16	17	17
65–79	12	12	13
>80	4	4	4

All data from Eurostat.

Table 2.2   Gross domestic product (at market prices, in million ECU/EU)

	1991	1994	1997	2000
EU-15	5,779,473	6,334,523	7,287,921	8,524,371
UK	836,147	878,109	1,171,548	1,547,903
	(−1)	(5)	(3)	(3)

Percentage change on previous period – constant prices (in brackets). All data from Eurostat.

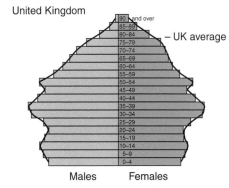

United Kingdom

Source: Office for National Statistics. Census 2001

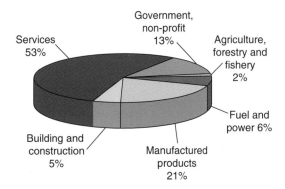

Figure 2.3   Economic structure (gross value rates as % of sectors, 1995, UK). All data from Eurostat

governments, has not changed this central tenet of free enterprise.

After 9 years of growth in the 1980s under the government of Margaret Thatcher, the UK went into a recession in the early 1990s but, as Table 2.2 illustrates, 1993–1994 saw a significant rise in real gross domestic product (GDP). Since then, economic growth has been gradual.

Historically, the manufacturing sector was the basis of economic strength, but this sector has declined steadily over the years. A significant share of GDP has been taken by services, particularly financial services (Figure 2.3).

Table 2.3   Cost-of-living comparisons in 2000 (Brussels = 100[1])

Food and non-alcoholic beverages	Clothing and footwear	Housing, water, electricity, gas and other fuels	Furnishing, household equipment and maintenance	Health
111	83	312	125	118

Transport	Recreation and culture	Education	Alcohol and tobacco	Communications
129	114	114	181	96

Hotels, cafes and restaurants	Miscellaneous		*Total*	*Total excluding rents*
129	144		160	119

All data from Eurostat.

Table 2.4   Working days lost in all industry due to labour disputes (per 1000 employees)

	1986	1987	1988	1989	1990	1991	1992	1993	1994	1995	1996	1997
EU-15	:	:	226	170	153	99	118	73	114	:	:	:
UK	90	164	166	177	182	83	34	24	30	13	19	:

":" Data not available.

Table 2.5   Working days lost in manufacturing industry due to labour disputes (per 1000 employees)

	1986	1987	1988	1989	1990	1991	1992	1993	1994	1995	1996	1997
EU-15	:	:	226	157	179	143	118	113	105	:	:	:
UK	185	125	280	138	178	43	19	25	12	13	18	:

All data from Eurostat. ":" Data not available.

Cost-of-living indices in the UK are around or above the average of the EU, except for housing, where the UK is particularly expensive (Table 2.3).

Legal, institutional and political environment

The UK is a parliamentary Monarchy. There is in Great Britain a strong sense of continuity between the past and the present. For instance, the constitution is unwritten and resides in judicial precedents. Thus, the constitution is based on traditions, which may be changed by Acts of Parliament, rather than a written constitution. The Parliament consists of the House of Commons and the House of Lords. The latter chamber mostly has a consultative role and its functioning is under review. Some powers have been devolved to a new independent Parliament for Scotland and a Welsh Assembly. Two parties have dominated the political scene since the 1920s, the Conservative and the Labour Party.

Much of the UK's employment legislation was consolidated in the 1990s by Acts of Parliament (the 1992 Trade Union and Labour Relations Act and the 1993 Trade Union Reform and Employment Rights).

As illustrated in Tables 2.4 and 2.5, in recent years, labour disputes have had a diminishing impact on the disruption of working days.

Labour market

Over 27 million people are in employment in the UK, the highest number of people in employment since data began to be collected in this form in 1959, with the vast

---

[1] Cost-of-living comparison is carried out by calculation of index numbers (Brussels = 100) based on (a) prices of a shopping basket of over 3000 goods and services, (b) expenditure patterns of international officials and (c) exchange rates. All information was correct on 1 July 1996. Figures come from work by Eurostat in the field of cost-of-living adjustments to salaries of EU officials. Staff regulations fix indices for Belgium and Luxembourg at 100. Hence indices are available for all EU capitals except Brussels and Luxembourg. Country codes refer to the capital city.

Table 2.6   Persons in employment (million)

	1986	1987	1988	1989	1990	1991	1992	1993	1994	1995	1996	2000
	24.4	24.8	25.7	26.6	26.8	26.2	25.8	25.5	25.7	25.9	26.2	27.7*
1985 = 100	100.4	102.2	105.7	109.4	110.3	107.9	106.1	104.9	105.7	106.8	107.8	

All data from Eurostat. * Data from Summerfield and Babbs (2003).

Table 2.7   Persons in employment in different sectors (thousand)

	1987	1989	1991	1993	1995	1997	2000
Industry	8.084	8.607	8.107	7.443	7.079	:	7.024
Agriculture	583	593	593	519	533	:	424
Services	16.010	17.190	17.264	17.361	18.203	:	20.190

All data from (Eurostat). ":" Data not available.

Table 2.8   Unemployment rate (%)

1987	1990	1993	1996	1999	2000
11	7	11	8	6	6

All data from Eurostat.

Table 2.9   Unemployment rates (%)

	UK	EU-15
Women unemployed	5	10
Men unemployed	6	7
Long-term unemployment (as % of all unemployed)	28	45

All data from Eurostat.

Table 2.10   Employment rate by gender (%, 2000)

	UK	EU-15
Women	65	55
Men	78	73

All data from Eurostat.

majority of jobs in the service sector (Tables 2.6 and 2.7). Compared to the rest of the EU, in 2001 the UK had one of the highest employment rates after Denmark, Sweden and the Netherlands.

Unemployment rates are relatively low. An interesting feature of the UK economy is that more women participate in the work force than on average in the EU, and that the unemployment rate for women is lower than that for men. EU averages present a reversed picture (Tables 2.8–2.10).

Hourly labour costs in the UK tend to be lower than European averages except for Ireland, Greece, Spain and Portugal (Tables 2.11 and 2.12).

The breakdown of labour costs in the UK is also favourable to business. Indeed, indirect labour costs are low in relation to those of other EU countries (Table 2.13). The proportion of the social security costs as a percentage of indirect costs is one of the lowest in the EU.

In addition to the above, the British have a tradition of working long hours with averages significantly higher than the EU norm (Table 2.14).

Education system

In the UK, education is compulsory from the age of 5–16. Education is free in state schools, although a number of private schools also exist. Pre-primary school (nursery education) is underdeveloped. Consequently, the private sector provision in the form of playgroups has grown – facilitating the greater participation of women in the workforce. Additionally, recent policy for funding 2.5 hours a day for pre-school children has reduced childcare costs.

The participation rate of 16 and 17 years old in full-time non-compulsory education is rising, but remains low compared to European standards. The levels of education of people aged 25–59 also remain lower in the UK than in the rest of EU. National Vocational Qualifications (NVQs) were introduced in the 1980s and offer a framework of competency-based qualifications. Current government policy is based on encouraging a voluntary approach to training in the workplace (Table 2.15).

Table 2.11   Average hourly labour costs[2] (manual and non-manual workers) in total industry

	1988	1989	1990	1991	1992	1993	1994	1995	1996
Ecu	10.97	11.61	12.2	13.57	13.11	12.8	13.75	13.43	13.93

All data from Eurostat.

Table 2.12   Monthly earnings: non-manual workers (Ecu)

	1986	1987	1988	1989	1990	1991	1992	1993	1994	1995	1996
In industry	1337	1533	1771	1849	2020	2148	2158	2158	2140	2104	2348
In retail trade	875	1001	1172	1211	1319	1416	1419	1402	1469	1390	1535

All data from Eurostat.

Table 2.13   Structure of labour costs (%) in total industry (1995)

Direct cost	Indirect cost	Social security as part of indirect cost
84	16	13

All data from Eurostat.

Table 2.14   Number of hours usually worked per week: full-time employees

	1988	1991	1994	1997	2000
EU-15	40.7	40.3	40.3	42.1	41.7
UK	43.7	43.4	44.7	44.9	44.2

All data from Eurostat.

Table 2.15   Percentage of population aged 25–64 completing at least upper secondary education, 2000

<Upper secondary education	Total (25–59)	25–29	30–34	35–39	40–44	45–49	50–54	55–59	60–64
EU-15 (women and men)	64	76	73	70	66	62	55	51	45
UK (women and men)	81	90	89	86	83	79	72	64	67
EU-15 (women)	61	77	73	70	64	58	50	45	37
UK (women)	77	90	88	85	79	74	65	56	56

All data from Eurostat.

References

Eurostat, Statistical Office of the European Communities (eds.) (2002) *Eurostat Yearbook 2002, The Statistical Eye on Europe 1990–2000*, Office for Official Publications of the European Communities, Luxembourg.

Summerfield, C. and Babb, P. (eds.) (2003) *Social Trends*, No. 33, London: The Stationery Office.

REPUBLIC OF IRELAND

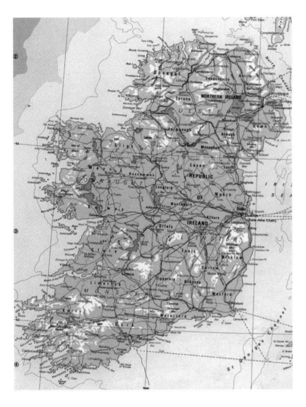

Area	68,890 km^2
Population	3,626,087 inhabitants
Density	52 inhabitants per km^2
Capital and population	Dublin (953,000)
Other major cities and population	Cork (218,000) Limerick (79,000) Galway (57,000)
Official languages	Irish and English
Religions	92% Roman Catholic 3% Church of Ireland 5% Others

Topography and climate

The Republic of Ireland comprises approximately five-sixths of the island of Ireland. Northern Ireland, a constituent part of the UK of Great Britain and Northern Ireland, makes up the remaining north-eastern part of the island. It is situated on Europe's western seaboard, just west of Britain and separated from it by the Irish Sea.

The relief of the island comprises a generally mountainous coastal area and a flatter inland region. The western and southern coasts which face the Atlantic are mostly rural and indented. The highest mountain peak is Carrantouhill (1040 m) in the south west. Peat bogs account for almost 10% of the landmass. There are numerous small islands particularly on the Atlantic coast but only a minority remain populated all year round. The Shannon river at 354 km is the longest river on the islands of Ireland and Great Britain. It dominates much of the centre of the country and has a number of large lakes on its course.

Ireland's situation, in the western Atlantic and on the route of the Gulf Stream, is the dominant influence on its climate. It has a mild, temperate, moist climate.

Rainfall, carried by the prevailing westerly winds is well distributed throughout the year. Given that no part of Ireland is more than 100 km from the sea, the climate is relatively uniform throughout the country. January

Figure 2.4

and February are normally the coldest months with temperatures in the range of 4–7°C. Snow falls on occasion during the winter months but is rarely prolonged or severe. July and August are normally the warmest months with average temperatures in the range of 14–16°C. Rainfall is lowest on the east coast and highest on the west coast.

A homogenous nation?

Despite its relatively recent arrival as an independent nation, Ireland has an ancient history and rich literary, oral, and artistic traditions. The island of Ireland was ruled by Britain for approximately 600 years, much of which was marked by various uprisings and struggles for independence. Ireland is thus a comparatively new nation state, achieving partial independence from Britain in 1921 and only becoming a Republic in 1949. It is also a small country comprising some 68,890 km² with a population of 3.7 million or 1% of the population of the EU. Ireland has been a member of the United Nations since 1955 and the EU since 1973.

Over 90% of the population are Roman Catholic. The other main religious group are Protestant, including Church of Ireland (Anglican), Presbyterian and Methodist denominations. Until recently, Catholicism has played a key influencing role in Irish society. This was particularly manifest in the Catholic church's role in education, its influence on political decision-making and in broader moral values. The country is predominantly English speaking although a substantial number of people can also speak Irish (Gaeilge), the country's native tongue. However, the use of Irish as an everyday language is confined to a small minority of the population, mostly in the west and south-west of the country.

The Republic of Ireland has traditionally been quite a homogenous nation. The population is predominantly of Celtic origin and, up to recently it did not have any significant cultural and/or religious minorities. However, the period since independence has seen dramatic changes in Irish society, most notably over the last decade which has been characterised by rapid economic growth, a reversal of population decline and considerable inward migration. Thus Ireland has seen the return to the country of many of its citizens who emigrated in earlier decades and, for the first time, experienced a growth in the number of foreign nationals seeking to live and work in Ireland. The rapid pace of economic development and increasing affluence in Irish society has sparked increasing debate on economic and social issues, such as environmental concerns, racism and increasing materialism in Irish society.

Principal characteristics

Figure 2.5 and Table 2.16[1] show the relative position of the Republic of Ireland in relation to other European countries on a number of standardised items.

People

Possibly the most remarkable feature of Ireland's social and economic history was the dramatic decline in the country's population from the mid-1800s, with a decrease from over 6 million in 1841 to some 3.5 million in 1991. The country's current population density of about 53 people per km² represents just over half of what it was in the early 1840s, when the whole island had an estimated population of over 8 million. The "great famine" of 1845–1848, stemming from disease among the staple potato crop, saw between 1 and 2 million die and another 2 million emigrate. This spate of emigration continued for over a century and apart from the post famine period was also particularly high in the 1950s, with over 2% of the total population leaving the country in some years. This situation has now significantly reversed and the country is experiencing significant levels of net immigration (Figure 2.6).

Looking at recent trends we find that Ireland's population remained effectively static through the 1980s but started to increase towards the end of the decade and over the 1990s. However, Ireland's population of approximately 3.7 million people remains the second lowest in the EU. Ireland also has a relatively young population but, as in other EU member states, the number of children is falling due to a somewhat declining birth rate. However, the birth rate remains above the EU average.

---

[1] All statistics from Annual *Eurostat* Yearbooks published by the Office for Official Publications of the European Communities, Luxemburg. Most data for this chapter from *Eurostat Yearbook 2002: The Statistical Guide to Europe Data 1990–2000, 1987–1997*. Brussels: Office for Official Publications of the European Communities. Other data from previous yearbooks.

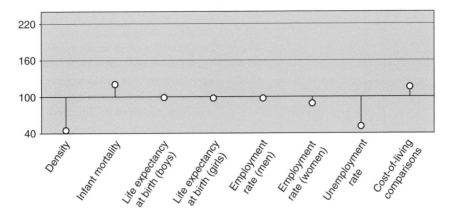

Figure 2.5   Principal characteristics in relation to EU-15 = 100

Table 2.16   Underlying table for "Principal characteristics in relation to EU-15"

	EU-15	IRL*	Relation (IRL/EU-15) × 100
Density (inhabitants per km²) Year: 1997	117	53	45.3
Infant mortality (per thousand live birth) Year: 2000	4.9	5.9	120.4
Life expectancy at birth (boys; years) Year: 1999	74.9	73.9	98.7
Life expectancy at birth (girls; years) Year: 1999	81.2	79.1	97.4
Employment rate (men; %)	70	68	97
Employment rate (women; %) Year: 1997	50	45	89
Unemployment rate (%) Year: 2000	8	4	51
Cost-of-living comparisons (total value; B = 100**) Year: 2000	B = 100	116	116

All data from Eurostat.
* IRL = Ireland.
** Based on cost-of-living in capital city of each country, with Brussels = 100.

Table 2.17   Population by age (% of total population)

Age (years)	Ireland		EU-15 2000
	1987	2000	
<15	29	22	17
15–24	17	17	12
25–49	31	35	37
50–64	12	14	17
65–79	9	9	13
>80	2	2.5	3.7

population. Between 1981 and 1996, the Irish population aged nearly 3 years leading to an average age of 33.6 in 1996 compared with 30.8 in 1981 (CSO, 1998). This is unlikely to have any impact in the short term but, as the average age of the working-age population moves closer to the 50s, this will have significant implications for HR, particularly in terms of succession planning, training/retraining, rewards and so forth. Furthermore, as the population ages, and should the birth rate continue to fall, the dependency ratio will increase, as greater numbers depend on the shrinking economically active cohort. It appears however, that a significant ageing (or "greying") of Ireland's workforce will not occur for at least another 20 years (Table 2.17).

In the Republic of Ireland, the average number of people per household is 3.3. As in the UK this figure has been shrinking over recent decades: the equivalent figure in 1981 was 3.6. We can also cite similar reasons in explaining this trend: more people are now living on their own (20% in 1991 as opposed to 17% in 1981). However, the numbers living alone remains significantly smaller than in the UK. Ireland has also

The Irish workforce will continue to expand in the medium term as those currently of school-going age enter the labour market. However, as in many other EU countries, there is evidence of some ageing of the

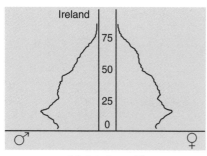

All data from (1)

Population by gender 1901–1996

Total population (persons)

Year	Total	Males	Females
1901	3,221,823	1,610,085	1,611,738
1911	3,139,688	1,589,509	1,550,179
1926	2,971,992	1,506,889	1,465,103
1936	2,968,420	1,520,454	1,447,966
1946	2,955,107	1,494,877	1,460,230
1951	2,960,593	1,506,597	1,453,996
1961	2,818,341	1,416,549	1,401,792
1971	2,978,248	1,495,760	1,482,488
1981	3,443,405	1,729,354	1,714,051
1991	3,525,719	1,753,418	1,772,301
1996	3,626,087	1,800,232	1,825,855

Figure 2.6   Population by gender 1997 (% of total population). *Source*: Central Statistics Office

seen an increase in the number of couples without children (up from 130,000 in 1981 to 145,000 in 1991) and in the number of single parents. In 1981, Ireland had 77,000 single women with children but by 1991 this figure had increased by 22% to 94,000.

Economy

Ireland is a classic example of a small open economy which is heavily export dependent (exports account for over 60% of GNP). Ireland was among the first of a group of EU member states to join the Economic and Monetary Union (EMU) in January 1999. Ireland is also a late developing economy with most industrial activity occurring since the 1960s.

Although experiencing initial development immediately after the independence period and during the 1960s, the Irish economy has struggled for much of its existence. Indeed by the mid-1980s the country had become locked in deep recession and faced effective economic bankruptcy. However, since then, the country has undergone a remarkable economic transformation and over

the past decade is one of the world's most successful and fastest growing economies. Expansive growth in the Irish economy over recent years continues apace. Real GDP growth rates since 1994 have averaged out at 9% a year (10% in 1998) or almost four times the EU average (Economist Intelligence Unit, 1999). Growth in the Irish economy has been fuelled by a very rapid growth in exports of goods and services. The numbers at work are growing by at least 4% a year (5.5% in 1998) and the standardised unemployment rate has fallen below the EU average (10%) and currently stands at less than 6% (and falling), which is the lowest it has been since 1979. Industrial production in Ireland has been impressively high when compared to other EU countries. The bulk of total manufacturing production, which increased by 17% between 1997 and 1998, can be attributed to the strong performance of a small number of high technology sectors dominated by foreign multinationals, particularly pharmaceuticals (production almost doubled between 1996 and 1997), electrical engineering, office equipment and the production of data processing machinery including computer components. Traditional indigenous sector growth is more modest, but still strong at approximately 4% in 1998.

Over the decade of the 1990s Irish Government Debt has fallen significantly: public debt as a share of GNP has fallen from 110% in 1988 to 66% in 1997 (Tansey, 1998).

In terms of international competitiveness, the World Competitiveness Yearbook 2002, ranks Ireland as the 10th most competitive world economy (down from 7th in 2001 and 5th in 2000). This fall is partially explained by Ireland's exposure to the technology sector and to international trade, which suffered severe setbacks over the recent past.

Despite strong growth in output and employment during the 1990s, inflation generally remained below the EU average. However, the recent past has seen a sharp and significant increase in Irish inflation and the prospect of high levels of wage increases, combined with spiralling property prices, may fuel inflationary pressures

Table 2.18   Gross domestic product (at market prices, in million Ecu/EU)

	1991	1994	1997	2000
EU-15	5,779,473	6,334,523	7,287,921	8,524,371
Ireland	38,648	46,148	70,608	103,470
UK	836,147	878,109	1,171,548	1,547,903

even more and thus represent a major threat to the Irish economy's recent success. We have also seen that unemployment has fallen significantly in recent years, with skill shortages in many sectors of the economy. Again the recent economic downturn has eased these shortages. However, in the longer term some commentators fear that decreased labour supply may arrest Ireland's economic growth and, particularly, its capacity to attract foreign direct investment (FDI) (see Tansey, 1998).

A key result of these developments is that Ireland can no longer be ranked as one of the poorest countries in the EU. As we can see from Table 2.19, Ireland has effectively caught up with many of its hitherto richer European counterparts. This table also demonstrates that the traditionally significant income gap between Ireland and the UK effectively disappeared.

Using 2000 figures, we find that the overall cost-of-living in Ireland is expensive (Table 2.20). This is particularly the case in relation to utilities and alcohol/tobacco.

Table 2.19 GDP per capita in selected countries 1961–1997*

Year	Ireland	Britain	Germany	Spain	USA
1961–1970	60.5	112.5	118.4	67	171
1971–1980	62	100.5	116	74	149
1981–1990	66	100	116	71	143
1991	76	97	105	79	137
1992	79.5	98	108	77	136
1993	83	99	108	78	141.5
1994	88	98	110	76	142
1995	95	98	109	76	140
1996e	101	99	109	77	141
1997p	104	100	109	77	140

(* GDP per capita with EU average = 100; e = estimated; p = projected).
Source: Tansey (1998) (based on Eurstat and Directorate General II, EU Commission data).

Legal, institutional and political environment

Political and judicial system

The Irish political system, a parliamentary democracy, is prescribed by the Constitution of 1937 (*Bunreacht Na hEireann*) which provides for a national parliament, defines the structure of the courts and details the fundamental rights of Irish citizens. The constitution can only be altered with the approval of the people through a referendum.

Ireland's bicameral Parliament (*Oireachtas*) consists of a directly elected President and two houses: *Dail Eireann* (lower house) and *Seanad Eireann* (upper house). The current President is Mary McAleese. The Presidency, a non-political position, is largely a figure-head position. Mary McAleese is Ireland's second female President, succeeding Mary Robinson who was elected to the post in 1991. Effective political power rests with *Dail Eireann* (lower house) and the office of *Taoiseach* (Prime Minister). Elections must be held at least once every 5 years and take place under a system of proportional representation.

Ireland's two major political parties, *Fianna Fail* and *Fine Gael*, are based on divisions between parties which supported and opposed the Anglo-Irish Treaty of 1921: *Fianna Fail* opposing the Treaty and *Fine Gael* a descendant of the party supporting the Treaty. By and large the major political parties in Ireland are quite centrist in orientation. Ireland has had a remarkably stable political system since the early turmoil of the 1920s. The centrist *Fianna Fail* party has been the dominant power in Irish political life. However, it last formed a single party Government in 1977 and since then the country has been governed by coalitions or minority governments led by either *Fianna Fail* or *Fine Gael*.

Table 2.20   Cost-of-living comparisons 2002: Dublin compared to EU (Brussels = 100)

Food and non-alcoholic beverages	Clothing and footwear	Housing, electricity, water, gas, fuels	Furnishing, household equipment and maintenance	Health
105	66	162	112	114
Transport	Recreation and culture	Education	Alcohol and tobacco	Communications
116	93	75	189	85
Hotels, cafes and restaurants	Miscellaneous		*Total*	*Total exc. rents*
116	88		116	103

Table 2.21   Working days lost in all industry due to labour disputes (per 1000 employees)

	1986	1987	1988	1989	1990	1991	1992	1993	1994	1995
EU-15	–	–	226	170	153	99	118	73	114	–
Ireland	30	72	224	100	266	62	177	327	378	133
Germany	1	1	2	4	15	6	60	3	9	8
UK	90	164	166	182	83	34	24	30	13	19

Table 2.22   Working days lost in manufacturing industry due to labour disputes (per 1000 employees)

	1986	1987	1988	1989	1990	1991	1992	1993	1994	1995	1996
EU-15	–	–	226	157	179	143	118	113	105	–	–
Ireland	189	450	237	98	735	59	42	41	31	66	24
Germany	2	3	4	6	10	13	24	7	15	–	–
UK	185	125	280	138	178	43	19	25	12	13	18

Table 2.23   Persons in employment (million)

	1987	1988	1989	1990	1991	1992	1993	1994	1995	1996	1997
Ireland	1.08	1.09	1.095	1.13	1.13	1.15	1.155	1.21	1.26	1.31	1.37
UK	24.8	25.7	26.6	26.8	26.2	25.8	25.5	25.7	25.9	26.2	26.6
EU-15	–	–	–	–	–	–	–	–	–	149.1	150.1

The current Government consists of a centrist/right wing coalition of *Fianna Fail* and the Progressive Democrats. The *Taoiseach* is Bertie Ahern, leader of Fianna Fail.

Judicial authority in Ireland is vested in the Supreme Court, the High Court, a Court of Criminal Appeal, a Central Criminal Court, Circuit Courts and District Courts. The Supreme Court is the court of final appeal and has the power to play a key role in upholding and interpreting the Constitution. Judges are appointed by the president on the recommendation of the Government.

Labour disputes

As we can see in Tables 2.21 and 2.22, the period since the late 1980s has seen an increase in labour disputes. This increase is related to the buoyancy in economic activity and increased worker demands for improvements in pay. Much of this increase can be attributed to a small number of large-scale disputes, which – because of the relatively small scale of the Irish labour force – can add significantly to the level of days lost due to strike activity in any one year. The disproportional impact of one or two large disputes thus helps explain the large

year on year fluctuations in dispute activity in Ireland. For example, one large dispute such as those affecting a large company (e.g. Waterford Crystal in 1990) or a large occupational group (e.g. Nurses in 1999) impacts dramatically on Irish strike figures in that particular year. Over recent years, we have seen an increase in strike activity in the public sector and some decrease in the private sector (particularly in relation to working days lost).

Labour market

By EU standards, Ireland's employed labour force is extremely small with numbers employed accounting for just less than 1% of the EU total. However, the Irish labour market is currently a very dynamic one which, in recent years, has been primarily characterised by significant growth in the number of labour market entrants and a huge increase in demand for labour. Between 1980 and 1996, Irish non-agricultural employment growth of 26% exceeded that of the EU (7%) and the US (15%) (Table 2.23).

The transformation from an effectively stagnant and under-developed economy in the late 1950s to one characterised by industrial expansion and rapid economic growth, has wrought extensive change in employment

Table 2.24 Persons in employment in different sectors (thousand)

	1987	1989	1991	1993	1995	1997	2000
Industry	310	314	328	313	349	391	476
Agriculture	170	169	158	151	151	149	130
Services	598	609	644	688	757	829	1050

Table 2.25 Unemployment rate (%)

1987	1990	1993	1996	1998	1999	2000
17	13	16	12	8	6	4

Table 2.26 Unemployment rates in Ireland, UK and EU-15, 2000

	Ireland	UK	EU-15
Women unemployed (%)	4	5	10
Men unemployed (%)	4	6	7
Long-term unemployment (% of all unemployed, 1997 figures only)	57	39	49

Table 2.27 Average hourly labour costs (manual and non-manual workers) in total industry. Ecu

	1990	1992	1994	1996
Ireland	11.64	12.8	13.23	13.90
UK	12.2	13.11	13.75	13.93
Germany	20.08	23.14	26.14	26.5
Portugal	3.57	5.55	5.45	6.06
EU-15	–	17.68	19.05	20.10

All data from Eurostat.

Table 2.28 Structure of labour costs (%) in total industry (1996)

	Direct cost	Indirect cost	Social security as part of indirect cost
Ireland	83	17	14
Germany	74	26	24
Portugal	75	25	20
UK	84*	16*	13
EU-15	75	25	23

* 1995 figures only.

Table 2.29 Number of hours usually worked per week: full-time employees

	1993	1997
EU-15	–	42.1
Ireland	44	43.2
Germany		41.7
UK	44.5	44.9

Source: Labour Force Survey results, 1997: Eurostat.

structure. Possibly, the most significant long-term trend in this regard is the progressive fall in the numbers working in agriculture. We have also seen a decline in some of Ireland's traditional industries and a dramatic rise in employment in the service sector, particularly private services. Of the current labour force of 1.6 million people, approximately 8% are employed in agriculture, 29% are employed in industry and the remaining 63% are employed in services (Table 2.24).

Over recent years, the largest share of employment creation was accounted for by growth in the services sector. However, employment growth in manufacturing and construction sectors has also remained strong. Unemployment, a traditional problem in the Irish economy and the source of large scale emigration from the country over many decades, has also fallen significantly in recent years (from 18% in 1986 to just over 4% in 2000) and skill shortages have emerged in some sectors of the economy (Table 2.25). Indeed, a number of commentators fear that decreased labour supply may arrest Ireland's economic growth and, particularly, its capacity to attract FDI.

As noted earlier, unemployment levels in Ireland have continued to fall rapidly and are now (2002) just over 5%. Unemployment rates for men and women are quite similar and below the EU average (Table 2.26).

Average hourly labour costs in Ireland are similar to those prevailing in the UK and are well below the EU average (Table 2.27). However, Irish labour costs are generally above those in less developed EU countries, especially Greece and Portugal.

Indirect labour costs in Ireland are well below the EU average and are similar, though slightly above, UK levels (Tables 2.28 and 2.29). As in the UK, the Irish tend to work longer hours than the average in the EU-15.

Education system

Education in Ireland is primarily based on a free state school system and is compulsory for all children between 6 and 15 years of age. Three distinct levels of schooling exist within the Irish educational system: primary level, post-primary/secondary level and tertiary or third level education. Primary education covers a period of 8 years (4–12) and is typically provided by national schools, which are state-aided parish denominational schools established under diocesan patronage. Pupils normally transfer to post-primary/secondary education at the age of 12 and as a matter of course (there are no state examinations at this level). As in the UK, pre-primary education is poorly developed in Ireland and is largely dependent on private sector provision.

A distinctive feature of the Irish educational system remains that, while the State bears the bulk of the cost of running schools, the vast majority of both primary and second level schools are denominational. At primary level this is almost universal, while at second level, there are secondary schools which are privately owned (in the main by religious orders), and vocational, community and comprehensive schools which are publicly owned. Today, three in every five students attend secondary schools, only one in four attend vocational schools, and one in seven attend a comprehensive or community school. Two state examinations exist at second level: the Junior Certificate which is taken after 3 years of study and, in general, marks the end of compulsory schooling, and the Leaving Certificate (upper secondary/senior cycle) which is typically completed 2 years later. Traditionally, second level education was largely characterised as classical-academic in orientation and was generally intended to prepare students for third level education and white collar occupations. Vocational schools were seen to provide a more technically oriented education and practical training in preparation for subsequent employment. However, economic growth in the 1970s and 1980s highlighted the necessity to match education with the needs of the economy and we have witnessed some movement away from the traditional perspective on education, to a more applied focus in second level education.

Provision of public sector education at third level in Ireland is divided between three institutional sectors: (a) Higher Education Authority (HEA) Institutions comprising the Universities, National College of Art

and Design, and the National College of Surgeons; (b) Vocational Colleges and Institutes of Technology and (c) the Teacher Training Colleges. Arts, natural science, commerce/business and engineering are the most popular courses at undergraduate level, while post-graduate activity centres around the sciences. The distribution of students in full-time third level education is represented in Table 2.30.

Participation at third level is determined by a points system, based on Leaving Certificate examination results and, while entry to some programmes of study is more difficult in terms of the number of points required, in general, demand for third level education outstrips the supply of places available at the various third level institutions. The total number of full-time students at third level has increased significantly over the last number of years (in excess of 40% since 1990).

In evaluating participation rates in full-time education, it is evident that, while participation is virtually complete in the 5–14 year age group, outside of compulsory schooling, Ireland rates relatively poorly at the higher levels of educational attainment, particularly in completion figures for upper secondary education (see Tables 2.31 and 2.32).

A combination of limited third level places and, until 1996, the prohibitive costs associated with attending third level institutions (most notably tuition fees which have now been abolished), may partly explain Ireland's lower representation at third level education, while the

Table 2.30   Distribution of students in third level education

Institution	Full-time enrolments	Part-time enrolments
State aided		
Universities	58,090	8426
Teacher Training Colleges	547	
Technological Colleges	41,000	12,561
National College of Industrial Relations	567	1808
Aided by other state departments	758	
Non-aided		
Religious Institutions	1254	
Royal College of Surgeons in Ireland	1003	
Other	4282	
Total	**107,501**	**22,795**
of which aided by State	100,204	

Source: Department of Education Statistical Report 1996/1997.

Table 2.31   Percentage of population aged 25–29 completing upper secondary education, 2000 (%)

	Total (25–59)	25–29	30–34	35–39	40–44	45–49	50–54	55–59	60–64
EU-15 (women and men)	64	76	73	70	66	61	55	52	64
Ireland (women and men)	49	69	62	57	50	39	36	32	27
UK (women and men)	81	90	89	86	83	79	72	64	67
EU-15 (women)	61	77	73	70	64	58	50	45	37
Ireland (women)	53	73	67	61	52	42	39	34	28
UK (women)	77	90	88	85	79	74	65	56	56

Table 2.32   Percentage of the labour force 25–64 years of age by the highest completed level of education (1995)

	Early childhood, primary and lower secondary education	Upper secondary education	Non-university tertiary education	University-level education	Total
North America					
Canada	19	29	32	19	100
US	11	52	9	28	100
Pacific Area					
Australia	42	31	12	16	100
Korea	39	41	x	20	100
New Zealand	36	37	16	12	100
European Union					
Austria	24	66	2	7	100
Belgium	37	32	17	14	100
Denmark	33	44	7	16	100
Finland	30	47	10	13	100
France	25	54	9	12	100
Germany	12	62	11	15	100
Greece	52	26	8	15	100
Ireland	**45**	**29**	**12**	**13**	**100**
Italy	56	33	x	11	100
Luxembourg	63	21	x	16	100
Netherlands	31	43	a	27	100
Portugal	76	10	4	9	100
Spain	64	15	6	16	100
Sweden	24	47	14	15	100
UK	19	57	10	14	100
Other OECD countries					
Czech Republic	12	76	x	12	100
Norway	15	53	12	20	100
Poland	21	64	4	12	100
Switzerland	15	61	14	10	100
Turkey	76	15	a	9	100
Mean	**35**	**42**	**10**	**15**	**100**

Source: OECD Database.

relatively young minimum school leaving age (15 years) might explain lower showings at second level. It must also be recognised that free second level education was only introduced in Ireland 32 years ago and thus many of the individuals represented in the figures here may not have been able to avail of either second or third level educational opportunities. However, it is also clear that participation rates for younger people are higher than ever before and continue to increase. In comparison with those who have completed third level education in the OECD countries, it would appear that Ireland fares positively against many of her EU counterparts. Here again there is evidence of increased participation among the younger age categories.

The link between education and employment is well documented, where the attainment of educational qualifications critically impacts upon one's ability to successfully gain and retain employment. The latest OECD report on education (1998) argues that many of the benefits of education cannot be quantified and that social cohesion, rather than narrow economic gain, is the greatest prize for societies in which all citizens use learning to become more effective participants in democratic, civil and economic processes (see Heraty, 1998). Indicators from the OCED (1998) Education report associate higher levels of education with higher earnings, a lower chance of unemployment and more skills that yield social advantage. This link is evidenced in the most recent Irish labour force survey, which suggest that individuals who possess no post-primary qualification are six times more likely to be unemployed than are those with a third level qualification. In the case of those who do find employment, the remuneration they receive is very often far lower than those with higher qualifications. Education and earnings are thus positively linked, and so the earnings advantage of increased education would appear to outweigh the costs of acquiring it.

REFERENCES

Central Statistics Office (CSO) *Labour Market Surveys 1970–1998*. Dublin: CSO.

Eurostat Yearbook (2002) *The Statistical Guide to Europe Data 1990–2000*. Brussels: Office for Official Publications of the European Communities. Other data from previous yearbooks.

Economist Intelligence Unit (EIU) (1999) *Country Profile: Ireland*. London: Economist Intelligence Unit.

Economist, The (1988) A Survey of the Republic of Ireland. Poorest of the Rich. *The Economist*, 306(7533): 1–26.

Economist, The (1997) Green is Good – Advantages of Ireland as a Host For DFI. *The Economist*, 343(8017): 21–24.

Eurostat, Statistical Office of the European Communities (eds.) (2002) *Eurostat Yearbook 2002, The Statistical Eye on Europe 1990–2000*, Office for Official Publications of *the European Communities, Luxembourg*.

Heraty, N. (1998) The Irish labour market in perspective. In: Gunnigle, P. (ed.), *The Irish Employee Recruitment Handbook: Finding and Keeping a High Quality Workforce*. Dublin: Oak Tree Press.

OECD (1998) *Education at a Glance*. Paris: OECD.

Tansey, P. (1998) *Ireland at Work: Economic Growth and the Labour Market 1987–1997*. Dublin: Oak Tree Press.

HRM IN THE UNITED KINGDOM AND THE REPUBLIC OF IRELAND

HISTORICAL BACKGROUND

A comparison of HRM in the UK and Ireland should be revealing for a number of reasons. Given that Ireland only achieved independence from the UK in 1921 and inherited much of the UK's legal tradition, public service structures and managerial conventions, it is inevitable that the evolution of HRM there paralleled, in part at least, developments in the UK.

For many years the two countries' labour markets have also been closely linked. This primarily involved labour flows from Ireland to the UK, particularly from the mid-nineteenth century to the early 1990s. More recently we have seen a considerable levelling off in labour flows between the countries, as economic activity in Ireland increased and employment opportunities there grew dramatically. Other important aspects of human resource (HR) which link both countries include the fact, that a number of UK-based trade unions operate in Ireland, while the two countries also share the same professional human resource management (HRM) body – the *Chartered Institute of Personnel and Development* (CIPD).

On the other hand, there are important contrasts. While both countries joined the European Economic Community at the same time, Ireland has adopted a stance more favourable to EU integration than its larger neighbour, a fact most evident in Ireland's acceptance of the Euro and the UK's resistance to it. Over the past 20 years or so, industrial relations in the two countries have followed somewhat different trajectories. While Ireland embraced a form of national social partnership agreements, as a means of promoting economic development, the UK effectively jettisoned this approach in favour of a return to enterprise-level collective bargaining.

Despite these differences, however, trade union density has declined significantly in both countries to the extent that there are now large tracts of the private sector that are overwhelmingly non-union in both jurisdictions.

THE HR FUNCTION AND ITS INVOLVEMENT IN STRATEGY

In tracing the development of the HRM function in the UK and Ireland from the 1950s to the early 1980s we note that HRM practice progressively conformed to what has been called the "pluralist tradition". This approach is grounded in the acceptance that a conflict of interests exists between management and labour, and a reliance on collective bargaining as the primary means of resolving it. Industrial relations were the main HR activity and priority of HR practitioners, whose role incorporated much workplace bargaining with trade union representatives. The key goal was industrial peace and this provided emergent HR (then mostly called "personnel") departments and practitioners with a more central management role, albeit a largely reactive one.

We have of course seen this pluralist model come under increasing challenge in recent decades. The stimuli for this change are found in most developed economies and stem primarily from increased competitive pressures on organisations, coupled with particular social changes. Developments in the UK and Ireland have witnessed major changes in approaches to workforce management, most notably manifest in declining union density and influence, greater employer/enterprise-level autonomy in HRM and significant organisational restructuring. When these developments are combined with labour market changes such as a general decrease in unemployment in the UK and Ireland and greater use of atypical employment forms, we find that HRM, long viewed as a lower order management/strategic concern, has become an area of considerable strategic concern, with much discussion about its potential to affect bottom-line performance.

The increased significance of HRM is reflected in the increasing professionalism of the HR function in both the UK and Ireland. In July 2000, the Institute for Professional Development (IPD) was granted charter status in recognition of its professionalism and its distinctive knowledge and competence. The CIPD, as it is now known, is Europe's largest professional body representing those who specialise in the management and development of people. The unique situation exists

whereby members in both countries are covered by this one organisation. The CIPD is dedicated to promoting best practice HRM and its members are committed to a Code of Professional Conduct. Membership has been steadily growing in both countries, with a combined membership currently of 110,000. The Republic of Ireland has experienced a massive 360% growth in membership since 1990. Most new members gain their professional qualification via the standardised programme run by colleges and universities across the UK and Ireland. The existence and operational practices of this professional body are consequently a significant factor in shaping the development and professionalisation of HRM practice in both countries.

A critical tenet of much recent HRM literature is the extent to which HR represents a decisive strategic issue for organisations. It is argued that organisations need to integrate HR considerations in their strategic decision-making and develop comprehensive and complementary Personnel/HR policies that support business strategy (see e.g. Beer et al., 1984; Fombrun et al., 1984). The Cranet findings indicate that in the UK senior HR specialists have a seat on the board of directors (or the equivalent body in the public sector) in just half of the organisations surveyed (see Table 2.33). The percentage is almost exactly the same as a decade ago. Data from the UK's workplace employee relations' survey, which asked individuals at workplace level to estimate whether their most senior HR specialist was so represented, indicate a similar picture (Cully et al., 1999). The situation is much the same in Ireland, where the percentage, has also remained relatively static over the decade at roughly 50%.

It is difficult to see how the HR function could be playing a more strategic role when in many cases it remains un-represented on the main decision-making forum of the organisation. However, it could be argued that influence is exercised in different ways and through different mechanisms. In this respect our data also investigated the degree and the nature of the HR function's

Table 2.33 Senior HR specialist represented on board of directors over the last decade (% of organisations)

	UK			Ireland		
	1992	1995	1999/2000	1992	1995	1999/2000
Yes	52	54	49	53	55	49
No	48	46	51	47	45	51

Table 2.34   Stage at which personnel/HR is involved in the development of corporate strategy over the last decade (% of organisations)

	UK			Ireland		
	1992	1995	1999/2000	1992	1995	1999/2000
From the outset	53	57	54	50	56	56
Through consultation	32	29	32	31	27	32
On implementation	8	7	8	10	11	7
Not consulted	7	7	6	9	6	5

involvement in strategy development. Table 2.34 sets out the nature and level of the HR function's involvement in strategy development. In the UK only just over half of the most senior HR managers/directors are consulted from the outset on the creation of corporate strategy: almost exactly the same as a decade earlier. Again, the Irish data indicates more or less exactly the same levels. Overall, the picture emerging suggests that despite all the rhetoric, the formal position and the influence of the HR function on corporate strategy development remain somewhat mixed.

THE ROLE OF LINE MANAGEMENT IN HRM

Just as wars are too important to be left to generals, perhaps HRM, as suggested by Beer et al. (1984), is too important to be left to the HR department. The role of line management in HRM has been much discussed over the last decade (see e.g. Brewster and Söderstrom, 1994; Heraty and Morley, 1995; Legge, 1995; Brewster et al., 1997; Thornhill and Saunders, 1998; Larsen and Brewster, 2003). Clearly the most common pattern is the sharing of decision-making on HR issues between HR specialists and line management. However, differences can and do arise in the relative weight of decision-making undertaken by both stakeholders, depending upon which aspect of HRM is examined.

Table 2.35 captures an important indicator of HR policy sophistication, namely, where primary responsibility for policy decisions on key aspects of HR strategy lie. Over the decade the picture that emerges in the UK and Ireland is one of continuity rather than change in this respect. Despite the relative stability of the *primary* responsibility for decision-making, on key HRM activities, the Cranet findings indicate an overall pattern of increased line management involvement in HRM

decisions throughout the 1990s. Our data suggest that during the 1990s primary responsibility for major policy decisions on pay and benefits, recruitment and selection, training and development and industrial relations rested largely with the HR department in consultation with line management. Where increases in line management responsibility in these areas did occur, the extent of the increases appears to be limited and incremental (Mayrhofer and Brewster, 2000). Drawing on the 1999 data in the UK/Republic of Ireland comparative context, a relatively stronger line involvement in recruitment is seen in Ireland; with roughly 10% of organisations indicating that line managers have sole responsibility for recruitment and selection.

Data from the three rounds of the survey also indicate some increase in line management responsibility in operational areas of HR activity (see Table 2.36). In particular in the domain of pay and benefits, line management responsibility in Ireland has effectively doubled over the decade. A somewhat different picture can be seen in the UK, where increased line involvement appears limited to the area of recruitment and selection. In general the data show an increase in line management responsibility for core HR activities despite the fact that quite a high percentage of respondents in both countries have also indicated no change in levels of responsibility. Concomitantly, we find no evidence of complete devolution to line managers but rather the specialist HR function retains considerable input into, and responsibility for, core HRM activities.

Organisations have become leaner after a decade of downsizing, new technology has been introduced and "overhead" departments have been under pressure to prove themselves (Sparrow and Hiltrop, 1994). This has heralded an era of at least a rhetoric of outsourcing of HRM activities. This takes the form of contracting

Table 2.35 Changes in primary responsibility for major policy decisions on key aspects of HRM over the last decade (% of organisations)

	UK			Ireland		
	1992	1995	1999/2000	1992	1995	1999/2000
Responsibility for recruitment						
Line management	6	4	4	11	7	11
Line management with HR department	39	37	32	23	32	25
HR department with line management	44	46	48	50	46	42
HR department	11	12	15	16	16	21
Responsibility for training						
Line management	4	4	4	8	6	9
Line management with HR department	27	29	30	18	29	26
HR department with line management	58	57	54	60	56	49
HR department	10	10	13	14	9	15

Table 2.36 Changes in line management responsibility (% of organisations)

	UK			Ireland		
	1992	1995	1999/2000	1992	1995	1999/2000
Line management involvement with pay and benefits						
Increase	26	26	22	12	19	23
Same	66	70	73	85	75	75
Decrease	7	4	5	3	6	2
Line management involvement with recruitment and selection						
Increase	32	36	39	31	38	46
Same	60	59	55	64	57	49
Decrease	8	5	6	5	4	5
Line management involvement with training and development						
Increase	47	49	47	43	52	55
Same	45	47	47	55	44	39
Decrease	8	4	5	1	4	6
Line management involvement with industrial relations						
Increase	25	24	24	36	31	37
Same	69	71	72	63	63	59
Decrease	6	4	4	1	6	4
Line management involvement with workforce expansion/reduction						
Increase	31	32	27	25	31	32
Same	64	65	68	73	65	66
Decrease	5	3	4	1	4	2

out to suppliers, for example, using recruitment agencies, or changing individual employment contracts in order to hire people as consultants rather than employees (Richbell, 2001). All this might suggest that HR departments would also become smaller and that outsourcing of HR activities would increase. Our data shows that in the UK almost all HR departments make use of external providers. However, the size of the HR departments relative to the size of the organisation has barely changed in the last decade. In the UK, one HR staff

member now supports 76 employees, very similar to the figure a decade ago (Van Ommeren and Brewster, 2000). There is evidence from the latest round of the survey, of increased outsourcing of HRM activities by Irish organisations, with almost 50% indicating an increase in their use of external providers during the last 3 years.

The findings in this section indicate a trend towards greater strategic integration of HR policies and practices. The data show that in just under half of respondent organisations the HR department is represented on the board of directors and is actively involved in strategy formulation. This is combined with a gradual move towards devolving HR activities to line management. The challenge for the future appears to lie in sustaining a balance between strategic and technical roles, and shifting from being a provider to being an enabler in HRM, particularly in facilitating organisational change. This will most likely involve the use of core HR staff, while outsourcing appropriate activities and concurrently devolving responsibilities to the line and to employees.

RECRUITMENT AND SELECTION

Both the UK and Ireland are characterised by tight labour markets: in the UK, in 2002, the level of unemployment remained relatively unchanged from the previous year at 5%, while in Ireland it was 4.4%, up from 3.7% in April 2001 (CSO, 2002). A number of changes have taken place in both countries, in the 3 years since the last round of the survey, which have affected the state of the labour market quite significantly. Two important events – the foot-and-mouth crisis and the aftermath of "9/11" – have had similar economic repercussions in both the UK and Ireland. These include crisis in the financial markets, a fall in tourism and related activities, and an increase in unemployment. These have been particularly acute in Ireland, where, owing to the large number of US-owned multinational corporations (MNCs), redundancies have become commonplace. Despite these changes, the labour market remains a challenge for recruiters, the key areas for organisations in terms of recruitment and selection being sourcing, attracting and assessing suitable employees. It is argued that recruitment and selection decisions are the most important of all managerial decisions since

they are a prerequisite to the development of an effective workforce, while the costs of poor recruitment and selection can be significant and long-lasting (Lewis, 1984; Plumbley, 1985; Smith and Robertson, 1993). We may divide the process into two distinct phases: recruitment, which is concerned with attracting a group of potential candidates to apply for a given vacancy, and selection, the process of choosing the most suitable candidate for employment from the recruitment pool.

Perhaps the most important decision facing recruiters is whether to recruit internally, from those already employed by the organisation, or to source from the external labour market. This decision in recent years has been affected by the tight labour market. Traditionally speaking, the relative merits of an internal and external labour market focus have been seen as somewhat of a "mixed bag" by UK and Irish organisations. On the one hand, an internal labour market emphasis is regarded as cost-effective, both in terms of eliminating the need for external advertising/sourcing and also in terms of reducing the induction or settling in period, and is considered good HR practice, acting as a positive motivator for current employees. In addition, it adds credibility to employee development initiatives. On the other hand, it limits the potential range of candidates, over-reliance on it can lead to a lack of new ideas and perspectives, it has the potential to increase the importance of internal politics, and it can discourage those who are not selected. The choice between sourcing internal and external candidates is particularly important in regard to management cadres.

Table 2.37 shows the main ways in which managerial vacancies are filled by organisations in the UK and Ireland. Three notable trends are discernible from this data. First, it appears that UK organisations have a

Table 2.37   Recruitment methods: use of internal mechanisms for filling managerial vacancies (% of organisations)

	UK			Ireland		
	1992*	1995	1999/2000	1992	1995	1999/2000
Senior management		65	57		60	53
Middle management		82	78		78	69
Junior management		87	75		82	60
Total managerial only*	87	78	70	74	74	61

* This question in 1992 was not separated by different managerial levels (one category of "managerial"): S3V4a1 and S3V4b1 recoded as "internal" category. 1995/1999 figures are added together and divided by 3 for average figure as comparison.

greater propensity than their Irish counterparts to use internal sources for managerial recruitment. This might be explained by Ireland's younger demographic profile and the dramatic expansion in economic activity in Ireland in recent years. On the supply side this has led to a significant increase in new entrants into the managerial labour market, while on the demand side organisations experiencing rapid growth clearly have a need for new managerial recruits. The second important trend is the increase in the use of external sources in both countries. One reason for this may be the growing competitive pressures on organisations that may force them to identify and attract "new blood" from outside the organisation to help meet the competitive challenges facing their organisations. The final trend apparent from the data is that internal sources are more commonly used for recruiting middle and junior management than for senior management positions. It seems that in sourcing their top-level managers, organisations in both countries are increasingly looking outside their existing managerial pool.

The *Cranet-E* study also looked at the main steps organisations are taking to improve their recruitment and retention efforts. Re-training and enhanced pay and benefit packages seem to be the most common approaches. The number of organisations recruiting abroad is particularly extensive in Ireland and may reflect the tightening in the Irish labour market during the 1990s and a related employer focus on enticing some of the Irish diaspora back to the country.

Selection tools available to organisations range from the more traditional methods of interviews, application forms and references, to more sophisticated techniques such as psychometric tests and assessment centres. Storey (1992) suggests that developments in the realm of selection in the UK lend some support to those who propound the HRM thesis, where a key feature has been the increase in selection testing, designed explicitly to assess behavioural and attitudinal characteristics. Table 2.38 provides information on the use of a variety of selection methods in UK and Irish organisations.

The selection interview is arguably the most widely studied – and criticised – of all selection instruments. The available research evidence on the interview as a selection tool is far from favourable. Among the common criticisms are that it lacks reliability and predictive validity, and that interviewers are prone to inaccurate recollection, making "snap" judgements and subject to "halo and horns" effects (Plumbley, 1985). Despite these criticisms, the interview continues to be widely used by Irish and UK organisations, being the third most popular selection tool (behind reference checking and application forms) among the organisations studied. In 1999, almost 90% of respondents in Irish organisations reported using the interview, whether one-to-one or panel. The survey findings indicate that the panel interview is a more commonly used selection tool in Irish organisations than in its EU counterparts, with 54% using this type of interview, compared with the EU average of 21%.

The reliability and validity of application forms, as a discrete selection tool, have similarly been tested, and it is widely held that they are open to misinterpretation, particularly in respect of their potential for allowing applicants to portray a false persona (Muchinski, 1986). Our findings indicate that approximately six in every ten organisations use application forms for all appointments. References feature as the most popular selection tool, despite the fact that their predictive ability is low (about 0.13 against a perfect prediction of 1.0: Smith and Robertson, 1993). In 1999/2000, references were used by almost three-quarters of both UK and Irish organisations for all appointments. Evidence from all three rounds of the survey demonstrates considerable reliance on references as a selection tool by Irish organisations, notwithstanding the criticisms expressed in the literature.

Turning to what might be seen as more sophisticated selection tools, many commentators support the use of assessment centres (which typically have a prediction rate of 0.6) and psychometric testing (with a prediction range of between 0.3 and 0.6) as consistently more valid behaviour predictors, which are ideally suited as a pre-selection device (see e.g. Muchinsky, 1986; Terpstra, 1996). The use of these techniques has traditionally been low both in the UK (Robertson and Makin, 1986) and Ireland (McMahon, 1988), and the survey findings show little change in this pattern. However, the diffusion of such techniques is somewhat higher among UK organisations, for all appointments, most particularly with respect to psychometric testing. With regard to assessment centres, 27% of UK organisations and 13% of Irish organisations used this method for some appointments. The data suggest that the application form, the interview (mostly on a one-to-one basis) and reference checks remain the most commonly used selection methods in both the UK and Ireland.

Table 2.38   Selection methods: use of different methods for every or most appointments (% of organisations)

	UK			Ireland		
	1992*	1995	1999/2000	1992*	1995	1999/2000
Interview panel						
Every appointment	71	29	38	86	44	54
Most appointments		20	16		28	19
Some appointments			20			115
One-to-one interviews						
Every appointment	N/I	42	43	N/I	36	35
Most appointments		19	17		13	14
Some appointments			13			17
Application forms						
Every appointment	96	70	67	91	61	57
Most appointments		19	17		23	17
Some appointments			8			13
Psychometric testing						
Every appointment	45	5	7	29	4	4
Most appointments		12	10		11	7
Some appointments			34			31
Assessment centre						
Every appointment	18		1	7	3	0
Most appointments		3	6		12	1
Some appointments			25			12
Graphology						
Every appointment		1		1	3	1
Most appointments					2	
Some appointments						1
References						
Every appointment	92	73	79	91	73	75
Most appointments		17	11		20	15
Some appointments			5			6

* This question in 1992 asked which are *regularly* used (so compare this figure to "Every, Most" and "Some" appointments). N/I = category not included.

TRAINING AND DEVELOPMENT

An organisation's employees are increasingly considered as essential competitive resources which, if developed effectively, will contribute significantly to the achievement of strategic business goals (Beaumont, 1993). Traditionally, competitiveness was achieved through financial efficiency, marketing capability or technological innovation (Heraty and Morley, 1997). The various environmental changes faced by organisations in recent years, including globalisation and the rapid growth in the use of information technology, have produced an increased focus on training and development in both the literature and practice of HRM. According to Garavan et al. (1995) failure to acknowledge that employee training and development is a key factor in establishing and maintaining the effectiveness of the organisation will inevitably damage its productivity and competitiveness, and consequently its future success.

One measure of training and development activity is the amount of money spent on it. However, this measure is problematic, partly because organisations have differing interpretations of what constitutes training expenditure and those reported expenditures can be difficult to interpret (Morley et al., 2001). Nevertheless the evidence from the Cranet survey (Table 2.39) indicates that two-thirds of respondent organisations in the UK and Ireland invest between 1% and 5% of their annual wage bill in training and development. More significantly, there has been a substantial rise since 1992 in organisations reporting a spend of between 3% and 10%.

Irish organisations tend to spend proportionately more on training and development than their UK counterparts. In 1995, the Irish organisations studied were spending an average of 4% of annual salaries on training. However, by 1999/2000, their levels of investments had almost levelled out, with the UK being only marginally higher (3%).

The nature and extent of the changes that have taken place in the level of spending on training are by no means clear-cut. The trend is towards an increase in total training expenditure. This is highlighted by the fact that the percentage of those indicating that they spend less than 1% on training has fallen significantly in both the UK and Ireland over the last decade. Organisations in the service sector, in UK and Ireland, tend to allocate a more generous budget to training and development. For instance, in 1999, UK organisations in financial services spent 4% of annual salaries on training. In Ireland, organisations in "other services" spent up to 5%. This probably reflects the extent of development in the Irish economy, which now hosts a large number of high-technology firms.

A feature of expenditure on training and development in the UK and Ireland illustrated by the data, is that it is distributed unequally across employee grades. Indeed, research consistently shows that managers and professionals receive on average 5 days' training per year compared with 3 days for clerical and manual

employees. This finding highlights the fact that in UK, companies HR development priorities are set at the top of the organisation, so that people at the top benefit more widely from investments in training and development. Such a trend runs counter to the premise that customer-facing employees, who are often at the bottom of the organisational structure, are critical to organisation success. The conclusion has to be that a gap exists between theory and practice and that organisations in the UK are relatively more generous about investing in their top people. In Ireland, the difference between upper and lower levels is less marked (see Table 2.40).

Given the important role accorded to the training and development of employees in achieving organisational goals, the data revealed in the Cranet survey raises the question as to why other EU counties invest more heavily than Ireland in training and development. Comparing the EU average for the number of days' training received by professional/technical staff to Ireland's data, we see that Ireland has the lowest number for both professional/ technical and clerical staff (5% and 3% respectively, with the EU average at 6% and 4%, respectively). In addition to this, almost one-third of Irish respondents indicated that they spend less than 2% on training. This analysis is further reinforced by the survey results, revealing that the proportion of days' training is also relatively low in relation to the importance attached to training and development in the literature. This appears to be especially the case in relation to management categories.

Data from the survey suggest that Irish organisations spend more on training and development than their UK counterparts. They also tend to spread their training more equally among the various grades of employees. However, UK organisations appear to be more thorough in their use of diagnostic tools. The Cranet survey shows that 83% of UK organisations monitor the effectiveness of the training they provide, while only 72% do so in Ireland. It is interesting

Table 2.39 Proportion of annual wage bill spent on training and development

(%)	UK			Ireland		
	1992	1995	1999	1992	1995	1999
<1	21	17	7	22	19	8
1–1.9	29	33	32	31	22	24
2–2.9	20	20	23	18	23	24
3–4.9	16	15	21	14	16	21
5–9.9	11	11	13	14	13	18
>10	4	3	4	1	7	3

Table 2.40 Mean number of training days received by staff category

	UK			Ireland		
	1992	1995	1999/2000	1992	1995	1999/2000
Management	5	4	5	6	5	5
Professional/technical	5	4	5	6	5	5
Clerical	3	3	3	3	3	3
Manual	3	2	3	4	3	4

to draw the parallel between the results on "systematic analysis of training needs" (UK: 82%, IRL: 73%) and the "monitoring of training effectiveness" (UK: 83%, IRL: 72%), which are very similar. The conclusion must be that although Irish organisations appear more generous in their training expenditure, UK organisations are more scrupulous in identifying training needs and monitoring results.

PERFORMANCE AND REWARD MANAGEMENT

The management of remuneration, it is argued, is a necessary condition of successful management of the employment relationship. The rationale for this appears to lie in the traditional notion of pay as the indicator of an individual's worth to an organisation. It is widely maintained that the management of rewards and performance needs to be consistent, and there should be some degree of synergy between the two if they are to achieve improvements in organisational productivity and performance. As far as reward management is concerned, recent developments in the HRM literature on organisational systems and structures point towards the word "pay" being replaced by the word "reward" (Armstrong, 2001). This indicates a much broader approach to the issue of remuneration. An organisation's reward system is a powerful indicator of its approach to workforce management (Gunnigle et al., 1997). Constituent elements of the reward package include both financial and non-financial benefits. The financial element comprises basic pay, additional pay and indirect pay (including pensions). Non-financial rewards focus on an individual's need for recognition, personal development and achievement.

Significant pay differentials still exist. For example, in the UK, men's incomes outstrip those of women at all ages, particularly at the peak average income which is nearly twice as high for men as for women (Office for National Statistics, 2000). Pay differentials are also marked between different grades of staff, most notably between management and manual employees. In Ireland, despite the fact that the Anti-Discrimination Pay Act came into force in 1974, women earn on average only 85% of men's wages (Coughlan, 2002). The introduction of a minimum wage, which came into effect in 1999 in the UK and in 2000 in Ireland, much later than similar schemes in many other European countries, has made very little difference to this pattern. (Since the UK, unlike many other countries, including Ireland, had no national agreement during the 1990s to balance employment against wage restraint, the "employees share" of GDP remained broadly constant.)

Direct financial rewards – including basic pay and premium elements such as incentive pay, overtime, allowances and bonuses – form the largest proportion of the reward package for employees in the UK and Ireland. In 1998, in the UK, 14% of gross average weekly earnings of male manual employees and 3% of male non-manual employees were made up of overtime alone, demonstrating also the degree of potential variability in a person's earnings. Indirect rewards, such as a pension scheme, company car, educational support, shares, childcare provision, health insurance, sick pay, subsistence expenses and relocation expenses, are also a significant part of reward systems and in many cases the government offers tax incentives for the use of such rewards. Such schemes may also provide incentives for employers: e.g. UK employers can claim nursery provision costs against tax, and can reclaim value added tax on subsistence expenses. These are often seen by organisations as an opportunity to display a sense of caring for the well-being of employees, and may be offered as incentives in addition to current market rates.

In the UK in the 1980s and 1990s large companies moved away from national negotiations, so that company-wide, or even site-level agreements became the norm. At the beginning of the 1990s, national or industry-wide pay setting was still common for manual staff; but by 1999, the company/division level was the most frequently used for all grades of staff. In Ireland, however, the situation is very different. There is widespread and increasing use of national bargaining for most grades of staff, with the general exception of managerial remuneration, which is largely settled on an individual basis. The Irish system is significantly different in this respect from the UK. Since 1987 wage levels and pay increases have been determined by a series of social partnership agreements, developed and agreed by the government, the Irish Congress of Trade Unions and the Irish Business and Employers Confederation. Centralised bargaining is therefore the dominant means by which pay is determined for professional, technical, clerical and manual employees.

Of course, many factors play a part in determining pay, among them the size of an organisation's workforce, ownership, geographical spread, the labour market, skill specialisation, sector and unionisation. So, even a clear national trend is not necessarily reflected across all sectors or sizes of organisation.

During the 1980s in the UK, there was an increasing focus on augmenting the level of reward available to individual "high achievers", with an associated rise in the use of variable pay and benefit schemes, particularly merit or performance-related pay. This rise applied to an extensive range of grades, from managerial to non-manual grades and some manual grades as well, although the introduction of such pay schemes in the public sector was slower than in the private sector. Spurred by government tax incentives, methods of rewarding employees through financial participation such as profit sharing and share ownership opportunities, have also increased in both countries. In particular, governments have been keen to support such schemes as a means of encouraging the development of an enterprise culture. Previous rounds of the Cranet survey have indicated an increase in variable pay in Ireland in recent years, which is consistent with the European trend (Morley and Gunnigle, 1997). Data from the 1999/2000 survey indicate a continuation of this trend, with 41% of Irish respondents suggesting that the proportion of non-money benefits in the total reward package had increased.

In 1999/2000, over three-quarters of UK organisations reported using variable pay schemes, though only about a third report an increase in their use over the last 3 years. The situation was similar in the two earlier phases of the survey, when respectively three, and almost four, out of ten respondent organisations reported an increase in their use of variable pay over the previous 3 years. Compared to the use of variable pay, nine out of ten organisations reported that they offered family-friendly benefit schemes, with one in four reporting an increase in their use over the last 3 years, and one in fifteen reporting a decrease. The use of non-money benefits is continuing to grow. In the UK and Ireland, non-financial benefits typically include workplace childcare, childcare allowances, career break schemes and extended maternity and paternal leave. The greatest areas of change during the 1990s have been in the use of maternity and paternal leave, fuelled by increasing trade union and political demands and legislative changes

during the period. The split between public and private sector organisations in the use of non-money benefits is very noteworthy. In 1999, public administration organisations were more than three times as likely to offer family-friendly non-money benefits than companies in the industrial sector.

Share schemes and profit sharing vary considerably by country (Pendleton et al., 2002). Traditionally in Ireland, interest in share ownership schemes has been relatively low, despite the provision of tax relief to encourage their adoption by employers (Morley and Gunnigle, 1997). The Irish data reveal little change in the use of share options since the 1992 survey; and where used, it is most likely to occur among managerial grades (Table 2.41). During the 1990s the use of employee share options decreased in the UK by some 10%, as economic circumstances worsened. Managerial grades continue to be the group most likely to be offered such schemes.

Profit sharing has a slightly lower coverage than share option schemes among managerial staff in both countries. But for all grades, profit sharing is used to about the same extent today as at the beginning of the decade. In the most recent round of the survey, the percentage of Irish organisations reporting the use of group bonus schemes has remained at roughly 22% for both managerial grades and professional/technical grades. The use of group bonus schemes for managerial, professional and clerical staff has increased throughout the decade in the UK, with about four in ten organisations using group bonus schemes for managerial staff in 1999/2000.

In both the UK and in Ireland, the use of merit or performance-related pay has traditionally been the preserve of managerial and professional staff. However, there has been a marked reduction in the use of merit or performance-related pay for managerial, professional and clerical staff in the UK during the 1990s, as indicated by the data in Table 2.42. Our data suggest that merit/performance-related pay remains a common feature of organisational life in Ireland, with almost half of all respondents indicating that merit-based pay structures operated in their organisations. The traditional pattern of using merit or performance-related pay primarily among managerial grades remains. The 1999/2000 results reveal a fall in the use of merit/PRP schemes in Irish organisations, similar to the picture in the UK. This may have been linked to academic scepticism about the effectiveness of such schemes given the

Table 2.41   Share options, profit sharing, group bonus schemes and merit/performance-related pay (% of organisations)

	UK			Ireland		
	1992	1995	1999/2000	1992	1995	1999/2000
Incentive schemes offered to managers						
Employee share options	37	31	32	28	26	24
Profit sharing	26	27	24	15	23	17
Group bonus	25	26	33	16	22	22
Merit/performance-related pay	65	63	49	52	58	47
Incentive schemes offered to professional/technical staff						
Employee share options	29	22	23	16	15	16
Profit sharing	21	23	22	11	17	17
Group bonus	18	18	24	14	19	19
Merit/performance-related pay	52	49	40	44	51	41
Incentive schemes offered to clerical/administrative staff						
Employee share options	25	19	20	10	11	12
Profit sharing	19	22	21	11	16	16
Group bonus	14	15	20	11	19	15
Merit/performance-related pay	42	41	33	27	39	31
Incentive schemes offered to manual staff						
Employee share options	23	17	17	10	9	9
Profit sharing	17	19	18	11	13	13
Group bonus	25	17	19	17	19	15
Merit/performance-related pay	21	22	22	12	16	15

Table 2.42   Merit/performance-related pay by staff category (% of organisations)

	UK			Ireland		
	1992	1995	1999/2000	1992	1995	1999/2000
Management	65	63	49	52	58	47
Professional/technical	52	49	40	44	51	41
Clerical	42	41	33	27	39	31
Manual	21	22	22	12	16	15

lack of correlation between performance pay and performance, or to the fact that they invariably increase wage bills. Ironically, in view of the pressure on the public sector to "learn from the private sector", as the private sector abandons such schemes, pressure is growing in the public sector for their introduction.

According to our most recent data, about two-thirds of managerial and professional/technical staff are covered by an appraisal system, with a significant proportion of manual grades also covered. This increase in manual grades has been accompanied by a drop in coverage of the numbers of other staff categories.

The management of performance is a key variable in organisational effectiveness, and in view of the strategic pressures facing organisations, it is becoming increasingly evident that as organisations seek to improve productivity and growth, they will concurrently attempt carefully to monitor employee performance (Morley et al., 2002). In the UK, there is discussion as to whether appraisal should be linked with pay, and there is much debate as to the issue of assessment vs. development in relation to the link between pay and performance. Performance appraisal is however linked to pay currently in about a third of organisations in the UK. In both the UK and Ireland performance appraisal is widely practised, although there are large variations in its application to different staff categories (Table 2.43). In recent years in the UK and Ireland, there has been a trend towards making appraisal schemes more inclusive and extending them to clerical and manual staff.

Table 2.43   Appraisal system for staff categories (% of organisations)

	UK			Ireland		
	1992	1995	1999/2000	1992	1995	1999/2000
Management	N/A	90	92	N/A	77	64
Professional/technical	N/A	87	90	N/A	70	61
Clerical	N/A	76	85	N/A	61	58
Manual	N/A	50	68	N/A	37	38

In the UK the sector most likely to use appraisal schemes for all grades of staff is the services sector, although other sectors are not very far behind. In Ireland, it is considerably more often the industry sector that operates appraisal schemes. In Ireland, successive rounds of the survey have indicated that the private sector uses performance appraisal far more extensively than the public sector. One possible explanatory factor is the presence of MNCs. Ireland is significantly more reliant on foreign-owned (particularly US-owned) industry than the UK – or indeed any other EU country; and MNCs are more likely to apply performance appraisal systems across grades (Morley and Gunnigle, 1997). Previous survey data have revealed that private-sector multinationals of comparable size were more than twice as likely to operate an appraisal system for all employee grades. It is not surprising to find that the same applies to the 1999/2000 data.

When we look at how the performance appraisal process is conducted we find that, in both the UK and Ireland in 1999/2000, the most common participants were the immediate supervisor, the employee and, in about two-thirds of cases, the next-level superior. The use of peers, subordinates and customers in the process is minimal, with only one in ten organisations using these alternatives in the UK and one in five in Ireland. In the UK a small but increasing proportion of organisations has introduced 360-degree feedback. In 1995 only 2% of organisations used this tool, but by 1999, this had increased to 4%. The main stated purpose of performance appraisal in the UK in 1999 was to assess individual training needs. Next was the assessment of the promotion potential of employees. Assessment of organisational needs was a stated aim in just over half of organisations in the middle of the 1990s, and has been increasing since.

Patterns of reward management have been changing in recent years. However, big differentials remain in the availability of reward schemes for the various staff categories. This applies to both pay and non-pay benefits. There is also a large variation in the locus of pay determination, depending on factors such as industrial sector and company size. Performance appraisal similarly shows substantial variation in application between staff grades, despite efforts over recent years to make schemes more inclusive.

EMPLOYEE COMMUNICATIONS AND THE ROLE OF TRADE UNIONS

Industrial relations and aspects thereof, such as the role of internal communications, have undergone significant change in both the UK and Ireland over the past two decades. These changes have taken place against a background of continuing decline in trade union density and the concomitant growth in non-union firms. However, there are significant differences in the industrial relations systems of the two countries. In this context three aspects of Irish public policy are noteworthy: (i) support for trade unions and collective bargaining and the promotion of centralised "social partnership" agreements; (ii) a strong emphasis on attracting foreign investment; (iii) constitutional support for freedom of association. As mentioned in our introduction, government approaches to industrial relations in both countries were grounded in the voluntarist tradition, characterised by a "hands off" policy and a minimal legislative and procedural framework for collective bargaining. The election in 1979 in the UK of the Thatcher-led Conservative government marked a significant departure, with subsequent years witnessing a series of initiatives designed to curb trade union influence, decentralise wage determination and generally ensure greater market influence on wage levels and other industrial relations outcomes. In contrast, successive Irish Governments since 1986 have actively championed a series of centralised agreements between the social partners, covering both pay increases and a range of economic and social policy issues such as welfare provision, employment creation and tax reform.

A second area of contrast is the attraction of FDI. As noted earlier, while both countries actively pursue this policy goal, Ireland relies much more on foreign-owned (particularly US-owned) industry than the UK (see Gunnigle and McGuire, 2001). In the HR sphere it is clear that multinational firms have acted as an important mechanism for innovation in management practices, particularly in the diffusion of new HRM techniques and in expanding the role of the HR function. However, it is also clear that they pose industrial relations challenges, specifically in their ability to switch the locus of investment and also to adopt industrial relations styles that defy the pluralist model. In Ireland, we have seen a dramatic growth in non-union approaches over the past decade. This is particularly the case in the manufacturing sector where most new firms are non-union (Gunnigle et al., 2002).

A final area of contrast relates to the existence of a written constitution in Ireland, and specifically its support for the principle of freedom of association. Article 40.6.1 of the Irish constitution provides for the right of individuals to form or join associations or unions. However, beyond this constitutional support for freedom of association, there is no statutory provision for trade union recognition in Ireland. This means that although workers have constitutional support to join trade unions, there is no legal obligation on employers to recognise or bargain with such unions.

Using data from 1999/2000 we find that trade union density[1] in Ireland was 45% (Gunnigle et al., 2002). This represents a fall of some 17% since 1980 when union density in Ireland reached its highest point at 62%. The Cranet data (see Figure 2.7) provide us with additional insights into the operational role and impact of trade unions. The most recent survey finds that union penetration in respondent organisations is reasonably high with over half reporting union membership levels of 50% or greater of the workforce. However, when we look at the longitudinal trend in

[1] Trade Union density: percentage of unionizable employees who are trade union members.

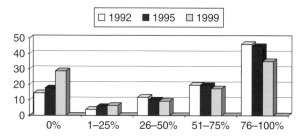

Figure 2.7 Trade union density in Irish organisations 1992–1999

union penetration, the picture is not nearly as positive. Rather what we find is a pattern of declining union penetration: over the period 1992–1999 we find that the numbers of respondent organisations that reported that 50% or more of their workforce were trade union members had fallen by 13%. As might be expected, trade union penetration in Ireland remains highest in the public sector. While the numbers of public sector organisations reporting low or zero levels of union membership is minuscule, four in every ten private sector organisations report an absence of union membership while a further one in five report membership levels of 50% or less.

In 1999/2000 eight in ten respondent organisations recognised trade unions. Looking at the longitudinal pattern we find a trend of declining levels of union recognition: in 1992 over 80% of respondent organisations recognised trade unions while by 1999/2000 this had fallen by some 14% (Table 2.44). Combining these findings with other research on union recognition in Ireland, such as that relating to union recognition in new start-ups or the incidence of strike action over union recognition, there is clear evidence of increasing employer resistance to union recognition (Gunnigle, 1995; D'Art and Turner, 2001; Gunnigle et al., 2002; Roche, 2001).

Union membership figures for the UK in 2001 were 29% compared to 38% in 1991, a fall of 17% over the 10-year period (Brook, 2001), although the numbers were beginning to turn upward in the opening years of the twenty-first century.

As well as "hard" indicators of trade union density and recognition, it is also useful to explore management perceptions of the influence of trade unions in their organisations. Table 2.45 presents a picture of relative stability in relation to perceived union influence. In 2000, some 37% of UK and 43% of Irish respondents

Table 2.44   Trade union recognition in Ireland in larger organisations 1992–1999

Trade union recognition	1992	1995	1999/2000
Yes	83% (186)	80% (205)	69% (296)
No	17% (38)	20% (50)	31% (132)

Table 2.45   Change in trade union influence (% of organisations)

	UK			Ireland		
	1992	1995	1999/2000	1992	1995	1999/2000
Increased	4	4	7	9	6	17
Same	42	58	44	67	68	45
Decreased	54	37	21	23	26	17

report that the influence of trade unions in their organisation has remained the same over the past 3 years. However, if we look only at those organisations where a change in the level of trade union influence was reported, we find that this is more likely to result in a decline rather than an increase in union influence. The decline in union influence is most marked among UK organisations. It is plausible to argue that this reflects the more hostile environment faced by UK trade unions during the period of Conservative governments of Margaret Thatcher and afterwards. This period saw a forthright onslaught on trade unions and a series of legislative changes aimed at reducing trade union influence at national and enterprise level. By contrast, when we look at the Irish context we find a more benign environment for trade unions as they have become progressively more integrated into national level decision-making on economic and social issues. This is not to say, however, that all is well for trade unions in Ireland. As we have demonstrated, there is considerable evidence of antipathy to trade unions at workplace level, most notably in new greenfield-site organisations (McGovern, 1989; Gunnigle, 1995; Gunnigle et al., 1997). However, many of these organisations employ less than 200 workers and because of their "newness" and "smallness", do not feature in our findings. Over time, though, it is plausible to argue that the dramatic growth of non-union approaches in Ireland among newer organisations will lead to a fall in trade union influence at enterprise level on a scale similar to that reported for UK organisations.

It can be argued that effective communication is at the heart of effective HRM and has the potential to foster greater commitment and act as a significant predictor of job satisfaction, and can help to improve internal control and facilitate the development of strategy (Morley et al., 2000). An important theme therefore in the literature is the suggestion that employers have sought increasingly to communicate directly with employees and at the same time reduce their reliance on indirect communication via trade unions or other representative organisations (see e.g. Bacon and Storey, 1993; Salamon, 1998). This theme is aptly captured by Salamon (1998: p. 365) who argues that "Since the early 1980s there has been a shift in the emphasis of organisational communication away from "disclosure" of information to trade unions in support of the collective bargaining process, and towards "dissemination" of information to employees in order to secure their greater involvement in and identification with the organisation's interests and objectives". In some quarters, this shift is viewed as part of a managerial strategy to adopt a more individualist "employee" relations orientation which may simultaneously involve attempts to bypass or marginalise trade unions at workplace level (see e.g. Kochan et al., 1986; Blyton and Turnbull, 1994; Gunnigle et al., 1997). In the 1999/2000 round of the survey almost two-thirds of respondent organisations reported an increase in direct communication with employees. Communication via computer mail had grown by 69%.

A related issue is the actual content of management–employee communications. The Cranet study explored the extent to which senior management communicated formally with employees about business strategy and financial performance (see Table 2.46). The findings indicate a high level of communication over strategy with management and professional/technical grades, but much lower levels of communication with clerical and manual grades. In the 1999/2000 survey, just 29% of both UK and Irish organisations reported that they communicate about strategy with manual grades. The contrast between higher- and lower-level employees is less pronounced in relation to communication on financial matters. Here we find that larger proportions of manual and clerical categories are briefed on financial matters: in 1999/2000 60% of UK and 42% of Irish organisations reported that they communicate on financial matters with manual grades. In general, it appears that UK organisations place more emphasis on

Table 2.46 Formal communication on business strategy and financial performance (% of organisations)

	UK			Ireland		
	1992	1995	1999/2000	1992	1995	1999/2000
Professional briefed						
About strategy	59	72	65	65	73	62
About finance	70	78	78	65	65	69
Clerical briefed						
About strategy	33	49	46	43	54	44
About finance	53	61	65	41	52	48
Manual briefed						
About strategy	28	41	37	42	43	32
About finance	48	52	55	35	42	37

communicating financial data to employees than their Irish counterparts. However, the respondent organisations report more extensive briefing for higher-level employees in both countries with little evidence of any change in this pattern.

National statistics and data from the CUL study present a mixed picture of trade union penetration in Ireland. Looking at trends in regard to aggregate levels of trade union density we find a steady decline since 1980. A similar picture emerges from our review of trade union membership levels within organisations. However, our data also indicate that larger organisations experience reasonably high levels of union penetration. And the findings on employee communication highlight a continuing move towards direct communication with employees, especially in the area of financial information.

ORGANISATION OF WORK: FLEXIBLE WORKING PATTERNS

Increasing flexibility at enterprise level has been one of the key themes of HRM debates in the UK and Ireland since the beginning of the 1980s. Of particular relevance has been the model of the "flexible firm" (Atkinson and Meager, 1984; NEDO, 1986) put forward by British researchers to make sense of the changes they felt were taking place at enterprise level there. The model has stimulated considerable debate among British and Irish academics both about the nature of empirical evidence of changes in employment practices and the social desirability of such a model of employment (see e.g. NEDO, 1986; Pollert, 1987; Morley et al., 1995; Brewster, 1998; Heraty, 1999).

Flexibility has been lauded as the cost-effective use of HR from a managerialist perspective. However, proponents of greater equality at work, particularly in relation to gender, have also championed the cause of flexibility (Laufer, 2000). Forms of employee-led flexibility include family-friendly policies and reflect changing social trends and values, with employees less willing or less able to work a conventional full-time nine-to-five working day. Both Ireland and the UK have seen a large increase in the number of women in the workforce since the 1980s. This is particularly striking in the area of part-time work which allows a woman to balance the dual burden of family and work responsibilities (Fynes et al., 1996).

However, changes in Ireland have been more dramatic than in the UK. In Ireland, just over one quarter (28%) of women of working age were active in the labour market in 1971, compared to the current situation, where more than 50% are part of the labour force (Coughlan, 2002). In the UK, part-time employment has a much longer history, even though there too, part-time work has increased during the 1990s.

If we look at the share of part-time employment in the total labour force, part-time employment in Ireland has grown by almost one-third since 1992. In the UK on the other hand it grew by just 15% in the same period. This is partly a reflection of different patterns of economic development in both countries. The economic boom experienced in Ireland during the 1990s has led to a rapid expansion of service sector jobs, which are much more likely to offer part-time employment. At the same time, employers are discovering the benefits of part-time working in terms of cost-effective use of

Table 2.47   Change in use of flexible working arrangements (% of organisations)

	UK			Ireland		
	1992*	1995	1999/2000	1992*	1995	1999/2000
Part-time working						
Increase	41	52	56	35	49	62
Same	42	38	35	30	25	21
Decrease	8	5	4	5	5	2
Not used	8	5	5	30	20	16
Temporary/casual work						
Increase	41	62	51	42	55	58
Same	35	29	35	41	31	30
Decrease	19	5	9	10	5	6
Not used	5	3	6	7	9	6

* 1992 data included "Don't know" category, which was selected out.

Table 2.48   Proportion of workforce on non-standard contracts (part-time and temporary)

	UK			Ireland		
	1992*	1995	1999/2000	1992*	1995	1999/2000
No part-timers employed	4	4	4	19	20	14
>10% of part-timers	27	31	33	15	11	19
No temporary workers employed	5	4	5	14	12	8
>10% of temporary workers	7	12	14	14	22	21

* 1992 figure is the missing value, since a "not used" option was not included.

labour in the face of often more competitive market conditions. Part-time employment in the UK tends to be more polarised between sectors and companies. Part-time employment in manufacturing is actually lower in the UK than in Ireland. On the other hand, the biggest employers of part-time workers in the UK are public administration, schools, social services and much of the health service.

In the three successive rounds of this survey, both UK and Irish respondents have indicated a continuous increase in the use of flexible working arrangements such as part-time working and temporary/casual work. In Ireland, the most marked increase over the last decade has occurred in the area of part-time work, where there have been significant increases – from 35% in 1992 to 62% in 1999, which is well above the EU average of 47%. Further evidence of this trend is apparent from the data in Table 2.48, which also shows the increasing use by employers in both countries of both part-time and temporary contracts. Irish companies however are much more likely to have over 10%

of their workforce on temporary contracts, almost twice as many as in the UK.

SUMMARY

Given the historical background, geographical proximity and cultural connections of Ireland and the UK, it is not surprising that the Cranet surveys have revealed more similarities than differences between the two countries. In relation to the role of the HR function, the data show a relatively strong strategic positioning of HRM in both UK and Irish organisations; with roughly 50% of respondents in both countries indicating a place on the board for the HR function. We have also seen some increase in involvement of the HR function in corporate strategy formulation among Irish organisations. Turning to the role of line management in HRM, the findings from Irish respondents do indicate an increased role for the line manager in the areas of recruitment and training and development. However, it is also clear that much of the responsibility for the execution of many of the key HR activities is shared between line management and the HR function, with no evidence in either country of a complete devolvement of responsibility to line managers. The challenge for the future appears to lie in sustaining a balance between strategic and technical roles, and shifting from being a provider, to being an enabler in HRM, particularly in facilitating organisational change. This will most likely involve the use of core HR staff, while outsourcing appropriate activities and devolving responsibilities to the line and to employees.

As to the recruitment and selection process, a variety of methods continue to enjoy popularity in both countries. In relation to the filling of managerial vacancies, the latest round of the survey indicates that for the most part, junior and middle management vacancies were filled from the internal labour market, while senior management positions were as likely to be filled externally as internally. Information was also sought from organisations on the frequency of use of different selection methods in making appointments generally. The evidence here suggests that recruitment and selection practices have remained relatively unchanged since 1992. The results seem to re-affirm the continuing popularity of traditional selection techniques such as the interview, the application form and the reference, despite their reported unreliability and invalidity. On the whole our findings indicate relatively little use being made in either Ireland or the UK of what are generally considered as more sophisticated selection tools, namely assessment centres and psychological testing.

In relation to evidence gathered from the Cranet survey on organisational training and development, the trend since 1992 has been an increase in investment in the training and development of employees in both Ireland and the UK. Unlike some of our European counterparts, Irish companies are not legally required to invest a minimum proportion of annual turnover on employee training and development. The result of this policy is evident in the survey findings, in that Irish organisations fall well below their European counterparts in relation to financial investment in their employees, both in actual percentage of turnover spent, and number of days' training given. Considering the important role accorded to the training and development of employees in contributing to the attainment of strategic business goals, the challenge facing practitioners is to ensure that all training and development activity meets the organisation's requirements.

In respect of the management of rewards in organisations, the Irish system is unique in that wage rates for most non-managerial employees are determined via centralised bargaining at national level, with managerial pay determined largely on an individual basis. Our data point to a pattern of relative stability in the area of compensation over the three rounds of the survey, particularly in the use of profit sharing and share options. Merit/performance-related pay continues to be the incentive used most frequently by Irish organisations, with the performance appraisal remaining a typical feature of organisational life. These schemes, now common for managerial employees, are less widespread for other grades.

The area of employee relations and the nature of management–employee communication provides us with an insight into the role and impact of trade unions. The 1999/2000 findings indicate that union penetration is reasonably high in Ireland; however, data from the three successive rounds of the survey together, expose a pattern of falling union penetration in Irish organisations.

Turning to the area of flexible working practices, in the three successive rounds of the survey, both UK and Irish respondent organisations have reported a continuous increase in the use of flexible working arrangements, in particular, non-standard contracts. In Ireland the most significant growth has been in the use of part-time work. Since the 1992 survey the number of organisations reporting an increase in the use of part-time workers has almost doubled. Further evidence of this trend is apparent in the significant rise in the number of Irish organisations reporting greater than 10% of the workforce on non-standard contracts. A number of factors can be seen to have led to the adoption of these particular flexible working arrangements, including changing aspirations and demographics, and the drive for competitiveness. In the light of the recent global economic uncertainty, mass redundancies and widespread workforce restructuring, a continuing increase in these forms of working arrangements seems likely.

HRM IN ACTION

PERFORMANCE IMPROVEMENT IN THE UK – AND THE LINK TO HARD HUMAN RESOURCES

Performance management has been a key feature of the debates in HRM in the UK over recent years. From its early manifestions in the form of the annual appraisal, it has through the 1990s and early years of the twenty-first century come to be recognised as a key aspect of integrated HR approaches. The development of performance management, away from a once a year appraisal, to an involving (and hopefully motivating) business-driven process, has been well documented – see for e.g. Armstrong and Baron (1998). At the same time as this development of the approach, advances beyond HR (e.g. government performance targets) have seen a popularisation of measurement cultures. Within organisations following predominantly US management trends this has been reflected both within the work of HR itself, with an increasing emphasis on the bottom line, and also within the design of many performance management processes.

The example presented below describes how an organisation operating within the UK embraced the move towards what Storey (1989) has described as "hard" approaches to HRM. The approach outlined was recognised as ambitious and complex, both in terms of its philosophy and the technology-based support it deployed. It should not therefore be seen as "typical" practice at the current time, in particular in relation to its inclusion of a forced distribution curve. Although popularised by Jack Welch at GE, a recent survey within the US (see Lawler and McDermott, 2003) suggested that 80% of respondents were deploying this approach to no or little effect.

Management of the case study company, Christian Salvesen, were very mindful of the potential impact this might have on morale when phased into operation. For this reason they sought as much as possible to emphasise the developmental aspects of the process and the key role of effective leadership towards this end. Their inclusion of 360 style feedback and competencies is also described below and these aspects, along with a link to reward are more commonly to be found within UK performance management implementations.

Students might want to think about:

1. The challenges of designing the rigorous performance standards required to underpin such an approach.
2. What will happen if and when the company decides to follow through on the vitality curve approach?
3. What might be the challenges and benefits around the proposed 360 degree approach for managers? What is the likely reaction from those involved?

Christian Salvesen is a European logistics organisation based in the middle of the UK, employing 15,000 staff and operating in nine countries across 200 sites in the UK, Belgium, France, Germany, Ireland, the Netherlands, Italy, Portugal and Spain.

In 1999 business results were poor and despite an excellent year in 2000 the downward trend re-emerged in 2001 and looked set to continue in 2002. At the end of January 2003, 30 members of the Senior Management team met to discuss and work on developing ideas for urgently improving the organisational performance of the company. A nine-person strong, cross-disciplinary group was established to look at ways of improving organisational performance. They represented the main divisions, general managers, finance and HR.

The core principles for the project were defined as:

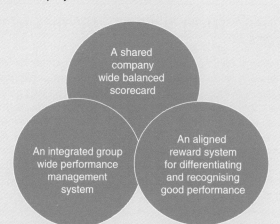

The group were influenced by Jack Welch's ideas of the "vitality curve" and as a result it was decided to seek to implement more effective performance measures around a balanced scorecard, to allow for accurate differentiation between staff. The intention was to "raise the performance bar" by eliminating the bottom 10% of performers each year.

What emerged from the design meetings of the core performance improvement team?

Beneath these "headline" measures, eight KPI's or key measures were translated across the 4 scorecard categories. These key measures became the improvement numbers and targets for every part of the business, from Group to Division and Regions, through to Site levels. As a result, everyone within the business knew the targets and what was being expected from them for this year.

Essentially a fairly "hard" approach to performance management emerged, with a primary focus on the "what" of performance. The "how" was also included via a new leadership competency model, which was to form a 10% element of the final review.

The core business imperatives were captured as being:

Finance	– Improve group return on capital (ROACE) by improving profit and using less capital
People	– Improve employee effectiveness and contribution through reduced turnover, absenteeism, accidents and improved management capability
Customer	– Improve customer sales and margin growth Improve customer satisfaction through the achievement of agreed terms of service delivery, with reduced claims, credit notes and queries
Operations	– Improve the cost of operations and transactions against the revenue achieved

Implementation details

The balanced scorecard was "rolled-out" initially to 250 managers in the higher managerial grades. It was supported by a new performance management process, underpinned by a revised reward architecture aiming to:

- link individual performance contribution to overall company performance contribution
- assess individual manager performance contribution across all 4 scorecard categories
- differentiate between performance in terms of three types across the peer groups (the top 20%, middle 70% and bottom 10%).

The new reward system was designed for introduction for 1 year into the new balanced scorecard performance approach. This was in order to give the business 1 year to become familiar with the process before any hard monetary rewards were associated with it. The new bonus system was underpinned by weightings which stressed the importance of the achievement of financial measures.

Category	Bonus weighting (%)
Finance	45
People/employee	25
Customer	15
Operations	15

In addition the new reward system was designed so that it would only pay out if overall company performance reached a pre-defined percentage of the target levels. This percentage could be set at the beginning of each year.

The list below summarises the process which was rolled out at Christian Salvesen:

Performance appraisal implementation process

1. Business scorecard objectives/targets set.
2. Objective setting exercise – individual sets personal objectives against the scorecard targets.
3. Individual requests and identifies six feedback respondents.
4. Individual organises the anonymous feedback gathering process from their six feedback respondents.
5. Individual has 1:1 feedback sharing interview with an external coach/consultant.
6. Appraisal meetings with line managers take place and overall performance agreed.
7. Business scorecard targets set for 2003/2004.

Implementation support

The impetus behind this performance initiative at Christian Salvesen came from the Chief Executive himself. As a result, there was never any doubt as to the degree of support from the top. Even with such a high degree of commitment, the implementation of such a different approach to people management within a fairly "traditional" organisation required considerable planning and resources. It was decided to support the objective setting, balanced scorecard and the roll-out of leadership element via automated software.

In the first instance an e-learning approach was deployed, supported by HR, around objective setting. This equipped managers to set personal scorecard objectives against

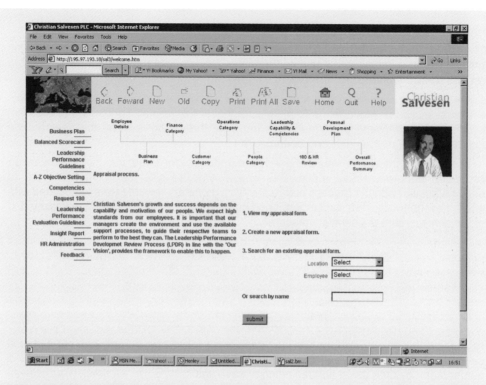

their business unit's overall scorecard objectives – an illustrative example of this is provided below:

Illustrative objective

DIVISIONAL SCORECARD – PEOPLE KPI: Staff turnover

Improve staff retention throughout the division by 15% by March 2003.

PERSONAL SCORECARD

Target objective: Develop and action a plan to measurably improve employee morale in the Logistics Project Team by end of March 2003.

Performance objective milestones:

1. Conduct structured focus groups with team members in order to identify morale issues and suggestions for improvement   Q1
2. Review turnover data and reason for leaving for 2000–2001 so that the top 5 reasons are clearly identified   Q1
3. Develop an action plan with actions, timings and costs and obtain sign off from Logistics Director and HR manager so that improvement is in plan   Q1
4. Work with HR training manager in order to produce individual training plan for each team member and present to team   Q1
5. Schedule monthly team meetings, set up agenda and actions file – in order to ensure importance and regularity of communications   Q1
6. Design and run a team building event and produce action plan in order to address issues raised during event   Q2

7. Conduct mid-year review of training plan and turnover stats and conduct mini employee survey within team in order to identify degree of improvement   Q3
8. Review T&D plan in order to identify areas to be carried over to 2004   Q3
9. Conduct Attitude Survey in Team in order to review end of year t/o stats   Q4
10. Present results of "morale improvement" project to Senior Management Team at December management meeting so that they can evaluate progress   Q4

Once produced the objectives were entered into the automated system which supported the whole performance management process, linking together the scorecard, business unit objectives and leadership capability element. The "how" or behavioural element has been captured via a 180 degree feedback process, with each manager receiving feedback from five direct reports and their line manager.

Interestingly, although the 180 degree feedback element accounts for only 10% of the total performance evaluation, it was one of the aspects that caused most disquiet. Managers were concerned about its apparent "subjectivity" and worried how they might in reality fare in the giving and receiving of "personal style" feedback. As a result the feedback process was designed to be as objective as possible. Composite feedback collating the views of all the nominated reviewers was prepared for each manager by the HR department. In addition, a follow-on discussion to review the feedback, was available for each manager, with an external consultant.

In summary, Christian Salvesen are pleased with their innovative and technologically supported solution, though they acknowledge that it is a "top down" approach in place of a bottom up paper approach. Although they needed to "outsource" the technology-supported element, they feel they have succeeded in the first part of their performance project – determining the business objectives and scorecard through top management buy-in, rather than via consultancy intervention.

References

Storey, J. (1989) (ed.) *New Perspectives on Human Resource Management.* London: Routledge.
Armstrong, M. and Baron, A. (1998) *Performance Management: The New Realities.* Wimbledon: CIPD.
Welch, J. (2003) *From the Gut.* New York: Headline.
Lawler, E.E. and McDermott, M. (2003) Current performance management practices: examining the varying impacts. *World at Work Journal,* 12, 2003.

This case was prepared by Elizabeth Houldsworth, Henley Management College, UK.

REPUBLIC OF IRELAND

Outsourcing HR at Alogar Ltd: A Case Vignette

Background

Alogar Ltd. is a US-owned multinational subsidiary located in Ireland. It is a leading designer, manufacturer and vendor of precision high performance electronic components. Its products are sold worldwide through a direct sales force, third-party industrial distributors and independent sales representatives. The company has its headquarters in the USA and has a number of manufacturing facilities spread across the globe. In addition, they have direct sales offices in over 15 countries, including the US.

The company employs in excess of 1000 people in Ireland, accounting for approximately one-tenth of its workforce worldwide. It operates in a highly competitive and dynamic marketplace, with both the company and its management conscious of the fact that organisational change and adaptation are necessary in order to remain competitive in this industry sector.

The HR function at Alogar Ltd.

Within Alogar, the HR function consists of six people, headed by the HR manager. The core functions carried out by this department include recruitment and staffing, compensation and benefits, training and development, HR information systems and employee relations. Their primary client group consists of over 1000 employees located throughout the company campus, which covers a number of separate buildings. Designated HR specialists are attached to specific areas of operation and are tasked with influencing and supporting each area's unique needs.

The role of the HR function in this organisation is guided by their mission statement which states:

> Our mission is to influence and support our stakeholders to achieve their desired results. We will achieve this through the development and continuous improvement of our processes and services in a spirit of teamwork and partnership.

This appears to be driven by the executive management team's vision of a company culture that is focused on stakeholder (customers, employees and shareholders) satisfaction, achieved through continuous improvement in value added activities. Additionally, there is considerable focus on continuing development throughout the company, where teams involving a cross section of the workforce tackle problems that range from broad environmental concerns to improvements in individual processes and equipment efficiency.

In 2001, the Benchmark Plan (BMP) was launched in Alogar. It defined the key elements of HR, elements that HR either owns or has significant input into. The BMP provided the genesis for some wide-ranging structural and operational changes within the HR department. The decision to use an external provider for the recruitment of manufacturing team members (MTMs) is an example of one such change.

The recruitment process

The recruitment and selection activity in this organisation was divided into two areas: direct and indirect recruitment.[1] A HR specialist was assigned the responsibility for the recruitment and selection of people to work directly in the manufacturing process – MTMs. The recruitment procedure for MTMs involved a number of stages. Once the company received an application for a position, the details were entered into the HR information system. Standard acknowledgment letters were then sent to all applicants. Those whose particulars met the specific criteria for MTM positions were contacted by

---

[1] Direct recruitment – employees working directly in the manufacturing process. Indirect recruitment – employees working in manufacturing support functions including HR, Finance, Production control and Information technology.

phone by a designated member of the recruitment team. They were invited to take part in the selection process, which involved psychometric testing and a first interview with a HR specialist for that area. On successful completion of both these stages, reference checks were completed. The candidate was then required to complete a company medical examination and take part in a second interview conducted by another HR consultant. Job offers were then made to successful candidates.

Rationale for the outsourcing decision

As was indicated earlier the 2001 BMP was the catalyst for a number of structural and operational changes within the HR department. The benchmarking plan was strongly associated with influenced by David Ulrich's publication "Human Resource Champions". According to the HR manager:

> The first thing that drove our need to look at outsourcing would have been the influence of David Ulrich.

One of the fundamental elements of Ulrich's work to which the HRD subscribed was the concept of becoming a "Strategic Partner". A central tenet of the strategic partner role is to design HR strategies to align with the core business objectives of the organisation. Strategic outsourcing was viewed as a process to facilitate such an objective. The HR manager believed that strategic outsourcing would enable the HRD employee's to concentrate on core competencies, thus facilitating the increased support of the organisation's core business.

A primary driver for the strategic outsourcing of specific elements of the direct recruitment process was to increase "responsiveness". From an organisational perspective this element of the recruitment process was highly unpredictable, according to the HR manager:

> The reality is we needed none (people) for six months and we needed one hundred (people) for the next month, so it was totally non linear, as these things are, in terms of demand.

Regarding the strategic outsourcing of the direct recruitment, he uses the analogy of a "Grand Prix" driver coming in from the track for a "Pit Stop": its all about the shortest turnaround time. This analogy is also used with respect to the HRD and direct recruitment, in that you have:

> Twenty-five people all waiting around for most of the race waiting for the driver to come in for eight seconds' work (HR manager).

The HR manager believes that the HRD has achieved increased flexibility, through the ability of strategic outsourcing to administer resources to direct recruitment, which are hard, fast and focused:

> That is the prime reason we went into it, and that's primarily what we are getting out of it (HR manager).

The second driver for strategic outsourcing is attributed to the then HR director. Thus, in the HR director, the HRD had an executive with purpose and the ability to direct and authorise activity – a champion.

Allied to the BMP was the construction and issue of a new and revised "Vision" statement for HRD. The HR manager spoke of the vision statement with respect to strategic outsourcing:

> Yes, that would have started it, but to be entirely honest it did not drive it from the start.

The mission statement was holistic in that it evolved into a "Shared Vision" to enable "The people in the HR function to 'Fit' into that role". Again there is a strong association with the reviewed literature; it can be argued that a vision permeates every stage of the strategic outsourcing process, from the earliest establishment of the relationship through writing and monitoring of the contract.

Looking at the decision and drive towards strategic outsourcing and possible links to overall corporate strategy, the HR manager believed that there was no direct link when the process started but: *funnily enough I would say it probably is fitting in right where we are now.* This is in reference to the global downturn in the semi-conductor industry.

> *Strategic outsourcing allows the HRD to participate more efficiently in the continuous focus on costs and service – principally their monitoring and reduction.*

According to the HR manager by adding value and increased service standards of core-competencies *We have tried to take the drudge work out of it, and keep the Silverware.*

Strategic outsourcing eliminates the non-core administration activities associated with the direct recruitment function, which are viewed by the HRD as *quite time consuming from an internal point of view.* This aspect of strategic outsourcing is believed to be of great benefit to the HRD in this organisation. There was a significant administration burden associated with the direct recruitment activity prior to outsourcing. In addition to the significant investment in man-hours and related costs, the selection rate was only 5% of all applicants, thus for every five people recruited by the HRD 100 applications had to be processed.

Criteria for selection of the outsourcing vendor

Having developed a strategic plan, vision and the rationale for strategic outsourcing, the HRD now focused in on the process and criteria for vendor selection, to provide the outsourcing services. The ideology through which the HRD filtered the selection process was simply "Quality". According to the respondent: "the criteria for selection from our point of view was quality of service and the ability to deliver".

The aspect of cost with respect to vendor selection was secondary, the process was put out to tender and the vendor chosen *was not actually the cheapest quote.*

The HRD were looking for the right "Fit", as it was not just quality, but *perceived level of quality* that was paramount. Also according to the respondent: *we went with what we thought were the competencies of the vendor.*

Thus this drive for quality, competency and "Fit" was so strong that the HRD were put to some significant inconvenience, in that the successful outsourcing vendor was based in a different city, but the determination to find and develop a vendor that could service the HRD's unique needs and requirements overcame this geographical barrier.

Management of the strategic outsourcing relationship

The first step undertaken for the management of the relationship was the documentation of the entire direct recruitment process by HRD. The logic being that the outsourcing vendor would know exactly what was expected of them. This also highlighted exactly the HRD's new responsibilities towards the direct recruitment function.

Thus the macro's for the management of the relationship were in place before the process was enacted: *Everybody was very clear what it is they had to do* according to the

HR manager. This approach was followed by monthly on site face-to-face meetings with the vendor to monitor the process and deal with any issues or problem areas. Currently, this has been reduced to monthly conference calls as the relationship has progressed. Allied to the above was the dedication of a HR consultant to the outsourcing relationship. Thus there was constant interaction in terms of quality and service in the day-to-day operational context.

Difficulties encountered

The respondent points out that "Trying to get the vendor to understand our requirements and the particular type of person we need adds another layer of complexity". This specific communication problem led to a high level of "rejects" at final interview stage – the stage when the HRD re-entered the direct recruitment process. This resulted in an increase in the time factor as "it took another layer of intensive communication to get it right" according to the respondent.

Metrics: pre- and post-strategic outsourcing

A detailed cost analysis has not been undertaken but the perception is that strategic outsourcing is more expensive than the previous in-house direct recruitment process. According to the respondent: "My inclination is that at the moment, for the actual man-hours of work that people do, it probably is more expensive". The HR manager does state that if responsiveness were to be factored into a cost analysis that it may actually reduce direct recruitment costs.

With respect to overall staff turnover in direct recruitment, there has been a slight reduction, but according to the HR manager *I most definitely would not attribute it to anything to do with outsourcing*. His view is that the reduction is for economic reasons linked to the global downturn in the semi-conductor industry and the resulting loosening of the labour market.

In these terms there are periods through the year when HRD is not billed, however in the short-term HRD pays a premium for the flexibility of a strategic outsourcing service, but according to the respondent *That's not the point*. The ability to apply strong, hard and fast resources coupled with the flexibility it affords, balances the costs out in the respondents view.

The future

The HR manager's view of the future of strategic outsourcing of the direct recruitment process is a pragmatic one. The future of strategic outsourcing is linked to the shifting priorities of the HRD and, the external business environment of the organisation as a whole. He says:

> There could come a time when responsiveness is no longer a major issue for us, in which case we may decide to go back into our slower steadier model of lets do it internally.

This pragmatic approach highlights their understanding of not only where the HRD "Fits" within the overall organisational business strategy, but also the adaptability of the department to utilise the best possible strategies that suit the real time in which they operate.

Case questions

1. Discuss the implications of the decision to outsource the direct recruitment activity on the key stakeholders groups involved.
2. Evaluate the relative advantages and disadvantages of strategic outsourcing for this organisation.
3. What is your view on the process used for choosing an outsourcing vendor?

This case was prepared with the assistance of Michael O'Brien University of Limerick

LEARNING QUESTIONS

1. "Given the historical background, geographical proximity and cultural connections of Ireland and the UK, it is not surprising that the Cranet surveys have revealed more similarities than differences between the two countries". Critically analyse this statement.
2. An important component of the HRM literature over the past decade is the devolution of HRM responsibilities from the HR function to line management. How can the data from the Cranet E surveys inform our assessment of the current situation in the UK and Ireland?
3. Discuss and evaluate the different approaches in the use of reward systems in the UK and Ireland, and their effects.
4. Critically evaluate the flexible firm model as an accurate representation of current employment conditions in the UK and Ireland.
5. The Irish system of remuneration is unique in that pay for most non-managerial employees is determined via centralised bargaining at national level, with managerial remuneration determined mainly on an individual basis. Identify the benefits and drawbacks of this system to the employee, the employer and the government.
6. "An organisation's reward system is a powerful indicator of its approach to workforce management and has meaning to the employee precisely because it conveys information about important aspects of employment other than pay". Critically analyse this statement.
7. Relative to other European countries, the UK and Ireland invest less in training and development. Discuss the possible causes for this divergence and its effects.
8. The extent of trade union recognition and membership and the nature of management–union relations are seen as key indicators of management approaches to, and changes in, employee relations. How do the data from successive rounds of the Cranet survey in the UK and Ireland inform our thinking on this issue?

REFERENCES AND SOURCES

References

Armstrong, M. (2001) *A Handbook of Human Resource Management Practice*, 8th edn. London: Kogan Page.

Atkinson, J. and Meager, N. (1986) *Changing Patterns of Work*. London: IMS/OECD.

Bacon, N. and Storey, J. (1993) Individualization of the employment relationship and the implications for trade unions. *Employee Relations*, 15(1): 5–17.

Beaumont, P. (1993) *Human Resource Management: Key Concepts and Skills*. London: Sage.

Beer, M., Spector, B., Lawrence, P.R., Quinn-Mills, D. and Walton, R.E. (1984) *Managing Human Assets: The Groundbreaking Harvard Business School Program*. New York: The Free Press/Macmillan.

Blyton, P. and Turnbull, P. (1994) *The Dynamics of Employee Relations*. London: Macmillan.

Brewster, C.J. (1998) Flexible Working in Europe: extent, growth and challenge for HRM. In: Sparrow, P. and Marchington, M. (eds), *HRM: The New Agenda*. London: Pitman.

Brewster, C. and Söderstrom, M. (1994) Human resources and line management. In: Brewster, C. and Hegewisch (eds.), *Policy and Practice in European HRM*. London: Routledge.

Brewster, C., Larsen, H.H. and Mayrhofer, W. (1997) Integration and assignment: a paradox in human resource management. *Journal of International Management*, 3(1): 1–23.

Brook, K. (2001) Trade Union Membership: an analysis of data from the autumn LFS. In: *Labour Market Trends*, 110(7). London: Office for National Statistics.

Central Statistics Office (CSO) *Labour Market Surveys 1970–1998*. Dublin: CSO.

Coughlan, A. (2002) *Women in Management in Irish Business*. Dublin: IBEC.

Cully, M., O'Reilly, A., Woodland, S. and Dix, G. (1999) *Britain at Work: 1998 Workplace Employee Relations Survey*. London: Routledge.

D'Art, D. and Turner, T. (eds.) (2001) *Irish Employment Relations in the New Economy*. Dublin: Blackhall.

Economist Intelligence Unit (EIU) (1999) *Country Profile: Ireland*. London: Economist Intelligence Unit.

Eurostat, Statistical Office of the European Communities (1999) *Eurostat Yearbook: A Statistical Eye on Europe 1987–1997*. Brussels: Office for Official Publications of the European Communities.

Edwardes, M. (1983) *Back from the Brink*. London: Pan Books.

Fombrun, C.J., Tichy, N.M. and Devanna, M.A. (1984) *Strategic Human Resource Management*. New York: Wiley.

Fynes, B., Morrisey, T., Roche, W.K., Whelan, B.J. and Williams, J. (1996) *Flexible Working Lives: The Changing Nature of Working Time Arrangements in Ireland*. Dublin: Oak Tree Press.

Garavan, T.N., Costine, P. and Heraty, N. (1995) *Training and Development in Ireland: Context, Policy and Practice*. Dublin: Oak Tree Press.

Gunnigle, P. (1995) Collectivism and the management of industrial relations in greenfield sites. *Human Resource Management Journal*, 5(3): 24–40.

Gunnigle, P. and McGuire, D. (2001) Why Ireland? A qualitative review of the factors influencing the location of US Multinationals in Ireland with particular reference to the impact of labour issues. *Economic and Social Review*, 32(1): 43–67.

Gunnigle, P., MacCurtain, S. and Morley, M. (2001) Dismantling pluralism: employee relations in Irish Greenfield sites. *Personnel Review*, 30(3): 263–279.

Gunnigle, P., Morley, M. and Turner, T. (1997) Challenging collectivist traditions: individualism and the management of industrial relations in Greenfield sites. *Economic and Social Review*, 28(2): 105–134.

Gunnigle, P., Morley, M., Clifford, N. and Turner, T. (eds.) (1997) *Human Resource Management in Irish Organizations: Practice in Perspective*. Dublin: Oak Tree Press.

Gunnigle, P., O'Sullivan, M. and Kinsella, M. (2002) Organised Labour in the New Economy: Trade Unions and Public Policy in the Republic of Ireland. In D'Art, D. and Turner, T. (eds.) *Irish Employment Relations in the New Economy*, Dublin: Blackhall Press, pp. 222–258.

Gunnigle, P., Turner, T. and Morley, M. (1998) Employment flexibility and industrial relations arrangements at organization level: a comparison of five European countries. *Employee Relations: The International Journal*, 20(5): 430–442.

Heraty, N. (1999) The Irish labour market in perspective. In: Gunnigle, P. (ed.), *The Irish Employee Recruitment Handbook: Finding and Keeping a High Quality Workforce*. Dublin: Oak Tree Press.

Heraty, N. and Morley, M. (1997) Training and development. In: Gunnigle, P., Morley, M., Clifford, N. and Turner, T., with Heraty, N. and Crowley, M. *Human Resource Management in Irish Organizations: Practice in Perspective*. Dublin: Oak Tree Press.

Kochan, T.A., Katz, H.C. and McKersie, R.B. (1986) *The Transformation of American Industrial Relations*. New York: Basic Books.

Larsen, H.H. and Brewster, C. (2003) Line management responsibility for HRM: what's happening in Europe? *Employee Relations*, 25(3): 228–244.

Laufer, J. (2000) A search for equality but enduring differences. In: Davidson, M.J. and Burke, R.J. (eds.), *Women in Management Current Research Issues*, Vol. II. London: Sage.

Lawler, E. (1986) *High Involvement Management: Participating Strategies for Organizational Performance*. London: Jossey-Bass.

Legge, K. (1995) *Human Resource Management: Rhetorics and Realities*. London: Macmillan.

Lewis, C. (1984) What's new in selection? *Personnel Management*, January.

McGovern, P. (1989) Union Recognition and Union Avoidance in the 1980s. In: *Industrial Relations in Ireland: Contemporary Issues and Developments*. Dublin: University College Dublin, 1989.

McLoughlin, I. and Gourlay, S. (1992) Enterprise without unions: the management of employee relations in non-union firms. *Journal of Management Studies*, 29(5): 669–691.

McMahon, G. (1988) Personnel selection in Ireland: scientific prediction or crystal ball gazing? *IPM News*, 3(3): 20–23.

Marchington, M., Wilkinson, A. and Ackers, P. (1993) Waving or drowning in participation, *Personnel Management*, March: 47–48.

Mayrhofer, W. and Brewster, C. (2000) *Finally on their own? The changing role of functional specialists in Europe – conceptual and empirical considerations*, paper presented to the annual conference of the Society for Industrial and Organizational Psychologists, New Orleans, April.

Millward, N., Stevens, M., Smart, D. and Hawes, W.R. (1992) *Workplace Industrial Relations in Transition*. Aldershot: Dartmouth.

Morley, M. and Gunnigle, P. (1997) Compensation and benefits. In: Gunnigle, P., Morley, M., Clifford, N. and Turner, T., with Heraty, N. and Crowley, M., *Human Resource Management in Irish Organizations: Practice in Perspective*. Dublin: Oak Tree Press.

Morley, M. and Heraty, N. (1995) Line managers and human resource development. *Journal of European Industrial Training*, 19(10): 30–42.

Morley, M., Gunnigle, P. and Heraty, N. (1995) Developments in flexible working practices in the Republic of Ireland: research evidence considered. *International Journal of Manpower*, 16(8).

Morley, M., Gunnigle, P., Heraty, N. and Garavon, T. (2001) Human Resource Development: Sectoral and intervention Level Evidence of Human Capital Accumulation. *Journal of European Industrial Training*, 25(2/3/4): 48–229.

Morley, M., Gunnigle, P. and Turner, T. (2001) *The Cranfield Network on Human Resource Management Survey Executive Report*. University of Limerick: Employee Relations Research Unit.

Morley, M., Mayrhofer, W. and Brewster, C. (2000) Communication in organizations: dialogue and impact. In: Brewster, C. and Larsen, H.H. (eds.), *Human Resource Management in Northern Europe: Trends, Dilemmas and Strategy*. Oxford: Blackwell.

Muchinski, P. (1986) Personnel selection methods. In: Cooper, C. and Robertson, I.T. (eds.), *International Review of Industrial and Organizational Psychology*. New York: John Wiley.

OECD (1998) *Education at a Glance*. Paris: OECD.

Pendleton, A., Poutsma, E., Brewster, C. and Van Ommeren, J. (2002) Employee share ownership and profit sharing in the European Union: incidence, company characteristics and union representation. *Transfer*, 8(1): 47–62.

Plumbley, P. (1985) *Recruitment and Selection*. London: Institute of Personnel Management.

Pollert, A. (1987) The flexible firm: a model in search of reality (or a policy in search of a practice)? *Warwick Papers in Industrial Relations*, (19): December.

Robertson, I.T. and Makin, P. (1986) Management selection in Britain: a survey and critique. *Journal of Occupational Psychology*, 59: 45–57.

Roche, W.K. (2001) Accounting for the trend in trade union recognition in Ireland. *Industrial Relations Journal*, 32(1): 37–55.

Richbell, S. (2001) Trends and emerging values in HRM: The UK scene. *International Journal of Manpower*, 22(3): 261–268.

Salamon, M. (1998) *Industrial Relations: Theory and Practice*. Hemel Hempstead, UK: Prentice-Hall.

Smith, M. and Robertson, I.T. (1993) *The Theory and Practice of Systematic Staff Selection*. London: Macmillan.

Sparrow, P. and Hiltrop, J. (1994) *European Human Resource Management in Transition*. Hemel Hempstead, UK: Prentice-Hall.

Storey, J. (1992) *Developments in the Management of Human Resources*. Oxford: Blackwell.

Tansey, P. (1998) *Ireland at Work: Economic Growth and the Labour Market 1987–1997*. Dublin: Oak Tree Press.

Terpstra, D. (1996) The search for effective methods (employee recruitment and selection). *HR Focus*, 17(5): 16–18.

Thornhill, A. and Saunders, M.N.K. (1998) What if line managers don't realise they're responsible for HR? Lessons from an organization experiencing rapid change. *Personnel Review*, 27(6): 460–476.

Van Ommeren, J. and Brewster, C. (2000) *The Determinants of the Number of HR Staff in Organizations: Theory and Empirical Evidence*, SWP 12/99, Cranfield Working Paper.

3

The Netherlands and Germany: Flexibility or Rigidity?

Bart Dietz, Job Hoogendoorn, Rüdiger Kabst and Anja Schmelter

INSTITUTIONAL BACKGROUND

FEDERAL REPUBLIC OF GERMANY

Area	357,022 km^2
Population	82,558,000 inhabitants
Density	231 inhabitants per km^2
Capital and population	Berlin: 3,388,000 (2002)
Other major cities and population	Hamburg (1,726,000) Munich (1,230,000) Cologne (1,017,000) Frankfurt (641,000) Dresden (474,000)
Official language	German
Business languages	German and English
Religions	33% Roman Catholic 34% Protestant 1% Jewish 32% Others

Topography and climate

The Federal Republic of Germany is situated in the centre of Europe. It has nine neighbours: Denmark, The Netherlands, Belgium, Luxembourg, France, Switzerland, Austria, the Czech Republic and Poland. The longest distance from north to south is 876 km, and from west to east 640 km. The total length of the country's borders is 3758 km. Germany was one of the six founders of the European Union (EU) in 1957.

Figure 3.1 The Brandenburg Gate in Berlin – symbol of German unity

From north to south Germany is divided into five regions with different topographical features: the North German Plain, the Central Upland Range, the terrace panorama of the southwest, the Alpine foothills in the south and the Bavarian Alps. In the north are dry, sandy lowlands with many lakes as well as heaths and moors. The Central Upland Range divides northern Germany from the south. The Alps between Lake Constance and Berchtesgaden is limited to the Allgäu, the Bavarian Alps and the Berchtesgaden Alps.

Germany is situated in the moderately cool west wind zone between the Atlantic Ocean and the continental climate in the east. Sharp changes in temperature are rare. During winter, the average temperature lies between 1.5°C in the lowland areas and −6°C in the mountains. During the warmest month of the year, July, temperatures are between 18°C in low-lying regions and 20°C in the sheltered valleys of the south.

Federal states

The Federal Republic of Germany consists of 16 federal states known as "Bundesländer" (capitals shown in parentheses): Baden-Württemberg (Stuttgart), Bavaria (Munich), Brandenburg (Potsdam), Hessen (Wiesbaden), Lower Saxony (Hanover), Mecklenburg-Western Pomerania (Schwerin), North Rhine-Westphalia (Düsseldorf), Rhineland-Palatinate (Mainz), Saarland (Saarbrücken), Saxony (Dresden), Saxony-Anhalt (Magdeburg), Schleswig-Holstein (Kiel) and Thuringia (Erfurt). Berlin, Bremen and Hamburg are city-states.

Until Germany was reunited in 1990, the Federal Republic consisted of 11 states which had been created in the former Western occupation zones and had adopted democratic constitutions between 1946 and 1957. In the Soviet-occupied zone, which later became the German Democratic Republic (GDR), five states were likewise formed, but these were soon replaced by a centralised administration. After the first free election in the former GDR, on 18 March 1990, five new federal states were created with boundaries largely conforming to those of the period prior to 1952. On 3 October 1990 the GDR, and hence the states of Brandenburg, Mecklenburg-Western Pomerania, Saxony- Anhalt and Thuringia, joined the Federal Republic of Germany. At the same time, Berlin East was merged with Berlin West.

Principal characteristics

Table 3.1 shows the position of Germany in relation to other European countries on a number of standardised items.

People

Germany has a population of approximately 82 million (including 7.3 million foreigners) and is one of the most densely populated countries in Europe. The population is distributed very unevenly. The western part of Germany is much more densely populated than the eastern part. Of the 19 cities with more than 300,000 inhabitants, two are in the eastern part of Germany. Nearly one-third of the population live in the 84 large cities with more than 100,000 inhabitants. But the majority of people in the Federal Republic live in small towns and villages. Despite increases in the number of births over the last years, Germany has one of the lowest birth rates in the world. The population increase after the Second World War was mainly due to immigration (Figure 3.2).

Table 3.1   Principal characteristics in relation to EU-15

	EU-15	Germany	Relation (Germany/EU-15) × 100
Density (inhabitants per km^2) Year: 2002	116	231	198.3
People having completed at least upper secondary education (%) Year: 2000	64	82	128
Life expectancy at birth (boys; years) Year: 1999	74.9	74.7	99.7
Life expectancy at birth (girls; years) Year: 1999	81.2	80.7	99.4
Employment rate (men; %) Year: 2000	72	73	100
Employment rate (women; %) Year: 2000	54	58	107
Unemployment rate (%) Year: 2000	8	8	96
Cost-of-living comparisons (total value; $B = 100$) Year: 2000	$B = 100$	107	107

Age (years)	1987 (%)	2000 (%)	EUR-15 (2000) (%)
<15	16	16	17
15–24	16	11	12
25–49	36	38	37
50–64	18	19	17
65–79	11	13	13
>80	3	3	4

Source: Eurostat Yearbook 2002.

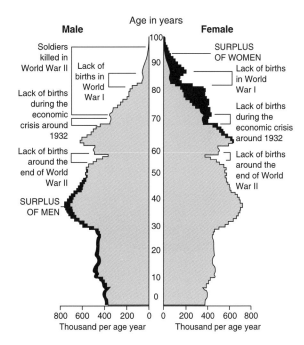

Figure 3.2   Age structure of the population of Germany on 31 December 2000

Economy

Germany is one of the world's leading industrial countries. Its economy is ranked third after the USA and Japan, and in terms of world trade it holds second place. In 2000, the gross domestic product (GDP) came to a record of EUR 2026 billion, which equals a per capita amount of EUR 23,540. As the world's second largest trading nation, Germany is deeply integrated into the global economy and highly dependent on foreign trade. The mainstay of the German economy is industry, although its importance has declined markedly in recent years as a result of structural change. The public and private service sectors increased their share considerably.

Since the Second World War the Federal Republic has developed a socially responsible market economy, in which the state plays a mainly regulatory role (Figure 3.3).

Living in Germany in comparison to other EU countries is slightly more expensive (see Appendix 1). In the majority of the areas compared the cost of living in Germany is higher than in the rest of the EU. Outstanding is expenditure on health – almost 50% higher than in other EU countries.

Legal and political environment

The German political system is based on the following principles: Germany is a republic and a democracy; it is a federal state based on the rule of law and social justice. Its republican system is reflected in the name "Federal Republic of Germany". The head of state is the elected Federal President. Responsibility is entrusted to

the legislature, the executive and the judiciary. The two chambers, Bundestag and Bundesrat, are the legislative bodies of the Federal Republic. The main functions of the Bundestag, apart from legislation, are the election of the Federal Chancellor and the scrutiny of the Federal Government. Through the Bundesrat, the states participate in the legislation and administration of the Federation, and in EU matters. The Federal Government participates in the legislative process mainly by introducing bills and issuing ordinances on the basis of specific legal authorisation. It consists of the Federal Chancellor, who is elected by the Bundestag on the proposal of the Federal President, and the Federal Ministers who are appointed and dismissed by the Federal President on the proposal of the Federal Chancellor.

The main parties in Germany are the Christian Democrats (CDU), the Social Democrats (SPD), the Free Democrats (FDP) and the Greens (Die Grünen). After the CDU and FDP together had ruled Germany for 16 years, in 1998 the Social Democrats, with the Greens, took over. They were re-elected in 2002.

Labour market

Between 1950 and 1992, the number of gainfully employed persons in the old states increased from 21.2 to 29.5 million (average figure for the year). It thereafter declined, reaching 27.9 million in 1997. In 1998 it rose again slightly. In the new states, employment fell by about 3.6–6.2 million between 1989 and 1993 as a result of the crisis precipitated by the transition to a social market economy. This drastic reduction in the number of jobs temporarily came to a halt at the beginning of 1994. In 1995 a total of 6.4 million people were employed, but by 1997 the figure had dropped again to just under 6.1 million. The total figures for Germany are shown in Table 3.2.

Government policy in the western part of the country after 1982 initially improved the conditions for economic growth and considerably reduced the obstacles to employment (Table 3.3). By 1991 unemployment

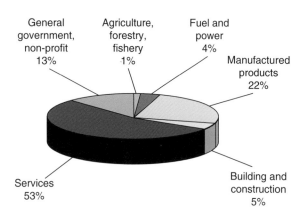

Figure 3.3 Economic structure of Germany. *Source*: Eurostat Yearbook 2002

Table 3.2 Persons in employment

Year	1991	1992	1993	1994	1995	1996	1997	1998	1999	2000
People (in million)	40.1	40.1	40.2	40.2	40.1	40.0	40.3	40.3	40.5	40.3

Source: Federal Statistical Office Germany Yearbook 2002.

there had dropped to 1.7 million, but – largely as a consequence of the 1992/1993 recession and the period of sluggish growth that followed – it began to rise again, reaching an average of 3.0 million in the year 1997 (Table 3.4). In the course of 1998, unemployment declined.

Hourly labour costs in Germany are higher than the European average. This might partly be due to the relatively strong position that trade unions occupy in Germany. Agreements on pay, working hours, holidays and general working conditions are freely negotiated between labour and management, who are often called "social partners" in Germany. Their central organisations – the trade union and employers' associations – play an important role.

Educational system

As an industrial country that is short of raw materials, Germany is largely dependent on a skilled labour force and therefore invests heavily in education. In 2000, public spending alone on educational institutions totalled approximately EUR 68.1 billion.

Because of the cultural and educational autonomy of the federal states the German school system is quite heterogeneous. The different school types are classified into a higher scheme, determined by the conference of the ministers of cultural and educational affairs, to make them comparable. A distinction is made between general education and vocational education. School attendance is compulsory for 9 years (in some states 10). Thereafter pupils have to attend at least a part-time vocational school (Berufsschule) until they reach the age of 18. Attendance at all public schools is free.

Kindergartens are not part of the state school system but fall under child and youth services. Most of them are run by churches, charitable organisations and municipalities, some by firms or associations.

Most institutions of higher education in Germany belong to the states. The higher institutions are self-governing. The mainstays of the tertiary education system are the academic universities and equivalent institutions. Courses culminate in a master's degree (Magister), a diploma or a state examination (Staatsexamen). After that, further qualification is possible up to doctorate level or a second degree.

Table 3.5 indicates how important education in Germany is. In all age groups German people have a superior education than the EU average. *Sources*: Eurostat Yearbook 2002; Federal Statistical Office Germany Yearbook 2002.

Table 3.3 Persons (in thousands) in employment in different sectors

	1990	1995	2000
Agriculture	1081	1134	985
Industry	11,619	12,883	12,180
Service	16,301	21,765	23,187

Source: Eurostat Yearbook 2002.

Table 3.4 Unemployment rate

Year	1993	1994	1995	1996	1997	1998	1999	2000	2000	
									Men	Women
Per cent	8	8	8	9	10	9	9	8	8	8

Source: Eurostat Yearbook 2002.

Table 3.5 People aged 25–64 having completed at least upper secondary education (%, 2000)

	Total (25–64)	25–29	30–34	35–39	40–44	45–49	50–54	55–59	60–64
EU-15	64	76	73	70	66	62	55	51	45
Germany	81	84	85	85	84	83	80	77	71

Source: Eurostat Yearbook 2002.

KINGDOM OF THE NETHERLANDS

Area	34,006 km^2
Population	15,983,000 inhabitants
Density	470 inhabitants per km^2
Capital and population	Amsterdam: 735,328 (2002)
Other major cities and population	Rotterdam (952,665) The Hague (440,000)
Official language	Dutch
Business languages	Dutch and English
Religions	31% Roman Catholic 21% Protestant 4% Muslim 4% Others 40% No religion

Topography and climate

The Netherlands is a country situated on the western side of Europe. It has three neighbouring countries: Germany, Belgium and Luxembourg. Most of its largest cities, like Amsterdam, Rotterdam and The Hague, are located near the Atlantic Ocean, on the western side of the country. Together with Belgium, France, Germany, Italy and Luxembourg, the Netherlands was one of the initial founders of the EU, established in 1957 in Rome.

The Netherlands has a cool west wind coming from the Atlantic Ocean. During the summer, with an average temperature of 16.6°C, it is moderately warm. During the winter the average temperature is 2.2°C.

Provinces

The Netherlands is divided into 12 provinces. Originally there were 11, but in 1970 land was irrigated and a new province, Flevoland, was born. In addition to these provinces, the Dutch Antilles and the island of Aruba also belong to the kingdom of the Netherlands. Each of the

Figure 3.4   The "Oranjes", National Dutch Soccer Team

provinces has its own government. However, the central government in The Hague makes the main decisions.

Principal characteristics

Table 3.6 shows the position of The Netherlands in relation to other European countries on a number of standardised items.

Table 3.6   Principal characteristics of the Netherlands in relation to EU-15

	EU-15	The Netherlands	Relation (The Netherlands/EU-15) $\times$ 100
Density (inhabitants per km^2) Year: 1999	118	467	395.76
People having completed at least upper secondary education (%) Year: 2001	64	67	105
Life expectancy at birth (boys; years) Year: 2000	75.3	75.7	100.5
Life expectancy at birth (girls; years) Year: 2000	81.4	82.80	98.3
Employment rate (men; %) Year: 2001	73	83	113
Employment rate (women; %) Year: 2001	55	65	119
Unemployment rate (%) Year: 2001	7	2	33
Cost-of-living comparisons (total value; B = 100) Year: 2000	B = 100	114	114

Source: Eurostat Yearbook 2003.

Table 3.7   Age structure of population

Age (years)	1990 (%)	2000 (%)	EU-15 (2002) (%)
<15	18	19	17
15–24	16	12	12
25–49	38	39	37
50–64	15	17	17
65–79	10	10	13
>80	3	3	4

Source: Eurostat Yearbook 2002.

People

The Netherlands has a population of approximately 16 million. At 470 inhabitants per km^2, its density is the highest in Europe. The population is unevenly distributed, the western part of the Netherlands being much more densely populated than the eastern part.

The Netherland's birth rate is about the average for European countries. After the Second World War there was a large increase in the population, and birth rates were high. In the first decade of this century, the population is ageing, and by 2014 some 25% of the population will exceed the age of 65 (Table 3.7).

Economy

The economy of the Netherlands is commonly characterised as an "open economy" in which foreign trade plays a central role. In 2000, the GDP at market prices (GDP) was EUR 408.089 billion. In purchasing power standards (PPS) per head, this represented EUR 26.310. Together with Sweden, the Netherlands shows the smallest discrepancy between the richest and the poorest among its regions. Some examples of large Dutch multinational firms are: ABN Amro, Unilever and Shell. The state plays a main regulatory role in the market economy. Different governmental organisations like NMA and OPTA have the responsibility for maintaining a fair and liberal market economy in the Netherlands.

Gross value added at current prices and current exchange rates (Breakdown of economic sectors) (Figure 3.5).

Generally speaking, the cost of living in the Netherlands is somewhat higher than the EU average. Expenditure on housing, water, electricity, gas and other fuels is noticeably higher (71%) than the average.

Legal, institutional and political environment

The Netherlands is a constitutional monarchy based on the rule of law and social justice. Queen Beatrix is formally the head of the government, and is routinely involved in political decision-making.

Responsibility is entrusted to the organs established by the constitution for this purpose: the legislature, the executive and the judiciary. These are called the "Trias politica".

The legislature consists of two chambers. The second chamber consists of 150 persons and is chosen directly by the people entitled to vote. The first chamber consists of 75 persons and is chosen indirectly during other elections. Every 4 years elections are held and people can choose the party or person of preference.

The party, or coalition of parties, that receives more than half of the 150 seats in the second chamber forms the government and develops governmental policy for a 4-year period. Ministers are selected from these parties. The main political parties in the Netherlands are the Christian Democrats (CDA), the Social Democrats (PvdA) and the Liberal Party (VVD).

Labour market

As in most other European countries, the main part of the Dutch labour force works in the service sector (Tables 3.8 and 3.9).

During the last decade unemployment in the Netherlands fell, but forecasts for the near future are not bright. Statistical studies expect the unemployment rate to grow in the coming years, mainly because of the high cost of labour and relatively low levels of consumer confidence (Table 3.10).

Hourly labour costs in the Netherlands are higher than the European average. This might partly be due to the strength of the trade unions in the Netherlands. Agreements on such topics as pay, working hours, holidays and general working conditions are negotiated between management and workforce, who are often called "social partners". A vital role in these negotiation processes is played by the centralised organisations of unions and employers.

Educational system

In comparison to other EU countries the educational level of people in the Netherlands is average. The cultural and educational character of Dutch schools is quite homogeneous. There are two main types of school: Christian schools and public schools. There is also a small number of schools outside the mainstream (such as Muslim schools). The government, in the form of the minister of education, has the main responsibility for educational standards in all schools.

School attendance is compulsory for a period of 8 years. Thereafter, pupils must attend at least a part-time vocational school until the age of 18. After secondary school, they can choose to pursue university study (Table 3.11). Most institutions of higher education in the Netherlands belong to the state. Only a few universities are self-governing.

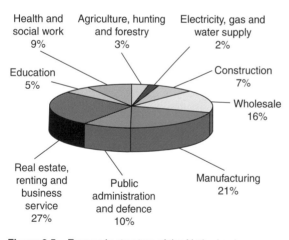

Figure 3.5 Economic structure of the Netherlands.
Source: Eurostat Yearbook 2002

Table 3.9 Persons (in thousands) in employment in different sectors

	1990	1995	2000
Agriculture	297	252	240
Industry	1648	1535	1582
Service	4229	4788	5516

Source: Eurostat Yearbook 2002.

Table 3.8 Persons in employment

Year	1992	1993	1994	1995	1996	1997	1998	1999	2000	2001	2002
People (in million)	10.3	10.4	10.5	10.5	10.5	10.6	10.6	10.7	10.7	10.8	10.8

Source: CBS statline.

Table 3.10   Unemployment rate

Year	1993	1994	1995	1996	1997	1998	2000	2000	
								Men	Women
Per cent	7	7	7	6	5	4	3	2	4

Source: Eurostat Yearbook 2002.

Table 3.11   People aged 25–64 having completed at least upper secondary education (%, 2000)

	Total (25–64)	25–29	30–34	35–39	40–44	45–49	50–54	55–59	60–64
EU-15	66	76	73	70	66	62	55	51	45
The Netherlands	66	76	74	71	68	63	60	55	53

Source: Eurostat Yearbook 2002.

HRM IN GERMANY AND THE NETHERLANDS

INTRODUCTION

Organisational flexibility is commonly associated with economic success and competitiveness, whereas rigidity has negative connotations. Organisations are expected to overcome rigidity so as to survive in volatile, competitive and ever-changing markets. In the face of globalisation and rapid technological change, flexibility has become a virtue. From a labour market perspective, flexible working patterns provide an opportunity for employers to draw on elements of the workforce which would otherwise not be available, such as employees with children, elderly or disabled people or people who prefer to spend less time on their job (Brewster et al., 1997). Especially in economies with high unemployment, rigidity of the labour market is often seen as the main barrier to reducing unemployment. Although flexibility is a frequently discussed issue, there is still no widely accepted definition.

For those writers concerned with manufacturing industry (e.g. Katz, 1985; Piore and Sabel, 1985; Kern and Schumann, 1987), new technology is the key to a more flexible form of production and thus a response to rapid market changes. This stream of literature focuses on production systems rather than employment; however, it indicates that a more skilled, motivated and flexible workforce is crucial to an organisation's flexibility.

The importance of employees and human resource management (HRM) is stressed even more in the work of Atkinson (1984, 1985), who has developed a model of "the flexible firm". He identifies different forms of flexibility. Numerical flexibility refers to the adjustment of the level of labour input to meet fluctuations in output (Atkinson and Meager, 1986). Functional flexibility is "the ability to adjust and deploy the skills of its employees to match the tasks required by its changing workload, production method and/or technology" (Atkinson and Meager, 1986). To reinforce numerical and functional flexibility, pay and financial flexibility is suggested.[1]

Both approaches, however, highlight the importance of employees and HRM with regard to an organisation's flexibility.

ANALYSIS

HRM appears to be an important means of adjusting the organisation to an ever-changing environment. To achieve competitive advantage an organisation needs not merely to react to new situations, but to shape the organisation in accordance with future demands. An organisation might even be able to influence external developments.

---

[1] We do not consider the fourth form of flexibility, distancing, here.

The extent of an organisation's flexibility can be influenced by HRM. The significance attached to the HRM function and its role in strategic planning, recruitment, personnel development, performance evaluation and remuneration, as well as employee participation and patterns of work, are HRM features that are likely to have an impact on organisational flexibility. In comparing Germany and the Netherlands, we aim to discover whether country-specific aspects also affect labour rigidity. Furthermore, we shall see whether organisations in the two countries tend to diverge or whether they become more similar.

The role of the HRM function

For most organisations, the employees constitute the most expensive part of their operating costs. Kara, Kayis and O'Kane (2002) refer to workers as the "most flexible resource". The significance actually attached to employees might be reflected in the role the HRM function plays in an organisation. As a core function, HRM should be represented on the board of directors. Where the head of human resource (HR) is a board member, management is more likely to focus on employees' needs and abilities in leading the company (Table 3.12). Moreover, if its head serves on the board the HRM function receives top management information more quickly and more extensively and thus can react faster.

Compared to other EU countries, where on average 57% of organisations have the head of HRM on the main board of directors, both the Netherlands and Germany score relatively low. Whereas in Dutch organisations the proportion with the head of HRM being a board member has remained more or less stable over the last decade, the proportion of German organisations with a head of personnel on the main board has risen sharply. When we look at the educational background of the head of HRM, major differences between the Netherlands and Germany appear.

In 1999/2000, almost 70% of German heads of personnel held a university degree (most of them in business studies or economics), but less than 40% of their Dutch colleagues (40% of those who did held a degree in humanities or fine arts). In view of the comparatively high degree of professionalisation, the proportion of German HRM executives with board membership is lower than one would expect.

More than half the organisations in both countries do not seem to have a close link between the corporate management and the personnel function. This might indicate a negative impact on an organisation's flexibility. To further investigate this aspect, we take a closer look at the status and role of the HRM in relation to corporate strategy.

HRM strategy

The aim of flexibility is to adjust employees quantitatively and qualitatively to the current situation, or, more proactively, to future situations. Thus it is necessary both to integrate HRM into the strategy development process and to conduct HRM strategically. An organisation's strategy is based on the one hand on the own resources it commands and on the other on the possibilities and constraints of its environment. When changes occur in the environment, the organisational strategy must be adjusted accordingly. Furthermore, strategic planning is supposed to anticipate the development of an organisation's environment. The integration of HRM is achieved by involving in the strategy formulation process those who are responsible for personnel.

So how is this related to organisational flexibility? HRM may be crucial as it can counterbalance the tendency towards increased bureaucracy that occurs when organisations grow and age, and in this way it is directly linked to organisational flexibility (Butler et al., 1991). Integrating the personnel function into the strategy formulation process is expected to contribute positively to an organisation's flexibility, because opportunities and potential bottlenecks arising from HRs are taken into consideration. Thus the strategy can be adjusted to an organisation's human capital, or the measures necessary to adapt HRs to an envisaged strategy can be taken into account during the planning process. In both cases, integrating the HRM function into the strategy formulation process is likely to increase flexibility (Table 3.13).

Table 3.12 Does the head of the personnel/HRs function serve on the main board of directors or equivalent (% of organisations)?

	Germany (%)			The Netherlands (%)		
	1991	1995	1999/2000	1991	1995	1999/2000
Yes	31	39	46	44	42	41

In the Netherlands, the relatively low representation of the head of HR on the board of directors is compensated for by a higher level of involvement of the HR department in the general strategy formulation process compared to Germany. In this respect, Dutch organisations are slightly above the European average (93%). However, the proportion of German organisations in which the HR department is integrated into the strategy formulation process from the outset is higher compared to the Dutch. To shed more light on these contradictory findings we need to take the size of the organisation into consideration. In Germany, there appears to be a positive relationship between the number of employees and the integration of HRM into strategy development. This pattern is not obvious for Dutch organisations. Apart from that it can be assumed that the integration of the personnel function into the strategic planning process corresponds with the existence of an HR strategy in the organisation. In Germany, 35% of the organisations do not have an HR strategy, whereas in the Netherlands 85% have a written or unwritten HR strategy.

To determine the status of the personnel department within an organisation, one can examine the distribution of responsibility for major HR-related functions. Table 3.14 suggests how responsibility for training has changed over the last decade.

In both countries we see a tendency towards decreased sole responsibility of the HR department for

training activities. In both countries nowadays more than 80% of HR departments share responsibility with line management. Whereas the HR department in Dutch organisations has historically worked in co-operation with line management, the responsibility of German HR departments changed in recent years. In the beginning of the 1990s 40% of the German HR departments still had sole responsibility for training; however, this number fell to 8% in 1999/2000.

As to flexibility, we may assume that close collaboration between line management and the HR function exerts a positive effect on an organisation's flexibility, because the personnel function is able to design training and development according to the needs identified by line management.

Recruitment and selection

The recruitment and selection process forms an essential starting point in providing flexibility. A volatile organisational environment requires quantitative adjustments, i.e. people are laid off and hired frequently. This would seem to call for cheap and easy-to-handle cheap selection methods. On the other hand, in terms of functional rather than numerical flexibility, recruitment and selection is supposed to provide well and broadly educated employees who are able to adjust to changing tasks and situations. Thus sophisticated selection practices are appropriate.

It is important to be able to recruit and retain the best human capital available externally or internally. Table 3.15 shows how many Dutch and German organisations have introduced the mechanisms mentioned to recruit or retain employees.

Compared to Swiss, Norwegian, Irish and French organisations the Germans and Dutch rarely recruit abroad. Retraining is used frequently in Dutch organisations (also compared to other European countries),

Table 3.13 Stage at which HR is involved in development of corporate strategy

	Germany (%)	The Netherlands (%)
From the outset	59	44
Through consultation	20	39
On implementation	7	13
Not consulted	14	4

Table 3.14 Change in responsibility of line management (training)

	Germany (%)			The Netherlands (%)		
	1991	1995	1999/2000	1991	1995	1999/2000
Line management	8	10	7	6	12	11
Line management with HR department	20	40	45	35	52	56
HR department with line management	32	39	40	46	32	26
HR department	40	11	8	13	4	7

Table 3.15 Mechanisms introduced for the recruitment/retention of employees

	Germany (%)	The Netherlands (%)
Recruitment abroad	16	16
Retraining	37	67
Increased pay	37	40
Relocation	7	10
Marketing and image	60	29

Table 3.16 Mechanisms introduced for the recruitment/selection of employees

	Germany (%)	The Netherlands (%)
Application forms		
Every appointment	34	54
Most appointments	16	12
Some appointments	8	10
Few appointments	7	5
Not used	34	20
Assessment centre		
Every appointment	0	1
Most appointments	4	8
Some appointments	24	63
Few appointments	20	10
Not used	53	17
Psychometric tests		
Every appointment	0	1
Most appointments	1	6
Some appointments	8	34
Few appointments	9	18
Not used	82	42
References		
Every appointment	6	5
Most appointments	14	10
Some appointments	36	42
Few appointments	30	17
Not used	14	27

whereas it is unusual for German organisations (only Czech organisations use retraining less frequently). In contrast, German organisations are among those who use marketing to recruit and retain employees often, whereas the use of marketing in the Netherlands corresponds to the European average.

When it comes to retraining employees, Dutch organisations appear to be more flexible (in terms of functional flexibility) with regard to adjusting qualifications and skills to new jobs compared to their German neighbours. It could be that German employees are less often willing to do a job that does not match their current skills.

Organisations in the two countries are quite similar with regard to the frequency with which they use interviews (either panel or one-to-one). There are differences, however, concerning the practices listed in Table 3.16. Every second Dutch organisation uses application forms for every appointment, but only one-third of all German organisations do so. Assessment centre and psychometric tests appear to be more popular in the Netherlands than in Germany. In contrast to that, German organisations rely more heavily on references than the Dutch.

Training and development

As mentioned earlier, training and education are instruments for achieving functional flexibility as identified by Atkinson and Meager (1986). Training and education provides employees with the ability to perform more tasks and functions. An educational structure with an adequate percentage of highly educated employees makes it possible for the organisation to change activities with negligible effect on the composition of the labour force. Thus training and education can enhance flexibility. The result of training and education is a multifunctional workforce. According to Van den Beukel and Molleman (1998), "the most notable driving force behind multifunctionality lies in the necessity for organisations to respond quickly to the often capricious demands of customers. Organisations expect employees to play a significant part in ensuring that 'Whatever a customer orders is delivered tomorrow, if not today.'"

Ebeling and Lee (1994) see one advantage of a multifunctional workforce as the increased capacity to deal with absenteeism. "Should an employee be ill or have a day off, rather than his or her work being put on hold and perhaps also delaying consequent steps in the production process, the task of the absent worker can be assigned to a multiskilled colleague". Multiskilling can also be of benefit in the event of high levels of turnover, because empty positions can be filled without much trouble. Clark (1993) found that the need for multifunctionality was not based on fluctuations in the supply of labour (due to absenteeism), but on a low or tight staffing level. This notion is supported by Van den Beukel and Molleman (1998, p. 305), as they state that "Because the organisation was under pressure to reduce labour costs, staff levels were kept to a

The necessity of multifunctionality

Constraining forces

1. Quality of working life
   - Stability valued
   - 'Rights in the job'
   - Individual preferences
2. Quality of work
   - Specialist knowledge
   - Suitability of worker

Constraining forces

3. Skill retention
4. Costs of training
5. Social psychological issues

Driving forces

1. Volatile and uncertain market
   - High occurrence of changes in production
   - Shifts in demand
2. Fluctuations in supply of labour
3. Quality of working life
   - Number of skills increased
   - Understanding and involvement of process
4. Functional or heterogeneous grouping
5. Quality of product and process
6. Tight staffing levels

Figure 3.6 Multifunctionality: driving and constraining forces

Table 3.17 Proportion of wage bill spent on training and development

(%)	Germany (%)	The Netherlands (%)
<1	14	5
1–1.9	29	27
2–2.9	23	26
3–4.9	15	19
5–9.9	15	15
>10	5	8

Table 3.18 Number of training days received by staff category

	Germany	The Netherlands
Management	5	5
Professional/technical	5	6
Clerical	3	3
Manual	2	4

minimum and it was therefore essential that employees were trained in many different areas."

In addition to driving forces, there are also several constraining forces for multifunctionality achieved through training and development, as shown in the Figure 3.6 (Van den Beukel and Molleman, 1998). Because companies are faced with limitations in financial resources, an obvious constraint is the cost of training. A secondary constraint is that senior workers (i.e. those with a longer history in the company) settle themselves in stable jobs, and are less likely to move to other tasks (or rotate their jobs). These employees seem to develop a belief that they have earned certain rights in a job through their seniority (Carnall, 1982).

Obviously every person has different preferences and some people are simply better at certain tasks than others. Clark (1993) called this "horses for courses". This principle limits multifunctionality, because employees may be doing tasks that they simply do not like or to which they are not suited. There is also the danger that extensive training in multiple fields will result in the loss of specialist knowledge. Because this can never be the company's intention, this can also be considered as a constraining power. Related to this is the issue of skill retention: maintaining a skill is difficult if there are not enough opportunities to practise it. An example of social psychological issues would be that the distribution of tasks among the team would be perceived by some as unfair and demotivating (Kerr, 1983).

It is important to notice that although the need for functional flexibility may be high, companies not only identify the constraints from a managerial perspective (concentrating on organisational flexibility and cost issues), but also realise that employees are affected in terms of quality of working life.

Table 3.17 indicates the proportion of their wage bill that German and Dutch companies spend on training and development. It shows that the percentages in most cases are virtually the same in both countries. There are significant differences, though, in the highest and lowest category. Fourteen per cent of the German companies spends less than 1% of their annual wage bill on training and development, as opposed to 5% of the Dutch companies. And 8% of the Dutch firms seem to spend more than 10% of their annual wage bill on training and development compared to 5% of the German firms.

Table 3.18, which lists the number of training days received by each staff category, underlines the slightly more intensive training in Dutch companies. Dutch firms either match, or score more highly than, their German counterparts.

In the manual labour category a noticeable difference can be found between the scores of the German and Dutch firms, 2 and 4 days per year respectively. The training and development of manual labour seems to be regarded as less relevant in Germany compared to the Netherlands. This phenomenon can be explained in two ways. On the one hand, the German labour market is currently experiencing a relatively large supply side surplus. In the Netherlands the opposite is true, increasing the demand for multiskilled employees. On the other hand, the German dual education system may provide a basic training for manual workers, in particular for the so-called "Facharbeiter", reducing the need for training activities in this staff category.

As well as the volume of training provided, the effectiveness of the training also needs to be taken into account. For instance, the cost of training might be higher in one country, or the training programmes themselves might differ in quality as between countries.

Performance measurements and rewards

Both managers and academics frequently argue that performance-oriented remuneration increases flexibility. The employee receives feedback on his or her performance that enables him or her to adjust the level of effort necessary to reach previously defined goals. Moreover, individual behaviour can be aligned to organisational objectives. Performance measurement and associated rewards may sensitise employees to market demands – which again increases flexibility because new trends and developments may be detected earlier.

Although companies in both countries show a tendency towards using performance-related pay regardless of employee level (Table 3.19), the trend in the

Netherlands has been slightly stronger during the last decade. In Germany, performance-related pay for clerical staff is more frequently used than in the Netherlands, whereas merit-related remuneration for management is more common in Dutch organisations.

More noticeable differences between the two countries exist with regard to the use of appraisal systems. More than 80% of Dutch organisations use appraisal systems for all kinds of employees. In Germany, only every other organisation uses appraisal systems for manual and clerical workers. The proportion of German organisations with appraisal systems for professional or technical staff and management averages 60%.

Employee communication and the role of trade unions and works councils

Union influence and the existence of works councils are connected to organisational flexibility in two ways (Table 3.20). In the first place, trade unions monitor the effects of flexible work on society and individuals. Secondly, trade unions need to adjust their services to be able to look after the interests of flexible workers (Valverde et al., 1997).

Nearly every German and Dutch company has a works council. Thus in comparison to the EU average, employee interest can be taken for granted and is institutionalised. As can be seen from Table 3.21, union influence is more or less stable. About two-thirds of German and Dutch companies report no serious changes in union influence.

Table 3.20   Presence of works council

	Germany (%)	The Netherlands (%)	Other EU (%)
Yes	96	91	69

Table 3.19   Use of merit/performance-related pay by staff category (% of organisations)

	Germany (%)			The Netherlands (%)		
	1991	1995	1999/2000	1991	1995	1999/2000
Management	21	19	31	20	37	48
Professional/technical	40	36	44	26	40	47
Clerical	35	34	42	23	30	37
Manual	32	28	36	27	31	36

As shown in Table 3.22, Dutch and German firms communicate financial results and strategy issues to nearly all managerial employees. However, differences can be noticed in respect of the other employee groups. Whereas Dutch and German companies report quite similar findings with regard to briefings about financial results, Dutch firms demonstrate a higher propensity to inform their professional, clerical and manual employees about strategy issues than German firms.

Organisation of work: flexible patterns of work

Flexible work patterns are likely to be the core feature in overcoming organisational rigidity. From an economic point of view, flexible working practices are considered to be a powerful means of reducing unemployment and tapping into new segments of the labour market (Brewster et al., 1997). Non-traditional contracts provide the opportunity for numerical flexibility within an otherwise rather rigid labour legislation. More than in other HR areas, flexible work patterns are determined by external factors like labour law or the external labour market. Thus country-specific differences are very likely.

As illustrated in Table 3.23, in Dutch companies a higher proportion of the workforce is employed on temporary/casual work contracts than in German companies. To put it another way, temporary/casual employment is more common in the Netherlands than in Germany. As the law in respect of temporary employment is rather restrictive in Germany, these results are not surprising.

Because of the increasing use of temporary workers by employment agencies in the Netherlands, Dutch labour law was revised in 1998 to introduce the so-called "flex law". This was designed to enhance and clarify the rights of the temporary worker. The flex law regulates the rights of temporary workers who work for employment agencies and are sent to client organisations on a temporary basis. As a consequence of this legislation, the judicial position of the employee grows stronger as the labour relationship develops over time.

When we look at the use of part-time arrangements as depicted in Table 3.24, we can conclude that part-time employment has been relatively stable in Germany over the last decade. In the Netherlands, however, the situation has been quite dynamic. Part-time employment in Dutch companies has increased in comparison with other types of employment contract. It is now much more common in Dutch companies than in German companies.

Table 3.21   Trade union influence: analysis of recent changes

	Germany (%)	The Netherlands (%)
Influence has increased	13	16
Influence is the same	69	63
Influence has decreased	18	21

Table 3.22   Percentage of firms that formally communicate financial results and company strategy to employees

	Germany (%)			The Netherlands (%)		
	1991	1995	1999/2000	1991	1995	1999/2000
Management briefed						
About strategy	94	92	93	96	99	97
About finance	90	96	93	94	98	93
Professional briefed						
About strategy	31	41	45	73	83	68
About finance	71	76	80	73	80	70
Clerical briefed						
About strategy	13	21	25	28	42	41
About finance	55	67	64	44	47	42
Manual briefed						
About strategy	7	11	15	27	40	38
About finance	43	49	50	40	43	38

Table 3.23   Proportion of workforce on temporary/casual working arrangements

(%)	Germany (%)			The Netherlands (%)		
	1991	1995	1999/2000	1991	1995	1999/2000
<1	65	34	29	23	15	16
1–10	32	25	29	58	69	58
11–20	2	1	2	16	6	14
>20	1	2	2	3	2	7
Not used	0	38	38	0	8	5

Table 3.24   Proportion of workforce on part-time arrangements

(%)	Germany (%)			The Netherlands (%)		
	1991	1995	1999/2000	1991	1995	1999/2000
<1	11	9	14	17	4	2
1–10	65	63	61	61	42	35
11–20	17	16	14	10	21	21
>20	7	12	11	12	33	42

CONCLUSIONS

Europe's labour markets have undergone a substantial change during recent years. Evidence from the Cranet survey suggests that a clear majority of employers in Europe report that the range, extent and use of flexible working hours and contractual arrangements have been increasing (Valverde et al., 1997). However, while there is a common trend towards increased flexibility across Europe, the nature and extent of flexible working practices vary by country. It is important to understand the various forms of flexibility, the purposes they serve, and the way in which they are integrated within the national context.

There seems little doubt that companies regard flexibility as an important contributor to competitiveness. However, flexibility is not necessarily a panacea for companies – it inevitably involves problems. It may create problems in communicating with employees who may never all be together at one time or it may generate feelings of suspicion or unfairness between increasingly disparate groups of employees. Disaffected or uninterested workers may generate substantial friction for employers. For employees, flexibility may also lead to uncertainty of income and job security.

However, flexibility may also produce benefits for individuals and for society at large. It can benefit employees by opening up opportunities to work as well as to balance work and family life. Flexible working patterns may provide additional opportunities to work, can enable family income to be supplemented and may allow work to be fitted in with family responsibilities. Society can benefit from having more people in the labour market.

Flexibility remains a controversial issue. The coming years will show whether it proves to be a panacea or a danger to organisational and individual health.

ACKNOWLEDGEMENTS

The authors would like to thank Drs. Chris van Saaze and Arjen Mackaay for their insightful and valuable contributions.

HRM IN ACTION

GERMANY: VOLKSWAGEN'S PROJECT 5000 × 5000 – STRIVING FOR FLEXIBILITY IN GERMANY

Industry background

One of the pillars of the German economy is the car industry. More than 700,000 people work in that industry, with a further 1,000,000 employed indirectly.

Car manufacturers, however, operate in a difficult competitive environment characterised by an existing overcapacity and a decline in new vehicle registrations. The car industry faces growing pressure to cut costs and raise productivity. At the same time, customers expect vehicles that suit their individual needs and make ever-increasing demands with regard to safety and quality. Consequently, car producers are being forced more and more to operate flexibly.

In view of these challenges, the rather restrictive German labour legislation and high labour costs constitute a heavy burden on German car production.

Volkswagen

One of the world's leading car manufacturers is the German-based Volkswagen AG (VW). Founded in 1938, Volkswagen has become the largest automobile manufacturer in Europe, with a market share of 30% in Germany and 12% worldwide (in 2002). In 45 plants across the world, more than 5 million vehicles per year are produced. Almost 325,000 employees (more than 50% of them in Germany) produced sales revenues of approximately 87 billion EUR in 2002.

One notable feature of Volkswagen is that the state of Lower Saxony is a major shareholder, exerting a significant influence on strategic decision-making. Furthermore, trade union membership is comparatively high, about 90% of the workers being members of IG Metall. As a result of the company's history and the influence of trade unions and work councils, VW is characterised by a co-operative and consensus-oriented corporate culture.

In an effort to reconcile market pressures and its social responsibility as one of Germany's biggest employers, VW has developed new employment models aimed at increasing flexibility while retaining or even creating jobs in costly German production sites. In 1993, to help cope with the recession in the automobile market, VW introduced a 4-day-week combined with reductions in employees' annual income.

Project 5000 × 5000

Not expecting the market demand for automobiles to grow substantially, Volkswagen has decided to achieve organisational growth by expanding its product range. It has entered the high-growth segment of the MPV (multipurpose vans) market by introducing the Touran in 2003. Despite high labour costs and rigid labour legislation, VW decided to produce the van in Germany instead of building a production facility in a country with lower hourly wages and social contributions. In order to stay competitive, VW founded Auto 5000 GmbH as a pilot project in August 2001. In this "company within the company" the Touran (and in the future also the new Minibus) will be produced on the basis of a new type of organisation and a labour model unique in Germany. In the face of increasing unemployment, the public, press and government responded positively to the idea of hiring and training 5000 unemployed to produce the van. The trade union, however, forced

Volkswagen to enter fierce negotiations over the new model since its working conditions would fall short of those laid down by the standard collective agreement between VW and IG Metall. Initially, agreement seemed impossible. However, under pressure from public and media, the parties resumed negotiations and reached a new agreement in August 2001.

The agreement comprises four main features:

1. Employment of 5000 unemployed people.
2. Payment of 5000 DM (2301 EUR) monthly.
3. 35 working hours per week.
4. HR development.

Employment of 5000 unemployed

The first stage provides for 3500 unemployed people to work in Wolfsburg on the production of the VW Touran. In 2005 another 1500 unemployed are due to be contracted for the production of the Microbus. Volkswagen regards this is an important signal for the labour market in the light of continuing redundancies in other large companies.

With the support of the Federal Employment Office, potential employees are encouraged to apply via the internet. The extensive selection process covers an applicant's profile, online qualification tests and an assessment centre. Volkswagen wants to hire the best-qualified and motivated personnel regardless of their previous jobs or educational and vocational background.

Compensation

Every employee receives a monthly basic salary of 2301 EUR and a yearly minimum bonus of 3068 EUR. In the 6-month probationary period employees will receive less. Auto 5000 GmbH employees have the chance to earn more if they reach the breakeven point. They receive a share in the profits dependent on the previous year's business results.

In Germany, employers who hire unemployed people may apply for a subsidy from the Federal Employment Office. Thus Volkswagen may expect to reduce labour costs further in the initial stage by means of substantial state grants.

Working hours

The value-creating, regular hours of work amount to a yearly average of 35 h per week. Depending on factory capacity utilisation, working time may increase to 42 h per week. Hours of overtime are credited to the employee's time account, which is generally balanced out with leisure time. Overtime will be paid only if additional work is due to defective material or is the fault of the organisation. Production will take place in three shifts per day on up to 6 days per week. On up to 30 Saturdays per year, Auto 5000 GmbH may introduce a late shift. In addition to the working time of 35 h, the agreement with the union provides for 3 h of qualification per week; of these, 1.5 h are remunerated and 1.5 "donated" by the employee.

HR development

The concept of "From talent to an automotive engineering specialist" represents the way new employees are able to continuously obtain further qualifications before and after the start of production. The process can be divided roughly into two stages: learning the basic prerequisites to fulfil tasks within Auto 5000 GmbH and subsequent life-long learning in the course of day-to-day work.

In the first 9 months, Auto 5000 GmbH employees will be carefully prepared for the challenges they will face in the factory; this will be accomplished by completing training which qualifies them for general industrial work and, subsequently, for automotive engineering specifically. In the second stage, the employees learn continuously and directly in the manufacturing process. If, for example, the employees find that they are unable to eradicate a malfunction which occurs during manufacturing, they are offered qualification modules developed on-site. Over a 2-year period employees may acquire an approved mechanic's certificate especially developed for this purpose.

Conclusions

All in all, Project 5000 × 5000 appears to represent an innovative model. The German government considers it a ground-breaking approach, the media give it positive exposure and more than 3000 previously unemployed have been chosen out of more than 40,000 and have started to produce the Touran. Some trade union representatives and associations of unemployed, however, are still reluctant to use the model in other companies or to see it as generally applicable. The debate about the merits and consequences of 5000 × 5000 will continue.

THE NETHERLANDS: FURNIFASHION'S PART-TIME FACTOR – FLEXIBLE WORKFORCE AT ANY COST?

Furnifashion[1] is a globally operating chain of retail outlets, selling a very diverse range of products consisting of thousands of furniture-related items. Worldwide, the Swedish furniture giant employs about 10,000 employees, distributed across 45 locations, 35 of which are situated near large urban areas in northwest Europe. In 2002 its total revenues were 5 billion EUR. In the Netherlands, where its self-service formula was a huge success, Furnifashion employs 984 employees in five outlets. The numbers of employees in Amsterdam, Rotterdam, the Hague, Utrecht and Arnhem are respectively 244, 235, 207, 166 and 132.

About half of the staff work part-time; their average age is 28 years. The salary system has 18 levels within the context of the collective labour agreement and 7 outside this agreement. On average there are nine remuneration plateaus per salary level, whereby each transition to another plateau represents a 2% increase in salary.

In 2002, 50% of all employees had not yet reached their appropriate salary maximum. Employee turnover at Furnifashion was 9% in 2001 (the same as in 2000); for 2002 a similar turnover rate was expected. Absence due to illness was 10% in the two preceding years and was also expected to remain the same in 2002. The percentage of female employees was 75%.

For 2002, projected turnover was 302 million EUR with an expected net profit of 7.5 million EUR. For 2003, a revenue growth of approximately 6%, with similar profit, is forecast. Costs of goods sold in 2003 are expected to increase by 1%, as in 2001 and 2002. A relatively large portion of the products is acquired in Eastern European countries.

---

[1] Furnifashion resembles a well-known Dutch department store. The figures given have been altered to maintain anonymity.

Wage costs, 30.1 million EUR in 2002, are restricted by corporate headquarters to a maximum growth of 3%, leading to 31 million EUR. Furnifashion operates a rigorous budgeting system, which is also applied to wage costs. Every case of expenditure exceeding budget must be reported to corporate headquarters immediately.

At the end of 2002 an agreement was struck concerning the renewal of the collective labour agreement as of 1 January 2003. The new collective labour agreement was to be valid for 2 years (1 January 2003–31 December 2004). Except for an incidental rise in wages of 2% on 1 January 2003 and 2% on 1 January 2004, the negotiations concerning the collective labour agreement resulted in a (fully paid) reduction in working hours from 40 to 38 per week. It was agreed that hiring new staff would only occur "when needed and possible". However, no recruitment quota for additional personnel were determined. In addition, it was agreed that adjustment for inflation (expected to be 2%) would be sacrificed in return for this reduction in working hours.

During this period, Furnifashion's operations in the Netherlands were underperforming when compared to most of their European counterparts. Apparently the other European Furnifashion companies are more successful in job restructuring (outsourcing employee tasks to customers) and in improving labour productivity and cost control. The standard deviation of the average turnover per labour hour in particular is much higher in Holland than, e.g. in Sweden and the UK, where relatively more part-time workers are used. Furnifashion's opening hours in the Netherlands (60 h a week, including one evening a week and one Sunday per month) are comparable to opening hours in other countries. Distribution of sales over the week (Monday 7%, Tuesday 9%, Wednesday 16%, Thursday 17%, Friday 23% and Saturday and Sunday 28%) is also similar to those in other European countries.

Because of the perceived underperformance in the Netherlands, Furnifashion corporate headquarters have asked the international HRM staff for assistance. The task of the HRM staff is to provide support in identifying possible causes of the unsatisfactory performance and to suggest improvements that could help the Dutch management.

The objective of such improvements is for Dutch Furnifashion subsidiaries to be able to match the performance standards of the best of the European outlets. (Furnifashion is capitalised at 75 million EUR, with a balance sheet total of 150 m EUR.) The international HRM staff at corporate headquarters has identified a non-compliance of the Dutch operations with the "Samen Act" (a law to promote participation of ethnic minorities in the Dutch labour market). Currently less then 4% of Dutch Furnifashion employees come from ethnic minorities, whereas the Act prescribes that 7% of the workforce should be of an ethnic minority background.

The problem that Furnifashion faced in the Netherlands was to adapt the availability of the workforce to the daily fluctuations in revenues. It proved impossible to achieve a satisfactory balance between customer presence and staff presence, especially during the "slow" days of the week (Monday, Tuesday, Wednesday mornings and Thursday). The concentration of customer demand on Wednesday afternoon, Friday, Saturday and Sunday could not be matched by a sufficient staff presence.

An analysis was carried out in which turnover per opening hour was monitored, as well as employee presence per hour. Changes in rates of occupancy were calculated. It was concluded that the problem could be solved only by increasing the number of part-timers.

Furnifashion therefore increased the ratio of part-time workers, thus gaining flexibility. They decided that out of the total recruitment mix, 80% should be part-time employees. In addition, they established a target whereby at least 7% of the total recruitment mix should have a background as prescribed in the "Samen Act".

This resulted in *more flexibility*, *better financial performance* and *increased productivity* as part-time staff proved to be more willing to work additional and more flexible hours when required. Replacing full-timers by part-timers also contributed to an improvement in net profit and a better return on equity. Thanks to these satisfying results and relatively large financial borrowing capacity, Furnifashion has recently been able to open three new department stores in the Netherlands. The new strategic HRM policy allowed Furnifashion to exceed the norms of the "Samen Act" with 10% of ethnic minority staff. In addition, the yearly attrition of 9% was replaced by a recruitment of 6%, reducing the wage bill by 3%.

A minor disadvantage of this strategy was that there were relatively high numbers of new (part-time) staff members requiring training and education to prepare them for their tasks. However, the savings made by reducing the number of full-time staff outweighed this.

This case aims to demonstrate that by improving flexibility, firms can improve their financial performance. And by reinvesting some of the resulting gains, they can create new employment. A firm's ability to adapt to alterations in its environment depends to a large extent on the nature of its workforce and its acceptance of managerial policies designed to enhance flexibility. As companies are increasingly forced to be "lean and mean", a strategic HRM policy towards part-time and temporary staff becomes crucial.

TEACHING QUESTIONS

1. Taking into account the German labour market and industrial relations, what are the innovative aspects of the 5000 × 5000 project?
2. Do you consider Auto 5000 GmbH to be flexible with regard to their HRM practices? Why or why not?
3. In what way does Volkswagen rely on the German education system in hiring people regardless of their prior job experience?
4. Do you think the concept of Auto 5000 GmbH may be transferred to other countries?
5. In 2003 the availability of staff declines, due to personnel turnover and shortening of the obligatory labour week. How can Furnifashion make an appropriate assessment of the proportion of the lost workforce that needs to be re-installed?
6. How many full-time employees should Furnifashion employ in 2003? And which selection criteria would deserve a more focused attention?
7. Based on what information would you be able to judge whether the productivity target is reasonable?
8. How should local Dutch Furnifashion management operate, in case corporate headquarters have the opinion that the targeted goals are unreasonble?
9. How would you distribute the cumulative wage sum? Would you spend it all on hiring new staff?

REFERENCES

Atkinson, J. (1984) Manpower strategies for flexible organizations. *Personnel Management*, August: 28–31.

Atkinson, J. (1985) *Flexibility, uncertainty and manpower management.* Report 89 Brighton, Institute of Manpower Studies.

Atkinson, J. and Meager, N. (1986) *Changing working patterns: How companies achieve flexibility to meet their needs.* National Economic Development Office.

Brewster, C., Mayne, L., Valverde, M.A. and Kabst, R. (1997) Flexibility in European labour markets? The evidence renewed. *Employee Relations*, 19(6): 509–518.

Butler, J.E., Ferris, G.R. and Napier, N.K. (1991) Strategy and human resources management. *South-Western Series in Human Resources Management*: 215–294.

Carnall, C.A. (1982) Semi-autonomous work groups and the social structure of the organization. *Journal of Management Studies*, 19: 277–294.

Clark, J. (1993) Full flexibility and self-supervision in an automated factory. In: Clark, J. (ed.), *Human Resource Management and Technical Change*. London: Sage Publications.

Ebeling, A.C. and Lee, C.Y. (1994) Cross-training effectiveness and profitability. *International Journal of Production Research*, 32: 2843–2859.

Kara, S., Kayis, B. and O'Kane, S. (2002) The role of human factors in flexibility management: a survey. *Human Factors and Ergonomics in Manufacturing*, 12(1): 75–119.

Katz, H.C. (1985) *Shifting Gears: Changing Labour Relations in the US Automobile Industry.* Cambridge, MA: MIT Press.

Kern, H. and Schumann, M. (1987) Limits of the division of labour. *Economic and Industrial Democracy*, 8(2): 151–170.

Kerr, N.L. (1983) Motivation losses in small groups: a social dilemma analysis. *Journal of Personality and Social Psychology*, 45: 819–828.

Piore, M.J. and Sabel, C.F. (1985) *The Second Industrial Divide: Possibilities for Prosperity.* New York: Basic Books.

Valverde, M.A., Kabst, R., Brewster, C. and Mayne, L. (1997) Conclusion: the flexibility paradox. *Employee Relations*, 19(6): 596–608.

Van den Beukel, A.L. and Molleman, E. (1998) Multifunctionality: driving and constraining forces. *Human Factors and Ergonomics in Manufacturing*, 8(4): 303–321.

4

Austria and Switzerland: Small Countries with Large Differences

Christiane Erten, Guido Strunk, Jean-Claude Gonzalez and Martin Hilb

INSTITUTIONAL BACKGROUND

REPUBLIC OF AUSTRIA

Area	83,858 km²; 2.6% of EUR-15 area	**Other important cities and population**	Graz (302,210) Linz (211,021) Salzburg (143,978)
Population	8,069,000; 2.2% of EUR-15 population,	**Official language**	German
		Business languages	German and English
Density	96 inhabitants per km²	**Religions**	78% Roman Catholic
Capital and population	Wien (Vienna): 1,606,843 (1998)		5% Protestant 17% Others

Figure 4.1   Wiener Zentralfriedhof (Central churchyard in Vienna)

Topography and climate

The Republic of Austria extends over 573 km from west to east and over 298 km from north to south. It has an area of about 84,000 km, a resident population of about 8 million and a density of 96 inhabitants per km^2. Austria is bordered on the west by Switzerland and Liechtenstein, on the north-west by Germany, on the north by Czech Republic, on the east by Slovakia and Hungary, on the south-east by Slovenia, and on the south-west by Italy. Austria joined the European Union (EU) on 1 January 1995.

The major types of the Austrian landscape are the gneiss and granite plateaux of the Bohemian Massif in the north, the foothills of the Alps and the Carpathians which lie to the south and south-east of that plateaux, the Alps (60% of the area), the Vienna Basin in the north-east and the edge of the Hungarian Plain in the east and south-east. The Bohemian Massif is a forested highland region, whereas the lowland region of Austria, including the Vienna Basin supports the main agricultural activities in Austria. Numerous streams (e.g. the Danube river) and steep topography provide a large potential for hydro-electric potential. Austria produces about one-tenth of the world's magnesite, a principle source of magnesium.

The east and north-east belong to the dry continental Pannonian climate zone. The Alps and the western gneiss and granite plateaux form part of the humid-cool to humid-cold Alpine region. At the foothills of the Alps as well as in valleys in the south and the south-east it is dryer and warmer.

Principal characteristics

Austria consists of nine Bundesländer (federal states). Vienna, the capital of Austria is home to several important international organisations (one of the three United Nations headquarters, OPEC, etc.) and also a major centre for tourism. Formerly an important industrial centre, it is increasingly concentrating on the service sector.

Table 4.1 shows Austria's situation in relation to the EU. Below average is the infant mortality and the unemployment rate, above average is the employment rate for women and the standard of living.

Special features

The contemporary cultural milieu of Austria has a rich heritage: architecture and poetry, medicine and science and especially music. Great Austrian composers include Mozart, Hadyn, Schubert, the Strauss family, Schoenberg, Berg and von Webern. Writers of international reputation are, e.g. Grillparzer, Nestroy, Raimund, Hofmannsthal, Musil, Handke and Bernhard. Vienna's art galleries are well known for their wealth of old masters.

Within the last 25 years environmental awareness has increased considerably in Austria. Nature conservation policies have become very important. As agricultural and regional policies have a direct impact on the natural resources of a country, systematic checks are carried out to ensure that projects do stick to the protective measures taken in this field. Many public organisations have persons in charge of solving environmental problems which have been caused by the organisation itself.

Table 4.1   Austria's situation in relation to the EU

	EU-15[1]	Austria	Relation (Austria/EU-15) $\times$ 100
Density (inhabitants per km^2) Year: 1997	116	96.1	82.8
Infant mortality[2] (per thousand live birth) Year: 1997**	5.5 5.0 (1999)	4.7 4.4 (1999)	85.5 88.0 (1999)
Life expectancy at birth (boys; years) Year: 1997**	74.0 74.6 (1998)	74.2 74.7 (1998)	100.3 100.1 (1998)
Life expectancy at birth (girls; years) Year: 1997**	80.5 80.9 (1998)	80.5 80.9 (1998)	100.0
Marriage (per thousand people) Year: 1997**	5.0 5.1 (1999)	5.1 4.9 (1999)	102.0 96.1 (1999)
Divorces (per thousand people) Year: 1997**	1.8 1.8 (1998)	2.2 2.2 (1998)	122.2
Population increase (average increase between 1986 and 1996; % per year) Year: 1996	0.376	0.623	165.7
Net migration (per 10,000 people) Year: 1996	2.0	0.6	30.0
Employment rate (men; %) Year: 1998**	71	76	108
Employment rate (women; %) Year: 1998**	51	59	115
Unemployment rate (%) Year: 1998**	10	5	47
Cost-of-living comparisons (total value; $B = 100^3$) Year: 1996	$B = 100$	114.7 110.0 (1998)	114.7 110.0 (1998)

All data from (1), except * from (2) and ** from (3).

---

[1] EU-15: Total of the 15 EU Member States of the European Union (Belgium, Denmark, Germany, Greece, Spain, France, Ireland, Italy, Luxembourg, the Netherlands, Austria, Portugal, Finland, Sweden and the United Kindom).

[2] Infant mortality is the mortality of live-born children who have not yet reached their first birthday. It is computed as the ratio of deaths of children under 1 year of age to the number of live birth in a certain calendar year.

[3] Cost-of-living comparison is carried out by calculation of index numbers (Brussels = 100) based on (a) prices of a shopping basket of over 3000 goods and services, (b) expenditure patterns of international officials and (c) exchange rates. All information is at 1 July 1996. Figures come from work by Eurostat in the field of cost-of-living adjustments to salaries of EU officials. Staff regulations fix indices for Belgium and Luxembourg at 100. Hence indices are available for all EU capitals except Brussels and Luxembourg. Country codes refer to the capital city.

Age (years)	1986	1999	EU-15 (1998)	Women (% of age group)	
<15	18	17	17	49*	
15–24	17	12	13	50*	
25–49	34	39	37	49*	
50–64	16	17	17	51*	
65–79	11	12	12	61	
>80	4	3	4	71	
				Over all: 52*	

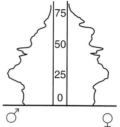

All data from (1), except * from (8); figure from (1).

Figure 4.2   Population by age and gender (% of total population).

Population

Although net migration (immigrants minus emigrants) has fallen continuously a population growth can be observed. In general it can be stated that the ageing of the population has accelerated. Increased longevity in the last 50 years reflects the high welfare standard reached in Austria. As can be seen in Figure 4.2 elder people (aged 50 and over) form an increasingly large part of the population. This is due to a drop in fertility and a decline in mortality. Furthermore, the figure shows very clearly that the life expectancy of women is increasing dramatically with advanced age.

The average Austrian household is 2.5 persons. Thirty per cent of the households consist of only one person and only about 55% of all couples do have children.

Legal, institutional and political environment

Austria is a democratic federal republic. The chancellor heads the Council of Ministers. The president acts as head of state with primarily ceremonial functions. For a long time, the Austrian Social Democratic Party, has been the major political organisation in the country. Currently, two other important parties – the Austrian People's Party (Christian Democrats) and the Liberal Party – form a coalition government with the social democrats and the green party in opposition. Traditionally, the public sector is of great importance in Austria. This has been emphasised in the 1970s where under the rule of the social democrats this sector has been expanded. In recent years, however, there are many moves towards privatisation of formerly public sector areas, e.g. telecommunications or railroads. Nevertheless, many of the economic leaders in Austria

still are directly or indirectly linked to the political system via the political parties. Thus, much of the social elite is also formed via the political system.

The social-welfare system provides earnings-related benefits for old people, work injury, illness, permanent disability, maternity and death. Especially the maternity leave is with 2 years longer than in most of the other European countries. Furthermore, there is the possibility to divide it between the couple, so that, e.g. both parents stay at home for 1 year each. Special programs also offer family allowances, unemployment insurance and benefits for war victims.

As shown in Tables 4.2 and 4.3 Austria has nearly no labour disputes in comparison to the EU. This is due to a very special Austrian system of decision-making, the so-called "social partnership".

Economy

Austria has a developed mixed free market and still partly government-operated economy based on services and manufactured goods. In 1999 the growth of the gross domestic product is with 2% little below the European average of 2%.

In Austria the gross national product (GNP) originates primarily from services (49%), followed by manufacturing (21%), and general governmental and non-profit activities (17%). Agriculture supplies only about 2% of the GNP. Overall, Austria's agriculture is well diversified, and provides a big proportion of domestic needs. Grape growing is the basis of a wine industry that also represents an important export factor. The principal products in manufacturing are machinery (including electrical), transport vehicles, metals (including steel), beverages and tobacco, textiles, chemicals and foodstuffs. Furthermore, tourism is an important

Table 4.2   Working days lost in all industry due to labour disputes (per 1000 employees)

	1986	1987	1988	1989	1990	1991	1992	1993	1994	1995	1996	1997
EUR-15	:	:	226	170	153	99	118	73	114	:	:	:
Austria	1	2	0	1	3	17	7	4	0	0	0	:

":" Data not available.

Table 4.3   Working days lost in manufacturing industry due to labour disputes (per 1000 employees)

	1986	1987	1988	1989	1990	1991	1992	1993	1994	1995	1996	1997
EUR-15	:	:	226	157	179	143	118	113	105	:	:	:
Austria	0	1	0	0	2	0	1	2	0	0	0	:

All data from (1). ":" Data not available.

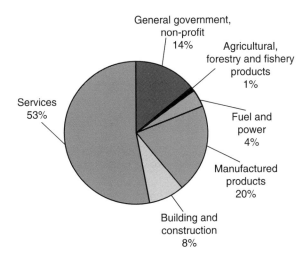

Figure 4.3   Economic structure (gross value rates as % of sectors, 1997, Austria). All data from (1)

part of the service sector in the economy and reduces the impact of foreign-trade deficits (Figure 4.3).

Exports consist primarily of machinery and transport equipment, manufactured goods, paper and paper products and chemicals. Germany is one of the most important importers of Austrian products. The transportation network is well developed. Railroads are still mostly government owned. The country has two principal Danube river ports, Vienna and Linz.

A cost-of-living comparison with the EU shows that in Austria prices for housing or transport are far above the EU average whereas clothing and footwear or household equipment seem to be rather cheap in comparison. On average it is more expensive to live in Austria than in many other European countries.

Labour market

Although the absolute number of persons in employment is rising, Tables 4.4–4.7 also show a rising unemployment rate, with women worse affected than men (6% vs. 4%). Furthermore, there are regional and sectoral disparities. Whereas employment in agriculture and industry is steadily declining, the service sector is becoming increasingly important, showing a continuing rise of employed persons.

The average hourly labour costs[4] (24.83 ECU[5]) have been rising continuously (Table 4.8). As they have reached a fairly high level in comparison to other

---

[4] Surveys of labour costs have been carried out since 1966 and at present are every 4 years. Data for intervening years are estimated by each Member State using a Eurostat updating method. The term "labour costs" is taken to mean expenditure by employers to employ workers. These costs can be subdivided into two main categories: direct and indirect. Direct costs are all earnings including earnings in kind. Indirect costs are mainly social contributions, whether statutory, conventional or voluntary.

[5] ECU: Until 31 December 1998 all data of national currencies were converted into ECU on the basis of market exchange rates. After the introduction of the Euro, conversion has been replaced by irrevocably fixed conversion rates.

Table 4.4   Persons in employment (million people)

1985	1986	1987	1988	1989	1990	1991	1992	1993	1994	1995	1996	1997	1998	1999
	3.3	3.3	3.3	3.4	3.4	3.5	3.5	3.6	:	3.2**	3.6	3.6*	:	3.7
100	101.5	102.0	102.1	103.6	105.7	107.7	109.5	110.5	:	97.0	110.5	110.5	:	114.2

All data from (1), except * from (8), ** from (10).
":" Data not available.

Table 4.5   Persons in employment in different sectors (1000 people)

	1986	1987	1988	1989	1990	1991	1992	1993	1994	1995	1996	1997	1998	1999
Agriculture	283	285	269	266	269	257	250	246	:	:	269	249*	:	229
Industry	1240	1240	1240	1240	1260	1280	1260	1260	:	:	1096	1070*	:	1094
Service	1750	1760	1790	1830	1880	1920	2020	2050	:	:	2253	2290*	:	2354

All data from (1), except * from (8).
":" Data not available.

Table 4.6   Unemployment rate (%)

1986–1992	1993	1994	1995	1996	1997	1998	1998		1997*
							Men	Women	
No data	4	4	4	4	4	5	4**	6**	29**

* Long-time unemployment (% of all unemployment).
All data from (11), except ** from (3).

Table 4.7   Persons in employment by age and gender (% of population in age group)

Age (years)	Total	Male	Female
15–24	55	59	51
25–49	83	91	75
50–64	45	57	33
>65	3*	4*	2*

All data from (1); year: 1999, except * from (8); year: 1997.

Table 4.8   Explanation of labour costs[4] (%, 1995)

	Direct	Indirect	Social security as part of indirect costs
All industry	75	25	18

All data from (1).

Table 4.9   Employees average hours usually worked per week (ISCO-88 (COM))[6]

Men	39.6 h per week (persons in full-time employment mostly (55%) work 40 h per week)
Women	34.7 h per week (persons in full-time employment mostly (58%) work 40 h per week)

All data from (8); year: 1997.

average hours usually worked per week are on average higher than in many other countries of the EU (Table 4.9).

Employee relations and trade unions

The Austrian system of employee relations is highly regulated in European comparison. In many ways similar to the German system, most of the important aspects of the working life are governed by tight

European countries and are considered to be not competitive there are political discussions on possible changes to this situation. The opening of the EU to the low labour cost eastern neighbours of Austria has made this issue increasingly important. On the other side, the

---

[6] ISCO-88 (COM): International Standard Classification of Occupations (ISCO) is used at European level by the EU statistic service – Eurostat. The last version is ISCO-88 (COM). It makes it possible to present coherent information about jobs and occupations.

regulations. For example, hiring as well as firing employees is controlled by clear rules.

The "Österreichischer Gewerkschaftsbund (ÖGB)" is the big Austrian trade union. It is a "unity trade union" which is organised along single unions that are sector oriented. Originally consisting of about 15 single unions in the last years these unions have merged into a smaller number of larger blocks, e.g. private sector employees. In practice, the ÖGB and its unions have a monopoly for negotiating collective agreements. These collective agreements form an essential building block of the employee relations system. Above them a number of legal acts form the arena within which collective agreements take place. In addition, agreements at the organisational level (Betriebsvereinbarungen) give the opportunity to taylor the more general rules and regulations to the specific situation.

For a long time, the Austrian system of social partnership as a specific way of handling conflicting interest at the societal level has been an important factor of social peace and economic growth. Because of the small geographic size and the strong link between economic, industrial and political actors the system of social partnership was able to prepare crucial economic decisions and support their realisation. Due to a number of factors, among them a tendency towards deregulation, the importance of the social partnership as a conflict regulation model has decreased.

Education system

Education in Austria is free and compulsory for children between the ages of 6 and 15 years. The first 4 years are the primary education (Volksschule). Then there is the choice between two major types of secondary schools. One leads to vocational training, the other to university. University education is publicly funded (tuition fees are about €700 per year) and without entry exams.

Table 4.10 Young persons (aged 15–24 years) in education (% rate of participation in education)

Age (years)	Total	Men	Women
15	96	96	96
16	93	94	92
17	90	92	88
18	74	77	72
19	55	54	55
20	38	37	39
21	34	36	33
22	33	34	31
23	29	31	27
24	25	26	24
All ages	56	58	54

All data from (8); year: 1997.

Table 4.11 Level of education of persons aged 25–59 years (%)

	Total	Men	Women
Third level education	9	10	8
Upper secondary level	66	72	60
<Upper secondary level	25	18	32

All data from (8); year: 1997.

As shown in Tables 4.10 and 4.11, in 1997 25% aged 25–59 years had completed only compulsory schooling, with a still higher figure for women (32%) than for men (18%). The education gap between women and men is steadily narrowing. Furthermore, the number of 24-year old persons which are still in education is rather high (25%) compared to other European countries. This is due to a university system where students are free to choose how many exams they will do within one semester. Therefore, a big number of students partly work and study only part time which means that they take a rather long time to finish their degrees.

SWITZERLAND

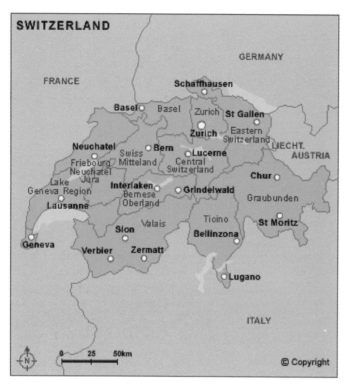

Area	41,293 km^2
Population	70,000 inhabitants
Density	185 inhabitants per km^2
Capital and population	Berne: 30,000
Other important cities and population	Zurich (84,500) Geneva (45,000) Basle (36,000) Lausanne (26,500) Lucerne (16,500)
Official languages	German, French, Italian and Romantsch
Business language	English
Religions	48% Roman Catholic 44% Protestant 8% Others (e.g. Moslem and Jewish)

Figure 4.4   Landesgemeinde

Topography and climate

Switzerland is located in the centre of Europe, sharing borders with Italy, France, Germany, Austria and Lichtenstein. Three quarters of the country are agriculturally productive, 28% being meadows and arable land, orchards and vineyards, 25% forests and 22% pasture. The climate is temperate but differs greatly from region to region.

Special features and principal characteristics

Switzerland's location and geographical structure (mountainous, with many small and often isolated valleys) are important in understanding its culture. The cultural mix of people with different languages, mentalities and religions has a long tradition. While it is difficult to generalise, the Swiss can be described as fairly pragmatic and consensus oriented, with a high commitment to federalism under the motto: "Small is beautiful and effective".

Table 4.12   Switzerland's situation in relation to the EU

	EU-15	Switzerland	Relation (Switzerland/EU-15) × 100
Density (inhabitants per km^2) Year: 2000	116	185	159.5
Infant mortality[7] (per thousand live birth) Year: 1997	5.5	4.8	87.3
Life expectancy at birth (boys; years) Year: 2000	74.0	76.9	103.9
Life expectancy at birth (girls; years) Year: 2000	80.5	82.6	102.6
Marriage (per thousand people) Year: 2000	5.0 5.1 (1999)	5.5 4.9 (1999)	101.0 96.1 (1999)
Divorces (per thousand people) Year: 2000	1.8 1.8 (1998)	1.5 2.2 (1998)	91.2
Population increase (average increase 1986–1996; % per year) Year: 2000	0.376	0.671	178.5
Unemployment rate (%) Year: 2001	10	3	25

Switzerland has four national languages which are spoken in different areas: German is the mother tongue of around 65% of the population, French 18%, Italian 10% and Romantsch 1%. Additionally, there are various regional dialects.

The share of foreigners has been growing steadily up to 20%. This is the highest percentage of a foreign labour force in Europe (Table 4.12).

Legal, institutional and political environment

The Swiss confederation, which was originally founded in 1291 out of the cantons of Uri, Schwyz and Unterwalden, has been a federal republic since 1848. Nowadays, Switzerland consists of 26 cantons (federal states). Each canton includes many communities. Berne is the capital of Switzerland, Zurich is its financial centre, and Geneva is home to about 30 important international organisations (such as IRC, WHO, ILO, WTO, the European HQ of the UN).

This excellent position is one of the reasons why leading international corporations have selected Switzerland as Headquarters Operations (e.g. Procter & Gamble selected Geneva as its second World Head Office in 1999, moving more than 1000 professionals to Switzerland).

Switzerland is a very federalist state based on the principle of subsidiary; only what the individual family cannot do, the community should do; only what the community cannot do, the canton should do; only what the canton cannot do, the federal state should do.

At each level the power is divided into three: an executive, a legislative and a judicial level. At the federal level, Switzerland is governed by a permanent coalition. The Cabinet (or Federal Council) consists of seven members (a coalition of the four largest parties, the Liberals, Christian Democrats, Social Democrats and People's Party) with representatives from the German, French and Italian speaking areas; each year, a new member of the Federal Council serves as president of the Confederation. The Federal Assembly (the Parliament) is divided into the Council of States (cantonal representatives), with 46 members, and the National Council (representative body of the people),

---

[7] See footnote 2.

with 200 members. The Federal Supreme Court located in Lausanne is the highest judicial power.

Apart from elections, Swiss citizens have two further means of directly influencing the legislative process, which are unique to Switzerland. First there is the possibility of submitting a people's initiative, with signatures from 100,000 enfranchised citizens collected within 18 months, to the Federal Council which has to accept it or to promulgate its own proposed legislation. To become law, the bill must be accepted by both Houses of the Federal Assembly. But the participation of the citizens goes beyond the right of initiative, also implying the right of referendum. If a bill ratified by the Federal Assembly would in any way permanently change the federal constitution, then it is subjected to an obligatory referendum of the citizens and cantons. The people can even make use of their right to a facultative referendum which is applied to bills not permanently changing the federal constitution. In that case 50,000 enfranchised voters or eight cantons may demand a referendum within 90 days. This system of individual initiative and responsibilities has helped create a lasting political and social stability.

The federal elections are conducted every 4 years. The last federal election took place in 1999. The results of the 1999 elections were the following for the major parties:

Party	In % of votes	In seats
Liberal Party (FDP + LPS)	23	44
Social Democratic Party (SPS)	22	51
Christian Party (CVP)	16	35
People's Party (SVP)	20	43
Ecologist Movement (GPS)	5	9

The four-party coalition has run the federal government for four decades. Two members from each of the FDP, SPS, CVP and one member of the SVP are widely known as the "magic formula". Those parties have kept their comfortable majority of three quarters of the 200 seats in the National Council.

Economy

The Swiss economy can be characterised by (Figure 4.5):

- A dominant export orientation.
- A strong and continuing tendency towards the services industry with over 60% of the GNP originating

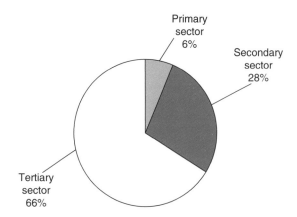

Figure 4.5   Structure of the Swiss economy. *Source*: Swiss Statistical Yearbook, 2002

from the services sector. The number of people working in the services industry has doubled with the success of Switzerland's finance business. The health sector is also substantial in size.
- A decentralised industry structure dominated by small and medium-size companies; only 0.2% of enterprises employ more than 500 people and on average the 245,000 companies employ only 12 people each.
- A specialisation in quality and high-tech goods.
- A full use of the labour potential, the economic activity rate of the population being higher only in the Scandinavian countries.

Labour market

Approximately 2.3 million of the working population are men and 1.3 million are women. Female participation rates to the labour market have increased slowly to about 40%; women continue to represent a labour reservoir.

Six per cent of the labour force are employed in primary production, 28% in manufacturing and 66% in services. The structure of the demand for labour will continue to shift towards the white-collar sector, in which more than twice as many as in the industrial sector are employed.

Switzerland is experiencing many of the same demographic changes as other European countries, especially regarding the economically active population between the age of 20 and 65, which continues to decrease; this fall has only partially been offset by immigration into

Switzerland. The ratio between the working and the non-working population will continue to decrease due to longer life expectancy, the falling birth-rate and the likelihood of a stricter immigration policy (Tables 4.13–4.15).

Table 4.13   Population by age and gender (% of total population)

Age (years)	2000	EU-15 (1998)	Women (% of age group)
<19	23	17	49
20–39	29	13	50
40–64	33	37	50
65–79	11	17	57
>80	4	4	67
			Over all: 51

Source: Switzerland Statistical Yearbook, 2002.

Table 4.14   Working days lost in all economic sectors due to labour disputes (strikes and lock-outs; in absolute number of days)

	1997	1998	1999	2000
Switzerland	435	24,719	2675	3894

Source: Switzerland Statistical Yearbook, 2002.

Table 4.15   Working days lost in all economic sectors due to labour disputes (strikes and lock-outs; per 1000 employees)

	1997	1998	1999	2000
Switzerland	0.1	7.4	0.8	:

Source: Switzerland Statistical Yearbook, 2002.
":" Data not available.

Close to 4 million people are employed in Switzerland, most of them in the service sector, agriculture being the smallest sector (Table 4.16).

Education system

In Switzerland, a country with few natural resources, investment in human capital has always been of key importance. At all levels, Swiss teachers enjoy the highest wages worldwide. The Swiss approach to education is not geared to a "star system", but rather tries to mobilise every available skill. Active corporate industry and development programs take up the task of training and development once compulsory school education is completed.

Switzerland has a two-tier educational system, consisting of a vocational school career pattern and an academic career pattern (Table 4.17).

Due to the fact that most young people choose the vocational career path (by completing a technological, business or social apprenticeship), Switzerland has one of the lowest percentage of academics in Europe.

There are eight cantonal universities and two federal polytechnic institutes of higher education. The career path for university students is similar to that in other countries.

The apprenticeship system is not particular to Switzerland. On an apprenticeship programme, the student continues his or her studies for 2 days a week, while working to learn a trade for the remaining 3 days of the week. This programme lasts 3–4 years. This training is effective in the sense that many students who have completed an apprenticeship go on to climb the career ladder up to the very top. Thus they are demonstrating that learning by doing is an effective teaching method not only in Japan.

Table 4.16   Employment statistics

	1993	1994	1995	1996	1997	1998	1999	2000
Persons in employment (total; million people)								
	3.8	3.8	3.8	3.8	3.8	3.9	3.9	3.9
Persons in employment in different sectors (1000 people)								
Agriculture	176	162	168	175	179	181	187	181
Industry	1107	1090	1120	1079	1026	1018	1003	1035
Service	2556	1529	1515	1565	2600	2659	2683	2694

Source: Switzerland Statistical Yearbook, 2002.

Table 4.17   The Swiss educational system

Age	Vocational school career	Academic school career	Age
		University (Doctorate)	24–26
		University (Master's degree)	22 + 23
19–21	Vocational colleges (bachelor's degree)	University (Bachelor's degree)	19–21
16–18	Vocational apprenticeship	Cantonal high school	15–18
13–15	Secondary school	Secondary school	13 + 14
7–12	Primary school		7–12
5–6	Kindergarten		5–6

Source: Switzerland Statistical Yearbook, 2002.

The age of entry into the labour market depends on the path of education a person has chosen (see Table 4.17). University students usually enter the labour market at the age of 24–26. Under the Swiss military system men have an initial training period of 15 weeks at the age of 20 as military recruits, and a yearly 3-week refresher course for the next 8 years. Thereafter, there are periodical refresher courses until the age of 40 (45 for officers).

HRM IN AUSTRIA AND SWITZERLAND

INTRODUCTION

The following analysis will examine and document how human resource management (HRM) in two superficially "similar" countries nevertheless exhibit subtle, yet noticeable differences.

The two countries have a number of similarities:

- consensus orientation
- neutrality
- small
- no access to open sea
- part of the alpine arc
- both are different from Germany
- both have a highly developed apprenticeship program
- both have a dual-track educational system.

But they also exhibit substantial differences like, e.g. decision-making in politics, languages (Switzerland has four official languages; German is only one of them), the importance of the military system and army in Switzerland and its economic power in terms of multinational corporations.

Geographic and linguistic closeness are therefore no guarantee for cultural similarities. Leadership styles can serve as another example for differences: Austria manages by cooperation and formal titles, Switzerland by consensus and understatement. The following Figure 4.6 which also integrates Germany[1] as the third German speaking country gives an idea of the relationship between these three countries on a cultural level.

The reasons for a possible diverging scenario for (future) HRM developments primarily stem from two sets of considerations:

1. In Switzerland there is a substantially higher number of MNCs (the highest number per 100,000 inhabitants worldwide). Switzerland is home to the world HQ of several transnational corporations.[2]

[1] In terms of culture (behaviour, norms, etc.) West and East Germany still exhibit a lot of differences and therefore have to be featured separately.

[2] Based on a Financial Times report, 4 of the 10 largest transnational companies are Swiss, whereby Nestlé (managed by an Austrian) is the largest.

2. Unlike Austria, Switzerland chose not to become part of the EU. This might subject Austrian HRM practices to substantially different pressures for change.

This analysis is formulated on a macro level. The fine-grain picture that we witness requires a much more nuanced assessment than can be given within this book. However, our view is not an across-the-board univocal judgement. This is illustrated and further discussed in the following seven subchapters that have been chosen to be analysed.

Figure 4.7 presents an integrated HRM framework which serves as the basis of the analysis.

The framework comprises the following three elements:

1. A holistic corporate vision, which adds simultaneous value to customers, employees, shareholders and society, and serves as an effective basis for effective HRM.
2. A *cycle concept* of targeted selection, appraisal, reward and development of human resources (HRs) (important parts within Chapter 3).
3. Integrated feedback (identified by arrows).

The Cranfield study of HRM development within Europe (whose questionnaire is based on the integrated framework) indicates that there are considerable differences between the European countries. The extent of these differences depend among other factors on the level of strategic-orientation and decentralisation of the HR function to line managers.

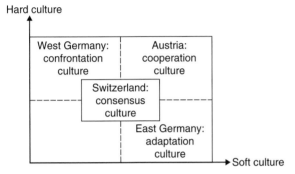

Figure 4.6   Conceptualised differences between German-speaking countries (Avery et al., 1999)

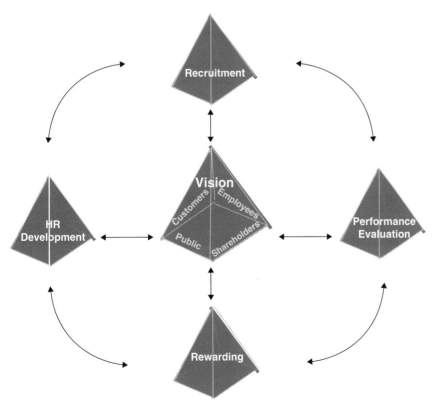

Figure 4.7   Integrated HRM framework (Hilb, 2002)

According to the data of the Cranfield European HRM survey that will be analysed in the next chapter, Austria and Switzerland are positioned differently in their HRM practices (see Figure 4.8)[3], using a different predominant style.

The results of the "European-HRM-Survey" depicted in Figure 4.8 can be summarised as follows:

- The majority of companies in, e.g., Germany support the *legalistic approach*. In terms of HRM this means that their central HRM departments predominantly deal with operative HR tasks (as they arise, without particularly involving line managers).
- Companies in, e.g., the Netherlands predominantly practice the so-called *Wild-West approach*. They tend to perceive the most important HR tasks as being decentralised from the line manager, whereby more often than not a standardised strategic orientation is lacking.
- Companies in, e.g., Austria tend to adopt strategic HRM concepts, whereby HRM functions are perceived as the core of the HRM department (*HR–Policy approach*).
- For example, Swiss companies often strive for an *integrated approach*. They attempt to strategically align HRM functions, allowing them to be decentrally implemented by line managers.

These trend-results do not infer that all organisations in every country fit the "typical mode": indeed there will probably be a range of all kinds of organisations in each country. The following chapter will demonstrate the national tendencies of Austria and Switzerland.

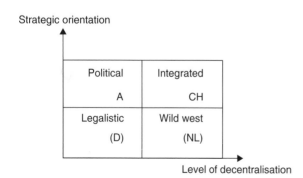

Figure 4.8   Development stages of HRM in Europe

---
[3] Hilb, M. (2002) *Integrated HRM*, 10th edn. Berlin 2002.

ANALYSIS

The HRM function: marginal or core?

Comparing HRM to the more old-fashioned personnel management we find that one of the most important distinctions between the two are considerations about a closer link of HRM to business strategy. But exploring empirical evidence we have to admit that this is largely a feature of the more prescriptive writing (Brewster, 1993: p. 38 ff, Brewster et al., 2000: p. 20); in reality, even in the US (Guest, 1990), such linking can hardly be found. Taking a closer look at Europe we see that due to very different legal and national frameworks such linkage – if existing – appears in many different ways like, e.g. legally required work councils or trade unions giving employees' representatives significant power. Another way to link HRM to top decision making-structures may also be the representation of the head of the personnel department in the main Board of Directors as well as his/her involvement in the formulation of a corporate strategy from the outset.

As for Austria Table 4.18 shows a dramatic change during the 1990s. Whereas in the beginning of the decade only a very small percentage of HR executives was represented in the main Board of Directors, we find a sharp increase in 1999; however, the numbers remain still about 10% below the European average. This positive development can be interpreted twofold: first of all there may be a shift in the importance attributed by Austrian organisations to the personnel function nowadays. Secondly, the result might indicate a change from a rather administrative function of HR towards a more strategic focus.

The Swiss development is in contrast to the Austrian trend. The decrease in the percentage of HR executives represented at the management board level could be a consequence of the globalisation, i.e. Americanisation of society in Switzerland.

Table 4.18   Does the head of the personnel/HRs function have a place on the main Board of Directors or equivalent? (% of organisations)

	Switzerland			Austria		
	1991	1995	1999	1993	1995	1999
Yes	58	61	53	26	No survey	42

Trying to predict the chance that the HR executives may be part of the main Board of Directors, we take a look at organisational details also collected within the Cranet survey. In Austria we find that bigger organisations with a rather high percentage of highly qualified professional/technical employees have a greater tendency to have HR executives on the main Board of Directors. Surprisingly, the number is correlated with the percentage of male employees whereas there is no relationship between the overall number of female employees within an organisation and the representation of the head of the personnel function in the main Board of Directors. This could relate to the top position of Austria in Hofstede's (1980) masculinity ranking.

HRM strategy: its status and role

There are innumerable examples of cases where corporate strategy decisions taken for pure business reasons but in ignorance of HR factors have failed because of that ignorance (Brewster and Bournois, 1993: p. 39). It is therefore important to explore the involvement of HRM in the development of corporate strategies.

Looking at Table 4.19 we find two contradictory results. The percentage of Austrian organisations involving HRM in the development of their corporate strategy from the outset is rather high, even higher than in Switzerland which showed a much higher percentage of HR executives being part of the main Board of Directors. On the one hand this may indicate that the personnel function is taken quite seriously within Austrian organisations. On the other hand we have to admit that the way of integrating HR people differs between countries, thus showing a different structuring of functions.

However, the share of organisations not integrating the HR function at all in the development of the corporate strategy is higher than in Switzerland and considerably higher than the EU average (7%), and this together with a general decrease of involvement during the 1990s, is worrying for Austria. But we can see that Switzerland also exhibits this general decrease of involvement. The view of many Swiss people on that development is that in booming times like the 1990s, HR is the 5th wheel of the carriage. The 1990s were the time of a technology-driven boom, and it is only recently that the new discourse about knowledge management has somewhat put again human beings "at the centre".

Recent developments towards new organisational forms show that many organisations are moving away from large, centralised (staff) units and assign more responsibility and resources to "local" or "front line" managers. One of the defining issues of HRM is about a balance of responsibilities between the HR department and line managers who are in day-to-day contact with their subordinates. Therefore, new challenges for the HR department and the need to document its contribution to the overall organisational success arise.

Answers to the question with whom the primary responsibility for major policy decisions on key aspects like recruitment and training lies, show over the past decade a slight development towards an increase in the responsibility of line management and line management together with the HR department (see Table 4.20).

Table 4.19   Stage at which HR is involved in development of corporate strategy (% of organisations)

	Switzerland			Austria		
	1991	1995	1999	1993	1995	1999
From the outset	55	55	49	60	No survey	59
Through consultation	23	20	25	18	No survey	17
On implementation	6	9	9	9	No survey	7
Non-consulted	15	16	17	12	No survey	20

Table 4.20   Responsibility for recruitment – primary responsibility for major policy decisions on key aspects of HRM (recruitment) (% of organisations)

	Switzerland			Austria		
	1991	1995	1999	1993	1995	1999
Line management	6	7	10	9	No survey	10
Line management with HR department	57	68	68	42	No survey	45
HR department with line management	34	23	20	40	No survey	38
HR department	3	2	1	9	No survey	7

This holds true for both countries but the extent of the assignment of responsibility to line managers varies with the subject.

Concerning the responsibility for training we have different results for Austria and Switzerland. In Austria there is an increase in the importance of line management which is even above the EU average (Table 4.21). Consequently the responsibility of the HR department alone or together with line management mark a decreasing tendency for recruitment and training. In Switzerland the importance of line management is decreasing whereas the working together of HR people with line managers seems to be enforced. Nevertheless the general trend is a weakening of the position of HR departments during the 1990s in both countries and across Europe.

As a reflection of this trend we can see that the performance of Austrian HR departments is not evaluated systematically. Only in about one quarter (24%) of organisations a systematic evaluation is being carried out. In doing so, primarily the views of top management are considered together with the views of line management.

Tables 4.22–4.26 take a closer look at changes of line management responsibilities over time for key functional areas of HRM.

First of all, we can see that in both countries about two-thirds of organisations do not show much change over the past decade. For the rest we can observe an increase in the responsibility of line managers in all categories. Interestingly this increase was higher at the beginning of the 1990s than at the end of the century.

Table 4.21   Responsibility for training – primary responsibility for major policy decisions on key aspects of HRM (training) (% of organisations)

	Switzerland			Austria		
	1991	1995	1999	1993	1995	1999
Line management	12	13	8	14	No survey	16
Line management with HR department	52	58	53	39	No survey	47
HR department with line management	31	25	33	35	No survey	30
HR department	6	4	6	12	No survey	7

Table 4.22   Pay and benefits – change in responsibility of line management in the last 3 years (% of organisations)

	Switzerland			Austria		
	1991	1995	1999	1993	1995	1999
Increase	34	31	33	27	No survey	20
Same	65	62	64	67	No survey	73
Decrease	1	7	3	6	No survey	7

Table 4.23   Recruitment and selection – change in responsibility of line management in the last 3 years (% of organisations)

	Switzerland			Austria		
	1991	1995	1999	1993	1995	1999
Increase	31	32	31	26	No survey	25
Same	65	59	65	63	No survey	66
Decrease	4	8	4	11	No survey	9

Table 4.24   Training and development – change in responsibility of line management in the last 3 years (% of organisations)

	Switzerland			Austria		
	1991	1995	1999	1993	1995	1999
Increase	49	46	43	43	No survey	38
Same	47	49	51	52	No survey	54
Decrease	4	5	6	5	No survey	7

Table 4.25   Industrial relations – change in responsibility of line management in the last 3 years (% of organisations)

	Switzerland			Austria		
	1991	1995	1999	1993	1995	1999
Increase	11	10	9	18	No survey	14
Same	81	85	84	76	No survey	81
Decrease	8	5	6	6	No survey	5

Table 4.26   Workforce expansion/reduction – change in responsibility of line management in the last 3 years (% of organisations)

	Switzerland			Austria		
	1991	1995	1999	1993	1995	1999
Increase	24	36	33	24	No survey	19
Same	65	57	61	65	No survey	71
Decrease	12	7	6	11	No survey	10

In Austria further in-depth analysis shows that there are no differences between public and private organisations.

Comparing Austria to the average of EU countries, the percentage of "no change at all" is higher whereas the increase of the responsibility of line management is on average lower. This might indicate a rather stable economic framework for Austrian organisations with traditional approaches still common in management and HRM.

Recruitment and selection

The organisation of recruitment and selection can be analysed through a few main items. Are recruitment and selection policies centrally or decentrally determined? Who are the main agents responsible for recruitment and selection? What are the most important selection methods for different staff categories? What is the temporal dimension of recruitment and selection, i.e. is recruitment based on manpower planning and the forecast of future skill requirements or not. For some of these issues we can offer data; others like the temporal dimension are well known (e.g. the lack of specialised IT people all over Europe).

If we take a look at how vacant positions are filled in Austrian organisations (Table 4.27) we see that at the end of the 1990s managerial vacancies at the middle and junior level are most frequently filled internally. Only senior managers are recruited with the help of head hunters and consultancies. The use of

Table 4.27   Recruitment methods: use of internal mechanisms for filling managerial vacancies (% organisations)

	Switzerland			Austria		
	1991*	1995	1999	1993	1995	1999
Senior Management	N/A	64	50	N/A	No survey	58
Middle Management	N/A	82	78	N/A	No survey	82
Junior Management	N/A	86	80	N/A	No survey	65
Total managerial only*	83	77	69	75	No survey	69

* The question in 1991/1993 was not separated by different managerial levels (one category of "managerial"): S3V4a1 and S3V4b1 recoded as "internal" category. 1995/1999 figures are added together and divided by 3 for an average figure as comparison.

advertisements in newspapers can be found less frequently in the case of senior managers compared to middle or junior managers. In general a tight labour market means that recruitment will increasingly be done externally. But furthermore we can state that recruitment practices are also dependent on the "public/private sector" variable. Recruiting abroad and marketing the organisation's image are significantly more frequently used by private companies than by public organisations.

In Swiss organisations we find a decreasing tendency of filling managerial positions internally. This might be again a reflection of the globalisation trend in the Swiss economy and science and therefore the especially high international orientation of the Swiss industry.

As for selection methods in Austrian and Swiss organisations Table 4.28 gives a good overview.

It immediately becomes clear that application forms, followed by one-to-one interviews, are the most important methods, used for every appointment in Austria. However, it is interesting to see that one-to-one interviews are much more common for every appointment in Switzerland than in Austria where only about half of the organisations make use of this method. This is below the European average of 55%. For Switzerland the "congenial", consensual Swiss culture leads to an emphasis of interpersonal factors, and this can best be satisfied with one-to-one, face-to-face interviews. Interview panels as well as references are also important in the selection processes of both countries.

In contrast to what might be assumed from the substantial body of literature on assessment centres, this method is used rarely and only for some appointments. Particularly striking is the rather frequent use of graphology (analysis of handwriting) in Switzerland, whereas in Austria this method is hardly used at all. The result in partly French-speaking Switzerland puts the country among those few, almost exclusively Francophone countries which make any significant use of graphology.

Training and development

With the increasing importance of concepts like the learning organisation, knowledge based society and a strong service and hi-tech sector, the training and development of employees has become a key factor for organisational success.

Table 4.29 gives an overview about the proportion of annual salaries and wage bill spent on training and development.

Obviously Swiss organisations are spending more on training and development than Austrian ones. This may reflect the fact that Austria has almost no global operating MNCs compared to Switzerland where we can find a lot of very big companies, especially among the pharmaceutical, food and financial services sectors. Furthermore, there is the importance of technological developments over the past 10 years leading to a need to get workers acquainted with those new technologies. As for Austria we have a slight positive trend towards more spending at the end of the 1990s which at least indicates the awareness of Austrian organisations concerning this increasing importance of training and development. Background information tells us that there are nearly no differences between public and private companies concerning the spending on training and development within Austria. Furthermore, there seem to be quite big differences between different organisations. Some organisations invest a lot in their HRs whereas others seem to offer nearly no training at all.

Table 4.28　Selection methods: use of different methods for every or most appointments (% of organisations)

	Switzerland			Austria		
	1991	1995	1999	1993	1995	1999
Interview panel	Not asked				No survey	
Every appointment		34	37			14
Most appointments		18	15			22
Some appointments		18	21			23
Frequently used (1993 only)				83		
One-to-one interviews	Not asked				No survey	
Every appointment		73	68			49
Most appointments		15	20			35
Some appointments		5	8			9
Frequently used (1993 only)				N/A		
Application forms	Not asked				No survey	
Every appointment		66	54			67
Most appointments		10	15			15
Some appointments		7	8			6
Frequently used (1993 only)				83		
Psychometric testing	Not asked				No survey	
Every appointment		14	6			6
Most appointments		4	7			11
Some appointments		15	23			12
Frequently used (1993 only)				32		
Assessment centre	Not asked				No survey	
Every appointment		1	1			1
Most appointments		0	2			3
Some appointments		11	24			19
Frequently used (1993 only)				18		
Graphology	Not asked				No survey	
Every appointment		4	1			0
Most appointment		4	2			0
Some appointments		37	25			1
Frequently used (1993 only)				9		
References	Not asked				No survey	
Every appointment		32	19			11
Most appointment		31	26			19
Some appointments		22	34			37
Frequently used (1993 only)				65		

Taking a look at the importance of training and development expressed in the mean number of training days received by staff category we find that between 2 and 7 days are dedicated to training in both countries (Table 4.30). Overall, in both countries the number of training days increases with a higher hierarchical level. Very positively for Austria is the fact the overall number of training days has also risen among all categories of employees.

Combining the fact that Austria is spending a smaller proportion of annual salaries on training and development than Switzerland together with the result that the number of training days received by staff category is higher gives us a better overview of the Austrian situation. On one hand we see that training and development is not underevaluated; we also know that a systematic analysis of training needs is carried out in 74% of the organisations. On the other hand we may argue that Austrian companies are spending their money more efficiently or we may assume that training on average is less expensive in Austria than in Switzerland. This might be one of the reasons why the monitoring of training effectiveness is less frequent (49%) in Austria than in other countries and clearly below the EU average.

Table 4.29 Proportion of annual salaries and wage bill spent on training and development (% of organisations)

	Switzerland			Austria		
	1991	1995	1999	1993	1995	1999
<1	20	20	19	30	No survey	20
1–1.9	28	25	29	36	No survey	36
2–2.9	21	22	23	12	No survey	14
3–4.9	20	16	11	11	No survey	17
5–9.9	8	11	10	11	No survey	10
>10	3	6	8	0	No survey	3

Table 4.30 Mean number of training days received by staff category

Mean	Switzerland			Austria		
	1991	1995	1999	1993	1995	1999
Management	6	6	5	6	No survey	7
Professional/ technical	4	4	4	5	No survey	6
Clerical	2	1	2	2	No survey	4
Manual	2	0	2	2	No survey	3

Performance measurements and rewards

Compensation management is closely linked to performance appraisal. Practices of both vary considerably across countries (Sparrow, 1999: p. 102 ff). In Austria merit/performance related pay is not very popular, not even at the management level.

Compared to Switzerland, Austria uses this form of remunerating its employees about one-third less frequently and is also clearly below the European average (Table 4.31). In most of the countries we find different forms of incentive schemes (employee share options, profit sharing, group bonuses, or performance related pay). Austrian managers are mostly in profit sharing schemes (45% in 1999) whereas merit/performance related pay is used for the other staff categories. However, across both countries a general decrease in the use of merit/performance related pay can be observed over the past decade. The only exception are clerical employees in Austria where companies use this form of incentive schemes more often at the end of the decade than in the beginning. If we take a look at differences in the public and private sector we find, not surprisingly, that many of the private sector companies use performance related pay whereas most of the public organisations do not.

In Switzerland the Americanisation of top executive compensation levels in many Swiss multinational companies has been criticised heavily by the mass media and the public. That contributed to a trend questioning the effectiveness of extreme performance-oriented compensation schemes and might be one of the factors for an also decreasing trend in Switzerland.

In line with the low importance of merit/performance related pay we also find a less frequent use of appraisal

Table 4.31 Merit/performance related pay by staff category (% of organisations)

	Switzerland			Austria		
	1991	1995	1999	1993	1995	1999
Management	65	79	63	40	No survey	38
Professional/ technical	66	78	71	38	No survey	36
Clerical	56	71	60	24	No survey	33
Manual	56	66	59	26	No survey	24

Table 4.32 Appraisal system for staff categories (% of organisations)

	Switzerland			Austria		
	1991	1995	1999	1993	1995	1999
Management	N/A*	89	93	N/A	No survey	68
Professional/ technical	N/A	94	95	N/A	No survey	62
Clerical	N/A	89	92	N/A	No survey	56
Manual	N/A	87	90	N/A	No survey	46

* N/A – Question not asked in 1991/1993.

Table 4.33 Change in trade union influence (% of organisations)

	Switzerland			Austria		
	1991	1995	1999	1993	1995	1999
Increased	18	7	9	14	No survey	9
Same	13	82	48	10	No survey	56
Decreased	69	10	21	75	No survey	18

systems in Austria as compared to Switzerland (Table 4.32). Focussing on the use of appraisal systems for Austrian managers at the end of the 1990s we find a percentage similar to the European average (68%); for the other staff categories in Austria the use of appraisal systems is clearly below the EU average. This relates to the fact that performance appraisal in Austria is much more often designated to determine individual (77%) and organisational (52%) training needs than to determine individual performance related pay (45%). In almost all cases, the immediate superior is contributing to the appraisal process.

Employee communication and the role of trade unions and work councils

Over the past decade the nature and context of industrial relations in Europe has undergone extensive change. Despite suggestions of convergence of industrial relations, particularly within the EU, substantial differences persist (Morley et al., 2000: p. 199 ff). Consequently, we have to keep in mind that the comparing of industrial relations systems and concepts is difficult across national boundaries. Comparing Europe and the US we find that in Europe the collective bargaining process is either viewed as some sort of class struggle between labour and capital or as a co-operative venture aimed at improving the benefits of their members through making their employers more effective, whereas in the US union leaders often have a zero-sum, economic, view of collective bargaining and lack ideological ideas.

Whereas in the beginning of the 1990s the influence of trade unions decreased significantly (Switzerland

69% and Austria 75%). Table 4.33 shows that at the end of the 1990s most of the surveyed companies report no further changes in the influence of trade unions.

The importance of communication in organisations is not confined to HRM. It could be argued that effective communication is at the heart of business success (Mintzberg, 1973). It has the potential to encourage greater commitment and is a good predictor for job satisfaction; it also facilitates every day work as well as important issues like, e.g. strategy development (Morley et al., 2000: p. 147 ff).

In order to examine formal communication practices on business strategy and financial performance we take a look at Table 4.34. First of all we find that in both countries over all staff categories there is much more information on financial matters than on strategy. For Austria this might be due to the fact that there is not a lot of strategic work and planning in general in most of the Austrian companies (as already described in Tables 4.18 and 4.19). Apart from that we can state a clear tendency of an increasing importance concerning the information about these two issues in both countries. At the end of the 1990s all staff categories are better informed about strategy and finance than in the beginning. This also may reflect the increasing importance of globalisation as employees increasingly need to be informed about the larger global context to best perform their day-to-day tasks.

However, there is also a very clear gradation over the different hierarchical levels in both countries. Whereas between 92% and 96% of the management personnel in Austria are informed about financial and strategic matters only 13–30% of the manual workers get information about these issues. The most obvious increase can be found in the category of Austrian clerical workers. For the management this is similar to the European average whereas the percentage of manual workers that are informed in Austria is clearly below

Table 4.34 Formal communication on business strategy and financial performance (% of organisations)

	Switzerland			Austria		
	1991	1995	1999	1993	1995	1999
Management briefed						
About strategy	89	98	95	91		96
About finance	91	92	93	89	No survey	92
Professional briefed						
About strategy	28	48	45	41		47
About finance	63	79	79	66	No survey	73
Clerical briefed						
About strategy	8	22	28	19	No survey	30
About finance	39	57	63	42		60
Manual briefed						
About strategy	9	21	27	9	No survey	13
About finance	38	54	61	25		30

the European average. In the category of professional and clerical staff Austria informs more about financial and less about strategic matters. Referring again to the results of Tables 4.18 and 4.19 this picture is probably more due to a lack in strategic planning as compared to many European countries than to a deliberate exclusion of employees. The "slope" of information is even more dramatic in Switzerland: in general, those at the bottom of Swiss organisations get little information about the financial situation or the strategy of their organisations.

Organisation of work: flexible patterns of work

Loss of competitiveness and persistent rates of unemployment are important arguments in favour of more labour flexibility. Therefore flexible patterns of work are of increasing importance all over Europe – but at different pace. We have to take into account that different legal frameworks offer quite different possibilities to organisations in designing their work organisations. Furthermore, we can assume that there are differences between public and private organisations which cannot be seen from the tables. But in general private organisations use most of the flexible working arrangements much more frequently than public organisations.

Looking again at Austria confirms the increasing trend in the use of flexible working arrangements which is way above the EU average of 41%. In contrast to Switzerland there is a clear increase in the use of

Table 4.35 Part-time working – change in use of flexible working arrangements (% of organisations)

	Switzerland			Austria		
	1991	1995	1999	1993	1995	1999
Increase	81	62	67	52	No survey	71
Same	16	32	30	40	No survey	25
Decrease	1	6	2	6	No survey	2
Not used	2	1	1	2	No survey	1

flexible working arrangements (part-time working) and a reverse trend for the decreasing development (Table 4.35).

However, still nearly half of the companies of the Austrian sample do not use flexible working arrangements (temporary/casual) at all and flexible working patterns apply only to a minority of employees in most Austrian organisations as compared to most other European countries. And this has not changed during the past decade (Table 4.36). This is also in sharp contrast to Switzerland where we find nearly the opposite situation. Only a small percentage of organisations do not use flexible working arrangements at all and this number has even decreased in course of the 1990s.

If we take into account the proportion of workforce on non-standard contracts (part-time) we find a similar situation (Table 4.37). On the whole we can state that there is a clear increasing trend of such part-time contracts in both countries. This brings Austria, having started from a very low level to about the same position

Table 4.36   Temporary/casual work – change in use of flexible working arrangements (% of organisations)

	Switzerland			Austria		
	1991*	1995	1999	1993*	1995	1999
Increase	58	42	53	21	No survey	28
Same	32	36	40	18	No survey	18
Decrease	5	17	3	12	No survey	6
Not used	4	5	3	49	No survey	49

*1991/1993 data included "Don't know" category, which was selected out.

Table 4.37   Part-time – proportion of workforce on non-standard contracts (% of organisations)

	Switzerland			Austria		
	1991*	1995	1999	1993*	1995	1999
No part-time employees	3	0	1	3	No survey	0
>10% of part-timers	37	41	51	15	No survey	36

* 1991/1993 figure for "no part-timers" is the missing value, since a "not used" option was not included.

Table 4.38   Temporary/casual – proportion of workforce on non-standard contracts (% of organisations)

	Switzerland			Austria		
	1991*	1995	1999	1993*	1995	1999
No temporary workers	4	6	7	27	No survey	57
>10% of temporary workers	4	3	7	2	No survey	8

* 1991/1993 figure for "no temporary workers" is the missing value, since a "not used" option was not included.

that has been already held by Switzerland at the beginning of the 1990s.

If we have a look at the proportion of workforce on temporary/casual contracts as shown in Table 4.38 we find some interesting differences.

Temporary/casual work arrangements seem to be much less used in Switzerland than part-time contracts. The small number of Swiss companies employing more than 10% of temporary workers is similar to

the Austrian situation. But the percentage of organisations having no temporary workers at all is very small and still increasing in Switzerland whereas in Austria the share of companies having no temporary workers at all has risen dramatically. This result goes in line with the picture we got from Table 4.36, showing that at the end of the century nearly half of the Austrian organisations did not use flexible-working arrangements at all. Apart from legal restrictions this result again relates to the impression that Austrian companies still follow rather traditional approaches in HRM.

Conclusion

As demonstrated in the previous sections there are large differences between these two small, neighbouring countries Austria and Switzerland.

In Switzerland, the political system is run according to a "magic formula", unchanged for more than 40 years. In Austria, the economic system is still determined to a certain extent by the "social partnership" model. Switzerland is home to the world HQ of several transnational corporations. Austria is member of the EU. Labour legislation, social and political thinking are different in both countries.

This different economic background may be part of the reason for the different results in many of the analysed domains:

- In contrast to the Swiss development we find an increasing number of Austrian organisations with their head of the HRs function represented in the main Board of Directors.
- The increase of the responsibility of line management is in Austria on average lower than in Switzerland.
- Swiss organisations show a decreasing tendency of filling managerial positions internally which again might be a reflection of the stronger globalisation trend of the Swiss economy.
- Swiss organisations spend more on training and development than Austrian organisations that however, show an increasing tendency.
- Merit/performance related pay is much less popular in Austria than in Switzerland. This is partly due to disadvantageous taxation legislation and can partly be attributed to the different economic background of the two countries.

- Although on an increasing development Austrian organisations still do not use flexible patterns of work to a significant extent.

Referring to the introductory notes we can summarise that the differences between the Austrian co-operative culture and the Swiss consensus culture can especially be found in the field of politics. In the field of HRM we often could observe a more HR-policy-oriented approach in Austria whereas Swiss companies seemed to strive for the integrated approach.

HRM IN ACTION

AUSTRIA: HRM IN AN IT ORGANISATION

Background information

IT AG-Austria[1] was established in Germany as family owned enterprise; 1987 an Austrian branch was set up which then in 1996 became the headquarters. After 2 years of preparation for the Initial Public Offering (IPO), the company was changed into a public limited company. IT AG-Austria is a service sector company and is divided into two major business units: it offers services in the field of IT and e-business as well as services in the field of telecommunications with an emphasis on internet technologies. In 2002 the company had branches in six countries with 10 locations and approximately 800 employees.

Table 4.39 shows a continuous increase in the number of employees until 1999, the date of the sale of the company to the market through the IPO; only afterwards due to the acquisition of companies we find a jump up of manpower by 60%. The founders always had in mind not to increase the number of employees too rapidly in order to ensure continuous integration and commitment of newcomers. Due to the problems of the whole IT sector the share value of the company is now only at about one sixth compared to the best prices of its shares. However, the management board considers the company to be a good medium-sized enterprise, part of the "true economy" and in contrast to many of the "new economy" start-ups that do not exist any more.

Table 4.39   Number of employees working for IT AG-Austria between 1996 and 2001[2]

	Development of turnover	Overall number of employees	Austria
1996		Approximately 160	
1997		Approximately 280	
1998	26, 12 Mio. Euro	320	164
1999	34, 49 Mio. Euro	484	214
2000	61, 36 Mio. Euro	771	233
2001 (1 half year)	33, 48 Mio. Euro	785	240

---

[1] Real name disguised for reasons of confidentiality.
[2] This case study is based on interviews with the head of the HRM department of the IT AG-Austria as well as on business reports; for 1996 and 1997 no official turnover figures had been available. Our thanks go to Christine Malle for providing this material.

Organisation

Until 1 year ago the hierarchy was very flat: management board, managers and subordinates. At the moment there are five levels: (1) a Board of Directors of four, (2) managers and for the sales as well as the research and development department, (3) team-leader, (4) key-account manager and (5) employees.

Project managers need soft skills and expertise. They have to manage different projects and teams; the teams are built according to the necessary expertises of a project and break up after having accomplished their tasks. Project managers are not supposed to become normal team members but keep their position.

Nowadays decisions are taken more centrally by the Board of Directors than in former times. But this is more due to the actual size of the company as well as to changes on the sales market than to the IPO.

The language of the group is German. Communication with branches is in English.

HRM in the IT AG-Austria

The HR function in Austria has been set up 7 years ago and is organised with a central group of five people. They are responsible for all areas of HR work apart from wage and salary administration. At the moment there is a development towards a centralisation of HR issues within the Austrian headquarters. However, the company tries to only centralise such issues that are suited for central handling. The head of department defines the following areas as most important HR issues:

- Promotion of HRM
- Research
- Recruitment/staffing practices
- Training and development
- Health and safety
- Outplacement
- Communication
- Event management

The head of the HRs function is not part of the main Board of Directors but he directly reports to the board. The HR department is increasingly involved in the development of corporate strategy from the outset on. This situation is in line with the results outlined in the first two tables in the comparative analysis.

Reorganisation of "internal" employee planning and staffing

Being part of the service sector the company considers their sales and HR department to be the most important ones. As soon as the sales department is ready to start a project, the HR function has to form the necessary team. But with the continuous growth of the company this "invisible" link becomes looser. Competencies and responsibilities are getting increasingly blurred.

In course of the actual reorganisation the company is establishing a resource deployment department, responsible for the best suited forming and support of project teams. Resource deployment managers are recruited internally from different specialist departments (e.g. data based management, customer relationship management, SAP, etc.) as well as externally. This reorganisation is in correspondence with the results in the comparative analysis above and points towards a slight increase in the responsibility of line managers within Austrian companies.

In the future the internal recruitment and support of employees is supposed to function more decentralised whereas the international HRM should be handled in a more centralised way; the following activities are planned: better communication through a common newsletter for the whole group, training and development programmes, competence development of high potentials and employees' representation. Outplacement and promotion will remain in the responsibility of the branches in different countries.

Communication

Communication and communication channels have changed. Electronic media and the intranet have become a main source of information. The newsletter for employees is available on the Intranet as well as in a paper version. It is edited by HR people but everyone is welcome to contribute, present ideas and share viewpoints with the management and other colleagues of the whole group. For example, quality managers are profiting from this opportunity and communicate important issues. Furthermore, the Board of Directors informs through this communication media about business strategy and also financial matters. The establishment of this newsletter as well as the clear development towards a planned and structured information policy within the IT AG-Austria again reflect the results that are presented in the comparative section "Employee communication and the role of trade unions and work councils".

Training and development

The introduction of new employees is based on ISO procedures. In organisations predominantly composed of experts employee development is one of the biggest challenges. The analysis of training needs is effectuated through formal career plans, and special individual interviews. Development and training is based on a three-level system.

Step 1

If one of the project team members has a problem or needs qualified help there is an immediate solution provided; this can be through the buying of books, software, or some training course. Books can be used personally and afterwards are returned to the company-owned library. Additionally also private investment in books and software is promoted.

Step 2

In collaboration with training institutions the HR department is organising courses that are open for all employees. The programme is adapted two times a year. These courses represent only a small amount of the training and development activities offered by the company.

Step 3

Here, we find the individual training which is based on formal career plans and individual interviews. Last year IT AG-Austria has got an award for its training and development efforts.

Working practices

Although flexible working arrangements are only allowed since the 1 January 2001 they already had been in use before. This is due to the IT sector where flexibility is helpful and necessary. However, the company emphasises that physical presence is important. There is a lot of big projects with team work and team responsibility requiring daily presence. Furthermore, two-thirds of the employees are on fixed-term contracts. Here, we are again in line with the results above: we find a trend towards flexible working arrangements but compared to other European companies within the IT sector the IT AG-Austria is still representing a rather conservative business model.

Compensation and benefits

The total reward package is in line with other companies of the sector. In course of the IPO an employee share options scheme has been set up. But due to Austrian taxation legislation such profits are under higher tax rates than private profits from speculation in shares. This means that the originally planned share options scheme is not yet implemented. In correspondence with the results, merit/performance related pay is not really used.

Summary

The HR function of the IT AG-Austria is a typical example of HRM in a private sector company in Austria at the end of the century. In key areas it represents most of the Austrian trends in HRM as shown in the comparative part of this chapter:

- Training and development is becoming increasingly important.
- Employee communication on business strategy is being expanded (newsletter and intranet).
- The use of incentive schemes is not very popular.
- Flexible working arrangements are not very wide-spread in private sector companies.

However, the HR function of the IT AG-Austria offers more: with a customer as well as employee-oriented focus it tries to ensure the functioning of important issues and the well-being of employees. Furthermore, there is a strong focus on international HRM and efforts to find the best way between a centralised and decentralised handling of different HR matters.

SWITZERLAND: CONTEXT MATTERS – THE SIGNIFICANCE OF THE UNIQUE MILITARY SYSTEM OF SWITZERLAND

The Swiss army is a purely militia force, based upon the principle of universal compulsory personal military service. This translates into the obligation for the majority of Swiss males, between the age of 20 and 32 (40 for officers), to serve every year in the army. At the end of their "active" duty, the soldiers retain the property of their equipment, including the rifle and 24 rounds. This institution influences the Swiss society in more ways than one would at first sight imagine: people from different regions come together for their basic military training and they get back together for their yearly repeat periods. This has a profound integrating effect on interpersonal relationships and carries over later on in work life.

1. In the military, a CEO may serve as a soldier and a blue collar worker as an officer. Back in civilian world, this change of roles translates into low distance between

executives and employees: Switzerland could then be described as a low "prestige-differential" society. This means that it would be externally very difficult to differentiate between people's position in society based on external indicators.

2. The fact that people meet regularly with people from different professions, regions and social backgrounds results in a low distance and consensus-oriented culture.

Switzerland is thus the embodiment of a profound paradox: a very hierarchical institution, such as the army, producing less distance between people. In turn, this constitutes an important contextual factor relevant for various leadership and HR tasks in Swiss companies.

TEACHING QUESTIONS

1. How would you characterise the two most important characteristics of HR practice in Austria and Switzerland?
2. Provide concrete examples of typical characteristics of the context of HR that would help somebody coming from abroad deal effectively with these realities?
3. Discuss the influence of the organisation's size and sector for HRM in Austria and Switzerland.
4. Try to find three main reasons for a possible diverging scenario of HRM developments in Austria and Switzerland.
5. Discuss the interplay between the military system and behaviour in business in Switzerland.
6. Depict a contrasting picture of the most important economic features of Austria and Switzerland.

REFERENCES AND SOURCES

References

Avery, G., Donnenberg, O., Gick, W. and Hilb, M. (1999) Conceptualized differences between German speaking countries. *Journal of Management Development*, 18(1).

Brewster, C. and Bournois, F. (1993) A European perspective on human resource management. In: Hegewisch, A. and Brewster, C. (eds.), *European Development in Human Resource Management*. London: Kogan Page, pp. 33–54.

Brewster, C. and Larsen, H.H. (eds.) (2000), *Human Resource Management in Northern Europe. Trends, Dilemmas and Strategy*. Oxford: Blackwell.

Dowling, P.J., Welch, D.E. and Schuler, R.S. (1999) *International Human Resource Management*, 3rd edn. Cincinnati, OH: South-Western College Publishing.

Guest, D. (1990) Human resource management and the American dream. *Journal of Management Studies*, 27(4): 377–397.

Hilb, M. (2002) *Integriertes Personalmanagement: Ziele-Strategien-Instrumente*, 10th edn. Neuwieds: Luchterhand.

Hofstede, G. (1980) *Culture's Consequences: International Differences in Work-related Values*. Beverly Hills: Sage.

Mayrhofer, W., Brewster, C. and Morley, M. (2000) The concept of strategic European human resource management. In: Brewster C. et al. (eds.), *New Challenges for European Human Resource Management*. London: Macmillan Press, pp. 3–33.

Mayrhofer, W., Brewster, C. and Morley, M. (2000) Communication, consultation and the HRM debate. In: Brewster, C., Mayrhofer, W. and Morley, M. (eds.), *New Challenges for European Human Resource Management*. London: Macmillan, pp. 222–245.

Mintzberg, H. (1973) *The Nature of Managerial Work*. New York: Harper & Row.

Morley, M., Brewster, C., Gunnigle, P. and Mayrhofer, W. 2000. Evaluating change in European industrial relations: research evidence on trends at organisational level. In: Brewster, C., Mayrhofer, W. and Morley, M. (eds.), *New Challenges for European Human Resource Management*. London: Macmillan, pp. 199–221.

Sparrow, P. (1999) International reward systems. In: Brewster, C. and Harris, H. (eds.), *International HRM*. London/New York: Routledge, pp. 102–119.

Sources for Austria Institutional Background

(1) Eurostat, Statistical Office of the European Communities (eds.) (2001) *Eurostat Yearbook 2001*. Brussels: European Communities
(2) ÖSTAT: http://www.oestat.gv.at (11.09.99)
(3) Eurostat: http://europa.eu.int (11.09.99)
(4) http://www.oesterreich.com (11.09.99)
(5) http://www.graz.at (11.09.99)
(6) http://www.ist.at/linz/ (11.09.99)
(7) http://www.magwien.gv.at (11.09.99)

(8) Eurostat, Statistical Office of the European Communities (eds.) (1998) *Labour Force Survey. Results 1997.* Luxembourg: Office for Official Publications of the European Communities

(9) Bamberger, R., Brunner, F., Lades, H. (1953) Die Welt von A–Z. Wien: Verlag für Jugend und Volk

(10) Eurostat, Statistical Office of the European Communities (eds.) (1996) *Labour Force Survey. Results 1995.* Luxembourg: Office for Official Publications of the European Communities

(11) WIFO: http://www.wifo.ac.at (17.09.99)

5

France and Belgium: Language, Culture and Differences in Human Resource Practices

Dirk Buyens, Françoise Dany, Koen Dewettinck and Bérénice Quinodon

INTRODUCTION

For historical reasons, and because they are neighbouring countries, France and Belgium have some close similarities. Indeed, Belgium was once a dependent province of France. And even though Belgium has been independent since 1831, French culture and institutions have influenced her significantly. In fact, French was the language of Belgian government, the upper classes, and secondary and higher education for more than a hundred years. Even today, for 32% of the Belgian population, French is the legal language. This group mainly lives in Wallonia, the southern part of Belgium. Fifty-six per cent of the population speaks Flemish (Dutch) and lives in Flanders, the northern part of the country. Eleven per cent of the Belgian population is legally bilingual.

As 43% of Belgians speak French, nothing could be more appropriate than thinking about a common model of human resource management (HRM) as between France and Belgium.

However, the emancipation movement of the Dutch-speaking majority in Belgium achieved momentum in the 1950s and continues to thrive. This emancipation movement has largely gained from the economic growth Flanders has experienced during that period. This evolution has caused a shift in focus from France to the Netherlands, also a Dutch-speaking neighbouring country, as the most important role model for the Flemish.

The intention of this chapter is to compare HRM practices in Belgium and France. We shall therefore focus on HR's role and strategic impact; employee relations and trade unions; recruitment; flexible work patterns; performance management and rewards, and training and development. However, because of the cultural and linguistic similarities between on the one hand Wallonia and France (Latin-European-oriented regions) and on the other hand Flanders and the Netherlands, we shall present research findings from France, the two different Belgian regions and the Netherlands. Consequently we aim to position our comparison in the "convergence versus divergence" debate.

INSTITUTIONAL BACKGROUND

FRANCE

Topography and climate

From the main mountain ranges (the Pyrenees to the south and the Alps to the east) to the lowland areas of Poitou-Charentes, the topography of France is quite varied. Nevertheless, two-thirds of the country is covered by rolling plains.

The climate of France is temperate. France has four subclimates: Atlantic from Cotentin to the Pyrenees, Continental from Cotentin to Vallée du Rhône, Mediterranean on the south coast and Corsica, and Alpine for the Alps and the Pyrenees.

Overseas territories

The fact that France has kept some possessions overseas appears an anomaly compared to other former European colonial powers. These possessions have three different statuses:

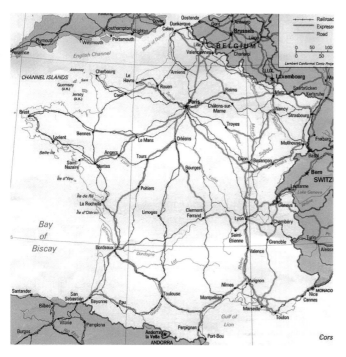

Area	543,965 km^2
Population	59,226,000 inhabitants
Density	109 inhabitants per km^2
Capital and population	Paris (2,152,423)
Other major cities and population	Marseille (800,550)
	Lyon (415,487)
	Bordeaux (210,336)
Official language	French
Religions	65% Roman Catholic
	7% Muslim
	2% Anglican
	26% Others

France has a central position in Europe; it is bordered on the west by the North Atlantic Ocean, on the south by Mediterranean Sea and on the north by the North Sea. The coastline is 11,000 km long.

France is bounded by Belgium, Luxembourg, Germany, Switzerland, Italy and Spain. It includes many islands of which the most important is Corsica.

- Overseas departments (DOM): French Guyana (157,500 inhabitants), Martinique (388,300), Guadeloupe (422,000) and Reunion (669,600).
- Overseas territories (TOM): New Caledonia (197,500 inhabitants), French Polynesia (220,000) and Wallis and Futuna (14,200).
- Territorial collectivities (CT): St Pierre and Miquelon and Mayotte (130,000 inhabitants).

Diverse cultural identity

France is characterised by a mixed cultural identity from its numerous regions, with their differing languages and habits. France also has people with origins in countries throughout the world (South Europe, Arabia, Africa, etc.).

Today's diversity reflects both the former colonial power of France and the tradition of welcoming foreigners. It is today a prosperous and modern European nation with significant international influence.

Principal characteristics

Table 5.1 shows the position of France in relation to other European countries in respect of a number of standardised items.

People

France is one of the four most populous countries in the European Union (EU). Over the last 50 years, its population has grown by 40%. This is due partly to natural increase and partly to migration before 1974. People are also living longer, as illustrated in Figure 5.2.

Economy

Historically, the manufacturing sector was the basis of France's economic strength but this sector has declined steadily over the year (Table 5.2). A significant share of GDP has been taken by services, particularly financial services.

The cost of living in France is generally higher than in the rest of the EU, except for health, clothing and footwear and communications where France is noticeably lower (Table 5.3).

Institutional and political environment

France is governed by the constitution of 4 October 1958 (revised in 2000) which established a parliamentary system. The President of the Republic, who is elected for 5 years (constitutional law of 2 October 2000) by direct universal suffrage, holds executive

Figure 5.1   Different views of Paris, France

Table 5.1   Principal characteristics in relation to EU-15

	EU-15	France	Relation (France/EU-15) $\times$ 100
Density (inhibitants per km^2) **Year: 1997**	**116**	**107**	**92.2**
Infant mortality (per thousand live birth) Year: 2000	4.7	4.6	97.9
Life expectancy at birth (boys; years) Year: 1999	74.9	74.9	100.0
Life expectancy at birth (girls; years) Year: 1999	81.2	82.4	101.5
Employment rate (men; %) Year: 2000	72	69	82
Employment rate (women; %) Year: 2000	54	55	99
Unemployment rate (%) Year: 2000	8	10	114
Cost-of-living comparisons (total value; B = 100[1]) Year: 2000	B = 100	105	105

All data from (1).

Age (years)	France (%) 1986	France (%) 2000	EU-15 (%) 2000
<15	21	19	17
15–24	16	13	12
25–49	34	36	37
50–64	16	16	17
65–79	10	12	13
>80	3	4	4

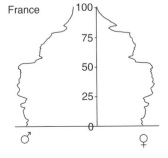

Figure 5.2   Population by age (% of total population)

Table 5.2   Persons in employment in different sectors (thousand)

	1990	1995	2000
Industry	1394	1080	971
Agriculture	6629	5946	6152
Services	13,758	15,019	16,256

All data from (1).

Table 5.3 Cost-of-living comparisons in the EU (2000, Brussels = 100[1])

Food and non-alcoholic beverages	Alcoholic beverages tobacco	Clothing and footwear	Housing	Household equipment
103	106	92	158	117
Health	Transport	Communications	Recreation and culture	Education
97	106	65	104	126
Hotels, cafés and restaurants	Miscellaneous	*Total*	*Total excluding rents*	
106	118	118	105	

Table 5.4 Gross domestic product (at market prices, at current prices and current exchange rates)

		1993	1994	1995	1996	1997	1998	1999	2000
1000 million ECU (nominal growth)	France	1089.4	1139.3	1188.1	1224.6	1241.1	1297.6	1350.1	1404.8
Yearly growth as % of previous year (real growth)	France	−1	2	2	1	2	3	3	3
	EU-15	−1	3	2	2	3	3	3	3

All data from (1).

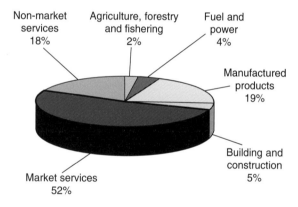

Non-market services 18%
Agriculture, forestry and fishering 2%
Fuel and power 4%
Manufactured products 19%
Building and construction 5%
Market services 52%

Figure 5.3 Economic structure (gross value rates as % of sectors, 1997, France). All data from (1)

Table 5.5 Persons in employment (million)

1990	1995	2000
21.8	22	23.4

All data from (1).

Table 5.6 Employment rate by gender (%, 1997)

	France	EU-15
Women	61	58
Men	75	78

All data from (1).

power jointly with a prime minister whom he chooses himself. Legislative power belongs to the French parliament which is composed of two houses: the Senate (often called the "upper house") elected by indirect universal suffrage and renewed by one-third every 3 years; and the National Assembly elected for 5 years by direct universal suffrage.

Labour market

Over 23 million people are in employment in France, the vast majority of jobs being offered by the service sector (Table 5.5).

The French unemployment rate remains one of the highest in Europe though it has been decreasing since 1998. An interesting feature is that more women participate in the work force than the average in the EU (Table 5.6). But the unemployment rate for women still remains higher than that for men (14% in 1998 against 10%) (Table 5.7).

Hourly labour costs in France are comparatively high, especially indirect costs, which are among the highest in Europe (Table 5.8). This is mostly due to social security costs (Table 5.9).

Table 5.7   Unemployment rate (%, 2000)

1990	1991	1992	1993	1994	1995	1996	1997	1998	1999	2000
9	10	10	12	12	12	12	12	12	11	10

	2000	
	France	EU-15
Women unemployed	11.5	9.7
Men unemployed	7.8	7.0
Long-term unemployment (as % of all unemployed)	40	45

All data from (1).

Table 5.8   Average labour costs (manual and non-manual) in total industry (1999)

	1992	1993	1994	1995	1996	1997	1998	1999
EU-15	17.68	18.33	19.05	19.47	20.10	20.97	21.45	21.5
France	19.12	20.27	20.90	21.59	23.11	23.35	24.10	23.8

Table 5.9   Structure of labour cost (%, 2000)

Direct cost	Indirect cost	Social security as part of indirect cost
67	33	29

Table 5.10   Level of education for the population aged 25–64 (%, 2000)

At least upper secondary education	Total (25–64)	25–29	30–34	35–39	40–44	45–49	50–54	55–59	60–64
EU-15 (women and men)	64	76	73	70	66	62	55	51	45
France (women and men)	62	79	74	68	62	60	54	48	39
EU-15 (women)	61	77	73	70	64	58	50	45	37
France (women)	59	79	74	67	60	56	49	43	32

All data from (1).

Education

In France, education is compulsory from 6 up to the age of 16. Education is free in state schools, although a number of private schools also exist. State pre-primary schools (for children from 3, sometimes 2 up to 5) are not compulsory but nursery schools must allow all the 3-year-old children of families who want their children to be educated in such structures.

The levels of education of people aged from 25 to 64 are at about the European averages (Table 5.10).

---

[1] Cost-of-living comparison is carried out by calculation of index numbers (Brussels = 100) based on (a) prices of a shopping basket of over 3000 goods and services, (b) expenditure patterns of international officials and (c) exchange rates. Figures come from work by Eurostat in the field of cost-of-living adjustments to salaries of EU officials. Staff regulations fix indices for Belgium and Luxembourg at 100. Hence indices are available for all EU capitals except Brussels and Luxembourg. Country codes refer to the capital city.

BELGIUM

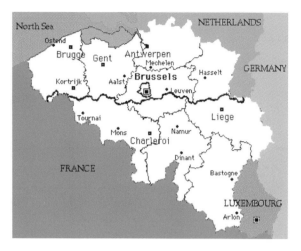

Area	30,528 km²; 1% of EU-15 area
Population	10,241,506; 3% of EU-15 population
Density	334 inhabitants per km²
Capital and population	Brussels (Brussel) 134,243 (1999)
Other important cities and population	Antwerp (447,632) Bruges (115,991) Ghent (224,074) Hasselt (67,777) Liège (187,538) Leuven (88,245) Mons (91,187) Namen (104,994) Arlon (24,6850
Official languages	Flemish (56%) French (32%) German (1%) Legally bilingual (11%)
Business languages	Flemish, French, English and German
Religions	75% Roman Catholic 25% Protestant or others

Belgium has an area of 30,528 km, a population of more than 10 million, and a density of 334 inhabitants per km². Flanders has an area of 13,522 km, Brussels 161 km and Wallonia 16,844 km. Belgium is bordered on the north by the North Sea and the Netherlands, on the east by Germany, on the southeast by Luxembourg, and on the southwest and west by France. French, Flemish and German are recognised as the official national languages. The northern region of Belgium is Flemish-speaking, the south French, and German is spoken along the eastern border. The capital, Brussels, is bilingual. Belgium is a member of the EU.

Topography and climate

Belgium is a small country in Northwestern Europe. "Belgium, heart of Europe" is not just a slogan: the geographical centre of the 15 countries of the EU is actually in Belgium, and more precisely in Oignies-en-Thiérache (Viroinval), in the province of Namur. Belgium is divided between two main areas occupied by the Dutch-speaking Flemings in the north and by French-speaking Walloons in the south.

Flanders, the northern, Dutch-language part of Belgium consists of flat coastal plains in the northwest. Flanders has about 64 km of coastline with beaches and dunes. Wallonia is bordered by France, Germany, Luxembourg and the Belgian region of Flanders. The northern section consists of low and very fertile clay plateaus, dissected by tributaries of the Meuse river. The southeast is dominated by the more rugged topography of the Ardennes. Much of the Ardennes consists

Figure 5.4   Atomium, Brussels

of wooded plateaus. In the far south is a region of low hills known as the Belgian Lorraine.

The weather in Belgium is largely determined by the movements of westerly maritime air streams. Atlantic depressions approach from the west and the southwest and create a changeable climate. Hence the climate is maritime, with mild winters and cool summers. The hottest month in Brussels is July, with an average temperature of 17.8°C. The coldest is January, with an average of 2.2°C. Extreme temperatures are rare. The annual rainfall is about 850 mm.

Federal state structure and provinces

Today Belgium is a true federal state, organised into three regions (Flanders, Wallonia and the Brussels Capital Region) and three communities (French-, Dutch- and German-speaking) each with their own legislative and executive power.

Principal characteristics

Figure 5.5 shows Belgium's principal characteristics as seen in relation to the EU: a very high population density and a rather low unemployment rate.

Special features

Through the centuries Belgium has been occupied and ruled in succession by different peoples, including the Romans, Germanic tribes, Burgundians, Spaniards and Austrians, resulting in a melting pot of cultures. Belgium bears more traces than any other country of the continuous exchange between Germanic and Romance cultures.

People

Population development

The total population of Belgium at the beginning of the twenty-first century was just over 10 million (2000: 10,241,506).

Economy

Belgium has an open economy which has encountered strong international competition. There is also a highly developed private enterprise economy which has capitalised on its central geographic location, its fast and efficient transport network, its diversified industrial and commercial base and its modern functional seaports

Table 5.11 Population by age and sex (% of total population)

Age (years)	1990	2000	EU-15 (2000)	Female per age group (%)
<15	18	18	17	49
15–24	14	12	12	
25–49	36	37	37	50
50–64	17	17	17	
65–79	11	13	13	60
>80	4	3	4	

All data from (1) and (2) and (3).

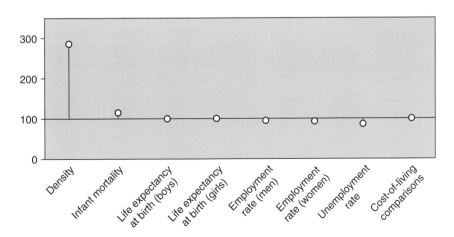

Figure 5.5   Principal characteristics in relation to EU-15 = 100

which form the magnetic poles of industrial growth. Flanders has the greatest seaport concentration in the world. As far as general cargo is concerned, Flanders seaports handle the highest volume on a worldwide scale. Industry is mainly concentrated in the Flemish area in the north, although the government is encouraging reinvestment in the southern region of Wallonia. Belgium has almost no raw materials. For that reason it must import substantial quantities of raw materials and export a large volume of manufactures. This makes its economy very dependent on the state of world markets. Two-thirds of its trade is with other EU countries. Hence the Belgian economy is also mainly an export economy. Its most important sectors are: the car industry, the steel industry, precious metals, plastics, electrical devices, fuels, chemical products, pharmaceutical products, carpets, food, furniture, clothing, paper, carton, glass, copper, rubber, photographic products and cinema (Figure 5.6).

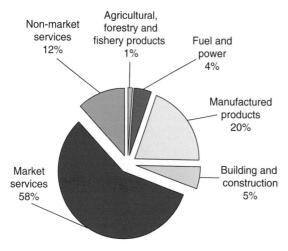

Figure 5.6   Economic structure (gross value rates as % of sectors, 1995, Belgium)

Belgium has a very low inflation rate, but a high governmental debt, which is however steadily decreasing. Over the past 30 years, Belgium has enjoyed the second-highest average annual growth in productivity among OECD countries (after Japan) (Table 5.12).

The cost of living equals the average of the EU.

Legal and institutional environment/political system

Belgium is a federal parliamentary democracy under a constitutional monarch. In a federal state legislative power is exercised on the one hand by the federal parliament, which consists of two bodies (the Chamber of Representatives and the Senate), and on the other hand by government ministers, who take full responsibility by countersigning the bills which have been adopted by the parliament and royal decree.

In 1993 Belgium completed its process of regionalisation and became a federal state consisting of communities (the Flemish Community, the French Community and the German-speaking Community) and regions (the Flemish Region, the Brussels Capital Region and the Walloon Region). As a result of the regionalisation there are now three levels of government: federal, regional and linguistic community. To some extent Belgian regions are similar to the American states or German "Länder". Belgium is further organised into 10 provinces and 589 communes.

Education

The level of education in Belgium today is one of the highest in Europe. The post-war educational system in Belgium was explicitly oriented towards raising the level of education of the population and the democratisation of education. Primary and secondary education

Table 5.12   Gross domestic product (at market prices, current series in 100 million EU)

		1990	1991	1992	1993	1994	1995	1996	1997	1998	1999	2000
		157	164	176	185	197	212	213	216	224	236	248
Percentage change on previous period (constant prices)	Belgium	3	2	2	−2	3	3	1	4	2	3	4
	EU-15	*	*	1	−1	3	2	2	3	3	3	3

All data from (1); * data not available.

became free and an extensive system of allowances and grants was introduced.

In higher education there are three types of award-granting institutions: universities, awarding first degrees, post-graduate and doctoral degrees; non-academic long-term institutions; and non-academic short-term institutions.

As in many other countries, the Belgian labour market is characterised by an increasing number of highly qualified entrants. Over the last few years there has been a considerable growth in business courses such as MBAs, and there is a large variety of other post-graduate studies. More and more students start a post-graduate course after acquiring their university degrees.

As Tables 5.13 and 5.14 show, in 1997 39% of people aged 25–59 years had completed only compulsory schooling, with a higher figure for women (40%) than for men (38%). The number of 24-year-olds still in education (20%) is not that high compared to other European countries.

Labour market

The unemployment rate in Belgium has improved slowly over the past few years (Tables 5.15–5.18). Belgium's unemployment rate in 2000 was 7%. However, there are marked regional differences. Rates in Wallonia and Brussels are two to three times higher than in Flanders.

Table 5.13   Young persons (aged 15–24 years) in education (% rate of participation in education)

Age (years)	Total	Men	Women
15	99	99	99
16	99	100	99
17	98	97	99
18	92	91	94
19	80	79	82
20	66	62	71
21	53	51	55
22	40	42	38
23	28	28	29
24	20	22	18
All ages	67	67	68

All data from (3); year: 1997.

Table 5.14   Level of education of persons aged 25–59 years (%)

	Total	Men	Women
Third level education	27	26	28
Upper secondary level	34	35	32
<Upper secondary level	39	38	40

All data from (3); year: 1997.

Table 5.15   Employment rate by age group (%)

	15–64			15–24			25–49			50–64		
	1990	1995	2000	1990	1995	2000	1990	1995	2000	1990	1995	2000
EU-15	*	60	63	*	37	40	*	74	78	*	47	49
Belgium	54	56	61	30	27	30	75	76	81	31	35	39

All data from (1); * Data not available.

Table 5.16   Persons in employment in different sectors (thousands)

	Agriculture			Industry			Services		
	1990	1995	2000	1990	1995	2000	1990	1995	2000
EU-15	*	7829	6767	*	44,751	45,668	*	95,474	105,300
Belgium	119	102	79	1113	1072	1064	2393	2619	2978

All data from (1); * Data not available.

Table 5.17   Unemployment rate (%)

	1990	1991	1992	1993	1994	1995	1996	1997	1998	1999	2000
EU-15	*	8	9	11	11	11	11	11	10	9	8
Belgium	7	7	7	9	10	10	10	9	10	9	7

All data from (1); * data not available.

Table 5.18   Persons in employment by age and sex (% of population in age group)

Age (years)	Total	Male	Female
15–24	32	35	29
25–49	84	94	74
50–64	37	51	24
>65	*	*	*

All data from (3); * data not available.

HRM IN FRANCE AND BELGIUM: LANGUAGE, CULTURE AND DIFFERENCES IN HR PRACTICES

THE ROLE OF THE HRM FUNCTION: MARGINAL OR CORE?

Over the past few years, there has been a significant increase in the importance given to the HRM function, especially in Belgium. The increasing number of HR directors that are board members indicates this change. Although this number has decreased slightly in Wallonia, it has increased in Flanders, so that the two regions of Belgium are now converging in this respect. France has the highest HR participation on the board of all the EU countries. Table 5.19 shows that HR participation in Belgium has shifted towards the French model, while we also notice that Flanders has moved away from the model of the Netherlands. However, this does not yet allow us to conclude that this is convergence: Dutch figures show that another, less centralised model still exists.

As far as the role of the HRM function is concerned, another point of discussion is the relationship that exists between the HR department and line managers. Should the HR department adopt a consultancy role and enable line management to take responsibility for the main HR issues (recruitment, training, etc.) or should it insist on remaining the party chiefly responsible for HR issues?

It is often said that highly compartmentalised, bureaucratic organisations, where the HR department exercises exclusive power and responsibility in HR matters, can no longer cope efficiently with the demands of a dramatically different environment (Heckscher and Donnellon, 1994). Although our data support the thesis of a high level of shared responsibilities between line management and HR departments, we see no significant increase in the level of shared responsibility between 1995 and 1999/2000. (We note however that this level was already high: about 80% of French, Belgian and Dutch organisations state that responsibility for training, e.g. was shared.) We even note a slight decrease in the level of sharing responsibilities in Belgium and the Netherlands as regards recruitment issues (Table 5.20). This trend applies to both Wallonia and Flanders without significant differences.

Almost half of the French organisations report an increase of the level of line management's responsibility for training. In contrast, where line management has the final word in terms of training (i.e. where line management is solely responsible or where it is responsible jointly with the HR department), we find that it has less responsibility than it did before (Table 5.21). It seems that the rhetoric of empowerment has reached French line management, but without any actual increase in the

Table 5.19   Proportion of HR directors who are board members

		Belgium							
France		Wallonia		Flanders		Total*		The Netherlands	
1995	1999/2000	1995	1999/2000	1995	1999/2000	1995	1999/2000	1995	1999/2000
83	88	88	81	51	78	56	78	41	41

* This "total" does not correspond to an average of the Walloon and Flemish figures for two main reasons:
1. There are many more Flemish organisations than Walloon ones.
2. The total includes the results of the English-speaking organisations.

Table 5.20   Responsibility for recruitment (1995 and 1999/2000)

	France		Belgium		The Netherlands	
	1995	1999/2000	1995	1999/2000	1995	1999/2000
Line management	5	3	9	7	12	7
Sharing of responsibility						
Line management with HR	41	34	38	31	56	44
HR with line management	51	56	43	43	26	30
HR department	3	7	9	19	5	19
Evolution of line management as the final authority		–		–		–17

Table 5.21   Responsibility for training (1995 and 1999/2000)

	France		Belgium		The Netherlands	
	1995	1999/2000	1995	1999/2000	1995	1999/2000
Line management	5	3	12	7	12	11
Sharing of responsibility						
Line management with HR	37	28	36	43	50	57
HR with line management	52	58	42	42	31	25
HR department	7	11	8	8	4	7
Evolution of line management as the final authority		–11		+2		+6

final level of decision-making power. A similar analysis applies to the figures concerning recruitment. In the other countries, there is a more pronounced trend towards line management's loss of final responsibility in recruitment decisions and a gain in responsibility in training decisions.

HRM STRATEGY: ITS STATUS AND ROLE

During the last 10–20 years, there has been a general decrease in the administrative practices of HR departments and a growing focus on specialist services in Belgium and perhaps elsewhere (Buyens and De Vos, 1999). As the economic environment becomes more complex, and an organisation's capacity to change emerges as a crucial issue, there is a growing emphasis on the strategic role of HRM in helping the organisation to survive (see e.g. Brown, 1991; Mabey and Salaman, 1995; Ulrich, 1997).

Holbeche's (1999) evaluation of HR's current strategic status does not paint a very positive picture. She describes the situation as follows:

"For years, Personnel has struggled to reinvent itself, to get closer to the customer, and to add value to the

Table 5.22   Involvement of HR in corporate strategy development 1999/2000

	France	Wallonia	Flanders	The Netherlands
From the outset	64	61	53	44
Consultative	20	18	28	42
Implementation	15	21	14	11
Not consulted	1	0	4	3

business. We are now supposed to be in the era of HR as a strategic business partner. The trouble is, the expectations of internal customers and of personnel specialists themselves about what HR can and should contribute may not have kept pace with the rhetoric. In many cases, HR professionals are still perceived to be primarily concerned with 'tea and sympathy' issues, or are expected to be 'fixers' of line management problems.''

(Holbeche, 1999: pp. 3–4)

As Table 5.22 shows, our figures on HR's involvement in corporate strategy development partly support Holbeche's view. In Flanders half of the respondents claim to be involved in corporate strategy development from the outset. In the French-speaking areas (Wallonia and France), this percentage is higher (six out of every ten organisations). If we compare the results for the four regions, we notice that the Walloon numbers are more in line with the French, while the Flemish numbers are more in line with those of the Netherlands. Indeed, it seems that within the French-speaking areas, HRM has made more progress at the strategic level. Filella (1991) had already come to a similar conclusion with regard to the Latin-European HR-model in his study.

These findings are in line with the importance of strategic considerations within the HR field. In France and Wallonia, fewer than one in ten of the respondents state that they have no HR strategy, while the corresponding percentages for the Dutch-speaking regions are about twice that high. However, in many cases, with the exception of the Netherlands, these policies are unwritten. Filella (1991) would argue that this difference is due to the importance of the oral tradition in the countries of the Latin model. We note also that unwritten strategies restrain senior executives in the department much less.

However, although HR seems to be involved in the formulation of corporate strategy, there is clearly a lack of focus in evaluating HR's performance. In Belgium, only half or fewer of the respondents state that the

personnel department's performance is evaluated. France and the Netherlands do even worse in this respect. Where HR's performance is evaluated, however, our data suggest that evaluation focuses on performance against objectives. Costs as such seem not to be the most important criterion. This may reflect a trend towards recognising HR as not being solely involved in managing the cost factor. This seems to be the case for all four of the regions examined here.

The analysis of HRM's status and role confirms that HR's strategic impact can be strengthened further. Although there are some differences between the regions involved, especially between on the one hand France and Wallonia and on the other hand Flanders and the Netherlands, the overall picture shows that HR's status is rather similar. The fact that HR still often lacks strategies to link its own activities to corporate strategy, and the observation that HR is not much involved in evaluating its own performance, undoubtedly help to explain HR's questionable status at the strategic level.

COMMUNICATION AND EMPLOYEE RELATIONS

Fuelled by the introduction of the new technologies, the volume of employee communication is still increasing. Table 5.23 shows that this development occurs primarily via written communication, team briefings and direct and personal contact.

Though written communication is still largely supported by traditional means, there has been a vast increase in the use of e-mail, both in Belgium (for more details on e-HRM practices in Belgium, see "HRM in action") as well as in France. However, there is still a substantial number of organisations in France and Wallonia (one-fifth in France, one-third in Wallonia) who in 1999/2000 were still not using e-mail to communicate with their employees. Thus, in the Latin-European

Table 5.23 How organisations communicate major issues to their employees: changes between 1996 and 1999/2000

	France	Wallonia	Flanders	The Netherlands
A. Change through representative bodies				
Increased	23	28	23	29
Same	68	62	56	59
Decreased	6	6	5	3
Not used	3	3	16	8
B. Change verbally directed to employees				
Increased	47	55	48	41
Same	48	45	48	54
Decreased	2	0	3	4
Not used	2	0	1	1
C. Change written to employees				
Increased	50	48	55	52
Same	44	45	42	45
Decreased	4	0	3	3
Not used	2	6	0	0
D. Change in use of computer mail				
Increased	66	43	69	69
Same	11	26	17	13
Decreased	0	0	0	1
Not used	23	32	15	18
E. Change in use of team briefings				
Increased	50	60	49	32
Same	44	33	39	64
Decreased	4	3	1	2
Not used	2	3	11	1

Table 5.24 Communication of business strategy and financial information (1999/2000)

	France	Wallonia	Flanders	The Netherlands
Management briefed about strategy	93	94	95	97
Professional staff briefed about strategy	50	45	60	70
Clerical staff briefed about strategy	32	27	45	41
Manual workers briefed about strategy	22	18	39	40
Management briefed about finance	94	97	95	95
Professional staff briefed about finance	72	67	65	71
Clerical staff briefed about finance	60	48	50	42
Manual workers briefed about finance	42	42	42	37

HR-model, one seems less attached to electronic means of communication. Traditional written communication increased in almost half the French and Belgian organisations between 1995 and 1999: so much for the paperless office!

Despite the increase in the use of electronic forms of communication, both team briefings and direct personal contacts have also increased for half the French and Belgian organisations. One conclusion that can be drawn from these figures is that electronic means of communications do not replace the traditional means, but that they create a supplementary channel to reach employees. This may have triggered a communication overload, as experienced by a majority of (especially information) workers.

With regard to top-down communication practices, we can readily observe that, particularly in the French-speaking regions (Wallonia and France), communication is highly targeted. Table 5.24 shows clearly that, for these companies, access to strategic communication is hierarchical. This is less true of the Dutch-speaking region. This may be attributed to cultural differences. As Hofstede (1980) found, these two regions differ significantly in their power-distance behaviour, which tells us about dependence relationships in a country. In small-power-distance countries (like the Netherlands) there is limited dependence of subordinates on bosses, and a preference for consultation. The emotional distance between the boss and the subordinate is relatively small: subordinates will quite readily approach and contradict their bosses. In large-power-distance countries (like France) there is considerable dependence of subordinates on bosses. The emotional distance between the subordinate and the boss is much wider: subordinates are unlikely to approach and contradict their bosses directly. This larger power distance may be partly reflected into a more hierarchical way of managing and communicating.

Access to financial information is far more common and democratic. While the hierarchy persists, the information gap between management and professional staff on the one hand and clerical and manual workers on the other hand is narrower, especially in France where management is twice as well informed about financial performance as manual labourers are (and four times as well informed about strategic plans).

The other aspect of vertical communication, upward communication, has remained relatively stable. As Table 5.25 makes clear, the immediate superior is still the most common vehicle for employees. However, some other modes of expression are also frequently used. Direct communication to senior managers is a very common practice in the three countries and its use continues to increase. In contrast, bottom-up communication through trade unions is also used by almost all organisations, though it has hardly increased during the last 3 years. The use of team briefing is on the increase for a third of the French companies and for nearly half of the Belgian companies, but is less frequent than these other forms.

It seems, therefore, that the traditional channels of bottom-up communication (through hierarchical or representative channels) are still very widely used. This is especially the case when compared to some other options, such as attitude surveys or suggestion schemes, which are less often used, especially in the French-speaking organisations.

In sum, the Cranet data on practices of communication show that the general trend is towards convergence

Table 5.25   How employees communicate their views to management: changes between 1996 and 1999/2000

	France	Wallonia	Flanders	The Netherlands
Direct to senior managers				
Increased	27	30	36	37
Same	60	61	55	53
Decreased	2	0	3	6
Not used	10	9	5	3
Through immediate superior				
Increased	19	31	47	38
Same	78	62	49	61
Decreased	3	3	2	1
Not used	0	3	1	0
Through works council				
Increased	21	34	20	33
Same	63	56	58	56
Decreased	14	6	10	9
Not used	3	3	12	2
Through workforce meetings				
Increased	28	44	31	34
Same	59	47	48	51
Decreased	6	0	5	5
Not used	7	9	15	10
Through team briefings				
Increased	35	47	45	26
Same	52	41	39	63
Decreased	3	0	0	7
Not used	10	12	15	5

between the regions: nowhere has the volume of communication diminished. But our data also highlight some cultural specificity: hierarchical channels are much more common in the French-speaking region.

THE INFLUENCE OF TRADE UNIONS: BIG DIFFERENCES BETWEEN COUNTRIES

Turning to the issue of representation, the Belgian and French situations are very different. In France, trade-union membership is traditionally low. In more than half the French companies the number of union members is under 10%. It is the lowest score among EU countries. In Belgium, however, about 58% of the organisations state that more than 50% of the workforce is unionised and more than 35% state that over 75% are union members (see Box 5.2).

Despite the huge difference in unionisation, syndic-alism is not decreasing in either Belgium or France. In fact, its influence has increased over these years. In Belgium, though, the influence of the unions differs very much between industries. This trend is similar for Wallonia and Flanders. Especially within the more traditional industries, like the steel industry, and in public organisations, union influence is considerable. The French social legislative background on the other hand can explain the weakness of union membership in France. Five unions are recognised for collective bargaining purposes regardless of the size of their membership (see Box 5.1), while many of the services undertaken by trade unions in other countries are carried out by the national welfare system in France. In fact, French unions offer no collective services. Thus, French employees do not feel the need to become union members.

BOX 5.1   FRENCH EMPLOYEE REPRESENTATIVE STRUCTURES

In France, employee representative structure is rather complex. There are four different structures:

- *Workforce delegates* (*délégués du personnel*) are compulsory for any enterprise or establishment with 10 or more employees. These delegates are elected by all the employees and are in charge of presenting individual and/or collective grievances of employees to management. They can also call in the labour inspectorate when they suspect the company is not abiding by the social and work laws. These delegates are not necessarily union members but they can be.
- *The works council* (*comité d'entreprise*) is compulsory for an enterprise or establishment with 50 or more employees. The works council is composed of employee members elected by their colleagues, and representatives from the trade unions (who play a consultative role), and is chaired by the head of the company (who does not take part in the majority of the votes). It has two main functions:
  - A consultative one in regard to an employer's decisions concerning the organisation of work and management.
  - An executive one in regard to social and cultural facilities for employees. Companies have a statutory obligation to fund their works council, which then decides how to allocate these funds.
- *The Workplace Health and Safety Committee* (CHSCT) is compulsory for companies with 50 or more employees. This committee is composed of the head of the company and employee representatives (works council members or the workforce delegates). It plays an essentially consultative role but must be consulted before every change that might affect working conditions. It also has the right to launch special investigations into industrial accidents and issue a notification of danger.
- *Trade union delegates*: every representative union has the right to nominate a delegate in each company with 50 or more employees. Union delegates are supposed to represent their unions but also employees for collective bargaining (in France there is at least one compulsory collective bargaining each year in every company over wages and working time). This is a rather complicated role to play since it involves reconciling the interests of different groups.

Only agreements signed by representative trade unions are legally considered effective.
There are two kinds of representative union:

- CFTC, CGT, CFDT, FO and CGC are recognised as representative unions no matter how many members they have in a specific company. This national representative role is due to historical reasons.
- The other unions (SUD, CNT, "*le Groupe des 10*", etc.) are not considered representative at a national level, hence they cannot negotiate national agreements. They can be judged however (by a legal tribunal) to be representative in a specific company. Several criteria, such as their historical role in the company and the number of members they have, must be taken into account to judge their representational validity.

This system can lead to a paradoxical situation where a significant agreement is reached between the head of a company and a union with very few members in the company. That is one reason why there is currently keen debate about an eventual reform of the system of representation in France.

BOX 5.2   THE BELGIAN SYSTEM

Like the United Kingdom, Belgium has a long history of trade unionism. Belgium was the first country on the continent of Europe to undergo an industrial revolution and the Belgian working class developed a strong belief in unionism. Trade unions can be considered as "de facto associations", under the terms of the Act of 24 May 1921 covering freedom of association. Three trade unions are considered to be representative in Belgium: a Christian one (representing about 50% of unionised workers), a socialist one (about 40%) and a liberal conservative one (about 10%) (Buelens et al., 1992). There is no single co-ordinating trade union body in Belgium, though there is an inter-professional body that provides general union services and logistical support for the occupational federations.

The three umbrella union organisations compete with each other at the national, regional and company level. Industrial relations are further organised around two functions: industrial negotiations and economic consultations. The table below summarises the situation:

Level	Situation	
	Negotiation	Consultation
National	National Labour Council (representing all groups)	Central Economic Council (representing all groups)
Sectoral	Representative Commission (representing all groups)	Professional Councils (representing all groups)
Company	Union delegations (representing unionised workers)	Company Council and Committee for Security and Hygiene on the workplace (representing all groups)

The distinction between negotiation and consultation is not as clear-cut as it would appear officially. At the company level, negotiation must occur with national and sector agreements and thus always implies greater demands on the company than at the other two levels. However, within a company, economic and financial matters are excluded from negotiations as being a prerogative of management, as are certain matters concerning social aspects that affect the organisation of production.

Belgian trade unions are not subsidised. As a result, their main source of funding is membership fees. This fee is determined by the professional union, and therefore varies depending on union, place and region. Usual trade union activities like defence of interests, trade union papers, documentation, information bulletins, social allowances, strike allowances, etc. are financed by members' contributions.

Trade unions in Belgium have to varying extents lost some of their support, social appeal and legitimacy and have consequently experienced a loss of power. As in other countries, trade unionism is on the defensive and the unions are in the extremely difficult position of having to reconcile the structural adaptation necessary in a competitive market place with the continuing need to defend their members' interests (Buelens et al., 1992).

RECRUITMENT AND SELECTION

The comparative figures on recruitment and selection indicate some notable differences between France, the two Belgian regions and the Netherlands. For example, internal mechanisms for filling managerial vacancies are very popular (Table 5.26). One important difference is that, whereas in both Belgium and France internal recruitment mechanisms are widely used for senior and middle management jobs, only about a quarter of the French organisations use internal mechanisms for junior managerial vacancies. The explanation lies in the French institutional context. In France, the educational system – with its unique system of selection via the "*grandes écoles*" (see Box 5.3) – provides the organisation with a breeding ground of junior managers (Barsoux and Lawrence, 1990). French HR managers rely on this prestigious source of new managerial blood, while their Belgian and Dutch colleagues rely more on promotion from the lower levels to secure the necessary inflow of management skills.

Table 5.26   Use of internal mechanisms for filling managerial vacancies 1999/2000

	France	Wallonia	Flanders	The Netherlands
Senior management	54	51	53	49
Middle management	70	67	69	75
Junior management	2	79	59	66

BOX 5.3   FRENCH ÉLITE SYSTEM: *"LES GRANDES ÉCOLES"*

As Barsoux and Lawrence showed (Barsoux and Lawrence, 1990), in France there are essentially two ways to become a manager (*cadre*): through the French educational élite system or through loyalty to a given company. Our data from the Cranet survey and a recent survey made by the APEC (*Agence pour l'Emploi des Cadres*) underline the importance of the "*grandes écoles*". According to the APEC (APEC, 2002) in 2001, 260,000 new managerial positions were created, less than a third of which were filled by internal promotion. This result, covering all categories of manager, is consistent with our findings: a large majority of organisations recruits their junior managers from the French educational élite.

French educational élite system ...

In France, there are two different channels for the higher educational system:
Universities accept all students who have succeeded in their secondary education and award diplomas at various levels (from 2 years of higher education to 8 years for a

doctoral programme). This system is not highly selective since there are now approximately 70% of each generation who have successfully passed through secondary education.

The so-called "grandes écoles" are engineering or business schools. Their method of recruiting students is highly selective: students are admitted through nationwide examinations after 2 years of "preparatory classes" where students are given a strong fundamental background in mathematics, human sciences (for business preparatory classes) or physics (for future engineers).

... that recruiters enjoy

A survey made by the APEC (APEC, 2001) among young "*diplômés*" from the engineering and business "*grandes écoles*" and undergraduates and graduates from university (4 years and more of higher education) highlights the disparities that exist between them.

Once they finish their studies, only about half of the undergraduates and graduates from university become managers whereas a large majority of the *diplômés* from a business school (73%) and almost all the alumni from an engineering school (94%) are given the status of "*cadres*".

Graduates from universities and "*grandes écoles*" are also privileged in terms of unemployment: in April 2001, 15% of the students who graduated from universities in 1999 were unemployed in contrast to the 5% of jobless alumni from engineering schools.

Table 5.27   Selection methods used (1999/2000)

	France	Wallonia	Flanders	The Netherlands
Interview panel				
Every appointment	6	0	25	33
Most appointments	4	5	16	16
One-to-one interviews				
Every appointment	92	82	82	77
Most appointments	7	12	13	9
Application forms				
Every appointment	81	71	71	47
Most appointments	10	18	10	14
Psychometric tests				
Every appointment	7	18	18	0
Most appointments	14	7	20	5
Assessment centres				
Every appointment	3	5	0	2
Most appointments	3	5	8	8
Graphology				
Every appointment	5	0	0	0
Most appointments	11	4	0	2
References				
Every appointment	25	19	6	4
Most appointments	28	11	11	11

When we look at the figures for selection methods, we notice some striking differences between France, Wallonia, Flanders and the Netherlands.

Table 5.27 shows that there are major differences in the use of interview panels as between the four regions and that there is a clear distinction between the French-speaking regions (France and Wallonia) and the Dutch-speaking regions (Flanders and the Netherlands). While four or five out of ten, respectively, of the Flemish and Dutch respondents use interview panels for almost every appointment, the corresponding percentages for Wallonia and France are significantly lower.

One-to-one interviews are used very frequently in the four regions. If we consider both interview techniques (interview panel and one-to-one interviews), we can conclude that one-to-one interviews are regarded as a more important selection technique than interview panels. This is true for all four regions. One conclusion could be that interview panels and one-to-one interviews are both very frequently used, probably as distinct phases of a single selection procedure.

The use of application forms, the second most popular selection technique for the countries involved, seems to correspond with country barriers. In France, application forms are used most frequently, while only half of the Dutch organisations use application forms for every appointment. In Belgium, the use of application forms is far more popular than in the Netherlands, but slightly less popular than in France.

Both psychometric tests and assessment centres are used frequently, though this is not well reflected in the table since they are only used for some appointments and not for every or most appointments. A possible explanation is that these selection tools are very frequently used, but only for a limited number of job categories (probably only for more senior posts) because of their cost. Assessment centres are used most in the Netherlands and least in France.

A country-specific pattern arises for the use of psychometric tests. These are most used in Belgium, less in France and hardly at all in the Netherlands.

Graphology, which attempts to learn about candidates through their handwriting, is not widely used except in France and is slightly more popular in Wallonia than in Flanders or the Netherlands. It seems that in the French-speaking areas graphology as a selection method is more commonly accepted.

References too are more popular in the French-speaking areas. Thus, for this category of selection tools, we again see that the figures for Wallonia are more in line with those for France, while the Flemish figures are more in accordance with the Dutch.

Overall, the most frequently used selection tools are: one-to-one interviews, application forms and references. These tools are known to have a certain proven efficacy. Such findings indicate that the more traditional selection tools are still very widely used. The French-speaking population seems to be more traditional in this respect

than their Dutch-speaking counterparts. With regard to the use of interview panels, assessment centres, graphology and references, the Walloon profile converges towards the French profile, while the Flemish profile has much in common with the Dutch profile. In the Dutch-speaking areas, joint selection decisions and the use of new selection tools (such as assessment centres) seem to be more popular than in the French-speaking areas. The results thus indicate that differences in the use of selection tools across the neighbouring countries are not very heavily influenced by country-specific factors, but rather by language or culture-specific factors.

ORGANISATION OF WORK: FLEXIBLE PATTERNS OF WORK

National governments and legislative institutions are keenly interested in establishing "atypical" and flexible working patterns that can have an impact on the unemployment rate and also on the basis of the social welfare system (Cranfield Network, 1996). In line with the hypothesis of convergence, one can assert that flexible working patterns should increase in every region we have studied (Boyer, 1989), because they are a means of containing wage costs and deploying resources more effectively. Hence, adopting an institutionalist's point of view, we can suppose that the determination of HR policies and practices in the three countries we have studied is strongly influenced by institutions like national regulatory structures. On the other hand, as flexible working practices have a direct impact on workers' and employers' habits and values, it is interesting to explore whether the substantial differences observed are due to national characteristics or to cultural differences between the French-speaking and the Dutch-speaking regions.

The figures for France, Belgium and the Netherlands confirm that the more traditional flexible working patterns are increasing everywhere (see Table 5.28).

Table 5.28   Evolution between 1995 and 1999/2000 of organisations where over 10% of employees are on flexible contracts

	France	Belgium	The Netherlands
Annual hours	+39	+4	−2
Part time	+5	+11	+13
Temporary	+4	+6	+16

Newer flexible employment patterns like home-based working and teleworking, despite the rhetoric, are still ignored by most organisations. Looking at annual hours, part-time work and temporary work, we see big differences in the forms of employment flexibility that are chosen.

The main differences between France, Belgium and the Netherlands are best explained by national specifics (especially legislation) rather than by cultural–linguistic reasons – a finding supported on a pan-European level by the work of Brewster and Tregaskis (2001).

PERFORMANCE MEASUREMENTS AND REWARDS

Today, performance appraisal is a central element in Belgian and French companies' strategic HRM. Although there is no universally accepted model of performance appraisal, it often includes a definition of the employee's objectives, monitoring and measuring of performance, feedback on results and, possibly, rewards and plans to improve future performance (Mabey and Salaman, 1995). Employee performance management systems are a widely discussed issue in contemporary HRM. For employees, performance measurement systems are important as they can provide valued feedback on their behaviour and performance. For the organisation, performance measurement systems are a helpful tool in guiding employees' behaviour and performance towards organisational objectives. As a result, the quest for a strategic HRM has boosted the interest in and the use of performance measurement and performance management systems in organisations.

Table 5.29 shows appraisal systems to be very widely used in the four regions and for all employee categories. One exception is the use of appraisal systems for clerical and manual workers in Wallonia. In France, management and professional workers are clearly more frequently guided by appraisal systems than their clerical and manual working colleagues. In this sense, we already see a distinction between the French-speaking and the Dutch-speaking countries. While the performance appraisal system seems to focus more on the management and professional employees in the French-speaking areas, all employee categories are equally involved in performance appraisal systems in the Dutch-speaking countries.

Unlike the very widespread use of appraisal systems, the system does not always involve incentive schemes related to performance. For example, where the French report that management appraisal systems are used in 87% of the cases, the same respondents state that only in 78% of the cases is the French managers' incentive scheme related to performance. In Flanders, the use of performance-related incentive schemes for managers is also significantly smaller than the use of management appraisal systems. Linking the use of performance-related pay with various employee categories, both in France and in Belgium, performance-related pay is mostly used for management functions and its use declines through professional workers, clerical workers and manual workers.

The immediate supervisor is undoubtedly the most frequently used source for evaluating employee performance. Employees themselves are the second most quoted contributors to the performance appraisal system (except for the Walloon sample). The contribution of subordinates, peers and customers is limited. Only a few organisations dare to use those sources as input for the performance appraisal system. It is striking to note that feedback from subordinates is almost never taken into account in performance appraisal systems. This potentially valuable and often surprising source of personal feedback seems to be neglected. Also, customers' feedback, another potentially interesting source, is not frequently used in Belgian, French and Dutch performance appraisal systems.

Table 5.29   Use of appraisal systems for different employee categories (1999/2000)

	France	Wallonia	Flanders	The Netherlands
Management	87	70	81	84
Professional	85	73	88	83
Clerical	76	48	82	84
Manual	69	43	76	83

In sum, in Belgium and France performance management is becoming more and more important. This trend can be understood in the light of the current HRM ambition to become a respected strategic partner in corporate matters. Performance management is the main vehicle for aligning individual employee behaviour and performance with the objectives developed at the strategic corporate level. Table 5.29 showed that differences between France, Wallonia, Flanders and the Netherlands are minimal in this area. The challenge to prove the added value of HRM seems to have a universal character in which regional, cultural or linguistic differences play only a marginal role.

TRAINING AND DEVELOPMENT

Training and development in France and Belgium are heavily influenced by national legislation. French legislation, e.g. imposes on companies a certain formalism in training and a minimum of 1.5% of the wage bill has to be dedicated to training or paid in "tax" (see Box 5.4).

BOX 5.4   EMPLOYEE TRAINING AND DEVELOPMENT IN FRANCE

Professional training in France is highly regulated. The French training system is based on a law voted in 1971 that:

- Establishes a statutory obligation for employers of companies with more than 10 employees to devote at least 1.5% of their wage bill to the funding of a continuing training system.
- Organises the continuing training system in two directions:
  - training specified in the company's "training plan";
  - training initiated by employees exercising their individual right to training and development.

The yearly company training plan

At least 0.9% of the wage bill (taken from the 1.5% that companies must devote to training and development) must finance the company's annual training plan. This plan must be designed to achieve the following objectives:

- Acquiring competencies currently lacking in the company, where that deficiency is affecting peformance.
- Preparing employees for the changes that will occur in their job (for instance the use of new technologies).
- Re-orienting the company's competencies panel.
- Adapting employees to cultural changes.

Every year, the nature and conditions of the training programmes that will form part of this plan are discussed between the company's management and the employee representatives committee. A review of the actions taken in the previous year and their costs must also to be presented to the employee representatives committee.

The individual's right to training

Company contributions are also used to finance the system to ensure the individual's right to training. This is composed essentially of two different kinds of training and development possibilities:

- *A day to undertake a skill assessment.* Every employee who has been working for more than 5 years, including 1 year in the company where they currently work, has the right to spend 1 working day carrying out a skill assessment. That is an opportunity to discuss their occupational and professional skills, employability and motivation, and on that basis to develop an occupational and if necessary a training plan.

- *Training leave*: Every employee who has been working at least 2 years, including 1 year in the company where they currently work, has the right to take a leave of absence (maximum 1 year) in order to train.

The employee is free to choose the theme of the training courses to be followed but the employer has no obligation to recognise the training in the form of, for instance, pay or grading.

A vocational training reform?

This system, which was set up in the early 1970s, has since shown that it is not totally adapted to modern economic and social developments. A recent investigation commissioned by the government makes clear that:

- The system has failed to achieve its original goal to fight against inequalities and French workers' "underqualification": great disparities still remain, for instance, "fewer than 3% of female blue-collar workers in SMEs with fewer than 20 employees have access to vocational training, as opposed to about 70% of male managerial staff in large companies with work-forces of over 2000" (ANPE, 2001).
- Although the training system recognises an individual's right to training and development, training issues are still understood more as a company interest than as a means for employees to develop their "employability".

For these reasons, the government has since asked the social partners to think about a reform that would lead to:

- an individual's entitlement to training which would be "portable": that means that even in a jobless period someone could undertake training;
- the recognition and validation of competencies and experiences acquired in professional life;
- greater possibilities of "co-investment" from the company and the employee through the individual entitlement to training

Table 5.30   Proportion of wage bill spent on training and development (1999/2000)

%	France	Wallonia	Flanders	The Netherlands
<1	0	35	22	5
1–2.99	27	38	28	51
3–4.99	38	12	27	19
5–9.99	31	12	17	16
>10	4	4	5	9

So, not surprisingly, we observe substantial differences between France, where almost three-quarters of the respondents report that they spend more than 3% of their wage bill on training and development, and Belgium, where only 28% spend more than 3% of their wage bill on training and development (see Table 5.30). Moreover, it is noteworthy that at least one-third of the French companies spend more than 5% of their wage bill on training and development, far beyond the legal minimum of 1.5%. It is as if the extra attention that the legislation

Table 5.31   Number of training days received by staff category (1999/2000)

	France	Wallonia	Flanders	The Netherlands
Management	6	5	6	5
Professional	5	4	6	6
Clerical	4	3	3	3
Manual	5	3	3	4

focuses on the subject makes spending in this area more legitimate.

As a consequence of the legislation, French employees are more likely to have been in training in 1999/2000. Whereas half of the Walloon, Flemish and Dutch respondents state that fewer than 40% of their employees have been involved in training in 1999/2000, 55% of French companies declare that more than half their employees have been trained.

It is interesting that French legislation surely contributes to diminishing the segregation concerning training as between management and professional workers on the one hand and clerical and manual workers on the other hand. In France, these last categories are almost as intensively involved in training as managers and professional workers (about 5 training days a year). In Belgium and the Netherlands, however, the differences between training involving managers and professional workers (about 6 days a year) are much greater than those involving clerical and manual workers (about 3 days a year). These figures make interesting reading in the light of the debate currently going on in France concerning the French training system, which is being blamed for increasing inequalities between staff categories.

To conclude, it seems that there are important national specifics in training and development: the differences we note between France, Wallonia, Flanders and the Netherlands are again best explained by national institutional differences rather than by linguistic, regional or cultural differences.

HRM IN ACTION

FRANCE

What is the future for the French elitism system?

One of the main characteristics of French HR practices and policies is elitism: in France young *diplomés* (almost invariably male) are often regarded as a class apart from other employees – a working "elite".

However, APEC (the public association that promotes employment for French managers) forecasts that by 2010 there might be a shortage of 440,000 *cadres* (as these people are called) in both the public and private sectors. This is due to the change in the age structure of the working population: it assumes that the system will survive unchanged.

This section discusses the possible new policies and practices towards other young people, as well as towards senior managers, that might weaken the hegemony of the "young *diplômés*". Is it the end of the French young *diplômés*' special status?

The origin of an elitist class at work[1]

Since the origin of the concept[2] young *diplômés* have made up a large proportion of the *cadre* class. The so-called "*30 Glorieuses*" (from the 1950s to the 1970s) were the golden age for the cadres: they were regarded as potential chief executives and their wages increased faster than prices. A *cadre* was seen as a "success" and the image of the "dynamic young cadre: HEC, IBM, marketing, BMW" become a part of the collective mind (Bouffartigue and Gadéa, 2000).

During the economic crisis of the 1980s and 1990s, the assumption of a privileged position for the *cadre* remained important: indeed whereas the total unemployment rate increased to 15% in 1994, it only reached 6% for the *cadres*. But at that time it became clear that the *cadres* did not all enjoy the same status or, at least, guaranteed employment (Dany, 2001). According to Pochic (2001), seniors (over 50 years old) were (and still are) twice as likely to be unemployed as the other *cadres* and if unemployment for male *diplômés* from the most prestigious *Grandes Écoles* (the *cadre* training institutes) did exist, they found another job much faster than others (certainly much faster than women with or without a diploma and older cadres).

So, it is not the *cadres* as a whole who should be considered an elite but the young male *diplômé* of one of the so-called *Grandes Écoles*. Indeed, as Bauer and Cohen had already shown in 1981, the first step in the French selection system for potential senior managers does not take place inside the organisations but outside: being a *diplômé* from a *Grande École* is a pre-requisite. This is still often the case: a recent article in a French magazine[3] states that France Telecom has constituted a pool of potential top managers by selecting 60 people (40 males and 20 females) from prestigious business and engineering schools, and another magazine[4] underlines the fact that at least 25% of the CEOs of the 400 biggest French organisations are graduates from the three most prestigious *Grandes Écoles* (Polytechnique, ENA and HEC).

But projections show that in future years there would not be enough *diplômés* to replace those top managers who retire. Consequently, if they want to fill the gap, organisations will have to change HR practices that until now have been concentrated on this group. Being a (male) diplômé of a *Grande École* might not be the only path to becoming a senior manager: there might be some chance for both young motivated people without a prestigious diploma and seniors who still want to climb the ladder.

Let's look at some examples of these practices.

HR policies and strategies to deal with the forthcoming scarcity of cadres

In order to establish a balance between managers who leave and those who enter the working world, two main policies are used:

- Recruiting from a wider pool, which implies being open to people from different backgrounds, not just the usual elite.
- Retaining seniors, which implies giving them motivating opportunities at work.

---

[1] See Bouffartigue and Gadea (2000); Boltanski (1982).

[2] We can date the origin of the cadres to 1937 with the creation of a special union for cadres: the CGC that is born from the contentions of the engineers who claim their differences from both the employers and the blue collars. See e.g. Bouffartigue and Gadéa (2000).

[3] *Entreprise et carrières*, "des femmes dirigeantes chez France Telecom", 14/05/2002.

[4] *l'Expansion*, "X, ENA, HEC, les bastions de l'élite résistent", 27/11/2002.

HR strategies and policies focused on newcomers

Recruitment on a wider scale

"For the last quarter of 2002, we plan to recruit 1700 employees. Next year, Crédit Agricole [one of the biggest French banks] expects to hire 5000 co-workers. Besides the development of our commercial approach, this is essentially due to necessary renewals of jobs left by those who had gone on early retirement." Explains François Xavier Heulle, HR director of FNCA, group Crédit Agricole.[5]

"Like the other big French and European companies, France Telecom faces an evolution of the pyramid of the ages of its employees which reduces the base. So, it is a necessity to make it look younger. Indeed, in the headquarters, the average age of the employees increases by 6 months every year... That is why, as in 2001, we should recruit this year about 2500 people (of whom 80% will be young graduates)." Bernard Bresson, HR director of France Telecom.

These two extracts from interviews run by the ANPE[6] show that for big French companies, the scale of recruitment has changed.[7] They now recruit more than a thousand employees a year. This is leading some of them to question their practices. Despite the fact that French companies may sometimes look archaic as regards their recruitment practices (see earlier in this chapter), more and more organisations, especially those involved in recruiting on a large scale, are interested in techniques that allow them to recruit many people in a short time. Among these techniques are e-recruitment and other possibilities the new technologies offer. Here are two examples taken from the press.

"The group [BNP Paribas, one of the biggest French banks] receives about 100,000 applications a year (about 8000–9000 candidates each month). More than a third are made via the Internet site and this medium is becoming more and more important ... We strongly advise students to send their CV by Internet. It is easier for us to enter them in our databases, and then to examine their candidature. The process is so much faster"

Explains Françoise Barnier, in charge of recruitment in France at the BNP Paribas group in "*La semaine de l'économie*" a broadcast on the 5th French channel.[8]

---

[5] These figures were still the official ones in September 2002, see Le Figaro, 02/09/2002.

[6] We have translated these interviews taken in the web site of the French employment agency, the ANPE: http://www.anpe.fr/actualite/interview/index.jsp

[7] According to *l'express* a French magazine 10 companies planed to hire more than 800 young graduates in 2002: Vinci (2500 young graduates), France Telecom (1600), Caisse D'épargne (1400), BNP Paribas (1200), Unilog (1100), Groupe Bouygues (1030), Thales (900), La Poste (900), Altran (850), Atos (800) see "Palmares 2002 des entreprises qui recrutent", L'Express, 21/03/2002.

One year later, in a context of economical uncertainties, figures were less optimistic but nevertheless, 10 companies still intended to hire more than 400 young graduates: Vinci (2500); Caisse d'épargne (1600), La Poste (1000), Unilog (700), Totalfinaelf (525), Auchan (500), Deloitte Touche (480), Accenture (450), Caisses régionales du Crédit Agricole (450), Groupe Bouygue (430); L'Express, 31/01/2003.

[8] This interview (in French) is also available on the net at the following address: http://www.france5.fr/semaineeco

Looking at the 2001 activity report of BNP Paribas, we can easily understand why recruitment is so important an issue: between 1999 and 2000 alone, 1859 employees retired (approximately 6% of its employees). As a consequence the number of *cadres* recruited increased from 754 in 1999 to 1753 in 2001!

The point for these organisations is to be able to recruit thousands of people within a year. That's why they require new technologies to be efficient. Keeping this in mind, we are not surprised by the lukewarm attitude of some recruiters to e-recruitment. That's the case for companies that receive via the net thousands of applications a day … For instance, the campus-manager of PPR (Pinault – Printemps – La Redoute) tells us that:

"In the beginning [when they started to use e-recruitment], every candidate's details were centralised on the group website. Then we printed them on paper and faxed them to our different subsidiaries: Conforama, Printemps, … it was in fact unmanageable".[9]

Being technically ready to organise recruitment on a large scale is not enough for companies. If they really want to attract thousands of applications, they surely have to open their recruitment process to people from non-traditional backgrounds.

Opening up recruitment to people from different backgrounds

"Publicis has a very open policy of recruitment. For instance, self-taught people, philosophy graduates, writers can be hired … The diploma is not necessarily "the" reference. However "diplomés" from business schools are pretty numerous." Comments on Publicis' recruitment policy made in La semaine de l'économie.[10]

"[Solvay] is well known and during the recruitment process the candidate realises that we really try to appreciate the man (or the woman, of course) and not only his/her diplomas …" Jean-Claude Gaudriot, HR director of Solvay, interview with media RH.

Figures from an annual survey run by APEC among young graduates from university and business and engineering schools partially support these assertions. The proportion who have achieved *cadre* status since their first job has indeed increased from 44% in 2000 to 51% in 2002. Although this increase is significant, they are still in a worse situation than the *diplômés* from business or engineering school, of whom approximately 90% achieve *cadre* status. Above all it is less secure: nearly a third of young graduates from university are on short-term contracts, whereas there are only 10% of *diplômés* from the *Grandes Écoles* who have not been hired on a long-term contract. This recent survey tends to show that although, little by little, differences between graduates and *diplômés* are diminishing the gap is still important and there might be still a long way to go before the reality matches HR managers' visions.

---

[9] Cited in *Courrier Cadres*, n°1398, May 2001.

[10] Interviews and comments made during the broadcaset *"la semaine de l'économie"* are available in French at the following web site: www.france5.fr/semaineeco

Organising vertical mobility

Thus, as Régine ADAMEC – HR director of Toys' "R" Us France – has said, another way to fill the *cadres'* vacant jobs is to promote *non-cadre* employees:

> *"Motivated people and not inevitably graduates are welcome. We can integrate them into our Geoffrey School – which is an internal school of training and development – and which in 4 years, at the rate of 4 days a month of training, enables an employee to become a shop director."* Régine ADAMEC, HR director of Toys' "R" Us France interviewed by media RH.[11]

Not surprisingly, this solution is favoured by companies that face difficulties attracting enough young *diplômés* and/or having to recruit numerous *cadres*. That is the case in the construction and banking sectors in which respectively nearly half and 38% of the jobs are filled by internal promotion.

> *What is clear is that we do not try to fill a vacancy but we hire an applicant for an "evolution". We search for future colleagues able to show rapidly their worth for a job and then capable of giving satisfaction in several posts in a few years … As our hierarchical lines are short a young cadre can soon be given important technical and managerial responsibilities.* Jean-Paul MOROVAL, DRH Ascométal, interviewed by media RH.
>
> *In 1992 the bank [BNP Paribas] created a learning centre at Louveciennes where around 400 trainees reside. In this centre, four different levels of training are delivered; from a vocational training certificate to a master's degree in banking. These qualifications are recognised at state level. In 2001, 817 trainees succeeded in obtaining their qualification as " cadre". In 2000, there were 780. Some of our most senior managers have followed this course."*
> Quoted from Entreprise et carrière, June 2002.

These statements tend to show that, in spite of the increasing use of a new transactional, short-term, psychological contract, some French organisations try to attract at least some specific groups on the basis of a long-term relationship.

Figures from APEC[12] lend support to these qualitative data: although less than a third of the appointments of *cadres* are currently filled by internal promotion, there was an increase in the use of internal promotion of 27% between 2000 and 2001 whereas, in the same period, the number of external recruitments increased by only 2%.

All the different approaches we have considered so far are designed to improve the way vacancies are filled. But another way to deal with the problem is to enhance the poor rate of activity of the 50–60-year-old *cadres*. Indeed, 62% of the cadres who are between 50 and 65 have stopped work.[13]

---

[11] Interviews run by médiaRH are available in french at the following address: www.mediaRH.com

[12] APEC, *cadroscopie 2002*.

[13] According to the figures of the AGIRC the "pension found" of the cadres, 38% of the cadres who are between 50 and 65 are actually working, 20.5% are unemployed, the others are on early retirement or retirement.

HR strategies and policies focused on leavers

That is why some organisations adopt special policies towards the career management of *cadres* who are over 50. Below are two different examples taken from the press: Boiron and Thales. Although both these companies are concerned about the management of senior executives, they have chosen different ways to "satisfy" their seniors. One company (Boiron) encourages people to stay longer by allowing them to work on part-time, whereas the other (Thales) tries to convince its *cadres* that their career is not finished at 50.

"The agreement made concerning the preparation for retirement has several goals. First it eases the cadre's leaving by offering him the possibility of working on part-time during the 6 last years of his career; then, it eases the forward planning of departures and the organisation of long periods of collaboration between the cadre due for retirement and the one who will replace him. And finally, it fits with the current credo that individual satisfaction is necessary for organisational performance." Example of the Boiron laboratories, quoted in the PhD project of Anne Claude Hinault, IRESCO[14].

In La Redoute, Axa and La Caisse d'épargne, employees who are 55 or older can also work on part-time and be paid at least 75% (in La caisse d'épargne) or 80% of their formal wage.

Other organisations have decided to motivate their seniors by offering them interesting career opportunities: for instance, Thales assumes that:

"From 2004 on, we will face an increased scarcity of qualified people. So it is in our own interest to keep our seniors motivated until the legal age for retirement … The biggest measures we have taken are about career management and training."

Thales has developed these following tools for seniors:

- *"careers interviews"* for people who are 45 or older: there they define the areas in which the *cadre* has a particular value to add (mainly areas requiring a detailed knowledge of corporate culture, audit exercises and projects involving the transmission of corporate knowledge);
- individual training plans.

Some of the measures that have been taken are even bolder, and the HR director of Thales France goes on:

"senior employees often constitute an extra cost for an organisation because they are among the best paid employees despite the fact that they have nearly no command of new technologies. That's why … we are looking to increase the variable part of their remuneration." Interview with Pierre Maciejowski in Entreprise et carrières.

According to recent research carried out by APEC and "*quinquadres*", ideas about senior managers are slowly changing. Indeed, when asked, recruiters do attribute some special capabilities to seniors: they are better able than younger managers to deal with conflicts, they are also better diplomats and their commitment and loyalty to the organisation are

---

[14] Available (in french) on the net at the following address: www.iresco.fr/labos/lsci/rite/membres/hinault.htm

stronger.[15] But despite these positive opinions, in 2001 only 3.4% of the *cadres* recruited were at senior manager level.

Is it the end of the young diplômés' special status?

According to the interviews we can read in the French media, there is no doubt that HR managers are willing to change the traditional French selection model. This assumes that they at least partially deal with the initial selection process internally instead of relying on the educational system as they used to do. In terms of HR practice this puts the emphasis on detection and selection tools such as, for example:

- *annual interviews with managers*
  Rhodia, for instance, uses individual interviews with an HR manager to assess the skills of each cadre evaluated according to the organisation's reference frame founded on the three great values of the company – "conquest, requirement and coherence". These values are developed into 12 "behavioural competences", among them autonomy, courage and the ability to motivate teams, which are important criteria for judging the potential of the cadre.
- *assessment of competences*
  One of the best ways to discover if an employee has the potential to become a top manager is to assess his or her competences in a "real-life simulation". For instance, each future director of a Carrefour supermarket has to pass a 1-day test during which they must cope with emergencies such as a strike, delays in delivery, fire in the supermarket and so on …
- *360-degree feedback evaluation*
  One of the methods used by Alcatel Alsthom to detect its "high potentials" is 360-degree assessment: the goal is to gather a variety of points of view of the manager's competences: Each of the assessors expresses his or her opinion of the employee's competences and professionalism.

But the fact that organisations will take increasing control of the selection process does not mean that young *diplômés* will no longer be perceived as "high potential". It is clear that they still have great assets such as:

- their social capital: the alumni networks of the *Grandes Écoles* are powerful and well organised and they provide the young *diplômé* with an advantage that graduates from universities do not enjoy.
- their great resistance to stress and capacity for working long hours. Young *diplômés* have been prepared through the preparatory school system to handle stress and long working hours. Since organisations often place "high flyers" in risky jobs with high stakes to assess their potential, it is clear that the "*young diplômé*" profile still matches some of the elements that companies are seeking. It seems likely that this peculiarly French way of organising their management groups will continue into the foreseeable future.

However, as EDF claims, "the *Diplômé* alone is not sufficient any more" and even if some *diplômés* are still in the organisations' pools of high flyers, other bright people will also be given the chance of inclusion in top management succession plans – a chance they did not have when being a *diplômé* from a prestigious *Grande École* was a prerequisite …

---

[15]*baromètre 2002* groupe Quinquadre et Apec.

References

APEC, *cadroscopie 2002,* 2002.
APEC and Groupe Quincadres, *Baromètre 2002: le recrutement et l'emploi des cadres de 50 ans et plus*, 2002.
Bauer, M. and Cohen, E. (1981) *Qui gouverne les groupes industriels.* Paris: Seuil.
Boltanski, L. (1982) *Les cadres, la formation d'un groupe social.* Paris: Editions de Minuit .
Bouffartigue, P. and Gadea, C. (2000) *La sociologie des cadres.* Paris: Repères-La Découverte.
Dany, F. (2001) La carrière des cadres à l'épreuve des dispositifs de gestion. In: *Cadres, la grande rupture*, sous la direction de Bouffartigue, P., Paris: Editions La Découverte.
Hinault, A.-C. l'individualisation des fins de carriers en entreprise. *Problématique de recherche*, available at the following address: *www.iresco.fr/labos/lsci/rite/membres/hinault.htm.*
Pochic, S. (2001) Chômage des cadres : quelles déstabilisations? In: *Cadres, la grande rupture*, sous la direction de Bouffartigue, P. Paris: Editions La Découverte.

Articles from French magazines

Courrier Cadres, no 1398, May 2001.
Entreprise et carrières, des femmes dirigeantes chez France Telecom, 14 May 2002.
Les Echos supplément management, Ressources Humaines: des parcours à risque chez EDF, 5 October 1999.
l'Expansion, X, ENA, HEC, les bastions de l'élite résistent, 27 November 2002.
L'Express, Palmarès 2002 des entreprises qui recrutent, 21 March 2002.
L'Express, Palmarès 2003 des entreprises qui recrutent, 31 January 2003.

Websites (in French)

www.mediarh.com: you can find every week an interview with the HR director of a big French company. For this chapter, we used:
- 5 questions à Jean-Paul Moroval, DRH du groupe Ascométal, available at the following address: www.mediarh.com/new/recherche.htm
- La chimie, interview de Jean-Claude Gaudriot, DRH de Solvay, available at the following address: www.mediarh.com/baro/solvay.htm
- 5 questions à Régine ADAMEC, DRH de Toys are Us, available at the following address: www.mediarh.com/new/recherche.htm

www.france5.fr/semaineeco: you can find every week an interview with the HR director of a big French company and analysis of some French companies' recruitment policies. For this chapter, we used:
- Publicis, bienvenue aux profils décalés, broadcasted the 21 October 2001, available at the following address: www.france5.fr/semaineeco/004219/2/30646.cfm

www.apec.fr: you can download all the research studies conducted by the APEC.
www.anpe.fr: this is the web site of the French association for employment, where you can also find interviews with HR managers, for this chapter we used:
- Interview with François-Xavier Heulle, responsable RH à la FNCA (Crédit Agricole), De réelles opportunités à saisir pour les nouveaux salariés, 15 October 2002. (www.anpe.fr/actualite/interview/actu_interview31.jsp).
- Interview with Bernard Bresson, directeur des Ressources Humaines de France Télécom: Découvrir des mondes très évolutifs, 02 September 2002. (www.anpe.fr/ actualite/interview/actu_interview28.jsp).

BELGIUM

E-HRM in Belgium

Some research findings and a real-life case at Belgacom

The so-called e-economy has made a significant impact on HRM and many newly developed IT applications have found their way into HR practice. In 2001, the HRM Centre of the Vlerick Leuven Gent Management School conducted a field study designed to learn more about electronic HR practices in the 100 biggest Belgian private organisations (based on the number of employees). Seventy per cent of them were willing to co-operate. The research focused on four specific areas within the HR function: recruitment and selection, learning, communication and administration.

In what follows, you will find our main observations on each of these topics. In addition, you will learn in more detail about e-HR practices at Belgacom. Belgacom is the main telecoms operator in Belgium and they have invested heavily during recent years in developing and implementing an e-HR strategy.

E-recruitment

It is clear that recruitment practices in Belgian organisations have been widely affected by the electronic evolution. Ninety-six per cent of the organisations surveyed state that they currently use some form of e-recruitment. Almost 87% make use of specialised job sites and place vacancies on their own company web sites. The companies appear very positive about this evolution. Almost half of the organisations say that using electronic means of recruitment makes it possible to shorten the recruitment process drastically and they see this as the main advantage. Twenty-four per cent also believe that the use of e-recruitment results in a steadier flow of candidates. However, this advantage can also turn into a disadvantage as it has become far easier for applicants to submit their CVs. This may result in a lower quality of CVs, less motivated candidates and extra time needed to process the extra load. On the other hand, not every applicant is Internet-minded, so that potential applicants may not be reached by electronic communication. Consequently, Belgian organisations like to use a multimedia approach in which the Internet is seen as a new, supplementary channel working alongside traditional recruitment modes.

E-selection

E-selection seems to be the least widespread electronic HR practice in Belgian organisations. Only 13% state that they use electronic selection tools. Of the non-users, 53% do not intend to introduce e-selection in the future. The primary reason is that Belgian selection practitioners prefer personal contact with the candidates. Another group of organisations (about 10%) say that they do not think about implementing e-selection since their selection is handled by a subcontractor.

There are some perceived weaknesses of e-selection. The first is that, because of the lack of personal contact, it is very difficult to find out whether a candidate's personality fits the organisational culture. Second, developing e-selection tools is very expensive. On the other hand, e-selection can be a very powerful tool for international selection assignments, though adequate and reliable software is still not readily available.

E-learning

E-learning can be defined as the systematic use of networked multimedia computer technologies to empower learners, improve learning, connect learners to people and resources supportive of their needs and integrate learning, performance, and individual and organisational goals. Almost 46% of the companies surveyed claim some experience of e-learning, though about one-fifth of these say that they are still in the start-up or pilot phase of the project.

E-learning courses can be supplied through the Internet, Intranet or on CD-ROM. Learners can access courses at their individual personal computer or in an open learning centre. Most of the Belgian companies, however, provide their e-learning courses via individual personal computers. Most courses supplied are technical courses, but computer-based learning is also used for language courses, specialised professional courses and IT courses.

Companies state that the possibility of learning "any time anywhere" and the efficiency of electronic learning are its most important advantages. Other advantages are an increased ability to take individual learning needs into account and cost savings. On the other hand, e-learning makes employees' progress much more difficult to control, coach, evaluate and follow-up. Furthermore, not every training course can be delivered electronically and not every employee is willing, ready or able to learn through electronic media.

E-communication

Most of the surveyed organisations have an Intranet. Intranet is seen as a powerful, easy-to-access and transparent communication channel. It is regarded as a very useful tool for sharing information on a large scale. Another advantage is that, with Intranet, information can more easily be kept up to date. If the Intranet is also used by the HR department, HR professionals say that a good deal of time can be saved inasmuch as employees may find answers to their HR-related questions directly on Intranet, without the need to involve the HR department. In this sense, the purely operational and administrative load on the department may be diminished, creating space for more strategically oriented activities.

Currently, in Belgian organisations the Intranet is used primarily for disseminating information. In a few cases, the Intranet is designed to empower employees to carry out some basic administrative transactions. Only two organisations mentioned that they are planning to develop an HRM portal through which employees will be given a full-service, interactive package.

E-HR administration

Seventy of the bigger Belgian HR departments have a personnel information system: 30% use a system developed in-house, the others use commercial packages (mostly as part of an integrated enterprise-resource-planning system like SAP or Peoplesoft). Organisations that have implemented a personnel information system successfully argue that its main advantages are the possibilities it offers for integration and better alignment of information streams (including worldwide) and the fact that information is much more easily available. Such systems also form a solid base for the execution and follow-up of personnel administration. On the other hand, some state that such systems can be very complex and consequently not always very user-friendly.

Conclusion

Our research has shown that most of the larger Belgian organisations have a positive attitude towards the use of electronic HRM applications. At the same time, we found that e-HRM practice in Belgium is still in its infancy. One reason for this may be that starting up an e-application involves substantial amounts of money, time and personnel. Once implemented, however, especially in organisations employing a significant number of people, economies of scale can be realised. This is because e-solutions can reduce costs as HR processes may be handled faster and more efficiently.

One important implication of the e-trend is that it forces HR into a new role. Responsibilities are transferred from the HR professional to the line manager or even the employee. One key question, therefore, is what the impact of E-mode is for the employees involved. How far are they prepared to work, to learn, and to be recruited and selected in this new way?

Another consequence is that less time needs to be spent on administrative and routine activities. Time will consequently become available for HR professionals to spend on strategic considerations. This implies a shift in the mindset of the HR professional.

E-HRM: A new way of working and living at Belgacom

Belgacom is the leading supplier of global telecommunication solutions on the Belgian market. The company is owned by the Belgian state (50% + one share) and ADSB, an international consortium. Belgacom's service portfolio consists of local, inter-city and international voice and data services, cellular telephone services, satellite, carrier and all Internet-related services.

Like other incumbent telecoms operators, Belgacom is experiencing the rapid development of technology in the sector and the resulting impact on products and services: the shift from voice to data (Internet), the boom in mobile communications and new fixed-telephony applications.

To enable Belgacom to adapt its human resources environment to technological changes in the telecoms world, especially those related to the rapid development of e-business, the BeST (Belgacom e-Business Strategic Transformation) Programme was launched in 2001. First and foremost, with this programme Belgacom wanted to equip as many as possible of its 23,000 employees to retain a position within the company and to adapt their training and technical knowledge to the continuously changing environment. More specifically, the programme aims to transform Belgacom into an electronically enabled company with the people, processes, technologies and capabilities required to conduct e-commerce.

One of the business imperatives for HR was the development of an e-HR strategy. In 2001 Hubert De Neve was hired as e-HR Strategy Director. In De Neve's view, e-HR implies a fundamental shift or a re-thinking of the role of the HRM-function. Through a consistent application of "self-service", employees are empowered to manage their own working lives and careers, supported by technology-based systems and tools. At the same time, the HR department is required to put all its effort into alignment with the business strategy.

To implement this strategy, De Neve set up a team of four project managers and two internal consultants. The team focused heavily on the construction of an employee portal site, considered as the "one-stop shop" for all employee-related concerns and activities. The basic feature of this portal is that it is designed entirely from an employee-centric perspective. It does not refer to internal units or departments and hence is completely transparent as regards the organisation's complexity. All its content is based on questions and requests as they occur in the daily life of an employee. This portal site is available to all employees and provides information and tools concerning administrative and other internal company services, productivity management, recruitment applications, training and development, career management and the like. The table below shows the main e-applications integrated into the site.

Employee administration services	• Communication • Personal data update • Benefit services • Company services (facilities, IT, etc.)
Management productivity	• Performance management • Change actions • Salary actions • Approvals (workflow applications)
Recruitment applications	• Job posting • Online application • Job requisitions
Training and development	• Competency management • Training planning • Enrolment • Distance learning • Career counselling
Work-life topics	• Well-being and safety • Psycho-social support • Family activities and allowances
Others	• Expense reimbursement • Purchase ordering • Commission tracking • Time recording • Corporate directory (Who's who?)

The main objectives of the site are to facilitate the employee's way of working while at the same time to reduce HR call and processing activities. By making information directly available to employees and enabling e-HR transactions, the portal site should reduce the incoming call and processing load for the HR department by 66%. When the portal site does not suffice to support the employee, a shared service centre is available to deal with further questions. Call centre technology and integrated case management tools are in place to handle an extra 28% of the incoming requests. This means that only for the remaining 6% of the incoming requests do individualised problem-solving and specialised advice need to be provided (where this used to be nearly 100%). This approach clearly means that more time becomes available for dealing with more value-adding activities by HR professionals.

Of course this e-HR roadmap requires a serious investment, for which business people expect a return. This ROI issue has clearly been confronted within Belgacom, which by itself was a significant change for managing the HR function. Let us look at a specific example that illustrates the activity-based costing model that has been applied for calculating the expected return. Each year Belgacom's HR department handles about 500 employee address changes. It was calculated that such a transaction takes about 50 min to process, involving at least 3 days elapsed time, resulting in an estimated labour cost per transaction of €19. Using self-service functionality, address change now takes only 12 min of processing time and a maximum elapsed time of 1 day, resulting in an estimated labour cost of €4.5. Thus, there is a cost saving of €14.5 per transaction and a cycle time reduction of at least 2 days. Taking into account the number of address changes and assuming an average hourly labour cost of €22.5, the total cost saving is €7250 a year.

Based on generally reported results of e-HR investment studies, Belgacom expects a significant ROI. In general, the implementation of e-HR aims at a 30% cost reduction for the HR-function. Process time should reduce by 36%. Return on investment is required to be about 17%; break-even should be reached within 18–36 months, depending on the project. As well as these financial implications, however, implementing e-HR should also result in improved service levels to (internal) customers, better and faster decision-making, and increased employee satisfaction leading to a better-performing workforce and reduced attrition.

Of course, implementing such an e-HR strategy does not only affect the role of the HR professional. All 23,000 employees are involved in this project as they are forced to become more pro-active in relation to their own work conditions and career. Also, the portal site provides managers with supporting tools that make them more effective in their people management responsibilities. Transferring HR responsibilities to line managers is of course a challenge on its own. Thus, launching such an e-HR strategy involves a huge change process in which both the HR department and its internal customers (employees and managers) need to adopt a new role. Therefore a large proportion of Belgacom's budget for this project (15%) is spent on marketing, communication and change management support: providing correct and timely information about the benefits for all stakeholders is key. And clearly this has not been done without success: 1 year of e-HR investment has already produced a shift: over 80% of HR transactions in Belgacom's ERP backbone system are currently carried out through the employee self-service portal.

CONCLUSION

In this chapter we tried to present a picture of HR practices in Belgium and France. We have also tried to determine whether these practices are more influenced by countries' legal frameworks or by cultural and linguistic elements. The Franco-Belgian case is very interesting in this respect as both countries have at the same time, both at the legal and at the cultural level, similarities and differences. HR-relevant legislation is in some areas very similar between France and Belgium (e.g. in the legislative framework for union representation) and in others very different (e.g. in the legislative framework for training and development). At the cultural level, the southern part of Belgium is very similar to France, while the northern part, Flanders, is very dissimilar and sees the Netherlands, a neighbouring country where the same language is spoken, as the most important role model. We therefore presented, where possible, the figures for France, two distinctive regions in Belgium – Wallonia and Flanders – and the figures for the Netherlands where relevant. More precisely, we aimed at positioning our comparison in the "convergence versus divergence" debate.

Based on the data presented in this chapter, we come to the following main conclusions.

Important technical and economic tendencies – like the adoption of an HR strategy, use of flexible work patterns, recruitment, employee relations, or appraisal system policies – display a similar evolution in the three countries. Without any doubt, because of the significant cost that the wage bill represents, and the obligation to be economically efficient that is imposed upon every organisation, HR policies converge.

National governments and legislative institutions are keenly interested in the HR practices of organisations because of their impact on the unemployment rate, economic growth and social welfare systems. So, not surprisingly, the legislative context is highly important for explaining some differences between states regarding flexible working patterns, training and development practices and trade-union membership. Moreover, specific aspects of the French educational system explain differences in figures relating to the recruitment of junior managerial staff.

The figures presented also support our assumption that cultural features exert a certain influence on HR practices. In 1991 Filella emphasised the importance of the oral tradition in the countries of the Latin model. This is still important in the French-speaking region, where HR strategies exist but are often only verbal. The French culture of centralisation still has an impact on HR practices. France is the region where, first of all, HR directors are board members, and where (in most cases) the HR department has the final say in matters such as recruitment and training. One interesting point is that, as far as centralisation is concerned, Wallonia does not seem to follow the French model. Our assumption about the possible impact of a "distance to power" behaviour (Hofstede, 1980) can still be supported if we pay attention to the figures for access to strategic communication. In Dutch-speaking organisations there are twice as many manuals workers with access to strategic communication as there are in the French-speaking region.

Finally, in the French-speaking regions, there is a tendency towards "archaism". First of all, it seems that the more traditional selection techniques are more widely used in the French-speaking regions in comparison with the Dutch-speaking regions, where newly developed tools like assessment centres are more widely used. Furthermore, figures concerning the use of e-mails, new channels of upward communication, or flexible working patterns, indicate that French-speaking regions do not have an avant-garde culture, while this is more the case in the Dutch-speaking regions.

Overall, it is clear that there are as many arguments in favour of the proponents of convergence as there are in favour of the proponents of divergence. On this question we can only agree with Brewster and Tyson (1991), who found it impossible to draw conclusions about this issue. We agree with them as well when they point out that "researchers who focus on the content of management tend to find similarities; researchers who focus on process tend to identify cultural variations" (Brewster and Tyson, 1991).

LEARNING QUESTIONS

1. How would you describe the status and role of HR in France, the Netherlands and Belgium (Wallonia and Flanders)? What would be your general conclusions?
2. It is claimed that there are big differences in trade union influence between France and Belgium. Explain and comment.
3. What is the influence of the French "*grandes ecoles*" on French companies' recruitment mechanisms?
4. Comment on the differences between France, Wallonia, Flanders and the Netherlands in their use of selection methods.

5. What would you conclude on the use of flexible patterns of work in the four regions? Are the noted differences due to national regulatory structures or are they due to cultural differences?
6. In both Belgium and France, performance management is becoming more and more important. Is this statement true or false? Comment.
7. Are differences in training and development between the four regions best explained by national institutional differences or by cultural, linguistic differences? Comment.
8. Why is a comparison of HR practices in France, Wallonia, Flanders and the Netherlands appropriate and interesting?

REFERENCES AND SOURCES

References

Adler, N.J. (1997) *International Dimensions of Organizational Behavior*, 3rd edn. Boston: Kent.

ANPE (French "Association nationale pour l'emploi des cadres") (2001) *La formation professionnelle est arrivée près de chez vous.* Paris, ANPE report.

Barsoux, J.-L. and Lawrence, P. (1990) *Management in France*. London: Cassell.

Bauer, M. and Cohen, E. (1981) *Qui gouverne les groupes industriels? Essai sur l'exercice du pouvoir, du et dans le groupe industriel*. Paris: Le Seuil.

Boyer, R. (ed) (1989) *The Search for Labour Market Flexibility: The European Economy in Transition*. Oxford, Oxford University Press.

Brown, D. (1991) HR is the key to survival in the 90's. *Personnel*, 68: 5–6.

Brewster, C. and Tregaskis, O. (2001) Adaptive, reactive and inclusive organisational approaches to workforce flexibility in Europe. *Comportamento Organizacional e Gestão*, 7(2): 209–232.

Brewster, C. and Tyson, S. (1991) *International Comparisons in Human Resources Management*. London: Pitman Publishing.

Buelens, M., De Clercq, J., De Graeve, B. and Vanderheyden, K. (1992) Belgium. In: Brewster, C., Hegewish, A., Holden, L. and Lockhart, T. (eds.), *The European Human Resource Management Guide*. London: Academic Press, pp. 42–79.

Buyens, D. and De Vos, A. (1999) The added value of the HR department. In: Brewster, C. and Harris, H. (eds.), *International HRM. Contemporary Issues in Europe.* London: Routledge.

Cranfield Network (1996) *Working Time and Contract Flexibility in the E.U.*, Report to DGV. Cranfield University Press.

Erez, M. and Early, P.C. (1993) *Culture, Self-identity, and Work.* New York: Oxford University Press.

Filella, J. (1991) Is there a Latin model in the management of human resources? *Personnel Review*, 20(6): 14–23.

Hofstede, G. (1980) *Culture's Consequences: International Differences in Work-Related Values.* Newbury Park: Sage Publications.

Holbeche, L. (1999) *Aligning Human Resources and Business Strategy.* Oxford: Butterworth-Heinemann.

Heckscher, C. and Donnellon, A.M. (eds.) (1994) *The Post-Bureaucratic Organization.* London: Sage Publications.

Mabey, C. and Salaman, G. (1995) *Strategic Human Resource Management.* Oxford: Blackwell.

Maurice, M., Sellier, F. and Sylvestre, J. (1986) *The Social Foundations of Industrial Power.* Cambridge, MA: MIT Press.

Rosenzweig, P.M. and Nohria, N. (1994) Influences on human resource management practices in multinational corporations. *Journal of International Business Studies*, 25(2): 229–252.

Sackmann, S.A., Phillips, M.E., Kleinberg, M.J. and Boyacigiller, N.A. (1997) Single and multiple cultures in international cross-cultural management research. In: Sackmann, S.A. (ed.), *Cultural Complexity in Organizations.* Thousand Oaks, CA: Sage Publications.

Sparrow, P. and Hiltrop, J. (1994) *European Human Resource Management in Transition.* New York: Prentice-Hall.

Ulrich, D. (1997) *Human Resource Champions: the Next Agenda for Adding Value to HR Practices.* Boston: Harvard Business School Press.

Source for France Institutional Background

(1) Eurostat, Statistical Office of the European Communities (eds.) (2002) Eurostat Yearbook 2002. A statistical guide to Europe. Data 1990–2000. Brussels: European Communities.

Sources for Belgium Institutional Background

(1) Eurostat, Statistical Office of the European Communities (eds.) (1997) Eurostat Yearbook '97. A statistical eye on Europe 1986–1996. Brussels: European Communities.

(2) Eurostat, Statistical Office of the European Communities (eds.) (2002) Eurostat Yearbook 2002. A statistical guide to Europe. Data 1990–2000. Brussels: European Communities.

(3) Eurostat, Statistical Office of the European Communities (eds.) (1998) Labour force survey. Results 1997. Luxembourg: Office for Official Publications of the European Communities.

Spain and Portugal: Different Paths to the Same Destiny

Rita Campos e Cunha, Carlos Obeso and Miguel Pina e Cunha

INSTITUTIONAL BACKGROUND

SPAIN

Area	504,782 km^2
Population	39,996,671 inhabitants
Capital	Madrid
Official language	Spanish
Religions	82% Catholic
	1% Islamic
	1% Protestant

Topography and climate

The Kingdom of Spain had a population of 39,996,671 in 2001. The country's land area is 504,782 km^2, most of which comprises highlands and tableland. Spain is the second highest country in Europe after Switzerland, with an average height of 600 m. The country is generally hot and sunny in the summer, although the north tends to be wetter and milder. This has proven a boon for tourism, which is Spain's main industry. Spain has international borders with Portugal (1232 km), France and Andorra (712 km) and Gibraltar (a little over half a mile).

Table 6.1 Couples without a child

	1992		2000	
	Only one member works	Both members work	Only one member works	Both members work
Spain	69.8	30.2	57.8	42.2
Portugal	41.0	59.0	35.3	64.7
EU mean	46.7	53.2	39.2	60.7

Source: Eurostat 2002.

Spain's gross domestic product (GDP) per capita was €15,300 in 2000 – 68% of the European Union's (EU) average of €22,500. The country's GDP at market prices was €608,789 million in 2000, of which 63% represented services, 16% industry, 8% construction and 4% agriculture.

For those born in 1998, life expectancy was 75.3 years for men and 82.2 years for women, slightly higher than the European averages of 74.6 years and 80.9 years respectively.

Spain is a constitutional monarchy. The country is divided into 18 regions, each with a measure of self-government and its own parliament. The devolved powers held by these regions vary widely, with the Basque Country and Catalonia enjoying greater autonomy than the rest.

Spain is officially a secular country although most of the population is Roman Catholic, albeit only 25% of the population attend church regularly. Other major faiths are Islam (400,000 believers) and Protestantism (350,000 believers).

The labour market

The introduction of the euro highlighted the need to speed up convergence in the EU's labour markets. These markets are currently characterised by considerable national differences.[1]

The activity rate in Spain according to the *Encuesta de la Población Activa* (EPA) (Active Population Survey)[2] was 52%, a figure 5% below the average for the EU. The activity rate has remained virtually static since 1976 (when it stood at 51%). The activity rate for men is currently 64% (slightly below the EU average) whereas that for women is just 40% – well below the EU average of 54%.

However, there is a rising trend in female employment. The female active population has grown by 80% since 1976, rising from 29% to 40% currently. Nevertheless, Spain still has a long way to go before it catches up with more advanced countries in this respect. We can see the effects of these trends and some of its consequences in the still important differential with the EU in respect of couples where both members work (Table 6.1).

According to the EPA survey, unemployment in Spain stood at 13% at the end of 2001 compared with an average of 8% in the euro zone. The unemployment rate for men was 9% whereas that for women was 19%. Youth unemployment (i.e. those aged under 24) was 24% compared with 16% in the euro zone and 15% in the EU as a whole. This figure rose to 31% for the 16–19 age group. The long-term unemployed (jobless for over 3 years) made up 14% of all those out of work.

The country's high unemployment rate continues to be a problem despite the fact that in recent years Spain has created more jobs in relative terms than any other EU country. Nevertheless, much of this employment is of a temporary nature. Youth unemployment is Spain's biggest challenge after female unemployment.

Types of employment contract

In November 2001, 32% of the country's 11,913,200[3] salaried workers were temporarily employed (the country has no fewer than 10 types of temporary employment contract). This was slightly less than the figure of 35% registered in 1995 but it is still much higher than the average for the EU (14%). One should note that

---

[1] Carlos Obeso (1998) La Europa social: políticas e instrumentos para la gestión del empleo. In: *El dilema de Europa*. Ediciones el bronce.

[2] *Encuesta de Población Activa. Instituto Nacional de Estadística*. Third Quarter 2001.

---

[3] EPA. *op. cit.*

temporary contracts are at least 10% higher than the EU average in 43 of the 59 activities listed in the Spanish employment classification. Of the 13,096,970 contracts registered at Spanish job centres (INEM[4]) from January to November 2001, only 9% were for permanent jobs. The remainder were temporary ones. Permanent contracts in November 2000 represented just over 9% of the total.

The distribution of temporary contracts varies by age and gender. According to a trade union report,[5] the private sector accounts for 80% of temporary contracts. The report also reveals that female temporary employment was 35% of the total, 4% higher than among men. This proportion rose to 69% for the under-24 age group.

An OECD[6] report shows that 27% of new employees had contracts of 6 months or less in 1995 compared with just 11% in OECD countries as a whole. Temporary contracts not only make up a high percentage of all jobs in Spain but also tend to be short-term ones.

EPA statistics reveal that in 2001, 31% of temporary workers had been with their companies for longer than the duration of their employment contracts. Spanish employers commonly flout the law by issuing temporary contracts, laying off employees and then re-contracting the same workers under yet another temporary contract.

In the third quarter of 2001 only 8% of those employed worked part-time compared with the European average of 18%. Of these part-time workers, 77% were women. Most part-time contracts also tend to be temporary ones (56% in 1999).

Even though part-time contracts have increased slightly over the last few years, they are nothing like as common as in other EU countries. There are various reasons for the low proportion of part-time work in Spain. In small firms, the kinds of jobs that would normally be done by part-time workers are often covered by extending the working day of temporary and (to a lesser extent) full-time workers.

Education and training

In 1997, 53% of the EU population aged between 50 and 59 lacked a certificate of secondary education.

The figure for Spain was 82%. For those aged between 40 and 49 the figures were 42% in the EU and 72% in Spain. For the group aged between 30 and 39 the EU figure was 33% compared with 55% in Spain. The smallest difference was in the group aged 20–29 (30% in the EU figure compared with 40% in Spain). The abysmal difference between Spain and the EU in the older age groups thus narrows in the younger ones. One can therefore say that convergence is taking place, if slowly.

A recent INE[7] study involved a survey of people aged between 16 and 35. The survey covered 60,000 households in which the respondents had stopped studying between 1990 and 2000. The results revealed that out of a total of 3,288,500 students, 6% stopped studying after primary school, 29% in the first stage of secondary school, 22% in the second stage and 43% after completing their university education. There are big differences between regions. For example, 66% of young people in the Basque Country finish their university education compared with just 33% in Castille-La Mancha and 33% in the Balearic Islands.

The picture is no brighter when one considers occupational training. According to Eurostat, the ratio of baccalaureate students to those taking occupational training was 42–58% in the EU as a whole. These figures are reversed in Spain (59–41%). The ratio of baccalaureate student to those taking occupational training is the lowest in the EU.

Labour costs

Labour costs in Spain are competitive with those in other industrialised countries. According to an INE (Spanish Statistics Institute) report published in the third quarter of 2001, the average monthly salary cost per worker was €1793.54. Of this figure, the salary component was €1334.33 while social security and other costs amounted to €459.21.

The average cost per hour worked was €10.37; however, this varied according to the sector concerned. The average for industry was €11.56, in the construction business €8.26 and in service industries €10.34.

The Spanish minimum wage is extremely low. Eight EU countries set a minimum wage. Spain's minimum wage is just 35% of average salary, 24% below the

[4] *Instituto Nacional de Empleo*. Statistics Series. November 2001.
[5] *Evaluación del acuerdo interconfederal para la estabilidad el empleo*. November 2000. CCOO and UGT.
[6] OECD. *Employment Outlook*, 1995.

[7] *Boletín de cifras, Instituto Nacional de Estadistica*. No. 6, 2001.

level considered acceptable under the European Social Charter.

Welfare provisions

Unemployment coverage in 2001 was about 50%, a figure which was substantially lower than that for 1993 (77%). There are various explanations for this dramatic fall in coverage but one of the most important concerns laws which impose more severe limits on eligibility for unemployment benefit. Those wishing to claim unemployment benefit must have made social security contributions for at least 1 year in the last 6 to be eligible. The requirement was previously 6 months' worth of contributions in the last 4 years.

The maximum unemployment benefit entitlement (i.e. for someone with two or more children who has made contributions for more than 6 years) was just €1113.20 in 2001. Given the prevalence of temporary jobs, few workers meet these tougher eligibility requirements.

Trade union membership

There were 2,249,400 trade union members in Spain in 1997.[8] Of these, approximately 35% were members of *Comisiones Obreras* and a further 35% of *Unión General de Trabajadores*. This means that just 18% of all employed salaried workers belonged to a trade union. This figure rises to 30–35% if one considers just public sector workers. The most important unions are found in the mining and steel industries. However, membership is generally in decline in these sectors – a trend which also holds true in the building and chemical industries. Union membership in banking, commerce and among the unemployed and pensioners is on the increase although one should note that the figures are still extremely low.

Spanish union membership is low compared with other EU countries. According to ILO data,[9] Spanish trade union membership was 11% in 1994 compared with 31% in Italy, 58% in Norway, 77% in Sweden and 38% in Belgium. Only France, with 6%, had a lower membership rate.

---

[8] Basically *Comisiones Obreras*, *Unión General de Trabajadores* and trailing some way behind in third place *Unión Sindical Obrera*. The remaining unions are all relatively small, except for ELA-STV in the Basque Country.
[9] ILO. *World Employment*, 1997.

Nevertheless, one should note that Spain is the EU country in which trade union membership is growing fastest. There was a 92% increase in membership between 1985 (835,000 members) and 1994 (1,606,000 members). Trade union membership rose 269% between 1985 and 1997.

Trade union influence is much greater than the number of union members would suggest. There are two reasons for this. The first is that unions are party to collective bargaining negotiations with companies and enjoy the same standing as works committees. The second is that in recent years agreements between unions and employers have subsequently been enshrined in legislation. Unions have thus strongly influenced the regulation of working conditions in Spain.

Collective bargaining agreements

There were 8,285,500 workers covered by collective bargaining agreements in Spain in 2000, representing almost 70% of the salaried workforce. Of these, 11% were covered by company agreements while the rest were covered by industry-wide agreements (the latter being the level at which trade unions negotiate).

Trade unions' participation in industry-wide collective bargaining gives them much greater influence than their membership figures would suggest. Another matter is whether unions actually exercise much power. The agreement signed in 2001 included salary increases which were set below inflation. The agreement signed by employers and trade unions indicates that wage rise in 2002 will be very modest. Whether these facts indicate trade union weakness or responsible negotiation is open to discussion.

Spain's convergence with the rest of Europe

Spain's labour market still exhibits serious shortcomings compared with other EU countries but the gap is narrowing. The European Commissioner for Employment, Anna Diamantopoulou, reprimanded the Spanish government in 2001 for: its failure to tackle high unemployment rates; the large number of temporary contracts; the parlous work situation of women, young people and the long-term unemployed; poor public employment services; and the country's woeful education levels. Some of these shortcomings have been illustrated elsewhere in this chapter.

PORTUGAL

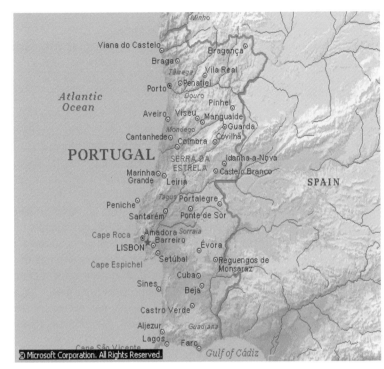

Area	92,082 km^2
Population	9,998,000 inhabitants
Density	108 inhabitants per km^2
Capital and population	Lisboa (Lisbon): (663,394)
Other important cities and population	Porto (400,000) Coimbra (150,000) Vila Nova de Gaia (247,500)
Official language	Portuguese
Business languages	Portuguese and English
Religions	97% Catholic 1% Protestant 2% Others

Portugal is a rectangle-looking country, in the western-most part of Continental Europe. It has an area of about 92,000 km^2, a resident population of about 10 million and a density of 108 inhabitants per km^2. Portugal is bordered on the north and east by Spain and on the south and west by the Atlantic Ocean. The Azores and the Madeira Islands, strategically located in the Atlantic, are an integral part of Portugal and considered as two autonomous regions. Portugal joined the EU on 1 January 1986.

Topography and climate

Portugal has a diversified landscape, with mountains and rivers marking their natural frontiers and a largely mountainous interior, although not very high. In the west and south, a large coastal plain is found, which is highly cultivated. The highest mountain range in mainland Portugal is Serra da Estrela, rising to almost 2000 m. In the Azores, Monte do Pico in Pico Island rises to almost 2400 m. Four great rivers cross Portugal, rising in Spain and emptying in the Atlantic: the Minho river, which forms part of the northern border, the Douro, with its steep sides cultivated with the vines that are used for the

Port wine and Porto (Oporto) at its mouth, the Tagus river (Tejo), the largest one, ends in Lisbon and the Guadiana river, which forms part of the south-eastern border, with Spain.

The climate changes according to altitude with high temperatures occurring only in the relatively low plains of the south. In the northern part of Portugal, average temperature is around 10°C and rainfall can be heavy. In the central part, between the Tagus and Douro rivers, temperatures average 15–16°C while in the southern part, the warmer and dryer one, average temperature is around 18°C. During the months of July and August there is virtually no rain throughout the country.

Diverse cultural identity

Portugal is an independent country since 1143, with steady continental borders defined since the fourteenth century. This fact and its linguistic unity, allow Portugal, therefore, to be considered as the oldest European country.

Portuguese culture has been deeply influenced by its history. What is now the Portuguese territory has been occupied by several different civilisations, such as the Romans, the Visigoths and the Moorish Muslims. In the fourteenth century, Portuguese Kings initiated a long-term expansion programme, through the oceans, to new continents. These two facts led to a cultural openness that resembles the idea of a melting pot and to frequent intercultural contacts all over the world. Due to these cultural and economic exchanges, several European traditions were introduced by the Portuguese, such as the "five o'clock tea" in England.

Portugal has been a member of the EU since 1986 and maintains close contacts with Portuguese speaking countries from different continents, particularly Africa and South America. Ethnic communities from these locations may be found in the mainland.

In summary, Portugal is an open people, influenced by the sea and the expansion history, being nowadays clearly oriented to its European heritage.

Table 6.2 shows the relative position of Portugal relative to the other European countries on a number of standardised items.

People

Portugal may be considered as an average European country relative to its population characteristics. The total population has been stable over the last decade, or even slightly decreasing. This current population stability may be attributed to the joint contribution of a declining birth rate, which is compensated by a

decrease in the Portuguese immigration rates, coupled with the fact that in the last two decades, Portugal has been receiving immigrants from African Portuguese speaking countries (Table 6.3).

People are nevertheless living longer, in particular women with a 79.1 year life expectancy, which is higher than men (72.0) (Table 6.2).

Economy

The Portuguese economy has been growing strongly (Table 6.3), in the last years, with falling interest rates and a low unemployment rate (4%). Despite widespread scepticism, the determination of officials to see Portugal become a full member in Economic and monetary union (EMU) from the start was unwaivering. The country qualified for the EMU in 1998 and joined with 10 other European countries in lauching the euro on 1 January 1999, meeting the Maastricht criteria relative to inflation, budget deficit, level of government debt, interest rates and the exchange rate (Table 6.4).

To face the budget deficit that has surpassed the Maastricht criterium, the new government raised taxes and initiated a strong campaign for cost cutting in Public Administration, as well as some structural reforms, such as the reform of the Labour legislation, which was approved by the Parliament in early January 2003. The main purpose of the new legislation is the introduction of some flexibility into a very rigid system, such as labour mobility, time flexibility and functional flexibility.

Table 6.2 Principal characteristics in relation to EU-15 = 100

Density	108
Infant mortality	5.94/1000
Life expectancy at birth (boys)	72.0
Life expectancy at birth (girls)	79.1
Employment rate (men)	76.2
Employment rate (women)	60.4
Unemployment rate	4.1
Cost-of-living comparisons	87

All data from Eurostat 2002.

Table 6.3 Population by age

Age (years)	Portugal (%)			EU-15 (%) 2000
	1987	1997	2000	
<15	23	17	17	17
15–24	17	16	15	12
25–49	32	35	36	37
50–64	16	17	17	17
65–79	10	12	13	13
>80	2	3	2	4

All data from Eurostat 2002.

Table 6.4 Gross domestic product (at market prices)

	1993	1994	1995	1996	1997	1998	1999	2000
1000 million ECU (nominal growth)	73.6	76.3	82.6	88.6	94.2	100.7	108.2	115.3
Yearly growth as % of previous year	−2	1	4	4	4	5	3	3
EU-15	−1	3	2	2	3	3	3	3

All data from Eurostat 2002.

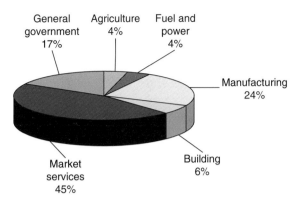

Figure 6.1   Economic structure (gross value added at current basic prices and current exchange rates, as % of sectors; 1999 Portugal)

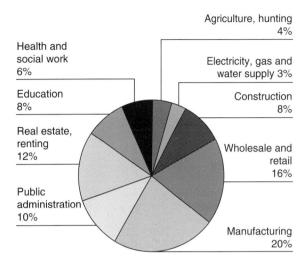

Figure 6.2   Economic structure in more detail.

Table 6.5   Cost-of-living comparisons in the EU in 2000 (Brussels = 100[1])

Food and non-alcoholic beverages	Alcoholic beverages and tobacco	Clothing	Housing	Furnishing, house equipment	Health	Transport
89	90	79	96	93	106	103

Communication	Recreation and culture	Education	Hotels, cafes and restaurants	Miscellaneous	*Total*	*Total excluding rents*
63	82	42	63	85	*87*	*84*

All data from Eurostat 2002.

Economic structure

By sectors, agriculture has been losing its weight in the GDP. Portugal is one of the leading producers of wine, particularly port wine, cork and olive oil. Manufacturing, on the other hand, is of increasing importance in the last decade and basically includes processed foods and canned fish, textiles and footwear, cork-based goods, paper, glass and pottery and wood. Foreign exchange receipts from tourism help to compensate for Portugal's trade deficit, being a very important sector for the country (Figures 6.1 and 6.2).

Privatisation has been a key element of economic policy for the last decade, reducing the public debt, cutting back the participation of the government in the economy, promoting the development of the local equity market and, in general, developing the efficiency of Portuguese economy.

The Portuguese cost of living is well below the EU's average (Table 6.5).

Legal, institutional and political environment

Portugal is governed under a constitution set up in 1976 after the restoration of democracy, and revised in 1982. Portugal is a republic with a President, popularly elected to a 5-year term, who appoints the prime minister, the country's chief administrative official. Legislative power is vested in a unicameral parliament, the Assembly of the Republic. Members of the Assembly are elected under a system of proportional representation and serve 4-year terms. The leading political parties in Portugal are the Social Democratic Party, the Socialist Party, the Communist Party and the Popular Party.

Labour market

Portugal has numerous labour market advantages, in part due to a greater national cohesiveness than many other European countries (Figure 6.3). There is a regular tripartite dialogue among the government, employers and the unions, a low level of unionisation and few work stoppages. Absenteeism is low and there is considerable labour mobility, which can be exemplified by

the move from agriculture employment to the services sector. Employment in agriculture fell from about 30% 20 years ago to 5% in mid-1990s. Workers have shifted mainly to the services sector, which now accounts for over 55% of employment (Tables 6.6 and 6.7).

Each year the government and the public sector unions decide on the wage guidelines for the coming year, setting the tone for the private sector, where agreements are made on an industry-by-industry level.

Portugal compares favourably with other countries in terms of unit labour costs and productivity, which went hand-in-hand with stronger economic performance.

The unemployment rate is one of the lowest in Europe (Table 6.8). During the course of 2000, Portugal scored one of the largest declines in the unemployment rate and recorded the fourth lowest jobless rate in the EU.

Hourly labour costs are the lowest in Europe, as well as mean monthly earnings, which is favourable to business (Tables 6.9 and 6.10).

The breakdown of labour costs in Portugal show a percentage of close to 25% in indirect costs, very similar to the Austrian situation (Table 6.11).

In addition to the previous factors, Portugal has an average number of working hours per week

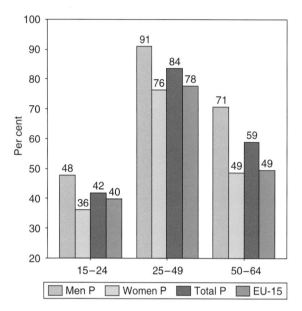

Figure 6.3   Employment rate of men and women (and total), compared to EU-15

Table 6.6   Persons in employment (million)

	1990	1991	1992	1993	1994	1995	1996	1997	1998	1999	2000
Portugal	4.6	4.8	4.5	4.5	4.4	4.4	4.4	4.5	4.7	4.8	4.9

All data from Eurostat 2002

Table 6.7   Persons in employment in different sectors (million)

	1990	1991	1992	1993	1994	1995	1996	1997	1998	1999	2000
Agriculture	0.8	0.8	0.5	0.5	0.5	0.5	0.5	0.6	0.6	0.5	0.5
Industry	1.6	1.6	1.5	1.5	1.4	1.4	1.4	1.4	1.5	1.5	1.5
Services	2.2	2.3	2.5	2.5	2.5	2.5	2.5	2.5	2.6	2.8	2.8

Table 6.8   Unemployment rate (%)

1990	1991	1992	1993	1994	1995	1996	1997	1998	1999	2000
5	4	4	6	7	7	7	7	5	5	4

	2000	
	Portugal	EU-15
Women unemployed	5	10
Men unemployed	3	7
Long-term unemployment (as % of all employees)	43	45

All data from Eurostat 2002

Table 6.9 Average hourly labour costs (manual and non-manual workers) in total industry

	1990	1991	1992	1993	1994	1995	1996	1997	1998
ECU	3.57	4.20	5.55	5.41	5.45	5.75	6.06	6.18	6.28

All data from Eurostat 2002.

Table 6.11 Structure of labour costs in total industry (%, 1999)

Direct cost	Indirect cost	Social security as part of indirect cost
75	25	20

All data from Eurostat 2002.

Table 6.10 Mean monthly earnings, in industry and services, in EU: 1998

Total	645
Men	723

All data from Eurostat 2002.

Table 6.12 Number of hours usually worked per week: full-time employees (1997)

EU-15	41.7
Portugal	42.0

All data from Eurostat 2002.

Table 6.13 Level of education for the population aged 25–59 (%, 2000)

<Upper secondary education	Total (25–64)	25–29	30–34	35–40	40–44	45–49	50–54	55–59	60–64
EU-15 (women and men)	64	76	73	70	66	62	55	51	45
Portugal (women and men)	22	38	26	20	21	17	14	12	11
EU-15 (women)	61	77	73	70	64	58	50	45	37
Portugal (women)	23	41	30	23	22	16	14	12	11

All data from Eurostat 2002.

(Table 6.12), higher than the EU norm, which is also contributing to the improvement of the country's economic performance.

Education system

Education in Portugal is compulsory until the age of 16. It is free in public schools that nowadays compete with private schools at all levels of education, from kindergarten to the university. Kindergarten was a priority for the previous government as well as creating the infrastructure for general access to this level. A national debate on the role and capacity of the school system to prepare people for the challenges of the information society is taking place. The previous prime minister, Mr. António Guterres, expressed the urgency of reforms when he referred to his "passion for education", which is shared by the current government. The figures reveal that education must in fact be a priority: the percentage of the population with upper secondary education is still very low when compared with the average EU countries, despite the improvement that is benefiting younger generations. Massive professional training programmes have taken place since the 1980s, in an effort to improve the intellectual capital of Portuguese organisations (Table 6.13).

HRM IN SPAIN AND PORTUGAL: DIFFERENT PATHS TO THE SAME DESTINY

Portugal and Spain have 1232 km of common borders but for years have been living, as it were, in social and political terms, with "their backs turned towards each other"; the consequence of centuries of warfare and colonial competition culminated in the Spanish invasion of Portugal in 1518.

Much of the modern history of the two countries shows strong similarities but these are only on the surface. Both countries suffered long years of dictatorship, from 1932 to 1968 in Portugal under the rule of Salazar, and from 1939 to 1974 in Spain under Franco. But even here there were differences. Franco came to power after a bloody civil war, Salazar as the aftermath of the 1926 military *coup d'état* against the parliamentary republic. The democratic opposition against Salazar was weaker in comparison with the opposition to Franco's revolt.

Both regimes were fascist by nature but their capacity to intervene in economic affairs was different. Salazar was ruling a backward agricultural country. Franco also inherited an economically depressed agricultural country but with two important industrial and well developed regions, the Basque country and Catalonia, which were politically difficult to control.

The consequence for Portugal was a quasi-pure corporatist regime where official unions played an important control role for the workers and where government bureaucracy was omnipresent. In Spain the situation, although similar in many ways, was different in some important respects. For 15 years following the civil war the fascist bureaucracy was impotent to rule the country. It was replaced by a technocratic-religious class, the Opus Dei. So in Spain, in contrast to Portugal, the corporatist state was of minor importance. This had the effect of strengthening the pressure towards modernisation, which had started in the early 1960s. Tourism played an important but not unique role in this development.

The francoist regime collapsed after Franco's death in 1975, evidence of its political weaknesses. In 1977, forced by a difficult economic situation and with many political and structural problems to resolve, the now legal political parties signed what was known as the "Moncloa Pacts", an economic and political agreement signed by all parties. The Moncloa Pacts were a consensual instrument that permitted the introduction of laws and reforms necessary for the future integration into the European Community: among others things, the reform of the labour law approved in 1978 in the Spanish Parliament under the name "*Estatuto de los Trabajadores*". The "Estatuto" has been reformed over the years but still now is the backbone of labour regulation.

The Moncloa Pacts were a political instrument that permitted a peaceful evolution to democracy. In this sense it was very positive. But since it was a consensual pact some major industrial reforms remained untouched until 1985 when entry to the European Community forced the socialist party to launch major industrial reforms that affected the nationalised coal and steel

industries. In this sense, the privatisation process was quicker and more profound in Portugal than in Spain.

Trade unions never played the same role in Spain as in Portugal. In Spain, illegal unions were already present by the end of the 1950s and although their leaders suffered imprisonment their influence impeded any authoritative role for the official unions, at least in the more industrialised part of the country. In Portugal opposition to the official unions was weaker, so state-approved corporate unionism was more important. The 1950s were marked by the beginning of the war in Africa and by a growing social discontent, which paved the way for a growing opposition movement. Companies did not feel the need for personnel specialists and universities offered no courses in this area. Personnel/human resource management (HRM) therefore remained a low-status administrative function, with a few exceptions among multinationals, which had personnel departments with non-bureaucratic tasks, such as development.

In Spain, the situation was somewhat different. In 1964, the AEDIPE, the Association for Personnel Managers, was created, with an interest in bringing together and disseminating what was known about personnel management, especially in the USA, France and the UK. At the same time some management and professional schools started courses in personnel management. It is difficult to ascertain how far this "scientific interest" influenced actual practices in companies. In any case it was an early starting point that facilitated the appearance of a group of few but good professionals who provided a different perspective from the current administrative and punitive view of personnel managers.

In 1974, the Portuguese regime was overthrown by a *coup d'état* that established a democratic regime. A pro-communist government was formed and the main sectors of the economy were nationalised. Owners and top managers were expelled from their firms, unions adopted a confrontational approach to labour relations and workers' councils were created in companies. Collective bargaining took on a central role, and lack of managerial expertise combined with politically based staffing practices and an absence of merit-based appraisal and pay to make organisations inefficient and unprofitable. Personnel management departments became more centralised and more important, increased their staff numbers and embarked on complex planning activities with little relevance to corporate strategy (and with no real impact on organisational performance), and on training to fill the gap left by the demise of technical/professional training schools and labour relations. During this period the human resource (HR) function was typically managed by law graduates.

In the late 1980s, coinciding with Portugal's entry into the European Community, a privatisation programme was started which has been ranked the third largest in the Western world, after the UK and New Zealand (Financial Times, 1995). With the privatisation programme, most companies underwent major restructuring, and the importance of the human factor was finally recognised, namely the need for talent, for open communication systems, for functional, numerical and financial flexibility and for customer-focused cultures. Due to productivity gains, many organisations started to pay above the collective bargaining rate, particularly for technical/professional staff, fringe benefits and incentives were introduced and unions lost much of their influence.

The privatisation programme introduced a higher level of competition, which created the incentives for managers to become more efficient and effective, establishing functional strategies that were consistent with the corporate strategy. The HR function was no exception, although there is still a long way to go, as we shall see in the following sections.

To sum up the national political and economic background, despite some apparent political similarities, the construction of modern Spain and Portugal followed different paths. The corporate state was a dominant force in Portugal until the 1974 revolution and a more modified influence in the case of Spain. For this and other reasons Spain developed, economically and politically, faster than Portugal until recent times, when integration into the European Community (1986) fuelled a convergence process not only between the two countries but among these countries and the rest of the Community.

Similarities and dissimilarities in HRM policies must be examined in the light of these different circumstances.

THE HRM FUNCTION: MARGINAL OR CORE?

One role of HRM in companies is to represent the function at Board of Directors level, not only for its symbolic meaning, but also for the potential power to

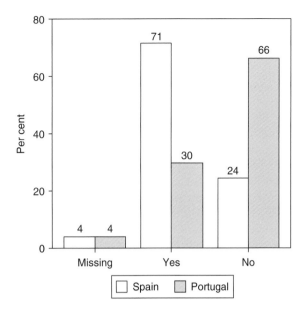

Figure 6.4   Chart 1 – Head of HR on board

allocate scarce resources. Being represented at board level probably gives the HR function a stronger political basis for developing and implementing coherent practices, as well as providing evidence of the role this function fulfils at the strategic level.

In this respect differences are apparent between Portugal and Spain, as indicated by Figure 6.4 (for the year 1999/2000). The proportion of Spanish organisations with HR representation on the Board of Directors is significantly higher than for Portuguese.

This situation is not very different from that which was obtained in the early 1990s, when this discrepancy already existed. Considering that, on average, 54% of the European organisations have board representation of this function, it is quite clear that Spanish organisations attribute a significantly higher importance to HR issues, while Portuguese organisations are still well below the European average. We must nevertheless be cautious about the Spanish figures. Commenting on the Cranet Report of 1995, Professor Josep Baruel of ESADE drew on data collected by the International Organisation Observatory to make the following comments (Baruel, 1996):

"... only 21% of the sample firms had a first-level director (who usually was a member of the board

of directors) who was solely responsible for HRM matters. In addition, 23% of companies had a first-line manager (usually on the board) with a broad set of responsibilities of which HRM was one."

From the above comments we can conclude that there are two possible explanations for the high level of board membership for Spanish organisations found in the Cranet survey: on the one hand that the Cranet sample comprises larger organisations, where HR managers have traditionally occupied a place on the board (mainly to control industrial relations), and on the other that these figures include board members with other responsibilities besides HRM. It is noticeable, though, that the Latin countries in general tend to have higher levels of at least formal board membership for the HR function.

With these comments in mind we can argue that the figures indicate a lack of managerial sophistication on the part of Portuguese and Spanish organisations in that they continue to regard the "hard" technical functions as the critical strategic areas rather than the "softer" ones such as HRM.

When not represented on the Board of Directors, responsibility for HR issues lies mainly with the Chief Executive Officer in both countries.

The most senior HR managers have a tenure of about 5 or 6 years in both Spain and Portugal and almost 90% have a university degree. Spanish managers have mainly an academic background in law and behavioural science, while Portuguese managers come mainly from business studies and behavioural science. The predominance of an academic background in law in the case of Spain reflects the important role played by the latter in managing industrial and labour relations, a consequence of many years of conflict and disputes (Gooderham et al., 1999) with trade unions and a juridical approach to industrial relations in the country. This is now changing, with new entrants tending to come mainly from a psychology background. On the other hand, the predominance of business studies and behavioural sciences in Portugal may lead us to expect that HRM will be enhancing its image and gaining strategic importance. It is noticeable that the HR function in Spain exercises little appeal to professionals with a business background. This reinforces the idea that, in spite of board representation, the HR function still plays a secondary role in Spanish organisations (Obeso, 2002).

HRM STRATEGY: ITS STATUS AND ROLE

Although in both Spain and Portugal almost two-thirds of organisations have a written corporate strategy, the involvement of the HR function in strategy development is somewhat different as between the two countries. In the last decade there has been a development in both countries towards a more active involvement, with the HR function making an input from the outset of strategy formulation. However, as Figure 6.5 demonstrates, in Spanish organisations the HR function is involved from the outset and then at the implementation stage (mainly in industrial relations, recruitment and selection and dismissal issues), while in Portuguese organisations there is less involvement from the outset, but more at a consultative level.

In Portugal, during the last decade, the HR function participated significantly more in the strategy formulation process, and the percentage of organisations where HR is involved only at the implementation level has been greatly reduced. Once again, it appears that HRM is becoming more strategically central, which may be linked to the rigidity of the labour laws in this country. The extreme difficulty of terminating work contracts leads to a careful consideration of all the personnel

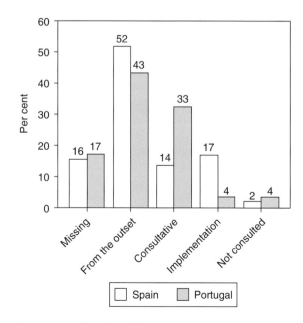

Figure 6.5 Chart 2 – HR involvement in corporate strategy

issues, from staffing to training and development or compensation.

These are countries where formalisation is often preferred. Hence in both countries the percentage of organisations with no reported HR strategy is quite small: 13% in Spain and 16% in Portugal.

In both countries, less than 50% of the HR departments have their performance evaluated. When evaluated, the main criteria used are performance against objectives and – to a lesser degree and only in Spain – cost-effectiveness. Once again, we may infer that in both countries the HR function is still not considered a critical success factor for the organisation.

Analysis of Figure 6.6 allows us to argue that there is a certain partnership between line management and HR departments in respect of major HR issues, such as pay, recruitment, training, industrial relations and workforce expansion/reduction, which is present in both countries. Portuguese line managers seem to have more autonomy in these issues than their Spanish counterparts, but we may speak of a shared responsibility. A qualitative analysis (Larsen et al., 2002) conducted in Summer 2002 suggests that Spanish companies have a dualistic perception of the responsibility of line managers. Although most of the companies surveyed agree that line management responsibility will grow in the future, there are companies which do not seem to advocate this development and do not seem to trust line managers to take on responsibility on HR areas. But all in all the trends for both countries suggest a growing integration of HRM and other functional areas in the organisation, increasing the probability of a more strategic and effective approach for the management of staff. Alternatively, the influence of the line in these areas may be seen as a continuing refusal to trust HR specialists to take responsibility in the interests of the business. We nevertheless believe that the first explanation is more likely to be the main reason for this partnership, and that HR managers are increasingly dedicating themselves to define the HR policies, to work on culture change, to build competence matrices and to specify priority areas of recruitment and training, at the same time reducing staff numbers in their own departments and making more use of subcontracting for the administrative aspects of personnel management. On the other hand, there were no significant changes over the last decade, which may be seen as a pattern in both countries. In this context it is noticeable

that in a small but growing number of Spanish firms the role of HR directors is changing, in function and name, towards a consultative role directed to general directors and line managers, with a focus on competence and development management (see Case History p. 187).

Recruitment and selection

Several methods may be used to improve recruitment or retention of employees, including recruiting abroad, retraining, increased pay, relocation and improving the organisational image. Figure 6.7 shows a similar pattern for Spain and Portugal, with the exception of retraining, which has been much more frequently used by Spanish organisations. Relocation and recruiting abroad are almost unused, probably for cultural reasons linked with the low mobility of people and the lower wage rates that may be offered in these two countries. In addition, at least in the Portuguese case, language may be a relevant issue, since there are few countries where Portuguese is spoken. In the case of Spain geographical mobility is extremely difficult (*Ministerio de Trabajo y Asuntos Sociales*, 2001) owing mainly to a sharp increase in housing costs (roughly 50% of workers' salaries goes to pay off the mortgage).

As discussed in the previous section, by and large, responsibility for recruitment and selection lies with line managers, in co-operation with the HR department. That fact, associated with the rigidity of labour laws (at least in Portugal) may account for the clearly more important role of retraining. It is a way to improve functional flexibility, since numerical flexibility is difficult to achieve. Increased pay is the second most used method, which is related to staff's increased skill qualifications and to the improvements in the economic situation these countries have experienced in the last decade.

Most Spanish and Portuguese organisations reported having either increased or maintained the number of employees, with only a small minority (6 and 9%, respectively) having experienced cuts during the previous 3 years. This represents a major change from 10 years ago, when 32 and 41%, respectively, of the Spanish and Portuguese organisations reported reductions in headcount. This positive outcome must be related to the economic situation and expectations of economic agents, particularly with the move to the euro system, but also with real improvements in organisational

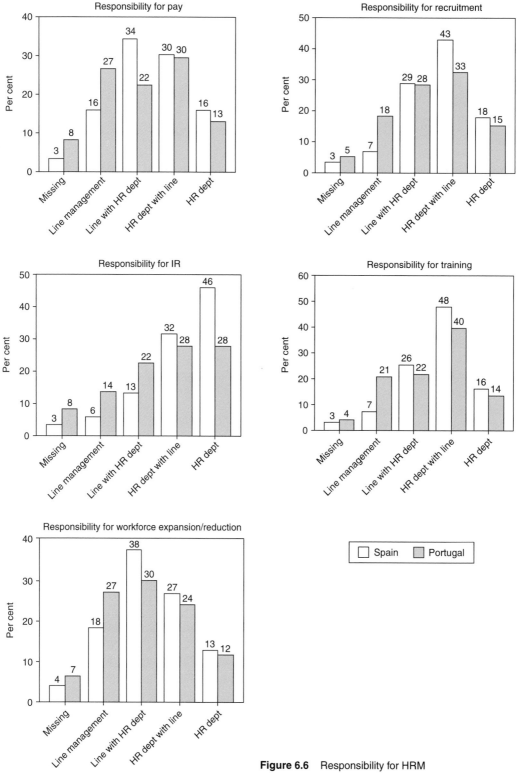

Figure 6.6 Responsibility for HRM

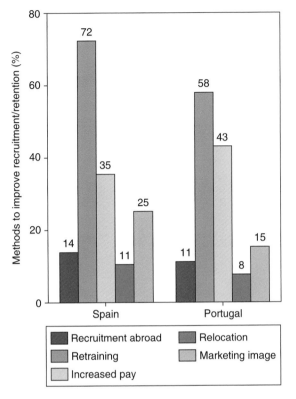

Figure 6.7   Methods of improving recruitment/retention of staff

most commonly used method, while for junior management, newspaper advertising is important. A comparison between the two countries reveals that Spanish organisations use internal sources of recruitment more than the Portuguese. This is the result of a bigger investment in human capital by Spanish organisations, over a longer period of time, whereby career development represents a strategic option and an instrument of flexibility. Figure 6.8 summarises these recruitment methods. Poor advancement opportunities may also be one of the reasons why Portuguese staff decide to leave the organisation.

Portuguese organisations covered by the survey report difficulties in recruiting and retaining professional staff in IT (31%), other professionals (50%) and manual workers (40%), while their Spanish counterparts report difficulties in retaining or recruiting professional staff in IT (29%) and other professions (33%). The other functional categories do not present a current threat for these organisations. A decade ago, Portugal was already experiencing problems with recruiting technical staff and Spain with managerial personnel. Portuguese organisations are increasingly using immigrant labour, both from former African colonies and, more recently, from east European countries. The latter, though performing lower status work, are nevertheless highly qualified and may in time come to be employed in higher-grade jobs.

Although these reported difficulties have eased somewhat because of the recession and the IT crisis in both countries, a Spanish report by Watson Wyatt (Jimenez et al., 2002) predicts recruitment problems in the coming years in almost all categories of workers, due to the end of new entrants arising from the baby boom of the 1970s. The fertility ratio in the year 2001 was 1.2 children for each woman, one of the lowest in the OECD countries.

As regards selection methods, Spanish and Portuguese respondents to the survey report a very similar pattern (Figure 6.9). In fact, we may distinguish two differences: one concerns the use of interview panels, which are used by twice as many Portuguese organisations as Spanish ones and the other concerns psychometric tests, which are more widely used by Spanish organisations.

Individual interviews are clearly the dominant selection method, used in both countries by more than nine out of every ten organisations. It is closely followed by application forms. References are also

efficiency and effectiveness, and with the enhancement of staff capabilities. The economic crisis of the early 2000s, however, is already reversing this trend. Organisations are restructuring and downsizing, unemployment is expected to rise (which may be a problem particularly in Spain, where this rate is much higher than the Portuguese one) and social friction is starting to show itself. In Portugal, for instance, industrial conflict is likely to grow as the government struggles to keep the public deficit within the parameters approved by the Stability Pact.

When managerial positions have to be filled, both internal and external recruitment sources are used by organisations in the two countries. There is a shared pattern in the preference for internal recruitment, like promotions, and less use of word of mouth, a discredited method in Spain – though not in Portugal, a small country where reliance on personal acquaintance (the *cunha*) is common. For senior and middle management positions, recruitment consultants are the second

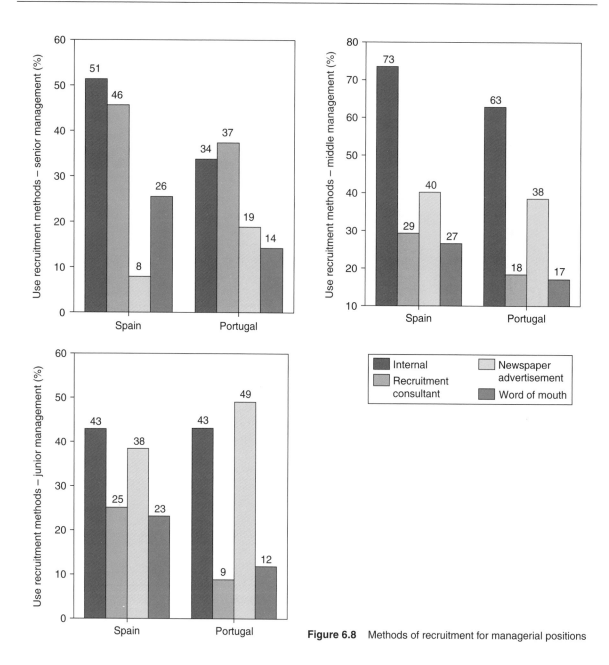

Figure 6.8   Methods of recruitment for managerial positions

equally widely used in the two countries. In Portugal, given the size of the country, people in general have extended networks (particularly managers) and it is very common to have managers call relatives or friends, in companies or even in universities, to get references on certain job applicants. Assessment centres are still a marginally used method, mainly in private multinational organisations. Relative to the data obtained 10 years ago, few differences are to be found, with the exception of increased assessment centre use in Portugal.

Training and development

Curious differences exist between Portugal and Spain regarding the status of training and development.

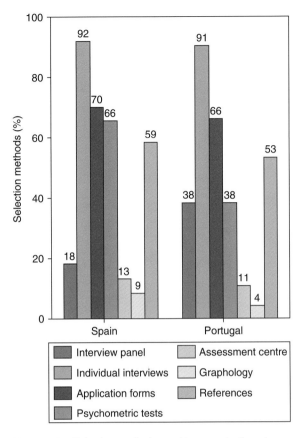

Figure 6.9   Selection methods used by organisations for some, most or every appointment

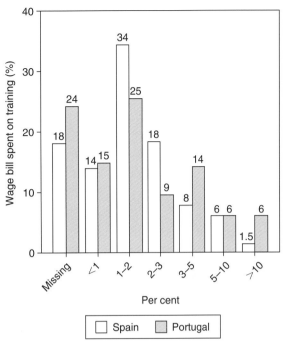

Figure 6.10   Proportion of wage bill spent on training and development

Starting with the percentage of the wage bill spent on training and development, the average for Spanish organisations is significantly lower than that for the Portuguese organisations, which have increased their investment in this area compared to 10 years ago (Figure 6.10).

This result points to a recognition of the need to improve employee skills and the consequent organisational investment. However, an analysis of the number of days' training received by staff category (see Figure 6.11), demonstrates that Spanish employees have attended a larger number of days of training and development.

The average proportion of Spanish employees receiving training was 51 vs. 37% for Portuguese employees, and they also had more days of training, which is particularly significant in the case of professional/ technical staff and clerical employees (ten vs. seven

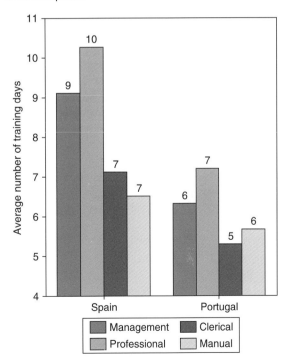

Figure 6.11   Average number of training days by staff category

and seven vs. five, respectively). Moreover, the average number of training days has increased for all staff categories in Spain, while this number has decreased in Portuguese organisations. This result suggests a more efficient use of investment in development activities by the Spanish organisations, but it could also mean that trainers are in greater demand in Portugal and therefore receive a premium.

To explore this issue further we looked at the percentage of organisations that report performing a systematic analysis of training needs and found that 81% of Spanish organisations do so, as against 71% of the Portuguese counterparts. On the other hand, for this analysis, Spanish organisations use business plans much more than the Portuguese ones (54 vs. 33%), as well as training audits (26 vs. 17%), management requests (73 vs. 56%) and employee requests (50 vs. 31%). Only the use of performance appraisal is similar for both countries – 44%.

We also analysed the degree to which organisations evaluate the effectiveness of training. In fact, more Spanish organisations evaluate training (75 vs. 64%). Criteria used also show some differences, since 89% of Spanish organisations report carrying out formal evaluations immediately after training either always or often (in most cases in the form of an evaluation survey by the trainee) vs. 37% of the Portuguese counterparts, while 80 vs. 53% (respectively) evaluate some months later. However, when asked whether training results are monitored a larger proportion of Portuguese organisations report doing so than Spanish (86 vs. 75% monitor behaviour change, 80 vs. 59% monitor results and 94 vs. 93% monitor training results, respectively). More Spanish organisations, however, evaluate training in terms of learning (53 vs. 42%).

Portuguese organisations seem to be more interested in evaluating the effect of training than the Spanish ones, which is understandable considering the investment involved. Spanish organisations, however, remain focused on the quality of learning (particularly short term), which requires a smaller evaluation effort.

In summary, although Portuguese organisations are making larger investments in the qualification of their HRs and in measuring the impact of these investments on organisational performance, which is a very positive sign, this investment seems less efficient than the Spanish one, perhaps because of a less systematic analysis of training needs as well as a less developed evaluation of the learning derived from training programmes.

Performance measurements and rewards

Variable pay seems to be on the rise in both countries, although in Spain the tendency is stronger than in Portugal. In the Spanish case since 1993 a growing number of companies have been applying different systems of variable pay. At present almost 70% of companies use it (50% in 1993), although the percentage of variable pay related to total pay remains the same as in 1993 (between 14 and 21% for functional managers). Figure 6.12 provides a snapshot of these trends.

The increase in the use of variable pay reflects a general tendency to relate pay to performance. However, if we observe the tendency in the sub-category of "merit pay" we notice important differences between the two countries. In Spain merit pay is concentrated in the management and professional strata and is on the decrease with the clerical and manual workers. In Portugal, when compared with 1992, merit pay is on the decrease for all categories of employees. Figure 6.13 reflects this evolution.

Merit pay is a sub-category of variable pay. It is a tool which is often clearly related to retention policies. The contradictory figures in the two countries, and the different trajectories of evolution, are the consequence of the disparate economic developments in the countries concerned. In Spain more than in Portugal this evolution has created an acute problem for recruitment and retention of managers and professionals which is reflected in the different use of merit pay. In Portugal, on the contrary, organisations needed to introduce financial flexibility, while at the same time they needed to recruit individuals capable of taking risks. The growing supply of first-degree courses in business, and of MBA programmes, has played a very significant role in providing organisations with a more dynamic and self-confident workforce, who feel motivated by bonuses and stock options.

However, questions have been raised about variable pay and particularly about its link to performance and about its effect on retention. The growth in variable pay has stopped or is reducing in other countries besides these two as firms find little correlation between the

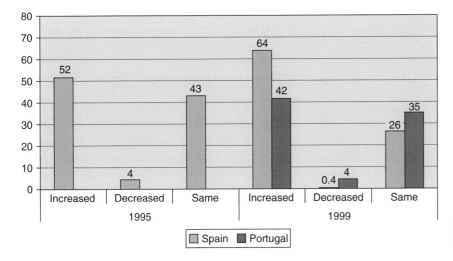

Figure 6.12 Change in variable pay over 3-year period (% organisations)

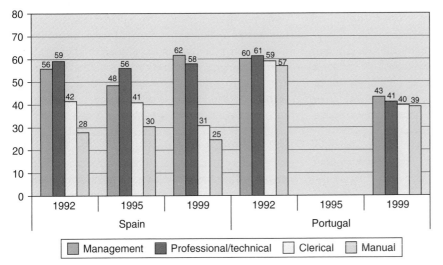

Figure 6.13 Merit/ performance related pay by staff category

increases in their wage costs and organisational performance. In addition, the economic recession that started in the year 2000 is casting doubt on the validity of variable pay as a retention method. In a recent survey (Walter, 2001) professionals in different sectors were asked about their preferences among 16 different retention policies used by Spanish companies. Fixed salary ranked third and variable salary fourteenth. Although more evidence is needed, these results may reflect the abuse, rather than the use, of variable pay, especially in periods of recession.

The relative importance of variable pay for clerical and manual workers in both countries is very much related to the difficulties of using performance appraisals fairly. In both countries performance appraisals are on the decrease, but this tendency affects mainly these two categories, reflecting line managers' lack of skill in conducting appraisals. In fact, this is a problem that HR managers commonly complain about without a positive response from managers. Training line managers on these issues is still a key objective for any company genuinely seeking to modernise its HR policies. In many organisations performance appraisal systems are still considered to be a chore and not a management tool, and that belief is rooted in the lack of valid appraisal criteria, the lack of properly trained appraisers and the quality of the feedback provided (see HRM in Action, Spain, p. 184).

Employee communications and the role of trade unions and work councils

In 1985 affiliation in Spanish trade unions was 19% of the total salaried work force, a low figure when compared with the European Community average. In Portugal affiliation was moderate, about 26%. Since then membership in Spanish trade unions has increased by 62%, the highest increase in the EU, while in Portugal there has been a decrease, by some 50%.

Although there are many reasons for this contradictory behaviour, the most important is the tendency in Spain, more so than in Portugal, to professionalise (to depoliticise up to a certain point) the trade unions. This tendency has helped the Spanish unions to formulate common policies, and to become more effective in the eyes of workers. It has also helped them to develop a more co-operative relationship with employers, a relationship that, amazingly, the government tried to reverse with the implementation of the *Real Decreto Ley* 5/2002 in an effort to regain control of HR regulation. The consequence was a general strike in June 2002 followed swiftly by the withdrawal of the law in question.

In general we can say that Iberian trade unions have suffered a steady loss of influence until 1995, regaining influence since then. This influence is more noticeable in the Spanish case.

The low level of unemployment in Portugal, for the last two decades, may be behind this low union influence. In addition, as pointed out by Sparrow and Hiltrop (1994), there appears to be a link between the overall level of militancy (as reflected in number of lost working days per 1000 workers, number of strikes and number of workers involved) and the level of unionisation. In Portugal levels of unionisation and militancy are similar, while in Spain there are very high levels of militancy combined with very low levels of unionisation. Another link pointed out by these authors refers to the type of national legislation governing labour relations, where countries with very high militancy rates (Spain having the highest) usually have more severe laws governing labour regulations.

Figure 6.14 shows the trend towards decreased influence in 1992 and increased influence in 1995 and 1999.

Union influence in both countries is concentrated on administrative and manual workers. The determination of pay at national or regional level, where unions negotiate, applies in both countries to about half the clerical workers, and two-thirds of manual employees. Fewer than a third of professional employees have their salaries set at this level in either country, and for managers the figures are 12% in Spain and 22% in Portugal.

In Spain more than in Portugal this national influence has increased substantially in the few years since the government empowered trade unions and employers' federations to negotiate general agreements, especially for labour contracts and for European funds for training. In Spain the management of European funds for training by employers' federations and trade unions

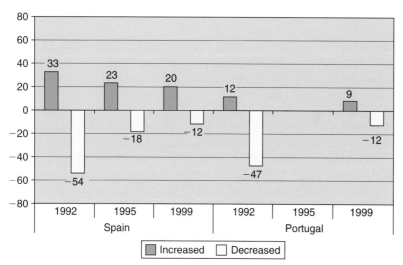

Figure 6.14 Change in trade union influence

came under investigation when the *Tribunal de Cuentas*, a governmental auditor, discovered irregularities in the use of these funds.

Works councils at company level, a quasi-union organisation, exercise different influence in the two countries. When comparisons are made for the year 1999 of the influence of unions and works councils in areas such as change processes, the differences between the two countries are significant (Table 6.14).

In Spain, trade unions and works councils play a more important role at company level than in Portugal. One important reason for this lies in the role played by illegal works councils during the Franco regime, without parallel in Salazar's Portugal, which was more dominated by corporate unions. In Portugal, and in addition to the comments presented above regarding differences in trade union influence, trade unions enjoyed a golden era after 1974 until the late 1980s, when a major privatisation programme was launched. Unions were dominated by a political/ideological

tendency, which ultimately led to a decline in their influence. As the economic constraints imposed by the single currency force the government to limit the public deficit, the social climate may become more difficult, perhaps once again paving the way for an increased influence of trade unions.

Organisation of work: flexible patterns of work

By the beginning of the current century Spain was established as the European champion in the use of temporary contracts, with an average of a third of all salaried workers compared with an average of 14% for the EU. Nor is there much evidence of any change (see Figure 6.15).

Spain has increased the use of flexible working practices since 1992 to a point where only 14% of the companies surveyed in 1999 reported not using flexible working compared with more than a third in Portugal.

The main increase in flexible arrangements in both countries was in temporary contracts. Figure 6.16 shows the differences between the two countries.

Although Portuguese organisations have increased the use of temporary contracts since 1992 and Spanish ones reduced the number (with an exception in the year 1995) the differences are substantial.

The use of temporary contracts in Portuguese organisations follows normal European standards. This is not

Table 6.14 Change in communication through trade unions/works councils (%, 1999)

	Spain	Portugal
Increased	22	9
Same	53	40
Decreased	16	13
Not used	9	38

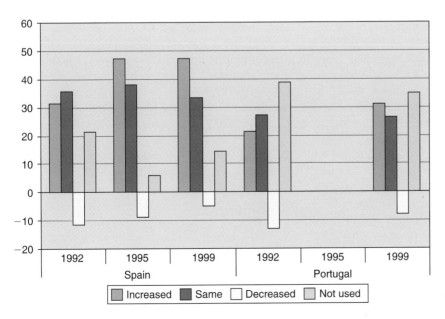

Figure 6.15 Change in use of flexible working arrangements

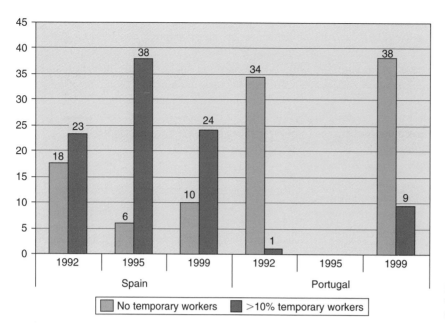

Figure 6.16 Proportion of workforce on temporary contracts

the case for Spain. One possible explanation for the Spanish figures is the cost of dismissal for full-time contracts, which amounts to 45 days' pay for each year of tenure. This cost has been reduced recently for certain new contracts and that has had some effect in reducing temporary contracts, though the figure still remains relatively high. Another (more plausible) explanation is the experience of compulsory full-time contracts for more than 40 years, the years of dictatorship. Seasonal contracts associated with the tourism sector may also help to account for the phenomenon.

The difficulty of dismissal (and the time taken up by the dismissal procedure), on the other hand, is one of the reasons why Portuguese employers have made extensive use of temporary contracts, since these provide a means of increasing labour market flexibility. However, a recent study by Varejão (2002) found that, like their counterparts in Italy, France and Germany, Portuguese organisations use fixed-term contracts for screening candidates for permanent jobs. They hire new workers on temporary contracts and evaluate the quality of their work to help them decide whether to offer them permanent contracts. This is quite common, for instance, in the recruitment of university graduates for organisations such as banks and insurance companies. In that sense, temporary contracts are stepping stones towards a permanent job, particularly for young workers. In Spain, however, studies indicate that fixed-term

contracts are involuntary, less well paid and with limited advancement opportunities (Adam and Canziani, 1998; Alba-Ramirez, 1998; Amuedo-Dorantes, 2000).

Part-time contracts are not widely used in either country – certainly below the European average. But we can observe differences, with a substantial increase in Spain and a more moderate use in Portugal. The explanation may be found in the still low proportion of female workers among the salaried workers in Spain. In Portugal, however, female participation in the workforce is more significant. In 2002, Portuguese female work participation was 60% (as against 40% in Spain) – well above the EU average of 53.8% (Eurostat, 2002). The small proportion of part-time contracts in Portugal and Spain is also probably associated with the need to have a full-time job, with the corresponding pay and social benefits. Organisations still do not feel the pressure to accommodate women's need for time flexibility. Figure 6.17 provides a picture of the situation in both countries (Figures 6.15 and 6.17).

Summary

We find commonalities as much as divergences among HRM practices in the two countries. Commonalities are the consequence of integration within the European Community/Union and an increasing, although for the moment still unbalanced, social and

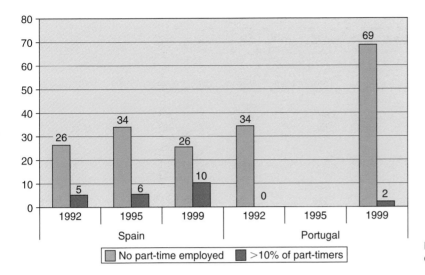

Figure 6.17   Proportion of workforce on part-time contracts

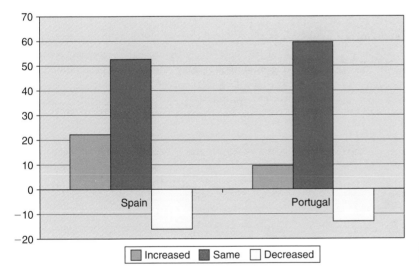

Figure 6.18   Change through trade unions/works councils, 1999

economic convergence in both countries. In 2001, Spain exported goods and services to Portugal to a value of 12,921 million euros, the third country after France and Germany. In the same year Portugal's exports to Spain reached 4777 million euros, making it the eighth country.

Forty years ago 100 Spanish firms were established in Portugal. In 2001, more than 3000 operated there. In the same year commercial contracts between the two countries increased by 30% relative to 2000. Almost half of Portugal's tourists are Spaniards

(5,500,000). Increasingly the same happens the other way round. In the year 2000, 3% of tourists visiting Madrid were Portuguese, the fourth country after Germany, the UK and France. Economic and social relations are also improving and that serves to reinforce convergence too.

But there are also dissimilarities. While the trend in both countries is towards contractual flexibility, temporary contracts are common in Spain but less so in Portugal. Unions are more influential in Spain than in Portugal. HR departments are more influential in

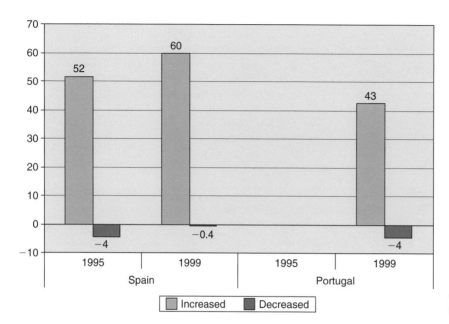

Figure 6.19   Change in variable pay over previous 3 years (% organisations)

Spain than in Portugal. However, training investment is higher in Portugal than in Spain.

The growing integration of the two economies encourages growing similarities, something we shall probably see more of in the future. For now, the HR function in these two countries seems to take different paths to achieving the same goal – gaining a strategic role and helping develop human capital, which is the core of social and economic development.

HRM IN ACTION

PORTUGAL

Novabase: creating a loyal workforce

This case history explores the interplay between leadership, structure and culture in a knowledge-intensive firm: Novabase. Novabase can be regarded as a successful firm in its industry, potentially providing valuable lessons for other knowledge-based companies. Its success can be measured in several ways. These include not only financial but also human criteria, with the company ranking fourth in a Portuguese survey of best companies to work for. Novabase considers that the efforts it has put into creating a loyal workforce have been well rewarded. Staff turnover is 13% – lower if only employees with permanent contracts are considered (8%). It is important to note that 66% of those who leave the company do so before completing a full year of work at Novabase. These figures are interpreted by the company as the result of a process of attraction–selection–attrition that contributes to cultural homogeneity (Schneider, 1987).

A brief description

Novabase was founded in 1989. It started as a technology supplier but evolved into an integrated IT services firm, operating in such areas as information technology, decision support systems, knowledge management, operational and office systems, supply chain management, marketing solutions and so forth. Its structure is of the network type, growing mainly through spin-offs. In recent years, however, and while preparing a successful IPO, Novabase also acquired several companies, complementing its previously existing areas of expertise. Since its foundation the company has grown significantly in terms of product diversification, size of workforce (over 700 at the end of 2001) and physical facilities. Despite these changes, the company has managed to retain the key features on which it was established, especially those related to its engineering-based knowledge and entrepreneurial culture. The success of the company can be illustrated by continued growth even in the face of market contraction: during the economic downturn of the first half of 2001 its sales increased by 108%.

Managing loyalty

This section describes the three interrelated processes used by Novabase to manage workforce loyalty: low-profile leadership, minimal structuring and a "high-profile" organisational culture.

Process 1

Low-profile leadership. The management of professionals in knowledge-intensive firms normally involves what may be described as low-profile leadership, i.e. leadership characterised by trust and remote control. These two terms are, of course, related. Remote control is only possible when there is enough trust. In this case, leadership can be viewed as embedded in and supported by the social system. In the case of Novabase, good leadership involves keeping a low profile: good leaders are not the owners of leadership but its facilitators. In this role, they are backed up by institutional and organisational factors, namely a strong set of cultural norms (arising from both the organisation and the engineering community) coupled with the powerful yet unobtrusive influence of minimal structures (which is discussed below).

Process 2

Minimal structuring. Given, on the one hand, the high levels of professionalism and expectations of autonomy and, on the other hand, the need for co-ordination, structures need to be carefully implemented. In this knowledge-intensive company, minimal structures embedded in the organisational system, and to a great extent internalised through practice, provide a valuable basis for organising (for an explanation of the minimal structure concept, see Kamoche and Cunha, 2001).

Minimal structures co-ordinate without constraining. They provide an unobtrusive means of co-ordination that relies on goals, deadlines and responsibilities. As discussed above, good leaders in this network seem to be those who are able to synthesise control and freedom, to co-ordinate rather than control: "There is autonomy and a good definition of roles. We know how to use roles without losing autonomy."

Process 3

High-profile organisational culture. Novabase manages culture so as to deal with two key issues: control and staff retention. Given the empty spaces of organising (Hatch, 1999) in the knowledge-intensive firm, reflected in the relative absence of structure and leadership, professionals in this firm are controlled and made loyal through a strong and shared organisational culture (normative compliance) as well as for utilitarian reasons (Etzioni, 1964).

In the case of Novabase, the cultural profile emphasises minimal structures, minimal familiarity and minimal stability. Hierarchy is rendered as invisible as possible and there is no dress code. The desired effects on employee loyalty seem to have been achieved, as demonstrated by the figures for staff retention and by being among the best companies to work for. According to the survey, the main advantage of working for Novabase is its "family spirit" and collaborative culture. One employee wrote in the 2000 annual report that this is the place "where friendships that go beyond professional relationships are made. It is not surprising that the word employee appears so often – you see, at Novabase, people really are important." Utilitarian compliance is mainly satisfied via "intrapreneurship", which is nurtured by the "adhocratic" culture. Performance measurement and reward systems are carefully managed, stock options are granted to employees, and motivation is managed, to a great extent, through the possibility of developing individual ideas with the support of the organisation.

SPAIN

New HR department at Garcia shoe stores

Garcia Zapatos is a small chain of shoe stores that sells only shoes produced by Garcia manufacturing. Garcia shoe manufacturing is located in Sabadell and has been a family business for 60 years. Until about 1990 the firm manufactured shoes primarily for the Spanish market. There were 150 employees, managed by seven people all related to the Garcia family. Because of its relatively small size and routine operation, Garcia's founder, Josep Garcia, did not even think about creating a department of HRM; he himself, along with his brother and a cousin, shared responsibility for whatever HR issues arose.

In 1995, Garcia's son Salva had just completed his business degree at ESADE Business School and joined the family business. Josep was very proud that his son had graduated from a prestigious university and entrusted him with significant responsibilities. These included managing the financial portfolio. However, given the pressures created by globalisation, he was also made responsible for expanding the operation and diversifying the business. About a year after joining the business he decided to expand from shoe manufacturing to shoe retailing. The idea was to set up numerous outlets in the vicinity of Barcelona where Garcia shoes would be sold directly to the customer at Garcia outlet stores. Within 4 years he had expanded from a single shoe outlet in Barcelona to 26 stores, of which 10 were in Barcelona and the rest in other cities in Catalonia. An average shoe store had a staff of between six and ten people including the store manager(s).

In the third quarter of 2000, the retail division employed a total of 210 people (about 30 managers and assistant managers and the rest sales personnel). Business was doing well. The only criterion that Salva Garcia applied to decide whether or not to keep a store open was profitability. A store that lost money for three consecutive quarters was closed down. During the 5-year experience in store retailing only on two occasions was a store closed and employees transferred to other stores. Success was partially due to the prices and the reputation for quality that Garcia manufacturing benefited from. The other reason for success was the careful selection of the store locations.

Problems in profitability began to surface during the fourth quarter of 2000 in the retail division and the effect spilled over into manufacturing as production was cut to reflect a decline in sales. The problem of poor profitability affected 16 of the company's 26 stores.

In analysing the situation, Salva Garcia found that the market had been infiltrated by cheaper shoes from the Maghreb and East European countries such as Poland and Slovakia, by increased local competition from another new shoe outlet store, and by the fact that Garcia had been unable to reduce its prices dramatically during the sale season. In addition Garcia noticed that, for the first time in the history of the company, absenteeism compared to previous years had increased – by an average of 3% (at the factory) and 9% (retail stores). Turnover, especially among store managers, had reached 33%, and many of the employees in the retail stores complained of being poorly informed about the company's ideas for the future and felt that they were inadequately trained in selling shoes and maintained that they were badly supervised by incompetent store managers.

Salva Garcia concluded that the principal reason for all these problems was the lack of sound HRM policies and practices. Up to that point, employee relations were managed by his father and a couple of other senior managers (all members of the family) with a very limited knowledge of HRM. To put matters right, he has decided to create a new department of HRM and has hired the recruitment consulting firm of Dolan y Salmeron Inc. to help him find a director of HRM to set up a new department and design sound HR policies and practices for both manufacturing and retail operations.

Case study questions

1. Does Garcia shoe manufacturing and retail need an HRM department? Justify your answer.
2. If you were hired as the new director of HRM at Garcia shoe manufacturing and retail, what would be the first steps that you would undertake? Why?
3. Indicate at least three different HR policies/practices for dealing with some of the current problems at Garcia shoe manufacturing and retail.

Case prepared by Simon L. Dolan

LEARNING QUESTIONS

1. How, and to what extent, has history influenced HRM in Spain and Portugal?
2. Is it possible to argue that one of these two countries is more advanced than the other in HRM? Explain what you mean by "more advanced" and provide evidence for your answer.
3. What role does the HRM function play in Spain and Portugal? What differences can you identify between the countries?
4. Explain the different situations of the unions in these countires compared to those in northern Europe where they have many more members.
5. Spain is a country of regions. How does this affect HRM in that country?
6. What explains the low take-up of some flexible working practices such as part-time working in Spain and Portugal? And what are the reasons for the comparatively high use of short-term contracts? Why do they differ between the countries?

REFERENCES

Anon (2001) *Encuesta de Calidad de Vida en el Trabajo. Ministerio de Trabajo y Asuntos Sociales.*

Adam, P. and Canziani, P. (1998) Partial deregulation: fixed-term contracts in Italy and Spain. Centre for Economic Performance, Discussion Paper no 306.

Alba-Ramirez, A. (1998) How temporary is temporary employment in Spain? *Journal of Labor Research*, 19: 695–709.

Amuedo-Dorantes, C. (2000) Work transitions into and out of involuntary temporary employment in a segmented market: evidence from Spain. *Industrial and Labor Relations Review*, 53: 309–325.

Baruel, J. (1996) in Clark, T. (ed.), *Human Resource Management*. Oxford: Blackwell.

Etzioni, A. (1964) *Modern Organizations*. Englewood Cliffs, NJ: Prentice-Hall.

Gooderham, P.N., Norhhaug O. and Ringdal, K. (1999) Institutional and rational determinants of organizational practices: human resource management in European firms. *Administrative Science Quarterly* 44(3): 507–531.

Hatch, M.J. (1999) Exploring the empty spaces of organizing: How improvisational jazz helps redescribe organizational structure. *Organization Studies*, 20: 75–100.

Jimenez, A., Pimentel, M. and Echevarria, M. (2002) *España 2010: Mercado laboral*. Watson Wyatt.

Kamoche, K. and Cunha, M.P. (2001) Minimal structures: from jazz improvisation to product innovation. *Organization Studies*, 22: 733–764.

Larsen, T., Andersen, H. and De Reyna, C. (2002) The future of the Cranet survey. Unpublished paper. ESADE. 2002.

Obeso, C. (2002) *Desde las aulas de ESADE: la función de RRHH*. AEDIPE. March.

Schneider, B. (1987) The people make the place. *Personnel Psychology*, 40, 437–454.

Sparrow, P. and Hiltrop, J.M. (1994) *European Human Resource Management in Transition*. Cambridge, UK: Prentice-Hall International.

Varejão, J.M. (2002) Fixed-term contracts, employment flows and productivity, paper presented in Conferência do Banco de Portugal. *Desenvolvimento Económico Português no Espaço Europeu: Determinantes e Políticas*, February, Lisbon.

Walter, O. (2001) *España: Factores de fidelizacion de los profesionales cualificados*. Departamento de Invstigación sobre management y liderazgo Otto Walter, España, SA.

7

Italy, Greece and Cyprus: HRM in the South-Eastern Mediterranean Corner of the EU

Nancy Papalexandris and Eleni Stavrou-Costea

INSTITUTIONAL BACKGROUND

ITALY

Area	301,243 km², 9.5% of EU-15 area
Population	57,680,000 (January 2000), 15.6% of EU-15 population
Density	191 inhabitants per km²
Capital and population	Roma: 2,460,000 (including suburbs: 3,810,000)
Other major cities and population	Milano: 1,183,000 (including suburbs: 3,753,000)
	Napoli: 993,000 (including suburbs: 2,985,000)
	Torino: 857,000 (including suburbs: 2,216,000)
	Palermo: 661,000 (including suburbs: 1,242,000)
	Genova: 603,000 (including suburbs: 913,000)
Official language	Italian
Religion	Catholic

Topography and climate

Located in southern Europe, The Republic of Italy is a peninsula stretching into the central Mediterranean Sea. It extends more than 600 km from east to west and more than 1300 km from north to south. To the north-west it is bordered by France (488 km), to the north by Switzerland (740 km) and to the north-east by Austria (430 km) and Slovenia (232 km). This territory also includes two small independent states (Vatican City and San Marino). The coastline is more than 7600 km long, half of which comprises the two islands of Sicily and Sardinia.

More than one-third of the country is mountainous (about 35% of the surface) while the largest part is hilly (42%). Plains extend over about a fourth of the territory, and are located mostly (71%) in the north-eastern region.

There are many lakes and rivers (the total water surface is 7210 km²), most of them positioned in the northern region, but only a few of them are notable and partially navigable. While intensive agriculture is practiced in the plains and on the hills, both the natural beauty of the country and the richness of its historical heritage represent a natural draw for tourism.

The climate is temperate: the northern barrier provided by the Alps protects Italy from the colder winds while the sea exerts a milder effect. However, there are marked differences between the south and the north, particularly in the winter season, whereas summers are warm and hot wherever. The average temperature in the summer is 24–26°C, in the winter varies between 2–6°C in north and 9–12°C in south. Prolonged periods of drought can occur in the southern regions during the summer months.

Culture

Italian culture can be considered less homogeneous in comparison with other European nations. One explanation sometimes advanced for this relates to the geographical territory under consideration. Italy is a long peninsula, with the distance between Palermo in the south and Milano in the north being longer than the distance between Milano and London!

Another explanation invoked here is historical: the making of Italy as we understand it today took many centuries and was completed only in 1871 with the reunification lead by the Kingdom of Piemonte and the declaring of Rome as the capital. At that time people who lived in the northern area could not even understand the language spoken in Sicily or Campania. Every region had a local dialect which was a mix of some ancient Latin with words and structures derived from the languages of the occupants (including French and Austrians in the North, and Spaniards and the Muslims in the South). In the words of Cavour, the prime minister of the time, "Made Italy, we have now to make the Italians!"

A process of cultural integration certainly was fostered by the state after the reunification. The result has been a common language and a largely common value set grounded in the Latin and Catholic tradition. However, the pre-existing cultural differentiation has not been completely overcome. For example, the entrepreneurial attitude is certainly much more diffused among the people who live in the north-east area compared to the south. In these areas in the eighteenth century the land was given to the farmers under an agreement called "Mezzadria": the landlord would take half of the harvest, the remainder was for the farmer and his family. This system stimulated innovation in production methods and allowed a more distributed process of capital accumulation and wealth generation. Conversely, in the South the feudal large estate system endured until reunification.

Principal characteristics

Figure 7.1 depicts the position of Italy in relation to other EU countries. The population density is very high, infant mortality is a bit higher than the EU average while life expectancy is on average. Some economic issues emerge clearly if one considers that the employment rate is lower than the EU average, especially for females, while the unemployment rate is high. Finally, the cost of living is on the European average and is lower than in other large countries such as Germany, France and Great Britain.

People

Italy is one of the most populated countries in the EU. The population exceeds 57 million living on an area of about $301,000 \, km^2$, similar to Arizona and Great Britain. Density stands at 191 inhabitants per km^2. The average number of people per household is 3.2. Life expectancy is pretty high – 76.1 years for men and 82.6 for women (about 15 months more than the European average). The population is growing at a rate of about 2%, mainly due to migratory flows (+2%), while the natural rate of growth is steady (−0.2%). In any case, the rate of growth is not sufficient to prevent the population from ageing (as is evident from the Table 7.1).

Economy

Italy has a diversified industrial economy with roughly the same total and per capita output as France and the UK. The economy remains divided into a developed industrial north, dominated by private companies, and a less developed agricultural south, with an average 20% unemployment. Over the past decade, Italy has pursued a tight fiscal policy and has benefited from lower interest and inflation rates. Public debt has also been reduced but some structural reforms are still needed. Priorities here include reforms aimed at reducing the high tax burden and overhauling labour market rigidities.

While historically, the Italian economy was a mix of private enterprise and national government ownership, in the last 5 years a massive programme of privatisation has been pursued. This programme has involved all major banks and large companies previously owned by the government such as ENI, TELECOM, ENEL and AUTOSTRADE. Consequently, the whole enterprise system is now largely private, with the government holding only minority share interests which will eventually also be sold.

The public sector accounts for a large proportion of the economy providing most of the health care, childcare, old-age care and education: some private companies entered in these business in the last years, and the state is favouring this process to raise competition and improve efficiency.

A well-known characteristic feature of the industrial structure in Italy is the very high proportion of medium size (<200 employees) and small (<20 employees) companies. Usually these companies are organised in networks around a larger focal enterprise which provides

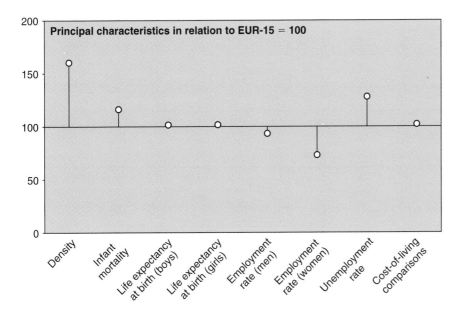

Figure 7.1 Principal characteristics in relation to EU-15: Italy

Table 7.1 Population by age (% of total population)

Age (years)	Italy		EU-15 2000
	1990	2000	
<15	17	14	17
15–24	16	12	12
25–49	35	37	37
50–64	18	18	17
65–79	12	14	13
>80	3	4	4

All data from (1). p. 19, 21, 23.

coordination. This gives to the system a very high level of flexibility and responsiveness. Two main reasons explain this industrial structure: (1) the lack of financial capital in a country that was a late comer in the industrial development; (2) a process of diffusion of technical competencies from the focal company into the surrounding geographical district which allowed the externalisation of lower value manufacturing activities to exploit the incentives.

With the exception of 1995, Italy's economic performance in terms of GDP growth has lagged behind that of its EU partners for the whole period 1994–2000 (Table 7.2).

GDP is primarily accounted for by services (68%), followed by industry (30%). Agriculture and breeding account for only about 2% of the GDP. Employment composition is slightly different with services accounting for 63%, industry 32% and agriculture 6%.

Given the lack of natural resources most raw materials needed by industry and more than 75% of energy requirements are imported. However, in 2001 exports (€ 240 billion) exceeded imports (€ 224 billion). Italy's positive balance of payments is particularly accounted for by engineering products, textiles and clothing, footwear, production machinery, motor vehicles, transport equipments, chemicals, food and beverages. The main trading partners are fellow EU members states including Germany (15%), France (13%), the UK (7%) and Spain (6%). A further 10% is accounted for by trade with the US.

A cost-of-living comparison shows that in Italy prices are on the EU average (Table 7.3). Only the costs of health care and housing (due to the very high cost of water, electricity and gas) are above the average, while communications, education, clothing and footwear are cheap compared to the other EU countries.

Legal, institutional and political environment

The Italian Republic is a parliamentary democracy. The government is appointed by the President of Republic and is responsible to a bicameral parliament, which

Table 7.2   Gross domestic product (at market prices). Current series in million (ECU/EUR)

		1994	1995	1996	1997	1998	1999	2000
1000 million ECU	Italy	863	839	971	1030	1069	1108	1166
Percentage change on previous period – constant prices	Italy	2	3	1	2	2	2	3
	EU-15	3	2	2	3	3	3	3

All data from (1), p. 160.

Table 7.3   Cost-of-living comparisons in the EU in 2000 (Brussels = 100)

Food and beverages	Alcoholic beverages and tobacco	Clothing and footwear	Housing, water, electricity, gas and other fuels	Furnishing household eq. and maintenance of house
101	105	82	117	108
Health 123	Transport 91	Communications 64	Recreation and culture 105	
Education 72	Hotels, cafes and restaurants 93	Miscellaneous goods and services 115	*Total* 102	*Total excluding rents* 97

All data from (4), p. 200.

Table 7.4   Persons in employment (million)

	1987	1988	1989	1990	1991	1992	1993	1994	1995	1996	1997*	2000**
	4.4	4.5	4.5	4.6	4.5	4.3	4.0	4.0	4.1	4.0	3.9*	4.1
1985 = 100	102.0	103.5	105.2	106.0	104.1	99.7	93.9	93.1	94.5	91.2	:	:

All data from (1, p. 296) except * from (2, p. 316) and ** from (4, p. 98). ":" Data not available.

consists of the Senate with 315 delegates (Senato della Repubblica) and the Chamber of Deputies (Camera dei Deputati) with 630 seats. The election system is complex with 75% of the seats being decided by a direct election majority vote system and the remaining 25% being decided by proportional representation election system.

The President is the head of the state, but with the exception of war and/or a serious institutional crisis, presidential functions are reduced to purely ceremonial ones.

Public administration is broadly organised along three institutional lines: national, regional and local. At the sub-national level, Italy is divided into 20 regions, 105 county council areas and 8100 municipalities. The regions administer health care and education, while the county councils have transport systems as their principal area of responsibility. The municipalities have the main responsibility for local services (e.g.

social welfare services, waste management, child care and care for the elderly).

The centralised national government aims ensure an equality of living conditions throughout the country transferring financial resources from the richest to the poorest regions, along with dealing with security, income tax collection and the building of large-scale infrastructure. Regions, councils and municipalities enjoy considerable autonomy and have some tax collection powers of their own. Councillors and majors are elected in direct local elections.

Labour market

Today (2002) over 23.4 million people are in employment in Italy and the vast majority of these jobs are found in the service sector (Table 7.4). The public sector is very large, employing around 32% of the workforce.

Table 7.5   Persons in employment in different sectors (thousands)

	1990	1991	1992	1993	1994	1995	1996	1997	1998	1999*	2000**
Industry	:	:	:	:	:	1065	1030	1000	:	1013	1005
Agriculture	:	:	:	:	:	135	130	127	:	121	120
Services	:	:	:	:	:	2933	2824	2785	:	2917	2998

All data from (2, pp. 316–317) except * from (3, p. 122) and ** from (4, p. 98). ":" Data not available.

Table 7.6   Employment rate of men and women 15–64 years (%, 2000)

	Men	Women	Total
Italy	68	39	53
EU-15	72	54	63

All data from (1), pp. 100–102.

Table 7.7   Unemployment rate total (%)

	1990	1991	1992	1993	1994	1995	1996	1997	1998	1999	2000
Italy	9	9	9	10	11	12	12	12	12	11	11
EU-15	:	:	:	11	11	11	11	11	10	9	8

All data from (1), p. 110. ":" Data not available.

Table 7.8   Unemployment rate: men, women, long-term (2000)

	Men	Women	Long-term (>12 months) as % of all unemployed
Italy	8.0	14.4	61
EU-15	7.0	9.7	45

All data from (1), p. 111, 113.

Table 7.9   Average hourly labour costs (manual and non-manual workers) in industry (ECU/EUR)

	1995	1996	1997	1998	1999	2000
EU-15	19.47	20.10	20.97	21.45	:	:
Italy	15.67	17.21	18.23	17.90	:	:

All data from (1), p. 213. ":" Data not available.

There is a trend towards a growth in the service sector, together with at declining number of people employed in industry and agriculture (Table 7.5).

As Tables 7.6–7.8 show, Italian men and women have a lower employment rate than the average in the EU. This is in part explained by a generous pension system which allows for retirement at an age of 55–56 years. While some restrictions has been applied to this in recent years, a more structural reform of the pension system is needed to raise the proportion of the population who are active in the labour force and also to deal with the ageing of the population.

The unemployment rate can be considered high compared to the EU average: a reduction has occurred in recent years (the 2002 rate is estimated at about 9%), but unfortunately long-term unemployment remains stubbornly high, especially in the South.

Hourly labour costs in Italy are lower than the average for the countries within the euro-zone (Table 7.9). As a consequence, manufacturing in some labour intensive industries remains reasonably competitive. Such work is also facilitated by very high level of availability of manual and technical skills among the Italian workforce and the subcontracting of lower value activities to small companies with fewer overhead costs.

Education system

Eight years of schooling are compulsory in Italy for all children from the age of 6. The first 5 years are spent at primary school and the following three at the first stage of secondary school. About 72% go on to the upper-secondary school (5 years), which is not currently divided into vocational or academic streams. Upper-secondary school also provides the basis for higher education which in Italy takes place in universities. All higher education, except for a few private universities such as Università Bocconi and Università Cattolica in Milan has traditionally been owned and funded by the state.

Unfortunately, only about 30% of students are able to complete their program and achieve the degree: this is due to a very selective approach in the higher education that has been in the past the basis for an effective

selection of the elites. This system is not reflecting any longer the main needs of the country: in 2000 a process of change was started to end up with a new system based on two layers of higher education, where only the second one will keep this very selective approach.

In the same time a reform was designed at the lower level of the educational system with the purpose of reducing the length until the upper-secondary school by 1 year and introducing a parallel vocational training system to raise the attendance.

As shown in Table 7.10, the percentage of people having completed at least upper-secondary education is lower in Italy than in the EU average, especially for women (Table 7.11).

Table 7.10　Level of education for the population aged 25–64 (%, 2000)

At least upper secondary education	Total (25–64)	25–29	30–34	35–39	40–44	45–49	50–54	55–59	60–64
EU-15 (women and men)	64	76	73	70	66	62	55	51	45
Italy (women and men)	45	63	55	52	51	44	34	27	21
EU-15 (women)	61	77	73	70	64	58	50	45	37
Italy (women)	45	66	58	54	49	42	30	23	17

All data from (1), p. 95.

Table 7.11　Underlying table for "Principal characteristics in relation to EU-15"

	EU-15	Italy	Relation (Italy/EU-15)*100
Density (inhabitants per km^2) Year: 2000	119	191	160.5
Infant mortality[2] (per thousand live birth) Year: 2000	4.9	5.7	116.3
Life expectancy at birth (boys; years) Year: 1999	74.9	76.1	101.6
Life expectancy at birth (girls; years) Year: 1999	81.2	82.6	101.7
Employment rate (men*; %) Year: 2000	72	68	93
Employment rate (women*; %) Year: 2000	54	39	73
Unemployment rate (%) Year: 2000	8	11	128
Cost-of-living comparisons (total value; $B = 100$) Year: 2000	$B = 100$	102	102

All data from (1).

HELLENIC REPUBLIC (GREECE)

Area	131,957 km^2
Population	10,964,020 (2001)
Density	83.1 inhabitants per km^2
Capital and population	Athinai (Athens) (c. 3 million)
Other important cities and population	Thessalonika (c. 1 million) Patras (c. 180,000)
Official language	Greek
Business languages	Greek, English
Religion	95% Orthodox Christian

All data from (1).

Topography and climate

Greece is situated in the southeast of Europe, in the eastern Mediterranean. The country's total area is 131,957 km^2. Greece is bordered on the north by Albania, Macedonia and Bulgaria and on the east by Turkey. Islands account for about 19% of its land area and there is a total coastline of 15,021 km. The great number of islands, and the fact that the country is largely surrounded by the sea, have provided Greece with special advantages. It is a predominantly agricultural country, cultivated land amounting to 30% of its total area in which part of its mountainous region is also included. Greece is also famous for its temperate Mediterranean climate. Winters are mild, with limited rainfall, and summers are warm, with much sunshine. Autumn is lengthy and mild, while spring is short and generally mild. The lowest

Figure 7.2 The ancient theatre in Epidavros

temperatures occur between December and February and the highest in July and August. The language is modern Greek, which has evolved over several millennia from ancient Greek. English, French and German are the main foreign languages spoken in Greece today and Greek schools are required to teach two of them, while Italian and Spanish are also studied at language institutes.

Principal characteristics

Figure 7.3 shows the position of Greece in relation to other European countries on a number of standardised items.

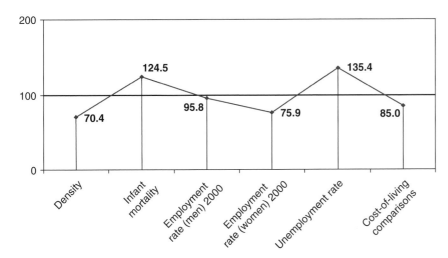

Figure 7.3 Principal characteristics in relation to EU-15: Greece. All data from (3)

Special features

Greek history dates back thousands of years and includes many great moments such as the birth of democracy in ancient Athens and the development of philosophy by Socrates, Plato and Aristotle. Some of the greater thinkers of all times such as Hippocrates, Thucydides and Sophocles were also Greeks. Glorious periods of history for Greece include the Macedonian Empire, during which Alexander the Great led the Greeks as far as India, and the Byzantine Empire, which lasted for almost a thousand years. This ended in 1453 AD when Greece came under the rule of the Ottoman Turks, which lasted almost 400 years. A long and hard-fought revolutionary war for national independence started in 1821 and finally, in 1828, Greece was recognised as an independent state. The 175 years of modern Greek history have witnessed many changes. In 1981, Greece became a full member of the European Community and in 2001 a member of the Economic and Monetary Union, replacing its currency the Drachma by the Euro.

People

Two demographic trends, found in all European countries and not just in Greece, are worth mentioning. The first is the ageing of the population and the decline in the number of births. It is estimated that in the next few years the number of deaths will be higher than the number of births. As can be seen from Table 7.12, older people (50+ years) form a large proportion (almost one-third) of the total population. Unfortunately it appears that the percentage of people under 15 years has fallen from 20 to 15%, which is also lower than the average in the EU. On the positive side, the table also shows that people are now living longer than 10 years ago.

The second trend is the increasing number of economic immigrants, especially from Asian and former communist countries. According to the last census, 797,000 immigrants are now living in Greece, and if undeclared immigrants are also included the actual number may be higher.

Economy

The Greek economy has gone through an important transitional phase, overcoming many of the problems of the past decades. The rate of inflation rate has fallen from two-digit figures in the 1980s to 3% currently and as a consequence interest rates have also declined. The Greek economy is converging with the rest of the European economies, as reflected in improvements in public debt and deficit. Another interesting point is the rate of increase in GDP, which is above the EU-15 average (Table 7.13). This growth could be partly attributed to the construction works now under way for the Olympic Games of 2004, which are to be staged in Athens.

Traditionally, the agricultural sector was the basis for the Greek economy, but structural changes in recent decades have resulted in the growth of the service sector, partly at the expense of the manufacturing sector.

Table 7.12 Population by age in Greece (% of total population)

Age (years)	Greece (%)		(EU-15) (%) 2000
	1990	2000	
<15	20	15	17
15–24	15	14	12
25–49	33	36	37
50–64	19	18	17
65–79	11	14	13
>80	3	4	4

All data from (2).

Table 7.13 Gross domestic product (at current prices and at current exchange rates)

		1991	1992	1993	1994	1995	1996	1997	1998	1999	2000
1000 million EURO (nominal growth)	Greece	73	77	80	84	90	98	107	109	117	123
Yearly growth as % of previous year (real growth)	Greece	3	1	22	2	2	2	4	3	3	4
	EU-15		1	20	3	2	2	3	3	3	3

All data from (2).

As Figure 7.3 indicates, a significant share of the GDP comes from services, especially tourism and the merchant marine.

Greek firms export mainly to European countries and to their Balkan neighbours. The principal exports are agricultural goods, food and drink products and other manufactured goods.

The cost of living in Greece is in almost every category lower than in most European countries (Table 7.14). At 2000 prices, Greece is the cheapest among all EU countries in the categories of "housing, water, electricity, gas and other fuels", "furnishing, household equipment and house maintenance", "health", "transport", "communications", "miscellaneous services" and expensive only in clothing and footwear.

Legal and institutional environment/political system

The Greek constitution, which in its earliest form dates back to 1822 and which was last revised in 2000, provides for a democratic government with legislative power exercised by a 300-member parliament elected every 4 years. The parliament elects a president for a 5-year term. Executive power is held by the president, the prime minister and the cabinet. The two most powerful parties that have governed Greece over the last 25 years are the Social-Democratic Party, "The Panhellenic Socialist Movement" (PASOK), and the Conservative Party, "New Democracy" (Nea Dimokratia), while the three other parties represented in parliament are the Communist Party of Greece (KKE), the "Coalition of the Left" (Synaspismos) and the Social and Democratic Movement (DIKKI). At the present time (February 2003) PASOK is the party in power.

Greece is divided into 52 districts and 13 geographical departments. The heads of these districts, as well as the mayors of every town, are also elected every 4 years. The Metropolitan region, which includes the departments of Athens, Piraeus and Eastern and Western Attica, contains over one-third of the country's total population. This region is also the administrative, financial and cultural centre of Greece. People vote every 5 years to elect 25 representatives to the European Parliament.

In Greece the judiciary is independent of both the executive and legislative bodies. The judicial system includes separate courts for civil, administrative, criminal and military cases. Civil cases are tried in the Civil Courts (i.e. the Court of First Instance and the Court of Appeal) and may ultimately be referred to the Supreme Court. Administrative matters (e.g. tax cases) are judged in the Administrative Court, the Administrative First Instance Court, the Administrative Court of Appeal and the Council of State (the supreme administrative court).

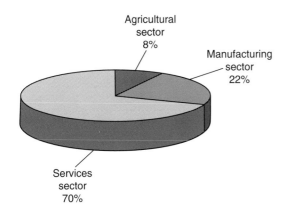

Figure 7.4   Economic structure, 2002. All data from (2)

Labour market

Recent developments in the Greek labour market include a decline in the number of people employed in

Table 7.14   Cost-of-living comparisons in the EU in 2000 (Brussels = 100)

Food and non-alcoholic beverages	Alcoholic drinks and tobacco	Clothing and footwear	Housing	Household equipment	Health	Transport
89	103	96	85	86	90	77

Communications	Education	Recreation and culture	Miscellaneous	*Total*	*Total excluding Housing*
58	59	105	75	85	83

Source: (2).

Table 7.15　Persons in employment (million)

1990	1991	1992	1993	1994	1995	1996	1997	1998	1999	2000
3.71	3.63	3.68	3.71	3.78	3.82	3.87	3.85	3.72	3.82	3.95

All data from (2).

Table 7.16　Persons in employment in different sectors (thousands)

	1990	1991	1992	1993	1994	1995	1996	1997	1998	1999	2000
Agriculture	889	807	804	791	788	780	784	765	889	780	671
Industry	961	933	933	899	894	886	885	866	961	886	888
Services	1867	1892	1942	2026	2104	2154	2199	2223	1867	2154	2387

All data from (2).

Table 7.17　Unemployment rate (%)

1990	1991	1992	1993	1994	1995	1996	1997	1998	1999	2000
6	7	8	9	9	9	10	10	11	12	11

All data from (2).

Table 7.18　Persons in employment by gender (%, 2000)

	Greece	EUR-15
Women	41	54
Men	69	72

All data from (2).

Table 7.19　Average hourly labour costs (manual and non-manual workers) in total industry

	1992	1993	1994	1995	1996	1997	1998
ECU	6.97	7.33	7.64	8.15	9.60	12.20	11.76

All data from (2).

Table 7.20　Structure of labour costs, total industry (%, 1999)

Direct cost	Total indirect cost	Employee's social security contributions
70	27	27

All data from (2).

farming and stock-farming and an increase in those employed in services. This trend, as illustrated in Tables 7.15 and 7.16, means that the role of agriculture is diminishing while the corresponding increase in the numbers employed in services brings the country closer to the norms for developed economies. An important feature of the Greek labour market is the high proportion of employers and self-employed people.

Unemployment in Greece, as shown in Table 7.17, is quite high and the latest figures indicate that at present it is above 10%, which means that about 500,000 people are without work. And as in most countries the unemployment rate for women (17%) is higher than that for men (7%) (Table 7.18).

Labour costs are rising steadily (Table 7.19), but are still the lowest (with the exception of Portugal) among European countries.

Although the data on the structure of labour costs (Table 7.20) are not up to date, the pattern of increase is quite close to the EU average.

Educational system

In Greece, compulsory education includes the 6 years of elementary school and the first 3 years of high school (mandatory education for students aged from 6 to 15). Those who wish to pursue their studies in higher education have to complete another 3 years of high school. Under the Greek constitution, education is free in state schools, in universities and in technical institutes, but there are also a number of private elementary and high schools, as well as a number of private post-secondary colleges. Courses last from 4 to 6 years in the universities and 3 to 4 years in the technical institutes.

Post-graduate courses are offered by all Greek universities; nevertheless Greece has the highest percentage in Europe of people studying abroad. Table 7.21 indicates that although in total the level of education in Greece is close to the average for Europe, the percentage of young people (25–29) with upper-secondary education is higher than the average European figure.

Vocational education is the responsibility of the Hellenic Manpower Employment Organization (OAED). Vocational guidance is provided through counselling, selection of candidates for training or re-orientation and information about occupations. Special programmes, sponsored by the Greek state and the EU, exist for the technical education of people aged 15–18 and the vocational education of adults 16–46 years old (Table 7.22).

Table 7.21 Level of education for the population aged 25–64 (in %, 2000)

>Upper-secondary education	Total (25–64)	25–29	30–34	35–39	40–44	45–49	50–54	55–59	60–64
EUR-15 (women and men)	64	76	73	70	66	62	55	51	45
Greece (women and men)	51	75	70	62	56	48	39	30	24
EUR-15 (women)	61	77	73	70	64	58	50	45	37
Greece (women)	49	79	72	61	55	45	35	25	18

All data from (2).

Finally, principal characteristics of Greece in relation to EU-15 are shown below (Table 7.22).

Table 7.22 Principal characteristics in relation to EU-15

	EU-15	Greece	Relation (Greece/EU-15) × 100
Density (inhabitants per km²) Year: 1999	115.2	79.4	68.9
Infant mortality (per thousand live births) Year: 1999	4.9	6.1	124.5
Employment rate (men; %) Year: 2000	72	69	96
Employment rate (women; %) Year: 2000	54	41	76
Unemployment rate (%) Year: 2000	8	11	135
Cost-of-living comparisons (total value; $B = 100$) Year: 2000	100	85	85

All data from (1) and (2).

THE REPUBLIC OF CYPRUS

Pronounciation Guide:
I beat   G Spanish fuego
E bet   D mother
A bat   th thesis
O bought kh Scots loch
U boot

ΚΥΠΡΟΣ   CYPRUS

Republic of Cyprus   Kipriakí Dimokratía   Kibris Cumhuriyeti
Area: 9,200 Sq.Km (3,600 Sq.Mi), 36% under foreign occupation
Population: 650,000   Capital City: Lefkosia (Nicosia)
Currency: Cypriot Pound

(C)1994 GAEPIS/Cosmos-FM
Distribute Freely
Διανομή Ελεύθερη
Alterations are prohibited
by Copyright Law

Area	9251 km^2
Population	793,100 (2001)
Density	85 inhabitants per km^2
	Note: Population includes the Turkish Cypriots but does not include Turkish settlers.
Capital and population	Lefkosia (Nicosia): 280,300 (2001)
Other important cities and population	Limassol (201,600)
	Larnaka (117,500)
	Pafos (67,600)
Official languages	Greek, Turkish
Business languages	Greek, English
Religions	77% Greek Orthodox
	18% Moslem
	5% Others

Cyprus has a rich cultural heritage. Nine of the island's Byzantine mountain churches and the entire towns of Kato Pafos, Palepafos and Choirokoitia have been included by UNESCO in its World Cultural Heritage List. In 1974, Turkey invaded Cyprus and continues to occupy 37% of the island. Economically and politically Cyprus has gravitated towards the European Union (EU). It has been accepted to become a full member of the EU by May 2004, with the hope that, through the political freedoms and safeguards it will acquire through such membership, Cyprus may recover from the wounds of the recent past and guarantee a prosperous and secure future for all its citizens.

Figure 7.5

Topography and climate

Cyprus is located in the eastern corner of the Mediterranean Sea. It is the third largest island (9251 km^2) in the Mediterranean. The nearest country to the west and north west of the island is Greece (the islands of Crete and Rhodes), with Turkey to the north and Syria, Lebanon and Israel to the east. To the south lies Egypt. The Mediterranean climate of the island is characterised by hot, dry summers and cool, wet winters. It is estimated that there are 300 sunny days each year.

Nicosia is located in the centre of Cyprus, but only 35 km from the sea. However, it has warmer summers and colder winters than the other towns of the island, which are positioned on the coastline. Nicosia is surrounded by two mountain ranges: the Troodos and the Pentadaktylos. Olympus, Troodos' highest peak, is 1951 m high while Pentadaktylos' highest point is 1000 m.

Special features

Cyprus's cultural heritage far outweighs its size. Its historical significance is evident from the vast number of ancient monuments and sites, castles and forts around the island. The island's strategic position at the crossroads of three continents (Africa, Asia and Europe) made it an object of invasion and conquest, but also a cultural and commercial meeting point. Prehistoric settlements date the start of civilisation on the island from the Stone Age (7000 BC). The discovery of copper on the island, as well as its agricultural and timber resources, attracted the Achaean Greeks at the end of the Trojan wars (about 1100 BC). They settled on the island, establishing the Greek heritage, language and civilisation that gave Cyprus its national and cultural identity over the centuries, in spite of the various other rulers the island has experienced. These included the Phoenicians, the Assyrians, the Egyptians, the Persians, the successors to Alexander the Great and the Romans, before Cyprus became part of the Byzantine Empire. Later came the Crusaders, the Frankish Louisianans and the Venetians, the Ottomans and the British. Cyprus gained its independence in 1960 after 3500 years of foreign rule. During all these years of foreign rule, the largest segment of the population of Cyprus (some 80%) retained its Greek identity, language and culture. In July 1974, after a short-lived military coup that overthrew the elected government, Turkey invaded Cyprus and since then 37% of the island has been occupied by Turkish troops. The catastrophic consequences of the Turkish invasion for the island's economy have been swept away over the past two decades by a rapid and sustained economic development, creating a service-based economy.

People

As can be seen from Tables 7.23–7.26, both birth rates and infant mortality rates have been declining over the last 5 years, whereas the percentage of the population between 15 and 64 and life expectancy (for both men and women) have been increasing. As a result, the Cypriot population is ageing at higher marginal rates year by year.

Furthermore, the life expectancy of Cypriots, regardless of gender, has been increasing throughout the past 15 years. Life expectancy among women is slightly higher than among men.

While life expectancy has been on the increase, death rates have been falling. In addition, infant mortality has been significantly reduced between 1993 and 2001.

The total number of births has decreased in the past 8 years, the percentage decrease ranging between 0.7 in 2000 and 7.5 in 1993. Nevertheless, the ratio between boys and girls has been steady.

The average Cypriot household comprises 3.06 persons and 87% of all couples have children.

Table 7.23   Population by age and sex, census years (% of total population)

Census year	Sex	0–14	15–64	>65
1976				
Total		**25**	**65**	**10**
	Males	26	65	9
	Females	25	65	11
1982				
Total		**25**	**64**	**11**
	Males	26	64	10
	Females	24	64	12
1992				
Total		**25**	**64**	**11**
	Males	26	64	10
	Females	25	63	12
2000				
Total		**21**	**67**	**12**
	Males	23	67	11
	Females	21	67	13

All data from (1).

Economy

The economic performance of Cyprus since 1974 has been extraordinary. Per capita GDP has more than tripled, reaching 12,534 EUR in 2001 (above that of several EU member states and the highest among the candidate countries to join the EU). Over the past decade, both inflation and unemployment were kept at very low levels, with inflation averaging 3.8% and unemployment below 3% for most of the 1990s. In 2001 inflation was

Table 7.24   Life expectancy at birth for males and females (in years)

Period	Males	Females
1985/1989	73.9	78.3
1987/1991	74.1	78.6
1992/1993	74.6	79.1
1994/1995	75.3	79.8
1996/1997	75	80
2000/2001	76.1	81

All data from (1).

Table 7.25   Death by sex and death rates

Year	Total	Males	Females	Death rate	Infant mortality
1993	4789	2540	2249	7.7	8.6
1994	4924	2564	2360	7.7	8.6
1995	4935	2614	2321	7.6	8.5
1996	4958	2649	2309	7.5	8.3
1997	5173	2737	2436	7.7	8.0
1998	5432	2908	2524	8.0	7.0
1999	5070	2599	2471	7.4	6.0
2000	5355	2846	2509	7.7	5.6
2001	4827	2565	2262	6.9	4.9

All data from (1).

Table 7.26   Live births by sex and birth rates

Year	Total	Males	Females	Birth rate	Change over previous year (%)	Masculinity proportion at birth
1993	10514	5442	5072	16.8	−8	51.8
1994	10379	5335	5044	16.4	−1	51.4
1995	9869	5152	4717	15.4	−5	52.2
1996	9638	4995	4643	14.9	−2	51.8
1997	9275	4719	4556	14.2	−4	50.9
1998	8875	4591	4228	13.4	−4	51.7
1999	8505	4312	4193	12.4	−4	50.7
2000	8447	4417	4030	12.2	−1	52.3
2001	8167	4201	3966	11.6	−3	51.4

All data from (1).

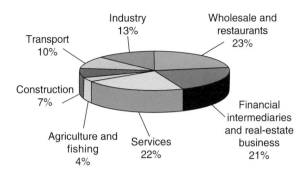

Figure 7.6   GDP by activity (at 2001 prices). All data from (1) and (2)

2% (well within the "Maastricht range") and unemployment 3%. Growth has remained strong in recent years, with 5% real GDP growth in 1999, 5% in 2000 (well above the European average of 3%) and 4% in 2001.

The impressive performance of the Cypriot economy has been driven mainly by the booming services sector (mainly tourism and financial services) as well as trade and the shipping industry (in 2001 trade and shipping together accounted for 66% of GDP). However, this makes the economy more vulnerable to external shocks. Moreover, because of its small manufacturing base, the country has a structural trade deficit. The current account deficit averaged 5% of GDP during 1997–2001 (Figure 7.6).

In 1998 the EU Commission decided to include Cyprus in the "fast-track" accession group. Accession talks have since become a catalyst for the advancement of structural changes, which were completed by December 2002. The most significant are the liberalisation of the capital account and privatisation in sectors such as telecommunications, energy and air transport. Fiscal consolidation remains the most important immediate task, as the budget deficit reached 4% of GDP in 2001 (well above the Maastricht reference rate of 3% of GDP).

Legal and institutional environment/political system

Cyprus is a republic with a presidential system of government. Under the 1960 constitution, executive power is vested in the President of the Republic, elected by universal suffrage for a 5-year term of office. The president exercises executive power through a Council of Ministers appointed by him or her. Each Minister is the head of his or her ministry and exercises executive power in respect of all issues within that ministry's domain.

Legislative power is exercised by the House of Representatives, consisting of 80 members (56 Greek Cypriots, 24 Turkish Cypriots) elected by proportional representation for a 5-year term. Since the Turkish invasion of 1974, the Turkish Cypriot parliamentary seats have remained vacant. Currently the members of the parliament come from eight different political parties namely, The Democratic Rally (DISY), The Progressive Party of the Working People (AKEL), the Democratic Party (DIKO), The Movement of Social Democrats (KISOS), The United Democrats (EDI), The New Horizons, The Movement of Ecologists and Environmentalists, and The Fighting Democratic Movement (ADIK).

Judicial power is exercised by the Supreme Court and the Districts Courts.

The basic objectives of government social policy are:

- To secure a minimum acceptable standard of living for all citizens, especially for those who do not participate – or participate to a limited extent – in the productive process.
- To achieve a more equitable distribution of the national income and of the tax burden, both between different income groups and regions. Special emphasis is attached to improving the income position of refugees.
- To implement and improve existing social programmes while preparing the introduction of new programmes, institutions and schemes.

Source: All data from (3).

Labour market

The relatively high rate of economic growth in 2001 has led to an increase in employment to 307,800 persons in 2001 compared to 301,800 in 2000 (see Table 7.27). Unemployment has fallen from 3% in 2000 – 3% of the labour force (or 9175 persons). Male unemployment was 2% (compared to 3% in 2000) and female unemployment 4% (5% in 2000).

As the Cypriot economy has increasingly come to rely on tourism and its services (financial or other) as the main engine of growth, employment in the tertiary sector has been steadily rising (see Table 7.28).

Table 7.27   Persons in employment (thousands)

Year	1989	1990	1991	1992	1993	1994	1995	1996	1997	1998	1999	2000	2001
People	246.7	253.4	254.2	265.6	265.3	272.8	283.8	285.2	286.1	288.8	294.7	301.8	307.8

All data from (4).

Table 7.28   Persons in employment in different sectors (%)

Year	1989	1990	1991	1992	1993	1994	1995	1996	1997	1998	1999	2000	2001
Primary (agriculture)	15	14	13	12	12	11	11	10	9	9	9	9	8
Secondary (industry)	29	29	29	28	27	26	26	25	24	23	22	21	21
Tertiary (services)	56	57	58	59	61	63	64	65	67	68	69	70	71

All data from (4).

Table 7.29   Percentage distribution of employees by monthly salary group and sex

Rates of pay per month in CYP*	1998			1999			2000			2001		
	Total	Male	Female	Total	Male	Female	Total	Male	Female	Total	Male	Female
Under 400	17	8	29	16	7	28	12	5	21	10	4	17
400–799	54	57	50	52	54	50	52	50	54	48	44	53
800–1199	18	21	13	19	23	14	21	26	14	24	28	18
1200–1999	10	13	7	11	13	8	14	16	10	15	19	11
≥2000	2	2	1	2	3	1	3	4	1	4	5	2

*CYP: Cyprus Pounds.
All data from (4).

As a result, employment in the agricultural and the industrial sectors has been falling.

Employment has been declining for the age groups between 15 and 29 years and 65 and above. The increase in employment has affected mainly the age groups between 30 and 64. Although employment in this age group has been rising for both genders, men are in general better paid than women (see Table 7.29).

Industrial relations and trade unions

Industrial relations in Cyprus have been very satisfactory since it became a republic in 1960. This is attributed to the responsible attitudes of both labour unions and employer organisations, which became particularly evident during the period following the Turkish invasion and occupation of the northern part of the island. It is also due to the government's policy of:

a. seeking the active participation of workers and employers in the formulation and implementation of social and economic policy, through tripartite bodies;
b. staying removed from disputes and promoting the idea that labour-management relations are first and foremost the business of the parties themselves;
c. producing procedural agreements for the settlement of disputes.

The economy has undoubtedly benefited from the close co-operation between the public sector and the social partners.

Table 7.30 Level of education by age group and sex (2002, percentage participation)

Age (years)	Less than upper secondary			Upper secondary			Tertiary		
	Total	Male	Female	Total	Male	Female	Total	Male	Female
15–24	49	58	41	40	36	43	11	6	16
25–34	17	19	15	42	36	42	41	39	43
35–49	30	27	33	40	40	40	30	32	27
50–59	53	47	59	27	29	25	20	25	15
>60	78	69	86	14	18	10	8	12	4

Educational system

Education in Cyprus is compulsory for children between the ages of 6 and 15 years (9 years in total). It comprises the primary school (6 years) and the *Gymnasium* (3 years). Then comes the upper-secondary level, which lasts for 3 years, from the ages of 15–18. This is divided into a general cycle (*Lykeion*) and a technical and vocational cycle (*Technical School*). The first offers optional subjects in five different branches (classical, science, economic, commercial and foreign languages). It also has three experimental comprehensive cycles (*Eniaio Lykeion*) where general and technical/vocational subjects are integrated.

The technical–vocational cycle comprises about 17 specialisations taught in 10 schools that are all based in large towns. The tertiary level comprises several institutions of higher education (8 public tertiary institutions and about 27 private ones) and, since 1992, the University of Cyprus. While the public institutions and the University of Cyprus require entry exams, the private institutions do not.

As Table 7.30 shows, in 2002 30% of people aged 35–49 years had completed only compulsory schooling, with a relatively higher figure for persons completing the upper-secondary level (40%). The percentage of young people in education falls below 50% at the ages of 19 and 20 years when they graduate from the upper-secondary level. At this age, all men join the army, which is compulsory for 26 months, while many women continue their education at a higher level. This is the reason for the higher participation rate of women than men at these ages. At the ages of 21 and 22, the participation rates for men and women are more or less comparable. At the age of 23 the participation rate for men is higher because by that age women graduate from tertiary institutions while men continue their education after finishing their army service.

HRM IN ITALY, GREECE AND CYPRUS: CURRENT POLICY AND PRACTICE

HISTORICAL BACKGROUND

Greece, Italy and Cyprus belong to the south-eastern Mediterranean region of Europe. They share a rich cultural heritage dating back to centuries BC as well as a sunny and warm climate, beautiful Mediterranean beaches and a plethora of archaeological sites. Furthermore, each of these countries has something unique to offer to the region, thus enriching its diversity and character.

In this chapter, after a brief overview of commonalties and differences in the cultural and geographic aspects of these three countries, we shall discuss their human resource (HR) practices and the ways in which these practices converge or diverge among the three countries.

The cultures in this region seem to have many similarities (Gentile, 1993; Verschuren et al., 1995; Leontidou, 1996). Much of the cultural heritage of Cyprus, Italy and Greece stem, to a large extent, from the historical ties that bond them. For example, during 1400 BC, the first of many waves of Greek merchants and settlers (Mycenaeans and Achaeans) reached the island of Cyprus, spreading the Greek language, religion and customs. They gradually took control and established the first city-kingdoms. By 50 BC the Hellenisation of Cyprus was complete, with 10 city-kingdoms. The cult of Aphrodite flourished in a period of great prosperity and the island became an important centre of the Greek world.

In a similar fashion, the Greeks arrived in Italy during the eighth century and established a number of colonies in the southern part of the Italian peninsula. Even though they did not reign for long, they influenced greatly the Italian civilisation. Later, Rome's conquest of Greece, through the three Macedonian Wars (215–146 BC), and the control of Asia Minor (133 BC) had a profound effect on the cultural development of the Roman world. This took the form of Hellenisation, which changed society and customs while handing on the inheritance of Greek civilisation to successive centuries.

In fact, in 330 AD Emperor Constantine moved the Capital of the Roman Empire to Constantinople, founding the Eastern Roman Empire which was renamed Byzantine Empire or Byzantium for short, by western historians in the nineteenth century. Byzantium transformed the linguistic heritage of Ancient Greece into a vehicle for the new Christian civilisation. Even though the Byzantine Empire fell to the Ottoman Empire in 1453 and the Greeks remained under the Ottoman rule for nearly 400 years, during this time their language, their religion and their sense of identity remained strong. On 25 March 1821, the Greeks started their war for independence, which they won and in 1830 the New Greek State was established.

Cyprus also became part of the Roman Empire between 58 BC and 330 AD and later, between 330 and 1191 AD, it became part of the Byzantium. Empress Helena, the mother of Emperor Constantine, visited the island and founded the Stavrovouni Monastery. Later on, between 1489–1571 the Venetians fortified the island against the Ottomans, building impressive walls around Nicosia and Famagusta, where the defences were considered works of art in military architecture. Around 1571, however, Cyprus, like Greece, fell under the Ottoman rule that lasted until 1878. After that time, the history of Greece, Cyprus and Italy continued to have much interplay.

An important part of the cultural heritage in this region is food. Even though the cuisine of Italy, especially southern Italy, has many unique features, it also has many features in common with Greece and Cyprus.

For example the history of Italian cooking begins with *Magna Grecia*, where the culture of the Greek colonies popularised the art. The daily fare was simple and sober but at banquets the food was more varied and plentiful and also took on ritual and symbolic meanings. In a similar fashion, Greek recipes and delicacies dominate Cypriot cuisine. Greece has a culinary tradition of some 4000 years. It was, in fact, a Greek, Archestratos in 330 BC, who wrote the first cookbook in History and let us not forget that cuisine is a sign of civilisation. Nevertheless, like most national cuisines, the Greek cuisine has not only influenced others, but also embraced ideas from its eastern and western neighbours.

Besides the cuisine, certain types of wine, olives and fruit are also considered indigenous features common to the Italian, Greek and Cypriot cultures. Of course the Cypriot and the Greek cultures are closer together than to the Italian culture in a number of aspects such as religion and language. To illustrate, the vast majority of Cypriots speak Greek and practice the Greek Orthodox religion, while the majority of Italians speak Italian, one of the neo-Latin group of languages, and practice the Catholic faith. But all three countries depend heavily on services and finance, many of which are related to tourism. Due to their sun, beautiful beaches and rich culture, these three countries (Greece, Cyprus and southern Italy particularly) attract millions of tourists every year, among the greatest proportions around the world.

THE BUSINESS SYSTEM

The business system of these three countries is shaped by many of the factors mentioned above, which over a long period of time created a related business climate. Specifically, their economy contains a large percentage of small entrepreneurial and family owned companies. In Greece and Cyprus more than 90% of companies employ less than 10 people (Labour Statistics, 1998; ICAP, 1999). In Italy, which is a much larger and industrially developed country, one can find smaller firms along with a number of large firms existing throughout the country but with more density in the highly developed Italian north.

Greece and Italy have also a number of larger firms, which for many years were managed in the same way as large patriarchal families, where members of the workforce and staff depended on the benevolence of the owner for their well-being. In those companies decision-making centred around one man, usually the founder/owner of the firm, who would refuse to delegate responsibility for fear of losing control over performance or results (Papalexandris, 1991; Corbetta, 1995). Given this form of managerial control, executives served rather as "assistants to" than as decision makers in their own right. While this tendency still exists today, market forces have urged even family owned firms to adopt more professionalised management systems.

The number of organisations in Cyprus with more than 200 employees does not exceed 300. Furthermore, the vast majority of smaller and larger organisations are family owned and controlled. Cyprus is among the countries that are preparing for entrance in the EU. Therefore, organisational and national competitiveness becomes even more important. According to the Cypriot Planning Bureau (PIO, 2000), the competitiveness of Cypriot products and services is suffering when compared to products of other countries. It is imperative for organisations in Cyprus to realise the fact that in today's environment and with the potential entrance of Cyprus in the EU, competitiveness becomes even more crucial. In turn, a number of challenges and opportunities evolve for Cypriot organisations (Stavrou-Costea, 2002). These include the highly increased numbers of working women, especially working mothers, increased divorce rates and the increased emphasis of Cypriots on their life outside work. In addition, Cyprus has become predominantly a service economy, relying mainly on tourism and financial services for its GNP (Kaparti and Mihail, 1996).

Today some signs suggest that business culture is changing in the region due to three factors: (a) the diffusion of "best practice" from multinationals operating in Greece, Italy and Cyprus, (b) the influence of management consultants and (c) the better trained new generation of managers. Furthermore, change has been achieved due to the increased global competition as well as the growth and development of the national economies. Finally, change has been initiated though greater availability of resources within these countries due to assisting their transition from mainly agricultural economies to industrialised and service oriented ones as well. Within this context, management among Greek, Italian and Cypriot firms realised that in order to compete in the new European market their management practices had to be improved.

The forces of competition are changing the public sector as well. For example, for the last 5–10 years (and for the years to come), many public corporations in Italy and Greece have been privatised and the structure of the economy has changed to a more market oriented one. In Cyprus, a number of governmental and semi-governmental organisations have been preparing for privatisation. The results of all these changes in the Greek and Cypriot economies are spectacular: new sectors are rapidly growing (e.g. telecommunications and information technology), products and services are exported in many foreign markets and in general the business climate in Greece and in Cyprus can be compared to that of most EU countries. Similarly in Italy, the economy shows very good rates of growth and of industrial modernisation. However, in Italy specifically, privatisation does not mean necessarily working according to market forces, since legislation and different regulatory restrictions limit liberalisation.

Despite the many similarities in the business system of Greece, Italy and Cyprus, a number of differences also may be reported. Two main differences have to do with country size and level of industrialisation, which is more advanced in the north of Italy. Yet all three countries are witnessing high rates of economic growth with Italy and Greece having joined the European Monetary Union (EMU) and with Cyprus having reached a stage where it fulfils all necessary economic requirements for becoming EU member.

HUMAN RESOURCE MANAGEMENT

The global and competitive market environments have led to new challenges for both organisations and individuals in them (Iversen, 2000). As a result, the workplace in Europe and other parts of the globe has faced some major changes the last 10 years. These are among many, the internationalisation of the economy, the workforce demography, the density and wider use of information technology and the continuous and rapid scientific and technological change. Also in recent years European countries have faced several common economic developments and structural transformations, like increased international competition and slower growth (Ferner and Hyman, 1992).

The aforementioned changes have had several consequences on the structure of organisations and the style of management, forcing organisations to realise the value of their HRs. They created the need for new structures and management practices which contribute to organisational commitment and flexibility whilst ensuring a long-term supply of employees with necessary competencies and skills (Beer et al., 1984; Iversen, 2000). HR managers must understand all these changes and develop the appropriate strategies in order to help their organisation to succeed.

Given these challenges, the main HRM practices among the three countries explored in this chapter are compared and contrasted diachronically. In addition, the figures reported by organisations in the Greece, Cyprus and Italy are compared to those of organisations in the EU as a whole for the 1999 round of the study. Even though the European scene is not homogenic and neither are organisational HR practices within the EU member states (Ronen and Shenkar, 1985; Sparrow and Hiltrop, 1994), these states do form a collective context, abiding to certain collective regulations, practices and norms (Thurley, 1990; Brewster and Tyson, 1991).

The role of the HRM function

Over the last few years many commentators have argued that the role of the HRM function should be more strategic, for organisations to gain a competitive advantage. It is supported that only through people can companies be able to compete in a global competitive environment (Pickles et al., 1999). Thus the HRM function must have a central role in this effort.

To what extent, however, has HRM been aligned with strategic planning in organisations? Brewster (1995) reports that the integration of HRM with business strategy is rare even among large organisations. Also, Down et al. (1997) claim that many management teams have had difficulty transforming HRM into a strategic function, leaving the HR department in most companies focused on administrative and clerical tasks. Many organisations tend to focus on the administrative aspects of the HRM function, due to difficulties they face in the integration of HRM to organisational goals (Down et al., 1997). As a result, they ignore the long-term perspective of HRs planning and set their sights too low, ending up with HRM strategies that are too functional, too operational, too narrow and too generic (Walker, 1999). In the end, such strategies fail to energise their managers in making necessary changes to achieve

competitiveness through people and often fade away or are replaced before they achieve any real impact.

A strategic approach to HRs demands HRM strategies which need to be integral to organisational strategies; pay attention to multiple levers for strategy implementation, including organisation, development, recruiting and staffing, rewards, performance and employee relations; provide for innovative ways to differentiate organisations in competitive markets; and establish a feasible implementation plan (Walker, 1999).

A way of measuring the role of the HRM function within the strategic context of organisations is by looking at its presence on the Board of Directors in the formulation and implementation of business strategy. Taking therefore the presence of the head of personnel on the Board of Directors as a proxy for the status and role of the HRM function, the evidence over the past 5 years shows that in the south-eastern Mediterranean Region, the role of the HRM function is not as strategic as expected (Table 7.31). The highest percentages are reported in Italy with approximately three-fifths of organisations suggesting representation of HRM on the Board of Directors.[1] In Greece, HRM presence on the Board of Directors includes only one-third of the organisations examined. Similarly in Cyprus, the head of HRs is represented on the board among one-third of organisations during 1999 even though such presence doubled since 1997. For smaller Cypriot organisations with employees ranging between 100 and 199, which is the vast majority of organisations on the island, the HRM presence on the board during 1999 was around 27%, a figure much smaller than the 1999 reported among their larger counterparts.

In addition to the above, the EU average during 1999 for the HR presence on the board is 54.5. Even though the EU average is also not as high as desired, it is easy to observe that, from the three countries, only Italy is above this average due to the different way Italian

---

[1] The Board of Directors is not the most appropriate phrase for the case of Italy. Among Italian organisations, HR is usually involved in what is called a management committee, which is in charge of managing the operational strategy of the company. The Board of Directors deals with the financial strategy and the management of external relations. Hence that board usually consists of external members to the organisation. In the case of family firms the board is made up primarily by family members and their advisors.

Table 7.31   Does the head of the personnel/HR function have a place on the main Board of Directors or equivalent?

	Italy		Greece		Cyprus		EU 1999
	1995	1999	1996	1999	1997	1999	
Yes	59.6	64.6	33.3	54.5	17.9	34.5	54.5
No	40.4	35.4	66.7	55.5	82.1	65.6	55.5

management approaches HR strategic involvement. Greece and Cyprus are quite below the average, but we can see that both countries are on the increase with Cyprus almost doubling its percentage from 1997 to 1999. Overall, EU organisations are larger and possibly have an organisational culture that is more professionalised than their south-eastern European counterparts.

HRM strategy

In a similar fashion to the role of HRM in organisations, the HR experts among south-eastern Mediterranean organisations are not as involved in the development of corporate strategy as desired. The highest involvement is reported consistently by organisations in Italy, either from the outset or through consultation. In Greece and Cyprus, such involvement takes place among half of the organisations from the outset. In addition, a relatively small but noticeable percent of organisations in Cyprus, Italy and Greece seem not to involve the HR function at all in the development of corporate strategy (Table 7.32).

Comparing the above countries to the EU as a whole, more Italian and fewer Greek organisations involve their HR experts in the corporate strategy from the outset than their EU counterparts (59%), while Cypriot organisations do so to a similar extent as their EU counterparts. Fewer Greek, Italian and Cypriot organisations involve their HR experts in the corporate strategy through consultation than their EU counterparts (24%), while more Greek and Cypriot organisations involve their HR experts in the corporate strategy on implementation than their EU counterparts (10%).

The high percent among Italian organisations may be due to the relationship of organisations with trade unions. Even though trade union involvement is very high among all three south-eastern Mediterranean countries examined in this chapter, the power of trade unions seems much stronger in Italy than in Greece or Cyprus. Trade unions in Italy have the power to close down

Table 7.32   Stage at which HR is involved in development of corporate strategy (1999)

HR involvement	Italy	Greece	Cyprus	EU
From the outset	72.0	47.6	58.3	58.5
Through consultation	20.0	16.2	16.7	24.1
On implementation	6.0	28.6	12.5	16.2
Not consulted	2.0	7.6	12.5	7.6

organisations, therefore through trade union involvement, HRM has to be consulted from the very beginning of the process. Nevertheless, this number still seems quite high for Italian organisations. In this case, Italian organisations seem to involve HR more than their EU, Greek and Cypriot counterparts. In a similar fashion, Italian organisations seem to involve more their HR experts in consulting on corporate strategy issues than their EU (8%), Greek (8%) and Cypriot (13%) counterparts. These results suggest that HR managers among Greek and Cypriot organisations, even EU ones, are not as involved in corporate strategy as their Italian counterparts.

Given the analyses in this section, HRM in Cyprus, Greece and even Italy seems to be at the stage where it needs to prove its utility in improving organisational effectiveness and profitability. It has yet to earn a seat at the senior management table as Pickles et al. (1999) described it, by helping to locate and implement the critical levers of change related to HRM and necessary for organisational success. Nevertheless, diachronically, progress seems to be noted in moving HRM towards acquiring a more strategic orientation among south-eastern Mediterranean organisations.

Recruitment and selection

Despite the inadequate involvement of HR on strategic decisions, it is evident that a co-operative relationship exists among HR specialists who have the expertise in selection and recruitment techniques and line managers who know better the skills needed to fill the vacancies in their department. The data presented (see Table 7.33) indicate that a crude dichotomy does not exist. In practice, it seems that a mutual responsibility exists between HR and line managers for selection and recruitment issues among the three countries. Only Cypriot organisations seem to lag a bit behind in this co-operative relationship.

The above results are also comparable to EU practices. More specifically, we see that the percentage among Greek organisations in relation to line management responsibility for 1999 is on the increase and higher than the EU average. That responsibility among Cypriot organisations dropped by 0.09%, but still remaining at the top of the three countries and well above the EU average. Furthermore, Italy's figure has dropped to zero. In relation to the co-operation between line management and HR management, we see that generally figures from all three south-eastern Mediterranean countries are close to the EU average, with Cyprus lagging a bit behind. Finally, in relation to the HR department's responsibility, all three countries have figures above the EU average, with Italy excelling with 24%.

Given the co-operation during recruitment between HR and line management diachronically, it is not surprising that the responsibility of line management for

recruitment and selection throughout the years has basically remained the same among organisations in all three countries. A symbiotic relationship may be imbedded in the south-eastern Mediterranean culture where people like to be involved, exchange ideas and interact highly.

In their co-operation during recruitment, how do line and HR managers fill managerial positions? As Table 7.34 shows, the most common practice is to fill managerial positions of all levels internally by transferring or promoting people who already work for the organisation. This reflects possibly a belief common among south-eastern Mediterranean business culture that the perfect candidate for a position is someone who has worked for many years for the organisation; therefore he/she is reliable and trustworthy for the position. It is also an indicator that many companies still use seniority-based systems. Furthermore, these data may indicate some form of loyalty between organisation and employees.

Despite the common trend among south-eastern Mediterranean countries, Italian organisations seem to fill managerial positions internally the least where Greek organisations seem to do so the most. Furthermore, Cypriot organisations show a decline between 1997 and 1999 in filling managerial positions at all levels internally. A similar yet smaller decline is also evident among Greek organisations, whereas internal promotions to vacant managerial positions have generally increased

Table 7.33 Primary responsibility for major policy decisions on key aspects of HRM (recruitment)

Recruitment	Italy		Greece		Cyprus		EU 1999
	1995	1999	1996	1999	1997	1999	
Line management	12.3	0	7.7	10.5	25.0	24.1	7.0
Line management with HR department	35.1	40.0	30.8	36.8	31.3	17.2	39.9
HR department with line management	33.3	35.7	44.2	36.8	25.0	37.9	42.5
HR department	19.3	24.3	17.3	15.8	18.8	20.7	10.7

Table 7.34 Recruitment methods; filling managerial vacancies internally

	Italy		Greece		Cyprus		EU 1999
	1995	1999	1996	1999	1997	1999	
Senior management	50.8	42.5	71.7	65.9	65.8	43.9	52.0
Middle management	50.8	65.8	84.9	79.5	81.6	53.7	76.3
Junior management	50.8	67.1	67.9	56.1	65.8	56.1	61.7
Total managerial	50.8	58.5	74.5	67.2	71.1	51.2	63.3

in Italy. This divergence may signal a persistence from the part of Italian organisations to traditional ways of filling managerial positions, while there is a slight shift from the part of Greek and Cypriot ones to search for the best candidates for those positions, regardless, whether they are recruited internally or externally. However, organisations reported in this table are the larger ones with over 200 employees. Among smaller Cypriot organisations for example, with employees ranging between 100 and 199, filling senior managerial positions internally still seems to be preferred.

Compared to EU practices reported in 1999, the percentages for Italian and Cypriot organisations in relation to filling senior managerial positions internally are below the EU average (52%) while the figures reported by Greek organisations are much higher. In filling middle and junior managerial positions internally, the EU averages are 76% and 62% respectively. In relation to middle management positions, we see that again the figure for Greek organisations is the only one above the EU average, while those of Italian and Cypriot ones are below. Notice that the percentage for Italian organisations is the only one on the increase since 1995. Finally, in relation to junior management positions, we see that the percentage reported among Italian organisations is the highest among the three countries; it is above the EU average and it is again the only one that increased since 1995.

The increase in middle and junior management positions makes sense for Italian organisations during the 1990s, due in part to downsizing and restructuring as well as the value of the job market (Camuffo and Costa, 1993; Regini and Regalia, 1997). However, less loyalty and greater mobility seems to exist in Italian organisations during the 1990s, especially among senior and junior management that is not well established within an organisation yet. The same case seems to exist among Cypriot organisations for all management levels. In turn, it is more usual that in Italy and in Cyprus, as opposed to the EU average, more middle managers would be recruited from outside an organisation. For companies located in dual/secondary labour markets in Italy and in Cyprus, one may still find greater loyalty due to the lack of options among management. That may be the reason for the percent of promotions among junior managers being above the EU average during 1999 in Italy. The figures for Greek and Cypriot organisations in respect to junior management promotions are below the EU average and they have decreased

since 1995. As far as Greece is concerned, these figures suggest that the sense of loyalty demonstrated for senior and middle management is not shared for junior management as well. The practice among Cypriot organisations seems consistent throughout all managerial positions, suggesting a greater emphasis on abilities and less emphasis on loyalty.

Convergence and divergence seem to exist also among Italian, Greek and Cypriot organisations in relation to the selection methods used in recruitment. While the application forms are among the most common methods used in all countries, the interview panel is most common among Cypriot organisations and the one-to-one interviews are most common in the other two countries. The rest of the selection methods are used at about the same levels in all three countries (Table 7.35).

From Table 7.35 we can highlight some comparisons between the countries reported and the EU as a whole. First, in relation to the use of interview panels, the percent for Cypriot organisations in *Every Appointment* is nearly 71%, while the EU average is only 21%. We get the same picture for Cypriot organisations from the *Every Appointment* practice in the second variable. We can also see that the figure for Italian organisations is 6%, almost 11% below the EU average. Internal panels are not so well known in Italian companies but they are more common among multinationals operating in Italy. In relation to the use of application forms, we see again a big difference between the Cypriot report in *Every Appointment* (81%) and the EU average that is 52%. In relation to psychometric testing, we have Cyprus again distinguishing itself. This time its average (12%) is below the EU average (22%) by almost 11%. As far as assessment centres are concerned, we have again a country percent that is below the EU average (23%) by almost 11%. Only this time it is Italy where only 12% of organisations reported using such centres. In relation to graphology tests, we see that all three-country figures are more or less very close to the EU average. Finally, in relation to the use of references we have Italian organisations (13%) below the EU average, while the other two countries' percents are almost 10% above it.

Given these results, it becomes apparent that organisations in these south-eastern Mediterranean countries rely on traditional methods of selecting their employees. Even though more advanced and reliable methods such as assessment centres and psychometric tests have been

Table 7.35   Selection methods; use of different methods for every or most appointments (%)

Selection method	Italy		Greece		Cyprus	
	1995	1999	1996	1999	1997	1999
Interview panel						
Every appointment	22	10	26	5	49	71
Most appointments	15	4	11	6	24	11
Some appointments	7	4	32	13	24	11
One-to-one interviews						
Every appointment	75	77	86	74	21	11
Most appointments	13	14	8	6	14	7
Some appointments	5	1	4	11	11	11
Application forms						
Every appointment	62	51	90	73	79	81
Most appointments	14	13	5	11	12	11
Some appointments	4	4	3	4	3	8
Psychometric testing						
Every appointment	5	8	13	13	5	4
Most appointments	3	10	27	10	10	7
Some appointments	3	23	27	14	10	11
Assessment centre						
Every appointment	3	6	9	4	0	4
Most appointments	5	3	6	4	5	0
Some appointments	3	12	9	14	15	11
Graphology						
Every appointment	0	1	2	3	9	0
Most appointments	0	1	1	6	9	0
Some appointments	0	4	1	7	5	4
References						
Every appointment	23	13	27	39	33	31
Most appointments	9	6	56	18	23	14
Some appointments	27	16	12	18	17	24

introduced in these countries, their use is not at all widespread although psychometric testing seems to be picking up in Italy. Such reliance on traditional selection methods may reinforce the need for the HR function to take on a more strategic role within organisations in the south-eastern Mediterranean region, linking selection to the other organisational functions and to the organisations long-term success (Terpstra, 1994; Pfeffer, 1995; Flanagan and Deshpande, 1996).

Training and development

In a fashion similar to the responsibility for recruitment, the responsibility for training is shared between HR specialists and line management (Table 7.36). Different from the case of recruitment, the main responsibility for training lies with the HR first and then with line management. Specifically, within the EU during 1999, the

shared responsibility between the HR department with line management averages 44%. In a similar fashion this type of shared responsibility is the highest in all three south-eastern Mediterranean countries. This indication is very encouraging for the role that HRM can play among south-eastern Mediterranean organisations in Europe.

While the joined responsibility between the HR department and line management was decreased in all three countries between 1995 and 1999, an analogous increase is noticeable in the role that line management has in co-operation with the HR department, in turn balancing the symbiosis between line and HRM. Nevertheless, the cases where the primary responsibility lies with the HR department alone seem to be above the EU average among Italian and Cypriot organisations, while those of Greek organisations are very close to the EU average. This average among Italian organisations

Table 7.36   Primary responsibility for major policy decisions on key aspects of HRM (training)

Responsibility for training	Italy		Greece		Cyprus		EU 1999
	1995	1999	1996	1999	1997	1999	
Line management	12.5	2.8	7.8	11.2	15.2	20.0	7.3
Line management with HR department	25.0	29.2	23.5	29.3	24.2	25.7	37.7
HR department with line management	51.8	41.7	54.9	48.3	51.5	40.0	43.6
HR department	10.7	26.4	13.7	11.2	9.1	14.3	11.4

showed a very large increase since 1995 while it showed an analogous decrease in the cases where primary responsibility was with line management alone.

Training is one of the more popular aspects of HRM. Companies usually present themselves as "learning organisations" or as employers that promote continuous training. The necessity of training is more than obvious: a well-trained workforce with updated skills and capabilities can be the basis of an organisation's sustainable competitive advantage (Huselid, 1995; Delery and Doty, 1996; Flanagan and Deshpande, 1996; Pfeffer and Veiga, 1999). But on the other hand some researchers argue that the reality of training is quite different from its rhetoric (Pfeffer, 1995). In reality, they argue, companies view training as a cost to be minimised and not as a long-term investment. What does CRANET research in Italy, Greece and Cyprus have to show about the rhetoric and the reality of training in organisations?

First, let us examine the amount of money spent on training annually. As Table 7.37 reveals, most organisations in Greece, Italy and Cyprus spend consistently more than 1% of annual salaries and wages on training. Furthermore, during 1999, 22% of organisations in Italy and 17% in Cyprus as well as 38% of organisations in Greece spent more than 2% of annual salaries and wages. In conclusion then, it seems that according to the survey, south-eastern Mediterranean organisations, with Greece spending slightly more, pay proper attention to training and their interest is more than rhetoric. A possible explanation for the higher percentage of Greece can be found in the great effort the country has placed on joining the EMU and the effort to take advantage of funds provided through the EU. Such funds were not yet available for Cyprus, however a semi-governmental organisation operates in Cyprus that

Table 7.37   Proportion of annual salaries and wage bill spent on training and development (1999)

(%)	Italy	Greece	Cyprus	EU
<1	26.3	20.3	37.9	12.9
1–1.9	40.4	26.6	31.0	27.3
2–2.9	12.3	16.5	13.8	20.1
3–4.9	10.5	21.5	3.4	19.4

funds training and development projects among Cypriot organisations. This organisation is called the Cyprus Human Resource Development Authority. As far as Italy is concerned, training is pretty much delegated to the HR function. So this is a sign that in Italy training is considerably more a tool rather than a strategic issue.

Compared to EU organisations as a group, the majority (47%) of which spend between 1 and 3% of annual salaries and wages on training, Italy, Greece and Cyprus seem to lag behind a bit. Consistently, the majority of organisations in the three south-eastern Mediterranean countries spend between less than 1 and 2% on training. It seems normal that all southern Mediterranean countries spend less on average than the EU as a whole, suggesting a greater cost than value orientation towards training among these countries.

It is also interesting to look at who benefits the most from training, in other words for which staff category companies allocate more resources for training. Evidence from the survey suggests that in Greece and Cyprus the management and professional categories receive more training than other staff categories. In Italy, no specific pattern is revealed, however an increase in all categories of training is noted between 1995 and 1999. As mentioned earlier, Italian organisations went through major restructuring as well as changes in the trade union system during the 1990s, which could account in part for this increase in training, especially among manual employees. The opposite may be observed for management and professional/technical positions in Greece and Cyprus, where their mean number of training days seems to fall diachronically. During the same time period, the mean numbers of training days for manual staff in Greek and Cypriot organisations have risen (Table 7.38).

The EU mean number of training days for management (5.7) and professional/technical (5.9) staff is higher than that of Italian but lower than that of Greek and Cypriot organisations. Differently from its south-eastern Mediterranean counterparts, management in Italy prefers to learn through "hidden" training such as experience, projects and consulting rather than formal training.

As far as professional/technical staff is concerned, the averages among Greek organisations are similar to those of managerial staff. The average for Italian organisations shows a large increase and is slightly below the EU average. The average among Cypriot organisations showed a small increase and is slightly above the EU average. In relation to clerical staff, the averages in all three countries are above the EU average. Additionally, those of Italian and Greek organisations showed an increase between 1995–1997 and 1999, in contrast to the average of Cypriot organisations. Finally, as far as training for the manual staff is concerned, the averages of all three countries showed an increase during this time period.

In the case of Cyprus, while Cypriot organisations pride for the overall emphasis they place on staff training and development as shown in the present study, serious questions are raised as to the effectiveness of such efforts. Specifically, few organisations have linked their training and development practices to management or career advancement. To illustrate, few organisations in Cyprus have implemented formal career plans, assessment centres, "high flyer" schemes or succession plans.

Furthermore, few organisations have committed to a written policy for management development (Stavrou-Costea, 2002). This is also true for Greece, although latest percentages show an increase over previous years.

Performance measurements and rewards

The link between performance (group or individual) and rewards has been a key theme in the new agenda of HRM. During the 1990s, collectively determined rewards as well as seniority-based systems of remuneration gave way to more variable forms of pay. Usually this happens, as organisations want to develop a flexible and committed workforce. By linking pay to performance, financial flexibility is achieved, while by rewarding the high performers better, commitment is generated, as employees realise that their effort is being rewarded (Pfeffer, 1995; Flanagan and Deshpande, 1996; Luthans, 1998).

The most common way of linking pay to performance is through an appraisal system, which is not only used for remuneration purposes, but also serves as a developmental tool. Indeed, as shown in Table 7.39, appraisal systems are quite popular and widespread among organisations in the south-eastern Mediterranean and are implemented among all staff categories. In Italy and Greece, their use declines for clerical and manual staff categories. In Cyprus, however, this trend is clear only for manual jobs. Even though Table 7.39 only

Table 7.39 Appraisal system for staff categories (1999)

	Italy	Greece	Cyprus	EU
Management	75.0	75.4	75.0	72.2
Professional/ technical	84.3	65.0	80.0	74.3
Clerical	66.7	66.4	80.5	67.3
Manual	43.3	55.2	50.0	56.4

Table 7.38 Mean number of training days received by staff category

Staff category	Italy		Greece		Cyprus		EU 1999
	1995	1999	1996	1999	1997	1999	
Management	3.5	4.2	8.8	7.4	7.8	6.8	5.7
Professional/technical	4.2	5.5	10.2	8.8	6.1	6.3	5.9
Clerical	3.2	5.6	6.4	6.5	5.0	4.3	4.0
Manual	1.9	4.8	2.6	4.0	1.7	3.6	3.5

reports the use of appraisal by larger organisations, such use is not much different for smaller Cypriot organisations with employees ranging between 100 and 199. For this latter group of organisations, the only noticeable difference with the larger Cypriot organisations is found in relation to manual staff. Specifically, the appraisal system for manual employees is used more by the larger (50%) than by the smaller (36%) Cypriot organisations. In such a case, it seems logical that smaller organisations may have fewer resources at their discretion and therefore have not yet professionalised their evaluation practices among manual staff.

During 1999, the use of appraisal systems for management is slightly higher in the above three countries than in the EU as a whole (72%). The opposite is true in relation to the appraisal system for manual staff, where the EU average is 56%. The use of appraisal system for professional/technical staff is higher in Italy and Cyprus but lower in Greece than in the EU (74%). Professional/technical appraisal in Italy takes place mainly through mentoring, while in Cyprus it is more formalised. A typical problem with appraisal in Italy seems related to leniency errors. In the Italian Catholic Church everyone is "good", so Italians are quite sceptical of performance appraisals. In turn, the interpretation of these systems in Italian organisations needs to be done with great caution. Furthermore, the appraisal system in Italy seems quite diffused, therefore its impact is not very high. A similar situation exists in the public sector of Cyprus, where the majority of employees receive very favourable performance evaluations. In Greece, especially for technical staff, formal performance appraisal is not always considered necessary, since results can be seen and provide evidence on overall performance. Also, professional staff in smaller companies enjoys high status, which makes formal appraisal inappropriate. The appraisal system for clerical staff is around 67% in the EU, a figure slightly higher than that

of Greek and Italian organisations but substantially lower than that of Cypriot ones. Overall, it seems that the larger Cypriot organisations have a well-established practice of appraising all staff categories. The question remains as to its effectiveness. As far as the private sector and the majority of semi-governmental organisations are concerned, efforts are continuously made to keep improving employee appraisal, demonstrating effectiveness in the appraisal system. However, appraisal in the Cypriot public sector needs serious improvements in order to become meaningful for employees and management as well as a useful link to the other HRM practices like compensation, training and development of staff.

Like performance appraisals, variable pay is quite widespread among organisations in Greece and Italy, but less common in Cyprus. However, one may observe a decline in overall variable pay at the manual staff category in all three countries. Nevertheless a noticeable proportion of lower staff categories does enjoy merit and performance related pay. Given these results, one could say that organisations in Italy, Greece, and less in Cyprus have included performance related pay among their pay options with Italy leading the way in the management and professional/technical staff category. Merit, like performance appraisals, is quite diffused in Italy. So most will enjoy merit in Italy as well (Table 7.40).

Compared to the EU practices during 1999, only Cypriot organisations use performance-related pay for management less than EU organisations (46%). As far as performance-related pay for professional/technical staff is concerned, Italian organisations use it more than EU organisations as a group (46%), while Greek and Cypriot organisations use it much less. Furthermore, an increase is noted among Italian organisations between 1995 and 1999, while Greek and Cypriot organisations decreased its use during the same period. The increase between 1995 and 1999 seems high compared to EU but it makes sense because merit became more popular

Table 7.40 Merit/performance related pay by staff category

	Italy		Greece		Cyprus		EU 1999
	1995	1999	1996	1999	1997	1999	
Management	42.4	74.0	43.4	59.1	28.9	24.4	45.7
Professional/technical	50.8	69.4	41.5	39.4	26.3	19.5	45.7
Clerical	30.5	45.2	45.3	40.9	21.1	14.6	36.8
Manual	25.4	17.8	43.4	27.3	10.5	9.8	28.1

Table 7.41   Change in trade union influence

Trade union influence	Italy		Greece		Cyprus		EU 1999
	1995	1999	1996	1999	1997	1999	
Increased	20.3	0	9.8	6.6	21.6	12.2	12.6
Same	67.8	68.1	65.9	48.4	64.9	78.0	55.9
Decreased	11.9	26.4	24.4	19.7	13.5	4.9	16.9

the past few years as a tool of managing restructuring during the 1990s.

The use of performance-related pay for clerical staff in the EU in 1999 is 37%, a figure higher only to Cypriot organisations, while the EU percent for manual staff is 28% which is higher than in all three countries. In fact, the use of performance related pay for manual staff in Italy, Greece and Cyprus has declined between 1995 and 1999. In Greece, a difference in the use of this practice can be found between smaller and larger firms in the sample. In smaller firms the prevailing family culture makes it difficult to reward excelling performance and an egalitarian pay system is most suitable. Compared to its southeast Mediterranean counterparts, the orientation of pay in Cyprus has remained stagnant in past practices. Performance related pay remains largely unutilised over the past 10 years. In fact, a decrease in its use at all staff categories may be noted between 1997 and 1999. However, if Cypriot organisations want to boost productivity, in order to compete more effectively within the EU and the global business arena, they will need to pay closer attention in motivating their employees through methods such as merit and performance related pay.

Industrial relations and employee communications

It is commonly accepted that for an organisation to have its employees committed and motivated, good employee relations are necessary (Pfeffer and Veiga, 1999). One way of looking at employee relations is through employee union representation. In Cyprus, union representation is very high. Specifically, 76% of organisations have reported that at least 75% of their employees belong to a trade union. Union participation in Italian and Greek organisations is much lower. In the former, the majority of organisations reported union representation among 11–50% of their employees and in the

latter only about 43% of organisations reported over 50% employee participation in trade unions.

Such representation among Italy, Greece and Cyprus has remained the same for the majority of organisations over the past years. It is surprising to see that in 1995 an increase in trade union influence among Italian organisations was noted, but this increase may be smaller than previous years for which we have no data. The trend is rather on the decrease than on the increase of unionism. Specifically, a decrease in representation is reported among a number of organisations in these countries, the largest of which is reported in Italy and the smallest of which is reported in Cyprus between 1995–1997 and 1999 (Table 7.41). In Italy, a crisis on trade unions started around 1982 and escalated around 1984, after which followed a constant decrease in unionism (Camuffo and Costa, 1993). These figures may signal a larger trend, also reported in the EU where the use of trade unions as a means of negotiating and establishing employee rights has been decreasing. To illustrate, in the EU as a whole, trade union influence during 1999 has decreased by 17% while it increased only by 13%.

The general decrease in trade union influence has been accompanied by an analogous increase in line management responsibility in respect to industrial relations. Even though this increase slowed down over the years, it is still higher than the decrease, which has also slowed down, in line management responsibility for industrial relations (Table 7.42). Nevertheless, the majority of organisations in Greece, Italy and Cyprus have not changed radically their line managers' responsibility concerning industrial relations. Furthermore, the increase noted is lower than the EU average increase reported in 1999 (19%), except in the case of Cypriot organisations.

The above analysis suggests that among Cypriot organisations especially, union representation remains high, in the traditional sense, from both sides of the employment relationship, supposedly protecting the

Table 7.42 Change in responsibility of line management in the last 3 years (industrial relations)

Industrial relations	Italy		Greece		Cyprus		EU 1999
	1995	1999	1996	1999	1997	1999	
Increase	26.4	11.9	25.5	16.1	22.9	22.2	19.0
Same	64.2	80.6	70.2	80.6	77.1	77.8	76.6
Decrease	9.4	7.5	4.3	3.2	0	0	4.4

Table 7.43 Formal communication on business strategy and financial performance during 1999 (%)

	Italy	Greece	Cyprus	EU
Managerial staff briefed				
About strategy	88	93	93	94
About finance	82	84	66	92
Professional staff briefed				
About strategy	62	19	39	54
About finance	47	33	27	72
Clerical staff briefed				
About strategy	21	21	20	33
About finance	16	42	17	57
Manual staff briefed				
About strategy	12	8	2	24
About finance	7	20	7	43

rights and responsibilities of both groups in organisations. However, few managers and employees have questioned the true strategic role of such representation for employee–employer relations as well as the improved participation of everyone towards organisational goals (Stavrou-Costea et al., 2000).

The fact that managers and employees have not explored adequately their employment relationship, not only in Cyprus but also in Greece and Italy, is shown in Table 7.43, indicating the ways in which top management communicates important information to the various categories of employees. As shown in Table 7.43, most communication regarding organisational strategy and financial information takes place consistently at the higher staff categories in all three countries under investigation. Furthermore, the level of communication seems to decrease as the staff category decreases.

Such results reinforce the persistence of management in these countries to traditional practices and methods. While in other parts of the globe issues such as participative management, quality circles and management by objectives are well embedded into organisational cultures (Lei et al., 1999), in Cyprus, Greece and Italy these issues are fundamentally ignored. These results also reinforce partial lack of understanding among management of these organisations in linking strategy to organisational performance at all levels of the organisation. In addition, they do pose a contrast in relation to variable pay and performance appraisals. Specifically, while proper attention regarding performance and variable pay is granted to employees at all levels, the same level of attention is not provided in relation to employee–management communication.

How do Cypriot, Italian and Greek organisations compare to their EU counterparts in 1999 when it comes to communicating their business strategy and financial performance? As far as communication among managerial staff is concerned, the EU average for both strategy and financial performance is comparable to Cypriot, Greek and Italian practices overall, with the exception of Cypriot practices regarding financial performance. Cypriot organisations do not seem as willing as their EU counterparts to communicate financial performance even to their managerial staff. This phenomenon at least among some businesses in the private sector in Cyprus may be due to their family nature, where information about financial performance remains strictly among family members.

At the professional staff category, while the EU average during 1999 regarding the communication of strategy is 54%, that of Greek and Cypriot organisations is much lower. The situation is worse regarding the communication of financial performance, where the EU average is 72% while in Greece, Cyprus and Italy that percentage is much lower. In a similar fashion, the percentages reported among Greek, Cypriot and Italian organisations regarding clerical and manual staff are much lower than those reported among EU organisations as a group. Overall, the EU averages reported, with the exception of those involving managerial staff, are low as well. While the sharing of key organisational information, such as strategy and financial performance, among all staff categories is critical in ensuring an organisation's long-term success (Pfeffer and Veiga, 1999), such sharing merits greater diffusion in Europe, especially its south-eastern Mediterranean edge.

Organisation of work: flexible patterns of work

The issue of flexibility has gained much attention over the last years, mainly for two reasons. First, new management theories emerged (i.e. the "flexible firm" theory) that proposed more effective ways of organising work and achieving better financial performance (Flanagan and Deshpande, 1996; Pfeffer and Veiga, 1999). Second, flexible-working arrangements seemed a good answer to rising unemployment (Luthans, 1998; Pfeffer and Veiga, 1999). Especially in Europe where unemployment is a major problem the last years, flexible-working schemes (e.g. part-time contracts and temporary/casual work arrangements) are becoming quite popular (Tregaskis et al., 1998).

However, the evidence presented in Table 7.44 suggests that in Greece, Italy and Cyprus flexible patterns of work are not very widespread. On the contrary few companies adopt large proportions of part-time or temporary workers. In Italy too, where part-timers are used quite a bit, the number of organisations that use over 10% of part-timers are few. These figures are not much different from EU averages reported in 1999 when it comes to temporary workers (11%). However, within the EU, the use of large proportions of part-timers is much higher (25%) than in Italy, Greece or Cyprus where the highest percentage reported is 11 among Cypriot organisations.

Not only are large proportions of part-time and temporary work arrangements used infrequently in the south-eastern European Mediterranean organisations of the study, but also an increase in their use is also smaller than expected (see Table 7.45). For example, in the EU during 1999 an increase of 47% in part-timers is reported. This figure is much higher than the increase reported in Cyprus (23%) and Greece (22%) and somewhat higher than the increase reported in Italy

Table 7.44 Proportion of workforce on non-standard contracts (%)

	Italy		Greece		Cyprus		EU 1999
	1995	1999	1996	1999	1997	1999	
Part-timers							
No part-timers employed	20	17	49	59	46	69	7
>10% of part-timers	13	6	11	10	8	3	25
Temporary/casual							
No temporary workers	65	64	35	58	37	33	25
>10% of temporary workers	2	3	6	9	9	11	11

Table 7.45 Change in use of flexible working arrangements (%)

	Italy		Greece		Cyprus		EU 1999
	1995	1999	1996	1999	1997	1999	
Part-timers							
Increase	43	37	18	22	28	23	47
Same	30	39	22	27	25	20	38
Decrease	7	8	6	4	0	3	6
Not used	20	16	54	47	47	54	10
Temporary/casual work							
Increase	14	29	16	17	29	43	41
Same	22	13	35	28	43	23	30
Decrease	4	2	10	4	3	9	8
Not used	61	57	39	51	26	26	21

(37%) during the same year. As shown in Table 7.45, the only country in which part-time is used – even in low proportions – by approximately 75–85% of organisations is Italy. In Italy, the use of part-time and temporary workers started between 1995 and 1999. After 1998–1999, there was a dramatic increase in such practices due to the change in the law to allow these non-standard contracts. Nevertheless, in the EU part-timers are used by over 90% of organisations, while in Cyprus fewer than 50% of organisations use such practices. Cypriot organisations may still be sheltered from low unemployment given that Cyprus is still a heavily regulated economy yet to join the EU (Stavrou-Costea and Mikellides, 2001b). However, in Greece and Italy, where unemployment is relatively high, the need for part-time arrangements appears quite strong.

In a similar fashion, temporary/casual workers show a lower use in Italy (43%), Greece (49%) and Cyprus (74%) against the EU as a whole (79%) during the latest report in 1999. Temporary employment in Italian organisations was not known before 1995. Differently from Italy, practices among Cypriot organisations are very close to the EU ones during the last report of 1999 and at similar proportions to the EU average (see Table 7.45 where 11% of organisations use over 10% of temporary workers). Why such a difference in regards to the use of temporary/casual work arrangements between Cypriot organisations and organisations from the other two south-eastern Mediterranean countries? The hiring process in Cyprus is quite cumbersome, especially for the governmental sector, therefore quite often temporary/ casual arrangements are preferred over regular employment. Furthermore, due to the island's heavy reliance on tourism, seasonal employees hired under a temporary basis are very common (Stavrou-Costea, 2002).

Besides part-time and temporary/casual employment, FWAs such as weekend work, shift work, overtime, flexitime, annual hour contracts, home-based work, teleworking, and subcontracting also exist. However, most organisations in the present study continue to utilise, without much adjustment, more traditional practices such as weekend work, shift work, overtime, seasonal and part-time employment. The majority of these organisations do not utilise flexible work schedules like fixed hour contracts, job sharing, home-based work or teleworking.

For example, at least 70% of Cypriot organisations use weekend work, shift work, overtime and subcontracting. However, few organisations use annual hour contracts (24% of smaller and 19% of larger ones), job sharing (20% of smaller and 13% of larger ones) and teleworking (5% of smaller and 9% of larger ones). Finally, fixed term contracts and flexible time are used in Cyprus by approximately half of the organisations in the sample.

In Greece flexibility still has a limited use. However, legislation which was passed recently in Greece will encourage employers to examine new forms of employment, while it is hoped that labour unions who are still against it will realise the advantages it offers in terms of work/family balance, fighting unemployment and improving competitiveness. It is strongly believed that flexibility and especially part-time work will be more acceptable if the general level of wages and salaries rises. As long as Greek employees are the lowest paid in Europe, they will oppose to anything that may imply loss of job security or reduction of pay.

In Italy the law has changed, allowing a wide adoption of temporary work arrangements. As a result, during 2000–2001 more new jobs were covered through temporary than traditional work arrangements, where eventually 80% of cases changed from temporary to permanent positions. A similar situation for temporary workers exists in the public sector in Cyprus, where many temporary or contractual employees eventually become regular employees.

Overall therefore, the role of HRM in Greek, Cypriot and Italian companies is considered more important than it used to. To illustrate, a large proportion of organisations in the sample include the person responsible for HRs in the Board of Directors. However, while the vast majority of HR managers are consulted regarding corporate strategy, their participation in the formulation of such a strategy from the outset is limited, suggesting that there is room for HR participation to be greater in the development of corporate strategy. The participation of line and HR managers in recruitment and selection seems quite stable and symbiotic. In most organisations joint responsibility between HR and line managers is the norm.

Even though many managers are sought from outside the organisation, especially in Italy and Cyprus, quite a common source of managerial recruitment in all three countries is the company itself, as firms often prefer to cover managerial positions with people who are already familiar with their business processes, policies and corporate culture. Beyond the preference for the internal labour market, the most commonly used selection methods in Italy and Greece include personal interviews and written applications forms followed by references. In Cyprus, the most commonly used selection methods are panel interviews, application forms and references. Graphology is rarely used in the South-Eastern Mediterranean, while the use of psychometric tests and assessment centres show some signs of increase.

The responsibility for training and development is in the hands of the HR department in collaboration with line managers. Training expenses exceed 2% of the annual soberest wage bill in almost one-fourth of firms in Italy and Cyprus and half of firms in Greece.

The use of formal systems of employee performance appraisal is widespread among all employee categories but with an emphasis on higher-ranking employees. The same holds true for performance-related pay, which is more widespread among managerial and professional/technical staff categories.

Employee relations have, at least for most firms, overcome the rivalry stage to reach that of peaceful coexistence. The importance of labour unions seems to be declining slowly but steadily. Flexible working patterns are still of limited use in the three countries. Some of them like job sharing, annual contracts and tele-working are the least common. Temporary, casual and part-time working are relatively more frequently used and they are gradually increasing. These two working patterns are expected to increase further, being considered as a means to raise the competitiveness of companies and to fight unemployment.

HRM IN ACTION

CASE STUDY 1: "LET'S GO TO PARADISE PLC." IN CYPRUS

The firm "Let's Go To Paradise Plc." is based in Nicosia and employs a total of 215 employees. It is specialised in organising traveller's excursions of all kinds in Cyprus and all around the world. The company is a public one and has entered the Cyprus Stock Exchange Market towards the end of the year 2000. The company's owner and major shareholder is also the Chief Executive Officer. Furthermore, two members of his family are also employed in the company. Particularly, his elder son is the Director of the Marketing Department and his younger son is the Director of the Accounting Department. The CEO's daughter decided to study interior design and to operate her own office. Despite that, she is part of the company's payroll and receives a salary from the company.

As it is well known, the Cypriot economy is based to a great extent upon tourist services. Companies in Cyprus that are employing more than 200 employees are less than 300 in total. The firm, "Let's Go To Paradise" is a member of an employers' union. Similarly, its employees are members of employee unions, like the majority of employees in Cyprus. Due to this all-embracing participation in unions, employees have fortified a number of fundamental rights and benefits, which are agreed each time through collective agreements. But in 2001, due to the facts that took place in the US on the 11th of September, the tourist sector suffered from a severe decrease. That was the main reason for the problems in the relations between employees and employers to sharpen.

The company operates an HR department, which occupies five employees. Although the head of the department has an MBA (Masters in Business Administration), he is not specialised in aspects concerning HRM. Additionally, his experience in such matters is very little, because by the time he finished his studies he was hired by "Let's Go To Paradise Plc." as a Sales Manager supervised by the Director of the Marketing Department. He was promoted to the HRM department because he had performed with excellence in his last working position.

Planning and major decisions concerning HRM issues up till now have been handled by the CEO who then informs the HRM director. In addition the HRM department functions are still performed in a traditional way and the hierarchical structure is still followed. For instance, communication of the decisions is done typically in a hierarchical top-down manner and in many cases it stops at the managerial level. Also, hiring new personnel is done by filling application forms and holding interviews. Promotions are granted on the basis of the years of service in the company, given the fact that the performance of the employee is satisfactory. In exceptional cases – like the one with the HRM director – promotions are granted based on the opinion of the CEO without the use of any formal procedures. Management thinks that such procedures are bureaucratic and time-consuming. Training and development of the employees is considered by the management as satisfactory due to the fact that all categories of employees have the opportunity to attend training seminars often held in Cyprus, when such seminars fall to the attention of the management. Such seminars are often funded by a semi-governmental organisation in Cyprus called "The Cyprus Human Resource Management Authority". The main purpose of this organisation is to develop and promote HRM related activities among Cypriot organisations. Finally, even though wages within the company are market driven (comparable to the market average), they do not include performance-based rewards.

The building that shelters the company is being renovated at the moment because it is very old. Some walls have been tore down and some others have been opened. Due to the renovation, the place is full of naked cables, boxes and dust. The outer walls of the building are being rebuilt and repainted. Even though required by law, the constructions manager does not require his workers to wear helmets when at work because it is too hot. Instead, he lets them wear a hat to protect themselves from the sun.

The new director of HRM, now that he has become acclimatised to his new role, was sitting in his new office and was thinking ways of improving his department's functions. Suddenly he remembered his friends who studied HRM. For that reason without wasting any time he gives a call to his friends and asks for their help. So he asks the following:

1. Point out to him the main HRM issues that need to be changed at "Let's Go to Paradise". Justify your answer.
2. How do these HR practices compare to overall HR trends in Cyprus? How different are practices at "Let's Go to Paradise" from the EU averages reported? How about those of Greece and Italy?
3. Recommend to him an action plan and introduce changes that concern HRM issues. Justify your answer.

CASE STUDY 2: TITAN, GREECE

Introduction

"TITAN Cement S.A." is a century old company and one of the 10 largest manufacturing firms in Greece. With stability and human-centred tradition and values, TITAN can be characterised as a creative, flexible and progressive firm, focused on technological innovation, with a well-established reputation in the Greek and International business context.

The company's strategic focus on the human factor has contributed to a great extent to its continuous growth and success. This can be seen in the following brief presentation of the history and business culture of the company, followed by its strategy in HRM matters.

Company history

1902: The first TITAN factory was established in Elefsina. It is the first cement factory in Greece, the Balkans and the east Mediterranean basin.
1912: The company's stock enters the Athens Stock Exchange.
1948: First exports abroad
1960: Extension of exports to the Middle East
1962: Second TITAN factory established in Salonica
1966: Third factory in Drepano of Peloponese
1976: Fourth factory in Kamari, outside Athens
1988: Stations for cement distribution are established in the US and Europe
1992: Acquisition of cement factory in Roanoke, USA
1998: Acquisition of 48.6% of the shares of the Plevenski factory in Bulgaria. Acquisition of the majority of shares of the factory USJE in FYROM, near Skopie.
1999: Acquisition of the majority of shares of the Egyptian Beni Suef Cement Company
2000: Acquisition of the American company TARMAC. Major restructuring of the group
2001: Acquisition of the cement production factory in Kosjeric of Serbia
2002: Acquisition of cement production factory in Egypt

Today, TITAN produces the whole spectrum of building materials and deals with marine and land transfer. Its activities extend beyond the Greek territory, in the USA, the south-eastern Europe, the Middle East and several countries of the EU.

The company runs the following operations, across Greece:

- 4 cement producing factories
- 4 cement distribution centres
- 21 units of finished concrete
- 12 pits and mines
- 5 marine companies and 300 ships for the transportation of cement, concrete and inactive materials
- "Intermix", a production unit of finished plaster and other construction material
- "Infoplan", an IT company
- "IONIA", a company producing and trading chinaware

On a worldwide basis, TITAN is ranked among the 300 best "small companies" and it is one of the 100 most rapidly developing companies in the world, according to the results of a survey by Forbes Global Business and Finance (November 1998).

Social responsibility

In the beginning of the 1970s, TITAN has launched a programme for the protection and restoration of the environment in the regions where it operates. Today more than 800,000 trees have been planted and exhausted pits, working spaces and the territories around them were transformed into green zones.

As a result, TITAN has been awarded the ISO 14001 certificate for its System of Environmental Management, which is not common for Greek business practice.

Furthermore, in close collaboration with the local government, TITAN, with sensibility and responsibility gets actively involved into the life and problems of the local communities, in which its production units operate.

The company responds willingly, with material, technical or consulting assistance, to requests for assistance in various issues such as tree planting, road construction, water supply, irrigation, church, school or hospital building projects.

Business and HRM strategy

TITAN's strategy aims at the increase and improvement of its economic performance and at the strengthening of its position in the international cement industry sector. The company's business strategy is based on the following four principles:

- International expansion and transformation of the company into a strong global player.
- Full vertical integration.
- Improvement of cost efficiency/productivity.
- Excellence in HRM.

In order to cope with its geographic dispersion and its operational diversification, restructuring of the group according to the standards of a multinational company was decided. Therefore, TITAN was restructured using the criteria of geographical areas (Africa, America, Balkans and South East Europe) and of diversified products (cement, concrete and finished plasters).

An expert Staff Centre, coordinating the individual sectors and branches was established which proved of major importance in assisting the new organisational structure. The eight Central Divisions comprising the Expert Staff Centre include the new HRM Division, under the direction of Mr Elias Moschonas.

The HR division deals with the coordination of all activities concerning the HRs, which amount to 5000 employees (2500 of whom outside Greece). It should be stressed that the HR division does not interfere with the job of other departments of the group, but rather collaborates with them for attaining excellence in HRM. For the realisation of its work, the division is operationally linked to all HR departments, operating in various factories and units of the group.

It was evident for the new HR director that, having grown to such an extent, the company needed to focus on HRM issues, which should receive primary attention. Although changes in HR policies are usually viewed with scepticism by the majority of employees, an encouraging element in TITAN was the fact that being a growing and successful company, employees, even older ones, had faith in the company's management and were willing to accept new views and ideas.

Goals of the HRM division

The HRM division has taken up the responsibility for tracing the strategies and formulating policies which aim at the development of the HRs, in conjunction with the priorities and the goals of the group. In general, the idea that is being promoted is the creation within the company of a seedbed for future managers, either from current employees of the company or from outsiders, who possess satisfying educational background and personality traits. Those managers will cover the increasing needs of the business operations in Greece and abroad and will ensure the succession in key positions of the group in the future.

Therefore, the company is targeted to the recruitment, development and retention of the best managers in the market, for the group's present and future needs.

In the spirit of this philosophy, the HRM division aims at covering the following three pillars of action:

1. To promote TITAN as a preferable employer, within a very competitive environment.
2. To constantly develop the company's people and to provide them with opportunities for knowledge and development within the group.
3. To connect performance with rewards, so that further improvement of productivity is achieved.

Regarding the first pillar, it aims at developing systems of recruitment and selection, mostly for junior managers, who show a potential for developing into top managers. Major recruitment means include personal contact, published advertisement, contact with Higher Education Institutions, participation in career forums and use of the Internet. The company believes that promoting the company's image, can be achieved through communication of its successful business activities, in conjunction with its business values, thus making the company very attractive for young, highly capable managers.

The second pillar, the development of the company's staff, includes reliable processes of induction and assessment, as well as sophisticated programmes of career development and succession planning. For this, it is necessary to provide thorough theoretical and practical training to all employees. One way of achieving that is through job rotation of employees in diverse positions and tasks, from which they can acquire multiple and useful knowledge.

Regarding employee appraisal, at the end of each year employees are appraised by their direct supervisor and his next level superior, while particular care is taken so that the appraisal outcomes and the points requiring improvement are communicated to the employees.

Concerning career development and succession planning, the group mostly follows the policy of internal development and promotion from within, by covering top, critical positions with existing managers, at a 80/20 rate, rather than recruiting from the outside.

Finally, the third pillar of HRM aims at the planning of short-term and long-term incentives which encourage good working relations and ensure a low labour turnover. These incentives include the provision of performance-related rewards, like bonuses, profit sharing and stock options. About the latter, in particular, TITAN has been the first company that has implemented it in Greece, with the assistance of the Greek Ministry of Development. An additional, important incentive is company-sponsored retirement, life and health insurance plans, including hospitalisation.

It should be added that the workers and technical staff of TITAN (approximately 900 people), participate in profit sharing since 1998, according to a financial ratio that fluctuates each year with the economic results of the company. This new practice agrees with the culture of trust and the good employee relations that are promoted within TITAN. It aims at the constant improvement of competitiveness on the one hand and the employee satisfaction on the other, thus resulting in a "win-win" situation for both the company and its employees. In order to achieve that, it is important to follow constantly the developments in the market and to be flexible regarding adjustment of rewards to the levels prevailing in the labour market.

In order to accomplish the above-mentioned aims, it is necessary to fully understand the attitudes and needs of employees. For this purpose, an attitude survey is being executed every 2 years, in order to locate any sources of employee dissatisfaction and to find ways to remove them. In this way, it is attempted to reinforce the ties between employees and the company, through mutual trust and respect.

Joining the HR division in TITAN

In order for a junior manager to be integrated to the HRM division, he/she should have the following characteristics:

- *Knowledge of business environment*. This comprises the following two attributes:
  - Industry knowledge: In order to add value to the HRM division, it is necessary to know the business environment to understand its strategy and direction, as well as the risks, the challenges and the opportunities it faces.
  - Business culture–vision–values: It is important to comprehend the business culture, values and strategic vision of the company and be able to get it across to the rest of the employees.
- *Knowledge of the labour market*. One of the tasks of a person working in HR, is to possess current and reliable information about developments and changes in the labour market where the company operates. Thus, he/she will be able to fill vacancies of the company timely and effectively.
- *Attitude traits*:
  - Concern for the human factor/empathy. The person working in HR division should always get in the position of each employee and understand their problems, in order to provide the best solution, while convincing them of the honest concern for their problems.
  - Perception of the "wider image". A common mistake that managers do is that they focus on their immediate activity issues and ignore the rest of functions that other departments have taken up. In this way, they create "functional silos" that seriously endanger the overall functionality of the company. Therefore, managers in HR should realise that showing interest in the overall function of the company and keeping good relations with other departments is one of their main obligations.
  - Self-motivation and patience. As the results at which the HR department aims usually appear in the long-run period, HRM is a far-sighted task with many difficulties and without direct rewards. This is because the human factor is most unpredictable and difficult to manage. Therefore, managers in HR should be able to maintain their patience and aspirations.
  - Staff vs. line function. Finally, managers in HR should realise that HRM is a supportive function, which can only rely on persuasion, since it does not have the line authority to change the way things are done. In other words, it should be a factor of balance among top management, employees, society and the labour market.

Conclusion

To sum up, TITAN is a successful company, characterised by the willingness to innovate, to improve and engage in new activities. Its basic source of inspiration and strength lies in its personnel. That is the reason why the human factor is a critical asset for the company. In its attempt to recruit, develop and retain employees of high potential, the company has created in 2000 a new HR division, which handles personnel issues at group level, through policy suggestion and the formation of a business culture aiming at the achievement of the Group's business goals. So far, results are very satisfactory. The company is celebrating its first centenary and its financial performance and levels of employee satisfaction show that its business restructuring, with its focus on HRM issues has proven beneficial for the company's future. Figure 7.7 shows the main target and pillars of HRM in TITAN:

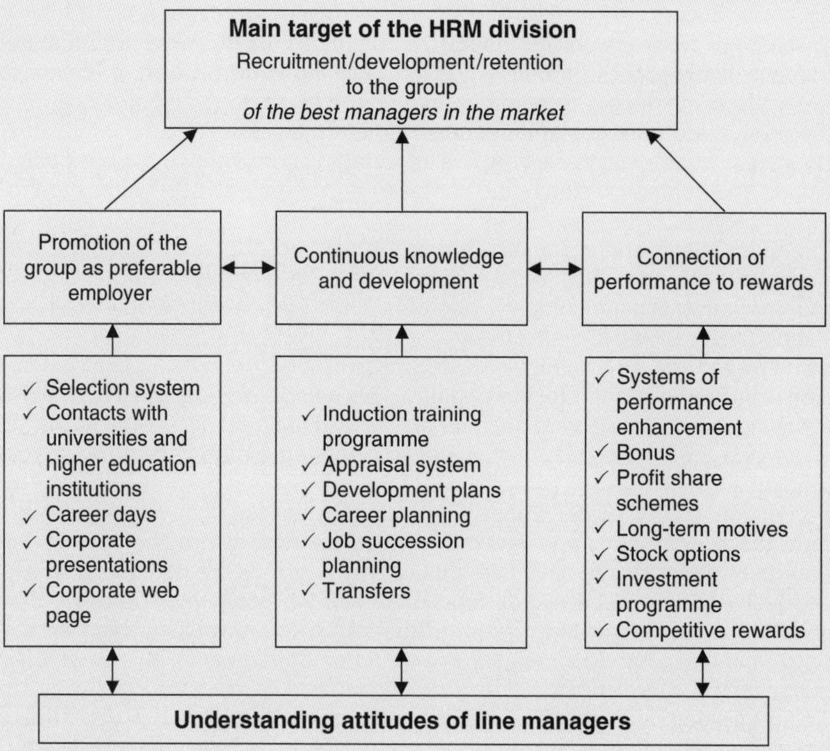

Figure 7.7   Pillars of HRM in TITAN

Case questions

1. Was the creation of the expert staff centre necessary for the restructuring of TITAN? Give your comments.
2. Write the mission statement for the HRM division of the TITAN company.
3. Make a brief job description for (a) a junior HR manager, working in the TITAN's HR division and (b) a junior assistant in the personnel office of a TITAN's Cement factory outside Athens.
4. As a young graduate, which would you consider the main advantages for working in a company like TITAN?

CONCLUSIONS

While HRM practices in Cyprus, Italy and Greece show many common characteristics, they also have a number of differences. These differences however are what make each of these countries unique in their use of HRM practices.

From the inter-country and intra-country comparison of CRANET data on Greece, Cyprus and Italy one may conclude that among firms in the sample, HRM is moving slowly away from its administrative to a more strategically oriented role. This includes the improved role of professionals in the field, the link of HR practices to the firm's strategy, the higher involvement of HR practitioners in strategic decisions, the higher involvement and collaboration with line managers. Furthermore, the slow though steady move towards more flexibility, more use of training, more performance linked rewards, show the tendency to adapt to international trends in the field. These findings from organisations in the south-eastern Mediterranean region of Europe are in accordance with practices of the northern European countries toward extensive training and development, increased flexibility and line management involvement (Brewster, 1999).

Developments in Greece are largely due to external environmental factors that dictate the move towards more competitive and goal oriented policies and practices in HRM. External competition, participation in the EMU and the higher educational level of professional management point to the need within Greek organisations to focus on the strategic alignment between HR strategy and business strategy as well as to adopt more value adding methods and techniques by HRM (Papalexandris, 2001).

Developments in Italy are also due to the same reasons as in Greece but also to internal competition since the highly developed Italian north provides a benchmark for other companies around Italy. Italy is defined as a dual economy, with two geographical regions, north and south. For example, Lombardia is the second richest region in the EU in terms of per capita income. In fact, the richest regions in Italy created a Federation to promote their business in the world. In southern Italy, however, 35% of unemployment exists among younger people. In addition dualism exists between multinational companies operating in Italy (especially in Rome and Milan) and national Italian companies (situated mostly in local countries). In turn, HR practices between the two groups of companies differ substantially. A third dichotomy (which also exists in Cyprus) is between lifetime employment, which is by law in Italy for companies over 15 employees (after a 6-month trial period) and outsourcing. Due to the high commitment required by employers towards their regular employees, many companies prefer small external suppliers rather than hiring internally.

Developments in Cyprus are to a very large extent due to the country's preparation for joining the EU in 2004 and its high adaptability to guidelines provided by the EU (Stavrou-Costea and Mikellides, 2001a). Due to the preparations to join the EU, Cyprus is called to face its political history as well as its current political situation, where over 37% of its territory has been under Turkish occupation since 1974. This political problem has had a serious impact over the years not only on Cypriot culture, but also on Cypriot business and economy. Furthermore, over the past 20 years, the Republic of Cyprus has become a good place for multinationals and offshore companies operating in the region to flourish. In turn, these firms operate quite differently from local organisations, raising the professionalism of HRM practices. The results reported show encouraging signs for organisations in Cyprus. Nevertheless, HR managers among Cypriot organisations need to bring their practices more in line with corporate strategy. They need to incorporate a long-term orientation, enhancing management's ability to bring the necessary changes in achieving organisational competitiveness. HR practices need time to be developed and to be employed so that they will have the desired results. The main focus of strategic HRM is on integrated combinations of HRM practices. In such a case, Cypriot HR managers need to be innovative. Such innovations may be derived from any of the HRM practices and may provide the opportunity for organisational competitiveness in attracting and maintaining the most suitable and effective human capital. Unless HRM takes on a leading role among Cypriot organisations, their chances for success in a European or a global context may be seriously impeded (Stavrou-Costea, 2002).

The picture presented so far, although quite encouraging, largely reflects the situation among larger, well-managed, modern and innovative firms in the three countries. The HR practices of smaller firms (less than 200 employees) that constitute over 90% of firms in the three countries are not systematically organised and they are more likely to vary depending on the owner-manager's will (Stavrou-Costea et al., 2000). However, very promising developments arise for these firms to acquire greater HR professionalism from the increased training opportunities available to them through training centres as well as consultants who are either former HR executives of larger companies, academics in HRM, or associates of international HR.

Having reached the end of this chapter we can conclude that despite differences among Greece, Italy and Cyprus as well as between these countries and countries in the greater European Union group, HR in the three countries follows the trends towards a more profession-alised, strategic and systematically organized HRM in line with the region's economic conditions and environ-mental constraints.

TEACHING QUESTIONS

1. What courses of action would you recommend to organisations in Cyprus, Greece and Italy in rela-tion to temporary work arrangements as reported in this chapter?
2. Why is HR less involved in the development of corporate strategy among organisations in Greece and Cyprus than in Italy?
3. Why has the increase in line management's respon-sibility in respect to pay and benefits as well as workforce expansion/reduction fallen between 1995–1997 and 1999 in all three countries?
4. Why do you believe exists a symbiotic relationship between HR and line management when it comes to major policy decisions on key aspects of HR among all three countries?
5. Why do Greek organisations compared to Cypriot, Italian and EU ones during 1999, consistently use a greater number of days on training across staff categories?
6. Why do Cypriot organisations compared to Italian and Greek ones during 1999, utilise the smallest proportion of annual salaries and wage bill spent on training and development? What could the Cyprus Human Resource Development Authority possibly have to do with it?
7. Why is the appraisal system for clerical staff among Cypriot organisations so well enforced in compari-son with Italian, Greek and EU ones?
8. Why is performance-related pay among managerial and professional/technical staff not widespread among Cypriot organisations, compared to Italian and Greek ones?
9. How could Greek, Italian and Cypriot organisa-tions improve their communication practices in relation to organisational strategy and financial performance?
10. Overall, which are the HR practices in Cyprus, Greece and Italy that, compared to the EU, could be substantially improved?

ACKNOWLEDGEMENTS

Our appreciation to the Cyprus HRM Association, the Cyprus Productivity Centre, especially Maria Mikellides, and the University of Cyprus for their col-laboration, assistance and support. Our appreciation as well to our colleague Francesco Paoletti at Università degli Studi di Milano-Bicocca for his valuable insight regarding the situation in Italy.

REFERENCES AND SOURCES

References

Beer, M., Spector, B., Laurence, P., Mills, D. and Walton, R.E. (1984) *Managing Human Assets.* New York: Free Press.

Brewster, C. (1995) Towards a "European" model of human resource management. *Journal of International Business Studies*, 26(1): 1–22.

Brewster, C. (1999) Strategic human resource management: the value of different paradigms. *Management International Review*, 45.

Brewster, C. and Tyson, S. (1991) *International Comparisons in Human Resource Management.* London: Pitman.

Camuffo, A. and Costa, G. (1993) Strategic human resource management – Italian style. *Sloan Management Review*, 34(2): 59–68.

Corbetta, G. (1995) Patterns of development of family busi-nesses in Italy. *Family Business Review*, viii(4): 255–266.

Labour Statistics 1998 (2000) Statistical Service of the Republic of Cyprus, Series II, Report No. 17.

Delery, J.E. and Doty, D.H. (1996) Modes of theorizing in strategic human resource management: tests of universal-istic, contingency, and configurational performance predic-tions. *Academy of Management Journal*, 39: 802–835.

Down, J.W., Mardis, W., Connolly, T.R. and Johnson, S. (1997) A strategic model. *HR Focus*, 74(6): 22–24.

Ferner, A. and Hyman, R. (1992) IR on the continent: a model of co-operation? *Personnel Management*, 24(8): 32–35.

Flanagan, D.J. and Deshpande, S.P. (1996) Top management's perceptions of changes in HRM practices after union elections in small firms: implications for building competi-tive advantage. *Journal of Small Business Management*, 34: 23–35.

Gentile, E. (1993) Impending modernity: fascism and the ambivalent image of the United States. *Journal of Con-temporary History*, 28: 7–30.

ICAP (1999) Greece in Figures, Greek Financial Directory.

Huselid, M.A. (1995) The impact of human resource management practices on turnover, productivity, and corporate financial performance. *Academy of Management Journal*, 38: 635–672.

Iversen, O.I. (2000) Managing people towards a multicultural workforce. An investigation into the importance of managerial competencies across national boarders in Europe – differences and similarities. Presented at the *8th World Congress on Human Resource Management*.

Leontidou, L. (1996) Alternatives to modernism in (southern) urban theory: exploring in-between spaces. *International Journal of Urban and Regional Research*, 20: 178–196.

Luthans, K. (1998) Using HRM to compete in the 21st century. *Management Quarterly*, 38: 17–23.

Kaparti, D. and Mihail, A. (1996) *The Effect of Cultural Factors on the Behaviour of the Cypriot Consumer*. Senior Thesis, University of Cyprus, Nicosia, Cyprus.

Lei, D., Slocum, J.W. and Pitts, R.A. (1999) Designing organisations for competitive advantage: the power of unlearning and learning. *Organisational Dynamics*, Winter: 24–29.

Papalexandris, N. (1991) A comparative study of human resource management in selected Greek and foreign-owned subsidiaries in Greece. In: Brewster, C. and Tyson, S. (eds.), *International Comparisons in HRM*. Great Britain: Pitman Publishing, pp. 145–158.

Papalexandris, N. (1993) Human resource management in Greece. In: Brewster, C. and Hegewisch, A. (eds.), *European Developments in HRM*. Great Britain: Kogan Page, pp. 163–180.

Papalexandris, N. (1997) Human resource management in Greece: a European comparison, paper presented in *Conference European HRM: Trends and Challenges*, Athens, October.

Papalexandris, N. and Chalikias, J. (2001) Changing picture of HRM functions among Greek firms in the 90's: intercountry and intracountry comparisons. Paper presented at *Global Human Resource Management Conference*.

Pfeffer, J. (1995) Producing sustainable competitive advantage through the effective management of people. *The Academy of Management Executive*, 9: 55–70.

Pfeffer, J. and Veiga, J.F. (1999) Putting people first for organisational success. *The Academy of Management Executive*, 13: 37.

Pickles, L.J., Bookbinder, S.M. and Watts, C.H. (1999) Building the HR value chain. *Employment Relations Today*, 25: 21–23.

Regini, M. and Regalia, I. (1997) Employers, unions and the state: the resurgence of concertation in Italy? *West European Politics*, 20(1): 210–229.

Ronen, S. and Shenkar, O. (1985) Clustering countries on attitudinal dimensions: a review and synthesis. *Academy of Management Review*, 10(3): 435–455.

Sparrow, P.R. and Hiltrop, J.M. (1997) Redefining the field of European human resource management: a battle between national mindsets and forces of business transition? *Human Resource Management*, 36(2): 201–219.

Stavrou-Costea, E. (2002) The role of human resource management in today's organisations: the case of Cyprus in comparison with the European union. *Journal of European Industrial Training*, 25(6–7): 261–269.

Stavrou-Costea, E., Pattouras, P. and Mikellidou, M. (2000) The role of human resource management in Cyprus: challenges and opportunities for the new millennium. In: *Human Resource Management – An Important Factor for European Integration*. Varna, Bulgaria: CRANET.

Stavrou-Costea, E. and Mikellides, M. (2001a) Human resource management as a source of organisational competitive advantage in the private and public sector: model development and a case empirical investigation. In: *Human Resources Global Conference*. Barcelona, Spain: ESADE.

Stavrou-Costea, E. and Mikellides, M. (2001b) The role of flexible work arrangements towards organisational competitiveness: the case of Cyprus in comparison with the EU. In: *CRANET Conference 2001: New Dimensions in Human Resource Management*. Nicosia, Cyprus: CRANET.

Terpstra, D.E. (1994) HRM: a key to competitiveness. *Management Decision*, 32: 10–15.

Thurley, K. (1990) Towards a European approach to personnel management. *Personnel Management*, 22(9): 54–58.

Tregaskis, O., Brewster, C. and Hegewisch, A. (1998) Flexible working in Europe: the evidence and the implications. *The European Journal of Work and Organisational Psychology*, 7: 61–78.

Verschuren, M.W.M. et al. (1995) Serum total cholesterol and long-term coronary heart disease mortality in different cultures: twenty-five-year follow-up of the seven country study. *The Journal of the American Medical Association*, 274: 131–137.

Walker, J.W. (1999) What makes a great human resource strategy? *Human Resource Planning*, 22(1): 11–14.

Sources for Italy Institutional Background

(1) Eurostat, Statistical Office of the European Communities (eds.) (2002) Eurostat Yearbook 2002. The statistical guide to Europe. Data 1990–2000. Brussels: European Communities.

Sources for Greek Institutional Background

(1) ICAP (2002) Greece in figures. Athens: ICAP.

(2) Eurostat, Statistical Office of the European Communities (eds.) (2002) Eurostat Yearbook 2002, The statistical guide to Europe. Data 1990–2000. Series: "Panorama of the EU". Brussels: European Communities.

Sources for Cyprus Institutional Background

(1) Statistical Abstract (2001) Statistical Service of the Republic of Cyprus.

(2) International Monetary Fund, Public Information Notice (PIN) No. 00/67, August 24, 2000.

(3 http://kypros.org/PIO/politics/parties/index.htm (12/12/2001).

(4) Labour Statistics (2001) Statistical Service of the Republic of Cyprus.

(5) Cyprus Labour Force Survey (2001) Statistical Service of the Republic of Cyprus.

8

Denmark and Norway: Siblings or Cousins?

Anna Patricia Rogaczewska, Henrik Holt Larsen, Odd Nordhaug,
Erik Døving and Martin Gjelsvik

INSTITUTIONAL BACKGROUND

DENMARK

Area	43,093 km^2 (excluding Greenland and The Faeroe Islands)
Population	5,313,577 inhabitants
Density	123 inhabitants per km^2
Capital and population	Copenhagen (1,069,813)
Other major	Aarhus (216,564)
cities and population	Odense (144,940)
	Aalborg (119,431)
	Esbjerg (73,350)
Official language	Danish
Religion	90% Protestant-Lutheran 10% Others (20+ recognised religious denominations)

Topography and climate

Denmark, situated in Northern Europe, is the oldest monarchy in Europe. Denmark is composed of the peninsula of Jutland, which borders on Germany in the south, and many smaller islands, the two largest being Zealand and Funen. The Kingdom of Denmark also includes the partly independent overseas territories of Greenland (area 2,166,086 km^2 and population 56,076) and the Faeroe Islands (area 1399 km^2 and population 44,801). Both these countries have home rule, although

each elects two representatives to the Danish parliament and they rely heavily on block grants from Denmark for their economic existence.

Denmark proper is small. Although being one of the smallest countries in Europe, Denmark has a total of 7400 km of coastline because of its many islands, 400+ of which 90 are inhabited. Most of the countryside is made up of rolling cultivated farmland, with low hills, lakes and woodlands. Denmark is a lowland, the highest point being no more than 173 m (Yding Skovhøj). Most of the land is a raised sea bottom moulded by the great Ice Ages into a mild, undulating landscape which is among the most intensively cultivated areas in Europe.

Figure 8.1 Borsen – The Old Stock Exchange in the centre of Copenhagen

The climate is influenced by the Gulf Stream from the west. It is temperate with the mean temperature ranging from 0°C in winter to 17°C in summer. In normal summers, the temperature rises occasionally to 30°C, and winter temperatures below −20°C are rare. The annual rainfall averages about 700 mm.

Principal characteristics

Seen in relation to the European Union (EU) the following shows some of the statistic characteristics of Denmark (Figure 8.2).

Culture

Denmark is culturally strongly influenced by its neighbouring countries, the United Kingdom, Germany and the other Nordic countries. Since the time of the Vikings the Danish Kingdom has proved to be strong and self-confident, interacting vigorously with the rest of the world. Due to the history and size of the country the Danes attach a huge significance to their national identity but without closed to the outside. Denmark has long and proud traditions in the area of music, theatre and film. The Nordisk Film Kompagni, founded in 1906, is the oldest film company in the world still in operation, and directors such as Bille August and Lars von Trier have distinguished themselves and Danish films internationally. Denmark offers a generous level of public subsidies

for culture and arts, from the professional companies down to the amateurs and children.

Danes have an informal approach to life at personal as well as business level. Denmark is regarded as a welfare state, with one of Europe's highest rates of spending on health care and education. A lot of these fundamentals in the Danish culture and society are in some way related to two significant issues in the latter Danish history. First the co-operative movement, starting in Jutland in 1870–1880 when a group of farmers jointly formed a co-operative dairy, a successful model which was broadly adapted and the basis of Denmark's important export-oriented agricultural sector. Secondly is the tradition of adult education, started by the priest and author N.F.S. Grundtvig. His ideas created special high schools where adults could attend courses for a period of 3–6 months, focusing on cultural or specific issues. The ideas of Grundtvig has since spread to many other countries. Danes often perceive Grundtvig to be the father of modern Denmark in terms of morale, values and democratic perception.

People

The Danish population is very homogeneous when compared with many other European countries. The number of foreign nationals has risen rapidly in recent years, however, because of a liberal attitude towards granting political asylum. Denmark also gives one of

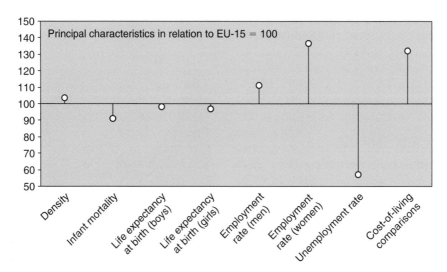

Figure 8.2   Danish characteristics in relation to the EU-15. All data from (1); except density, infant mortality, life expectancy at birth for boys and girls data from (2)

Age (years)	Denmark (%)		EU-15 (%) 2000
	1990	2000	
<15	17	18	17
15–24	15	12	12
25–49	37	36	37
50–64	15	19	17
65–79	12	11	13
>80	4	4	4

All data from (1).

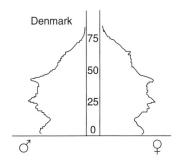

Figure 8.3   Population by age and gender (% of total population)

the highest percentages of aid in the world to developing countries.

Along with industrial development and economic transformation, Denmark's age distribution has changed in recent decades. During the last 10 years the proportion of population in the 0–24 age range fell from 32 to 30%. Over the same period the population aged between 25 and 64 increased from 52 to 54% (Figure 8.3).

More than a million of the population is below 17 years of age. Similarly, more than a million of the population is over 60. The size of the active population (those in work plus the unemployed) is thus about 3 million persons. Most of them live in towns and urbanised districts. There are almost 2.9 million households, of which over 645,000 families have children under the age of 18. An increasing number of individuals, almost 1.4 million adults, live on their own, with about 118,000 of them having children. In 1998, the population increased by 19,000 people. Immigration (net) to Denmark accounted for 11,000 of this increase. Immigrants and their descendants accounted for 6.8% of the total population. Most of these new citizens are of Turkish or Yugoslavian origin.

The Danish welfare model offers several benefits and Danes are entitled to a wide variety of services. Thus, citizens have the right to free education, health care, retirement pension payments plus a wide variety of extra allowances depending on circumstances.

The Danish welfare model is being widely discussed these years as demands rises and public service is perceived declining as it is becoming more and more difficult to accommodate all the needs of all citizens. Cutbacks are increasing in the public sector and even though the Danes continue to be willing to pay very high personal income tax to maintain the welfare

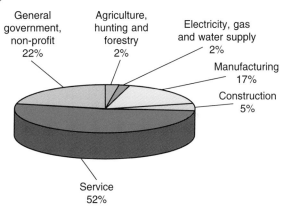

Figure 8.4   Economic structure (gross value rates as % of sectors, 2000, Denmark). All data from (1)

system, the balance between costs and service and issues like care taking and immigrants are heavily discussed.

Economy

Traditionally Denmark is an agricultural country, but in recent decades the economy has assumed a more complex form, dominated by manufacturing and a large service sector. Thus (Figure 8.4), 75% of the workforce is now employed in the service sector, which accounts for around 67% of GDP (Table 8.1).

Despite the fact that in the past couple of years Denmark has experienced recessive tendencies as the rest of the world economy, in a broad long-term perspective for the last decade the Danish economy may be characterised as stable and healthy. Hence, for the past 10 years Denmark has recorded a balance of payments surplus due to an acceleration of exports. For 1999 and 2000 the growth rate was 2.1 and 3.2%, respectively.

Table 8.1   Gross domestic product

		1990	1991	1992	1993	1994	1995	1996	1997	1998	1999	2000
1000 million ECU (nominal growth)	Denmark	105.0	108.4	113.7	118.5	128.0	137.8	144.2	149.2	155.9	165.4	176.5
GDP at market prices	Denmark	1.0	1.1	0.6	0	5.5	2.8	2.5	3.0	2.8	2.1	3.2
Percentage change on previous period – constant prices	EU-15	–	–	1.3	−0.4	2.8	2.4	1.6	2.5	2.9	2.6	3.3

All data from (1).

Table 8.2   Cost-of-living comparisons in the EU in 2000 – Denmark (Brussels = 100[1])

Food and non-alcoholic beverages	Alcoholic beverages and tobacco	Clothing and footwear	Housing, water, electricity, gas and other fuels	Furnishing, household equipment and maintenance of house	Health
134	134	81	155	117	125

Transport	Communication	Recreation and culture	Education	Hotels, cafes and restaurants	Miscellaneous goods and services
151	68	120	121	121	154
				Total	*Total excluding rents*
				132	127

All data from (1).

This compares with an average growth rate for the EU of 2.6% in 1999 and 3.3% in 2000.

A cost-of-living comparison with the EU shows that Danish prices are generally well above average, apart from clothing and footwear and communications (Table 8.2). This indicates that Denmark is one of the most expensive countries to live in compared to many other European countries.

The Danish Tax System is heavily debated these years, as a heavier tax burden is placed on both consumers and business life. This is due to the increasing pressure on the financing of the welfare state. One important reason for this is demographic change as described earlier, which, in the absence of reforms, will lead to a heavier tax burden. Another challenge to the existing tax system is growing internationalisation, which may threaten some of the existing tax bases. Latest reports from the Danish Economic Council indicate that the Danish economy is expected to move into a period of somewhat lower growth rates than was experienced in the nineties. These expectations are due to a slow down in the growth of domestic demand and exports grow-ing at a weaker pace after almost unprecedented high growth in the late 1990s.

Legal, institutional and political environment

Denmark is the oldest kingdom in Europe, with an unbroken line of kings and queens since Gorm the Old became the first king in about year 936. On 5 June 1849, King Frederik VII gave into pressure from different interest groups in society and allowed Denmark a free constitution and a two-chambered parliament was established. Since 1849, Denmark has been a constitutional monarchy. The Danish constitution was changed in 1953 with the result that the parliament now consists of just one chamber. In relation to this, a law was introduced that allowed the female gender to lead the monarchy and be heir to the throne. Denmark's legislative powers lie jointly in the hands of HM Queen Margrethe II and the Parliament.

The Danish Parliament – called Folketinget – has 179 members with 175 from Denmark, 2 from Greenland and 2 from the Faeroe Islands. Elections take place at least every 4 years and a party must have at least 2% of the popular vote in order to have seats in the Parliament. Private citizens have the right to vote at the age of 18. The Parliament controls the governmental ministries and the legislative process. Once the Parliament has passed a bill, the Queen's signature is required before it becomes law.

Denmark is divided into 275 municipalities and 14 counties. Every 4 years, local elections take place. At the municipal level, the local governments are responsible for social services such as schools, libraries, nurseries, day are, public facilities, heating, electricity and water. The county governments hold responsibility for the regional services such as hospitals and health insurance, roads, high schools and some of the educational programs.

As described later, labour disputes are generally rare in Denmark (Tables 8.3 and 8.4).

Labour market

Like the rest of Europe, during the past decade Denmark has suffered from a very high unemployment rate (Tables 8.5 and 8.6), but in recent years this has declined to a more acceptable level. Danish wages appear relatively high compared to other European countries, a factor which has often been considered a threat to Danish competitiveness on the world market. However, unlike most European countries, Denmark has virtually no welfare pension or other contributions paid by employers as a normal, compulsory part of the cost of labour and total labour costs (Tables 8.7–8.9) are on a level with the average for EU member states.

The Danish labour market operates with a clearly defined organisational structure based on collective agreements that have contract status, and a comprehensive mediation system exists to settle disputes with minimum delay. This means that major industrial conflicts are very rarely seen in Denmark, and despite a high level of trade union membership – 75% of the workforce – unofficial disputes are also rare.

The Danish labour force declined in size during the 1990s, even though demographic changes would have

Table 8.3   Working days lost in all industry due to labour disputes (per 1000 employees)

	1990	1991	1992	1993	1994	1995	1996	1997	1998	1999	2000
EU-15	153	99	118	73	114	:	:	:			
Denmark	42	30	27	50	33	84	32	:			

All data from (1). ":" Data not available.

Table 8.4   Working days lost in manufacturing industry due to labour disputes (per 1000 employees)

	1990	1991	1992	1993	1994	1995	1996	1997	1998	1999	2000
EU-15	179	143	118	113	105	:	:	:			
Denmark	102	95	79	159	103	210	102	:			

All data from (1). ":" Data not available.

Table 8.5   Unemployment rate (%)

1990	1991	1992	1993	1994	1995	1996	1997	1998	1999	2000
7.7	8	9	10	8	7	7	6	5	5	5

	2000	
	Denmark	EU-15
Women unemployed	5.3	9.7
Men unemployed	4.2	7.0
Long-term unemployment (as % of all unemployed)	20	45

All data from (1).

Table 8.6 Employment rate by age and gender (%)

Age (years)	Women			Men		
	Denmark		EU-15 2000	Denmark		EU-15 2000
	1990	2000		1990	2000	
15–24	62	64	37	68	70	43
25–49	81	81	67	88	89	88
50–64	53	60	39	72	70	61

All data from (1).

Table 8.7 Average hourly labour costs[2] (manual and non-manual workers) in industry (ECU)

	1990	1991	1992	1993	1994	1995	1996	1997	1998	1999	2000
Denmark	17.19	18.07	19.28	:	:	:	22.99	23.45	24.45	25.67	:

All data from (1). ":" Data not available.

Table 8.8 Structure of labour cost in % (total labour costs = 100) (1999)

Direct costs	Employers' social security contributions	Other costs
92	6	2

All data from (1).

Table 8.9 Number of hours usually worked per week: full-time employees (2000)

	Full-time	Part-time
EU-15	41.71	19.6
Denmark	40.6	19.8

All data from (1).

meant an increase of around 150,000 persons if labour market participation rates had remained the same. Instead, participation declined steadily.

Private sector employment, which increased rapidly in the latter part of the 1990s, is expected by the Danish Economic Council to remain almost constant in the coming years. The forecasted moderate increase in total employment is thus exclusively due to an expansion in the number of jobs in the public sector. This slow growth in employment, in combination with a small increase in the size of the available labour force, will result in a small increase in the rate of unemployment.

Education system

Denmark has a universal system of free education. According to the Danish Constitution, all children of compulsory education age have a right to free education in the Folkeskole – municipal basic school offering 9 years of comprehensive primary and lower secondary education, an optional pre-school class and a supplementary optional 10th year. In 1994, a new Act on the Folkeskole came into effect, which contains innovations in a number of fields. Fundamentally, the "Folkeskole" must have room for all, and all pupils shall be entitled to instruction and to showing their abilities in the broadest sense of the word. The main element of this new act is the abolishment of the course division after the 7th form and the consequent introduction of differentiated teaching. Recent years have seen comprehensive reforms in the entire education system. The common denominator is modernisation of the courses of education, greater freedom to reign for the institutions and a more efficient financial control (Table 8.10).

Approximately 52% of the population has taken some form of vocational training, and around 18% of the population has attended an institute of higher education. Moreover, great emphasis is placed on lifelong access to education. Denmark is particularly noted for producing highly skilled technicians and engineers. An interesting feature in this respect is that per capita Denmark has perhaps the largest PC ownership in the world (various surveys indicate around 50%).

Table 8.10   Level of education for the population aged 25–64 (%, 2000)

>Upper secondary education	Total (25–64)	25–29	30–34	35–39	40–44	45–49	50–54	55–59	60–64
EU-15 (women and men)	64	76	73	70	66	62	55	51	45
Denmark (women and men)	80	87	87	81	81	81	78	74	64
EU-15 (women)	61	77	73	70	64	58	50	45	37
Denmark (women)	78	89	86	83	79	79	76	66	56

All data from (1).

Universities are situated in Copenhagen, Aarhus, Roskilde, Odense and Aalborg, and there is a university centre in southern Jutland. In addition, there are two specialised centres of university rank in the Copenhagen region, namely the Technical University of Denmark and the Royal Veterinary and Agricultural University. Other centres include business and technical colleges, and other specialist institutions.

Denmark's international outlook means that the population commands excellent language skills, English virtually being considered a second language. In the south of the country almost everyone also has at least a basic knowledge of German as a consequence of the great interaction with northern Germany. In addition, among the younger generation it is common to be skilled in several European languages, such as German, French and Spanish.

NORWAY

Area	323,758 km² (excluding Svalbard and Jan Mayen)
Population	4,552,000 inhabitants
Density	14 inhabitants per km²
Capital and population	Oslo (512,600)
Other major cities and population	Bergen (233,300) Trondheim (151,400) Stavanger (109,700) Kristiansand (74,000)
Official language	Norwegian
Religions	87% Protestant-Lutheran 13% others (10+ recognised religious denominations)

Source: Statistics Norway

Topography and climate

The Kingdom of Norway occupies the western and northern parts of the Scandinavian peninsula as well as the Jan Mayen island and the Svalbard archipelago in the North Atlantic. Norway borders on Sweden (1619 km² common frontier), Finland and Russia to the East; the mainland is surrounded by ocean to the North, West and South. The Treaty of Svalbard grants to Norway "full and absolute sovereignty over Svalbard", though Norway is under obligation to give citizens of the signatory countries equality in matters relating to economic activities. Fortifications and naval bases are prohibited, and the islands are not to be used for the purposes of war. About 60% of Svalbard is protected (national parks).

Norway is a spacious and mountainous country. Norway's total area (including Svalbard and Jan Mayen) is slightly larger than Germany's and somewhat smaller than Sweden's. Although the net continental coastland is only 2650 km (excluding fjords and bays), the total continental coastline is about 25,000 km, and coastline of islands has been estimated to about 58,000 km. The Norwegian mainland includes numerous fresh-water lakes (about 5%), forests (25%) and a mere 3% farmland. Mountains constitute about 50% of the mainland, including some 3000 km² of glaciers. The climate is influenced by the Gulf Stream from the west. Most of mainland Norway consequently has a temperate, coastal climate with the mean temperature ranging from −4°C in the winter to 17°C in the summer, and moderate to heavy precipitation all seasons. The interior of northern and eastern Norway does however have a dry continental climate with warm summers and cold winters. In normal summers, the temperature rises occasionally to 30°C, and winter temperatures below −20°C are rare along the coast. Three-quarters of the population lives along the coast.

Principal characteristics

Table 8.11 shows some of the main characteristics of Norway as compared to EU average.

Culture

Norway is culturally strongly influenced by its neighbouring countries, especially its Nordic neighbours. The Scandinavian languages, a branch of the Germanic family, are very close and Scandinavians can easily understand each other. In fact, written Norwegian is virtually identical to written Danish. Norwegians have

Table 8.11   Key figures comparison, Norway and EU

	Norway	EU-15	Norway as % of EU-15 average
Population density	14	119	12
Infant mortality	3.8	4.9	78
Life expectancy at birth (boys)	75.6	74.9	101
Life expectancy at birth (girls)	81.1	81.2	100
Employment rate (men)	83	72.4	115
Employment rate (women)	75	49.7	151
Unemployment rate	3.6	8.2	44

Source: Eurostat.

an informal approach to life both at a personal and even business level. Norway is a welfare state, with one of Europe's highest rates of spending on health care and education. Nowhere else are the unfortunate and feckless so generously treated. The tradition of adult education originated in Denmark by the priest and author N.F.S. Grundvig. His ideas created special high schools where adults could attend courses for a period of 3 to 6 months, focusing on cultural or specific issues. Although few Norwegians attend church regularly, the moral legacy of Lutheranism remains strong – modesty and hard work are still basic virtues.

People

The Norwegian population is generally homogeneous compared to many European countries, during the last three decades this picture has changed somewhat. Important minorities are the ancient Sami people of the North and the Pakistanis that arrived during the 1970s. Statistics Norway classifies about 7% of the population as immigrants, a large proportion of these are from Sweden, Denmark and other North European countries. In addition, there are some refugees originating from Vietnam, Bosnia, the Middle East and Somalia.

Along with industrial development and economic transformation, Norway's age distribution has changed in recent decades. During the last 10 years the proportion of population in the 0–24 age range fell from 35 to 32%. Over the same period the population aged 25–64 increased from 50 to 52% (Table 8.12).

About one million of the population is below 17 years of age, whereas about 750,000 of the population is over 64. The size of the active population (those in work plus the unemployed) is thus about 2.8 million persons. Three-quarters of the inhabitants live in towns and urbanised districts. There are almost 2 million

households, of which over 560,000 families have children under the age of 18. An increasing number of individuals, almost 850,000 adults (19% of the population), live on their own, about 100,000 of these have children. In 2001, the population increased by 20,000 people. Immigration (net) accounted for 8000 of this increase. In terms of welfare provision, Norwegian citizens have the right to free education, health care, retirement pension payments plus a wide variety of extra allowances depending on circumstances.

Economy

Approximately 100 years ago Norway was one of the poorest countries in Europe, but today it has evolved into a modern, prosperous nation. Norway is now one of the wealthiest countries in the world benefiting in particular from the development of offshore oil and gas reserves. Currently, Norway is the world's third largest oil exporter behind Saudi-Arabia and Russia, and produces close to 25% of all energy in EEA.[1] As can be seen from Figure 8.5, the Norwegian economy is characterised by a huge offshore sector. Norway is also the dominant fishery nation, accounting for about one-quarter of all catches and aquaculture production in Europe. Year 2000 was the 10th year of consecutive growth in consumption and gross domestic product

Table 8.12 Population by age (% of total population)

Age (years)	Norway (%) 1990	Norway (%) 2000	EU-15 (%) 2000
<15	19	20	17
15–24	16	12	12
25–49	36	36	37
50–64	14	16	17
65–79	13	11	13
>80	4	4	4

All data from (1).

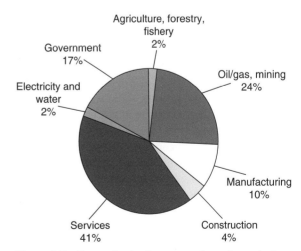

Figure 8.5 Economic structure, gross domestic product by sector, 2000. *Source*: Statistics Norway

---

[1] Calculated at oil equivalents. *Source*: Eurostat.

Table 8.13 Gross domestic product (at market prices at current prices and current exchange rates)

		1990	1991	1992	1993	1994	1995	1996	1997	1998	1999	2000
1000 million Euro (nominal growth)	Norway	90.9	95.2	97.6	99.1	103.6	112.1	124.0	136.7	131.7	144.1	175.6
Yearly growth as % of previous year (real growth)	Norway	2	3	3	3	6	4	5	5	2	1	2
	EU-15	3	3	1	−0.4	3	2	2	3	3	3	3

All data from (1).

(GDP) and for the first time Norway passed Switzerland in terms of GDP per person at purchasing power parities, but still behind Luxembourg and the US.[2] Dominant sectors in the economy include natural resource exploitation (oil/gas, forestry and fishery), shipping, heavy industry related to natural resources and more recently an expanding service sector. Thus, 74% of the workforce is employed in the service sector (including government) that accounts for around 60% of GDP.

Norway has also recorded high budgetary surplus during the last years, currently at around 15% of GDP and estimated at 10–15% for the coming years (Table 8.13). In order to manage this extraordinary cash flow, the authorities have created the Government Petroleum Fund and each year some part of the surplus is transferred to the Fund and invested in companies abroad. Recent estimates indicate that the Norwegian economy is expected to move into a period of moderate growth rates of between 1 and 2%.

Legal, institutional and political environment

Norway's history is entwined with the history of the other Scandinavian countries. For more than 400 years Norway was controlled by Denmark. In 1814, having allied themselves with Napoleon, Denmark lost Norway to Sweden according to the peace treaty of Kiel. During the intermezzo that occurred, Norway claimed independence and a constitution became finished at the constitutional assembly at May 17. When the Kiel treaty was finally implemented (by a Swedish invasion), Sweden accepted the May 17 constitution and Norway accepted the Swedish king as head of state. Norway's political institutions and nationalistic

Table 8.14 Working days lost due to labour disputes (per 1000 employees)

	1997	1998	1999	2000	2001
EU-15	73	114	:	:	:
Norway	3	127	3	219	0

Source: Statistics Norway, Eurostat. ":" Data not available.

movement emerged during the nineteenth century, and in 1905 Norway peacefully withdraw from the union.

The national legislature or parliament, Stortinget, has 165 members directly elected by proportional representation for a 4-year term. There is no right of dissolution between elections. Citizens have the right to vote at the age of 18. Although not explicitly written into the constitution, Norway is by precedence a parliamentary democracy. The Parliament controls the governmental ministries as well as the legislative process. While Norway remains a monarchy, the King's role is however merely ceremonial.

Norway is divided into 434 municipalities and 19 counties – including Oslo, which is a combined county/municipality. Every 4 years, local elections take place. At the municipal level, the local governments are responsible for social services such as schools, libraries, nurseries, day-care, public facilities and water. The county governments hold responsibility for the regional services such as roads, industrial policy, high schools and some other educational programs (Table 8.14).

Labour market

Unlike most of Europe, Norway has not suffered from high unemployment rates during the recent years. Long-term unemployment is now at a mere 5% of all unemployed. Currently, there are about 2.3 million

---

[2] *Source*: The Economist.

Table 8.15 Employment by sector, 2002 (1000 persons)

Agriculture, forestry, and fishery	86	4%
Oil/gas and mining	35	1%
Manufacturing	289	13%
Electricity and water	14	1%
Construction	157	7%
Services, exlc. government/non-profit	834	36%
Government and non-profit	868	38%
Total	2286	100%

Source: Statistics Norway.

Table 8.16 Unemployment rate 1997–2002 (%, annual average)

1997	1998	1999	2000	2001	2002
4	3	3	3	4	4

Source: Statistics Norway.

Table 8.17 Unemployment rates by age, gender and long-term unemployment (%, annual average)

	Norway 2001	EU-15 2000
All	4	8
Women unemployed	3	10
Men unemployed	4	7
Age 16–24	11	16
Long-term unemployment* (as % of all)	10	45

* 12 months or more.
Sources: Eurostat, Statistics Norway.

Table 8.18 Average hourly labour costs, comparison with select countries (US$, at current exchange rates)

	1998	1999	2000	2001
Czech republic	2.1	2.1	2.0	2.2
Denmark	22.7	23.0	20.4	20.7
Germany	26.8	26.2	23.0	23.0
Norway	24.0	24.5	22.6	23.2
Spain	12.1	12.1	10.9	10.9
Sweden	22.1	21.6	20.2	18.4
UK	16.4	16.6	15.9	15.8

Note: For production workers. Includes pay for time worked, other direct pay (e.g. holiday pay), employer expenditures on legally required insurance programmes and other labour taxes.
Source: The Economist.

Table 8.19 Number of hours usually worked per week

	Full-time	Part-time
EU-15	41.7	19.6
Norway	39.3	22.1

Source: Eurostat.

persons employed in Norway, which is 83% of all men and 75% of all women aged 25–66 (Tables 8.15–8.17). The Norwegian labour force, as well as labour market participation, inclined slowly in size during the 1990s. Norwegian wages – as well as current wage increases – are relatively high compared to other European countries, a factor which has often been considered a threat to Norwegian competitiveness on the world market. Labour costs are about 10% higher than in Denmark, and about two times higher than in Spain (Tables 8.18 and 8.19). Indirect labour costs such as social security accounts for approximately 20% of total labour costs.

Educational system

Norway has a universal system of free education. All children of compulsory education age have a right to free education in the municipal basic school offering 10 years of comprehensive primary and lower secondary education. Primary and lower secondary education in Norway is founded on the principle of a unified school system that provides equal and adapted education for all on the basis of a single national curriculum. As a result of Norway's scattered population, 40% of primary and lower secondary schools are so small that children of different ages are taught in the same classroom. Primary and lower secondary levels are often combined in the same school.

GDP (7%) is devoted to the educational sector, of which around one-fifth is spent on higher education. The educational level in Norway has increased substantially during the last decades. Currently 54% of the population has taken some form of vocational training, and around 26% of the population has attended an institute of higher education. The percentage of with at least upper secondary education is the highest in Europe (see Table 8.20). Moreover, there is an increasing emphasis on lifelong access to education.

Table 8.20   Level of education for the population aged 25–59 (%, 2000)

At least upper secondary	Total (25–64)	25–29	30–39	40–49	50–59	60–64
EU-15 (women and men)	64	76	71	64	53	45
Norway (women and men)	86	93	92	87	76	67
EU-15 (women)	61	77	71	61	48	37
Norway (women)	85	95	94	86	74	62

Source: Eurostat.

Universities are situated in Oslo, Bergen, Trondheim and Tromsø. In addition, there are specialised university institutions notably the Norwegian School of Economics and Business Administration and the Agricultural University of Norway. These are engaged in both research and teaching, and offer undergraduate, graduate and doctoral programs. Other centres include state university colleges, generally offering shorter courses of a more vocational orientation within, e.g. business, engineering, nursing and teaching. In addition, state colleges offer undergraduate courses interchangeable with those offered by the universities. Norway's international outlook means that the population commands excellent language skills, English virtually being a second language. In addition, among the younger generation it is common to be skilled in other European languages, such has German, French and Spanish, and virtually all Norwegians understand both spoken and written Swedish and Danish.

HRM IN DENMARK AND NORWAY: CURRENT POLICY AND PRACTICE

INTRODUCTION

In this chapter we shall compare essential human resource management (HRM) aspects in the two neighbouring countries Denmark and Norway. Both historically and culturally these countries have much in common and display numerous similarities. For many decades, trade unions have enjoyed an influential position in Scandinavia and still act as important power players in society and business. These cultures have also been characterised by profound egalitarian values which have contributed to keeping the wage differentials very limited and which have been accompanied by a low power distance. Despite these important similarities, Denmark and Norway differ substantially when it comes to their relationship and commitment to a wider European economic and political cooperation. Like Sweden and Finland, Denmark is a member of the EU, whereas Norway is not. However, there are no substantive reasons to believe that this difference will have a strong impact on the HRM regimes within the two countries. Another difference that may, however, have an impact on HRM practices in companies is the fact that Norwegian business life is much more dependent on the extraction and sales of raw materials in the form of, e.g. oil, gas and fish than is the Danish economy.

THE STRATEGIC IMPORTANCE OF HRM

As in most other developed economies, in Denmark and Norway over the past 15 years there has been a profound interest in and attention devoted to HRM as a field of practice and a theoretical discipline (Nordhaug, 1987, 1993; Nordhaug et al., 1997; Rogaczewska et al., 1999; Larsen, 1999, 2001a, b; Brewster and Larsen, 2000). This is a development that a posteriori mainly reflects the transition of economies based on manufacturing industries into economies relying heavily on service and knowledge based enterprises. As service, know-how, core competences, networking, knowledge and learning have been increasingly recognised as core assets in the "knowledge based economy", the competitive strength of the Danish and Norwegian economies in general and organisations in particular is associated with the ability to attract and develop human resources

(HRs) (Brewster and Larsen, 1993; Brandi et al., 2001; Larsen, 2001c, d; Nordhaug, 2002a). Consequently from the mid-1960s there has been a shift from a more "production function-oriented approach", stressing the deployment of raw material, machinery and human capital in the most optimal way to an emphasis on the strategic importance of managing HRs.

Although this tendency seems most prominent in knowledge intensive, service oriented or high technology producing companies, it has been the most important single driving force for the development of a HRM concept in Denmark and Norway. This is a development which also is reflected in the nomenclature relating to work life organisation where the concept of HRM in large part has substituted personnel management. (The conceptual differentiation between HRM and personnel administration or personnel management has been thoroughly elaborated elsewhere, e.g. Nordhaug, 1993; Gennard and Kelly, 1994; Brewster and Larsen, 2000; Larsen, 2000a; Storey, 2001)

As a consequence of the increasing awareness and acknowledgement of HRs as cornerstones in companies in regard to sustain and gain market shares, much attention has been devoted to the *strategic* role of HRM and the need for a closer interdependency between business strategy and HRM (Nordhaug et al., 1997; Rogaczewska et al., 1999; Nordhaug, 2002b). In this contextual setting, the organisations' ability to attract, develop and nurture the right portfolio of competence carriers becomes key for the feasibility of pursuing specific business strategies. Leaving room for discussion about the actual causality between HRM strategy on the one side and business strategy on the other, there is today little disagreement about the fact that inevitably, and to an increasing extent, HRM and business strategy are mutually interdependent and often very intertwined.

The conceptualisation of SHRM, strategic HRM, as well as the strategic foundation of the HR function is a recurrent theme in recent HR literature (Fombrun et al., 1984; Nordhaug, 1987, 2002b; Bamberger and Meshoulam, 2000; Greer, 2001). There are numerous ways in which HR issues can be included into corporate strategy (see Brewster et al., 2000 for a broad elaboration on the relationship between HRM and the process of strategic management). Moreover, there are also differences in the ways in which HRM is integrated into the overall strategic processes of the organisation. Notwithstanding the differences in approaches to SHRM,

it is commonly accepted that in order to fully exploit the potential benefits from integrating HR considerations and business strategy, HR has to play a prominent role in strategic decision-making. Using the findings from the Cranet Survey as a basis, we shall now take a closer look at aspects relating to more formal and direct HR participation in the strategic decision-making processes of companies in Denmark and Norway, respectively.

THE ROLE OF THE HRM FUNCTION: MARGINAL OR CORE?

One way of studying the strategic importance of HR in the organisation goes through looking at the formal representation of the head of HRM on the main Board of Directors or the top management group in the company. The empirical results for Denmark and Norway are shown in Table 8.21.

In appears that in roughly two-thirds of the organisations in Norway the head of HRM is represented in the top management team, and we also see that this proportion has remained fairly stable from 1992 to 1999. We also see that the Danish situation in this respect is one characterised by stability over time. However, there is a significantly lower proportion of representation in the top management group than in Norway, approximately one-half of the organisations. We also note that although there has been a slight increase from 1995 to 1999 in both countries, in Denmark as well as in Norway there has been a *decrease* in the absolute number of organisations with HR representation on the board for the period as a whole. Evidently, in Denmark there are still many organisations where the HR responsible does not *formally* play a strategic role, a tendency, which becomes even more evident when comparing Denmark with a range of other countries in the Cranet Survey. Actually, Denmark is among the countries exhibiting the lowest direct participation of the HRM head on the top management team or

Table 8.21   Does the head of the personnel/HRs function have a place on the main Board of Directors or equivalent?

	Denmark			Norway		
	1992	1995	1999	1992	1995	1999
Yes	56	47	52	75	67	69
No	44	53	48	25	33	31

Table 8.22   Stage at which HR is involved in the development of corporate strategy

	Denmark			Norway		
	1992	1995	1999	1992	1995	1999
From the outset	47	43	47	65	62	65
Through consultation	31	30	29	24	24	19
On implementation	15	18	15	8	10	12
Non-consulted	7	8	9	3	3	4

Board of Directors. Additionally, in Denmark data also show that where there is no HR specialist on the board, the managing director on the main board has the responsibility for HR issues.[1]

At first glance, it is difficult to see how HR can play a more strategic role when the head of the function is not represented in the forum where key strategic decisions are made. Yet, there may be other ways of securing that HR aspects are taken care of and included in the strategic decision-making. For instance, it can be a strength as well as a weakness that the managing director has the responsibility for HR issues. That is, HR influence can be exercised in different ways and through different organisational and managerial mechanisms. Whether such mechanisms are more or less used in Denmark compared to other countries is, however, at present beyond our knowledge.

The Cranet Survey also opens up the possibility for investigating the nature and depth of the strategic role played by the HR function in other regards. Table 8.22 outlines the HR function's involvement in strategy development.

In both countries the level and stages at which HR involvement takes place in business strategy development has been rather stable over the period as a whole. More specifically, we see that less than half of the Danish organisations with a corporate strategy consult the HR specialist from the outset. In Norway, this is the case for approximately two-thirds of the organisations. This is a similar pattern compared with what we just saw for representation in the top management team. Moreover, not only has the number of Danish organisations where HR specialists are not consulted in the strategy development process at all increased over the

decade, it is also significantly higher than in Norway. Hence, in roughly 10% of the Danish organisations HR specialists are not consulted at all when it comes to the development of a business strategy.

This in turn accentuates the question whether there is any correlation between the presence of the head of HRM on the Board of Directors on the one hand, and early involvement of HR specialists in the development of corporate strategy on the other? In Denmark, HR influence from the outset *does* reflect HR board-level involvement, i.e. if the head of HRM is represented on the main board, there is a higher propensity to consult HR specialists from the outset in the development of corporate strategy (Rogaczewska et al., 1999). Nevertheless, it is important to stress that the correlation is not universally applicable to all participating countries. Research has shown, that for instance in Sweden there is no significant positive correlation between having HR representation on the board and HR specialists being consulted from the outset when it comes to the development of a corporate strategy (Lindeberg and Månson, 2000).

SHRM – THE EMPEROR'S NEW CLOTHES?

What are the implications of these findings for the role played by HRM in Danish and Norwegian organisations? Admittedly, all in all the Danish data leave us with a rather gloomy picture suggesting that when it comes to the formal position and influence of the HR function on business strategy development there is "much talk – less action". (Or, as we shall see below: "Little talk, little (or: some?) action"!) Denmark ranks in the bottom half both when it comes to on board representation and (early) involvement in corporate strategy. But is this to say that HR is not recognised as having strategic importance in Danish organisations at all and that its role is marginal?

---

[1] This is the case for roughly two-thirds of the organisations which do not have HR representation on the board (The Danish Cranet-E Survey, 1999).

First, we have to ask ourselves to which extent HR representation and HR consultation in business strategy formulation is an appropriate single standing measure of how much attention and priority HR is *actually* given in the organisation. It is our impression, that an understanding of specific national and organisational cultural and institutional characteristics may be needed in the interpretation of how HRM is actually exercised in Danish organisations.

The Danish labour market is characterised by a relatively low degree of hierarchical structure, "authority by title" and power distance. This in turn means that although the head of HRM frequently does not have a seat on the Board of Directors, she/he may still have the credibility to exercise and incorporate her/his ideas at different levels of the organisation since they do not need to be accounted for and executed at the top management level. In addition, as we shall see later, there seems to be a widespread, "collective ownership" to HRM in Danish companies, which, for instance, is expressed in the high level of line manager responsibility for HRM.

The hypothesis of a low degree of hierarchical structure is also in part supported by the fact that there has been a radical increase in the number of organisations with a written HR policy.[2] Hence, over the period 1995–1999 there has been an increase by almost 33% in the number of organisations having elaborated a written HR policy. A fairly low degree of hierarchical structure *might* reflect itself in explicit policies that everyone can adhere to. But there are other and probably more vital explanatory variables for this dramatic increase in organisations with a written HR policy. In 1999, the Danish economy and employment rate was highly expansive (a tendency which has now reversed) and the lack of qualified people in most sectors positioned recruitment and retention as a core challenge for most organisations. The challenge of hiring competent people and retaining them in the organisation has been reinforced by very small cohorts of educated young people entering the labour market, the increasing emergence of new organisational forms, and a general increase in the demand for competence in using new generic technologies (Larsen, 2001c). The Cranet Survey data show that when asked about the

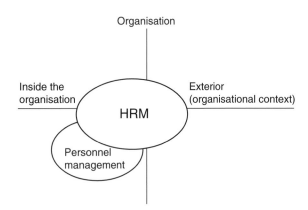

Figure 8.6 HR and the organisations image

methods for recruitment/retention of employees, the number of organisations indicating the importance of the organisations' *image* has more than doubled from 1995 to 1999.

This leads us to believe, that Danish organisations seem very aware of the importance of being able to create an identity and retain an image as an attractive work place. In this sense, HR policy has become vital in marketing the organisations' image; from having been an individual-oriented internal matter of the organisation, there seems to be an emerging symbiosis between the organisation's image, its identity and its HR policy. In this respect it can be argued that Danish HR policy has moved "out" of the organisation and become a vital cornerstone in shaping the perceptions of the organisation's image. This might explain the dramatic increase in the number of organisations indicating that they have a written HR policy. Graphically, this can be expressed in the way as shown in Figure 8.6.

As mentioned previously, the focus of Personnel Management has almost exclusively been on the individual, as well as intra-organisational processes (except for the recruitment of new employees from "the outside world" and "sending back individuals to the world" (due to retirement, termination, resignation, etc.). In contrast, HRM is incorporating the synergy between the individual and the organisation, for instance as it is seen in the interaction between individual and organisational learning. In addition, HR plays a key role in forming the identity and image/reputation of the organisation. This implies that the HRM concept presumes a synergy between intra- and extra-organisational features and processes.

---

[2] In 1995, 42% of the organisations indicated having a written HR policy, whereas this was the case for 55% of the organisations in 1999.

Another interesting feature of the Danish labour market is a large predominance of SMEs. More than 97% of Danish organisations have less than 100 employees, and more than 80% have less than 50 employees (Larsen, 2000b). Whereas large organisations often call for structure and formalisation, this is typically a less prominent feature of SMEs. Therefore, it could be argued that whereas it makes sense to measure HR influence by HR representation on the board in large corporations, this may be misleading in SMEs. In many SMEs top management will only consist of one or a few directors who each are responsible for a variety of fields of expertise including HRM. If this is the case, it is unlikely that HRM will stand out as a single discipline with representation on the board. An argument, which is also supported by the fact, mentioned earlier, that in those organisations where there is no HR specialist on the board, the managing director on the main board has the responsibility for HR issues. This does not necessarily mean that HRM is taken less seriously than when a formal HR function is established.

With the risk of idealising small organisations, other studies (source) have shown that smaller organisational units are more likely to be characterised by a high degree of responsibility feeling, lower degree of sickness absence, and higher degree of loyalty. Tentatively it may be argued that these organisations in larger part are characterised by a culture where HR and people-related issues are intrinsically incorporated at all levels of the decision-making processes and therefore do not necessarily call for a position at the top management level.

However, the factors that have now been mentioned in relation to Denmark, are basically the same in Norway. There we also find a large number of micro firms and small companies. Likewise, the power distance is very low. So given these similarities, the differences in formalisation of SHRM must have other causes. One factor that may explain some of these discrepancies, is a possible difference relating to the influence of US management theories and practices. Norwegian business schools have traditionally had very strong ties to US business schools and universities, whereas Danish business schools have had a much stronger orientation towards continental Europe. And we know that SHRM is in large part a US "invention". Moreover, it was launched at a fairly stage in Norway, which may contribute to explaining its substantial dispersion among work organisations (Nordhaug, 1987).

LINE MANAGEMENT AND HRM

With HRM gradually substituting personnel administration or personnel management, the relationship between the HR function and line management, with its generation of new demands and challenges for both parties, has been given much attention. Undisputedly, there is a widespread tendency in Europe to allocate HR responsibilities to line managers. This tendency has been strongly supported by international survey results (Brewster and Larsen, 1992, 1997; Brewster and Söderström, 1994; Brewster et al., 2000).

Earlier studies have shown, that compared to the other participating countries in the Cranet Survey Denmark ranks very high when it comes to allocating to line managers responsibilities or tasks that were formerly the burden of HR or personnel specialists. Over the last decade Norway has also moved in this direction. From having been ranked in the lowest end in 1991, Norway made some giant leaps in 1992 and 1995 and has now moved into a middle ranking. The 1999 figures for Norway seem to reinforce this ongoing pace whereas in Denmark, within most HRM areas (see Table 8.24), except for compensation and industrial relations, the level now seems to have stabilised.

Table 8.23 captures the development in the location of the *primary* responsibility for policy decisions on two key aspects of HRM, i.e. recruitment and selection together with training and development. In the latter area, Norwegian work life has undergone a major change when it comes to the role of the line managers. The number of Norwegian organisations confirming that the primary responsibility for these issues is now assigned to line managers has almost quadrupled from 1995 to 1999. Although not equally strong, the trend as to recruitment and selection goes in the same direction.

Whereas in Denmark there has been a gradual and consistent move in the direction of line management taking over the "former" responsibilities of the HR department, the data from the last round of the Cranet Survey seem to indicate that the level now seems to have been stabilised. More specifically, we see an indication of the HR responsibility being given "back" to the HR department or rather, that line management and the HR department increasingly make *joint* decisions on major policy decisions. Hence, in Denmark in both areas of consideration, we witness an increase in the number of organisations indicating that major policy

Table 8.23　Changes in primary responsibility for major policy decisions on key aspects of HRM

	Denmark		Norway	
	1995	1999	1995	1999
Recruitment and selection				
Line management	33	24	16	22
Line management with HR department	44	49	55	55
HR department with line management	19	22	27	22
HR department	4	5	2	2
Training and development				
Line management	29	23	12	41
Line management with HR department	41	44	44	46
HR department with line management	25	25	38	11
HR department	5	8	6	2

Table 8.24　Changes in line management responsibility and involvement

	Denmark			Norway		
	1992	1995	1999	1992	1995	1999
Pay and benefits						
Increase		23	31		31	36
Same		70	63		66	60
Decrease		6	6		3	4
Recruitment and selection						
Increase		25	25		46	49
Same		67	65		49	49
Decrease		8	10		5	2
Training and development						
Increase		35	31		50	51
Same		56	58		47	45
Decrease		9	11		3	4
Industrial relations						
Increase		15	24		18	24
Same		78	68		78	70
Decrease		7	8		4	6
Workforce expansion/reduction						
Increase	29	22	16	20	30	27
Same	67	73	80	78	66	50
Decrease	5	6	4	2	5	23

decisions are made in joint efforts between line management and the HR department.

At the same, a decreasing proportion of organisations indicate that the sole responsibility lies on the line management.

Altogether this seems to suggest that the HR department in Denmark experiences a process of repositioning in relation to line management. Although it is tempting to conclude that the HR department now acts as an internal consultant to the line – the nature of the linkage between the two seems to be of a somewhat different character. Whereas the HR department might earlier have tried to redefine its role as one of an internal consultancy service to the line management, it seems more plausible that the HR department now has succeeded to genuinely become an influential partner to the line managers.

Finally, the data from the last rounds of the survey also indicate some interesting features in both countries when it comes to the development in line management involvement in particular areas of interest. In Table 8.24 we see, that in both countries there seems to be an increasing involvement of the line management on issues related to compensation and industrial relations. This may indicate that the countries are moving in a direction implying a stronger individualisation of work life, epitomised by individualised performance appraisals and compensation systems (Larsen and Bang, 1993). Another possible conjecture is that in many organisations trade union representatives have taken on a new role. Broadly speaking, Scandinavian work life has been characterised by a high level of cooperation and consensus seeking between employers and unions. As opposed to many other countries where the presence of unions is regarded as a threat to the autonomy of the top management, employers in the Nordic countries have demonstrated a broad acceptance and willingness to have a recurring dialogue with unions and their representatives. The emergence of the new HRM and SHRM paradigms has created a strong pressure on local unions to redefine some of their roles and become more strongly involved in HR issues. As we will argue later, there seems to be a strong indication that they have succeeded in these efforts to become more active partners in a running co-operative dialogue.

It is noteworthy that in Norway there has been a substantial decrease in the involvement of the line management in relation to expansion or reduction of the workforce, whereas this has remained remarkably stable in Denmark from 1992 to 1999. We are not able to explain this Norwegian development, but a possible explanation is that in a period of increasing competition to attract talents to the companies, earlier decentralisation of responsibilities to the line managers has been reversed. In other words, there is reason that there has been a conscious centralisation process driven by the tougher conditions in the labour market.

RECRUITMENT AND SELECTION

The Cranet Survey contains several questions about the application of a wide array of selection and recruitment methods. Among these is the use of internal labour markets or internal recruitment when filling vacant positions above the entry-level in the organisation. Table 8.25 shows the distribution for Norwegian and Danish organisations in respect to filling managerial vacancies.

The pattern is quite equal when we look at the senior management level in that close to one-third of the organisations actively use their internal labour markets. We

Table 8.25 Recruitment methods: use of internal labour markets when filling managerial vacancies

	Denmark		Norway	
	1995	1999	1995	1999
Senior management	35.0	27.4	31.3	29.3
Middle management	73.6	67.6	59.8	59.4
Junior management	77.4	65.9	69.6	68.6
Total managerial only	62.0	53.6	53.6	52.4

also see that this proportion more than doubles if we move down to the middle management level and junior management level. In Norway, there have not been any changes from 1995 to 1999, whereas in Denmark there has been a decrease in the application of internal recruitment mechanisms in the same period for all managerial levels. The major reason for this can be the fact that many companies underwent expansion and growth in this period, making it necessary to rely heavily on external recruitment.

When we study the use of various selection methods, both similarities and dissimilarities can be found. These are shown in Table 8.26. In both countries, interview panels are used for every appointment in about one-third of the organisations. There is a tendency that such panels are somewhat more frequently in Norway than in Denmark. On the other hand, one-to-one interviews are more common in Danish work life.

The use of application forms seems to be on approximately the same level in the two countries, although slightly more often used in Denmark. However, psychometric testing of potential candidates for filling positions is far more frequently employed in Danish than in Norwegian organisations. Almost one in ten units in Denmark report to apply such methods, against 4% in Norway. Concurrently, albeit the proportion is still low, there has been a remarkable growth in Norwegian organisations' use of psychometric tests from 1995 to 1999.

Assessment centres have not become rooted in Scandinavian work life, and as the table shows only very few organisations have used this selection method. This may primarily be due to the modest number of large corporations. Since assessment centres are costly and require economies of scale to be run in a financially responsible manner, there is reason to believe that they can be found almost entirely in big organisations employing thousands of people.

Table 8.26   Selection methods: use of different methods for every or most appointments

	Denmark		Norway	
	1995	1999	1995	1999
Interview panel				
Every appointment	30.1	34.3	22.1	33.2
Most appointments	23.7	20.9	34.7	39.8
Some appointments	14.7	11.6	28.2	15.9
One-to-one interviews				
Every appointment	30.8	30.6	20.8	21.4
Most appointments	22.8	19.6	17.8	13.7
Some appointments	15.5	16.6	19.1	17.0
Application forms				
Every appointment	26.7	23.0	36.9	24.1
Most appointments	10.2	10.5	10.8	13.5
Some appointments	14.6	20.2	10.5	8.3
Psychometric testing				
Every appointment	8.7	9.1	1.5	4.1
Most appointments	17.4	15.4	2.6	7.1
Some appointments	27.9	27.7	12.6	23.4
Assessment centre				
Every appointment	0.6	0	0	0
Most appointments	1.2	1.8	0	0
Some appointments	6.1	7.5	5.5	6.5
Graphology				
Every appointment	0	0	1.2	0
Most appointment	1.2	0	1.6	0
Some appointments	1.5	0	0.8	0
References				
Every appointment	17.3	21.1	43.7	53.7
Most appointment	36.4	40.4	41.0	40.3
Some appointments	35.6	31.3	13.1	5.6

Graphology is even less used in relation to recruitment and selection. It is much more frequently applied in countries such as Switzerland and France. Finally, we see that in Norwegian organisations reference checks appear to be the most applied among the methods that are listed in the table. More than half of them used such checks for every appointment in 1999, whereas the corresponding Danish figure was 21%. However, we see that Danish organisations use such checks frequently for "most" and "some" appointments.

COMPENSATION, PERFORMANCE AND UNION INFLUENCE

Some claim that there is currently also in Scandinavia a sweeping wind of individualisation in work life. Traditionally, in the Nordic countries pay has been based on collective agreements between employers and unions.

Still, the unionisation remains very high in international terms and consequently one should not expect any decrease in the dispersion of collective bargaining and compensation agreements. On the other hand, many new enterprises have been established both within the so-called new economy and within the service sector that have not been exposed to existing unions or attempts to start up new ones. In addition, many young people today require to be treated in differential ways according to their competency levels, work effort, individual performances and personal preferences (cf. Gooderham and Nordhaug, 2001, 2002; Larsen, 2001b; Raghuram et al., 2001; Gooderham et al., 2004).

Table 8.27 provides us with some of the answers to these questions. It is evident that the proponents of increasing individualisation of performance measurement or estimation and compensation seem to have gained terrain during the last decade. Both in Denmark and Norway there has been a remarkable growth in the proportion of organisations that apply performance-related pay systems. If we look at managerial jobs, the figures are nearly doubled from 1995 to 1999. The frequency of use is rather similar in the two countries, except for the fact that Danish organisations use performance-related pay for manual employees to a much higher extent than do Norwegian organisations.

These findings might lead someone to surmise that this clear indication of a soaring individualisation of rewards is a reflection of decreasing union influence, since unions are carriers of strong collective and egalitarian values. Let us have a closer look at this (Table 8.28).

The respondents were asked to indicate whether the influence of local unions on *their specific organisation* has increased, remained stable or decreased during the latest years. It is interesting to note that in the years preceding 1992, the managers filling out the questionnaires reported about decreased union influence in roughly about half of the cases. In 1999, these figures have shrunk to 14% and 6%, respectively. Particularly in Norway, there has been a notable strengthening of the influence and power of local trade unions throughout the whole period of the three surveys. The tendency is similar in Denmark, but weaker.

In summary, we seem to be left with a truly antagonistic pattern. The individualisation of rewards and use of performance assessment have increased substantially in both countries. At the same time, unions seem to have

strengthened their influence in work organisations. Perhaps this can be explained by unions' cooperating more closely with the management on HR issues, while union attitudes towards individualised elements of pay systems have softened over the years. We do not, however, at present possess empirical material that could shed light on this.

TRAINING ACTIVITIES AND EXPENDITURE

In the Scandinavian region there has been a longstanding debate on the significance of lifelong learning and competence development in work life and in the population at large. Although some estimates have been made (e.g. Nordhaug, 1997), there is still considerable uncertainty as to the exact amounts of resources and money that are actually spent on such development. One of the main reasons is of course that the amount of resources used on everyday learning through on-the-job training and exchanges with colleagues and customers/clients is extremely difficult to assess. This is by many believed to be the most important source of learning in modern work life (Larsen and Svabo, 2002). Along a similar vein, career development is in Scandinavia seen more as professional and personal growth (in any direction at any age), rather than as elitarian nurturing of a small group of individuals believed to possess management potential (Larsen, 1997, 1998, 2000c; Larsen et al., 1998) (Table 8.29).

Yet, we have some indications of the amounts of resources that are spent on various types of formal training for employees.

If we look at the number of workdays invested, it becomes evident that there are only tiny differences between Denmark and Norway. The number of days used on managers lies in the range between 6 and 6.5. Norwegian professionals and technical personnel seem to receive about 20% more training time than their Danish counterparts, whereas clerical employees seem to get more training than Norwegian ones.

The time used for training and development activities is of course an important indicator of how much money organisations spend on these activities. Table 8.30 contains further information.

Here, the expenditure on training and development is calculated as a proportion of the total salary and wage expenditures of the organisations in the survey.

Table 8.27   Performance-related pay by staff category

	Denmark		Norway	
	1995	1999	1995	1999
Management	14.4	28.1	13.4	25.2
Professional/technical	12.2	19.0	11.2	21.8
Clerical	9.0	14.6	8.1	11.3
Manual	12.2	18.0	10.6	8.0

Table 8.28   Development of trade union influence

	Denmark			Norway		
	1992	1995	1999	1992	1995	1999
Increased	11.7	15.6	21.4	34.2	27.1	24.3
Same	38.0	64.2	55.4	19.2	68.0	67.7
Decreased	50.3	20.2	13.9	46.7	4.9	6.4

It is important to note that the figures are not the average proportions across all aggregated organisations. It is the calculated mean of the proportions every organisation has reported in the Cranet Survey.

A remarkable result is that the percentage of organisations that spend 1% or less measured against their wage budgets has decreased dramatically, in Denmark from around 20% to a little more than 5%; and in

Norway from 37 to 12%. At the same time, Norwegian work life appears as more polarised than the Danish. Compared with Denmark, twice the proportion of the Norwegian organisations is located below the 1% measure, and almost twice the proportion is located above the 10% measure.

COMMUNICATION, STRATEGY AND PERFORMANCE

The concept of "collaborative HRM" has been developed to depict the use of active communication of strategic and financial matters and information from management to employees. Previous research has demonstrated that such HRM is more widespread in the UK and in Denmark and Norway than in countries such as Germany, France and Spain (Gooderham et al., 1999).

Table 8.31 reveals a picture where managers are thoroughly oriented about strategic and financial performance issues. This pattern has remained virtually unchanged during the whole period covered. One surprising finding is that both in Norway and Denmark, there has been a certain decrease in the proportion of organisations that regularly brief their professionals on such issues. This reduction is especially strong in Norway, and we see the same trend for clerical and manual employees. Such a development may indicate that some organisations have tried out new and expanded communication methods and channels but after evaluating these they have reduced the use of such methods.

Table 8.29 Mean number of training days received by staff category

Mean	Denmark			Norway		
	1992	1995	1999	1992	1995	1999
Management	6.1	5.2	6.1	6.5	6.2	6.5
Professional/ technical	5.7	5.1	6.5	7.9	6.3	8.0
Clerical	3.6	3.5	4.2	3.6	2.6	3.4
Manual	2.7	2.3	3.7	3.8	2.9	3.5

Table 8.30 Expenditure on training and development as a proportion of annual salaries/wage bill

(%)	Denmark			Norway		
	1992	1995	1999	1992	1995	1999
<1	19.6	19.3	5.3	36.8	31.4	12.2
1–1.9	32.2	29.8	28.2	22.5	29.0	27.8
2–2.9	28.6	22.9	31.4	10.4	14.5	20.5
3–4.9	10.6	14.5	14.9	12.6	11.8	14.1
5–9.9	6.1	10.9	15.4	11.5	8.2	16.6
>10	2.9	2.5	4.8	6.0	5.1	8.8

Table 8.31 Formal Communication on business strategy and financial performance

	Denmark			Norway		
	1992	1995	1999	1992	1995	1999
Management briefed						
About strategy	95.1	94.6	95.6	96.1	96.1	95.4
About finance	94.5	96.2	95.6	95.0	95.3	85.8
Professional briefed						
About strategy	53.2	59.6	51.7	64.6	74.9	54.8
About finance	76.9	73.8	72.6	74.3	75.7	58.6
Clerical briefed						
About strategy	40.1	49.4	45.6	51.1	61.5	43.1
About finance	72.3	68.4	72.6	66.8	70.4	61.5
Manual briefed						
About strategy	25.5	35.9	27.4	49.6	55.3	36.8
About finance	54.4	50.6	49.7	65.7	65.6	54.8

HRM IN ACTION

CASE STUDY 1: COOP DENMARK

Anders Bojesen, Copenhagen Business School

Introduction and background

Coop Denmark A/S is Denmark's leading consumer goods retailer and a subsidiary of the largest Scandinavian consumer co-operative Coop Norden AB. The Coop Norden group has an aggregate annual turnover in Denmark, Sweden and Norway of DKK 100 billion. Coop Norden was established on 1 January 2002 and is owned by KF in Sweden (42%), FDB in Denmark (38%) and Coop NKL in Norway (20%). Altogether the owners represent about 5 million members in the three countries.

The Danish retail market is dominated by three major operators – Dansk Supermarked, Dagrofa and Coop Danmark (hereafter Coop). This case study deals with HR issues and challenges in the latter. Coop employs around 28,000 people. It runs 660 shops in Denmark, plus 471 shops run on a franchise basis and holds a market share of around 38% in total. It operates different types of superstores, supermarkets, mini-markets and discount shops under the five brand names: SuperBrugsen, Dagli'Brugsen and LokalBrugsen (710 shops), Irma (64 shops), Kvickly and Kvickly xtra (86 shops) and Fakta (245 shops). In addition, the company runs a furniture chain, an electronic chain and is also engaged in the production of coffee under its own brand. Apart from the retail business many employees are hired into headquarter and supply functions like logistics, marketing or the Coop laboratory which is responsible for research in foodstuff, securing the high quality and control of all Coop brands and products. With this range of activities Coop is a powerful operator in the retail sector in Denmark, and it has maintained its high market shares and increased profits over the past decade.

However, the Danish consumer market is characterised by fierce competition resulting in increasing demands of professional and effective company management, a process that also has set its marks on the Coop organisation. In recent years, the organisation has been going through a modernisation process and in the near future one of the biggest challenges is to meet the entry of the German consumer conglomerate Lidl into the Danish market, which is expected early in 2004. *"Lidl's entry in Finland resulted in a price war, where they – by lowering the price levels by 2.5 per cent – increased competition dramatically from day one"* says Ebbe Lundgaard, Chairman of the Board of Directors.

Headed by the managing director Coop is divided into three pillars: Retail, Supply and Finance. The managing director, who is also group director for retail, has the overall responsibility for the five store chains plus the departments HR, logistics and marketing. Group director Supply takes care of all supply departments (i.e. category management), Coop laboratory, Coop brands, coffee production, etc. Group director Finance is in charge of the departments accounting, data, finance and group solicitor.

For this case study five persons have been interviewed. From headquarters interviews have been conducted with one recruitment manager, situated in cooperate HR, one Chief consultant also from HR, with the responsibility for management development, talent spotting and the effect of IT on HRs and one logistics manager (operations). From the shops one Kvickly store manager and one service function manager have been interviewed.

HRs in the organisational set-up: role and strategy

The HR department is jointly operated and provides services to the individual departments, shops and superstores. As the rest of the organisation, the HR department of Coop is in a transition phase. Traditionally, HR has been very focused on the administrative tasks, but there is a clear desire to make HR a strategic partner. *"I would say that 80% of our time still goes with administration. This leaves very little room for the consultancy role at least on a strategic level. We want to become a strategic partner, and we're working on it, but it's something we have to make ourselves worthy of."* (HR consultant)

Located in the basement, of the big headquarter building, the self perception of HR used to be "they" have to come to us, but today this internal attitude has changed totally. The real challenge now is to change the whole mindset about HR in the rest of the organisation: *"Personnel management has been thought of as a support function: When somebody calls, we should be there, but this is now changing. We don't have to be called upon, we will come anyway and we know our worth and what to offer"* (HR consultant). One of the key messages that HR wants to deliver to the rest of the organisation is that in order to survive the constant flux on the market, all departments and store chains need to develop the needed personal skills. HR knows what to do, but it is line management who has to take ownership of the personnel responsibility. Thus, it is stated in the internal "Business plan for Coop Denmark personnel 2003", p. 2: *"Emphasis on developing human resources has increasingly put the responsibility of HR in the hands of the line manager, which accordingly has implied a strengthened focus on each managers capabilities as a personnel manager and not only his professional skills."*

Another important part of the HR strategy is the use of IT. It is the clear strategy of Coop to automate as many of the heavy administrative duties as possible. In addition, an increasing part of personnel administration is to be decentralised to each operation unit, and thereby supporting the intention of raising joint responsibility for own data.

The HR director does not have a seat in the management committee, but he refers directly to the managing director.

Recruitment – centralised or decentralised?

Until recently the HR department was involved in most of the recruiting at managerial levels. Because the number of shops has increased dramatically (this year Coop is expecting the opening of 25–30 new Fakta shops), recruiting at the lower levels of the organisation has been decentralised to the shops and individual departments. The HR department is increasingly concentrating on the selection and recruitment of good store managers and equipping them with adequate skills and tools, so that they can handle the recruiting and development of their employees.

To understand the situation of the store managers it should be mentioned that Coop recently has cut down the management level in the superstores to four people. Besides the store manager, three functional managers, for each of the areas Service, Food and Non-Food perform the management team. Each functional manager is in charge of general management activities, stocking, control of resources, recruiting of staff, etc.

On the next level are a number of sales managers, who are responsible for a product group like groceries, delicatessen, bakery, fruit and vegetables, garments and ironmongery, and the cashier line. In the standard Kvickly superstores there are normally 6–9 product groups. The sales manager takes care of daily coaching of the sales assistants, clerks and part-time workers, and he/she is a major force in the creation of a sales space that is attractive to visit for the customers. The functional manager and his/her sales manager is a close team who together operate a product group. It is considered important that their personalities represent a good and complementary "match".

In the Kvickly departments the respondents expressed that especially the sales manager level needs more attention. *"Here we have had some difficulty in getting competent sales managers particularly in non-food/ironmongery. Perhaps we tend to forget what it takes to sell electronic hardware compared to canned tomatoes." "The sales manager level, just below the functional managers, has to have a better training, otherwise I'm afraid that within very few years we will have a serious recruitment and retention problem."* (Superstore manager)

Respondents gave the impression that customers in general expect the salesman to give top-service and to have detailed knowledge about all products. In that sense CD-players, Cameras and kitchen machines are more complicated and demanding to sell than, e.g. canned food, or toilet paper.

In general Coop is striving hard to get "the right man in the right place", but the low or stagnant growth in the workforce is a big challenge in the retailing business where the situation is characterised by increasing number of shops, extended opening hours, low status and wage levels that are not all that handsome, at least for some parts of the workforce in the shops. Moving to higher positions is nearly the only way of getting wage increases. The pay policy is closely coordinated with the management development programmes, so as to create consistent incentives throughout the system. HR is working on the dissemination of clearer career paths, apart from positions in line management.

Training and development

The enterprise runs a course and conference centre in the provincial town of Middelfart where most of the training takes place. Although teaching capacity is sometimes invited in from the outside, the majority of the management training is deeply internally integrated and organised.

From the very beginning of company history training has been in focus: *"In 1932, a training course of around 9 months was mandatory, this goes to show that for Coop training has always been a natural basis for every day work."* (HR consultant)

A recent initiative to get new employees properly introduced and start training from the very beginning is the "housecoach" system. Every new employee is met by a housecoach and is sent on an introductory course together with other new hires, before he/she has the first working day. In addition, it is the housecoach who introduces the newcomer to colleagues, working routines, etc. *"This is a good concept. On a long-term basis we can see that there is less panic when new employees arrive – it is valuable."* (Superstore manager) Subsequent to the interviews a welcoming CD-R has been produced to replace the introductory course.

A restraint for training and development is when the different chains find difficulties in meeting the budget. Due to the heavy competition on the retail market there is a constant pressure for more effective and rational product handling to raise productivity, a fact that the Kvickly chain recently experienced when they had to cut down 240 jobs.

One way in which Coop is handling the dilemma between budget constraints and the need for constant development (as mentioned in the annual business plan and the staff policy) is by using the latest technology. An e-learning tool is a new concept for store managers to train their employees. The training in Coop values and mission is delivered to all employees on a CD-R. *"The tool is really good, it is fantastic that we can do it ourselves. I hope that we will see more of this in the future."* (Superstore manager) The tool aims at employees at all levels. A total score is given and that is mentioned as a great feature, which suits the "business acumen" culture in Coop perfectly.

Talent management

Coop has consolidated a comprehensive management training programme aimed at the nursing of management talents at all managerial levels. The keen emphasis on management talents is due to the fact that the performance of these people are immensely important for the firm's financial results. Managers who do a good job and who are able to motivate the staff efficiently and develop new leaders are most valuable for the enterprise.

A recent study of 13 talents in Coop showed that talents have very high demands for their managers and that the crucial factor for developing talent is the managers ability to coach and support. *"We were surprised, how decisive (for the success of the talent, edt.) it is to match the right managers and employees. It is perhaps obvious, but one does not always think about it."* (Recruitment manager)

Apart from revealing that it is the *relation* between manager and talent that is the key to success, the study also showed some general features about talents in Coop:

The talents are all, committed employees who:

- Have a constructive and positive attitude to work.
- Posses a competitive and winning mindset.
- Are keen to set goals and determined to reach them.
- Are open-minded, give their opinion and values honesty.
- Are happy to have many social contacts, and like to see themselves as being extrovert.
- Are very motivated to work – emphasise their drive.
- Seek challenges, are eager to learn, demand development, and like to come up with new ideas for problem solving.
- Take pride in – and are pleased with – doing a really good job.

Source: Coop Talent Analysis, 2003

Motivating the staff

An average Kvickly superstore has around 100 employees, but only about 50 of those are working full-time. The large number of students and part time workers in the stores is a special management challenge in order to install team spirit and effective and positive working culture. The goal of making everybody feel a valuable part of the same team is to some extent reached by paying attention to small daily issues and to praise, when a job is done well, says the functional manager. *"One thing is to set a good example, taking the first step, another is to support social arrangements as a bowling night etc."* (Functional manager) To motivate is perhaps one of the most important skills possessed by a manager in the retail business and to be able to motivate, you have to have humour and good listening skills.

Teambuilding is another activity used by Coop to motivate employees, it usually takes place once a year, held in each department. Especially when restructuring is undertaken, or departments are united, this way of motivating is valued as being successful.

One simple tool that has found widespread use in the shops is the "under or above the line" principle. Basically it is a rhetoric from a management course, where the Kvickly managers were trained in how their management style affects employees and management peers. *"When you're above the line you show a positive attitude, impacting your surroundings – pulling them above the line too, seeing every problem as a challenge. But if you are under the line you show a general negative attitude, pulling everybody down and that affects colleagues, working climate and the level of customer service etc."* (Functional manager) The culture and attitude Coop is striving for can be pictured by a quotation from the Danish humorist Robert Storm P.: "Problems of all kind are solved within five minutes, miracles take a little longer … ".

Conclusion and challenges for the future

Coop is in an organisation in a transition phase. The interviews revealed three major challenges for the future which will determine whether Coop can continue to be a market leader, keep the pace and still be successful or whether it must eventually face the defeat to their competitors. Those challenges are:

- Management
- Service
- Professional standards.

Coop has a constant need for good managers and to this point they have been able to attract the right talents, but it is a constant challenge, on a changing market. Even though talent development is given top priority, time pressure and the strong focus on the operation of the business are big restraints in developing good talents. *"It is often difficult to find the time to send people on courses – we don't have the resources to do it."* (Superstore manager)

From 1998–2001 five new directors have been hired into the organisation, indicating a shift in management effecting the entire organisation. *"In the last three years the management board has succeeded in sending clear messages and creating a more visible profile internally as well as externally."* (Logistics manager) Some respondents gave the impression that there is a "generation gap" in management, there are two groups: (a) under the age of 40 and (b) above 50 approaching 60. *"The young managers have a lot of energy, are very motivated and they merely respect you for your own opinion – they have the commercial responsibility. Those above 50 are members of the board or sit in staff functions having the overall responsibility."* (HR consultant) One aspect of the Coop organisation is alterations in top management – another is the changing market conditions.

The consumer market in retailing is characterised by a growing internationalisation, increasing price pressure, new technological breakthroughs and to some extent new life patterns and consumer preferences. These changes in market conditions call for new technical solutions, clearer company profiles and a shift from national focus to an international orientation. With the creation of Coop Norden in 2002, the organisation has taken a powerful and necessary step towards the future.

The Coop name (and organisation) is a new design, but has a long history rich in tradition. The unique co-operative FDB culture endures for better or worse. It still is a political organisation encompassing two cultures "the support base" consisting of headquarters and supply functions and "the shops" with all the store chains. To bridge these two cultures and setting uniform standards will be an important task in the years to come.

References and Sources

Coop Denmark: *Forretningsplan for Coop Danmark Personale 2003* (Business Plan for Coop Denmark Personnel 2003)
Coop Denmark: *Årsrapport 2002* (Annual Report 2002)
Coop Talent Analysis 2003
Five interviews with one Recruitment manager, HR consultant, Logistics manager, Superstore manager and one Functional manager, Coop Denmark, Denmark
Ørskov, Stig: *Forbrugerkongen*, Politiken 25.05.03, 6. sektion, forsiden (Newspaper article)

CASE STUDY 2: FROM PROGRAM TO CULTURE: A NORWEGIAN HRM PROJECT

Martin Gjelsvik and Odd Nordhaug

Introduction

The institutional rules of Norwegian banks were turned upside down in the latter part of the 1980s. The deregulation and liberalisation of the financial markets swiftly and radically altered the rules of the game in the banking industry. This development coincided with a serious downturn of the economy, causing big losses for the banks. The case presented here deals with a bank and its people that survived what may be coined a close-to-death experience, as the bank was on the verge of bankruptcy in 1991. Since then, the bank, with its roots back to 1839, has reinvented itself through a strong belief in linking its over-all strategies to an HR policy of continuous enhancing the knowledge and skills of the employees, close and long-term customer relations and a strong physical presence in the region. The bank has become a learning organisation where management consciously facilitates and encourages learning opportunities.

What was then conceived of as a program or a project, is today a continuing process to leverage the knowledge and skills of all employees; and turning those competencies into sales and solid profits. The story focuses on the introduction and implementation of an organisational development program that has been running for 12 consecutive years. The latter part of the article tells the story of how this program in itself has been reinvented to serve the needs for the organisation and its people.

To better appreciate the story here being told, a brief description of the bank's cultural context is provided.

Cultural context

In this chapter we briefly describe the historical and cultural context to better understand the Norwegian industrial and labour markets. On reading this chapter, have in mind that the context is under transformation with a stronger belief in market solutions and great individual differentiation. During the period after the Second World War, Norway has mostly been ruled by social democratic governments. The party has advocated social equality as an over-arching value, and until recently, favoured nationalised industries. The other ruling parties, the Conservative Party and the Christian Democratic Party, compared to the dominant European scene, pursued a policy which has not been unaffected by mainstream egalitarian values.

The emphasis on equality, or more precisely the absence of great inequality, has gone hand in hand with a very high unionisation, and powerful local and national unions that have played, and still play, active parts on the public arena. In banks and insurance companies, the principle of job security was regarded as sacred until the end of the 1980s. Hence, downsizing and outsourcing has not been deemed necessary, and the banks would rather find alternative solutions when change of business strategies and cost cutting during economic recessions were on the agenda.

Owing to these egalitarian values and the strong unions, wage differentials have stayed relatively small. In addition, employees and unions in many industries have resented individual performance assessments, and compensation has to a substantial degree been determined through collective bargaining.

Traditionally, Norwegian banks were among the most conservative work organisations in the country. This is partly due to their shelter from competition through cartel agreements that determined the interest rates and prices. The cartel arrangements were given the blessings of most politicians and public authorities and were not considered illegitimate by most people at that time. Starting in the 1980s, these rules of the game have changed dramatically. These changes offered new business opportunities for the financial industry. New products and new markets were opened. Put differently, the temptation to stretch for opportunities beyond the competencies of the employees and the capabilities of the organisation was great. When this temptation became a reality and uncovered in the late 1980s and the beginning of the 1990s, it is easy to understand why investments in knowledge and skills became a viable competitive strategy.

The bank's strategy

In the following we present the bank's business proposal and strategies to explicate how the organisational development program fits with the overall HR policies and overall strategies. In the annual report from 2000, the bank presents itself as follows.

Business idea

SpareBank1 SR-Bank shall

- be conceived of by the customer as the recommended and preferred partner;
- offer competitive financial products and services that meet the needs of the customer;
- offer its products through modern, easily accessible and local distribution channels, which ensure that the customer receives good quality and service;
- secure the bank's position as the recommended and leading bank by ensuring that its employees are customer oriented and qualified;
- actively participate in the effort to strengthen growth and development within its market, SpareBank;
- be a profitable and independent bank with local ties, and shall be a regional alternative to the competing financial corporations through the SpareBank 1 alliance.

Operations

SpareBank1 SR-Bank is today organised into five districts with headquarters in Stavanger with 50 offices. The group also consists of the bank's two subsidiaries; a real estate agency chain and a finance company. The bank is part of the SpareBanken1 Group and the SpareBank1 Alliance. The SpareBank1 Group is presently the fourth largest banking and financing group in Norway and commands NOK 180 billion in total assets. The total assets of SR-Bank were close to NOK 44 billion at the end of 2000.

The SpareBank1 alliance

In 1998 SpareBank1 and Sweden's second largest bank, FöreningsSparbanken AB, decided to enter into a strategic alliance. The alliance is a Scandinavian banking and product alliance where SpareBank1 banks in Norway and FöreningsSparbanken AB (publ) in Sweden collaborate through the jointly owned SpareBank1 Gruppen AS. The agreement with FöreningsSparbanken strengthens the regional competitiveness and we have access to expertise and capital that enables us to compete with the other major Norwegian and Scandinavian banks in our market.

We note the strong people orientation in the assertion that *"SpareBank1 SR-Bank is first and foremost the people who work there – and the people we work for"*. Furthermore, we recognise the strong belief in physical presence and the closeness to the customer. Thirdly, through the alliance and their subsidiaries, the bank has ample and strongly competitive opportunities for product development.

In their primary market the bank commands a 50% market share. In 2000, the bank acquired 8000 new customers, consolidating its position as the region's leading bank for both private customers and business and industry. The growth in deposits and lending was substantial, 15% and 20% respectively. A 70% increase in commission revenues from the sale of insurance and securities, adds to the bank's profits and constitutes tangible proof of the bank as a sales- and customer-oriented organisation.

In the annual report of 2000, the managing director states that *"We believe that the relationship between customer and bank is founded on personal contact, mutual respect and confidence. Therefore, we have never been interested in following a strategy that would replace personal contact with automation"*

Loyal to this strategy, the bank has chosen a relatively expensive distribution strategy. The customers will be able to choose between the bank's network of offices, telephone service and the Internet bank. The strategy entails a very high level of service and access to competent personnel.

SESAM

The decision to keep and develop the branch network was first taken back in 1989, and has been confirmed through the crisis in 1991–1993 and the recent technology development with the appearance of Internet banks. The challenge thus became to generate higher revenues, which was more a dream than a reality. Bank employees were not primarily sales people. On the contrary, the most prevalent motive for seeking a job in a bank had traditionally been the desire to obtain a stable income and a secure job.

To include the broad branch network as a part of the bank's strategy was not an obvious decision. The issue of the distribution network was in 1989 the subject of a heated debate. The branch network occupies considerable resources and incurred a major part of the fixed costs. An advanced and well-functioning ATM (automatic teller machines) network together with an electronic payment transfer system significantly reduced the customers' needs to visit the bank in person. Consequently, there were several good reasons for downsizing the branch network. The recommendations from the experts and consultants were also straightforward: Get rid of the brick and mortar!

In the internal discussion, two opposing points of view were present:

1. The bank needs to cut costs. Since the branch network incurs large costs, it must be reduced as much as possible. This is also in line with what our competitors are doing. The basis for this line of reasoning is purely cost oriented. The contribution of bank employees to revenues was not taken into consideration.
2. The branch network, including both the physical and HRs it comprises, represents a unique competitive advantage. No competitor has a similar distribution system. Such an advantage must be developed and exploited, not dismantled.
3. Associated with the argument above, a humanistic point of view was present at that time: We are responsible for our employees and their jobs. The challenge is: How can we use these strategic resources more efficiently than in the past?

When the smoke subsided, the two latter points of view surfaced as winners. However, the distribution network had to become modernised both physically and by enhancing the employees' communication skills and product knowledge. At his point in time, there was no appreciation of crisis and real need for change. The necessity for change was recognised neither by employees nor by a large number of bank managers. The ideals of improving the knowledge and competence of employees as well as providing high quality were easily agreed upon, but the process of transforming these ideas and intentions into practical actions gave rise to considerable differences of opinion. There were disparate views regarding the need for change in recruitment policy, career procedures and reward systems. The new ideas collided head-on with the dominant logic of the old way of doing bank business and customer service.

The former status of lending is quite illustrative. In determining the salary of employees working for the retail market (individuals and households), the traditional practice involved linking salary to the amount of loans the employee was authorised to grant. Lending was "good", it implied more authority and power vis-a-vis the customer, it provided status within the organisation, and it meant more pay at the end of the month. Lending was associated with more status than deposits, which in turn ensured more status than working with payment transactions. "Sales" was a four-letter word.

A common in-a-nutshell description of bank employees engaged in work with private customers was "order takers". This kind of reactive work behaviour was adequate as long as there was no reason for a customer to frequent more than one bank; as long as the customer, regardless of the service required, had to physically visit the bank. In the not too distant past, the banks offered the same products to practically identical prices. In addition, switching costs were high. But the bank market had now changed radically. The main questions were now these: How could a sales-oriented culture be developed? How could prevalent attitudes and work behaviour be changed? What kind of knowledge and skills do the employees and managers need? Do we have any tools or systems to aid us in this process?

The internal answers were far between. For several years the management had preached "we must get better at selling" and "we must become better at understanding customers' needs". There was no end to what the employees had to get better to. But can anyone be expected to improve without having the relevant tools or instructions indicating *how* this is to come about?

The notion of "needs-oriented sales" was introduced to distance the employees from the common perception of an aggressive insurance salesperson; a salesperson more interested in his or her bonuses than in the customer's needs. "Soft sell" was the buzzword, the starting point was always to meet the customer's actual needs. People had to be convinced that "overselling" would backfire in the form of complaints about poor and sloppy financial advice.

The HR department assumed responsibility for arranging sales courses. These courses were typically 1 day or weekend courses aimed at teaching employees various sales techniques. However, this approach was unsuccessful. The reasons were plenty. The courses were not specifically directed at sales in banks: the ideals and techniques were copied from traditional retail business. The concepts of "soft sell" and the focus on long-term customer relations were not at the forefront. Moreover, it had to be acknowledged that courses that were not part of a larger organisational context would easily result in only short-term enthusiasm among the participants, at best. The need for structural changes that could facilitate for learning with lasting effects through organisational capabilities such as improved routines and revised computer programs became increasingly evident. The instructor's job was completed when the course was completed; he or she had no responsibility for neither the use nor implementation and follow-up of the individual learning that had taken place. And there was no system to indicate what had been learned and if the performance in any substantial way was improved. The bank had to realise that they did not possess the knowledge or skills to design and implement a system to develop radical changes in the organisation to change attitudes and business processes.

Initial steps through knowledge imports

At his time the manager of the retail market came across a sales training program that seemed suitable for the task. On a business trip to the US for quite other purposes, he was introduced to a program with a good track record in US financial institutions. In a persuasive and entertaining 45 min, the designer of the product package convinced the astonished bank manager of its relevance also for a Norwegian savings bank.

On his return to the bank, efforts were made to spread the enthusiasm. Needless to say, this turned out to be rather difficult. Comments such as "this will be expensive" and "the US is different from Norway" were indications of profound scepticism. On the other hand, the program was tailor-made for banks; it could pride itself of an outstanding track record. It had gradually evolved through practical experience and testing. The program was not "theory", a well-known taboo in the banking business; it represented condensed practice. Not only was it practice, it was real banking practice!

After a year's tug of war within the organisation, a contract was signed. By that time the American developer of the program had visited the bank twice. His presentations combined with internal alliance building, the marketing manager and manager of HRs were early converts, did persuade top management. A decisive prerequisite was a translation of the program not only into Norwegian language, but into the bank's own culture and intentions as well.

American businesses, not least in the banking industry, are characterised by a higher degree of management by directive than are businesses based on the more participative Scandinavian model. Therefore, bank employees in the US typically have less autonomous jobs than their Norwegian counterparts. Empowerment has a long tradition in the Norwegian work place. Employee behaviour was at the time directed more through detailed manuals than through development oriented, co-operative projects. This is illustrated by the fact that the bank's management was a far more active and visible participant at all stages of the project than was management in the US. They became actively engaged in the training programs, used and disseminated the "new language" and discussed further development of the project in the top management team.

A new position as coordinator for the entire program was established on a contract basis. The coordinator, an external consultant and the bank manager in charge of the retail market division completed an intensive two-week training session in the US. It was at this time the program was "Norwegianised". The entire and very comprehensive program was reviewed and scrutinised in great detail, and the two representatives from the bank were in charge of adapting the program to allow for local Norwegian conditions. The main challenge for the consultant was to become familiar with the program and to be up-dated on pedagogical matters.

There was another important reservation regarding the project. Relying largely on detailed manuals and use of consultants in the training sessions, the program was explicitly built on behaviouristic theory and assumptions, an observation made by management as well as some employees. In this context, conflicts could be eliminated with a reference to SESAM as an authoritative source. This provides considerable opportunity for managerial manipulation of employees. A renowned organisational psychologist was asked to consider the ethical implications of the project. His advice was that the program was ethically sound given that the employees were informed about the measures taken and the tools to be used.

The explicit face

Having been "Norwegianised", the program was introduced in 1989. The target group was all employees in the retail market division, including managers at all levels. More than 500 employees were involved. The program thus constituted a comprehensive organisational development process.

The primary objective was to offer a tool and a learning environment that provided understanding and opportunities to utilise the process of communication between the customer and the bank employees providing services to the customer. The aim was to develop the skills to determine the customer's present and future needs and to suggest the right products and services to fill these needs.

The sales and organisational development project was labelled SESAM, the Norwegian acronym for *"Salg Er SAMarbeid"* (sales equals cooperation). The emphasis on the collaborative aspect was related to the customers' tendency to perceive the bank branches as one single bank. The customer wants to be recognised, regardless of whom they approach in the bank. Therefore it became crucial to stress the significance of intra-organisational cooperation, also across departmental boundaries. For example, information about the customer must be exchanged and made available to all customer service and support personnel.

The SESAM project had a long-term perspective. The organisation was to be transformed from an "order-taking station" into a "proactive sales train". Notwithstanding, the process was called a project, indicating a temporary perspective. The process consisted of a number of training manuals defining the new roles of employees and managers combined with 2–3 days training sessions. Inspired by Nonaka and Takeuchi (1995) the introductory year may be called the explicit face. The new roles and the related necessary skills were explicitly formulated in manuals. The training sessions were designed to transform this explicit knowledge into practice. The employees were expected to learn the content in the manuals in two ways, by repeating their contents, and by internalising the content through learning by doing. The latter process, internalisation, embodies explicit knowledge into tacit knowledge (Polanyi, 1966). By introducing the tacit aspect of knowledge, Polanyi pointed to the fact that "we can know more than we can tell". Tacit knowledge is difficult to verbalise and deeply rooted in and individual's action and experience as well as in the ideals, values or emotions he or she embraces. When knowledge becomes internalised into employees' and managers' tacit knowledge bases in the form of shared mental models or know-how, it becomes valuable assets both for the individual and the organisation. This internalised knowledge may be deepened and broadened through interaction with colleagues.

Below we offer detailed descriptions of two of the new roles, the one for tellers and the one for the manager of the retail division. Thus, we illustrate their complementarities. Each individual employee's role was defined through the so-called "winning plays". These plays were used for tellers, customer service representatives (financial advisors) and support personnel. All levels of management were also equipped with winning plays, from the first-line managers ("sales leaders" in the new language) to the managing director. The sales manager of a bank outlet (for instance the local branch manager) was familiar with his subordinates' wining plays. Conversely, employees also knew their superior's winning play. Thus, the different levels could check each other, and measures were generated so that everybody could continuously perfect his or her role performance.

The new role for the teller was defined in this way:

Winning play for tellers

1. Greeting and presentation:
   - Greet the customer politely so that he or she feels important and welcome.
   - Look up, smile and establish eye contact.

- Even if you are busy with something else, greet the customer by saying something, nodding or waving.
- Ask how you may be of assistance.

2. Carry out the customer's wishes:
   - Deal with the customer's requests in a competent and polite fashion.
   - Use your knowledge to deal with requests, be precise and effective.
   - Address the customer by name.
   - Draw the customer into conversation – establish contact.

3. Uncover needs:
   - Discover what PNO's[1] a customer may have, show interest and consideration.
   - Comment as you serve the customer.
   - Listen for sales opportunities in what the customer says.

4. Give recommendations:
   - Find out which service best suits the customer and recommend it.
   - Explain the solution.
   - Use brochures actively.
   - Recommend that the customer talk with a member of the customer service personnel.

5. Refer the customer to relevant colleagues:
   - Use a customer presentation card.
   - Write the customer's name, the services you suggested and your name on the card.
   - Enclose your business card and any other relevant documents.
   - Refer the customer to the right person.
   - If possible, escort the customer and introduce him or her.
   - If you are unable to escort the customer, explain who or she is to see and give the customer the customer presentation card.

6. Conclusion:
   - Thank the customer politely, using his or her name.
   - If possible, shake hands.
   - Welcome the customer back and offer your help in the future.

The winning play revealed a very important and previously controversial point for the tellers' role. The tellers themselves were not asked to cross-sell, they were asked to refer the customer to a customer service representative if an opportunity for cross-selling arose. However, the tellers have previously responded negatively to any suggestion that they assume a more proactive attitude towards sales. They claimed that sales activity would "only lead to long line at the counters". The management had until now been unable to provide any specific suggestions as to how these two seemingly conflicting demands, prompt service and active cross-selling, could be met simultaneously. The paradox had finally been resolved, and the tellers' attitudes towards sales immediately became more positive.

The second example of a winning play was designed for the general manager of the retail market division. Note the hierarchical system of roles and the complementarity of the roles.

---

[1] PNO: Problems, Needs and Opportunities. The rationale is that the customer comes to the bank with a problem that may be transformed into a need, which is a sales opportunity for the bank.

Winning play for the division general manager

1. Define and communicate the results you expect from each manager:
   - Establish "winning plays for sales managers" as a standard for sales management and training.
   - Set targets together with the managers.
   - Obtain acceptance for expected actions and set targets, both for superiors and subordinates, so that the desired behaviour is measurable.

2. Be a good example:
   - Practice what you preach.
   - Be optimistic and enthusiastic.
   - Practice the three C's (Competence, Courtesy and Consideration).

3. Empower your employees:
   - Share information.
   - Arrange monthly follow-up meetings with your managers.
   - Give your managers opportunities for individual development.
   - Delegate authority and responsibility.
   - Listen! Listen! Listen!

4. Build team spirit:
   - Set goals and map progress for the region.
   - Communicate goals and results.
   - Do not forget the humorous side of things.

5. Check on your expectations:
   - Execute hands-on management by visiting the local banks and branches.
   - Review the local bank's results monthly with each manager, using the sales reports.
   - Ask the customers if they are satisfied with the bank.

6. Reward and recognise:
   - At your monthly meetings, reward and recognise those who have achieved good results.
   - Reward and recognise both individual employees and teams.
   - Express your approval for a well-done job on a daily basis.
   - Catch your employees doing a good job.

Performance evaluation

Considerable emphasis was placed on measurable behaviour. Behavioural change was to be observed and reinforced through various forms of rewards: attention, praise and prizes. Reinforcing positive behaviour was a priority. During the first year, managers were instructed not to react negatively towards those employees that did not succeed. Realising that the project would lead to considerable changes in behaviour, the first year was designated to be a trial-and-error period. Employees being unable to adjust during this period were helped to overcome their problems in their current job position or transferred to another job.

"Catch your employees doing a good job" was the slogan that expressed the positive team spirit the organisation sought to nurture. This proved to be a great challenge, especially for managers. Contrary to the American or southern European spirit, Norwegians are introvert and seldom brag about the peers. Even if you believe your are good at something, you are not supposed to show it.

The bank had virtually no experience in sales and performance evaluation. Sales measurement at the individual level, with an accompanying reward system, was a central element in the American version of the program. This part of the program was de-emphasised because:

- American business is more individual oriented.
- American motivational theories are frequently based on a conception of the individual as an inherently egoistic and materially oriented being.
- Participation in the project would be motivating in itself. Higher sales would provide the necessary basis to ensure the survival of more of the existing jobs.
- Measuring individual sales could result in overly aggressive, short-term sales, leading to deterioration of good customer relations. The bank's goal was to develop stable long-term customer relationships.

Employee sentiments were mixed. Many wanted to demonstrate and visualise their own skills, e.g. as expressed in sales figures. Others, particularly the more union oriented, were sceptical. They partly expressed concern with the assumed "weak" performers, and partly argued on the basis of their natural right to stick to the main provisions of the National bank Agreement, which prohibited individual performance measurements. Evaluations conducted at the group level were accepted, on the condition that nothing could be traced back to the individual employee. The bank's management contested this formal argument, however, since the point in question was included under the main section in the National bank Agreement dealing with electronically based systems. The management claimed that registration using an electronic medium was forbidden, while manual recordings and measurements were allowed.

Many possible avenues to compromises were attempted. One suggestion was that manual measurements of individual employee performance could be carried out at the workplace and the results then collected by the closest line manager. Union representatives opposed this suggestion, even though the employees in many divisions found this solution desirable. However, the management was not interested in letting the issue evolve into an open conflict. A project that otherwise had been so positively received was not to be spoiled by a feature not considered vital to the success of the project.

Ultimately, the following agreement was reached: each individual employee should manually record his or her own sales figures every week. These were in turn registered on a form without specifying the respective persons. The sales manager added up the figures and calculated the results of the branch/department. The individual could benchmark herself against the calculated average sales scores.

Each subunit's results (or in the new terminology: the results of the single sales office) were then collected centrally and published every month for the entire bank. These figures formed the basis for the selection of a *Sales Office of the Month*. This recognition consisted of a symbolic sum of money and considerable positive PR in the Bank Newsletter. Similarly, each year the bank rewarded two prizes as Sales Office of the Year and Sales Manager of the Year. Furthermore, the sales offices achieving their sales targets were eligible for membership in the "Hundred Percent Club", which was restricted to those offices that reached their predetermined sales targets. Thus, virtually all performance measurement took place at the branch office or team level. The only individual reward, "Sales Manager of the Year", was based on a number of qualitative criteria and was awarded by a committee.

An equally contentious issue was the question of *what* ought to be measured or evaluated. The bank's management ultimately decided the issue, on the advice of the project coordinator and the head of the retail market division. Ten representative products were chosen, partly on the basis of their measurability, partly on the basis of their importance to the bank. The product selection was also designed to grant all bank offices equal opportunities to reach the targets. (Too much priority on deposits, e.g. would put the offices that primarily sold loans at a disadvantage.)

The development of sales targets and subsequent rewards undoubtedly had an effect on sales. This was not a function of the material goods accruing to the winners of the competitions. The positive recognition, the chance to be the centre of the new rituals, and the internal competition between similar offices were the essential elements. A sales office could, e.g. aim to be better than other offices of the same size or others operating in the same market.

During the first year, the level of the fixed sales targets was determined locally, without any particular influence or help from the bank's headquarter. As could be expected, this led to certain instances of tactical budgeting. During the course of the year, however, this became a somewhat awkward and embarrassing matter, as a couple of offices were constantly being named sales office of the month even though their results were mediocre. In the subsequent year, this practice was then changed. Each individual sales office presented its target figures to the regional administration, which coordinated the figures for that region. At the next step, the five regions were coordinated by the bank's headquarter. A number of key figures were set up as guidelines, e.g. it was considered reasonable to expect that an equal percentage of a bank's salary account customers used a cash card. In several areas such "objective" criteria were used.

It had thus taken the bank 2 years to establish a simple system for performance measurement that most employees and interest groups could accept. A crucial cultural barrier had been overcome, but in such a way that the new system could be integrated into the established culture without directly challenging the culture.

Branches and departments: the new learning communities

The responsibility for training employees at the operational level was assumed by their immediate superior, the sales manager. An external consultant trained the 60 sales managers. He was also in charge of training 20 bank employees to act as on-the-job instructors. These instructors assisted the sales manager in their training of their personnel.

Initially, the on-the-job instructors and sales managers completed a 5-day course with the consultant, the coordinator functioning as his assistant. At the operational level, a session spanning 2–3 days, depending on the specific job category, was implemented. It was only at this initial stage that the training took place off site. At later stages all groups had 1-day sessions once every 6 months. These meetings functioned partly as a forum for mutual exchange and information, partly as a corrective to activities that had been put into effect, and partly as an introduction to new activities.

However, the most important and encompassing learning process took place in the local branches and support departments. The sales managers were responsible for arranging weekly personnel meetings. These meetings were held in the morning before the bank opened the doors for customers. Typically they lasted for half an hour. The meeting followed a fixed pattern in 1-month periods. Two meetings were designated for ser-vice improvement, one meeting for product knowledge, and one for presentation and discussion of sales targets. The cycle was repeated every month. This responsibility was a new challenge for the sales manager, and the quality and results of the meetings varied greatly.

Some attempts were made to avoid the meetings altogether on the grounds of practical excuses, but no deviation from the plan was accepted. Management simply required that these arrangements were part of the sales managers' job, something he or she was committed to through SESAM.

The weekly meetings were regarded an appropriate vehicle to institutionalise the learning process at the organisational level as well as with the individual employee and manager. It was an important tool for the transition from project to organisation, from experiment to organisational routine. Learning was to be an organisational capability to leverage the competitive position of the bank.

The weekly meetings were always based on local experiences. Employees were encouraged to present good or bad examples of customer service or responses. These examples served as the basis for a discussion of improvements, changes, needs for new system solutions and advertising material. This institutionalised arena for learning through experience transfer was also important for political and ethical reasons. Local learning based on the team's own experience could serve as an important counterbalance to the more centralised and behaviourist learning model on which the project was originally founded. This local learning, which became increasingly significant, led to a "democratisation" of the organisational development that took place, and successful agendas for weekly agendas for weekly meetings were exchanged among the sales manager.

The weekly meetings represent a telling example of what Nonaka et al. have coined the "socialisation" process in the knowledge creation spiral (Nonaka and Takeuchi, 1995). At the individual level explicit knowledge (the SESAM manuals and the winning plays) was internalised through learning-by-doing in their respective jobs and communications with customers and peers. Explicit knowledge becomes embodied in new skills and attitudes, and gradually part of the individual's automatic routines, and thus made tacit. Since tacit knowledge is context specific and difficult to formalise, transferring tacit knowledge requires sharing the same experience through joint activities and spending time together. Thus, the weekly meetings became an important supplement to the formal training sessions. The combined learning arenas facilitate the blend of internalisation and socialisation processes that allow for leveraging both from the explicit and tacit knowledge potential.

As we will see in the following chapters, learning from experience has become the dominant knowledge creation method in the bank. Gradually, the explicit and formal manuals have been replaced with broad socialisation processes across all levels of the bank.

Twelve years later: best practice in practice

Twelve years after the introduction, the program is still healthy and running, an extraordinary achievement in itself. The program has survived three managing directors. All three have been enthusiastic about the program. Furthermore, today the program is expanded to involve the whole organisation. The reason is not hard to explain: the bank can pride itself by stunning results. Within the alliance of regional savings banks, SR-Bank outperforms the others in sales results. These internal bench markings are valid indicators of the program's success as the differences in results occur within a corporation with the same strategy, the same product mix, common plans for implementations and simultaneous product launches. As indicated above, although the basic beliefs and elements are the same, the program has undergone a transformation. Today all training sessions are based on the employees' own experiences.

In 1989 the program was introduced to transform bank employees from order taking to proactive selling. Today this is no longer an issue. The employees have all learned how to sell and the managers at all levels know how to motivate their employees to do just that.

In fact they are themselves part of the sales force. The program's content and intentions has become an integral part of the culture of the bank. The sales program is perceived as a "cultural development program". This is underscored by the fact that whereas the program initially included the retail bank, today the entire bank is involved. Corporate banking and all service functions are engaged in the program, not only to improve sales but also to develop a common culture and a common experience-oriented knowledge base. This implies that the program comprises 700 employees in 50 branches in five districts.

In other words, while the program is still running at unabated speed, the goals and intentions have changed. Initially, the goal was to learn new roles. The role of the teller was transformed to the role of the proactive financial advisor and seller of products and services. The present objective is to improve the performance of the existing roles, not to create new ones. The challenge is how to pose the most relevant questions to the customer to discover and fill present and future needs. Experience transfer is the main mechanism. The present managing director wants to see *"best practice in practice"*.

The transformation of a program to a culture

When SESAM was introduced in 1989 no one could imagine it still running more than 10 years later. Certainly, the intentions were long term, and everybody expected that instilling a sales culture would be a hard struggle. But what is long term when it comes to organisational change and development programs? They often come and go with new bosses and new trends in the market of superfluous consultancy fads.

The first test of the viability of the program came with the new managing director of the bank in 1991. The main structure of the program was then in place, including the rather cumbersome negotiations with the union as to performance measurements and the policies towards those employees that did not want to change their roles. The new director was recruited outside and was new to the finance industry. At the time of his entry, the bank was next to bankruptcy.

Contrary to the development in other banks in similar situations, he decided to keep all the bank branches as a strategy to stay close to the customer through human interactions. He threw the axe at the staff functions instead, which he cut by 25% virtually overnight. The return on the investments in the ensuing fixed costs associated with the branches and its employees had to be earned by leveraging the sales. He soon became convinced of the potential of the SESAM program, and dedicated much of his time to be visible at their training sessions and ceremonies. His message was clear and simple: "We have SESAM, let's use it, and let's install great ambitions for ourselves and our customers."

The managing director strengthened the importance of performance measurement and was a vigorous advocate for a strong sales culture. With the financial performance of the bank as the immediate backdrop, the message was appealing and easy to grasp. Without increased sales efforts and proven results, bank offices had to shut down and employees laid off. The position as SESAM manager became a 2-year assignment job with high status. The right candidate was handpicked from the high ranks of the bank hierarchy. The fact that the position had been occupied by bank managers proves the point. SESAM provides an arena where talented people are allowed to test their ambitions and competencies. It is an extremely visible and transparent position that brings you in contact with most employees and managers in the organisation.

Initially the creator of the original American version behind SESAM took part in the implementation of the program in the bank. Especially he met with the board and the management team to explain the philosophy and intentions of the program. A Norwegian consultant was also hired to run the training sessions the first couple of years. However, after

4 years the external consultants were ousted. They had played an important role, but their roles were no longer needed for the new cast. This evidences the new pride and self-confidence the success of the program fostered. The sales performance was surprisingly successful and sustainable, and the financial results more than indicated that the bank and the employment was no longer at stake.

As described above, the program formally consisted of written routines of roles and processes. The goal of the training sessions was to transform this explicitly formulated information into practical knowledge and skills for sales managers, financial advisors, tellers and support people. In daily language, "theory" should be converted to practice. This "theory" was imported through external consultants and those bank employees that had been acquainted with the program and its systematic approach in the US. After 3–4 years, this theory could no longer inform practice in the bank. "Theory" had become practice. The winning play (ref) is no longer in use as an explicit template, the routine has become an internalised competence.

Learning from theory is replaced by learning from practice. Only good and bad experience from practice could further improve practice. It was time for the bank employees to take charge of the program and the further development of the organisational culture of their work place and their common learning arenas.

This development coincided with the coming of the next managing director. As a former member of the Board of Directors, he was well acquainted with SESAM and its performance and its significant impact on the economic results of the bank. His vision was formulated in his view of SESAM as the vehicle for "implementing best practice in practice". What is needed in the present stage of the continuing process is learning arenas where the employees can share and reflect upon their own experiences. Two formal arenas serve this important purpose: the weekly local meetings at the branch under the leadership of the sales manager, and the training sessions under the leadership of the SESAM manager.

Learning with pleasure and fun has become the guiding principle at the training sessions. The sessions combine fun and play with learning from experience. The good and personally experienced story may carry loads of tacit knowledge across to colleagues. This requires a caring and open atmosphere at the sessions where employees use their courage to share failures as well as successes. The sales culture has become more differentiated than the traditional banking culture, where rule following was the hallmark of quality. When following predefined roles and routines is the most important rules of the game, it is difficult to differentiate between the excellent and the average employee. Today, you are encouraged to do your utmost, and you are allowed to show that you are indeed way above the average. The present managing director is also visible at the training sessions, where he insists that the employees tell how good they are.

New roles in a new culture

Sales leaders

The bank manager, who used to be an administrator controlling that the employees did in fact follow the rules and routines, is today a sales leader. The role of the bank manager includes the role of the sales leader. Contrary to widespread present management rhetoric, middle managers play a major role in the development of the bank and its prevailing culture. All bank managers are also expected to perform as sales leaders. They are not allowed to withdraw to their paper work in secluded offices. They are expected to serve as a good example as a sales leader and a relentless motivator of his or hers colleagues.

Sales managers are evaluated on an annual basis. Two dimensions are important:

1. Sales results over time.
2. Feedback from the employees, by means of an annual internal appraisal and analysis. The analysis includes leadership and organisational qualities like climate, job satisfaction, openness and trust. In addition a score of his or hers individual capacity is provided.

In other words, the sales manager's performance is evaluated along quantitative sales statistics and more qualitative dimensions at both the organisational as well as the individual level. If the sales manager does not perform as expected, he or she will be offered other opportunities in the bank.

The managing director

The managing director is actively supporting the program. He often takes part in the training sessions, and challenges the employees to propose chores for him do in order to support them in their daily tasks and struggles. He frequently asks "What can I do to make you perform a better job?" And the employees are responsive: "We want better systems, we need more people, and we want a more visible leader." He invites to a dialogue with the employees, and he listens to the stories of the employees. In the sessions the employees tell juicy stories to transmit their views of being an employee in the bank and what is on the mind of the customers.

The managing director is part of the process and the employees have learned to expect exactly that. He takes care not to control the process. He puts his head on the block in the same token as the sales managers and employees in their common efforts to improve their sales capabilities and relational processes. This is the logic of the "training arm" illustrating that the strength of the arm is dependent on everybody playing their respective roles to serve the customers.

The bank has been blessed with down to earth and practical managing directors that give credibility to their presence in the SESAM process. Their changing role is a demanding challenge. The role of the coach and visible supporter is very different from the controlling and distanced bookkeeper and the commander of detailed work instructions. Bank employees will easily unmask window dressing and empty rhetoric.

The SESAM learning structure

The program is managed by a SESAM leader. The position is an appointment for 2 years and is highly regarded within the bank culture. In recent years bank managers have served as managers and motivators for the program. The position may serve as a career opportunity, which is evidenced by the fact that former SESAM leaders now command positions as bank managers. Others view the position as a brake from a long-held job, witnessed by the present SESAM leader who is recruited from a position as a bank manager. The SESAM leaders may choose to go back to their former job or head for an alternative position.

The SESAM manager coordinates all the activities at the bank level. That includes the management and administration of two central and very comprehensive activities that encompass all managers and employees it the bank: training of sales managers and financial advisors/sellers. The first three activities below reach across the bank, fostering experience transfer and knowledge dispersions across branches and departments. The two latter activities are part of the daily routine within the local or regional structure:

1. Training of sales managers: Twice a year the sales leaders gather for 1½ days training sessions. The groups include branch managers, bank managers and department

managers in the retail bank. The sessions focus on central themes that differ from session to session depending on perceived challenges at the time of the gathering. Five sessions are orchestrated, one for each region. The 1 ½ days format is consciously chosen as a means to further develop the social relations between the managers from different branches of the region.

2. Training of financial advisors: All the financial advisors and sellers meet twice a year for a 1-day training session. They gather in groups of 25 people across the bank. In sessions led by external consultants, the participants focus on the sales process. With more than 600 financial advisors, tellers and support people, approximately 25 meeting are held annually. The external consultants are aided by the SESAM manager at all meetings.

3. Training of team leaders: In the larger bank branches, the financial advisors are organised in teams. The team leaders have no personnel responsibility, they are engaged to motivate for sales. These jobs are coined "performance positions" as they command additional wages. The teams are interdisciplinary as the members hold complementary competencies like financing, savings, insurance and payment transactions. The team leaders have this year been offered 1 ½ days training in how to coach their sales group. These training sessions will continue twice a year in the future.

4. Regional meetings: The regional bank manager has monthly meetings with his/hers local sales leaders (branch managers). The bank is divided into five regions and the regional bank manager is responsible for the activities in his/her region.

5. Local meetings: The sales managers conduct weekly sales meetings with the local advisors and sellers. The sales manager is typically identical with the branch manager. Presently there are 70 branches with comprehensive responsibilities for the sales. The agenda at these weekly consists of three fixed themes:
   a. Presentation of the sales results.
   b. Sales training. Each branch has adopted it own model according to their own needs and opportunities in the market. The market knowledge is local, hence a locally developed model for training.
   c. Product training.

The weekly, local meetings have become an integral part of the organisational routines. Everybody knows what is expected. The SESAM managers may show up on some of the meetings to be informed and pick up clues to explore in common training sessions. It's worth mentioning that these meeting have been part of the internal rules of the game for 10 years. It took some time to have them introduced and actually implemented, today their relevance is no longer disputed.

The SESAM structure

The SESAM manager does not work all by himself. He reports to a steering committee that includes the directors of the retail and corporate market, the marketing and the HR manager. This group makes the formal decision as to the content of the SESAM program and training session. Before a proposition is presented to this committee, a broad process has taken place. First, the SESAM manager consults with top management and the marketing and the HR department. Even more important, resource groups representing all organisational levels and geographical areas of the bank, respond to where they feel the competitive pressure and the need for more knowledge and training. They are also consulted on the methods to be used at the training sessions, the need for external consultants, etc. The SESAM manager sets off the resource groups and presents the proposed content of the next sessions to the groups before the final decision in the steering committee. This embracing process ensures that the goals and processes of the next training sessions are firmly rooted in the needs and experiences of the employees as well as with the strategies of management.

Performance measurement

Performance measurement has become an integral part of the SESAM program since its first introduction in the bank. At that time measuring sales ran contrary to the existing bank culture. The initial steps included discussions and negotiations with the union, which expressed skepticism. Management partly shared some of the reluctance, being aware that the program has its origin in the US with very different traditions. The negotiations with the union settled for a compromise: sales at the branch level was accepted, but individual sales should not be reported.

A selection of products is being measured. In accordance with the principles of the "training arm" the branches decide on which products and services after a consultation with the marketing department and the top management group. The range of products is small, because the organisation wants to focus on some initiatives. Typically these will coincide with marketing campaigns, seasonal sales or the utilisation of new technologies such as Internet banking. The mix of products may change from one-quarter to another and products may have differentiated relative weights.

The sales performance is in turn related to economic incentives through an elaborate system: on a monthly basis branches that reach their sales budgets receive NOK 400 per employee. Branches that achieve their quarterly budgets are granted a bonus of NOK 1500 per employee. The budgets and sales goals are stipulated on the basis of a combination of three factors: the bank's overall ambitions, the average of similar branches, and the local conditions and opportunities. Thus, a centrally prepared algorithm is used to define differentiated goals for the respective branches.

Note the absence of individual rewards. An internal competition is introduced between the branches by rewarding the five best performing branches with NOK 3000 per employee, the next five branches (number 6–10) are granted NOK 500. In addition to these regular bonuses, economic incentives are used for certain campaigns. All in all the employees in the best sales branches may pocket the equivalent of €3000 annually. Roughly speaking this adds another 10% to their wage.

To avoid complacency the bank has implemented various schemes for benchmarking at three levels:

- Internally between the branches of SR-Bank.
- Between SR-Bank and the other member banks of the savings bank alliance.
- Nationally through Gallup polls.

The effects of the economic aspects of the program are indisputable. Statistics from the bank alliance document beyond doubt that SR-Bank is the superior sales organisation. According to the bank, the SESAM program claims the honor. (The banks within the alliance market the same products in very similar markets, so internal factors are the most obvious candidates for good explanations.) All experience also testifies to the fact that those products and services that are included in the SESAM measurement scheme outperform those that are not included. As explicated above, the same product may be part of measurement system for some periods to be excluded in other periods. Again, the bank witnesses that the sales increase in the inclusion intervals.

Above we hinted that performance measurement was a controversial issue at the start-up of the SESAM program. It still is, but with a different set of reasons. As described above, the economic incentives do make a difference to your wage. The continued skepticism is today rooted in the *short-term* character of economic incentives. On the other hand, the bank wants *long-term* customer relations. Consequently, the bank is witnessing the paradox that short-term successes may harm their long-term goals. Reports reveal several examples of too aggressive selling. The sales philosophy tells the employees that their products and services are supposed to be solution-oriented, lasting sales; based on the discovery and mapping of the present and future needs of the customer.

Much to the surprise of management; economic, external incentives are very effective motivational factors. Strong emotional and competitive forces are set in motion. Paradoxically, the training sessions put much effort into discussions of the "good examples of what we are not supposed to do". Management is presently trying to balance these unintended consequences by stressing ethics and norms as the most viable basis for customer relations. A balanced scorecard has been introduced to include these features in a broader measurement system.

Looking back to the introduction of SESAM, it was explicitly stated that the model of aggressive insurance salespersons was discarded. Instead, the bank introduced the term "soft selling", underscoring the intention of avoiding obtrusion and pushing sales to reach short-term performance goals. The success of SESAM is in this respect close to becoming the best intentions' enemy.

The future: improving best practice

The SESAM program has a 12 years track record in the bank. Will it go on forever? The answer is most likely yes. It is no longer conceived of as a program; it is the way the bank carries on with its primary business and customer contact. The bank persistently argues that it has taken 6–7 years to implement the present sales culture. The employees have internalised the knowledge and skills that make them successful in the competitive banking environment. It has never been considered to drop the program. So what are the issues to be resolved in the future? The SESAM manager lists the following:

- The conflict between short-term performance measures and the goal of long-term and profitable customer relationships needs to be resolved. Solutions are not obvious. A potential path is to focus on the *drivers of sales*, not the actual sales output. Sales referrals, teambuilding and the quality of the financial advice may serve as potential candidates. Needless to say, the discovery and documentation of such drivers are no easy task.
- Developing the role of the sales leader. The sales leader is the key performer on the stage of sales actors. They need to internalise their role and the expectations from management, employees and customers. The sales leader has the responsibility to define the right quality of their services and employees to serve their local market effectively. To become a better leader they must command the courage to become more explicit on their feedback to the sales force.

This leads to the third issue of:
- Goal and development assessment talks with the employees, including the ability and courage to raise difficult issues and resolve controversies.
- Develop the human and social relations at the work place and within the sales teams. A caring organisation is the best basis for open and honest experience transfer and knowledge creation.
- Develop stretch targets. Stretch targets go beyond the budgets and reflect hopes and ambitions of teams and individuals. In peoples' efforts to reach such targets the bank is

tolerant of failures. The main point is to make people more creative and ambitious in what they want, and how they imagine getting there.

Teaching assignments

1. The SESAM program was modified on the basis of a belief that it was not fully compatible with the culture of Norwegian work-life. Discuss the degree to which the program could be adapted to a selected bank in your own country and, if needed, outline which adjustments should then be made to make the program more compatible with the local conditions.
2. Discuss courses of action that can be taken by higher-level managers who want to obtain top management support and commitment to an organisational development program that these managers consider vital for aligning the organisation and its competence base with a radically changed strategy involving a shift from internal to external focus.
3. Discuss whether the bank could have used economic incentives and rewards more actively in order to increase the sales of credits more effectively.
4. Explain which types of incentives that in your opinion should have been used as well as how a tailored reward system should have been designed.
5. The bank chose to implement the SESAM program in order to accomplish realignment of its competence base to the new strategy. However, an important question relates to what the bank alternatively could have done to promote such realignment. Suggest and discuss at least two alternative ways that could have been considered from the wide range of organisational and HRM measures that can be applied to promote this type of realignment.

References

Nonaka, I. and Takeuchi, H. (1995) *The Knowledge-Creating Company: How Japanese Companies Create the Dynamics of Innovation.* New York: Oxford University Press.

Polanyi, M. (1966) *The Tacit Dimension.* Gloucester, MA: Peter Smith (reprinted 1983).

CONCLUSIONS

The chapter describes HRM in two fairly similar countries, Denmark and Norway. They are both highly developed knowledge and service-based economies (in contrast to dominance of manufacturing industries), albeit Norway has a strong emphasis on extraction of energy and minerals as well as fishing. The analysis of HRM in Denmark and Norway shows two very similar economies, both very dependent on a highly skilled work force and with HRM as an important catalyst for the utilisation of HRs. In this sense they are very good examples of why the need for "inventing" a new and more updated concept (i.e. HRM) to replace the traditional concept of Personnel Management has occurred during the last two

decades. The fairly narrow perspective of Personnel Management, aiming (almost exclusively) at attracting, retaining and developing individuals, has proven to be insufficient to explain the complex interaction between individuals, jobs and organisations in a knowledge economy. Immaterial production – whether it is service, administration or "selling" information and know-how – makes human behaviour (in the form of competence and commitment) a competitive strength – and hence a strategic factor. This somewhat reduces the distinction between overall organisational strategy and HR strategy. Organisational excellence is achieved through HR initiatives – in contrast to an economy dominated by manufacturing companies where the physical properties of the manufactured products typically determine the competitiveness of the companies.

The proportion of companies where the head of the personnel/HR function has a place on the main board has remained stable in Denmark as well as Norway, although the proportion of companies in which this is the case, is higher in Norway than in Denmark. Along a similar vein, the involvement of HR from the outset in the development of corporate strategy is more common in Norway than in Denmark. Thus, in this respect, Norway and – in particular – Denmark are not "full-blooded" textbook examples of HRM. This can be interpreted as "room for improvement" of Danish and Norwegian HRM practice – or, in contrast – as an ability to maintain a critical distance to fads and hype in the HRM area, and a courage to not just follow the politically correct rhetoric of mainstream HRM thinking. A third explanation is somewhat more pragmatic, i.e. that fact that most Danish and Norwegian companies are fairly small and hence find it difficult to implement the "jewellery" of modern HRM thinking. In any case, the general picture is two economies where HRs are taken seriously and invested in, where competence (development) is of ultimate importance, where "eye contact" is established between the employee and the line manager, where organisational structures are fairly flat, and where – consequently – individuals are dealt with as individuals and are assigned responsibility for their own job to a fairly high extent.

HRM strategy and practice is associated with features of the national cultures (egalitarian values, for instance), thus identifying what could be called "collective ownership" to HRM in Danish companies – and to a somewhat lesser extent in Norway. The collective ownership is expressed in high level of line manager responsibility for HRM, the involvement of employees in HR issues and heavy emphasis on the development of competence and commitment of the employees. Collaborative HRM also implies the use of active communication of strategic and financial matters from management to employees.

Compared to the other participating countries in the Cranet Survey Denmark ranks very high when it comes to allocating to line managers responsibilities for HRs. Over the last decade Norway has also moved in this direction. The 1999 Cranet figures for Norway seem to reinforce this ongoing pace whereas in Denmark, within most HRM areas, except for compensation and

industrial relations, the level now seems to have stabilised. It should be added that line management and the HR department increasingly make *joint* decisions on major policy decisions.

Both countries are moving in a direction implying a stronger individualisation of work life, epitomised by individualised performance appraisals and compensation systems. Hence, both in Denmark and Norway there has been a remarkable growth in the proportion of organisations that apply performance-related pay systems. This significant increase in individualisation of rewards and use of performance assessment has gone *hand in hand* with a strengthening of the influence of the unions. However, the emergence of the new HRM and Strategic HRM paradigms has created a strong pressure on local unions to redefine some of their roles and become more strongly involved in HR issues.

The HRM scene in Denmark and Norway is not the same, however. Going back to the title of the chapter, the two countries are – in their approach to HRM – cousins rather than siblings. HRM in Denmark is less formalised, structured, and top-heavy than the Norwegian HRM environment, reflecting a slightly more informal, spontaneous and ad hoc flavoured national culture than the Norwegian national culture. Alternatively, as it has been suggested in the chapter, Norway is perhaps more influenced by US HRM thinking than Denmark which is leaning more towards the European scene.

It should not be disregarded, however, that the institutional background, history and language are very similar in the two countries. Despite the – moderate – differences in industrial pattern (with more emphasis on heavy industry, raw materials and energy in Norway) the two countries have a lot of similarities. As it has been seen, the actual HRM tools used are similar, the workforces are similar (including the high proportion of women in the workforce), and in both countries there is a high level of unionisation. Albeit this could in itself impede the individualisation of employment conditions, this has not been the case. Unions have increasingly realised that their prime role is *not* to act, negotiate and decide *on behalf of* the members, but – in contrast – provide the framework for – and help the members to choose and pursue what is – appropriate working and employment conditions for themselves.

In short, the two countries reflect many of the core features of the HRM concept, but not in the orthodox meaning of the field. To a fairly high extent the main elements of HRM (including the strategic HR orientation and a dynamic division of labour between the employee, the line manager, the HR function and top management) are found in Danish and Norwegian companies. The picture has been fairly stable during the 1990s, partly due to the fact that the HRM orientation was already fairly significant at the entry of the decade.

REFERENCES AND SOURCES

References

Bamberger, P. and Meshoulam, I. (2000) *Human Resource Strategy: Formulation, Implementation, and Impact.* Thousand Oaks: Sage.

Brandi, S., Hildebrandt, S. and Nordhaug, O. (2001) kompetansegullet@det.nye.arbeidsliv. (Goldcollars@the. new.worklife). Oslo: Cappelen Akademisk Forlag.

Brewster, C. and Larsen, H.H. (1992) Human resource management in Europe: evidence from ten countries. *International Journal of Human Resource Management,* 3(3): 409–434.

Brewster, C. and Larsen, H.H. (1993) Human resource management in Europe: evidence from ten countries. In: Hegewisch, A. and Brewster, C. (eds.), *European Developments in Human Resource Management.* London: Kogan Page.

Brewster, C. and Larsen, H.H. (1997) Integration and assignment: a paradox in human resource management. *Journal of International Management,* 3(1): 1–23.

Brewster, C. and Larsen, H.H. (eds.) (2000) *Human Resource Management in Northern Europe. Trends, Dilemmas and Strategy.* London: Blackwell.

Brewster, C. and Söderström, M. (1994) Human resources and line management. In: C. Brewster and A. Hegewisch (eds.), *A Policy and Practice in European Human Resource Management.* London: Routledge.

Brewster, C., Larsen, H.H. and Mayrhofer, W. (2000) Human resource management. A strategic approach? In: Brewster, C. and Larsen, H.H. (eds.), *Human Resource Management in Northern Europe. Trends, Dilemmas and Strategy.* London: Blackwell, pp. 39–65.

Fombrun, C., Tichy, N.M. and Devanna, M.A. (1984) *Strategic Human Resource Management.* New York: Wiley.

Gooderham, P. and Nordhaug, O. (2001) Elite graduate expectations. *European Business Forum,* 5(6): 54–57.

Gooderham, P. and Nordhaug, O. (2002) Are cultural differences in Europe on the decline? *European Business Forum,* (2), 8, 48–53.

Gooderham, P., Nordhaug, O. and Ringdal, K. (1999) Institutional and rational determinants of organizational practices: human resource management in European firms. *Administrative Science Quarterly,* 44(3): 507–531.

Gooderham, P., Nordhaug, O., Birkelund, G.E. and Ringdal, K. (2004) Job values among future business leaders: the impact of gender and social background. *Scandinavian Journal of Management* (in print).

Greer, C.R. (2001) *Strategic Human Resource Management. A General Managerial Approach,* 2nd edn, Upper Saddle River, NJ: Prentice Hall.

Larsen, H.H. (1997) Do high-flyer programmes facilitate organizational learning? *Journal of Managerial Psychology,* 12(1): 48–60.

Larsen, H.H. (1998) *Towards an Interactive Career Model. Dualities in the Relations between Individuals and Organizations,* Vol. I and II. København: Handelshøjskolen i København, 684 s.

Larsen, H.H. (1999) HRM: En udisciplineret disciplin eller en disciplinerende disciplin ...? *Økonomi & Politik,* 72(4): 10–17.

Larsen, H.H. (2000a) HRM og strategi: Et umage par? I xxxxxx (red.): *Strategi og anarki,.* København: Nyt fra Samfundsvidenskaberne, s. 185–204.

Larsen, H.H. (red.) (2000b) *Menneskelige ressourcer – den mindre virksomheds konkurrencekraft.* København: Nyt fra Samfundsvidenskaberne.

Larsen, H.H. (2000c) In search of management development in Europe: from self-fulfilling prophecies to organizational competence. In: Brewster, C., Mayrhofer, W. and Morley, M. (eds.), *New Challenges for European Human Resource Management.* London: Macmillan, pp. 168–196.

Larsen, H.H. (red.) (2001a) Human Resource Management i modlys – spydspidser og dilemmaer. Dansk Management Forum og Handelshøjskolen i København.

Larsen, H.H. (2001b) Noget for noget – rekruttering og fastholdelse af unge højtuddannede. København: Berlingske Tidende og Nyt fra Samfundsvidenskaberne.

Larsen, H.H. (2001c) Recruiting and retaining the digital generation. *European Business Forum,* (6) Summer: 57–60.

Larsen, H.H. (2001d) *Human Resource Management – Trends and Dilemmas.* Copenhagen: Institute of Organisation and Industrial Sociology, Copenhagen Business School.

Larsen, H.H. and Bang, S. (1993) Development dialogues – an alternative to performance appraisal systems. In: Shaw, B., Kirkbride, P.S. and Rowland, K.M. (eds.), *Research in Personnel and Human Resources Management,* (Suppl. 3): 171–188. Greenwich, CT: JAI Press.

Larsen, H.H. and Svabo, C. (red.) (2002) *Fra kursus til kompetenceudvikling på jobbet.* København: Jurist- og Økonomforbundets Forlag.

Larsen, H.H., London, M., Weinstein, M. and Raghuram, S. (1998) High-flyer management development programs: organizational rhetoric or self-fulfilling prophecy?

International Studies of Management and Organization, 28(1): 64–90.

London, M., Larsen, H.H. and Thisted, L.N. (1999) Relationships between feedback and self-development. *Group and Organization Management*, 24(1): March, 5–27.

Nordhaug, O. (1987) Strategisk personalledelse (*Strategic Human Resource Management*). Oslo: Tano Forlag.

Nordhaug, O. (1993/2002) Målrettet personalledelse (*Goal-Oriented Human Resource Management*). Oslo: Scandinavian University Press.

Nordhaug, O. (1997) Kompetanse i norsk arbeidsliv (Competence in Norwegian work life). In: Nordhaug, O. (ed.), *Kompetansepolitikk 2000+* (*Competence Policies 2000+*). Oslo: Tano Aschehoug.

Nordhaug, O. (2002a) *Kunnskapsledelse* (*Knowledge Management*). Oslo: Scandinavian University Press.

Nordhaug, O. (2002b) *Strategisk personalledelse* (*Strategic Human Resource Management*). Oslo: Scandinavian University Press.

Nordhaug, O., Larsen, H.H. and Øhrstrøm, B. (1997) *Personaleledelse – en målrettet strategiproces* (*HRM – a Targeted Strategy Process*). Copenhagen: Nyt fra Samfundsvidenskaberne.

Raghuram, S., London, M. and Larsen, H.H. (2001) Flexible employment practices in Europe: countries versus culture. *International Journal of Human Resource Management*, 12(5): 738–753.

Rogaczewska, A.P., Larsen, H.H. and Skovbro, C. (1999) Cranet-E undersøgelsen 1999. HRM i danske virksomheder på tærsklen til et nyt årtusinde. København: Dansk Management Forum & Handelshøjskolen i København.

Storey, J. (ed.) (2001) *Human Resource Management – A Critical Text*, 2nd edn. London: Thomson.

Sources for Denmark Institutional Background

(1) Eurostat, Statistical Office of the European Communities (eds.) (2000) *Eurostat Yearbook, A Statistical Eye on Europe 1990–2000*. Brussels: European Communities.

(2) Eurostat, Statistical Office of the European Communities (eds.) (1997) *Eurostat Yearbook, A Statistical Eye on Europe 1987–1997*. Brussels: European Communities.

9

Sweden and Finland: Small Countries with Large Companies

Tina Lindeberg, Bo Månson and Sinikka Vanhala

INSTITUTIONAL BACKGROUND

SWEDEN

Area	411,000 km², 13% of EU-15 area
Population	8,861,000 (January 2000), 2% of EU-15 population
Density	22 inhabitants per km²
Capital and population	Stockholm (718,500) (including suburbs: 1,588,000)
Other major cities and population	Göteborg (454,000) (including suburbs: 773,800) Malmö (248,000) (including suburbs: 506,300)
Official language	Swedish
Religion	Protestant

Topography and climate

The Kingdom of Sweden is located on the Scandinavian Peninsula. It extends 499 km from east to west and 1572 km from north to south. To the west it is bordered by Norway (1619 km) and on the east by Finland (586 km). The coastline is 2181 km long.

Approximately half of the country is forested. There are mountainous areas, about 10,000 lakes, and a number of big rivers. Ten per cent is farmland and about 55% is forest, which makes Sweden one of the most forested countries in Europe. In the southern part of the country there are wide plains, upon which highly productive agriculture is practised.

The climate is temperate, with marked differences between the south and the north. Winters are usually cold, while summers can be warm and sometimes hot. The average temperature in the summer is 16–18°C and in the winter −2°C. Sweden has around 100 days with snow each year.

Culture

Compared to many other European countries Sweden has a fairly homogeneous culture with one language, around 90% of the population belonging to the Lutheran Church, peace since 1814, a long tradition of constitutional monarchy as well as strong democratic and social values. Sweden has historically close cultural, political and social relations with its Nordic neighbours Denmark, Norway, Finland and Iceland.

Principal characteristics

Figure 9.1 shows the relative position of Sweden in relation to other European Union (EU) countries on a number of standardised items. The population density is considerably lower than average (only Finland has lower), infant mortality is the lowest in the EU, the employment rate for women is higher and the unemployment rate lower than average. The cost of living is fairly high.

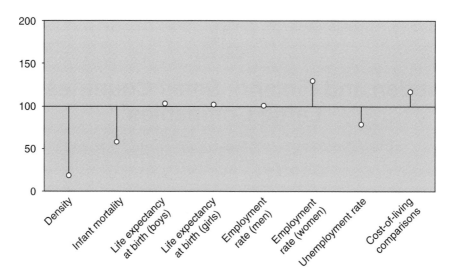

Figure 9.1   Sweden relative to the EU-15

People

Sweden is one of the least populated countries in the EU. The population is just below 9 million and the area 411,000 km², similar to California, Spain or Thailand, resulting in a population density of 22 inhabitants per km². Life expectancy is high – 77.4 years for men and 82.0 for women. These figures are higher than the European average – 2 years more for men and almost 1 year for women. Although it is often not realised, since the 1940s, immigration has accounted for more than 40% of the country's population growth (Table 9.1).

In Sweden the average number of people per household is 2.0. This figure has been the same since the middle of the 1990s. During the same time the EU average has decreased from 2.5 persons per household to 2.4.

Economy

The Swedish economy is a mix of private enterprise and national government ownership. More than 90% of the industry is privately owned. The public sector accounts for a large proportion of the Swedish economy and has a sizeable impact on the country's economic situation. The public sector provides the infrastructure, e.g. communications and energy supply, as well as most health care, childcare, old-age care and education.

A characteristic feature of the industrial structure in Sweden is the high proportion of very large companies

Table 9.1   Population by age (% of total population)

Age (years)	Sweden		EU-15 2000
	1990	2000	
<15	18	19	17
15–24	14	12	12
25–49	35	34	37
50–64	15	19	17
65–79	14	12	13
>80	4.2	4.9	3.7

All data from (4), p. 19, 21, 23.

(>500 employees) that employ 37% of the industrial workforce (1989), and the small proportion of companies with less than 20 employees (6% of the industrial workforce 1989).

The growth of the gross domestic product (GDP) has been below the European average in recent years (Table 9.2).

The GDP originates primarily from services (44%), followed by manufacturing (21%), general governmental and non-profit services (26%). Agricultural, forestry and fishery products supply only about 2% of the GDP.

Today, the engineering sector is the most important part of Swedish industry and accounts for the main part of employment in the manufacturing sector. Other expanding sectors are chemicals and pharmacy,

Table 9.2   Gross domestic product (at market prices, current series in million Ecu/EU)

		1994	1995	1996	1997	1998	1999	2000
1000 million Ecu	Sweden	174.2	183.6	206.3	210.8	213.7	226.5	246.6
Percentage change on previous period – constant prices	Sweden	4.1	3.7	1.1	2.1	3.6	4.1	3.6
	EU-15	2.8	2.4	1.6	2.5	2.9	2.6	3.3

All data from (4), p. 160.

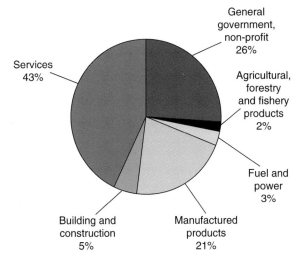

Figure 9.2   Economic structure (gross value added at market prices, at current prices and current exchange rates as % of branches, 1996). All data from (2), pp. 236–241

IT-technology and telecommunications, the design of advanced processes, energy and environmental products.

Export industries are today dominated by around 20 large corporations which have established subsidiaries and joint ventures all over the world. More than 50% of the cars that Volvo and Saab manufacture in Sweden are sold abroad. Other traditional export products are ball bearings, separators, wood and paper, chemicals, tools and telephones. New sectors are IT with Sweden being one of the leading countries in the world, pharmaceuticals and the production of popular music. Also technological know-how, as well as modern service ideas such as IKEA furniture and Hennes & Mauritz fashion have become expanding export products of great international interest (Figure 9.2).

A cost-of-living comparison with the EU shows that in Sweden prices, on average, are higher than in the EU (Table 9.3). This is the case for all groups of commodities except clothing and footwear. The prices for education and health as well as for alcohol and tobacco are far above the EU average.

Legal, institutional and political environment

Sweden is a constitutional monarchy with a parliamentary democracy. The government is appointed by and is responsible to the parliament (*Riksdagen*) with 349 delegates, elected by popular vote on the basis of proportional representation. The king is still the head of the state, but his functions are reduced to purely ceremonial ones.

The public sector has three levels of governing institutions: national, regional and local. At the sub-national level, Sweden is divided into 21 counties, 20 county council areas and 290 municipalities. The county councils have health care and transport systems as their principal areas of responsibility. The municipalities have the main responsibility for social welfare services, child-care, education and care for the elderly. Municipalities enjoy considerable autonomy and far-reaching powers of their own. Local self-government councillors are elected in direct local elections and municipalities have independent powers of taxation.

A Swedish model?

The question of whether there is such a thing as a "Swedish model" has been discussed since the 1930s. There has also been divided opinion about what this model is supposed to mean and whether it should be considered something positive or not.

The concept was originally used in reference to developments in the Swedish labour market during the 1930s. Unions and employers successfully managed to avoid both labour disputes and state intervention. *The Saltsjöbaden Agreement* of 1938 established a labour–employers bargaining system that worked smoothly for several decades. The Swedish trade union movement

Table 9.3   Cost-of-living comparisons in the EU in 2000 (Brussels = 100)

Food and beverages	Alcoholic beverages and tobacco	Clothing and footwear	Housing, water, electricity, gas and other fuels	Furnishing, household equipment and maintenance of house
128	173	89	147	116
Transport	Health	Transport	Communications	Recreation and culture
112	179	118	79	120
Education	Hotels, cafes and restaurants	Miscellaneous goods and services	*Total*	*Total excluding rents*
185	109	128	126	118

All data from (4), p. 200.

Table 9.4   Working days lost in all industry due to labour disputes (per 1000 employees)

	1986	1987	1988	1989	1990	1991	1992	1993	1994	1995	1996	1997
Sweden	171	4	203	103	191	6	7	54	15	172	:	:
EU-15	:	:	226	170	153	99	118	73	114	:	:	:

All data from (1), p. 309. ":" Data not available.

Table 9.5   Working days lost in manufacturing industry due to labour disputes (per 1000 employees)

	1986	1987	1988	1989	1990	1991	1992	1993	1994	1995	1996	1997
Sweden	3	11	666	41	8	5	0	182	29	13	0	:
EU-15	:	:	226	157	179	143	118	113	105	:	:	:

All data from (1), p. 309. ":" Data not available.

and its management counterparts became famous for their sense of responsibility and discipline. An important feature in this context was the system of centralised wage bargaining at the national level.

Later the term was applied to other areas too, especially to Sweden's domestic stability and its social welfare system. Two broad targets of economic and social policy seem to have been taken more seriously in Sweden after Second World War than in most other developed countries: *economic security*, including full employment, and *egalitarianism*, including both a general compression of income differences and the mitigation of poverty.

One important feature in the model has been corporatism; i.e. formalised co-operation between the state and various private organisations where the latter have been represented in various administrative and judicial government agencies, the most important organisations being the Swedish Employers Confederation (SAF) and the Swedish Confederation of Trade Unions (LO).

The Swedish unions had their highest level of power and influence during the 1970s when, often in informal but close co-operation with the government, they succeeded in getting a number of legal rights. Since the 1970s their active role seems to have decreased. The unions have had difficulties in creating a new role for themselves during the 1990s. The employer's federations, especially the SAF, have taken the initiative and led the way in important national discussions such as the European market and the single currency. The "Swedish model" is now being questioned more than ever before. Some argue that it is collapsing, others that it no longer stands for anything positive or uniform.

As illustrated in Tables 9.4 and 9.5, in recent years, labour disputes have had a diminishing impact on the disruption of labour days.

Labour market

Today (2002) over 4.2 million people are in employment in Sweden and the vast majority of jobs are found in the service sector. The public sector is large, employing around 35% of the workforce. In Table 9.6 we can see how the recession in the 1990s reduced the number of people in employment.

There is a trend towards a growth in the service sector together with at declining number of people employed in industry and agriculture (Table 9.7).

As Tables 9.8–9.10 show, Swedish men and women have a higher employment rate than the average in the EU. In Sweden the unemployment rate for women is lower than for men. EU averages present a reversed picture. Long-term unemployment in Sweden is considerably lower than in the EU.

Hourly labour costs in Sweden tend to be higher than the average for the countries within the euro-zone.

Sweden together with Belgium, Germany, Denmark, France and Austria, has the highest hourly labour costs in the EU (Tables 9.11 and 9.12).

The breakdown of labour costs in Sweden shows a large proportion of indirect labour costs, all of it consisting of social security costs (Table 9.13).

Sweden's number of hours usually worked per week for full-time employees are slightly less than the EU average (Table 9.14).

Education system

Nine years of schooling are compulsory for all children from the age of 6 or 7. The pupil spends his or her first 6 years at primary school and the following three

Table 9.6   Persons in employment (in million)

1985	1987	1988	1989	1990	1991	1992	1993	1994	1995	1996	1997*	2000**
	4.4	4.5	4.5	4.6	4.5	4.3	4.0	4.0	4.1	4.0	3.9*	4.1
100	102.0	103.5	105.2	106.0	104.1	99.7	93.9	93.1	94.5	91.2	:	:

All data from (1, p. 296) except * from (2, p. 316) and ** from (4, p. 98). ":" Data not available.

Table 9.7   Persons in employment in different sectors (1000 persons)

	1990	1991	1992	1993	1994	1995	1996	1997	1998	1999*	2000**
Industry	:	:	:	:	:	1065	1030	1000	:	1013	1005
Agriculture	:	:	:	:	:	135	130	127	:	121	120
Services	:	:	:	:	:	2933	2824	2785	:	2917	2998

All data from (2, pp. 316–317) except * from (3, p. 122) and ** from (4, p. 98). ":" Data not available.

Table 9.8   Unemployment rate total (%)

	1990	1991	1992	1993	1994	1995	1996	1997	1998	1999	2000
Sweden	2	3	6	9	9	9	10	10	8	7	6
EU-15	:	:	:	11	11	11	11	11	10	9	8

All data from (4), p. 110. ":" Data not available.

Table 9.9   Unemployment rate: men, women, long term

	2000		Long term (>12 months) as % of all unemployed
	Men	Women	
Sweden	6.0	5.8	31
EU-15	7.0	9.7	45

All data from (4), p. 111, 113.

Table 9.10   Employment rate of men and women 15–64 years (%, 2000)

	Men	Women	Total
Sweden	73	70	71
EU-15	72	54	63

All data from (4), pp. 101–102.

at the first stage of secondary school. About 95% go on to the upper secondary school, *the gymnasieskolan*, in vocational or academic programmes. The upper secondary school also provides the basis for higher education which in Sweden takes place in universities and university colleges. All higher education in Sweden, except for the Stockholm School of Economics, has traditionally been owned and funded by the state.

During the 1990s the whole Swedish system of education started to change with reforms occurring at all levels. Private or co-operative schools were introduced and universities and university colleges could become independent foundations.

Today there are seven universities (with most or all faculties), three technical universities, one special medical university, one university for agricultural sciences and a special school of economics. In addition to this there are about 25 regional or special university colleges all around the country, mainly for studies at undergraduate level in a variety of study programs or single disciplines.

As shown in Table 9.15, the percentage of people having completed at least upper secondary education is considerably higher in Sweden than the EU average, especially for women (Table 9.16).

Table 9.11   Average hourly labour costs (manual and non-manual workers) in industry (ECU/EUR)

	1995	1996	1997	1998	1999	2000
EU-15	19.47	20.10	20.97	21.45	:	:
Sweden	:	23.11	23.88	24.10	25.47	:

All data from (4), p. 213. ":" Data not available.

Table 9.12   Average gross monthly earnings of full-time employees in industry and services (ECU/EUR)

	1990	1991	1992	1993	1994	1995	1996	1997	1998	1999	2000
Sweden	:	:	:	:	:	:	2176	2245	2242	2351	2600

All data from (4), p. 208. ":" Data not available.

Table 9.13   Structure of labour costs in % in total industry (1996)

Direct cost	Indirect cost	Social security as part of indirect cost
72	29	29

All data from (2), p. 318.

Table 9.14   Number of hours usually worked per week: full-time employees

	1993	1996	1999
Sweden	:	41.4	41.3
EU-15	:	42.1	41.9

All data from (3), p. 131. ":" Data not available.

Table 9.15   Level of education for the population aged 25–64 (%, 2000)

At least upper secondary education	Total (25–64)	25–29	30–34	35–39	40–44	45–49	50–54	55–59	60–64
EU-15 (women and men)	64	76	73	70	66	62	55	51	45
Sweden (women and men)	77	87	88	85	79	76	72	67	57
EU-15 (women)	61	77	73	70	64	58	50	45	37
Sweden (women)	79	86	88	86	82	80	75	68	60

All data from (4), p. 95.

Table 9.16   Underlying table for "principal characteristics in relation to EU-15"

	EU-15	Sweden	Relation (Sweden/EU-15) $\times$ 100
Density (inhabitants per km^2) Year: 2000	119	22	18.5
Infant mortality^2 (per thousand live birth) Year: 2000	4.9	3.0	61
Life expectancy at birth (boys; years) Year: 1999	74.9	77.1	102.9
Life expectancy at birth (girls; years) Year: 1999	81.2	81.9	100.9
Employment rate (men; %) Year: 2000	72	73	100
Employment rate (women; %) Year: 2000	54	70	130
Unemployment rate (%) Year: 2000	8	6	71
Cost-of-living comparisons (total value; B = 100) Year: 2000	B = 100	118	118

All data from (4), pp. 36, 40, 100, 101, 110, 139, 200.

FINLAND

Area	338,127 km^2
Population	5,167,500
Density	17 inhabitants per km^2
Capital and population	Helsinki (555,500)
Other major cities and population	Espoo (213,300) Tampere (195,500) Vantaa (178,500) Turku (172,500)
Official languages	Finnish 6% Swedish
Religions	89% Evangelical Lutheran 1% Greek Orthodox 10% Others

Topography and climate

The Republic of Finland is situated in northern Europe, Fennoscandia, between the 60th and 70th parallels of latitude. Finland's neighbouring countries are Sweden, Norway and Russia. A quarter of Finland's total area lies north of the Arctic Circle.

Finland is known as a country of "thousands of lakes". Actually, there are some 190,000 lakes, and approximately as many islands. The main part of the country is lowland and covered by forests. As much as three-quarters of the country is forested. The highest mountains and hills are in Finnish Lapland.

The principal archipelago is the self-governing province of the Åland Islands off the southwest coast of the Finnish mainland.

Finland's climate is influenced by western maritime and eastern continental climates. The winters are normally cold and summers relatively warm, with marked differences between the south and the north of the country. The temperature often rises to +20°C or more in summer, and in winter −20°C is not rare. The mean temperature is about 5.5°C in southwest Finland, decreasing towards the northeast. The Baltic Sea, inland waters, and above all, the warming effect of the Gulf Stream from the Atlantic moderate the temperature.

Between east and west

Throughout her history Finland has been at the crossroads of western and eastern influences. Before the declaration of independence in 1917, Finland was for

100 years under Russian domination as a Grand Duchy of Russia (1809–1917) and before that for hundreds of years a part of the Kingdom of Sweden. During the period of Swedish domination, the Swedish legal and social systems and the Catholic/Lutheran Church became rooted in Finland, as well as the Swedish language in the southern and western part of the country. Eastern Finland, i.e. Karelia, became part of the Russo-Byzantine world embracing the Greek Orthodox Church. Finland's geographic position between eastern and western cultures, her domination by foreign powers, and defeat in the war against the Soviet Union, have left traces on Finnish culture, politics and mentality.

In 1995 Finland joined the EU and in 1999 became one of the first 11 member countries of the EU to adopt the single European currency, the Euro.

Principal characteristics

Figure 9.3 shows the position of Finland relative to the other EU countries. The population density is the lowest and infant mortality among the lowest in the EU. The women's labour force participation rate and the unemployment rate are above the EU average. Finland is a relatively expensive country; its cost-of-living index is at the same fairly high level as Sweden, but at a lower level than the UK or Denmark.

People

Finland is the seventh largest country in Europe and the least populated in the EU. The population is just over 5 million in an area almost as large as Germany, resulting in a density of 17 inhabitants per km². As a result of internal mobility, the population is concentrated in the southern part of the country. Approximately 62% of the population lives in towns and cities. The Finnish population is ageing. The demographic structure resembles that of most other industrial countries, with middle-aged groups predominating (see Figure 9.4). Women, on average, live longer than men and thus dominate the older age groups. Life expectancy is 81.0 years for women and

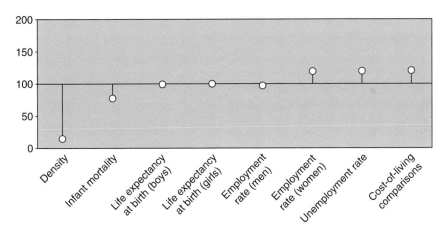

Figure 9.3   Principal characteristics of Finland in relation to EU-15 = 100

Table 9.17   Population by age (% of total population)

Age (years)	Finland 1990	Finland 2000	EU-15 2000
<15	19	18	17
15–24	13	13	12
25–49	38	35	37
50–64	16	19	17
65–79	11	12	13
>80	3	3	4

All data from (1).

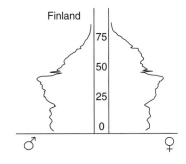

Figure 9.4   Age structure by gender

74.1 years for men, which are near the EU averages. Two out of three people aged 70 or over are women.

In Finland, the average number of people per household is 2.2 persons, which is a little lower than the EU average (1). One-person households in the EU are the most common in the EU Nordic countries, Finland, Sweden and Denmark. In Finland, 38% of individuals live on their own (1999), the EU average being 28% (1995). About 55% of all couples had children less than 18 years, and in 2000 almost every fifth family with children had only one parent (2).

Economy

Finland is a typical advanced industrial economy, with relatively stable GDP growth and relatively low inflation. The net wealth of Finnish households is at the average level for EU member states.

After growing steadily over a number of decades the Finnish economy fell into a deep recession in the early 1990s. GDP plummeted, as Table 9.17 illustrates, and unemployment soared to record levels. Waves of bankruptcy swept the business world. The latter part of the 1990s witnessed a rapid recovery, with GDP above the EU average.

Finnish GDP originates primarily from services (61%), followed by industry (35%) and agriculture (4%). The main exports are machinery and equipment, chemicals and metals, and timber, paper and pulp. Finland's main export partners are Germany (13%), Sweden (9%) and the UK (9%).

The engine of the Finnish economy has traditionally been the forest sector, with the sale of forest products, pulp and paper machinery. The second most important industry has been metal and engineering. In the 1990s the electronic and electrical industries grew to become the "third leg" of Finnish industry, and by 2000 was accounting for more than 30% of

Finnish exports. Today, the leading export is the mobile phone (Figure 9.5).

A characteristic feature of the Finnish industrial structure is the large number of small companies. As many as 92% of all conventional companies in Finland employ less than 50 persons, and only 0.1% employ more than 500 employees (3).

A cost-of-living comparison with the EU shows that Finland is among the most expensive countries to live (Table 9.19). Only in housing and education costs does Finland rank in the middle of the EU countries. For all other groups of products and services Finland is among the highest.

Legal, institutional and political system

Finland is a republic. The republican constitution adopted in 1919 vests sovereign power in the people, who are represented by a unicameral parliament (*Eduskunta*) with 200 seats. The president, who is elected by direct popular vote for 6 years, heads the republic. The country's foreign policy is the responsibility of the president.

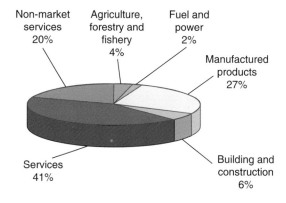

Figure 9.5   Finnish economic structure (gross value rates as % sectors, 2000). All data from (3)

Table 9.18   Finland's GDP (at market prices, at current prices and current exchange rates)

		1990	1991	1992	1993	1994	1995	1996	1997	1998	1999	2000
1000 million Ecu (nominal growth)	Finland	107.7	99.8	83.9	73.6	84.4	98.9	100.5	108.1	115.3	120.5	131.7
Yearly growth as % of previous year (real growth)	Finland	0.0	−6.3	−3.3	−1.1	4.0	3.8	4.0	6.3	5.3	4.1	5.6
	EU-15	3	3.4	1.3	−0.4	2.8	2.4	1.6	2.5	2.9	2.7	3.4

All data from (1).

The president and the parliament share legislative power. The largest political parties are the Finnish Social Democratic Party, the Centre Party and the National Coalition Party (Conservative). The government, headed by the prime minister, is responsible for the country's administration and must enjoy the confidence of parliament. Juridical power is vested in the independent courts of justice.

A Nordic welfare state

From the 1960s to the recession of the early 1990s, Finland was governed according to the ideals of the Nordic welfare state or the Nordic model. This meant several things including an expansion of the public sector, equality in social protection, a corporatist industrial relations system, relatively narrow salary gaps and high income taxes.

The core of the Finnish social protection system is to offer secure livelihood through comprehensive basic security and income-related benefits that guarantee the possibility of a reasonable level of subsistence. The benefits are partly universal and partly employment based. The system of universal social benefits means

that all residents are covered by basic pension, sickness and maternity benefits and also unemployment benefits. A fundamental principle of the Finnish social protection system is equality. Special attention has been given to the day care system for small children, which has enabled women to participate widely in working life. About 70% of mothers with pre-school children are in paid employment. All children under school age (7 years) have the right to municipal day care or their families can receive financial support for alternative arrangements.

Part of the Nordic model adopted in Finland is the corporatist – or tri-partite – industrial relations system involving negotiations between the employer and employee organisations and the government. The most notable feature of the Finnish industrial relations system is the role of centralised national agreements between employers' confederations and the labour unions. The industrial relations system partly explains the high level of strikes in some years (1986, 1990, 1991, 1994 and 1995). The second part of the 1990s saw a decline in strikes (Tables 9.20 and 9.21).

In the 1970s Finland was leading the world strike statistics with, e.g. 3282 strikes in 1976. With a few

Table 9.19 Cost-of-living comparisons in the EU in 2000 (Brussels = 100)

Food	Alcoholic beverages and tobacco	Clothing and footwear	Housing, water, electricity, gas and other fuels	Furnishing, household equipment	Health	Transport
114	174	93	134	114	143	121

Communications	Recreation and culture	Education	Hotels, cafés and restaurants	Miscellaneous goods and services	Total	Total excluding rents
76	121	89	118	124	120	115

All data from (1).

Table 9.20 Working days lost in all Finnish industry due to labour disputes (per 1000 employees)

	1986	1987	1988	1989	1990	1991	1992	1993	1994	1995	1996	1997	1998	1999	2000
EU-15	:	:	226	170	153	99	118	73	114	:	:	:	:	:	:
Finland	1353	64	88	98	446	230	41	10	309	512	9	48	60	9	109

":" Data not available.

Table 9.21 Working days lost in Finnish manufacturing industry due to labour disputes (per 1000 employees)

	1986	1987	1988	1989	1990	1991	1992	1993	1994	1995	1996	1997	1998	1999	2000
EU-15	:	:	226	157	179	143	118	113	105	:	:	:	:	:	:
Finland	2290	145	223	148	101	71	112	28	1040	29	22	58	43	23	330

All data from (1). ":" Data not available.

exceptions, strike rates have approached the European average since the late 1980s.

Labour market

Tables 9.22 and 9.23 illustrate the changes in the labour market over the last two decades. The number of people in employment dropped sharply with the advent of recession in the early 1990s, from 2.5 million in 1990 to 2.1 million in 1993. The decline was reversed in the mid-1990s, and since then the number of employees has been growing both in industry and services, though the number in agriculture is steadily falling.

Since the second half of the 1990s, the employment level in Finland has remained above the EU average, but below the Swedish level. The high employment levels in Finland and Sweden are due to high labour force participation rates for women (see Table 9.24).

Compared with other EU countries, unemployment (Table 9.25) is relatively high in Finland. Both men and women suffer from higher unemployment rates than the average in the EU. Since the peak year of 1994, the unemployment rate has been decreasing. However, in 2000 the official unemployment rate was still nearly 10%, and moreover, there are almost the same number of unemployed persons included in other statistics (e.g. employment training and unemployment retirement). However, long-term unemployment is somewhat lower in Finland compared with the EU average (Table 9.26).

The average hourly labour costs (ECU 20.90 in 1999) in Finland represent the EU-15 average. Labour costs fell during the recession owing to reductions in wages and salaries and other benefits. From 1994 on, the trend has been upwards (Table 9.27).

Table 9.22 Persons in employment (million)

1985	1986	1987	1988	1989	1990	1991	1992	1993	1994	1995	1996	1997	1998	1999	2000
	2.4	2.4	2.4	2.5	2.5	2.3	2.2	2.1	2.1	2.1	2.1	2.2	2.2	2.3	2.3
100	99.8	99.4	99.8	101.4	101.2	96.0	89.2	83.8	83.1	82.7	84.7	87.0	89.4	82.4	94.0

All data from (3).

Table 9.23 Persons in employment in different sectors (thousand)

	1986	1987	1988	1989	1990	1991	1992	1993	1994	1995	1996	1997	1998	1999	2000
Industry	589	569	553	561	556	502	453	424	426	572	579	593	614	637	643
Agriculture	266	251	238	218	207	198	187	173	167	170	159	153	144	144	142
Services	1205	1235	1268	1311	1318	1282	1217	1156	1149	1351	1384	1417	1458	1509	1545

All data from (1) and (3).

Table 9.24 Employment rate by age and sex (% of population in age group, 2000)

Age (years)	Total	Male	Female
15–24	45	47	44
25–49	81	86	77
50–64	58	59	56

All data from (1).

Table 9.25 Unemployment rate (%)

	1987*	1988*	1989*	1990	1991	1992	1993	1994	1995	1996	1997	1998	1999	2000
EU-15	:	:	:	:	:	:	11	11	11	11	11	10	9	8
Finland	5	4	3	3	7	12	16	17	15	15	13	11	10	10

All data from (1) except * from (3).

The breakdown of labour costs in Finland (Table 9.28) indicates a large proportion of indirect labour costs, most of which consist of social security costs.

Average working hours for full-time employees in Finland (Table 9.29) are less than the EU average.

Education system

In Finland, education is appreciated and trusted as a means, e.g. to meet international competition and to reduce unemployment. Finland's educational system is copied from Sweden. The comprehensive school is compulsory for the whole age group between 7 and 16.

Primary education covers the first 6 years, after which there are two alternative paths: senior secondary school or vocational school. Vocational, technical and professional education are provided mainly in specialised institutions. Higher education is the responsibility of 22 university-level educational institutions. The polytechnics represent a distinctive non-university sector of higher education. Education in universities and polytechnics is free of charge and publicly funded in Finland.

People are better educated in Finland than in the EU on average (Table 9.30). Both in Finland and in the EU, there is a clear trend indicating that the younger age groups are better educated than the older ones.

In 2000, there were 2.5 million people who had graduated from senior secondary schools, vocational or professional educational institutions or universities; 51% of them were women and 59% of graduates (matriculation examination) from senior secondary schools were women. Generally speaking, women are better educated than men in Finland. Only in the oldest age groups (56 years and over), do men have a better education (Table 9.31).

Table 9.26   Unemployment rate: male – female, long-term

	2000		Long-term unemployment*
	Men	Women	
Finland	9.0	10.6	24.6
EU-15	7.0	9.7	45.2

* As % of all unemployed.

Table 9.27   Average hourly labour costs (manual and non-manual workers) in total industry

ECU	1992	1993	1994	1995	1996	1997	1998	1999	2000
	17.56	15.68	17.64	20.36	19.65	19.76	20.24	20.99	:

All data from (1). ":" Data not available.

Table 9.28   Structure of labour costs in industry % (1998)

	Direct costs	Indirect costs	Social security as proportion of indirect costs
Total industry	76	24	22

All data from (1).

Table 9.29   Employees' average working hours per week (2000)

Full-time	40.9
Part-time	20.5

Table 9.30   Level of education of persons aged 25–64 years (%)

At least upper secondary education	Total (25–64)	25–29	30–34	35–39	40–44	45–49	50–54	55–59	60–64
EU-15 (women and men)	64	76	73	70	66	62	55	51	45
Finland (women and men)*	73	87	86	86	81	74	63	55	45
EU-15 (women)	61	77	73	70	64	58	50	45	37
Finland (women)*	75	90	89	88	83	76	64	56	44

* All data from (3).

Table 9.31   Principal characteristics in relation to EU-15

	EU-15	Finland	Relation (Finland/EU-15) × 100
Density (inhabitants per km²) Year: 2000	116	17	14.6
Infant mortality (per thousand live births) Year: 2000	4.9	3.8	77.5
Life expectancy at birth (boys; years) Year: 2000	74.9	74.1	98.9
Life expectancy at birth (girls; years) Year: 2000	81.2	81.0	99.8
Employment rate (men; %) Year: 2000	72.5	70.2	96.8
Employment rate (women; %) Year: 2000	54.0	64.3	119.1
Unemployment rate (%) Year: 2000	8.2	9.8	119.5
Cost-of-living comparisons (total value; B = 100¹) Year: 2000	B = 100	120.0	120.0

HRM IN SWEDEN AND FINLAND: CURRENT POLICY AND PRACTICE

HISTORICAL BACKGROUND

Sweden and Finland are neighbouring countries with a long shared history. Finland was part of the Kingdom of Sweden for almost 700 years, from the 1100s until 1809. The Swedish period strongly affected the basis of the whole Finnish society, its legal, social and the religious order, and rooted even the Swedish language in Finland. Then their paths separated. Finland was occupied by Russia and enjoyed the status of autonomous Grand Duchy in the Russian Empire until declaring independence in 1917. Between the world wars, the language issue, i.e. efforts to replace Swedish with Finnish as the official language, separated Finland from Sweden and the other Nordic countries. In the Second World War, Finland was fighting for its independence against the Soviet Union, while Sweden was one of the few European countries not militarily involved in the war. The result was that in the 1950s, while Sweden was acquiring the reputation of a welfare state, Finland was still recovering from the war.

Many of the similarities and commonalities between Sweden and Finland are explained by Nordic co-operation, which in its present form can be traced back to the early 1950s, when the Nordic Council[1] was founded. In a few years, the Agreement on a Common Labour Market was accepted, and the Nordic Passport Union was founded allowing free mobility across the borders of the Nordic countries. In the 1960s many Finns sought work in Sweden and took their families with them. Today there is a permanent Finnish minority of 350,000 people in Sweden – approximately the same number as the Swedish-speaking minority living in Finland.

During the first three or four decades after the Second World War economic and social development in Sweden and Finland as well as in other Nordic countries was rapid. The Nordic countries developed their own patterns of economic and social policy and labour relations, which were radically different from those in other Western countries. The concept of "the Nordic

---

[1] Official Nordic co-operation is channelled through two organisations: the Nordic Council and the Nordic Council of Ministers. Nordic Council was founded in 1952 as a forum for inter-parliamentary co-operation between Sweden, Denmark and Norway. Finland became a member in 1956.

model" was adopted to describe this Nordic approach. Originally the term "Nordic model" was used to describe the combination of welfare state ideology, social democratic dominance and the Nordic type of corporatism in labour market relations, i.e. the tri-partite negotiation network between the labour unions, the employer organisations and the state. In the 1980s the meaning of the Nordic model was broadened to include a shared cultural heritage, common values and a consensus-seeking approach in a mixed economy.

The economic prosperity of the 1980s was followed both in Sweden and in Finland by an extremely severe recession in the early 1990s. The shock was more moderate in Sweden; the simultaneous collapse of Finnish trade with the Soviet Union worsened the recession in Finland. The recession left two problems in Finnish working-life: high unemployment and a difficult working climate. In Sweden too many employees were laid off, both in the private and public sector. From 1992 to 1998 the labour market in Sweden was extremely tight. By the new millennium, the labour markets in Sweden and Finland had experienced something of a return to a more normal state of affairs.

Both countries joined the EU in 1995. After that, Finland joined the European Monetary Union, while Sweden did not fulfil the demands for joining. Sweden's being outside the common currency seems, however, not to have had any negative impact on the flourishing co-operation, with mergers and acquisitions, between large Swedish and Finnish companies.

Both Sweden and Finland are countries where the population is comparatively small and the economy depends to a great extent on international trade. In fact, the economy in both countries seems to follow the economic development of two telecom companies – Ericsson and Nokia.

From the point of view of human resource management (HRM), Sweden and Finland are expected not to differ radically from each other. This is because of the similarities in their industrial relations systems, labour legislation and social and political outlook.

ROLE OF THE HR FUNCTION

Board level participation by human resource (HR) managers in Sweden and Finland is relatively high, above the EU average. However, there is a significant difference between the countries (Table 9.32). The 1999 survey shows that in nearly 80% of the Swedish organisations the HR manager serves on the main board of directors or the equivalent; in Finland the percentage is 65.

There are no big changes over the past 10 years in board level participation in Swedish or Finnish organisations. However, comparison between Finnish public and private organisations revealed that in 1992 and 1995 the percentage was higher in the public sector organisations, while in 1999 the private sector exceeded the public organisations in respect of board level participation.

The responsibility for HR issues on the board, *if not the HR manager*, has changed in Sweden from mainly the administrative director to the managing director. This might indicate a change from an administrative focus in HR issues towards a more strategic focus. In Finland no such change is evident.

In a European context only France has a higher board level participation of HR managers than Sweden. Finland's level is above the EU average but not among the highest.

HRM STRATEGY INVOLVEMENT

In most organisations in Sweden and Finland, the person responsible for HR has been involved in strategy development either "from the outset" or through consultation (Table 9.33). The strategic involvement of HR "from the outset" is above the average in the EU. The trends have been similar in Sweden and Finland;

Table 9.32   Does the head of the personnel/human resources function have a place on the main board of directors or equivalent? (% of organisations)

	EU average 1999	Sweden			Finland		
		1992	1995	1999	1992	1995	1999
Yes	54.5	85	81	79	61	69	65
No	45.5	15	19	21	39	31	35

Table 9.33   Stage at which HR is involved in development of corporate strategy (% of organisations)

	EU average 1999	Sweden			Finland		
		1992	1995	1999	1992	1995	1999
From the outset	58	56	62	64	54	57	64
Through consultation	24	32	30	27	27	19	15
On implementation	10	7	4	4	11	12	14
Not consulted	8	5	4	5	8	12	7

Table 9.34   Primary responsibility for major policy decisions on key aspects of HRM (recruitment) (% of organisations)

	EU average 1999	Sweden			Finland		
		1992	1995	1999	1992	1995	1999
Line management	7	18	12	26	17	29	26
Line management with HR department	40	59	59	52	66	49	56
HR department with line management	43	23	29	20	15	18	14
HR department	11	0	0	2	2	4	4

involvement "from the outset" increased by about 10% in the 1990s. Involvement through consultation is higher in Sweden.

Swedish HRM seems somewhat more formalised than HRM in Finland or other EU countries. Three out of four Swedish organisations have a written personnel management/HR strategy, while in Finland the proportion is two out of three. In Sweden there was no real change in this from two earlier surveys (1992 and 1995), whereas in two earlier Finnish surveys the written HRM strategy was found only in half of organisations.

LINE MANAGEMENT INVOLVEMENT

Sweden and Finland have the highest rates of line management responsibility of all EU countries. A strong emphasis on line management responsibility in HR issues is general in the Scandinavian countries. With the exception of industrial relations, line management (alone or with the HR department) bears the primary responsibility for all major HR decisions. The independent role of the HR department is slight in both countries.

In more than half of Swedish and Finnish organisations responsibility is shared between line management and the HR function. In both countries, line managers alone tend to have a larger extent of responsibility concerning HR issues in public sector organisations than in the private sector. In private sector organisations the most common practice is to give the responsibility to line management in consultation with the HR department.

In recruitment and selection, line management alone has the primary responsibility in about a quarter of organisations in Finland, according to the last two surveys (see Table 9.34). The percentage is higher in public organisations. In Sweden there has been quite a dramatic change from 1995 to 1999 in line responsibility. Shared responsibility between the line management and the HR department can now be found in over half the organisations in both countries through the 1990s.

The distributions for primary responsibility for training (Table 9.35) are similar to those for recruitment. The primary responsibility of line management for training in both Sweden and Finland is among the highest for any EU country in 1999.

In a quarter of organisations in Sweden and Finland line management alone had the principal responsibility for training in 1999. The figures are the highest in the EU. In almost half of the organisations the responsibility lies with line management in consultation with the HR department, which is also well above the EU average. It follows that the responsibility of HR department for training is among the lowest in Sweden and Finland.

The responsibility of line management during the last 3 years before each survey seems to have been

Table 9.35   Primary responsibility for major policy decisions on key aspects of HRM (training) (% of organisations)

	EU average 1999	Sweden			Finland		
		1992	1995	1999	1992	1995	1999
Line management	7	16	23	24	15	26	24
Line management with HR department	38	56	45	46	54	53	48
HR department with line management	44	26	31	26	28	18	24
HR department	11	2	1	3	3	3	4

increasing rather than decreasing. The increases have been more moderate in Finland than in Sweden. The 3-year period before 1992 saw a significant increase in line management responsibility in employee resourcing (recruitment, selection and redundancy) and training and development in Finnish organisations. In 1995 and 1999, line management responsibility increased most in training and development compared with other HR areas.

The general position of the personnel/HR department/function has been weakening during the 1990s in both countries. The performance of the personnel/HR department/function is not evaluated systematically. Only in a third of organisations has a systematic evaluation been carried out. When the personnel/HR department/function is evaluated, the views of top management are mainly considered together with the views of line management and employees.

RECRUITMENT AND SELECTION

The number of employees in large Swedish and Finnish organisations has more often been decreasing than increasing. Employee recruitment has not yet reached the difficult time that is predicted for when the baby-boom generation will have retired. In 1999, most organisations in both countries focus their efforts on existing employees either by retraining or by increasing pay and/or benefits (Table 9.36). In Finland, as many as three out of four organisations, and in Sweden half of the organisations, rely on *retraining*. *Pay and/or benefit increases* are second in importance and *marketing the organisation's image* is the third in importance in aiding recruitment and retention.

Most managerial positions in Sweden and Finland are filled internally (Table 9.37). This is especially true

Table 9.36   Have you introduced any of the following in relation to recruitment or retention? (% of organisations)

	1999*	
	Sweden	Finland
Recruiting abroad	9	9
Retraining existing employees	51	77
Increased pay/benefits	47	41
Relocation of the company	8	8
Marketing the organisation's image	26	32
Other – please specify	8	7

* Question not included in 1992 and 1995 surveys.

of middle and junior managerial positions, in which internal recruitment was practised in 70% of Finnish organisations, and even more often in Swedish organisations. In contrast, "only" half of senior managers were recruited from inside the organisation in Finland; in Sweden the proportion was even less in 1999.

The use of internal resources for recruiting managers in Sweden has decreased between 1995 and 1999 in all managerial groups, while in Finland there is no detectable change. The internal recruitment of senior and middle managers is in line with the EU average, while in the case of junior management Sweden's figure is the highest.

The most common method of recruiting a senior manager outside the organisation in Sweden is to use a search consultant or recruitment agency. The next most important channel was advertising in newspapers, which was used in 60% of the organisations in 1999. In Finland newspaper advertising, is in the top position, ahead of search consultants or recruitment agencies.

Table 9.38 reports the use of selection methods in Swedish and Finnish organisations. The most important

Table 9.37   Recruitment methods: use of internal mechanisms for filling managerial vacancies

	EU average	Sweden			Finland		
		1992*	1995	1999	1992*	1995	1999
Senior management	52		58	42		54	54
Middle management	76		85	74		72	73
Junior management	62		90	81		75	69
Total management*			78	66		67	65

*Question in 1992 was not separated by different managerial levels. Data are missing.

Table 9.38   Selection methods: use of different methods for all or most appointments (% of organisations)

	EU average	Sweden			Finland		
		1992*	1995	1999	1992*	1995	1999
Interview panel							
Every appointment	21		13	12		9	12
Most appointments	17		19	27		31	23
Some appointments	17		18	23		32	27
Frequently used* (1992 only)		69			99		
One-to-one interviews							
Every appointment			73	66		59	57
Most appointments	61		14	21		27	25
Some appointments	18		8	7		10	16
Frequently used* (1992 only)	9	N/A			N/A		
Application forms							
Every appointment	52		77	40		42	39
Most appointments	16		20	19		24	28
Some appointments	8		3	7		11	11
Frequently used* (1992 only)		14			81		
Psychometric testing							
Every appointment			3	6		6	13
Most appointments	6		3	15		12	22
Some appointments	9		26	46		18	36
Frequently used* (1992 only)	22	24			74		
Assessment centre							
Every appointment	2		0	0		1	1
Most appointments	4		1	2		3	3
Some appointments	23		8	13		12	7
Frequently used* (1992 only)		5			17		
Graphology							
Every appointment	1		0	1		0	0
Most appointments	2		0	0		1	1
Some appointments	6		1	1		1	1
Frequently used* (1992 only)		0.3			3		
References							
Every appointment	28		55	67		9	6
Most appointments	17		37	32		29	28
Some appointments	27		6	1		42	44
Frequently used* (1992 only)		96			61		

*Question in 1992 asked which are **regularly** used.
N/A = category not included in 1992.

is one-to-one interviews, which is used in most or all appointments in over 80% of organisations in both countries, corresponding to the EU average. Second in importance are application forms in both countries. Application forms are used in two out of three companies in Finland and somewhat less often in Sweden in 1999. The use of application forms in Swedish organisations (in every appointment) dropped from 77% in 1995 to 40% in 1999.

Graphology as a selection method plays no role in Sweden and Finland, and assessment centres are likewise unimportant.

The use of references in every appointment differs dramatically as between Sweden and Finland. In Sweden 67% of organisations use references in every appointment, while the corresponding figure for Finland is only 6%. The Swedish percentage is among the highest in the EU and the Finnish among the lowest. Other selection methods (interview panel and psychometric testing) are seldom used in every appointment but more frequently in some appointments.

TRAINING AND DEVELOPMENT

Training and development are highly valued in Finland. However, when we compare training and development costs in Sweden and Finland we find that the Swedish organisations tend to spend a larger percentage than

Finnish organisations (Table 9.39). As many as one-third of the Swedish organisations spent over 5% on training in 1992–1995. This number has increased to 36% in 1999. In 1992–1995 half of the Finnish organisations, and in 1999 approximately 40%, spent less than 2% of their annual salary and wage bill on training and development. In Sweden fewer than 30% of organisations belong to the "less than 2%" group.

There is a slight trend towards more investment in training towards the end of the 1990s in Finland. In Sweden the distributions remain relatively stable.

When we look at training in terms of the number of days received per staff category, the general observation is that the amount of training varies hierarchically from 3 days for manual employees to 6–7 days for management in 1999 (Table 9.40).

The differences between the two countries are relatively small. The average number of training days received by management and professional/technical employees is one day higher in Finland. Compared with the other EU countries the Swedish and Finnish figures represent the averages.

A systematic analysis of training needs is carried out in 74% of the organisations in Sweden and in 69% of those in Finland. In the 1995 survey the respective percentages were 87 and 65%. Since 1995 the difference in systematic analysis of training needs between the countries has decreased.

Table 9.39 Proportion of annual salary and wage bill spent on training and development

(%)	EU average 1999	Sweden			Finland		
		1992	1995	1999	1992	1995	1999
<1	12.9	10	9	4	16	21	13
1–1.9	27.3	18	18	24	35	30	28
2–2.9	20.1	20	22	18	20	23	21
3–4.9	19.4	21	21	19	19	15	25
5–9.9	15.6	22	22	28	9	8	12
>10	4.9	9	7	8	1	3	2

Table 9.40 Mean number of training days received by staff category

Mean	EU average 1999	Sweden			Finland		
		1992	1995	1999	1992	1995	1999
Management	5.7	7	6	6	7	6	7
Professional/technical	5.9	5	4	6	6	5	7
Clerical	4.0	3	3	5	4	4	5
Manual	3.5	3	3	3	3	2	3

PERFORMANCE MEASUREMENT AWARDS

Table 9.41 shows that merit/performance-related pay schemes are used more frequently in Finland than in Sweden. In fact, Sweden has the lowest rate of use of such schemes among all EU countries for all categories except manual staff. Finland has the highest rate in the EU in the manual staff category and is close to the EU average in the other categories.

Merit/performance-related pay schemes are relatively widely used in Finnish companies. The differences between staff categories are not wide, ranging from 35 to 43%. From 1992 to 1999 the role of merit/performance-related pay has strengthened in Finland. For other incentive schemes there is a clear trend covering all employee groups, with a drop in 1995 and an increase in 1999.

In Sweden in 1999 merit/performance-related pay schemes are used for managers in one out of five organisations, which is a large increase compared to 1992. For professional and clerical staff it is used in fewer organisations. There has been no serious change from 1992 to 1999 in these staff categories. The tradition in Sweden and also in Finland, has been one of central agreements on wages, allowing little freedom to adapt salaries to individuals. However, there are moves towards a more individual approach in both countries.

The application of appraisal systems is much higher in Swedish organisations than in Finnish, according to both the 1995 and 1999 survey (Table 9.42). The rate in Sweden is high compared to the EU average and is the highest when it comes to professional and clerical staff. In both countries manual workers are the staff category least included in appraisal systems. This is often the largest category of staff. With managers or supervisors commonly responsible for more than 100 employees, it is virtually impossible to conduct appraisal discussions with every employee, especially if the aim is to carry out at least one such discussion per employee per year.

In Finland there is an increase in the use of appraisal systems from 1995 to 1999. In 1999 close to half of the organisations used appraisal systems for manual staff and half used it for other employee groups.

There has been a significant increase from 1995 to 1999 in appraisal systems in Sweden as well. This is true for all staff categories. Sweden has the highest rate in the EU in 1999 for professional and clerical staff categories. The high rates are partly explained by a slightly different use of the performance appraisal in Sweden, where it is used more as a tool for general evaluation of the employee, as well as the job situation. It also serves as a discussion of future development needs and is not focused on formal performance measurement.

Table 9.41   Change in merit/performance-related pay by staff category (% of organisations)

	EU average 1999	Sweden			Finland		
		1992	1995	1999	1992	1995	1999
Management	47	12	14	20	31	27	35
Professional/technical	46	9	11	12	32	31	43
Clerical	37	8	10	12	26	35	38
Manual	28	26	26	16	24	35	40

Table 9.42   Change in appraisal system for staff categories (% of organisations)

	EU average 1999	Sweden			Finland		
		1992	1995	1999	1992	1995	1999
Management	72	N/A	87	89	N/A	37	47
Professional/technical	74	N/A	83	94	N/A	46	52
Clerical	67	N/A	83	95	N/A	43	51
Manual	56	N/A	63	80	N/A	34	42

N/A–Question not asked in 1992.

Employee relations

Union membership rates are high in Sweden and Finland compared to other European countries. In Sweden there has been a drop in union membership rates since 1995 (Table 9.43). According to the Cranfield survey in 1999 the union membership rate is between 76 and 100% in 61% of the organisations. In 1995 this was the case in 93% of the organisations. The survey also shows that the public sector organisations have a considerably higher membership rate. According to the Swedish practitioners panel large older organisations – mainly state-owned organisations or large industrial conglomerates – tend to have a higher union membership rate among their employees.

The trend towards lower unionisation in Finland has not been so clear as in Sweden. According to 1999 survey, in 71% of organisations the unionisation rate was between 76 and 100%. In 1992 the proportion was 78%. As in Sweden the public sector organisations in Finland have a higher membership rate than the private sector ones. Unionisation in Finland is strongly related to the unemployment benefit system.

At the beginning of the 1990s there was a drastic drop in trade union influence in both countries. A remarkable proportion of organisations in Sweden and Finland reported in 1992 that trade union influence had decreased over the previous 3 years. Most organisations in both countries reported that trade union power remained the same in the 1995 and 1999 surveys. Only a few organisations saw an increase in trade union influence in 1999, and both countries are below the 1999 EU average ("increased" in 13% of the organisations). However, unionisation is far more extensive in Sweden and Finland than other European countries.

Communication   Formal communication is practised to a high degree in Swedish and Finnish companies (see Table 9.44).

In Finland, as Table 9.44 shows, a higher proportion of the employees are informed about financial issues than in Sweden, except for managers, where there is no big difference. Sweden and Finland have the highest rates in the EU, according to the 1999 survey, when it comes to communicating information to employees in all categories.

Table 9.43   Change in trade union influence (% of organisations)

	EU average 1999	Sweden			Finland		
		1992	1995	1999	1992	1995	1999
Increased	13	11	8	8	18	13	5
Same	56	28	74	68	24	72	74
Decreased	17	60	17	23	58	15	18

Table 9.44   Change in formal communication on business strategy and financial performance (% of organisations)

	EU average 1999	Sweden			Finland		
		1992	1995	1999	1992	1995	1999
Management briefed							
About strategy	94	96	98	98	98	97	95
About finance	92	98	96	98	93	93	94
Professional briefed							
About strategy	54	45	58	70	87	86	84
About finance	72	65	68	83	90	92	94
Clerical briefed							
About strategy	33	44	60	66	50	62	65
About finance	57	75	76	84	84	90	88
Manual briefed							
About strategy	24	37	52	50	42	57	56
About finance	43	68	67	68	82	86	79

Both vertical and horizontal communication have been increasing in the Finnish organisations. In respect of strategy, almost all managers, and about 85% of professional/technical staff, are normally briefed about it; clerical and manual staff are somewhat less often informed. In contrast, financial results are communicated to almost all staff, and four out of five employees are briefed about the organisation of work. There were significant changes in the communication channel between different survey rounds. In 1992 a big increase was noted in the use of representative staff bodies and direct verbal and written information, while in 1992 computer/e-mail systems were much more widely used.

When it comes to communication between employers and employees in Sweden the trend is towards an increase in information flow – both top-down and bottom-up. The results show that nearly all managers receive information about strategy. Not surprisingly, professional and clerical staff are informed to a lesser extent and only about half the manual workers are informed about strategy. A larger number of employees are informed of the financial situation than of strategy.

In Sweden there is also an increase in the number of organisations that perform attitude surveys, from 29% in 1995 to 42% in 1999. This is often connected to the introduction of new management control systems such as Balanced Scorecard (BSC).

Sweden and Finland are two countries with a more democratic approach to organisations, which is true for most northern European countries, especially the Nordic countries (Brewster and Larsen, 2000). In terms of management, e.g. there is a low power distance, which means that the hierarchical distance between the boss and the subordinate is small (Hofstede, 1984). And there are statutory requirements that strongly support the practice of keeping employees informed. This could help to explain the higher levels of formal communication.

FLEXIBLE PATTERNS OF WORK

Tables 9.45–9.48 show the position in respect of different aspects of flexible working. In Sweden flexible working patterns are becoming more widespread. However, in most organisations they apply only to a minority of the employees. The expected increase in tele-working has not occurred, according to various studies. There are a number of obstacles to this form of work, including lack of technical equipment in the homes of the employees, insufficient follow-up at work, jobs that require a presence at the workplace and people's desire to see and meet other people. Another possible obstacle in Sweden is related to the insurance issues concerning, for instance, workplace safety.

According to the survey, the use of flexible patterns of working over the past 3 years more often increased than decreased in Finnish companies also. The flexible patterns that increased most are part-time work, flexitime and fixed-term contracts. However, it is difficult to

Table 9.45 Change in use of part-time working (% of organisations)

	EU average 1999	Sweden			Finland		
		1992*	1995	1999	1992*	1995	1999
Increase	47	14	12	10	23	46	64
Same	38	60	61	60	44	28	29
Decrease	6	26	26	28	6	3	1
Not used	8	1	1	1	26	23	6

* 1992 data included "Don't know" category, which was selected out.

Table 9.46 Change in proportion of workforce on part-time contracts (% of organisations)

	EU average 1999	Sweden			Finland		
		1992*	1995	1999	1992*	1995	1999
No part-timers employed	7	1	0.5	1	6	23	8
>10% of part-timers	25	50	26	37	6	7	9

* 1992 figure for "no part-timers" is the missing value, since a "not used" option was not included.

Table 9.47 Change in proportion of workforce on temporary/casual contracts (% of organisations)

	EU average 1999	Sweden			Finland		
		1992*	1995	1999	1992*	1995	1999
No temporary workers	25	3	3	1	6	26	24
>10% of temporary workers	11	13	9	19	4	7	6

* 1992 figure for "no temporary workers" is the missing value, since a "not used" option was not included.

Table 9.48 The nature of the change in temporary casual contracts

	Sweden			Finland		
	1992*	1995	1999	1992*	1995	1999
Increase	33	56	45	19	38	21
Same	42	30	44	26	28	61
Decrease	21	9	8	47	12	11
Not used	4	6	4	8	22	7

* 1992 data included "Don't know" category, which was selected out.

say whether flexible patterns of working are widely used in Finnish companies or not. Nearly all organisations use at least some fixed-term contracts and 80% use shift work, while most organisations do not use such flexible working arrangements as tele-working, home-based work or annual hours contracts.

Traditionally, part-time contracts have not been much used in Finland. More than half of larger organisations had none or less than 1% of the workforce on a part-time basis in 1995, even though nearly half of the companies reported that the use of part-time working had increased during the 3 years before the survey. The use of part-time employees has increased substantially from 1995 to 1999. There were only 6% of organisations not using part-time contracts at all in 1999, while in 1995 the proportion was 23%. According to all three surveys, there were fewer than 10% of organisations in which the proportion of part-time employees was over 10%. Compared with other Nordic countries, where women normally work part-time, Finnish women have traditionally worked full-time. This applies equally to women with pre-school children.

In Sweden part-time contracts are a very common form of working arrangement, and have been for many years, especially in the public sector health care organisations, which employ many women. In Sweden it is mainly women who work part-time and the employment rate for women is higher in Sweden than in most

countries. This is one explanation for the frequent use of part-time contracts. In 37% of the organisations in Sweden the proportion of the workforce on part-time is over 10%. This is higher than the EU average of 25%, but far below the Netherlands, which has the highest rate in the EU (63%). In Sweden many employees in the health care sector are working part-time involuntarily and want to increase their working hours to full time, which they have done to a certain extent. This explains part of the decrease in employees on part-time contracts in Sweden over the past 10 years.

Temporary/casual contracts are used more in Sweden than in Finland. One out of five Swedish organisations have more than 10% of the workforce on temporary/casual contracts. Like part-time contracts, temporary/casual contracts are not widely used in Finland. About 25% of organisations had no temporary/casual workers at all.

If we compare all the EU countries, Sweden is close to Spain, which has the highest proportion of organisations with more than 10% of the employees on temporary contracts (24%). In fact, Sweden has the lowest value in the EU for "not used", with only 1% claiming that they use no temporary contracts at all.

The increase in temporary/casual contracts is greater in Swedish organisations than in Finnish and has been since the 1992 survey. The 1999 EU average increase is 40% and Sweden's is more than that.

In Finland one organisation out of five reported that the use of temporary/casual contracts was increasing and one organisation out of ten reported that its use was decreasing during the 3 years before the survey in 1999. A remarkable drop in the use of temporary/casual workers was found in the 1992 survey. This is due to the recession, which was especially abrupt in Finland. Temporary and casual employees had to leave first. The same pattern is seen for Sweden, which also experienced a deep recession at the beginning of the 1990s. In general, flexible working arrangements tend to be more common in Sweden than in Finland.

HRM IN ACTION

CASE STUDY 1: FÖRENINGSSPARBANKEN/SWEDBANK

FöreningsSparbanken is one of the largest banking groups in the Nordic area. At the turn of the year 2001–2002 the group had approximately 16,000 employees, of whom 9500 were in Sweden. The group has about 4.1 million private customers in Sweden and 3.2 million in the Baltic States. Independent savings banks and partly owned banks have an additional 1.7 million private customers.

At the beginning of the 1990s a number of banks in Sweden suffered from an economic crisis. As one of the results Sweden's co-operative banks were restructured and merged into one banking corporation, Sparbanken Sverige, and the workforce was reduced by almost 25%. In 1994 Sparbanken Sverige shares were listed on the Stockholm stock exchange. Some years later, the bank merged with another bank, Föreningsbanken, resulting in 139 local banks employing some 12,000 people in 1997. FöreningsSparbanken was born.

FöreningsSparbanken is still organised as a network of branches divided into 95 local banks. Today the bank's products and services are distributed through approximately 550 branches in Sweden. In addition the independent savings banks and partly owned banks have another 330 branches.

At 31 December 2001, the bank had a balance sheet total of 107 billion Euros, deposits of 27 billion Euros and loans totalling 76 billion Euros. Operating profit for the year 2001 was 900 million Euros, return on equity 15%.

Role of the HR function

FöreningsSparbanken has a stakeholder model involving four stakeholders:

1. The customers
2. Society
3. The shareholders
4. The employees.

The HR function perceives its role in the organisation as being to support the business while taking account of all four stakeholders. The core challenge is to make sure that employees are successful in their contacts with the customer. The HR function believes they are regarded by most people in the organisation as an important contributor to the core business. Their role has changed over the past 10 years from being a service function taking care of wages and other administrative activities towards working in a more strategic manner to support business.

The focus of HR has changed from the individual towards the organisation – even though the HR philosophy emphasises that the organisation consists of its individual constituents. Hence the individuals are also in focus. So is the competence of the individuals. The focus has also changed from an internal towards a more external view. Today the HR function has a stronger customer focus than some years ago. This change in perspective is illustrated in Figure 9.6.

The HRM focus is moving from an internal individual perspective towards a more external organisational perspective (Larsen, 1999).

The strategic influence of the HR function is strong in this organisation. The HR director is a member of the executive board of 12. The HR function's board representation has been the same since 1992 and the way HR issues are handled is very much a matter for the HR director. In other words it is an individual as well as an organisational issue.

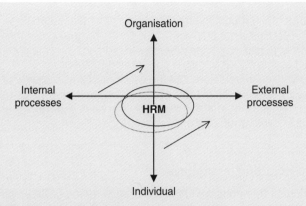

Figure 9.6   The customer focus of the HRM function (Larsen, 1999)

Organisation

HR is organised as a central group function, with a staff of nine. They deal with strategic HR issues working closely with top management.

Routine HR work is performed by a shared service function that sells its services in the organisation. This function operates in four different areas:

1. Administrative services, such as wages.
2. Recruitment and competence analysis.
3. Training.
4. Management and leadership development.

Sixty people work in this function, serving about 10,000 employees – the total operation in Sweden. The group as a whole employs around 16,000.

Responsibility for HR issues

Most of the work referred to as HR is performed in the line. Line managers have a clear responsibility to carry out HR work. The HR function acts as a supporting unit. This way of organising the HR work was introduced in 1992–1993. The HR function was at this point slimmed down from 280 people to 80.

This development corresponds with the Swedish result from the Cranet survey that shows the size of Swedish HR departments diminishing between 1991 and 1999. The idea of devolving HR responsibility to line management is another clear trend in Swedish Cranet data during the 1990s. The bank has come far in this process. Strategic HR issues, however, are kept at the central level of the organisation. This also confirms a trend in the Swedish data from 1992 to 1999/2000. HR policies are increasingly being determined at the central level of the organisation. There was a strong trend towards decentralisation in the early 1990s in Sweden which has disappeared over the past 7 or 8 years.

Training and competence development

The most important HR issues in the bank today are attracting, recruiting, developing and retaining staff. The biggest challenge lies in developing the existing staff. During the year 2001 approximately 80% of all employees took part in some form of training.

In the Swedish part of the group, the total training investment amounts to nearly 33 million Euros, or nearly 3000 Euros per employee. This figure includes direct training costs as well as the employee's time and sometimes meals and lodging. The time spent on competence development represents 2% of available annual working hours.

FöreningsSparbanken emphasises that the way to success leads through its employees' knowledge of their customers. It is crucial to give the right service to the right customer. Therefore the most important area for training in the bank is development of the employees' competence in dealing with the customer.

Measuring and reporting intangibles

As a consequence of the economic crisis in the early 1990s great emphasis was placed on analysing the market as well as decentralising the organisation. So as to be able to control the decentralised organisation the bank introduced a new management control system. Its aim was to create a control system that reflects the present, the past and the future. The model (see Figure 9.7) focuses on measuring and understanding intangible assets and it consists of three main parts: *Human Capital* (HC), *Market Capital* (MC) and *Profitability*. Fundamental to the development of the new control system was the belief that good management and empowered workers affect the entire human capital value. This, in turn, generates high market capital that results in higher profitability.

The *MC* is a concept reflecting how satisfied customers are with the company and how loyal they feel towards it – for instance, whether they are actively searching for alternatives.

The *HC* dimension measures the notion of *empowerment*, i.e. what employees want to do, what they can do, and what they actually do in relation to the business. The bank selected four key domains to measure HC: meeting with customers, competence, organisation and leadership.

The tool as a whole is co-ordinated by the HR group function where they also operate the HC part of the instrument. The other parts are operated by the Business Control and Marketing units. The results of the systematic measurements are incorporated into a large database. Of particular interest are the interrelationships between HC, MC and Profitability.

How to attract new employees

Marketing the organisation to potential employees is achieved mainly by marketing the organisation's values and image. The bank has a long tradition and its history goes back

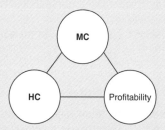

Figure 9.7   The management control model of FöreningsSparbanken – "Tool for the future"

to 1820. In marketing its image the bank highlights its attitude towards its employees. There is a clear development focus, where competence development possibilities are strongly emphasised. The HR philosophy clarifies what the bank can offer its employees and what it demands from them. The goal of the bank was to feature in the list of the 20 most interesting workplaces in a survey carried out among students. This objective was reached in 2001 and the bank is currently in eighteenth place.

Union influence

Since 1993 there has been a unique relationship between the union and the employer in the bank. The principle of negotiation is no longer applied. This is a break from the traditional industrial relations model in Sweden. The new co-determination agreement (*Insight, Involvement, Responsibility*) signed by the bank and the Union of Financial Sector Employees' local organisation in November 2000 was implemented throughout the Swedish part of the group during 2001. The agreement is based on the so-called process principle, in which union representatives take part in management decisions. The basic idea is to involve all employees closely in the group's development. Union representatives are represented on all the main organs of the organisation such as the management team, steering committees, etc.

Communication

The main method of communicating important information to employees has changed from paper to the electronic media. The chief source of information is the Intranet. The information policy allows the employee to access any information available on the Intranet. The aim is to be a transparent organisation. The employees can present ideas and their viewpoints to management through special e-mailboxes. The present CEO of FöreningsSparbanken visits one of the local bank offices every week.

Summary

The HR function of FöreningsSparbanken seems to be business oriented and influential at the strategic level. The HR department has a customer focus as well as an employee focus. The bank represents several trends of HR work seen in the Nordic countries such as:

- Extensive line management responsibility for HR issues.
- Slimming down of HR departments.
- Increasing investment time and money in employee training.
- Shift of HR policy-making from local to central level.
- Measuring and reporting on intangible assets.
- Change in union influence towards a more process-based, consensual approach.

CASE STUDY 2: VTT TECHNICAL RESEARCH CENTRE OF FINLAND

VTT Technical Research Centre of Finland (VTT)[1] is a contract research organisation involved in national and international assignments providing a wide range of technology

---

[1] The case description is based on the following sources of data: Tiittula (1994 and 1996), VTT's Annual Reports and internet material and articles and material distributed by Mr. Risto Suominen, HR Director of VTT and Suominen (2000).

and applied research services for its clients, private companies, institutions and the public sector. VTT is a governmental research institute responsible to the Ministry of Trade and Industry. It had undergone several major organisational changes, from a typical state bureaucracy of the early 1940s to a modern expert organisation with 3000 employees and a turnover of over 200 million Euros in 2001. The role of governmental funding has been decreasing, to about 30% of turnover in 2001. Most of the funding comes from domestic private and public organisations, and from abroad.

VTT's vision is to be a pioneer of technical expertise on an international scale and thus enhance the success of Finland. The vision includes three strategic targets: raising competitiveness, the VTT brand and employee management to new international levels. According to the company's mission statement, VTT's aim is to enhance the competitiveness of industry and other business sectors, and thereby improve social well-being through creating and applying technology. The main research fields are nuclear energy, energy production, emission control, systems and models, paper and mineral industries and materials and chemicals. The company serves over 5000 domestic and foreign customers.

From a government organisation to a modern high-tech research institute

The Technical Research Centre of Finland was founded in 1942. The background of the foundation was the decision to activate the national research system in Finland. From the beginning, VTT had close ties with the Helsinki University of Technology, which furthered the development of VTT into a first-class research institute. VTT started with a team of nine research scientists, and its activities remained on a modest scale until the 1970s. In 1970 the number of employees was 680. Until the early 1970s, VTT was managed like a government organisation. The company was divided into 27 laboratories, all directly responsible to the president of VTT. Managerial control was based on hierarchy and specialist knowledge, employee recruitment was determined by formal qualifications, and salaries reflected the rigid civil service salary scales with no reference to the performance of individual employees, teams or laboratories.

In spite of its governmental status, VTT has been able to develop relatively flexible policies to meet the challenges of the external environment. For example, the laboratories have been responsible for their results since the late 1970s, and VTT's central administration has systematically sought means to increase the proportion of market-based financing. This was part of the general trend prevailing in the public sector towards improving performance by imitating the structures and practices of private companies.

One of the most dramatic periods in the history of VTT was the year 1994, when a wholesale organisational change was carried out. The 27 laboratories were replaced by nine new profit centres and two service units: the VTT information service and the VTT internal service centre. VTT adopted a more business-like mode of management. In the process of re-organising, the number of employees was cut by 250 (9%). The procedure was exceptional: all employment relations were cut and then the research staff of the new profit centres were invited while support and administrative staff were required to apply for their prior or newly-formulated jobs.

The latest organisational changes took place in 2000–2001, when reforms and new practices were introduced in response to changes in the operating environment and the revision of VTT's strategy. The purpose of these changes was to strengthen the knowledge base and internal interaction, to improve customer service and to enhance VTT's competitiveness.

HRM in VTT

In an expert organisation like VTT, human resources are literally the most important resource. It means that HRs and HRM must be developed and refined in line with the strategic targets of the company. This kind of thinking is, however, quite novel in VTT. In addition to customers and owners, employees are an important stakeholder group. The position and value of HRM have been strengthening in the 1990s. The challenges for HRM lie in the nature of the organisation, its history as a state bureaucracy, the dominance of an engineering culture and the need to increase the level of competency in the organisation.

Background

By the 1970s VTT had reached a size that made it necessary to systemise and develop tools for personnel management. The company started local collective bargaining agreements in 1972, extensive employee training was organised from 1973 on, a company-wide co-operation system was established in 1977, joint performance evaluations were started in several laboratories at the beginning of the 1980s and opportunities to enhance doctoral studies were increased. The first employee attitude survey was carried out in 1990, and it is repeated every 2 or 3 years. Since 1995 VTT has published a separate annual personnel review.

Structure of employees

At the end of 2001 the total number of employees in VTT was a little over 3000. Employees are highly educated, with 67% of them holding an academic degree, and 19% a licentiate or doctoral degree.

The ageing of the population is a societal problem and one that affects large organisations too. In VTT the age structure of employees must be seen as a problem. The mean age is 41 years, and the two largest age groups are 40–44 and 45–49 years (see Figure 9.8).

VTT is primarily an expert organisation. More than 80% of its employees are research scientists and other research staff. The proportion of administrative, office and IT staff is relatively low (Figure 9.9).

VTT is a typical engineering organisation in the sense that the most common academic degree is engineering (one-third of employees) and two out of three employees are men. Even though the majority of employees, especially in the more senior positions, are men, gender imbalance involves no problem in VTT. The biased gender structure is seen as a result of biased educational choices by men and women.

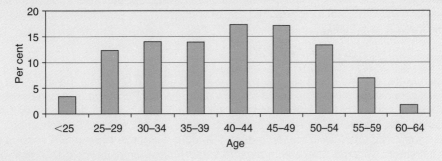

Figure 9.8   Employee structure by age

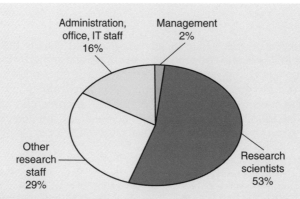

Figure 9.9 Employee structure by function

HRM strategy and policy

VTT established its first HRM strategy in 1996, and it was renewed in 2001. The HRM strategy is derived from the company strategy, and it involves the strategic decisions necessary to guarantee the competence and performance required. The target of the HRM strategy is an efficient, learning and satisfying organisation. This target is approached by eight "strategies":

1. VTT's vision, values and strategy.
2. Competence management.
3. Management of information and interaction.
4. Active development of work communities.
5. Successful recruitment.
6. Knowledge management.
7. Efficient performance management.
8. Supportive feedback and rewards.

The role of HRM policy is to specify the minimum level of HRM. This in itself is normally not enough to be sure of surviving the competition. That is why the HRM strategy and related development targets are needed.

The *HR review* is a link between short-term and long-term targets. The HR review involves the quantitative and qualitative structure of employees and describes the state of the work community. It serves as a basis for future plans and decisions. The first HR review was drawn up in 1995. Several surveys and other measures are used to gather the yearly data for the review. Employee satisfaction, motivation, attitudes and commitment are all seen as important factors to measure and improve. The EQA criteria were included in the measures in 2000.

Organisation of HRM

As part of the organisational change process in 2001, VTT's corporate management and internal services were combined to form a new unit called VTT Corporate Management and Services. In addition to corporate management, this new unit includes, among other things, HR and Legal Affairs, which consists of HRs, Legal Affairs and Internal Service Unit.

Responsibility for HRM is shared among the top management group, HR experts and line managers, which is the case in most of larger Finnish organisations. The profit units are responsible for the management and development of their own employees in order to ensure the necessary competence and performance level. The corporate level (top management together with the HR manager) is responsible for general HRM policy. The line managers are responsible for routine HR procedures, which in VTT are grouped into seven categories: employee planning, staffing, empowerment and support, employee development, performance evaluation and feedback, rewards and employee reorganisation.

Employee planning and staffing

Line managers are responsible for evaluating future staffing needs in line with the company's strategic targets. Employees are recruited from both inside and outside the company, with a preference for internal recruitment. However, a relatively high employee turnover (8.5% in 2001) means that new employees must be sought in the external labour market also. Recruitment is a decentralised activity, in which the line managers can call on the HR unit for support.

The induction phase is regarded as important in VTT. Every new employee is allocated a person responsible for his or her induction. A well-planned induction has been found to reduce short-term employee turnover. However, there are disturbing signs of a "quitting peak" after 2 years in the company. Normally such a peak would be expected after 3–4 years.

Empowerment and support

Employee involvement in the decision-making related to their own work is an important part of direct communication between the subordinate and his or her superior or between a team or group and its superior. Employees have their representative in the top managerial group of the profit unit.

Employee development

In an expert organisation employee development is highly important. The purpose of employee development is to support employees and motivate them towards better results and increased competence. This involves personal/team targets, performance evaluation, feedback and employee reward and also employee development. Each line manager is responsible for the development of his or her own employees. Employee development in VTT covers the whole spectrum of techniques from training planning and support for post-graduate studies to employee rotation and learning on the job. An example of a special training initiative offered in 2001 is the VTT Executive Programme, in which about 90 employees in executive positions received training aimed at creating a uniform management culture.

Evaluation and rewarding

The results of management system involves a relatively complicated evaluation of results as a basis for rewarding employees. The measures used derive from the BSC approach. The reward system comprises the following elements: (a) basic salary, merit increase and result-based profit; (b) suggestion profit, invention support, support for internal entrepreneurship; (c) career development support, knowledge development support and other rewards.

Employee re-organisation

Working at VTT involves working on projects. It means that new employees are recruited where possible on a temporary basis. However, one of the company's policies is to try to guarantee continuity of employment. That means that all the time employee relationships are ending and new projects are starting. Employee re-organisation is an important part of the line manager's work in trying to align the organisation's goals with the individual employee's. The challenge to management is to generate and maintain employee motivation.

Conclusions

VTT is an example of a public organisation that was managed like any state bureaucracy and has undergone huge changes on the way to its present position as a leading technological research institute in Finland. Public funding has become a basis for ensuring that VTT has the capacity to develop its own core expertise.

In terms of HRM, VTT is an example of vigorous development in the 1990s with conspicuous success: in 1999 VTT Construction, which is a profit unit of VTT, won the HRM quality competition based on the EQA criteria. In developing its HRM, VTT has applied benchmarking but also focuses on identifying own core competencies.

The key features of VTT's HRM are:

1. Emphasis on line responsibility.
2. Use of strict performance evaluation and related reward systems.
3. Importance of employee development.
4. Systematic use of measures of HRM.
5. Efforts to streamline HRM processes.

There are, of course, serious challenges also in VTT's HR function. They are related to processes and people: change management, the efficiency, learning and welfare of employees, and the handling of basic issues. VTT has performed well in the area of SHRM, while in the area of change management there is still much to do. The company's values need some clarification, and employee welfare, which is a concern in all Finnish organisations, needs special attention in VTT too. The fact that much still remains to be achieved can be regarded as a virtue, because the continuous development of HRM is a competitive advantage for any company in both the domestic and international markets.

CONCLUSIONS

Sweden and Finland, together with the other Nordic countries, Denmark, Norway and Iceland, form a relatively homogenous group in spite of different positions in respect of EU membership, participation in the European Monetary Union and membership of NATO. Sweden and Finland in particular have much in common, starting from the history of hundreds of years under the same regime and resulting in similar educational systems, labour legislation and industrial relations systems and corporate management. And it is not surprising that the three Cranet surveys reveal more similarities between the countries than differences.

The position of HRM in Swedish and Finnish companies is relatively strong; the board level participation of HR managers is quite high (above the EU average) and in most organisations the person responsible for HRM is involved in strategy development from the beginning of the process. In spite of the relatively strong formal position of HR managers, the power of line managers in HR issues has increased, as in the two case organisations described in this chapter. The extensive line management responsibility for HR is a distinctive feature of HRM in Sweden and Finland compared to other EU countries. In both countries, line management responsibility is somewhat higher in public organisations than in private companies. Line management responsibility in HR affairs has generally produced positive effects. There are, however, organisations in which the decentralisation of HRM has gone too far. It seems that organisations are now looking for the ideal way of balancing HRM between top management, HR specialists and line managers.

Training and development is a topic widely debated in Sweden and Finland. Both countries rely on increasing knowledge of employees. In Finland, however, training and development have assumed almost the status of a *mantra*. It is regarded as an answer to, e.g. the ageing of employees, the competitiveness of companies and the country, employee motivation and high unemployment. In spite of all the public discussion, Finnish organisations seem to spend less on training and development than Swedish organisations, and both countries are in the middle rank among EU members. There are, however, some signs of increasing training and development in Finnish organisations. Senior staff received more training in 1999 than in 1995, and this is especially true for professional and technical employees.

The third topic important to Swedish and Finnish companies and HRM is the flexible use of employees. Here Swedish and Finnish companies differ from each other. Swedish women have a long tradition of part-time working, while since Second World War the employment model for Finnish women has been full-time working. In both countries it has been seen as a question of women's equality in working life. However, the way it is seen is different in Sweden and Finland. The trend in both countries seems to be towards an increase in all kinds of flexible contracts, which makes managing employment relationships more complicated.

Although the position of HRM in Sweden and Finland is strong, the challenges it faces are formidable: how to meet the growing need of organisations for qualified employees and the qualifications of future employees, how to balance the demands of centralisation and decentralisation of HRM and how to resolve the contradiction between the needs of organisations for all kinds of flexibility and the needs of employees for stability and permanence in the employment relationship.

TEACHING QUESTIONS

1. What do you think are the biggest HR challenges facing Swedish and Finnish organisations?
2. a. In what main aspects/areas do HR practices in Sweden differ from those in the rest of Europe?
   b. In what main aspects/areas do HR practices in Finland differ from those in the rest of Europe?
3. An exceptionally deep recession in the early 1990s affected Finnish working life and HRM as well. Give examples of such effects.
4. What is the main explanation for the differences in employee flexibility between Sweden and Finland?
5. What makes employee relations so similar in Sweden and Finland?
6. Sweden and Finland both have a relatively high level of line management involvement in HR issues. What are the possible explanations for this?
7. In what sector (private or public) is line management responsibility for HR issues in Sweden and Finland larger?
8. What is a possible explanation for Sweden and Finland having the highest rates among the EU countries for communicating information to employees of different categories?
9. How do you explain the widespread use of performance appraisal in Sweden compared to Finland?

REFERENCES AND SOURCES

References

Brewster, C. and Larsen, H.H. (2000) *Human Resource Management in Northern Europe. Trends, Dilemmas and Strategy*. Oxford: Blackwell.

Hofstede, G. (1984) *Culture's Consequences: International Differences in Work-Related Values*. London: Sage.

Larsen, H.H. (1999) *Cranet-E undersøgelsen 1999, HRM i danske virksomheder*. Dansk Management Forum & Handeslhøjskolen i København.

Sources for Sweden Institutional Background

(1) Eurostat, Statistical Office of the European Communities (eds.) (1997) Eurostat Yearbook '97. A statistical eye on Europe. Data 1986–1996. Brussels: European Communities.

(2) Eurostat, Statistical Office of the European Communities (eds.) (1999) Eurostat Yearbook '98/99. A statistical eye on Europe. Data 1987–1997. Brussels: European Communities.

(3) Eurostat, Statistical Office of the European Communities (eds.) (2001) Eurostat Yearbook 2001. The statistical guide to Europe. Data 1989–1999. Brussels: European Communities.

(4) Eurostat, Statistical Office of the European Communities (eds.) (2002) Eurostat Yearbook 2002.

The statistical guide to Europe. Data 1990–2000. Brussels: European Communities.

Sources for Finland Institutional Background

(1) Eurostat, Statistical Office of the European Communities (eds.) (2002) Eurostat Yearbook 2002. The statistical guide to data 1990–2000. Brussels: European Communities 2002.

(2) Naiset ja miehet Suomessa. Sukupuolten tasa-arvo 2001:001. Helsinki: Tilastokeskus 2001.

(3) Statistical Yearbook of Finland 2001, Helsinki: Statistics Finland 2001, Vol. 96 (new series).

(4) Eurostat, Statistical Office of the European Communities (eds.) Eurostat Yearbook '98. A statistical eye on Europe 1987–1997. Brussels: European Communities 1999.

(5) http://www.finnfacts.fi/

Sources for Case Study 1

Webpage of ForeningsSparbanken:
  http://www.foreningssparbanken.se
Staffan Ivarsson, HR manager, Foreningssparbanken, Sweden.

Sources for Case Study 2

Suominen, R. (2000) Kun työsuoritus ratkaisee. *Työn tuuli* 1/2000, pp. 43–51.

Tiittula, P. (1994) Farewell to bureaucracy: Technical Research Centre of Finland as a pathfinder in management change. Acta Academicae Oeconomicae Helsingiensis, Series A:95. Helsinki School of Economics and Business Administration, Helsinki.

Tiittula, P. (1996) Yritysmäistyvä tutkimusorganisaatio. Helsingin kauppakorkeakoulun julkaisuja D-232. Helsinki.

http://www.vtt.fi/vtt/inbrief/

10

Bulgaria and Czech Republic: Countries in Transition

Josef Koubek and Elizabeth Vatchkova

INSTITUTIONAL BACKGROUND

BULGARIA

Area	110,993 km^2
Population	7,929,483
Density	71.5 inhabitants per km^2
Capital and population	Sofia (1,182,443)
Other major cities and population	Plovdiv (720,356) Varna (463,700)
Official language	Bulgarian
Religions	85% Christian Orthodox
	13% Muslim
	1% Catholic
	1% Protestant, Gregorian-Armenian, and Others

* Data by National Census, March 2001

Topography and climate

Bulgaria is situated in the eastern part of Balkan peninsula, at the natural crossroads between the east and the west, between Europe and Asia. It is bordered by Romania to the north, by the Black Sea to the east, by Turkey and Greece to the south, and by Macedonia, Montenegro and Serbia to the west.

The Bulgarian landscape is highly diverse. Its mountains – high and low, craggy and undulating – are divided in places by deep valleys or shallow river basins. The north is dominated by the vast lowlands of the Danube plains, the south by highlands and elevated

Figure 10.1   Alexander Nevski Cathedral, Sofia

plains. The average altitude of Bulgaria is 470 m and lowlands prevail.

Along the Black Sea coast to the east of Bulgaria, the 130 km of good, wide beaches are one of the country's main tourist attractions.

The capital of the country, Sofia, is at the foot of the Vitosha mountains (highest point, Cherni Vrah, 2290 m). The largest mountain range in Bulgaria is the Stara Planina or Balkan range, which runs right across Bulgaria from east to west dividing the country into two and giving the peninsula its name.

Bulgaria's climate is generally defined as moderate continental. In the southernmost regions of the country the influence of the Mediterranean is felt.

The influence of the Black Sea is limited to a narrow strip (200–300 km) in eastern Bulgaria. The higher mountainous regions have relatively low temperatures, heavy rainfall and continuous year-round snow.

The average annual temperature of the air in Bulgaria is 10.5°C (summer, 20–22°C).

In the winter, snow cover stays for long periods, creating favourable conditions for skiing.

Bulgaria has no very long rivers. However, it does have a relatively large number of rather unevenly distributed smaller rivers, which rise in the mountains and generally flow into either the Black or Aegean Seas. There are few natural lakes in Bulgaria, although there are 260 alpine glacial lakes, mostly in the Rila and Pirin mountains at altitudes of 1900–2400 m. The lakes and swamps along the Danube have been drained, with the exception of Sreburna lake, which has the status of an UNESCO reserve owing to its unique flora and fauna.

Bulgaria is one of the countries richest in thermal spas in Europe, ranking third after the Czech Republic and Spain in the number of mineral springs. These vary in mineral content and temperature (17°C to over 100°C in Sapareva Banya) and are thus used to treat a wide variety of ailments.

Bulgaria's rich biodiversity includes over 12,350 plant species and over 15,000 animal species, including many rare species. Three national parks and 89 reserves and other protected areas help to preserve this variety. Bulgaria has the largest number of biosphere reserves in the world.

Special features

As a country situated at the centre of the Balkan peninsula, Bulgaria is the natural link between Western and Central Europe and the Near and Middle East. Its history, economy and traditions connect it with Russia and the other Central and East European (CEE) countries.

Bulgarians are known for their intellectual curiosity and national pride. In the distant past, the land of the Bulgarians has experienced the Thracian, Hellenic, Roman and Slav civilisations. Some remarkable monuments and spiritual elements still remain and are embedded in modern Bulgarian culture.

Table 10.1 shows the position of Bulgaria in relation to other countries on a number of standardised items.

Population

The decline in population which became manifest in 1989 continues (Figure 10.2). In terms of population Bulgaria ranks 20th of Europe's 46 countries and is home to 1% of Europe's population. Life expectancy is increasing (see Table 10.2). The average life expectancy (Statistical Reference Book (NSI) 2001) in Bulgaria is 75.3 years for women and 68.2 years for men.

The average number of people per household is 2.76 (2001).

Economy

Following the launch of radical economic reforms in 1990, the 1998 gross domestic product (GDP) was only two-thirds of its pre-transition level of 1989. When the country failed to meet its debt service obligation in 1997 a currency board regime was introduced, pegging the Bulgarian lev to the German mark (replaced by the

Table 10.1   Principal characteristics in relation to EUR-15 = 100

	Density[1]	Infant mortality per 1000 live births[2]	Life expectancy at birth[2]		Employment rate[3]		Unemployment[3] rate (LFS)
			Boys	Girls	Men	Women	
BUL	74.6	14.4	68.2	75.3	41.8	35.8	19.5
Relation to EU	64.3	313	90.6	92.5	57.3	65.2	267.1

Source: Statistical Reference Book (NSI) 2001.
[1]1997 data; [2]1999 data; [3]2001 data.

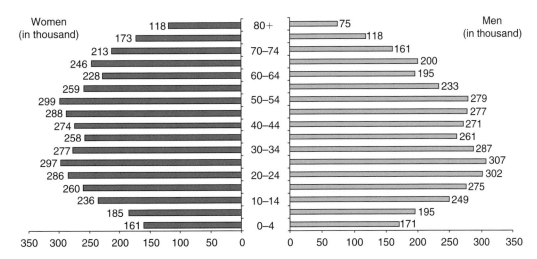

Figure 10.2 Population by age and gender (2001)
Source: NSI, 2003

Table 10.2 Population by age (% of total population)

Age (years)	Bulgaria		EUR-15 1997
	1986	2000	
<15	21	15	17
15–24	14	14	13
25–49	34	35	37
50–64	18	19	17
65–79	11	14	12
>80	2	3	4

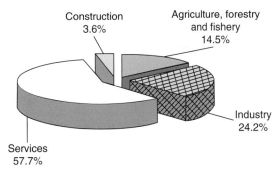

Figure 10.3 Economic structure (share of GDP by sector, 2001) *Source*: NSI, 2003

Table 10.3 Gross domestic product

	1993	1994	1995	1996	1997	1998	1999	2000
GDP-current prices in $ billion (nominal growth)	10.8	9.4	13.0	9.9	10.2	12.7	12.9	12.6
Real annual change (%)	−2	2	3	−10	−7	4	2	6

Source: NSI, 2003.

euro in 1999). The currency board system has brought stability to economic development, and during the second half of 1997 the GDP started to grow (see Table 10.3 and Figure 10.3).

The average monthly cost of living as of September 1999 is 114.74 euros (Figure 10.4).

Legal, institutional and political environment

The new constitution of the Republic of Bulgaria, adopted in July 1991, incorporates all the basic principles

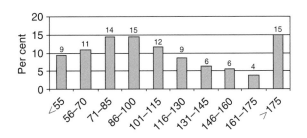

Figure 10.4 Households (=100) by monthly income per person (September, 1999). *Source*: Institute for Social and Trade Union Research

of modern constitutionalism. It provides for a multi-party parliamentary system and free elections on the basis of universal suffrage. Following elections, the largest parliamentary group is asked to form a government. A simple parliamentary majority is required to approve a government (Council of Ministers), and to pass normal legislation. A three-quarters majority is required to approve constitutional changes.

The president serves as head of state, and is directly elected once every 5 years for a maximum of two terms and is the Supreme Commander in Chief of the armed forces of the Republic of Bulgaria. He/she appoints the prime minister designate to form a government; schedules the elections for a National Assembly and for the bodies of local self-government and sets the date for national referenda, pursuant to a resolution of the National Assembly; and promulgates the adopted laws with a decree countersigned by the prime minister or the minister concerned.

Bulgaria is a parliamentary republic and the legislature is the country's basic power. The National Assembly is vested with the legislative power and exercises parliamentary control. Its mandate is for a term of 4 years.

The parliament consists of the 240-seat National Assembly. Members are directly elected for 4 years on the basis of proportional representation. Parties and electoral coalitions need at least 4% of the popular vote to qualify. Members of the National Assembly represent not only their constituencies but the entire nation. Members of the National Assembly act on the basis of the constitution and the laws and in accordance with their conscience and convictions.

The National Assembly elects permanent and ad hoc committees from among its members. It passes laws, resolutions, declarations and addresses. Any member of the National Assembly or the Council of Ministers has the right to introduce a bill. The State Budget Bill is drawn up and presented by the Council of Ministers.

The Council of Ministers is the principal body of the executive branch. Chaired by the prime minister, it initiates and implements the domestic and the foreign policy of the state, ensures public order and national security, and exercises overall guidance over the state administration and the armed forces. The prime minister designate is nominated by the largest parliamentary group and is given a mandate by the president to form a cabinet. The proposed Council of Ministers is elected by the National

Assembly. The activity of the Council of Ministers is under the direct control of the National Assembly. Individual ministers and the prime minister are obliged to answer questions and interpellations addressed to them by members of the National Assembly.

The statute and the competence of the local bodies of the executive branch depend on the territorial division of the Republic of Bulgaria.

Labour market

During the period 1989–2001 the total number of people employed fell by 1,425,000 as a result of the transition from a centrally planned to a market economy and the structural reforms taking place (Tables 10.4 and 10.5).

Unemployment is one of the most serious problems arising from the transition in Bulgaria. The number of registered unemployed reached a peak in 1993 with more than 600,000, representing a 16% unemployment rate (Table 10.6).

Measured by the ILO methodology, the number of unemployed exceeded registered jobless by 200,000, corresponding to a 21% unemployment rate. During the subsequent years, available unemployment data have been somewhat contradictory: while the registered data report strong fluctuations over the period 1994–1998, ending with an 11% decline in 1998, data provided by the Labour Force Survey (LFS) report a fall in unemployment until 1996 followed by an increase afterwards (Table 10.6).

During the last 13 years both the role and the structures of Bulgarian trade unions significantly changed. As a result of the privatisation, restructuring and fragmentation of the working force not more than 35–40% of the total amount of the employees are currently unionised (the data from the last census, 1999). Syndical pluralism is the typical model. Two big organisations have structures in nearly all industries and territorial regions of the country. Only these two organisations – "Confederation of the Independent Trade Unions in Bulgaria" and "Confederation of Labour 'Podkrepa'" – are represented in the social three-partied collaboration at national level. Besides there exist several small national trade unions: "Change", "Association of the democratic trade unions" and others. They cover roughly 3–4% of all unionised members (census 1999). There also exist

Table 10.4   Persons in employment (million)

	1993	1994	1995	1996	1997	1998	1999	2000	2001
Employment	3.221	3.241	3.282	3.285	3.157	3.152	3.088	2.980	2.968
1989 = 100	73.8	74.2	75.2	75.3	72.3	72.2	70.7	68.3	68.0
Employment-LFS	2.994	2.868	3.031	3.085	3.030	2.921	2.811	2.735	2.628
1993 = 100		95.8	101.2	103.0	101.2	97.6	93.9	91.3	87.8

Source: NSI, 2003; Labour Force Survey (for 1994).

Table 10.5   Persons in employment in different sectors (million)

	1993	1994	1995	1996	1997	1998	1999	2000	2001
Industry	1.178	1.128	1.103	1.083	1.010	0.965	0.891	0.844	0.832
Agriculture	0.712	0.751	0.782	0.785	0.800	0.825	0.795	0.781	0.767
Services	1.317	1.330	1.361	1.395	1.416	1.346	1.401	1.355	1.370

Source: NSI, 2003.

Table 10.6   Unemployment rate (%)

	1993	1994	1995	1996	1997	1998	1999	2000	2001
Registered unemployment	16	14	11	11	14	12	14	18	18
Unemployment-LFS	21	21	15	14	15	16	17	16	20

Source: NSI, 2003; Labour Force Survey (for 1994).

Table 10.7   Labour force structure by education (%)

	2000	2001
Higher	24	27
Upper secondary	58	56
Secondary, primary or lower	18	17

Source: NSI, 2003.

autonomous independent associations in various branches of industry, e.g. pilots, power engineers, policemen, etc.

Trade unions are well represented in the budget-funded organisations as well as in the state dominated ones or in organisations with prevailing municipal ownership. As a rule trade unions operate in the biggest and medium-sized enterprises, including multinational companies. Creation of trade unions in small and micro-firms as well as in the companies of the service sector (banks and distribution companies) is much more problematic.

Education

The Bulgarian constitution entitles every individual to free education. It is mandatory for children to attend school until they reach 16 years of age, i.e. until completion of their secondary education.

The school network in the country comprises of 4000 schools. These include municipal schools, schools administered by the Ministry of Education and Science, special schools and orphanages directly funded by the state budget and private schools. Over 1,100,000 students are educated in Bulgarian schools each year; teaching and non-teaching staff total 180,000.

In secondary education Bulgaria has introduced a 12-grade educational system. The legal starting age is 7 years for enrolment in the first grade – 6 years in certain exceptional cases.

In higher education there are 41 universities in the country, of which five are higher military schools and four are private universities. The higher educational system consists of three levels of achievements: bachelor's degree, master's degree and doctor's degree. The Law of Higher Education was amended in 1999. Paid-for education in public universities, introduced by a law passed in 1995, was abrogated and a uniform state fee was introduced for professional areas which amounts to 15% of the total sum required for the student's maintenance.

CZECH REPUBLIC

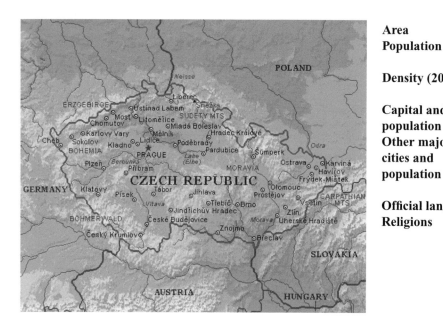

Area	78, 866 km^2
Population	10,230,060 inhabitants
Density (2001)	130 inhabitants per km^2
Capital and population	Praha (Prague): (1,169,106)
Other major cities and population	Brno (376,172) Ostrava (316,744) Plzeň (165,259) Olomouc (102,246)
Official language	Czech
Religions	59% Without confession 26% Roman Catholic 1% Czech Brothers Evangelical 1% Czech Husist 4% Others 9% Not declared

All data are from the 2001 census

Topography and climate

The Czech Republic has two kinds of regional division: the historical (Bohemia, Moravia and the south-east part of Silesia) and the administrative (Capital Praha and 76 districts, since 2000 established as 14 regions). It lies in the central part of Europe in the middle of the temperate zone of the northern hemisphere. The country's borders are with Poland (761.8 km), Germany (810.3 km), Austria (466.3 km) and Slovakia (251.8 km).

A major European watershed passes through the territory of the Czech Republic and separates the basins of the North, Baltic and Black Seas. The dividing node of the three seas is the mountain Králický Sněžník (1423 m above sea level). The principal rivers are the Labe (370 km) and the Vltava (433 km) in Bohemia, the Morava (246 km) and the Dyje (306 km) in Moravia, and the Odra (135 km) and the Opava (131 km) in Silesia and northern Moravia.

The climate in the Czech Republic is influenced by the mutual penetration and mingling of ocean and continental effects. The maritime effect is mainly felt in Bohemia, whereas continental climate effects have a bigger impact on Moravia and Silesia. The climate in the Czech Republic is influenced by its altitude and geographical relief to a large extent: 67% of the total area lies at an altitude of up to 500 m, 32% between 500 and 1000 m, and only 1% above 1000 m. The average altitude is 430 m. The highest point is 1602 m (Sněžka in the Krkonoše Mountains), the lowest 115 m (Labe river shore at Hřensko – a village on the German border).

Nationalities and culture

The most numerous national group in the Czech Republic are Czechs (94% of the total population). The national minorities are Slovakian (2%), Polish (0.5%), German (0.4%), Gipsy (0.1%) and others (1%), 2% are not declared. The number of foreign citizens having permission for temporary living and working in the Czech Republic is about 125,000, of whom about 24,000 are citizens of the Slovak Republic living on Czech territory.

The culture of the Czech Republic has been influenced by very close contact with some other European cultures (particularly German, Italian and French) during about 1300 years. On the other hand, Czech culture and science have significantly contributed to the European scene. First of all, there are numerous Czech composers (e.g. Benda, Mysliveček, Smetana, Dvořák, Janáček, Martinů, Mahler and Friml) whose works are an established element of European culture. Many Czech painters (Hollar, Mucha, Kupka, Šíma, Muzika, Kubín/Coubine, Filla, Čermínová/Toyen and others) and writers (especially Čapek, who – among others – coined the word "robot", the Nobel Prize laureate Seifert, Kundera and Hašek) achieved international recognition. As for Czech scientists, one could mention Komenský/Comenius (pedagogy), Purkyně (the cell), Ressel (the first ship's propeller), Jánský (blood groups), Hrozný (language of ancient Hittites), Hrdlička (origin of American Indians), Heyrovský (Nobel Prize for the discovery of polarography) or Wichterle (inert material used for contact lenses). Prague has the oldest university in Central Europe (founded in 1348) and the university has been a centre of education not only for Czechs, but for many other nationals. And of course the Reformation started in the Czech Kingdom at the beginning of the 15th century (Jan Hus), when the first Protestant church was established.

Principal characteristics

Table 10.8 shows the principal characteristics (2000) and the position of the Czech Republic relative to the averages for European Union (EU) countries.

Population

In terms of population size and density, the Czech Republic ranks 12th and 13th respectively in Europe, but the population has been declining during the 1990s. This has been caused by a continuing and relatively rapid fall in the birth rate, a fall which was not matched by the decrease in the mortality rate. On the other hand, life expectancy has increased steadily, from 67.6 years (men) and 75.4 years (women) in 1990 to 71.5 years (men) and 78.2 years (women) in 2000 (Table 10.8). The proportion of old people in the population continues to grow (Table 10.9).

The average number of people per household is at present 2.4, while in the period 1980–1991 it was 2.6. There was some decrease in the proportion of complete families (from 66% in 1980 to 62% in 1991 and to 54% in 2001) and an increase in the proportion of non-complete families (from 8% in 1980 to 11% in 1991 and 13% in 2001) and single households (from 24% in 1980 to 27% in 1991 and nearly 30% in 2001).

Economy

The Czech economy has changed radically since the beginning of the 1990s. State and co-operative

Figure 10.5   A view of Prague Castle and the Charles Bridge

Table 10.8   Principal characteristics in relation to EUR-15 = 100

	Density	Infant mortality per 1000 live births	Life expectancy at birth		Employment rate*		Unemployment rate
			Boys	Girls	Men	Women	
CZ	130	4.1	71.5	78.2	63.4	48.3	8.8
Relation to EU	112.0	83.7	95.5	96.3	87.6	89.8	107.3

*Employed from population 15 and more years.

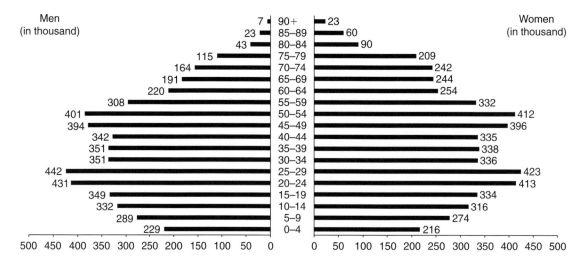

Figure 10.6   Population by age and sex (1 March 2001)

Table 10.9   Population by age and sex (% of total population)

Age (years)	1986	1996	2001 (census data)		EUR-15 2000
			Total	Women (%)	
<15	23	18	16	49	17
15–24	14	16	15	49	12
25–49	36	36	36	49	37
50–64	16	16	19	52	17
65–79	10	11	14	60	13
>80	2	3	2	70	4

organisations were privatised and the centrally directed economy was transformed into a free-market economy. Although most businesses are now private, the state is still a minority shareholder in several important companies. On the other hand, such activities as health services and education are mostly run by the public sector (Table 10.10).

Important recent developments in the economic structure include an increase in the proportion of services, fluctuations in the proportion of manufacturing and a decrease in the proportion of agriculture. Figure 10.7 presents a detailed picture.

The most important exports (2000) were machinery and transport equipment (45% of total value), manufactured goods classified chiefly by material (25%), miscellaneous manufactured articles (13%) and chemical and related products (7%). The same commodities

were the most important imports. The geographic orientation of the Czech export trade has changed substantially since 1990. While in the 1980s the most important part of Czech exports went to member countries of COMECON, particularly the Soviet Union, in 2000 the export trade was dominated by developed market economies (75% of total export value), particularly EU countries (69% of total export value). The most important export partner is Germany (40% of total export value). This reorientation of the export trade demonstrates the flexibility of the Czech economy.

Legal, institutional and political environment

The Czech Republic is a democratic state based on competition among all political parties respecting democratic principles and eschewing violence. Political power is based on free, universal, equal and direct suffrage by secret ballot. The constitution embodies the Charter of Fundamental Rights and Freedoms, protects minorities and guarantees the self-government (autonomy) of territorial autonomous units. There is a bicameral parliament consisting of the Chamber of Deputies with 200 deputies elected by proportional representation and the Senate with 81 senators elected by majority vote. The parliament has lawmaking power and elects the president of the republic. The president appoints the prime minister and individual members of the

Table 10.10   Gross domestic product (at current prices and current exchange rates)

	1990	1991	1992	1993	1994	1995	1996	1997	1998	1999	2000
1000 million CZK	626.2	753.8	842.6	1020.3	1182.8	1381.1	1567.0	1679.9	1820.7	1887.3	1959.5
Yearly growth as % of previous year (real growth)		1.2	1.1	1.2	1.2	1.2	1.1	1.1	1.1	1.0	1.0
1000 million ECU	17.1	20.6	23.0	29.9	34.6	39.8	45.5	46.8	50.6	51.2	55.0
Yearly growth as % of previous year (real growth)		1.2	1.1	1.3	1.1	1.2	1.2	1.0	1.1	1.0	1.1

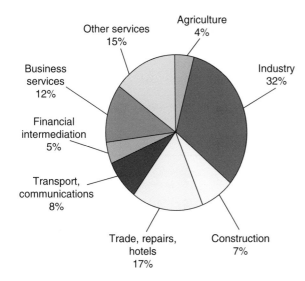

Figure 10.7   Economic structure (1998) (gross value rates as % of sectors, CzR 2000)

government proposed by the prime minister. The government is responsible to the Chamber of Deputies. The president of the republic also appoints, subject to the Senate's agreement, the members of the Constitutional Court, judges, the Council of the National Bank and the president and the vice-president of the Superior Office of Control (proposed by the Chamber of Deputies). She/he signs laws, with the right to refuse and send the laws back to the Chamber of Deputies. The Senate (Upper Chamber) is also entitled to send laws back to the Chamber of Deputies. Policy is implemented by the prime minister and the government. The government exercises extensive control of the national budget but in formulating economic strategy they must take account of the opinion of the independent Czech National

Bank, whose top management (the Bank Council) is appointed by the president of the republic. An Office of Ombudsman was recently established.

The political make-up of the current Chamber of Deputies is:

- Czech Social-Democratic Party – 74 deputies (32%).
- Civic Democratic Party – 63 deputies (28%).
- Communist Party of Bohemia and Moravia – 24 deputies (11%).
- Christian Democratic Union – Czech People's Party – 20 deputies (9%).
- Union of Freedom (Liberals) – 19 deputies (9%).

In the Senate, the 1998 election resulted in the following structure:

- Civic Democratic Party – 26 senators (32%).
- Czech Social-Democratic Party – 23 senators (28%).
- Christian Democratic Union – Czech People's Party – 17 senators (21%).
- Union of Freedom + the Civic Democratic Alliance – 11 senators (14%).
- Communist Party of Bohemia and Moravia – 4 senators (5%).

A by-election in 1999 produced one independent senator.

European principles have been introduced step by step into Czech employment law since 1990. Recently the process was completed by the ratification by parliament of the new Labour Code. The laws governing labour and employment are integrated with the laws concerned with social welfare and public health (old age pensions, disability pensions, widow's pension, death, sickness allowance and health care, maternity/

parental leave with allowance till a child is 3 years old, unemployment benefit, social aid, etc).

Labour disputes have been very rare in the Czech Republic. Their impact on loss of working days has been minimal and Czech statistics do not record such data.

Labour market

No conventional labour market existed before 1990, because labour activity was centrally managed and there was no unemployment. The real labour market appeared at the beginning of 1990s and therefore it is possible to analyse labour market data only since 1990 (Tables 10.11 and 10.12).

The unemployment rate was relatively low till the mid-1990s, but recently it has been increasing. While at the end of 1990 there were only 39,000 unemployed persons (1%) and 58,000 vacancies, at the end of 2000 there were 457,000 unemployed persons (9%) and 52,000 vacancies (Tables 10.13 and 10.14).

Hourly labour costs in the Czech Republic have been much lower than the European average (Tables 10.15–10.17).

Education

Education in the Czech Republic is free in public (state) schools at all levels, but there are some private schools (as a rule at secondary or tertiary level), and these

Table 10.11   Persons in employment (million)

1990	1991	1992	1993	1994	1995	1996	1997	1998	1999	2000
5.1*	5.0	4.9	4.8	4.8	4.8	4.8	4.8	4.7	4.7	4.6
100.0*	98.1	96.1	94.1	93.3	94.6	94.9	93.8	92.3	89.0	87.2

* Calculated from not-rounded data.

Table 10.12   Persons in employment in different sectors (thousand)

	1990	1991	1992	1993	1994	1995	1996	1997	1998	1999	2000
Agriculture*	820	:	:	:	441	405	390	358	340	324	311
Industry**	2241	:	:	:	1963	1987	1980	1961	1921	1835	1798
Services***	2291	:	:	:	2481	2619	2675	2628	2612	2604	2620

* Primary sphere – agriculture, hunting, forestry, fishing, mining and quarrying.
** Secondary sphere – industry (excluding mining and quarrying).
*** Tertiary sphere – all other branches.
Note: The data for 1990 were recalculated using methodology applied since 1994. ":" Data not available.

Table 10.13   Unemployment rate*

	1990	1991	1992	1993	1994	1995	1996	1997	1998	1999	2000
Per cent	0.7	4.1	2.6	3.5	3.2	2.9	3.5	5.2	7.3	9.4	8.8

	2000 (31 December)	
	Czech Republic	EU-15
Unemployment rate (women)	10.6	9.7
Unemployment rate (men)	7.3	7.0
Long-term unemployed**	38.4	45.2

* Out of the total labour force available, 31 December.
** Persons unemployed more than 12 months as a percentage of the total number of unemployed. The proportion of persons unemployed more than 9 months was 46% and the proportion of persons unemployed more than 6 months was 56%.

Table 10.14   Employment rate by sex (2000, 31 December)

	Czech Republic*	EU-15
Women	46.2	53.8
Men	64.7	72.4

*Lower employment rate in the Czech Republic is influenced by lower pension age (men 60 years; women 55–57 years – by number of children).

Table 10.15   Average hourly labour costs (manual and non-manual workers in total industry)*

	1990	1991	1992	1993	1994	1995	1996	1997	1998	1999	2000
CZK	:	:	:	51.17	56.91	66.82	80.08	86.10	101.36	107.63	116.32
Ecu	:	:	:	1.50	1.67	1.95	2.36	2.41	2.79	2.93	3.27

*Estimate based on average monthly labour costs. ":" Data not available.

Table 10.16   Monthly earnings: all workers*

	1990	1991	1992	1993	1994	1995	1996	1997	1998	1999	2000
In industry CZK	3410	3972	4805	5893	6888	8148	9587	10726	11859	12671	13573
Ecu	93.1	108.5	131.2	172.8	202.2	237.5	283.1	299.6	328.0	343.5	381.3
In retail trade** CZK	:	:	:	:	:	5915	6847	7706	8601	9353	10186
Ecu	:	:	:	:	:	172.4	202.2	215.3	237.9	253.6	286.1

*There are no published data on monthly earnings of non-manual workers.
**Data for period 1990–1994 are for total trade only. ":" Data not available.

Table 10.17   Structure of labour costs in total industry (%, 2000)

Direct cost	Indirect cost	Social security as part of indirect cost
64	36	26

require the payment of some fees. Even private primary and secondary schools, though, receive some funding from the state budget. Kindergartens are for children between 3 and 6 years of age, but they are not compulsory. The basic (primary) education is 9 years long (from 6 to 15 years of age) and it is compulsory. However, some pupils are allowed to enter a "gymnasium" (i.e. school of secondary general education) after 5 or 7 years of basic school. There are three kinds of secondary education in the Czech Republic: The gymnasiums (mostly 4 years of study, but also 6 or 8 years of study) provide general education of a higher level and are the normal preparation for study at university or for work in administrative jobs. The secondary technical schools (mostly 4 years of study, but also 2 or 3 years of study) are specialised (machinery, construction, chemistry, transport, health, economics, etc.) and prepare young people for technical or lower managerial positions or for study at university. Secondary vocational schools (mostly 3 years of study, but also 1, 2 or 4 years) prepare young people for skilled manual jobs, but graduates of 4-year courses are allowed to continue their study at universities. Graduates of the 4-year courses at all three kinds of secondary schools with the equivalent of General Certificate of Secondary Education (GCSE) "A" levels are allowed to continue their studies at university or at higher professional schools. The universities provide programmes at bachelor level (3 years of study), master level (another 1 or 2 years of study) and post-graduate doctoral level (3 years of study). The higher professional schools provide 2 or 3.5 years' study specialising in a particular profession (Tables 10.18 and 10.19).

A notable trend in the Czech Republic is the steadily increasing proportion of young people participating in secondary and tertiary education. Younger age groups are much better educated than the older ones. For example, the number of university students in 2000 was 207,000, an increase of 75.4% on the 1990 figure of 118,000.

Table 10.18 Proportion of population with tertiary education in the age group 25–59 years

	25–29	30–34	35–39	40–49	50–59	Total (25–59)
Men	11.8	13.9	15.9	15.2	13.7	14.1
Women	12.5	13.1	13.9	11.4	6.8	11.4

Source: Census Data, 2001.

Table 10.19 Labour force structure by education (%, 2000)

Highest attained education	Total	Men	Women
Compulsory (basic)	10	8	13
Secondary vocational and technical	44	51	34
Secondary vocational with GCSE	2	2	1
Secondary technical with GCSE	29	24	35
Secondary general with GCSE	4	2	6
University	11	12	10
Without education and not identified	0.2	0.2	0.2

Sources:
Statistical Yearbook of the Czech Republic 1990–1999.
Praha, Český statistický úřad (The Czech Statistical Office) 1990–2002.
Population Census Data 2001.
Internet Czech Statistical Office.
Eurostat.

HRM IN BULGARIA AND CZECH REPUBLIC

INTRODUCTION

Bulgaria and the Czech Republic were members of the Council for Mutual Economic Assistance (CMEA) until its termination in 1991. Politically and economically both countries were strongly dependent on the former Soviet Union. Overcoming this dependence has been accompanied by increased collaboration with the developed European countries. In the course of this transition economic, political, social and legislative changes have greatly influenced the development of HR practices.

Significant historical, economic, social and cultural differences between the two countries exist. While Bulgaria has been relatively detached from West European trends of development, the Czech Republic has been a participant and contributor to them throughout its history – with the exception of a period of 42 years after the Second World War. During the inter-war period the territory of what is now the Czech Republic contained some of the most industrialised and developed regions of Europe. In spite of the respective situations of both countries, there were some differences in their contacts with the Western Europe. The Czech people had much greater opportunities than the Bulgarians to be informed about, and to observe, West European practices. The Czech Republic enjoyed other advantages that affected the transformation process after 1989: an entrepreneurial tradition and the entrepreneurial spirit of the people, the knowledge and skills of the labour force, the relatively good technological condition of companies and infrastructure, foreign-investment-friendly legislation, closer proximity to the West European countries and a government that achieved membership of the OECD and NATO, as well as convergence with EU rules.

The different situations in Bulgaria and in the Czech Republic have inevitably influenced the nature of HRM in both countries. Czech organisations were in a position to adopt progressive personnel management methods applied during the inter-war period. They could learn quickly from the experience of West European, US and Japanese organisations by means of intensive training of Czech managers and personnel specialists both abroad and in the Czech Republic, as well as by imitating the practices employed in the foreign-owned companies doing business in the Czech Republic. The relatively small volume of foreign investments, and the smaller number of multinational companies operating in Bulgaria since 1989, created less favourable conditions for modernising HR practices in that country. Currently, the Bulgaria and Czech republics are among the group of new countries scheduled to join the EU.

The following analyses are based on the results of the two most recent surveys, conducted in 1996 and in 1998, within the framework of the Cranfield Project on European Human Resource Management, in Bulgaria and in the Czech Republic. The 1998 Bulgarian and Czech data are compared with the averages for EU member countries participating in the Cranfield Project (the data were calculated by the Centre for European Human Resource Management, Cranfield University). Because the numbers of respond- ents in individual EU countries were very different in the 1999/2000 survey (e.g. more than 20% of all EU respondents were from the UK, while the percentage of respondents from the other countries did not exceed 9%, with the minimum about 2% respondents from Italy), the simple average was used for the comparison. Because any average could be influenced by extreme values and by variability in individual national data, the tables provide information about the extreme values as well as the pertinent countries.

ANALYSIS

The HRM function: marginal or core?

The most important asset of any organisation is its people, with their competencies, potential, motivation and commitment. This asset, though, can be fully exploited only through an appropriate and professional system of people management, which in turn depends on the professionalism, recognition, reputation and status of the HRM function.

The HRM function can operate efficiently only insofar as it is involved in the process of strategic decision-making and is treated as a business partner and a contributor to organisational value. The formal status of the head of HRM can be considered as an indicator of the professionalism, recognition and reputation of the

Table 10.20   Percentage of organization where the head of the HR function serves on the main board of directors (valid %)

Answer	Bulgaria		Czech Republic		EU* extremes (1998–1999)		EU average
	1996	1999	1996	1998	Maximum	Minimum	
Yes	45	30	60	60	88 (F)	30 (P)	55
No	55	71	41	40	71 (P)	12 (F)	46

* F: France; P: Portugal.

HRM function, as can its involvement in the process of strategic decision-making. This status is assessed by observing the place that the function occupies vis-à-vis the main Board of Directors or the equivalent organisational managerial body (Table 10.20).

Formulating organisational strategy assumes more and more importance in the light of the accelerating structural changes taking place in the transitional economies. In such conditions the very survival of the organisation depends on the successful adaptation of the workforce to the requirements of the market environment.

The percentage of Czech organisations where the head of HR serves on the main Board of Directors is not only much higher than the percentage of Bulgarian organisations, but higher than the average for EU countries. In addition, the trend is towards an increase in the number of Czech HR managers participating in the top managerial bodies. According to the survey, Bulgarian HR managers are losing these positions.

Is the role of the HR function and its head so important in the Czech organisations? On the one hand an increasing role and recognition of HR function can be found in some organisations but, on the other hand, it seems that the presence of HR heads on the main Board of Directors is a tradition inherited from the former system. HR or personnel departments in Czech and Bulgarian organisations replaced the so-called personnel and cadre departments. Under the Soviet system, the activities of heads of the personnel and cadre departments were largely dependent on Communist Party control. Their role was to transmit the key political decisions. Consequently, the heads of these departments were the most powerful individuals in the organisations and they were members of top authorities. The transformation of former personnel and cadre departments removed the old-timers and obsolete

practices from these departments, but the tradition that HR heads served on the main Board of Directors survived. However, it seems that this practice became less and less important, as opposed to the new approach to the HR function, which was strengthening the membership of HR in the top decision-making body. This trend is supported by the fact that, when the head of HR does not serve on the main Board of Directors, or where no HR department exists, it is the chief executive or managing directors who most frequently takes responsibility for personnel issues.

Both surveys show a delay in the constitution of HRM departments in Bulgarian organisations compared to the EU countries. And the most recent data confirm this trend – only 71% of Bulgarian companies have HRM departments. This is a result of the process of dynamic restructuring and downsizing as well as of the still inadequate recognition of the importance of a specialist department for organisational competitiveness.

The status of HR management depends considerably on the competencies of their staff. These competencies are much lower in Bulgaria and in the Czech Republic than in EU countries as a whole. This situation results from the fact that the management of people was not determined by market principles in these countries in the period from the beginning of the Second World War until the beginning of the 1990s. During that time the education and training of HR/personnel management specialists in Bulgarian and Czech organisations was based on autocratic models and approaches. Thus they suffered from a lack of specialist skills and knowledge, while the newly educated ones did not possess the necessary knowledge, skills or experience. During the process of the HRM transformation in the first half of the 1990s HR/personnel positions were staffed either by people with some experience of personnel administration (personnel record-keeping, reward administration, labour economy, labour organisation, training) or by those with powerful protection from top managers (particularly where senior HRM positions are concerned).

The result of such "transformation" can be illustrated by the fact that only one-third of the most senior Czech personnel/HR managers in 1993 had had any previous experience in HR/personnel management at the time of their appointment. Such managers comprised about 45% of all senior personnel/HR managers in Czech organisations in 1996 and 48% in 1998. The data for Bulgaria are similar. Thus the proportion of experienced HR managers in both countries is substantially lower than the average for EU countries. Consequently, the level of their competence raises the question of whether they are the right business and strategic partners for their colleagues in top management.

When it comes to the experience of HR/personnel managers as measured by the time spent working in personnel/HRs or training, a convergence of Czech data towards the EU average can be observed. Using time as a measure could be misleading, however, because of differences in the nature of the HR/personnel job, in the context and in the practices used in particular organisations and countries. Many of the Bulgarian and Czech respondents reporting more time working in HR/personnel positions were probably employed in the so-called personnel and cadre departments, in personnel administration departments or in labour and wage departments during the period of communist rule. Their experience with HRM as such is not so long – which suggests that Bulgarian and Czech personnel managers are less prepared to apply modern HRM methods. An analysis of their educational background shows that the percentage of respondents with a university degree in the Czech organisations is comparable with the average for EU countries, while in the Bulgarian companies it is much higher. In Bulgaria this result is based on the long-standing practice of ensuring a high proportion of the employed population with a university degree. In 1989 it was 13.7%, compared to 8.4% in the Czech Republic, 12.3% in Hungary and 10.5% in Poland (Employment observatory, Central and Eastern Europe, p. 29).

The point is that the academic field of study of respondents is not relevant to contemporary HR purposes. While the most typical academic fields of respondents in EU countries were business studies, social/behavioural and law, those of the Czech respondents were engineering (25% in 1996 and 28% in 1998), social/behavioural

(20 and 18%, respectively) and business studies/economics (18 and 14%, respectively). The most common academic fields of the Bulgarian respondents were economics (47% in 1996 and 53% in 1999), engineering (25 and 27%) and business studies (6 and 8%).

All the data support the idea that HR/personnel units in the Bulgarian and the Czech organisations were not adequately staffed and that could impede the implementation of advanced HRM practices. When most HR/personnel management units were staffed in both countries during the first half of the 1990s, the selection criteria for the people appointed were quite modest, because of the dearth of highly qualified professionals. Hasty decisions were made so as to provide a temporary solution. Employees with insufficient professionalism and competence have been surviving in their positions and they have been obstructing the young specialists with an appropriate academic background (e.g. business graduates with an HRM specialisation) who were hired. On one hand, HR units were formally staffed, on the other hand, people in HR/personnel positions who lacked the necessary competencies were afraid of the young specialists' competition. There were many examples of senior personnel managers preferring to hire somebody they perceived as not competitive and thus frustrating the careers of young graduates. Surprisingly, there were only small differences between internationally and locally owned firms in this respect. HR/personnel managers in multinational companies were a little more competent, owing mainly to their ability to communicate in a foreign language. There was one widespread negative effect – very often English terms, even when inexact, came into use, replacing the existing vernacular ones.

HRM strategy: its status and role

Modern HRM is a strategic activity. Its level is reflected in the involvement of the HR/personnel function in developing organisational strategy and in the existence of a written HR/personnel strategy.

Table 10.21 shows that the practice of HRM participation in the development of the corporate strategy in the Czech Republic is comparable with the average for EU countries. The percentage of organisations where HR/personnel management was involved from the very beginning in the process of strategy elaboration fell between 1996 and 1998, but that could be the

Table 10.21   Stage when HR/personnel is involved in development of corporate strategy (valid % of organisations having corporate strategy)

Stage	Bulgaria		Czech Republic		EU* extremes (1998–1999)		EU average
	1996	1999	1996	1998	Maximum	Minimum	
From the outset	39	43	55	54	72 (I)	44 (NL)	58
Consultative	18	18	23	29	41 (P)	15 (FN)	24
Implementation	39	29	17	11	29 (G)	4 (S)	10
Not consulted	5	10	6	6	20 (A)	1 (F)	8

* A: Austria; F: France; FN: Finland; G: Greece; I: Italy; NL: The Netherlands; S: Sweden.

Table 10.22   Percentage of organisations with HRM strategy

Form of strategy	Bulgaria		Czech Republic		EU+* extremes (1998–1999)		EU+ average
	1996	1999	1996	1998	Maximum	Minimum	
Yes, written	38	32	39	46	74 (S)	25 (Dw)	50
Yes, unwritten	31	32	31	31	44 (P)	15 (S)	29
No	23	23	20	17	33 (Dw)	9 (F)	18

* EU members (without East Germany) + Norway and Switzerland; Dw: West Germany; F: France; P: Portugal; S: Sweden.

result of different structures of samples. Bulgarian practice shows a tendency to convergence with the EU countries, but the level of participation of HRM units in the development of corporate strategy from the outset and at a consultative stage is for the time being much lower.

The second significant piece of evidence about the strategic role of the HR function is the existence of HR/personnel strategy (see Table 10.22). Different trends can be observed in Bulgaria and in the Czech Republic. While Bulgaria reported a greater decrease in the percentage of organisations with an HRM strategy (particularly in written form), there was a substantial rise in the percentage of Czech organisations with a written strategy. This indicates a convergence of Czech practice towards the EU average, while Bulgaria lags behind in this domain.

These observations raise an important question: are the content and quality of the HRM strategies among individual countries and individual organisations comparable? The Cranet survey does not answer this question, but it seems that the variations in content and quality of written or unwritten forms of these strategies may be significant.

An issue of great interest is whether the HRM strategy is translated into work programmes and deadlines

for the HR/personnel function. Unfortunately this question was asked only in the 1996 survey. The 1996 study showed that the strategy was translated into work programmes and deadlines in about 56% of the Bulgarian companies and about 72% of the Czech organisations with HR/personnel strategies (in EU countries it was 66%). If we assume that the situation has not changed significantly in 1998 or 1999, this would mean that HR/personnel strategies developed in planning documents in the Czech organisations was implemented more frequently than in EU countries on average and much more frequently than in Bulgaria.

Analysing the evaluation of the performance of HR departments yields some surprising results. The survey shows that the performance of these departments in both countries was systematically evaluated much more frequently than in EU countries on average. While in Bulgaria and the Czech Republic such systematic evaluation was performed in about 52% of organisations in 1998/1999, the average for EU countries was only about 39%. It is difficult to say whether this is connected with the emphasis on the HR function's importance and its contribution to business results or with some other reasons. Perhaps in these two countries, HR had to do more to prove its value. The most popular evaluation criteria were (as with EU

Table 10.23   Primary responsibility for major policy decisions (% of organisations)

Primary responsibility	Bulgaria		Czech Republic		EU* extremes (1998–1999)		EU average
	1996	1999	1996	1998	Maximum	Minimum	
Recruitment and selection							
Line management	35	27	24	5	26 (FN)	– (I)	7
Line management in cons. with HR department	43	50	14	35	56 (FN)	26 (IR)	40
HR department in cons. with line management	17	16	51	53	56 (F)	14 (FN)	43
HR department	5	7	11	6	24 (I)	2 (S)	11
Training and development							
Line management	44	29	19	7	24 (S)	3 (F)	7
Line management in cons. with HR department	30	40	11	30	56 (NL)	22 (P)	38
HR department in cons. with line management	16	18	57	52	58 (F)	24 (DK)	44
HR department	10	13	14	10	26 (I)	3 (S)	11

* DK: Denmark; F: France; FN: Finland; I: Italy, IR: Ireland; NL: The Netherlands; P: Portugal; S: Sweden.

countries) performance against objectives and internal measures of cost effectiveness, while external bench-marking of costs was not so frequently used.

One characteristic feature of modern HRM is the empowerment of line managers to decide HR policies. The data from the 1998/1999 survey show that the HR responsibility of line managers in Bulgaria, and to some extent in the Czech Republic, was greater than in EU countries on average. It is likely that this arises from the earlier approach to the role of the personnel department. During the period of centralised planning the "personnel and cadre departments" assumed more responsibility for the political loyalty and political control of employees, and for employment administration, than for decision-making in specific HR activities. May be it is a consequence of some kind of distrust of the ability of the HR/personnel department itself and particularly in the personnel specialists. It could also be connected with contemporary trends in devolving HR responsibility to line managers.

It is noticeable that in Bulgaria there is a very pronounced responsibility among line management for decisions in recruitment and selection and training and development (see Table 10.23). The Bulgarian figures are much higher than the averages for EU countries – higher, even, than the EU maximum. This phenomenon can be explained partly by the strong influence exerted by the still predominant former management practice in a centrally planned economy, where line managers were largely responsible for all HR policy

decisions. A positive change was under way during the period of the last survey – a closer co-operation between the HR department and line management, by which their responsibilities for policy decisions in the field of HRM were shared more equally.

As far as the Czech Republic is concerned, two groups of policy decisions are distinguished. The first one is: pay and benefits, industrial relations and work-force expansion/reduction – here, line management predominates. The second group, where the chief responsibility lies with the HR department, includes recruitment and selection, and training and development. This reflects longstanding Czech practice, because resourcing and training and development were centrally managed and consisted mainly of standard activities, while decision-making in the area of pay and benefits, especially variable components of pay, was devolved to immediate superiors. Traditional, line managers have been responsible for workforce expansion and reduction, but again there were some centrally formulated rules. As to industrial relations policy, some ambiguity is evident in both countries since the beginning of the transformation process. Under the earlier system industrial relations were controlled by the Communist Party, and the trade unions were merely another tool to control the employees. The situation after 1990 meant a new approach to all labour relations as well as to industrial relations. The terms used are a little vague and few people distinguish between labour relations, employment relations and industrial relations. Consequently, the high level of line management responsibility for industrial relations' policy decisions could mean a high level of responsibility for employment relations' policy decisions. It can explain the changes in line management's responsibility for industrial relations' policy decisions over the last 3 years as well.

Both Bulgarian (a little more) and Czech organisations report a substantial increase in line management's responsibility for pay and benefits and for workforce expansion or reduction, and some increase in their responsibility for recruitment and selection and training and development policy decisions (see Table 10.24). The proportions of Bulgarian and Czech organisations reporting increases were higher than the EU average (Table 10.24), notably in respect of pay and benefits and workforce expansion or reduction, but also in recruitment and selection and industrial relations policies. On the other hand, there was a smaller increase in line management's responsibility for development policy decision-making.

Line management's responsibility for major policy decisions over the last 3 years in Bulgaria and the Czech Republic reflected a mix: partly recent trends, partly traditional approaches to the role of the HR/personnel department, and – probably – partly insufficient professionalism, competence and active involvement on the part of the existing HRM departments.

Recruitment and selection

In Bulgaria the primary responsibility for recruitment and selection still lies with line management. The strengthening of the HRM department's position and its more active involvement in the corporate management should lead to more balance in their roles in this field. In the Czech Republic it is often the HR/personnel department that takes the leading role in this area. As has been mentioned, it is a surviving Czech tradition.

The transformation processes in Bulgaria and in the Czech Republic were accompanied by a substantial restructuring both in the national economy and in individual companies. The former socialist system of full employment proved, under market conditions, to have created overemployment. Consequently, there were mass redundancies during the early stages of transformation

Table 10.24 Changes in line management's responsibility for major policy decisions over the last 3 years (% of organisations)

Change	Bulgaria		Czech Republic		EU* extremes (1998–1999)		EU average
	1996	1999	1996	1998	Maximum	Minimum	
Pay and benefits							
Increased	63	44	43	44	60 (S)	15 (D)	23
Same	34	51	54	54	78 (D)	38 (S)	73
Decreased	4	5	3	3	10 (I)	1 (G)	4
Recruitment and selection							
Increased	49	36	32	32	50 (S)	17 (D)	29
Same	42	54	51	64	78 (D)	49 (NL)	65
Decreased	10	10	16	4	13 (I)	1 (S)	6
Training and development							
Increased	40	37	30	31	55 (IR)	27 (G)	41
Same	52	55	57	67	69 (G)	40 (IR)	55
Decreased	8	8	14	2	11 (DK)	1 (F)	4
Industrial relations							
Increased	34	36	19	25	38 (NL)	12 (I)	19
Same	62	55	68	74	85 (D)	59 (IR)	77
Decreased	5	9	14	2	10 (E)	2 (S)	4
Workforce expansion/reduction							
Increased	35	42	32	37	50 (NL)	16 (DK)	24
Same	49	44	65	61	81 (DK)	47 (NL)	70
Decreased	16	14	3	1	10 (A)	2 (IR)	6

* A: Austria; D: Germany; DK: Denmark; E: Spain; F: France; G: Greece; I: Italy; IR: Ireland; NL: The Netherlands; S: Sweden.

and thus it was relatively easy to recruit people not only for manual or clerical jobs, but also for professional, technical and managerial jobs. But some difficulties in recruiting people emerged at the beginning of second half of the 1990s in both countries. The situation changed under the influence of the growing requirement for skilled, motivated and competent people as a source of competitive corporate advantage. Companies faced difficulties in recruiting the relevant personnel. Consequently, the need to improve recruitment and selection policies and practices became pressing. The changing labour market forced managers to pay more attention to the employer's image and to introduce measures to increase corporate attractiveness.

The survey studied differences in recruitment and retention methods used, as well as tendencies in their application in the Bulgarian and Czech organisations. While in Bulgaria the most popular method remained retraining existing employees, followed by increased pay and benefits, the Czech organisations preferred increased pay or benefits, and they practised much more marketing of the organisation's image and recruiting abroad. Both the Bulgarian and the Czech data indicate some decline in the use of these methods between the two surveys. This can be accounted for by the difference in the structures of the samples in the two surveys. In the Czech Republic it seems that the need for people referred to had passed by the end of the decade and the situation had normalised, whereas in Bulgaria the need for relevant people became more and more acute.

As for the methods used, Bulgaria lags behind in introducing advanced European practices. The Czech companies seem to adopt some modern ones, above all the marketing of the organisation's image. This highlights the trend towards convergence with the practice in EU countries.

The most popular methods of recruiting manual and clerical employees in both countries were advertisements in newspapers, word of mouth and collaboration with Labour Offices (the state job centres).

As to recruiting professional and technical employees, particularly managers, the ways used are quite different. Managerial vacancies are filled frequently from internal sources in Bulgaria and mostly in the Czech Republic (see Table 10.25).

More than 50% of all managerial positions in Bulgaria in 1996 were filled by people working in the same company, while only 25% of the senior, 24% of the middle and 17% of the junior managers were recruited by external consultants. During the next period even fewer companies used their services, primarily because they were expensive and most Bulgarian employers were not used to relying on them. Another reason for this is the unprecedented availability of specialists in the field of recruitment and selection working in HR departments as a result of intensive management training during the last 10 years (Figure 10.8).

In the same period the external recruitment of managers increased. This tendency could be explained by the intention of newly privatised companies to redesign the whole managerial process and to attract highly qualified managers. The relatively stable practice of recruiting junior managers internally is a necessary and positive one, because it helps to retain promising young managers and provides more opportunity for career development. Taking into account the huge emigration of young Bulgarians this practice should be strengthened. Czech organisations in particular rely on internal sources: about two-thirds of senior management positions, more than four-fifths of middle management positions and about three-quarters of junior management positions are filled internally. This is much more than the EU average and much more than

Table 10.25 Internal mechanisms for filling managerial vacancies (% of organisations)

Sources	Bulgaria		Czech Republic		EU* extremes (1998–1999)		EU average
	1996	1999	1996	1998	Maximum	Minimum	
Senior management	50	44	68	68	66 (G)	7 (DK)	52
Middle management	58	54	95	85	82 (A)	62 (P)	76
Junior management	49	41	68	78	81 (S)	31 (F)	62

* A: Austria; DK: Denmark; F: France; G: Greece; P: Portugal; S: Sweden.

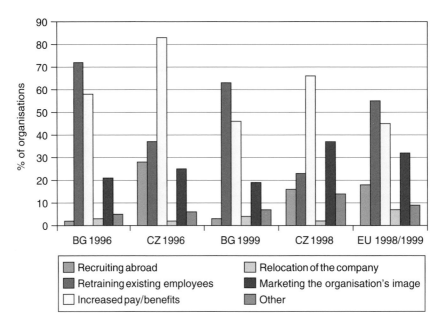

Figure 10.8   Different methods in relation to recruitment or retention (% of organisations)

in Bulgaria. The second most often used Czech way is advertising in newspapers, followed by collaboration with recruitment agencies (head hunters). In the case of middle and junior management positions it is word of mouth, which is much more frequent in Czech organisations than in EU countries on average. The relatively low use of recruitment agencies is a consequence of the cost of their services, as well as of some bad experiences with them. In both countries the recruitment agencies work much more often with international companies than with locally owned ones.

Comparison with the recruitment and selection practice in EU countries identifies two basic differences: companies in both countries rely less on recruitment agencies and more on word of mouth.

The most popular selection methods in Bulgarian and particularly in Czech organisations are application forms and one-to-one interviews. Graphology and assessment centres are the least popular. While Bulgaria reports less use of all the methods mentioned in the questionnaires except the assessment centre, the Czech Republic reports an increase in the popularity of interview panels and references.

It seems that the Czech organisations are gradually adopting EU selection practices, but this process

depends on the competence of HR/personnel departments, HR/personnel specialists and line managers. There is another reason for the unpopularity of modern selection methods in Bulgarian and Czech organisations: inadequate competence and professional capacity of an adequate number of existing recruitment and selection agencies and consultants. They prefer to recommend and apply selection methods that may not be very efficient for customers but yield more profit for themselves. Some agencies offer irrelevant methods, or do not customise them. Standardised "assessment centres", typology, graphology and dubious "personality tests" are all too common. Selection instruments are often taken from abroad and translated without being adapted to the local environment and national culture. In other words, commercial interests sometimes predominate over ethics and professionalism (see Table 10.26).

Training and development

During the last 10 years the idea that training and development can be an important competitive advantage has been gaining ground in all the transitional countries. There has been a tendency to increase

Table 10.26   Selection methods for every, most or some appointments (% of organisations)

Frequency	Bulgaria		Czech Republic		EU* extremes (1998–1999)		EU average
	1996	1999	1996	1998	Maximum	Minimum	
Interview panel							
For every appointment	14	3	6	4	54 (IR)	5 (G)	21
For most appointments	10	12	9	25	27 (S)	3 (F)	17
For some appointments	14	7	56	38	27 (FN)	4 (I)	17
One-to-one interviews							
For every appointment	45	28	68	57	92 (F)	30 (DK)	61
For most appointments	20	28	19	27	44 (A)	6 (G)	18
For some appointments	21	25	14	15	17 (IR)	1 (F)	9
Application forms							
For every appointment	54	35	71	81	82 (F)	23 (DK)	52
For most appointments	20	30	9	7	28 (FN)	10 (F)	16
For some appointments	17	25	14	6	21 (DK)	4 (G)	8
Psychometric tests							
For every appointment	8	6	3	3	23 (E)	1 (D)	6
For most appointments	5	4	16	9	25 (E)	1 (D)	9
For some appointments	11	9	23	35	46 (S)	7 (D)	22
Assessment centre							
For every appointment	–	1	4	1	6 (I)	– (D, DK, P)	2
For most appointments	–	1	4	2	8 (NL)	1 (IR)	4
For some appointments	–	5	–	6	63 (NL)	7 (FN)	23
Graphology							
For every appointment	3	1	–	1	5 (F)	– (A, B, D, DK, FN, UK)	1
For most appointments	–	–	–	–	11 (F)	– (A, DK, G, IR)	2
For some appointments	3	–	7	7	26 (F)	– (DK)	6
References							
For every appointment	25	10	9	9	79 (UK)	5 (NL)	28
For most appointments	16	22	26	27	41 (DK)	6 (I)	17
For some appointments	28	27	63	52	44 (FN)	1 (S)	27

* A: Austria; B: Belgium; D: Germany; DK: Denmark; E: Spain; F: France; FN: Finland; G: Greece; I: Italy; IR: Ireland; NL: The Netherlands; P: Portugal; S: Sweden; UK: United Kingdom.

investment in training, to develop new forms and methods for qualifications in personnel and to improve the efficiency of these activities. The effectiveness of training and development is closely evaluated in all the countries studied. This is reflected in the unprecedented increase in systematic training needs analysis as well as in measuring training outcomes in both countries. There are many possible reasons for this typically convergent tendency – the increase of investment in training, enhanced requirements for personnel professionals where international collaboration is demanded by the management of the multinational companies, the sudden shortening of the lifecycle of the modern professions among them.

Analysis of the data in Table 10.27 shows a positive tendency. In both countries the number of organisations devoting less than 1% of salary and wage bill to training and development has fallen sharply. In the same period in both countries the share of organisations spending from 5 to 10% has increased. In Bulgaria the greatest increase in investment in training was achieved by the group of companies allocating more than 10% – their share increases by 23 points. Thus in 1999 the proportion of Bulgarian companies with such a large training budget approached that of Portugal, which recorded the highest value for this indicator, and exceeded the average European level. In the Czech Republic the greatest increase in training investment was in the group of companies devoting between 1 and 2% of the annual salaries and wages bill to training.

Most Bulgarian and Czech organisations recognise the importance of training and development for their success, but they face problems in funding these activities. Managers often set other investment priorities (e.g. new technology) rather than investment in people. There is still a belief that it is the employee's responsibility to achieve, and subsequently to improve, their competence. Employers often overestimate the role of university and college education in creating completely relevant qualifications for their graduates and meeting specific corporate expectations. This mentality hinders the rapid modernisation of corporate training and development systems and partially explains the low level of investment in these activities compared to the average for EU countries.

The level of investment in training and development corresponds with the cost involved. In the two countries concerned some inexpensive but successful ways of developing employees are used. It is clear that the pressure to find cost-effective approaches has had a positive impact on corporate training practices.

The picture of corporate training and development in both countries can be enhanced by analysing the number of training days per year and per employee (see Table 10.28).

The values are rather higher in the Bulgarian than in the Czech organisations. Managerial and clerical staff in Bulgaria received more training in 1999, which corresponds with the need to improve the qualification of these staff categories and to meet current European criteria. In the Czech Republic all categories of staff except manual received less training. But organisations in both countries spent more days on training managerial and professional or technical staff than the EU average. As far as clerical and manual staff are concerned, Bulgaria spent much more time on training them than EU countries on average, while the Czech Republic adopted controversial practices. It seems that Czech organisations emphasise the training and development of managers and specialists as the key people, and they in turn become informal trainers of other categories of employees. It may be that the lower amount of clerical and manual staff is connected with the volume of informal training, which is traditional in Czech organisations, and with the somewhat different skill and education profile of Czech employees.

The hypothesis about the recognition of the pivotal role of employee training in a successful transition to a more effective HR management could be supported by the data about the proportion of organisations systematically analysing employee training needs. The percentage of the Czech organisations carrying out such analyses increased between 1996 and 1998 from 56% to 71%, thus reaching the average value of this indicator

Table 10.27 Organisations currently spending a proportion of their annual salary and wage bill on training (%)

Proportion of the annual salaries and wages bill (%)	Bulgaria		Czech Republic		EU* extremes (1998–1999)		EU average
	1996	1999	1996	1998	Maximum	Minimum	
<1	40	33	42	11	26 (I)	1 (F)	13
1–1.9	21	19	23	55	42 (E)	8 (F)	27
2–2.9	10	9	10	15	31 (DK)	12 (P)	20
3–4.9	7	13	10	10	38 (F)	10 (E)	19
5–9.9	14	17	7	7	31 (F)	2 (I)	16
≥10	7	9	10	2	9 (P)	2 (FN)	5

* DK: Denmark; E: Spain; F: France; FN: Finland; I: Italy; P: Portugal.

Table 10.28 Mean number of training days per year and by staff category (% of organisations)

Category	Bulgaria		Czech Republic		EU* extremes (1998–1999)		EU average
	1996	1999	1996	1998	Maximum	Minimum	
Managerial	7	8	9	9	9 (E)	4 (I)	6
Professional/technical	10	9	9	7	10 (E)	5 (IR)	6
Clerical	4	6	4	4	7 (E)	3 (IR)	4
Manual	7	5	2	3	6 (E)	2 (D)	6

* D: Germany; E: Spain; I: Italy; IR: Ireland.

in the EU countries. Obviously the Czech organisations are very interested in identifying training needs and they probably try to satisfy them, but only partly through formal (registered) training. During the period 1996–1999 the share of Bulgarian organisations performing such analysis changed from 42% only to 44%. Thus the level of this indicator still remains significantly lower than the minimum identified in EU countries.

There was a remarkable increase in the percentage of organisations monitoring the effectiveness of their training, both in Bulgaria and in the Czech Republic. The last survey, for 1998/1999, showed that for Bulgaria this indicator reached the EU average and in the Czech Republic it was even higher. Quite understandably, with inadequate financial resources the Bulgarian and Czech organisations are extremely interested in the effective allocation and utilisation of their training and development investments.

Performance measurements and rewards

The contemporary approach to performance management is making slow headway in Bulgarian and Czech organisations. This is due to a traditional attitude to performance appraisal: a reluctance on the part of managers to implement it. At the same time the employees regard such systems as hostile to them, and any formal performance appraisal is usually considered a pointless intervention. Most line managers believe that they are well informed about the performance of all their employees and there is no need for an appraisal system.

Consequently, merit/performance-related pay is mostly based on informal appraisal and often takes the form of piecework. But it seems that piecework has become less popular owing to the greater stress on quality and on changes in employee structures.

By contrast, the Czech organisations are rather above the EU average in their use of merit and performance-related pay, though, except for managers, they, like some other countries in Europe, are actually decreasing its use in some cases. As with the Bulgarian organisations, the systems used tend to be simple and informal.

The survey data show a fall in the use of merit/performance-related pay between 1996 and 1998/1999 in both countries, with the exception of payment for Czech managers (see Table 10.29). In Bulgaria the percentage of organisations offering merit/performance-related pay is considerably lower than the average for EU countries. Manual staff remuneration is an exception – for this category it is used in nearly 42% of the Bulgarian organisations. The Czech data indicate higher values for this indicator than EU averages. In Bulgaria, and more particularly in the Czech Republic, these forms of pay are primarily offered to manual and technical staff and relatively seldom to managers, while the EU average results show quite the opposite. This could be explained by the emphasis of the former system on quantitative performance records and the popularity of piecework. It is hoped that a more intensive use of this form of motivation for managerial staff will increase the effectiveness of their work.

Tabel 10.29 shows an interesting relationship. In EU countries the greater the responsibility of the position, the more its pay depends on performance. Most European organisations prefer to motivate their managers and professionals through merit/performance-related pay but rely less on this instrument to influence the behaviour of clerical and manual staff. In the Bulgarian and the Czech organisations this dependence is the other way round. Week dependency of managerial remuneration on the final corporate results is widely discussed in Bulgaria. This fact is one more reason, which proves the popular hypothesis that the

Table 10.29   Merit/performance-related pay offer to different employee categories

Employee category	Bulgaria		Czech Republic		EU* extremes (1998–1999)		EU average
	1996	1999	1996	1998	Maximum	Minimum	
Management	31	28	51	58	77 (F)	20 (S)	47
Professional/technical	48	40	70	64	69 (I)	12 (S)	46
Clerical	40	30	70	64	45 (I)	12 (S)	37
Manual	53	42	70	70	40 (FN)	15 (IR)	28

* F: France; FN: Finland; I: Italy; IR: Ireland; S: Sweden.

quality of managerial work in the newly market oriented countries is still not recognised as a factor of the effectiveness.

The survey data provide evidence of a growth in variable pay during the 3-year period preceding the last survey. But the reported extension was more pronounced between 1993 and 1996 (for Bulgaria in 67% of organisations and for the Czech Republic in 60%) than between the last two surveys (Bulgaria 46% of organisations and the Czech Republic 51%). In general, the last survey indicates a higher rate for introducing variable pay in Bulgaria, and more especially in the Czech Republic, as compared with the EU average of 42% of organisations. This could be due to a lower level of satisfaction about the results of such payments. Unfortunately, this hypothesis cannot be verified from the survey data.

In spite of the negative attitude towards the effectiveness of formal appraisal systems among Czech managers and employees, there has been some increase in the percentage of organisations applying them to managerial, professional/technical and clerical staff, while changes concerning manual staff are very slight (see Table 10.30). In Bulgaria a trend towards a more widespread use of such systems for clerical staff can be observed, accompanied by a constant level in the appraising of manual staff.

There are two differences between Bulgaria and the Czech Republic in this field. The Bulgarian organisations use appraisal most frequently for manual and professional or technical staff, while managerial appraisal is rare. The Czech organisations prefer a somewhat different approach. Their systems are aimed first of all at managerial and professional or technical staff. Evaluating manual staff is not a priority. The Czech model is similar to the EU average model and it seems that there is some convergence of the Czech practice towards the EU's position. This trend may perhaps be influenced by

more intensive contacts with west European practice and by the predominance of international companies in the Czech sample. In this regard, it is arguable whether the Czech data represent the situation that exists in the locally owned companies.

The most active formal contributors to performance appraisal in both countries are immediate superiors, followed by next level superiors and the employees themselves. Customers are very often involved in the process of evaluation in Bulgaria. In 1996 about 28% of Bulgarian organisations used customer feedback for such purposes – the highest European value of this indicator. Consequently, a process of attempting to link behaviour to the most relevant markets had been developing in Bulgarian organisations. Subordinates, peers and customers are more popular as contributors in Bulgarian than in Czech organisations. Comparing the latest data with 1996 shows a narrower scope of contributors to this activity in both countries. There is a substantial difference between Bulgaria and the Czech Republic on the one hand and the EU average on the other: while about 54% of organisations in EU countries consider the employee as a formal contributor to the appraisal process (in fact, the second most important one), the employee performs this role in only 24% of Czech organisations (third most important) and in 17% of Bulgarian organisations (fourth most important contributor). The role of the employee in the appraisal process is regarded as passive.

In both countries the appraisal process is most frequently used to determine individual performance-related pay (47% of Czech organisations and 38% of Bulgarian ones). The results of appraisal processes are less often used for identifying training needs, promotion potential, career development and organisation of work in both countries in comparison with the average for EU countries. In this area, too, the Czech Republic is closer to European practice than Bulgaria.

Table 10.30   Percentage of organisations with an appraisal system

Employee category	Bulgaria		Czech Republic		EU* extremes (1998–1999)		EU average
	1996	1999	1996	1998	Maximum	Minimum	
Managerial	46	40	56	60	92 (UK)	47 (FN)	72
Professional/technical	59	59	51	61	94 (S)	48 (DK)	74
Clerical	45	52	46	48	95 (S)	46 (E)	67
Manual	62	63	29	38	82 (NL)	32 (DK)	56

* DK: Denmark; E: Spain; FN: Finland; NL: The Netherlands; S: Sweden; UK: United Kingdom.

Employee relations and the role of trade unions

One of the biggest challenges for countries in transition is the democratisation of management, including communications within the organisation and in industrial relations. Transforming the authoritarian management style inherited from the centralised planning tradition is a difficult and time-consuming process.

The 1996 survey showed that the popularity of organisational communication policies in Bulgaria and in the Czech Republic is similar to that in organisations in the EU countries. Written policies predominate. In this respect the Czech companies report their greater willingness to develop non-written policies, compared to Bulgarian ones. An increasing diversity and range of approaches to organisational communication is a common tendency. However, the changes in communication models appear to be slow and unconvincing. The facts are that:

- In the developed European countries every second organisation during both survey periods increased its range of oral direct communication between managers and staff – in our two countries the direction of change is the same, but only half as many organisations are involved.
- The same is true of changes in the use of representative bodies, computers and e-mail.
- In conformity with predominant European practice, written communication declined in Bulgarian companies. By way of contrast, in Czech companies the use of direct written communications increased.
- The increased use of team briefings in the Czech Republic is also in line with the tendency of the EU countries, but in Bulgaria their use declined.
- The situation in respect of information flows from staff to management is different – here the Czech organisations show clear progress. Bulgaria, though,

has taken a step backwards in terms of management listening to the opinion and recommendations of their subordinates.

Employee communication and industrial relations are probably the least developed areas of HR/personnel management in the transforming countries, including Bulgaria and the Czech Republic. Employee relations is regarded as largely an administrative matter and is strongly influenced by the inherited conventions. The attitude could be described as "superior vs. subordinate" and "employer vs. employee" rather than "leader and collaborator" and "committed partnership of employer and employee". As concerns industrial relations, some animosity exists among both employers or managers (particularly in the private sector) and so-called "liberal" political parties towards trade unions. They are accused of "communist thinking" or "left-wing views" and are criticised for hampering economic progress. No wonder that in the Czech Republic even some international companies abuse the situation and try to exclude trade unions from their traditional "territory". There have been cases of management using pressure or even threats against people who wanted to establish or activate the company trade union organisation. Such an atmosphere leads to a long-term decline in trade union membership and influence. As for Bulgaria, most multinational companies report good collaboration with the trade unions.

Table 10.31 indicates that there was a more pronounced fall in the influence of trade unions in Bulgaria and in the Czech Republic than among the EU countries. But that could be the result of being at different stages in the process of change. It may be that the transforming countries are experiencing now the same reduction in trade union influence that the EU countries did in the past. The different shares of Bulgarian and Czech organisations where the power of trade unions became stronger eventually could be explained by

Table 10.31   Percentage of organisations where there has been a change in the influence of trade unions during the last 3 years

Change	Bulgaria		Czech Republic		EU* extremes (1998–1999)		EU average
	1996	1999	1996	1998	Maximum	Minimum	
Increased	21	11	9	7	24 (F)	– (I)	13
Same	54	41	62	55	74 (FN)	44 (UK)	56
Decreased	25	30	30	29	26 (I)	8 (B)	17

* B: Belgium; F: France; FN: Finland; I: Italy; UK: United Kingdom.

differences in the pressure from employers on trade union avoidance, the higher living standard of Czech people and their greater scepticism about the efficacy of trade unions. In spite of the attitude to unions referred to and their loss of influence, both countries recognise the legal right of employees to organise themselves. It means most Bulgarian (75%) and Czech (91%) organisations recognised trade unions for the purpose of collective bargaining in 1996 (there was no such question in the 1998/1999 survey).

The decreased trade union influence is reflected in the smaller impact made by collective bargaining on basic pay determination in both countries. In any case, the influence of collective bargaining in the Czech Republic is much lower than in Bulgaria and considerably lower than in the EU countries on average.

In the Czech Republic and the EU countries the role of collective bargaining in basic pay determination increases by employee category, from managers to manual staff. It is most important for manual staff basic pay determination and least important for managerial. The Bulgarian situation is quite different. Collective bargaining affects mainly the professional/technical and managerial staff's basic pay determination, but does not concern clerical and manual staff basic payment as much.

An analysis of organisational communication suggests that it is still strongly influenced by the concepts of centralised management and the totalitarian style. Democratic changes in the communication models are very slow. One important finding is that management in the transforming countries exhibit little faith in exchanging information with their employees, particularly with manual staff. Downward communication is much more common than upward communication.

Table 10.32 shows that – with the exception of Bulgarian management in 1996 regarding strategy – in both countries staff at management level in 1999/2000 received less formal information than in 1996 about the strategy and financial performance of their companies. Nevertheless, all employee categories in Czech organisations are better informed than in Bulgarian ones and nearly comparable with the average for EU countries. Czech managers fare even better in terms of strategic and financial information received, than their colleagues in the EU. In the Bulgarian organisations less formal information on strategic issues was provided to all staff. The only exception was professional/technical and clerical employees, who were better briefed about financial performance and organisation of work.

As has already been mentioned, downward communication in Bulgaria and, even more, in the Czech Republic is well developed. But it seems that managers do not pay enough attention to their employees' opinions and that they do not even recognise the need to develop more democratic communication practices.

The Cranet data do not enable us to identify the intensity or quality of the upward communication, they only show the methods used and the types of change that took place during the 3 years preceding the pertinent survey.

The most common ways in which employees communicate their views to management are through immediate superiors and directly to senior managers. Attitude surveys, suggestion schemes and regular meetings as well as team briefings are the least common communication models in Bulgaria and in the Czech Republic.

Table 10.32 Different categories of employees formally briefed about strategy and financial performance (% of organisations)

Employee category	Bulgaria		Czech Republic		EU* extremes (1998–1999)		EU average
	1996	1999	1996	1998	Maximum	Minimum	
Strategy							
Management	78	79	100	94	98 (S)	88 (I)	94
Professional/technical	67	43	70	61	84 (FN)	19 (G)	54
Clerical	30	20	41	34	66 (S)	17 (P)	33
Manual	17	11	30	31	57 (FN)	8 (G)	24
Financial performance							
Management	81	78	97	95	98 (S)	82 (I)	92
Professional/technical	59	60	51	62	94 (FN)	33(G)	72
Clerical	47	48	35	48	89 (FN)	16 (I)	57
Manual	31	26	19	30	79 (FN)	7 (I)	43

* FN: Finland; G: Greece; I: Italy; P: Portugal; S: Sweden.

The recent survey shows that in the Czech Republic all methods of upward communication except suggestion schemes have become more popular. However, Bulgarian organisations reported an increased use of only the two most frequent and traditional methods, i.e. through immediate superiors and directly to senior managers. Thus the changes in upward communication were more positive in the Czech Republic, indicating an extension in the variety of different ways of communicating and a tendency to adopt West European approaches.

Organisation of work: flexible patterns of work

Flexible patterns of work are gradually coming into use in the Czech and the Bulgarian organisations, but compared to the EU average their frequency is significantly lower. Some non-standard contracts, e.g. homebased work, tele-working or annual hours contracts are very rarely found. Fixed-term contracts and shift working are more popular in Bulgaria and in the Czech Republic than in EU countries on average. The most widespread non-standard contracts are part-time contracts and temporary/casual working arrangements (see Table 10.33).

In the EU countries part-time contracts are widely used, particularly among women. Employees in the transforming countries – even women – do not like such contracts. There are two principal reasons. First, family incomes are relatively low and are rising more slowly than the cost of living. Since part-time work means part-time pay, people simply cannot afford to work that way. The second reason is the unwillingness of employers to appoint people on such contracts, because the administrative complexity and fixed costs of part-time work are similar to full-time employee costs. Consequently, people are economically forced to accept full-time contracts and often when they would like to work part-time employers are not willing to allow it. While flexible staffing is becoming more popular in the EU countries, in the Czech Republic it is declining (see Table 10.34). Temporary/casual working

Table 10.33 Workforce on non-standard contracts (% of organisations)

Approximate proportion of workforce	Bulgaria		Czech Republic		EU* extremes (1998–1999)		EU average
	1996	1999	1996	1998	Maximum	Minimum	
Part-time contract							
No part-timers employed	55	52	3	6	69 (P)	– (NL)	7
10 and more % of part-timers	2	5	3	4	63 (NL)	2 (P)	25
Temporary/casual working arrangements							
No temporary workers	30	39	3	33	64 (I)	1 (S)	25
10 and more % of temporary workers	11	12	–	3	24 (E)	2 (DK)	11

* DK: Denmark; E: Spain; I: Italy; NL: The Netherlands; P: Portugal; S: Sweden.

Table 10.34 Use of flexible working arrangements over the last 3 years (% of organisations)

Change	Bulgaria		Czech Republic		EU* extremes (1998–1999)		EU average
	1996	1999	1996	1998	Maximum	Minimum	
Part-time contract							
Increased	10	7	6	8	76 (NL)	11 (S)	47
Same	28	35	57	62	68 (DK)	16 (P)	38
Decreased	10	12	37	24	29 (S)	– (NL, B)	6
Not used	53	47	–	6	68 (P)	1 (NL)	8
Temporary/casual working arrangements							
Increased	31	25	19	13	63 (NL)	17 (G)	41
Same	31	21	33	33	61 (FN)	13 (I)	30
Decreased	17	11	44	22	14 (F)	2 (I)	8
Not used	22	43	3	32	57 (I)	4 (S)	21

* B: Belgium; DK: Denmark; F: France; FN: Finland; G: Greece; I: Italy; NL: The Netherlands; P: Portugal; S: Sweden.

arrangements show a similar pattern. For example, in the Czech Republic they are applied mostly to the retired or to students.

Conclusions

Bulgaria and the Czech Republic are pursuing accelerating change in the field of HRs in order to achieve membership of the EU. The transformation process is complicated and inconsistent, strongly influenced by the economic development of the two countries, the intensity of economic and social contacts with the developed countries and the entrepreneurial environment and cultural characteristics of both countries. These factors are producing HRM policies and practices in the Czech Republic similar to those of the EU, more so than in Bulgaria. Thus the convergence process in Czech HRM is more pronounced.

By studying the surveys carried out in 1996 and 1998/1999, and the development of HRM practices, we can draw the following conclusions:

- Many positive trends in particular HRM activities are evident during the last 5 years of transition to a market economy in Bulgarian and Czech companies.
- The most significant progress has been in the field of training and development, especially among managers and professionals.
- The management of change is another domain in which great effort produced important successes.
- The strategic orientation of HRM has progressed, particularly in the Czech Republic.
- Merit- and performance-related pay have been much stronger influences on wage determination in the period in question.
- Progressive forms of flexible employment have been adopted slowly.
- The rate of change in the field of organisational communication is still unsatisfactory.

HRM IN ACTION

CZECH REPUBLIC: RATIONALISATION AND DOWNSIZING IN A STATE-OWNED COMPANY

LVZ in Kralovany was an engineering company with many satisfied customers both in the former Czechoslovakia and abroad in the 1970s and 1980s. The company produced a large assortment of machinery for other engineering companies, for the energy industry and for some other manufacturing companies. It specialised in big orders and often supplied all the machines and equipment for new shops and factories.

The company had about 5000 employees at the end of 1980s – mostly skilled manual workers and highly skilled and experienced professionals, technicians, engineers and workers. It consisted of several specialised units that provided nearly everything needed for its own functioning. In fact, it purchased only electrical motors, raw materials, energy and some semi-finished products.

But LVZ's markets changed substantially in the early 1990s. Domestic demand fell, and many foreign competitors entered the Czechoslovak market. LVZ lost its monopoly and local customers suddenly acquired considerable choice. Because the former system of central planning had forced them to purchase only LVZ products, they now preferred the novelty of foreign-made products. The reason was not the quality, technical inferiority or higher prices of LVZ products, but rather the extensive promotion practised by foreign producers (the management of LVZ did no promotion in the home market, where demand for their products was greater than they could satisfy – they therefore missed the opportunity). Moreover, the imported products were more attractively designed, and many Czech customers assumed that more attractive design meant better quality. It became fashionable to buy foreign-made products, access to which had been severely limited under

Communist rule. And last, but not least, Czech customers expected better service from foreign producers. At the same time, the LVZ lost most of its traditional markets in the former COMECON countries and it was not possible to compensate for this by increasing sales in the developing and West European countries, where LVZ products competed successfully because of lower prices, good quality and reliability.

LVZ's top management, facing a completely new situation, began to consider some measures aimed at rationalising the company's operations. They decided to reduce, or even eliminate, some activities and outsource them so as to reduce the hitherto broad range of products, to delayer and to reduce clerical staff.

A rationalisation group was established to deal with the problem. It comprised some top managers and selected middle managers. The group's mandate was to identify those activities and organisational units which would not be necessary for the future success of the company or could be not profitable. Some parts of the company would be closed down, others sold or privatised. As a start the group would suggest which parts and activities should be closed down immediately and which ones a little later, after the company had found alternative suppliers. The rationalisation process would consist of several stages.

The members of the group were asked not to tell anybody about their tasks before the project was completed and formally announced. Their work should take 2 months. Of course, during such a short period the members of the group could not analyse thoroughly all the relevant information, or even obtain it, so their proposals reflected their agreed views.

In spite of the instruction not to inform anybody about the project, LVZ employees gathered from different sources, notably the "grapevine", some vague information about what was being planned. Even though they had no certainty, they changed their attitudes to the company and many of them began to search for another job. They were not prepared to wait till the time came for mass redundancies, because they were afraid of the effect on the regional labour market. There was little unemployment in the Czech Republic then and jobs were not difficult to find. Some good skilled performers decided to resign and move to newly established small businesses in the region, while some of them set up their own small businesses.

The management made no attempt to retain any of those who left. In fact, they were glad, because it solved some of their potential problems over future dismissals. They failed to realise that the resignations involved mostly skilled workers, specialists, professionals, technicians and generally good performers, while the less skilled people and poor performers were waiting to see what would happen.

After 2 months the rationalisation group presented their proposals. Top management accepted the proposals and decided to dismiss, under the relevant articles of the Labour Code, all employees of those parts of the company being closed down. There was some surprise that all the employees concerned were to go – with no attempt to select the best employees or those who could be used in the other parts of the company. This approach was criticised as short-sighted. But management felt that their approach would cause less conflict and they wished to avoid any explanations about why one employee rather than another had been dismissed.

Of course, the company's employees realised that this was only the first stage of a downsizing exercise, but they had no way of knowing which activity or which part of company would be the next to go. They discussed these issues and considered their options. The uncertainty over the future resulted in more resignations, and because those were again the good and skilled people the process eroded the company's skills and performance base still further. There were even some managers who left the company, because they were unhappy about top management's decisions and didn't want to be associated with such an approach.

The second and subsequent stages of so-called rationalisation did not take place, because the exodus of so many people caused serious problems in maintaining the company activities. The management actions described resulted in a very bad image of the company as an employer, and it became increasingly difficult to attract and recruit the employees needed. And because the top management had not changed – even though the former state company had been privatised – people living in the region were not willing to join a company whose management had demonstrated such incompetence.

By the end of 1990s the company was in a very poor condition. It was forced to decline some lucrative orders because it lacked the staff necessary to fulfil them in time and to the standard of quality required. Employee compensation was affected, which made it difficult to attract staff. The continuing deskilling of the labour force meant a continuing deterioration in performance.

The LVZ case can be regarded as a typical example of the "transformation" of companies in post-communist countries, but it also serves as an example of the possible consequences of any delayering, downsizing and outsourcing exercise accompanied by poor managerial skills and bad communication with people.

BULGARIA: PROSOFT, A BULGARIAN SUCCESS STORY

The company

"The name ProSoft is the symbol of private business in Bulgaria. ProSoft became the symbol of entrepreneurship in high-tech industry as well. It does not rely on its past achievements, but actively seeks and always finds something new to offer on the Bulgarian IT market. ProSoft has always been one step ahead of our business development. It seems that our society and our business community are never prepared enough for the challenges and innovations that ProSoft offers."

Bojidar Danev, Chairman of the Bulgarian Industrial Association

ProSoft was founded in 1990 as a partnership with three owners. Its president and main shareholder, Julian Genov, is an IT engineer, nominated for the International WHO'S WHO of professionals for 2000. His PhD dissertation is on the "Transformation of the Organisation under the Conditions of Bulgarian Transition." Mr. Genov has carried out scientific research and written a number of publications on HRM. His report at the international congress IntEnt 2001 (South Africa) was entitled: *"National Culture and its Reflection on the Entrepreneurship in the Post-Communist Societies."*

The greatest ambition of ProSoft's managerial team from the very foundation of the company was "to change the way the IT business in Bulgaria is carried out." The innovative spirit of the firm, particularly in the field of HRM, has been manifested in various ways. Its first press advertisement for vacancies, quite unusual for the still predominantly autocratic management style of 1990, read: "If you meet our expectations, we shall go beyond yours."

In 1991 ProSoft opened branches in the eight largest Bulgarian cities. During the next year the company signed an official contract with IBM for distribution and training. New branches were opened. In 1993 assembly of the first branded personal computer ProSoft Terminator started. It became recognised as the leading Bulgarian brand-name computer and was the best-selling PC for the following 3 years.

According to a representative market survey of BBSS Gallup International conducted in the same year, the company was the leader in the Bulgarian market for personal computers and printers. It was recognised as the most popular office equipment provider. In 1994 ProSoft became an exclusive distributor for the whole range of printers of EPSON Deutschland GmbH and as the Bulgarian representative for DIGITAL EQUIPMENT. In 1995 a partnership contract was signed with Compaq. A special unit for servicing the biggest clients – ministries, banks and security companies – started functioning. The focus was on the effective support of people working with the company's products. During that year ProSoft successfully completed the first information projects of national importance. The sharp and deep economic recession of 1996/1997 forced the firm to adopt the only relevant strategy – survival. A large management training and development programme was undertaken with Phare support. October 1997 marked the end of the survival strategy and the beginning of the ProSoft's new expansion. The company acquired 33% of the shares of "2 Plus" – a partner of Hewlett-Packard in Bulgaria.

In 1999 ProSoft, which employed 140 people, was again recognised as the best Bulgarian IT company for that year.

The HR department and its policy

The HR department was established as an independent unit in ProSoft Holding in 1996. Its constitution followed a 6-year collaboration with HRM consultancy companies that had been established in 1990. In the beginning recruitment and selection were handled by external consultants – psychologists with both theoretical and practical experience.

The company's senior management is strongly committed to employee training and development. According to the ProSoft philosophy, it is human resources that create the products' added value and contribute to the company competitiveness.

The quality standard system ISO 9001 has been introduced into the company. This system requires training to be planned and delivered on an annual basis. In its 2000 version the whole training cycle was completed, including training needs analysis, evaluation of the training process and assessment of the effectiveness of training. Along with the quality standard ISO 9001, ProSoft works according to the principles of the standard "Investors in People" (see Figure 10.9).

The company's training system is based on modern scientific principles. Highly qualified professionals carry out the training. As a company that introduced the standard "Investors in people" ProSoft was included in a survey conducted by the American Society for Training and Development.[1]

The results from "1999 Measurement Kit" questionnaires – instruments for benchmarking and continuous improvement – showed that the company's activity in this field matches world and European standards. Data on similar organisations in Europe and 107 global IT organisations were compared. They showed that 41% of the companies taking part in the survey invested less than ProSoft in training. According to the results, ProSoft spent 71% of the European average for training per person and 62% of the IT industry average (Figure 10.10).

One important finding was that ProSoft spent more hours on training per eligible employee – 47.3 – than the average for the IT industry – 29.5 – and for Europe – 32.6 (Figure 10.11). Thus ProSoft invests much more in its people in order to improve their qualifications and to support their career development and self-realisation.

ProSoft trained 80% of its qualified personnel while the average percentage for the IT industry was 76% and for Europe 74% (Figure 10.12). The results of this survey demonstrate

---

[1] Training Benchmarking Report, ASTD, February 2000.

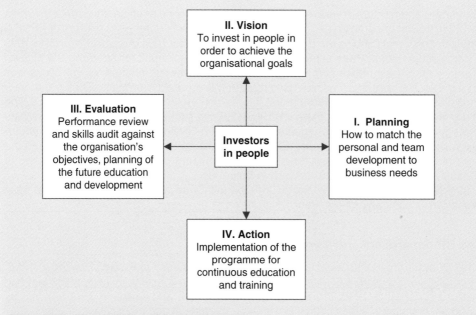

Figure 10.9 The "Investors in People" programme

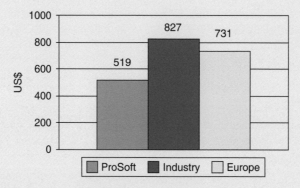

Figure 10.10 Total training expenditures per eligible employee (US$)

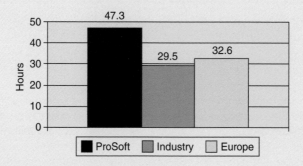

Figure 10.11 Total hours of training per eligible employee

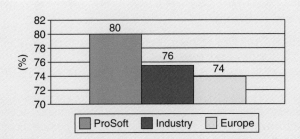

Figure 10.12   Percentage of eligible employees receiving training

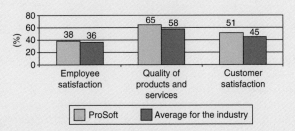

Figure 10.13   Improvement in organisational performance (1999 compared with 1998)

conclusively that the company performs to contemporary standards for the training of qualified personnel.

Figure 10.13 illustrates ProSoft's improvements in three very important areas – employee satisfaction (38% in 1999 compared with 36% in 1998), quality of goods and services (65% as against 58%) and customer satisfaction (51% as against 45%).

Similar results were reported in respect of the company's 20% growth in training expenditure in 1999 compared to the average for the industry – 20% – and for Europe – 16%. The same pattern applied to ProSoft's results for such items as work rotation and personnel participation in decision-making, individual development plans, etc. Most resources were invested in personnel training for product types – 20% (12% average for the IT industry and 8% for Europe). The conclusion can be drawn that personnel training and career advancement within the company are carefully planned.

The company had long ago recognised investment in training as one of the most important contributions to achieving organisational goals and acquiring competitive advantage. That was why its entire managerial team participated in the programme of the School of Management at the New Bulgarian University and the Open University in the UK. Constant improvement though training is a prerequisite for the fulfilment of ProSoft's next ambition – to be the first Bulgarian company to apply a European model for "Excellence in Business". It is considered that in order to succeed a company must achieve the status of "learning organisation". With this in mind the managerial team decided to observe the following principles:

- keeping a high rate of investment in training in compliance with corporate goals;
- planning carefully the development of individual and team skills and knowledge;
- elaborating and applying on a mass scale a well-thought-out programme for continuous training;
- systematic evaluation of the effectiveness of training, evaluation of progress in qualifications compared to goal attainment and added value.

HRM practices used in ProSoft

The methods used by ProSoft's Human Resource Department in their main areas of responsibility may be summarised as follows:

Recruitment

In recruiting staff the department regularly uses: media advertisements, advertisements in universities, personal recommendations, managers' and experts' personal contacts. Applicants are expected to present a motivation letter, Curriculum Vitae, documents certifying their educational attainments and any additional qualifications, and references or recommendations.

Selection

First stage

1. Analysis of the candidate's biographical data.
2. Telephone interview.
3. Completion of the application form.
4. Preparation of a shortlist of candidates for further participation in the selection process.
5. Feedback to all candidates who have participated in the selection process so far.

Second stage

1. Interview with a specialist from the HR department.
2. Language skills test.
3. IQ test.
4. Emotional intelligence test (for ability to work in a team).
5. Psychological tests.
6. Verification of references/recommendations.
7. Preparation of a shortlist of candidates for further participation in the selection process.
8. Feedback to all candidates who have participated in this stage of the selection process.

Third stage

1. Interview panel with the manager and specialists from the department where the vacancy exists.
2. Preparation of a shortlist of candidates for further participation in the selection process.
3. Feedback to all candidates who have participated in this stage of the selection process.

Fourth stage

1. Interview with the president of the company.
2. Final decision based on all results from the tests and interviews.
3. Feedback to all candidates who have participated in this stage of the selection process.

The selection methods applied in ProSoft differ from the common practice in Bulgaria, where IQ and personality tests are mostly used. Selection instruments also include modern competence measurement methods. The questionnaires test, among other factors, labour attitudes, abilities, achievements and motivation. Based on results from the questionnaires, the following three main indicators are used as criteria for the future performance of candidates:

1. The intelligence level (IQ), characterising the individual's potential. This is measured by the Catell test.

2. The level of emotional intelligence (EQ), showing the individual's adaptability to team-working and extent of integration into the organisation. The EQ measurement methods were developed by American psychologists. The authors used them to test 1000 managers, professionals and other employees from more than 100 organisations in the service, technology and industrial sector in the USA and Canada. The test has been modified for use in the UK, Europe, Japan and other nations and regions. The results form the basis for an individual professional profile, which, compared to the organisation's profile, may provide a successful predictor for effective completion of job assignments. This method has been applied for selection since 1997, ProSoft being the first company in Bulgaria to use it. Later on the method was standardised and adapted for use by other Bulgarian companies.

3. The motivation level (MQ) is measured by a combination of methods that identify the applicant's motivators and demotivators. The MQ level helps define the need for goal achievement. Standard interviews, traditional tests and the verification of the references usually provide information about the candidate's *ability* to do the job, whereas the MQ results show whether he/she will *actually* do it.

As well as those questionnaires and tests, the company is developing a method for measuring the individual's values. The aim is to differentiate between values that are relatively stable (universal and specific to the job) and those that result from economic and social changes. This will help to identify the main dimensions of the values influencing job performance. ProSoft pursues a policy of constant improvement and application of the most advanced approaches and methods, and invests in research in this field. The HRM directorate supports the belief that employee values are an important predictor for the quick and successful adaptation of newcomers to the organisation.

Taking into account the present social and economic situation in Bulgaria, there is enough evidence to assert that the competitiveness and added value of the company's products and services are to a significant extent due to its human factor, which is its most important strategic advantage over its competitors. The commitment of ProSoft's top management, and the company's extensive programme of employee training and professional development, are considered key factors.

Professional development and career management

The complex and dynamic nature of the work, as well as unceasing technological development, result in a continuous change in the knowledge and skills required. The pressure on employers to seek more flexible employees, willing to improve their competencies constantly, is intense.

HR management in ProSoft pays special attention to the key professionals. The different stages in an individual's career have been carefully analysed and career development counselling is provided. A career development algorithm developed by ProSoft's President Julian Genov is used (Figure 10.14).

Consultation

Consultation takes place at three levels:

1. Survey of the organisational climate, management and work practices in order to identify hidden and unexplored ways of improving efficiency and analysis of the results and submission of recommendations for managers and associates.

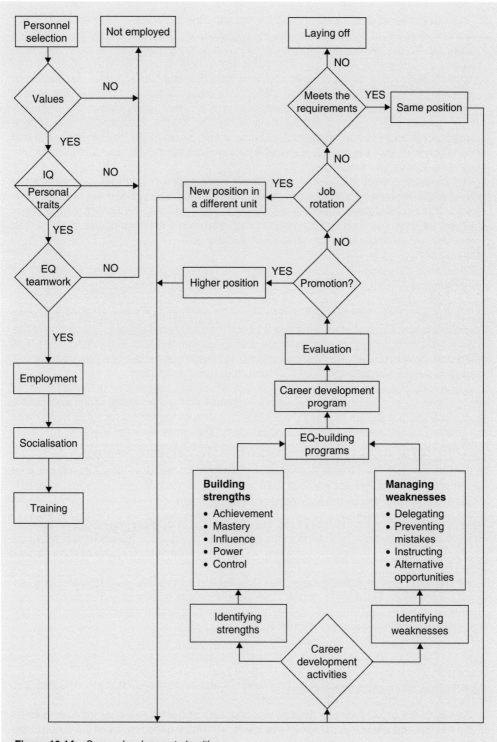

Figure 10.14   Career development algorithm

2. Individual consultations with managers with a view to optimising the organisational behaviour of associates.
3. Consultations on a specific problem.

Professional consultation contributes to a higher level of work satisfaction and reflects the associates' motivation and productivity.

Socialisation of new employees

The HR department uses a number of well-established methods to shorten the period of employee adaptation. ProSoft practice in this domain is based on the concept that the professional introduction of new associates minimises loss and stress and helps specialists to accept organisational realities more quickly. New specialists are introduced to their working team and to the organisational culture. They are provided with support in accepting their duties and responsibilities. The HR department routinely anticipates possible conflicts between old employees and newcomers and takes measures to prevent them.

Training and development

Training and development activities in ProSoft are directed at acquiring the knowledge and skills necessary to meet the immediate professional needs of associates. The usual practice is to involve lecturers from the same company or specialists in the relevant areas. Regular training courses are provided on the following topics among others:

- Professional skills and practices in different fields.
- Business communication.
- Negotiation skills.
- Conflict resolution.

Performance evaluation

HRM pays great attention to the functioning of the formal system of performance evaluation, which exercises an important influence on the organisation's psychological climate. In ProSoft the results of the evaluation are used for other HR activities – training, career development, promotion and compensation.

For the accreditation of technical experts, the company works with the authorised centres of MicroSoft, Novell, Compaq and others. The certificates received by the specialists from leading manufacturers are a proof of internationally recognised professional qualities.

One form of recognition for the work of ProSoft's teams and associates is the awarding of the annual prizes for achievement in different categories. This is the highest reward in the company. Nominees are selected by the employees themselves, who then choose the best of four or five contestants. The awards are announced at the annual meeting of the holding group on 9 January each year.

The problem

The meeting of the managerial team preceding the company's tenth anniversary provoked a stormy discussion. The team split into two groups supporting opposite positions on one important point – future investment in training. There were compelling reasons for radical change in corporate HRM policy and practice.

The immediate cause of the dispute was that two key employees had recently left the company, but the underlying reason was the high staff turnover rate, which had reached 20%. The director of the HR department reported that the maximum period key personnel were working for the company was 7 years. Only yesterday Gergana,[2] the marketing director, and Vassilka, the project manager, had left the company.

Gergana had worked for ProSoft for 6 years. She started her career when she was 26 years old. After 1 year she had eight subordinates. Over the period of her work with ProSoft a great deal was invested in her training. She attended English language courses at the British Council, she graduated from the School of Management in the Open University and attended many training sessions, seminars and conferences organised by partners Compaq and Epson. Every year the company spent 70% of her annual wage on training and education. Vassilka had worked for ProSoft for 8 years. A similar amount had been spent on her training.

Between Gergana and Vassilka there was a continuous silent conflict – both were very ambitious and tried to prove their importance to the company, and very often their activities were not coordinated with top management. In fact, they had sometimes represented their own decisions as having been made by top management. Because of this Gergana was in conflict with the financial director, who later left the company. Meanwhile Vassilka was obstructing the career development of Ivan – a young and very ambitious engineer. This made him leave the company too. When they took part in selection procedures both women tried to avoid appointing bright and talented applicants. It was this persistent conflict that led to their resignations. The company lost four highly qualified associates, in whom significant investments had been made. It was not difficult for them to find good new jobs, and they were all quickly recruited by multinational IT companies.

Every year on 9 January nearly all ProSoft's ex-employees attend an alternative party. Their conflicts are forgotten and they discuss the good old days when they worked at ProSoft.

---

[2] To protect privacy full names have not been used.

TEACHING QUESTIONS

1. Critically evaluate HRM policy and practice at ProSoft. Make a comparison in this field between ProSoft and an IT company from your own country.
2. How would you change this practice? What recommendations would you make to top management if you were an external consultant?
3. How could the company develop a successful policy for retaining their key personnel?
4. Comment on the conflict of interest between the four employees who left the company.
5. How would you suggest resolving the conflict?

REFERENCES

Brewster, C. and Koubek, J. (1995) Human resource management in turbulent times: HRM in the Czech Republic. *The International Journal of Human Resource Management*, 6(2): 223–247.

Brewster, C., Hegewisch, A. and Koubek, J. (1996) Different roads: changes in industrial and employee relations in the Czech Republic and East Germany since 1989. *Industrial Relations Journal*, 27(1): 50–64.

Koubek, J. (1995) Elevating the HR function. *People Management*, 27(July): 39.

Koubek, J. (1997) Human resource management in the Czech Republic. In: Hanel, U., Hegewisch, A. and Mayrhofer, W. (Hg.), Personalarbeit im Wandel. Entwicklungen in den neuen Bundesländern und Europa. München und Mering, Rainer Hampp Verlag 1997, pp. 95–113. Personalwirtschaftliche Schriften (herausgegeben von Dudo von Eckardstein und Oswald Neuberger), Band 11.

Koubek, J. (2000) Human resource management in transforming economy – convergency or divergency? (Example of the Czech Republic). *International Conference: HRM – an Important Factor for European Integration*, International Business School Transbusiness –E, Sofia.

Koubek, J. et al. (2000) The Cranfield project on European human resource management. *Acta Oeconomica Pragensia*, 8(4): 7–213.

Vatchkova, E. (1998) *Human Resource Management: European Comparative Researches*. University Press Stopanstvo, Sofia.

Vatchkova, E. (2001) Strategic human resource management and the integration of Bulgaria to the European labour market. *Round table, organized by Friedrich Ebert Stiftung*, Sofia, 5.07. 2001.

Vatchkova, E. (2001) The speed of changes – Bulgarian way to the integrated European HRM. *Vth Chemnitz East Forum: "Human resource management in transition"*, Chemnitz University of Technology, 21–23.03.

Vatchkova, E. (2001) Actual tasks of HRM in EU membership candidate countries (The examples of Bulgaria, the Czech Republic, Estonia and Cyprus). *Scientific International Cranet Conference: New Dimensions in Human Resource Management*, Nicosia, 08.11. 2001.

11

Estonia and Slovenia: Building Modern HRM Using a Dualist Approach

Ruth Alas and Ivan Svetlik

INSTITUTIONAL BACKGROUND

REPUBLIC OF ESTONIA*

Capital	Tallinn
Official language	Estonian
Area	45,227 km^2
Population	1,445,580 (1999 est.)
Currency	Eesti Kroon (EEK)
	1 kroon = 100 sent.
	(1 Euro = 15.65 EEK)

Topography and climate

Estonia is slightly bigger than Belgium, Denmark or the Netherlands. Almost half of its territory is forest and woodland. Nearly 1200 lakes (5% of the nation's area) dot the countryside, which is relatively flat – about two-thirds of the area lies less than 50 m above sea level. The highest point is Suur Munamägi, 318 m above sea level. The longest rivers are the Pärnu (144 km), the Kasari (112 km) and the Emajõgi (101 km). The largest of the lakes are Peipsi (3555 km^2, of which 1529 km^2 lies within Estonia) and Võrtsjärv (266 km^2). There are 1521 islands off Estonia's coast. The biggest are Saaremaa (2922 km^2), Hiiumaa (1023 km^2) and Muhu (206 km^2).

Estonia lies on almost the same latitude as southern Alaska, but thanks to the influence of the Gulf Stream, the climate is mild. The average temperature in the warmest month, July, is about 17°C; in the coldest, February, between −3.5°C and −7°C.

*The Estonian Institutional Background section was prepared by Maris Zernand.

Natural resources

The main natural resources in Estonia are oil shale and phosphorite. Oil shale is widely used as a fuel in power stations, and, to a lesser extent, in chemical industry. Estonia also possesses abundant deposits of peat, used in farming and as a fuel. There is limestone and dolomite, and even clay, which is used by the building industry. One of Estonia's most important resources is wood. Estonian forests are one of the main features of the country's national economy.

People

Estonians comprise 65% of the total population. Other ethnic groups include Russians (28%), Ukrainians (3%), Belarussians (2%) and Finns (1%). About one-third of the population (411,594) lives in Tallinn, the capital. Urban population comprises 69% of the total. Population density is 32.1 persons/km^2. Even when living in towns, Estonians still are close to the country.

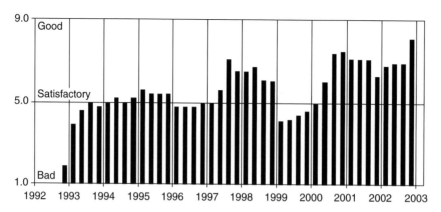

Figure 11.1   General economic situation. *Source*: Estonian Institute of Economic Research

Ethnically and linguistically, Estonians belong to the Finno-Ugric peoples, along with the Finns and Hungarians. The national character of Estonians has been shaped by the fate of the nation as well by the country's landscape. An Estonian prefers to manage on his own. An Estonian is usually sceptical by nature, tends to mock any kind of state authority and dreads superfluous sentimentality. The main religion is Lutheran, but there are also Orthodox, Baptists and others.

Political system

Estonia is a parliamentary republic. The Parliament (Riigikogu) has 101 members elected for a period of 4 years. Voting age is 18. Resident non-citizens are eligible to vote at local government elections. The head of state is the President, elected by the Riigikogu for a 5-year term. The head of government, the Prime Minister, is appointed by the President and approved by the Riigikogu.

Economy

Estonia is one of the most advanced emerging markets in central and eastern Europe. It has been an associated member of the European Union (EU) since 1995 and, together with nine other candidate countries, will become a full member in 2004.

Owing to rapid economic development, a liberal tax system and a highly favourable location, the country is at the heart of Europe's fastest-growing market, the Baltic Sea Region, which has a combined population of more than 90 million people. Estonia has become a central and eastern European leader in attracting foreign direct investments. The main sectors of the Estonian economy are oil-shale energy, telecommunications, textiles, chemical products, banking, services, food and fishing, timber, shipbuilding, electronics and transport.

The economic situation remained strong in recent years and while positive trends, are expected to continue the threats arising from a sluggish world economy, are significant. Loan demand is still strong and interest rates may rise somewhat (Figure 11.1 and Tables 11.1–11.3):

- 43% of the population are Internet users (EMOR, autumn 2002).
- 33% of the population have a computer at home, 68% of home computers are connected to the Internet.
- All Estonian schools are connected to the Internet.
- There are about 500 public Internet access points in Estonia, 36 per 100,000 people (one of the highest ratios in Europe).
- The number of Estonian web sites exceeds 1 million.
- Incomes can be declared to the Tax Board via the Internet.
- Expenditure incurred in the state budget can be followed on the Internet in real time.
- The government has changed Cabinet meetings to paperless sessions using a web-based document system.
- 43% of Estonian people conduct their routine banking via the Internet.
- 61% of the population are mobile phone subscribers.
- All of Estonia is covered by digital mobile phone networks.

Table 11.1   Key economic indicators

Key indicators	1996	1997	1998	1999	2000	2001
Mean annual population (million)	1.47	1.46	1.45	1.44	1.37*	1.36*
GDP at current prices (billion EUR)	3.4	4.1	4.7	4.8	5.5	6.1
Real growth of GDP (%)	4	11	5	−1	7	5
GDP per capita at current prices (EUR)	2300	2800	3200	3339	3986	4465
Annual FDI (million EUR)	116.0	236.1	515.8	284.3	435.1	597.8
Annual FDI per capita (EUR)	79	161	356	197	310	438
Consumer price index compared to previous year (%)	23	11	8	3	4	6
Unemployment rate** (%)	10	10	10	12	14	13
Average monthly wage (EUR)	191	228	263	284	312	352
Current account balance (% of GDP)	−9	−12	−9	−5	−6	−6
Deficit(−)/surplus of state budget (% of GDP)	−2	2	−1	−5	−1	1
Export (billion EUR)***	1.600	2.606	2.912	2.758	3.444	3.696
Import (billion EUR)***	2.485	3.940	4.306	3.865	4.614	4.798
Trade balance (billion EUR)***	−0.885	−1.334	−1.393	−1.106	−1.169	−1.101
Total government expenditures (% of GDP)	40	38	40	41	37	36

* Based on the 2000 population census.
** Unemployed/labour force according to ILO methodology.
*** Trade figures shown in general trade system.
Sources: Bank of Estonia, Ministry of Finance, Statistical Office of Estonia.

Table 11.2   GDP by main fields of economic activity
(as a % of total GDP)

Field of activity	1998	1999	2000	2001
Wholesale and retail trade	15	16	16	15
Manufacturing	15	15	17	18
Transport, storage and communication	12	14	15	16
Real estate, renting and business services	10	12	12	11
Construction	6	5	6	6
Financial services	3	4	4	4
Education	5	6	5	5
Agriculture and hunting	4	4	3	4

Source: Statistical Office of Estonia.

Table 11.3   Telecommunications and IT

	12/2000	12/2001	09/2002
Telephone main (fixed) lines per 100 inhabitants	35.9	34.9	34.3
Share of digital lines (%)	71	72	75
Number of mobile phone subscribers per 100 inhabitants	40.8	52	61

Sources: Estonian Telephone Company, Baltic News Service, Estonian Informatics Centre.

According to the RIPE Network Coordination Centre, Estonia has the highest Internet connected hosts/population ratio in central and eastern Europe and is also ahead of most EU countries.

Labour market

Wage policy is designed to maintain the international competitiveness of Estonia's exports by linking wages to productivity. Estonia has an educated, skilled and reliable workforce. The attitude of the labour force towards foreign investment is positive. Estonia rejoined the International Labour Organization in January 1992.

The following are some notable features of working life:

Length of working week	5 days
Length of working day	8 hours
Annual holidays	28 days
Age of retirement (men and women)	63 years

At the moment there is no compulsory unemployment insurance. However, those out of work are eligible to receive unemployment benefit (currently EEK 400) for a period of 6 months provided they have registered with the government.

Foreign citizens must apply for a work permit, holders of which have the same rights and obligations as residents.

The Estonian labour market has undergone great changes during the last decade. The number of employed has fallen continuously since the second half of the 1980s. At the beginning of 1998 the number of employed persons in Estonia was about 640,000; 200,000 fewer than in 1989. Over the same period the labour force participation rate fell from 77 to 64% and the employment rate from 77 to 58%. The most drastic changes occurred in 1993–1995, when unemployment grew from zero to its present level. From 1996 onwards a certain stability can be observed. The number of employed persons, the employment rate, the labour participation rate and the unemployment rate have all changed little since then. This suggests that important changes connected with transition in the labour market had been completed by that time. Of course, this does not mean that the changes have been completed altogether. The collapse of the Russian market in the late spring of 1998 had a serious effect on Estonian manufacturing in general and especially on the food industry exporting mainly to the eastern market. As yet no data are available on the extent of the resulting fall in employment and rise in unemployment.

Distribution of employment by fields of activity

Each year the distribution of employment by fields of activity draws closer to the employment structure of developed countries. The proportion of industry and, especially, agriculture in employment is falling while that of services is increasing. The greatest changes have occurred in the primary sector, where the share of agricultural workers in total employment has fallen. At the same time the proportion of the services sector is increasing. The shares of trade, financial services, real estate, government and education in the total employment rose. And in the future a further fall in agricultural employment and rise in employment in services can be expected.

The share of the private sector in employment was 69% at the beginning of 1998 and that of the public sector 31%. The proportion of private sector in employment has been continuously increasing: it was 24% of total employment in 1989, 39% in 1992 and 61% in

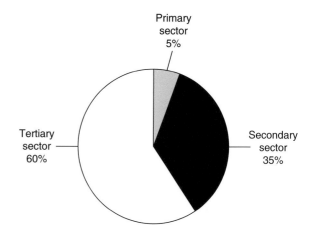

Figure 11.2   Distribution of employment

1995. In manufacturing the private sector accounted for only 9% in 1989 but for as much as 97% in 1998. The share of the public sector has decreased also in such fields as education and health care, although not at the same rate as in industry (Figure 11.2).

Of all those employed 91% are employees and 9% are entrepreneurs (including unpaid family members). A large proportion of the entrepreneurs are engaged in agriculture, where private entrepreneurship started 10 years ago. Entrepreneurs (farmers) make up nearly one-third of those engaged in the primary sector, while their share in the secondary sector is only 5% and in the services 7%. Still, as compared with developed countries the proportion of employees in Estonian agriculture is high and the proportion of entrepreneurs in industry and services can be regarded as small. Moreover, the growth in the proportion of entrepreneurs in employment has all but halted.

Unemployment

The number of employed, which was nearly 70,000 in spring 1998, has been quite stable since 1995 and unemployment has most probably increased because of the fall in the number of people seeking jobs at labour exchanges.

Fewer than half of the unemployed register at employment agencies as job-seekers: for example, in 1998 on average 32,000 people a month were registered, yet the "unemployment rate" was 4–5% (Figure 11.3).

Moreover, fewer than 18,000 people a month drew unemployment benefit. It is not easy to qualify for

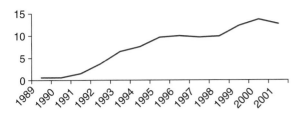

Figure 11.3   Unemployment rate (% aged 15–69)

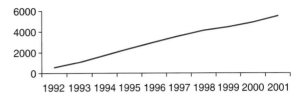

Figure 11.4   Average wage per month

unemployment benefit in Estonia: for example, to apply, one must have worked for at least half of the 1 year period prior to application. As a rule, the benefit is paid for 6 months, and since 1999 the rate has been 400 kroons a month (before then 300 kroons a month). Practically no unemployment insurance or other benefits are available in Estonia besides the state system. As well as unemployment benefit the employment agencies offer job-seekers some assistance that can be classified as measures of active labour policy: financial support to start one's own business (10,000 kroons were paid on one occasion), relevant training, and financial support for employers who hire an unemployed person whose competitiveness in the labour market is low (the handicapped, young persons between 16 and 20 years of age, persons who have less than 5 years before retirement age, people released from prison, etc.).

Surveys have shown that in Estonia unemployment is somewhat higher among men (10% at the beginning of 1998) than among women (9%). However, 60% of the job-seekers registered with employment agencies are women, which implies that women are more active in trying to find work through an employment agency. The number of people who have been out of work for a long time has been increasing steadily. While in 1995 the long-term unemployed accounted for 32% of all unemployed, in 1998 the figure was over 45%. This means that 30,000 people have not worked for a year or even longer. The situation is especially serious in rural areas.

Wage policy

In its transition to a market economy Estonia chose to pursue a liberal wage policy. Thus the government's interference in the wages of the business sector is limited to the establishment of minimum wages and adherence to the provisions of the wages law. The latter means

mainly that the employees as the weaker party in the labour market are given internationally acknowledged guarantees. In the regulation of wages in government and other public institutions (whose wage costs are established by the law on the state budget) the role of the government is much greater: it regulates the wages of about 10% of the employees. For these employees wages are based mainly on educational level required, while wage rates for all categories, and some requirements concerning the payment of wages, have been formally established. Special acts regulate the system of salaries of members of parliament, government officials, judges, public prosecutors and some other, mainly high-ranking, public servants.

The minimum wage set by the government since 2001 for full-time work is 1600 kroons a month. In 1995–1999 the minimum pay increased from 450 kroons a month to 1500 kroons. At present the minimum threshold above which any income is liable to income tax is 9000 kroons a year, or 800 kroons a month. Income tax is levied on all incomes above the minimum at a uniform rate of 26%. The tax is deducted from the wages and salaries paid by the employer. In addition, the employer pays a social tax, which is 33% of all payroll costs. This is used to cover the cost of pensions and health insurance.

In 1999 the average wage in Estonia was 4440 kroons a month (Figure 11.4). Over the period 1995–1998 the total rise in average pay was 78% (compared to a rise of 48% in the consumer price index). The increase in wages was higher than the rise in the CPI in all fields of activity without exception. In recent years the increase in wages has slowed down. In 1996 average wages increased by 28% as compared with the previous year and in 1997 by 18%, then in 1998 by 14%. There is a big difference between the wages in Tallinn and Harju County, surrounding the capital, on the one hand, and the remaining regions of Estonia on the other. Average wages in Tallinn and Harju County were over

5000 kroons a month in 1998. This figure is 1.7 times that of the county with the lowest level of incomes and the only one that is above the average for the whole country. The lowest average wages are in south-east Estonia, which is predominately an agricultural region. Moreover, as a result of uneven regional development (investment, especially foreign investment, tends to concentrate on Tallinn and its environments), the gap between earnings has been increasing. The lack of a uniform labour market has contributed to Tallinn's having become a place of work for some inhabitants from virtually every other region of Estonia.

Average wages in different fields of activity differ by a factor of more than three. Moreover, the difference between the lowest level, which is in agriculture (average wage 2506 kroons a month in 1998) and the highest, financial services (9025 kroons) has been growing. The same tendency can be observed in respect of earnings in financial services as compared to the average of the whole country. The wage differences between the sectors of the economy are considerably greater than would normally be due to differences in work and working conditions. It is worth mentioning that only hotels and restaurants (average pay in 1998 was 3382 kroons a month) and agriculture (2506 kroons) pay lower average wages than education (3382 kroons).

In some fields (construction and trade are the typical examples) what is known as "envelope pay" plays a significant role. There are different estimates as to the scale of the black economy in Estonia, but most probably it accounts for 15–20% of gross domestic product (GDP).

The average monthly net income per household member was 2000 kroons in 1999. Of this, income from wages or salaries amounted to 1214 kroons, or 61%. The second largest source of income was transfers from government – on average 27% of all disposable income. The average old-age pension was 1540 kroons a month in 1999. Of course, all these figures have increased from year to year. For example, the wage index increased about 7.5 times in the period 1992–1998.

In terms of income the population of Estonia could be categorised in the 1990s into three large groups: 5–10% are very wealthy, 15–20% are very poor and 17–80% are somewhere in between. Approximately one-third of the population's income is distributed among the tenth decile families. One-fifth of households (ninth and tenth deciles) earn almost half of the total. The first and the tenth decile differ sharply from the adjacent second and ninth decile. Those belonging to the first or ninth income deciles would have to cross a relatively higher barrier in order to reach the next decile than families in the other deciles. In order to move to an adjacent higher income decile, a household would need to increase its income by 10–20% in most cases, yet the difference as compared to the adjacent decile in the case of the first and ninth deciles is nearly double.

The place of a family in the hierarchy of income largely depends on how it is made up. A clear pattern emerges: the fewer children in the family, the higher income decile it occupies. From the eighth decile upwards, approximately half the households have dependent children. The number of children in the first income decile is approximately twice as high as that in the higher deciles. The most likely to find themselves in the lowest income decile are families with a single breadwinner, two or more children and economically inactive members.

REPUBLIC OF SLOVENIJA

Area	20,256 km^2
Population	1,989,000 (2000)
Density	98 inhabitants per km^2
Capital and population	Ljubljana: 270,441 (1998)
Other important	Maribor (131,110)
cities and population	Celje (49,317)
Official language	Slovene
Business languages	Slovene, English, German, Italian and Serbo-Croat
Religion	Predominantly Roman Catholic

Topography and climate

The Republic of Slovenia extends 248 km from west to east and 163 km from north to south. It is bordered to the west by Italy, to the north by Austria, to the east by Hungary, and to the south-east by Croatia.

Figure 11.5   Panorama of Ljubljana

Slovenia is in the first group of countries to become new members of the EU.

The Slovenian landscape is characterised by Alpine mountains, valleys and rivers in the north-west, which slopes down towards the fertile Panonian plain in the south-east, and towards the Karst and Adriatic coast in the south-west. It offers a unique combination of alpine, continental and Mediterranean climates and panoramas and a unique variety of species in a very small area (Figure 11.5).

Principal characteristics

The principal characteristics of Slovenia in comparison to the EU-15 are shown in Figure 11.6 and in Table 11.4. Slovenia has a relatively high employment rate of women and low unemployment. Population dynamics

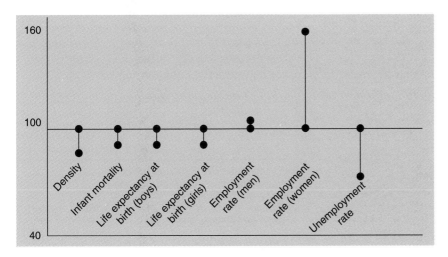

Figure 11.6   Principal characteristics in relation to EU-15 = 1000

are rather weak in terms of net (positive) migration, population growth, marriages and divorces as compared to the EU-15. Population density, which is lower than the EU-15 average, could be explained by the mountainous nature of the country.

Special features

Slovenia became an independent state only in 1991. For the previous 70 years it was one of the constituent parts of the first and second Yugoslavia. Between the two World Wars the western part was annexed by Italy. Earlier Slovenian ethnic territories belonged to the Hapsburg Empire. Although without a long political history, Slovene culture dates back to 1560, when the Bible was translated into the Slovene language. Culture is the main focus of Slovene identity. There are few nations with as many theatres and art galleries per 100,000 inhabitants as there are in Slovenia. The composer Jacobus Gallus, the mathematician Jurij Vega and the architect Jože Plečnik were all born Slovenians.

Apart from the Slavic culture, with strong Germanic and some Romance elements, Slovenia is characterised by its geographical position as a bridge between west and east, as well as between north and south, especially the Balkans. Slovenia could be described as a country of varieties: a variety of species and natural beauties, such as the Postojna cave with its so-called "human fish", a variety of historical monuments from the Roman period to the World Wars and a variety of industries from fine wines to software production.

People

The population of Slovenia has stabilised at slightly below 2 million. It is becoming old because of a combination of increased longevity, especially among women, and declining birth rates.

The average Slovenian household has 3.1 persons, with 18% having only one person; 72% of couples have children.

Economy

The Slovenian economy has been mainly privatised with the exception of banks, insurance companies and telecommunication, where privatisation has begun. There is still a strong public sector covering post, railways, health, education and social services. Since the recession caused by the break-up of the former Yugoslavia, the loss of markets in eastern Europe and the transition to a market economy was over, there has been a constant growth of 4% per annum in the period 1993–1999, which is well above the EU-15 average of 3%. GDP continues to increase at similar rates – 5% in 2000 and 3% in 2001.

The gross national product comprises services (58%), of which public services contribute 20% and other services 38%; manufacturing 38% and agriculture 5%. In comparison with the EU-15, services contribute less and manufacturing and agriculture more. Small businesses predominate: 92% of production units employ fewer than 50 people and 98% fewer than 249 (Table 11.5).

Slovenia exported 49% of GDP in 2000. The main economic partners are Germany, Italy, Croatia, Russia and Austria. In 1997, 37% of GDP (about two-thirds of all exports) went to the EU. The bulk of exported goods come from manufacturing: home appliances, cars, and electronic and pharmaceutical products. The road and rail networks, which have been extensively modernised, run largely from west to east and from north to south. The port of Koper is gaining in importance for the central European region.

Table 11.4 Population by age and sex (% of total population)

Age (years)	1986 (%)	1996 (%)	2002 (%)	EU-15 (1996) (%)	Women (% of age group)
<15	22	18	16	17	49
15–24	15	15	14	13	49
25–49	37	38	38	37	50
50–64	17	16	17	16	51
65–79	8	10	12	12	60
>80	2	2.4	2.4	3.9	72
Total					52

All data from (6), (8) and (9).

Table 11.5 Economic structure 1995 (as % of GDP, current prices)

	Slovenia (%)	EU-15 (%)
Agricultural, forestry and fishery products	5	2
Manufactured products, fuel and power	33	26
Building and construction	5	5
Services	38	52
General government, non-profit	20	15

All data from (2), (6) and (8).

Legal and institutional environment/political system

Until 1991 Slovenia was a part of the former Yugoslavia, where there was a one-party communist régime. Yugoslavia experimented with so-called "self-management", which was characterised by its humane face in comparison to other communist countries. However, it suffered a crisis because of increasing economic inefficiency and declining political legitimacy. In 1989 the transition process leading to a market economy and political pluralism started.

The Slovenian constitution introduced a division between legislative, executive and judicial power. Supreme authority lies with the National Assembly, composed of 90 representatives elected according to a combined proportional and majority system. Currently, seven political parties are represented in the Parliament. Four of them – Liberal Democrats, Social Democrats, People's Christian Party and the Party of Youth – form the central-left government. The prime minister is nominated by the president of the republic from within the strongest party and then elected, together with his or her cabinet, by the Assembly. The president of the republic is elected by popular vote for 5 years and has no executive power.

The main national projects in Slovenia have been the establishment of democratic institutions, privatisation as the basis for a market economy and economic restructuring, and implementation of the *acquis communitaire* on the way to EU membership, which is planned for Spring 2004. A well-developed social welfare system established in the socialist period has been preserved and adapted to the new circumstances. It provides for all the kinds of insurance and public services normally found in the developed central European countries. This has been made possible by a stepwise transition process and strong trade unions, who play an active role in the social partnership arrangements.

Labour market

Table 11.6 provides a picture of the labour market in Slovenia in comparison to the EU-15 averages.

Labour force participation rates in Slovenia are comparable to those of the EU-15. Women's participation on the labour market exceeds the EU average and is comparable to that of Scandinavian countries if we bear in mind that over 90% of women in Slovenia work full-time. In the year 2000 there was 5% of work-active population in the agricultural sector, 40% in the industrial sector and 55% in services (ESS, 2000). The percentage of self-employed varies between 11 and 12, and is close to the EU-15 average. The flexibility of the labour market is increasing, especially in the form of temporary employment, which accounts for about 12% of the work-active population. Three-quarters of new entrants are temporarily employed. On the other hand, part-time working has not been much used and is almost equally distributed among men and women. About 8% of the work-active population work part-time only.

Unemployment is below the EU-15 average and fell to 6% in 2001. While men were more affected at the beginning of the transition, women were in a worse position in 2001 with 6% unemployment. The labour force participation rate among older workers is low (in the age group of men 55–59 only 47% and in the age group of

Table 11.6   The main characteristics of the labour market

	1980		1990		1995		1999		2001	
	SI*	EU	SI*	EU	SI*	EU	SI*	EU	SI*	EU
Labour force participation rate as % of population 15–65 years	68	66	68	67	68	67	68	69	68	69
Female labour force participation rate as % of population 15–65 years	61	49	65	55	62	57	64	59	63	
Unemployment rate										
Men	2	7	5	6	8	9	7	8	6	6
Women	2	10	5	11	7	12	8	11	6	9

All data from (3), (7) and (8).
* SI = Slovenia

men 60–64 only 24% as compared to the EU-15 with 72% and 33%, respectively). Although general unemployment is not high it affects older and unskilled workers and youth disproportionately. Among the unemployed 57% were unemployed more than 1 year in 2000 as compared to 47% in the EU-15. Regional differences in unemployment remain very high.

The following data give some idea of labour costs and the cost of living:

- Average gross monthly earnings of all employees in industry and services were 809 EUR in 1999.
- GDP per capita was 9803 EUR in 2000.
- GDP per capita expressed in purchasing power parity was 15,585 EUR in 2000.
- GDP in purchasing power parity per capita in 2000 reached 69% of the EU-15 average.
- Hourly labour costs in industry in 1999 were 7.9 EUR.

The difference between the wage of an unskilled and a university-educated worker increased from a ratio of 1:2.8 in 1991 to 1:3.9 in 1997. The earnings of women in industry and services reached 90% of men's earnings in 1999.

Average usual weekly working hours fell from 43.9 in 1994 to 41.9 in 1998. Actual weekly working hours were 41.1 and 37.3, respectively.

Employee relations and trade unions

In respect of employee relations, Slovenia's present situation is a legacy of the system of self-management, which was concerned largely with macro-economic issues. The old trade union movement, now re-formed, is still the strongest workers' organisation. Some new unions appeared on the scene, of which three have been represented at national level. Trade unions are organised according to the economic sector. Their membership, after falling, stabilised in the second half of the 1990s and is now between 40 and 50% of the active working population (Stanojević, 2000).

Collective bargaining and social partnership have been gaining in importance. For example, trade unions are represented on several national bodies. As a result the number of days lost in strikes per 1000 employees fell from 189 in 1992 to 4.8 in the year 2000 (Stanojević and Vrhovec, 2001). In the second half of the 1990s growth in wages lagged behind growth in productivity. The self-management system created a sense of ownership among

employees. This is one of the reasons why, in more than half of the enterprises, workers and managers acquired a majority of the shares. However, the participation of workers at their workplaces remains weak in comparison to west European organisations (Stanojević, 2001).

Education system

Education in Slovenia takes place mainly in state schools. Compulsory education lasts 9 years, from age 6 to 15. Nearly all young people continue their education to secondary level. Of these, one-third go to general schools (gimnazia), and the others to different vocational schools for between 2 and 5 years. The dual system, similar to the German model, is one of the possibilities. Over 40% of young people go on to post-secondary education, i.e. universities and technical colleges. There are universities in Ljubljana and Maribor, with a third in the process of formation at the coast. Various colleges are located at other regional centres. A new element of education and training in Slovenia is the system of national qualifications.

Education in Slovenia is free for all young people up to master's degree level, which has been increasingly subsidised by the state. Where there are more applicants than places, selection is based on external examinations.

As shown in Tables 11.7–11.9, a sizable share of the young generation is engaged in education and training.

Table 11.7   14–19-year olds in education and training in 1996 (% of the population of the same age)

Age	Total	Men	Women
14	97	97	98
15	97	96	99
16	94	94	94
17	87	85	90
18	65	59	71
19	43	38	48

All data from (4).

Table 11.8   Educational attainment of 25–59-year olds in 1996 (% of population)

	Total	Men	Women
Tertiary	14	13	15
Upper secondary	59	64	53
Less than upper secondary	27	23	32

All data from (5).

Table 11.9   Principal characteristics of Slovenia in comparison to EU-15

Indicator	Slovenia	EU-15	Relation (SLO/EU-15) $\times$ 1000
Density (inhabitants per km², year 2000)	98	116	84
Infant mortality (per 1000 live births, year 2000)	5	5	94
Life expectancy at birth (boys) (in years for the period 1999–2000)	72	74	96
Life expectancy at birth (girls) (in years for the period 1999–2000)	79	80	98
Marriages (per 1000 people, year 2000)	4	5	76
Divorces (per 1000 people, year 2000)	1	2	56
Population increase (average increase between 1986 and 1996, v%)	1	1	82
Net migration (per 1000 people, year 2000)	1	2	35
Employment rate (men; %, year 2001)	68	71	102
Employment rate (women; %, year 2001)	59	51	152
Unemployment rate (%, year 2002)	6	10	77

At the age of 19 the vast majority are already at the post-secondary level and the percentage does not drop much until the age of 24. Men tend to leave education earlier than women. The effect is visible in the educational structure of the population, in which more women than men go on to higher education. However, the current educational structure of the Slovenian population is far from satisfactory. There are too few people with tertiary education and too many with less than an upper secondary one.

HRM IN ESTONIA AND SLOVENIA: CURRENT POLICY AND PRACTICE

HISTORICAL BACKGROUND

Estonia and Slovenia are two small and new countries situated in quite different parts of Europe. Before discussing HRM policy and practice in both countries, it is worth highlighting some of their common – and some different – historical, economic and social characteristics.

As to similarities, historically both countries belonged to bigger multi-ethnic states, Slovenia to the former Yugoslavia for more than 70 years and Estonia to the Soviet Union for 50 years. Both experienced a communist régime (Slovenia for 45 years and Estonia for 50), which influenced the culture of today's population and, more generally, the institutional structure. Both countries became independent at the beginning of the 1990s, Slovenia for the first time in modern history and Estonia for the second time, having been independent at the beginning of the twentieth century). Both countries now have established democratic political régimes and market economies. The identity of both countries has been cultural rather than political. Both are in the first group of countries to become new members of the EU.

In the last decade both countries have enjoyed steady economic growth leading to a rise in the service sector of the economy, though Estonia's share of active population in the service sector is larger. However, in recent times the employment situation in both has worsened. Labour force activity has shrunk. Unemployment is regionally unequally distributed and associated with low regional mobility. There are significant structural inconsistencies in the labour market.

There are also significant differences between the two countries. Estonia has a larger area and a smaller population, which exacerbates the problem of low regional mobility. In Estonia the population is concentrated in the main cities, while in Slovenia it is more evenly dispersed. In Estonia the dominant religion is

Lutheran and during the Soviet occupation the population became more varied with respect to ethnic composition. The Slovenian population, on the other hand, is predominantly Catholic and remains broadly homogeneous with regard to ethnicity.

Experiences with state control under communism also differed as between Slovenia and Estonia. Slovenia enjoyed quite a high degree of autonomy within a rather decentralised Yugoslav state, where quasi-markets and strong links with the western economies existed. This made the first steps to independence easier since the main social, economic and political institutions were already in place. Among communist régimes, the Yugoslav was one relatively liberal, which meant that there was less outside interference with an organisation's personnel policies. The situation in Estonia could be described as different: it enjoyed less autonomy within the Soviet state, and its economy was more strictly planned and less oriented towards the west. There was less freedom also to develop and pursue particular personnel policies within organisations. While in Estonia there was no official unemployment and therefore no experience of labour offices, conversely in Slovenia unemployment, although low, was recognised and labour offices were in place.

The transition towards a market economy in Estonia was quick and radical compared to the soft and slower approach in Slovenia. It was based on a weaker economy, with fewer medium and bigger enterprises than in Slovenia and also with a lower standard of living. As a consequence Estonia has attracted more foreign investment and has more unemployment. However, long-term unemployment is lower than in Slovenia.

The main hypothesis based on our analysis is that the similarities in size and political history have had less impact on the nature of HRM in the two countries than the starting points and speed of their economic transition, the scale of their service sectors, the size of their organisations, the professionalisation of HR and the cultural background.

ROLE OF THE HR FUNCTION

As Table 11.10 shows, there is a big difference between the two countries with respect to integration of the head of the HR function into the top management team. In Slovenian organisations they have been accorded a much more strategic role. The percentage of organisations having the head of the HRM function on the board

Table 11.10 Does the head of the personnel/HR function have a place on the main board of directors or equivalent?

	Slovenia	Estonia	EU average
Yes			
N	108	23	
%	57	34	54

of directors in Slovenia is close to the European average, while in Estonia it is not far above the minimum of 29% organisations reported in the Portuguese data. Where the HR manager does not participate in the top management team, the Chief Executive assumes responsibility for HR issues in most cases in both countries. Other directors or company secretaries are seldom put in this position. The difference between the two countries could perhaps be explained by a longer tradition of HR in Slovenian companies and also by their focused training based on specialist HRM undergraduate programmes that have been in place for over 30 years.

HRM STRATEGY INVOLVEMENT

Significant differences between the two countries exist also with respect to the involvement of responsible persons for HR in the corporate strategy, which is claimed to exist in a written form in 87% of Slovenian and 65% of Estonian organisations. A written HRM strategy exists in 54% of Slovenian and 38% of Estonian organisations. Consistent with the data in Table 11.11, Slovenian HR managers are more frequently involved from the outset of the strategy and in the implementation phase. On the other hand, Estonian HR managers are more often consulted. The performance of HR departments in both countries is systematically evaluated only in about one-third of firms, in Estonia more frequently than in Slovenia. However, the criteria for evaluation differ. In Estonian organisations performance against objectives is used in 63% of firms, external benchmarking in 9% and internal measures of cost-effectiveness in 27%. The corresponding percentages in Slovenia are 22%, 5% and 36%. This suggests that the performance of HR departments and the implementation of the company's HR strategy is better planned and controlled for in Estonian organisations, while in Slovenian it seems more implicit and left to the judgement of HR managers. Their participation in the top management seems to be taken as a sufficient guarantee.

Table 11.11   At what stage is the person responsible for personnel/HR involved in the development of corporate strategy?

	Slovenia	Estonia	EU average
From the outset			
N	99	24	
%	59	41	58
Through consultation			
N	19	17	
%	11	29	24
On implementation			
N	43	12	
%	26	20	10
Not consulted			
N	6	6	
%	4	10	8

Table 11.12   Primary responsibility for policy decisions on recruitment, selection, training and development

	Slovenia	Estonia
Recruitment and selection		
Line management		
N	20	9
%	11	14
Line management in consultation with HR department		
N	63	34
%	35	51
HR department in consultation with line management		
N	80	20
%	45	30
HR department		
N	16	3
%	9	4
Training and development		
Line management		
N	22	9
%	13	14
Line management in consultation with HR department		
N	56	33
%	32	50
HR department in consultation with line management		
N	80	24
%	46	36
HR department		
N	16	0
%	9	0

As the data in Table 11.12 reveal, line managers in Estonian organisations take much greater responsibility for recruitment, selection, training and development than HR departments. In Slovenia the situation is the opposite. In addition, the increase in line management responsibility for HR over the last 3 years has been

Table 11.13   Mechanisms introduced in relation to recruitment or retention of employees

Yes	Slovenia	Estonia
Recruiting abroad		
N	12	9
%	6	13
Re-training existing employees		
N	115	47
%	60	69
Increased pay/benefits		
N	89	48
%	46	71
Relocation of the company		
N	7	2
%	4	3
Marketing the organisation image		
N	47	27
%	24	40

lower than in Estonia. This indicates the strength of the HRM profession in Slovenian organisations and the orientation of Estonian organisations towards HRM as opposed to the traditional personnel function, which seems to be deeply rooted in Slovenian ones. In spite of the differences neither country falls out of the European range, where on the one hand there are countries where line management plays the primary role, such as Norway and Finland, and on the other countries where HR departments prevail, such as Israel and Spain.

RECRUITMENT, SELECTION, TRAINING AND DEVELOPMENT

Estonian organisations have been more active in the field of recruitment and retention of employees than Slovenian ones, as can be observed from Table 11.13. They also use a greater variety of selection methods with the exception of panel interviews. However, in both countries re-training of existing employees, increased pay and benefits and marketing the organisational image occupy the first three places. These differences seem to contradict the previous data. Stronger HR departments in Slovenian organisations do not show their professional activity to the extent that their weaker Estonian counterparts do together with their more active line managers. Perhaps newly developed HR departments in Estonian organisations are more prone to innovation than already established Slovenian ones. This difference may also reflect the speed of economic change and restructuring, which seems to be higher in Estonia than in Slovenia. It should be noted also that in both countries recruitment from abroad is

Table 11.14 Proportion of wage bill spent on training and development

Country order	Frequency	Per cent	Valid per cent	Cumulative per cent
Estonia				
Valid				
<1%	1	2	2	2
1–1.9%	17	25	33	35
2–2.9%	17	25	33	67
3–4.9%	9	13	17	85
5–9.9%	3	5	5	90
>10%	5	7	10	100
Total	52	77	100	
Missing	System	16	24	
Total		68	100.0	
Slovenia				
Valid				
<1%	40	21	30	30
1–1.9%	39	20	29	59
2–2.9%	27	14	20	79
3–4.9%	16	8	12	90
5–9.9%	6	3	4	95
>10%	7	4	5	100
Total	135	70	100	
Missing	System	57	30	
Total		192	100	

low in comparison to the most active European countries in this field, such as Ireland and Switzerland. Estonian organisations also use pay increments more than organisations in any other European country, which could be the consequence of a rapid economic development from relatively low starting point.

Estonian organisations spend a significantly bigger share of their wage bill on training and development than Slovenian ones (Table 11.14). In this respect Estonia compares favourable with the EU average. This could be linked to the wage level, which is lower in Estonia than in Slovenia. However, a more important factor seems to be the speed of economic restructuring, which is higher in Estonia and requires the labour market to be adjusted accordingly.

A third explanation may lie in the fact that Slovenian organisations often use their employees as trainers, which may keep the cost of training down. In spite of the differences between the countries their common characteristic is that their organisations invest in HRs far less than those in some other European countries such as France.

More days per year are spent on training in Estonian than in Slovenian organisations. This applies especially to Estonian managers and clerical workers, who spend

Table 11.15 Number of training days received by staff categories

	Slovenia	Estonia
Days on training		
Management		
N	167	50
Days	7	8
Professional/technical		
N	168	53
Days	6	7
Clerical/administrative		
N	160	41
Days	3	6
Manual		
N	145	40
Days	2	3

nearly as long on training as their counterparts in Bulgaria and Spain. A worrying figure is the number of days of training recorded for manual workers in Slovenian organisations, which is as low as in Germany and Switzerland where the workforce is already well trained. Managerial employees in both countries receive on average more days training that the average across the EU which stands at 5.7 (Table 11.15).

Table 11.16 Offering merit/performance-related pay for different categories of employees

Yes	Slovenia	Estonia
Merit/performance related pay		
Management		
N	117	24
%	61	35
Professional/technical		
N	135	34
%	70	50
Clerical/administrative		
N	115	21
%	60	31
Manual		
N	119	20
%	62	29

Table 11.17 The change of influence of trade unions on the organisation during the last 3 years

	Slovenia	Estonia
Increased		
N	40	5
%	21	8
Decreased		
N	21	5
%	11	8

REWARDS AND PERFORMANCE MANAGEMENT

Merit- or performance-related pay schemes have been much more widely used in Slovenian than in Estonian organisations for all categories of employee. This could be explained by the fact that performance appraisal systems are more common in Slovenia, which depend in turn on adequate professional support and can be developed and introduced over a longer period. In Slovenian organisations performance appraisal is used for management in 81%, for professionals and technicians in 82%, for clerical workers in 76% and for manual workers in 83% of organisations. The corresponding percentages for Estonia are 56, 65, 65 and 55. However, when it is used in Estonian organisations the appraisal depends less on superiors than in Slovenia and more on employees, subordinates, peers and customers. Appraisal systems in Estonia tend more towards the 360° approach than in Slovenia and are therefore more difficult to develop, implement and maintain. Its results in Estonian organisations are also more widely used, for example, for training needs analysis and work planning rather than for pay and promotion as in Slovenian ones.

In respect of their use of merit- and performance-related pay Estonian organisations are close to the Scandinavian tradition, where it is seldom used for any category of employees. On the other hand, Slovenian organisations resemble continental European ones, such as in Belgium, France, the Czech Republic and Austria. Underlying this contrast one could find perhaps the emphasis on teamwork and team achievement in the first group of countries and the emphasis on individual work and achievement in the second group. It is interesting to observe that Slovenian and Czech organisations use merit- or performance-related pay for manual workers much more than any other European country (Table 11.16).

EMPLOYEE RELATIONS

Trade unions in Slovenia are well organised and strong compared to the Estonian ones. As Table 11.17 shows, their strength has increased dramatically in the last 3 years, much more than in Estonia. The two countries belong to the opposite extremes of European countries: Slovenia to the group where trade union influence has increased most, such as Norway, France and Belgium, and Estonia to the group where it has increased least, such as Italy, Finland and the Czech Republic. However, the involvement of professionals, technicians and clerical workers in decision-making in the organisations of both countries provides a somewhat different picture (see Table 11.18). They seem to play a much more important role in all aspects of Estonian organisations than in Slovenian organisations. In Slovenia clerical workers especially are consulted less than anywhere else – even less than in Italy, Turkey or Israel. One might say that Slovenian organisations practise representative democracy, while in Estonian direct democracy is being used. This corresponds with the more pronounced HRM orientation of Estonian organisations.

This difference is confirmed by the data on how employees communicate their views to management. In Estonia the use of team briefings, immediate superiors and regular workforce meetings has increased most

Table 11.18 Employee categories formally briefed about the issues listed

	Slovenia	Estonia
Strategy		
Management		
N	178	63
%	93	93
Professional/technical		
N	88	41
%	46	60
Clerical		
N	10	24
%	5	35
Financial performance		
Management		
N	173	65
%	90	97
Professional/technical		
N	82	39
%	43	57
Clerical		
N	29	22
%	15	32
Organisation of work		
Management		
N	173	64
%	90	94
Professional/technical		
N	129	58
%	67	85
Clerical		
N	74	50
%	39	74

Table 11.19 Approximate proportion of workforce on part-time and temporary/casual work arrangements

	Slovenia	Estonia
Part-time		
<1%		
N	66	14
%	36	23
1–5%		
N	41	17
%	22	27
6–10%		
N	2	7
%	1	11
11–20%		
N	1	2
%	1	3
>20%		
N	3	4
%	2	7
Temporary/casual		
<1%		
N	67	13
%	38	22
1–5%		
N	44	4
%	25	7
6–10%		
N	8	3
%	5	5
11–20%		
N	2	
%	1	
>20%		
N	2	
%	1	

in the last 3 years. In Slovenia the biggest increases are reported for trade unions and workers' councils, senior mangers and attitude surveys. A coalition between management and workers' representatives seems to exist in Slovenian organisations, while in Estonian communication seems to be less structured and to be maintained by direct communication with various groups of workers. Because of the strong trade unions decisions on basic pay are normally made more centrally in Slovenia than in Estonia. This applies to the regional dimension as well as the organisational hierarchies (Table 11.18).

FLEXIBLE PATTERNS OF WORK

In terms of flexible working the two countries display quite different patterns. While in Estonia part-time is more often used for bigger percentages of employees, in Slovenia temporary and casual work takes this place. With respect to part-time Estonia demonstrates its north European and Slovenia its south European character. Neither of these forms of flexibility is as widely used as in many other European countries, however. It should be noticed also that in the last 3 years flexible work arrangements in general have expanded much more in Slovenia than in Estonia. In Estonia a number of flexible forms have been reduced rather than expanded. The exceptions are some of the newer forms of flexibility, such as flexi-time, fixed-term contracts, subcontracting/outsourcing, home-based work and tele-working, which in both countries are becoming more common. The first three have expanded more in Slovenia and the last two in Estonia (Table 11.19).

HRM IN ACTION

CASE STUDY 1: AS NORMA IN ESTONIA

The AS Norma group specialises in the manufacturing and sale of safety systems and components for cars, and the related research and development. The technologies used include metal processing, plastic moulding and galvanisation. At the end of 2000 the group employed 1049 people, including 836 in AS Norma itself. The shares of AS Norma are quoted on the main list of companies of the Tallinn Stock Exchange. AS Norma shares are also traded in on the stock exchanges of Frankfurt, Berlin, Munich and Helsinki.

History

The history of AS Norma dates back to the nineteenth century, when in 1884 an innovative way of packing fish in tins was started in Tallinn. The company has operated under the name of Norma since 1932.

The Republic of Estonia was occupied by the USSR in 1940 and the Soviet régime nationalised the country's entire industry.

In 1946 Norma employed 46 people. A new era in the company's history started in 1957, when it became the first factory in the Soviet Union to manufacture electric torches. In 1960 the company began making electro-mechanical toys. By the end of 1960 it employed 804 workers and a personnel department was established.

In the 1960s Norma introduced the technology for processing plastic materials. The company developed a new range of electrical and mechanical toys and by 1966 toys accounted for 62% of the total sales of the company. The company distributed its toys and torches all over the Soviet Union and in some western countries as well. By 1970 the company was employing 2100 people.

The manufacturing capability, the corporate structure and the skilled engineering and technical staff which had been acquired in the 1960s proved a good foundation for further development. Whereas the car manufacturing in all the developed countries increased rapidly, the growing number of traffic accidents called for the protection of drivers and passengers. Norma started to prepare for the development and mass production of a local unpatented type of car safety belt.

In December 1973 Norma launched its first batch of 6200 safety belts. This was followed by extensive growth and by 1974 the company was producing 440,000 belts per year. By the end of 1970s the company had introduced 23 different models and versions of safety belt and acquired the right to use the symbol "E" (Europe) awarded by international testing centres. By 1980 the company had made 16 million belts. By that time the company employed over 2500 workers and safety belts accounted for 72% of the total sales of the company. The company co-operated continuously with the car manufacturers at both local and international level.

In 1989 the process of *perestroika* began in the Soviet Union, and with the disintegration of the USSR the country found itself facing serious economic difficulties. There were problems with the supply of materials, shortage of cash, inflation and so on. State control prevented the flexible development of the company and it had to be restructured in line with the principles of the market economy. For this purpose the company opted for a "people's enterprise", which was the only suitable type of a company allowed by the law. In effect the state-owned company was taken over on a lease. Now the state was no longer responsible for the company's operations. The highest decision-making body was the Council of Representatives of the People's Enterprise, which also elected the day-to-day management. In 1991 the new type of a company employed 2938 people and it continued with this structure until 1994.

From the point of view of the development of the company, the formation of the people's enterprise proved a very positive step. It helped to weather the serious recession, allowed independence in decision-making and enabled the company to restructure in accordance with the principles of the market economy with minimum of loss. The company built up a homogeneous marketing service and tried to maintain and secure its positions in the eastern markets while also looking for opportunities to expand westwards. With the Russian authorities imposing double tariffs on Estonian imports, the company had to use sophisticated barter schemes when settling accounts with its eastern partners.

At about the same time Norma also started collaborating with a subsidiary of General Motors, Saab Automobile AB. Norma began supplying the company with plastic and metal car components. This was an essential move in the acquisition of basic expertise and in working with western car manufacturers. This experience demonstrated how much is needed to be done to improve the company's quality systems, efficiency and employee re-training so as to meet current standards in the industry.

Norma started to reconstruct its production units into achievement units. The first step was to establish a unified quality service (preparatory work was begun to certify Norma according to ISO standards) and a Department of Research and Development. All this was necessary if Norma was to become an equal partner with the western car industry to break into the western markets.

In 1994 the company's "people's enterprise" status began to hinder its further development. To gain a foothold in the international market, it had to change its legal status. So People's Enterprise Norma became a private limited company.

In 1994 the manufacture of safety belts accounted for 90% of total output. There were 94 different modifications of safety belts which all met European standards. Norma also achieved its first international recognition: the award of Supplier of the Year by GM for co-operation with Saab. In the same year Saab carried out the first quality audit in Norma, which was done in accordance with ISO standards.

In 1995 several production units became independent subsidiaries and many were closed down. Norma also established some joint-stock companies with its western partners. In 1996 the Articles of Association were harmonised with the Business Law. The former management (major shareholders) resigned from operational activities and started to represent the interests of shareholders on the board of the company. The shareholders elected a board of six members. AS Norma was re-formed as the AS Norma Group which started to function as a holding company. In 1996 the company began co-operation with an international certification firm Det Norske Veritas (DNV), in order to implement a quality system ISO 9000. From 5 August 1996 the shares of AS Norma have been quoted on the free-market list of the Tallinn Stock Exchange.

In 1999 there was a significant change in the composition of the shareholders. The majority shareholder AS Norma Group sold its 51% holding to a strategic investor Autoliv AB. This opened up new opportunities for Norma in securing a place in the future global car industry market.

AS Norma's net sales in the year 2000 were EEK 632.6 million, and net profit amounted for EEK 157.5 million. Exports made up 90% of the group's sales, divided as to 69% in the Russian market and 31% in the western market.

The development of personnel management

The Soviet period

In 1957 Norma employed the first specialist whose responsibility was to co-ordinate personnel work and the job title was commandant-manager. By 1960 the number of employees had increased to over 800 and there was a corresponding need for a centralised and systematic personnel management. The result was the formation of the Staff Department, which was reported directly to the General Director of the company. In 1975 the Staff Department became the Department of Staff and Technical Training. In the years 1960–1980 the number of employees in the Staff Department varied from four to five in addition to the Head of the Department. The main functions of personnel work in the Soviet era were:

1. training staff and upgrading their qualifications;
2. monitoring work discipline;
3. managing staff turnover;
4. planning the social development of the staff;
5. administering labour contracts and dismissal procedures;
6. ideological work; and
7. undertaking job satisfaction surveys.

The duties of the Staff Department did not involve the issues of payment.

The Staff Department dealt with the planning of specialist labour needs. Training was the responsibility of unit managers and special instructors, who did it in addition to their own work. Employees were trained either on-site or outside the company. On-site training was based on methodologies prescribed by the state or prepared by the Staff Department or instructors.

When the company started making safety belts in 1973, it faced a significant need for qualified staff. Many specialisms had to be trained for on-site, and to tackle the problem study rooms were set up in the production units.

The Staff Department kept records of work discipline, noting any violations committed by employees – absenteeism, breaches of public order, alcoholism, etc. Such violations were taken into account in determining employees' career advancement and wages.

In the 1970s staff turnover was relatively high – for example, in 1971, 499 employees left the company. The main reason for leaving was given as dissatisfaction with working conditions, living standards and wages. Norma's management understood the growing complexity of dealing with staff. The progress of science and technology involved changes not only in manufacturing techniques. There were also changes in the role played by people in the production process. The main emphasis was laid on the handling of new equipment and the awareness of staff. Unskilled manual work lost its primary status. In 1972 the company devised its first 3-year plan for social development, which involved technical progress, productivity and the development of employees' mental and physical well-being. The plan was based on a methodology devised by the Laboratory of the Scientific Organization of Work at the Bureau of Projecting and Technology of the Ministry of Local Industry of the ESSR. This methodology was well suited to Norma's needs. The main basis for the plan was a comprehensive questionnaire, which involved all units and all categories of employees. The questionnaire was designed to ascertain the employees' opinions about working conditions, wages and welfare. In the Soviet period this was a remarkably progressive move.

One part of the social development plan dealt with financial incentives and employee motivation, another with training, welfare, working conditions and holidays. During the Soviet period the wages of workers and salaries of engineering/technical staff were divided into several categories. To change them was a very complicated business – if not impossible. As the company expanded its production capacity, so it earned more money and enjoyed greater financial support from the ministry. The Department of Scientific Organization of Work and Wages devised a new bonus system, which enabled an extra bonus to be paid for meeting the prescribed work norms and quality standards. Bonuses were also paid for rationalisation, implementing new technology and saving.

The complex measures for improving working conditions and implementing new technologies proved fruitful. By 1980 the number of employees at Norma had reached 3112 (an increase of 980 as compared to 1971). Turnover had increased from 17.7 million roubles in 1972 to 82.2 million roubles in 1980. Productivity per person had tripled. There were 180 employees with higher education and 1320 with secondary or secondary-technical education. At the same time labour turnover had improved as well. In 1980 the number of employees who left the company voluntarily was 385.

As we have seen, part of the plan of social development involved the improvement of working conditions, the employee welfare and the organisation of holidays. The active participation of Norma's trade union should be noted here. This part of the plan dealt with building canteens, opening a medical dispensary, improving labour protection and improving the working conditions and holiday options (sanatoria, children's summer camps, etc.) of auxiliary staff. The response to the questionnaire revealed a growing satisfaction among employees with working conditions, training opportunities and wages. The main reasons for leaving the company were related to the welfare and living conditions of the employees.

We should not overlook the ideological work carried out with workers in a Soviet enterprise by Komsomol and other Communist party organisations, as well as several staff-related reports to ministries and party organisations. Part of this huge bureaucratic reporting was undertaken by the Staff Department. Luckily management at Norma in the Soviet era was dominated by economics rather than political ideology.

Despite the complicated economic and social situation at the end of the 1980s and the beginning of the 1990s – including the disintegration of the USSR and severe inflation – Norma continued training its employees in the light of their needs as well as the company's. The main emphasis was on the basics of contemporary economics, management, languages and computer skills.

In 1990, when the Soviet Union was disintegrating and state regulation of wages had disappeared, Norma started calculating wages on the basis of full-time work. The system of additional bonuses was terminated. All unit managers were given a budget for motivating employees to complete additional tasks. Payments were made on the order of the unit manager. Once a quarter all employees started to receive what was called a share profit, which varied with length of service and wages for the period. Of course the whole scheme depended on the financial performance of the company. Implementing the new payment system and labour contracts was the task of the Wage, Staff and Training Department.

The period of the Republic of Estonia

In 1991 the company became a "people's enterprise" and started to adapt its management structure to the demands of the market economy and contemporary management style. The total number of employees at that period was 2938. In 1991 the Staff and Training Department was renamed Personnel Department. For a short period (1991–1993) the Personnel Department and the Wage Department were both responsible to the Administrative Manager, but still as independent departments.

In 1994 the company created an HR Department, which was responsible to the General Director who appointed the Personnel Manager. The existing Personnel and Wage Departments (nine people in all) became part of the new HR Department. The prime duty of the HR Department was to develop a personnel policy which would support the company in the achievement of its strategic goals.

Personnel policy

In Norma personnel policy is divided into the following elements: wage policy and motivation; recruitment, development and training; the organisation of holidays. The HR Department began to rationalise wage policy through a comprehensive job appraisal, which was carried out by unit managers and personnel specialists. They used the Hay method, which was quite popular in the west.

A second stage of the appraisal was designed to evaluate the suitability of personnel to their jobs. Every employee was appraised by his or her direct manager. The next step was to compile job descriptions, which were written by unit managers and specialists.

After this preliminary work the company introduced a new wage system for office staff in 1995. It was based on a well-established methodology called *job-scales*. There are nine wage bands, according to the value of the work, and within each wage band five different levels of knowledge, skills and experience.

The new wage system proved efficient, but was not motivating enough. The efficiency of company operations had increased, but in line with the intensity of the work. By way of comparison: the number of employees in Norma in 1993 was 2099, which had fallen to 1580 people (1200 of them in the parent company) by the end of 1995.

The main motivational tool was a single bonus from the unit manager's dedicated budget. The challenge was to increase the interest of employees in the company's economic results while at the same time improving the efficiency of management and work. In 1996 Norma introduced management by results, which involved measuring the results of subdivisions. In 1997 the company organised a large scale on-site training session for managers on the management by results system. The next step was to develop plans for the subdivisions. Every employee had his or her own plan of achievement, which was drawn up during an interview with the division manager. The plans included measurable goals, which were appraised at the end of a fixed period.

During the second stage the Personnel Department developed a formula for relating wages to results. The payment or non-payment of the wage was to depend on the economic performance of the company and thus the contribution of all its employees. At the end of each quarter the board of the company decided on the rate of the wage by result as a percentage (the percentage of the division payment fund), which was the maximum to be used in the company. The rate for each subdivision depended on its own results. The manager of the subdivision allocated the wages of the subordinates. The salary of the subdivision manager was fixed by his or her direct superior. This system significantly improved employee motivation and the willingness to appraise the quality of work and analyse mistakes. The essence of Norma's personnel policy, as expressed in the second half of 1997, is as follows: *The aim of AS Norma's personnel policy is to find and retain the best specialists in their field, and sustain high motivation by competitive wage and personnel development programmes throughout the organisation.*

Another important part of personnel policy was development and training. At the same time as working out a new wage policy, Norma also started to design a new training policy. The goal of personnel policy at corporate level is to ensure, in all the subdivisions of AS Norma, the skills, qualifications, knowledge and motivation necessary to maintain the company's competitive advantage and continuous development.

The training activity is managed and co-ordinated by the Training Manager of the HR Department. The main responsibility for training lies with the subdivision managers. Training requirements are determined once a year, when the annual budget is discussed and the training budget is confirmed at the end of the year according to the funds available. One factor is the company's training capacity and the budget earmarked. Another is the training requirement identified by the subdivision managers in the process of drawing up the budget, based on the goals of the divisions and the specific needs of employees. The role of the HR Department is to reconcile these two elements and draw up the final training plan and budget. Every half-year there is an interim report on the implementation and achievements of the training programme. The companies providing the training are also assessed, on the basis of the results of the training.

Training and development also involve consulting with employees to ascertain their training needs; the development of an individual (supporting the studies of young people, study loans, etc.); exploring career opportunities (requirements) for the more talented employees; interviews with employees; questionnaires; etc.

The measures in place have improved both work quality and employee satisfaction and the company has rid itself of surplus staff. Labour turnover has also fallen significantly from 13% in 1997 to 4% in 1999. At the end of 1998 Norma employed 1386 people. The efficiency of the Personnel Department has also increased: in 1999 the HR Department employed five people compared with the earlier nine.

The company has changed the basis of its recruitment. Personnel selection in Norma is a process that involves three parties – the particular subdivision (or field), the Personnel Department and the applicant for the job. The task of the Personnel Department is to collect relevant information and ascertain the requirements of the subdivision and the applicants, i.e. to co-ordinate and systematise both supply and demand. To this end the company uses recruitment agencies, advertising and also the internal potential of the company itself. Competitions are organised to fill vacancies. The final decision about someone's transfer or recruitment lies in the hands of a subdivision manager or the director of the field of activity concerned.

Norma considers it essential to work with young people. It has become a tradition for the staff of the Personnel Department and the managers of subdivisions to attend the annual personnel fair "The Key to the Future". They try to determine the job expectations of young specialists and their suitability for the future requirements of the company. All job applicants are registered in the database of the company's HR Department. Another aspect of co-operation is to offer the university students the chance to undertake their internship with the company.

In 1999 the majority shareholding in the company was acquired by a strategic investor Autoliv AB and the assembly lines were transferred to Estonia. The company then began using placement tests when creating new jobs and recruiting new personnel. Some of the new employees are trained at the Swedish facilities. AS Norma carries out a labour market survey twice a year so as to be aware of the situation in the industrial market. The results of the survey are built into the payment system.

Holidays and pay are areas where the Trade Union of Norma (a member of the Union of Estonian Metalworkers) also plays an active role. Every year AS Norma and the trade union negotiate a contract covering working conditions and pay which sets out the exact arrangements for pay and holidays for the coming year. This contract also outlines the catering and welfare requirements of the employees.

In September 2001, AS Norma employed 1072 people. The majority (30%) are between 40 and 60 years of age. Thirty-one per cent have a higher or secondary-technical education. More than 50% of the employees have been with the company for more than 5 years. It is clear that the economic success of the company over last few years is due not only to its modern equipment and contemporary working methods, but also to its balanced and efficient personnel policy. Since 1994 the productivity of the average employee has increased by a factor of 2.8.

Among the company's traditions are: celebrating Christmas by organising a Christmas dinner; theatre visits; a summer camp for the children of employees; a Christmas bonus; a picnic in summer and a festive reception for employees with over 25 years of service.

CASE STUDY 2: THE MERCATOR GROUP IN SLOVENIA

Composed by Jana Lutovac Lah

The company

The Mercator Group is one of the biggest and most successful businesses in south-east Europe, already more than 50 years old. It is the leading trading chain in the Slovene market, the third largest foodstuffs dealer in the Croatian market and a prominent trader in the market of Bosnia and Herzegovina. It was during the period 1995–1998 that the changes in internal organisation, restructuring and adjustment to European models of trade organisation, as well as the adaptation to European financial, spatial and service standards occurred as part of the company's pursuit of its aim to maintain and strengthen what was the largest market share in the Slovene trade. Today in Slovenia 10 million customers make a purchase in one of Mercator's shops every month. It is Mercator's ambition to become one of the 20 largest trading companies in the world by 2003.

Mercator's main activity is trade. However, it is also engaged in industry, agriculture, service activities and restaurant and hotel management.

Mercator bases its business philosophy, strategy and targets on "the four S's": Satisfaction of the client (customer), Satisfaction of the employee (HRs), Satisfaction of the owners (shareholders) and Satisfaction of the business partners (suppliers and others).

The nature of the Mercator Group is represented by the following values:

- mutual trust and teamwork;
- ethical and moral values in reciprocal relationships;
- encouragement of creativity and managerial incentives for employees;
- continuous personal development of employees;
- the satisfied customer is the focus of all operations; the customer's requirements are continuously observed and the offer adjusted.

Among the company's strategic aims are ensuring the social security of its employees and care for the environment.

The mercator group in figures

Number of employees as at 31 January 2001: 13,692
Educational status of workforce:
- ISCED 2   14%
- ISCED 3, 4   80%
- ISCED 5, 6   6%

Market share in Slovenia:
- 1997   15%
- 2001   37% (plus 5% by franchise units)

Breakdown of products by origin:
- Home market   76% domestic goods
                       24% imported goods
- The new markets   40% Slovene products
                       40% local suppliers
                       20% imported goods

Net income sales in 2001: EUR 1275.3 million

Ownership of Mercator Group as at 31 December 2001:
- Natural persons   29%
- Legal persons   28%
- Kapitalska družba, d.d. (Capital Company)   17%
  - The Slovene compensation company   13%
  - Authorised investment companies   11%

HRM involvement in the management of the company

In the area of HRM the company's top management co-operates closely with the relevant specialists. All proposals made by the specialists regarding the development and planning of HR management are submitted for approval to the four-member board. In this way, for instance, projects such as the annual performance appraisal interview, employee satisfaction measurement, measurement of organisational climate and programmes for in-company training were endorsed by the board.

Basic HR strategy is to develop an organisational culture that will increase employee satisfaction. Among the activities designed to support this strategy are:

- Promoting the values, strategic aims and mission of the Mercator Group through education and training.
- Encouraging a positive management style that enables every employee to apply his or her knowledge, experience, skills and creativity at work, and at the same time to contribute to an atmosphere conducive to the achievement of targets on time and to a high standard of quality.
- Holding all managers accountable for the professional and personal career development of their employees, as well as providing for the social security of employees in accordance with their contribution to the achievement of the agreed targets.
- Strengthening the individual and collective motivation of employees through non-material incentives (praise and rewards, annual appraisal interviews, career schemes, formation of inter-functional teams, support for employee education, qualifications and knowledge transfers, and public recognition of individuals and teams for outstanding achievement).
- Encouraging trust and teamwork, mutual assistance and moral and ethical values in reciprocal relationships.
- Promoting the commitment of employees to:
  - mobility as regards work location locally and internationally;
  - project planning and task completion;
  - responsibility for their own development planning while respecting the company's interests;
  - achieving a higher level of education so as to maintain long-term professional and working competitiveness and improved social security.
- Continuous functional training and education of employees, according to the requirements of the retail trade, and the creation and maintenance of internal networks of trainers, mentors and lecturers for retail sales training.

Employee relations at Mercator are governed by the company's Collective Agreement. The management regards this as quite successful, in that all company–employee relations have been conducted within the legal framework. The agreement is re-negotiated every year, and there has been no serious conflict.

Recruting and retaining employees

At the end of each calendar year the HR sector distributes to all the directors and trading companies in the Mercator Group a questionnaire designed to determine the need for new employees (probationers, apprentices, etc.), as well as for training and education (scholarships for youth, education, functional training and qualification of employees). The plans are not fixed and cover all categories from retail sales staff to highly qualified employees.

Workers are recruited in four main ways:

1. Informal job applications (the company receives up to 400 applications for jobs every year, 50 of them from highly educated people).
2. Employment agency (for scholarship-holders).
3. A scholarship-holders base.
4. Mercator's senior directors' recommendations.

The board of management decides all clerical appointments that require ISCED 3 education level or above, following proposals from the HRM department and managers of the units that employ new employees. Manual workers are recruited by the HR officers and the managers of retail departments.

There is a steady turnover of shop assistants, where, because of the hours worked, the quality of life is gradually becoming worse. However, turnover among specialist staff is very low (in an average year only two or three young specialists leave the company).

Motivational techniques used to retain employees include: annual appraisal interviews, the possibility of additional education and qualifications, employee satisfaction measurement, sports and games involving teams from companies in the Mercator Group (culminating in an event called "the Mercatoriad"), supplementary pension schemes, medical check-ups and prizes for business achievement awarded two or three times a year.

In Mercator salaries are made up of six components:

- fixed salary;
- environmental factors (from 0% to 10%);
- other supplements (from −7% to +7%);
- promotion ladder (from 0% to 20% at the discretion of the board);
- success of business operations (from −15% to +15%);
- individual performance (from −15% to +15%).

Socially disadvantaged employees receive the company's social security benefit once a year, which represents 60% of the national average wage.

Employees consider Mercator to be an ethical and moral company fulfilling all its contractual obligations. They perceive a high correlation between their work efforts and their rewards. They claim that they can learn a great deal at Mercator, and that they are acquiring the most up-to-date knowledge. Of course, they are also motivated by the opportunities provided for training and education at work. The employees understand that only the best workers can be promoted, and that there is no possibility of promotion unless they attain a higher level of education. The importance of Mercator in the Slovene economy is another powerful tool of motivation: employees are proud to say they work at Mercator.

Training and education

Mercator's management are aware that employees welcome the opportunity to study and develop personally, as this reduces anxiety over their future employment prospects and increases their self-reliance. By helping employees to acquire qualifications and further education the company is enabling them to achieve a high level of professional and general knowledge, creativity and teamwork, to identify their personal aims in line with the company's development and to care for their personal growth and career development. At the same time engaging employees in the educational process helps the organisation to achieve strategically important goals such as the ability to adapt quickly to market changes, the capacity to make well-thought out business decisions and improved quality of work and services, as well as to increase employee satisfaction and motivation.

Thus for the year 2001 Mercator planned to educate and train 12,942 people. The actual number amounted to 17,497, or 135% of the planned number. In 2001, 16,180 employees were included in the processes of functional education and training, representing 122,907 training hours, or 9 hours per employee.

As well as functional training, which represents the most extensive and complex training activity, the following achievements were also recorded:

- 192 employees participated in educational programmes for working adults;
- 70 schoolboys/schoolgirls and students were awarded scholarships;
- 205 young people were taken into apprenticeship;
- 39 sector presentations were given to apprentices by managers or their closest colleagues, who also attended all the apprenticeship examinations – in their business units 75 apprentices completed their learning practice at the conclusion of their apprenticeship agreements;
- 775 training courses were organised for students of secondary-business schools, college students and scholarship-holders.

All functional education and training is evaluated on the basis of tests taken by the employees immediately at the end of the course.

Employee satisfaction and organisational climate

In 2001, the attitudes of Mercator's workforce were measured for the second successive year. Seven items were observed: satisfaction at work, sources of information, management style of immediate supervisor, the director's leadership style, trust in the CEO, trust in the board of directors, communications with immediate supervisor and corporate culture (attitude towards the company's business philosophy and priorities). The survey showed high levels of satisfaction with the internal working environment (nature of work, leadership, communications), and acceptance of organisational culture, which includes the values of long-term commitment, participation and development.

A positive organisational climate was also recorded in a nationwide research project carried out under the patronage of the Chamber of Economy of Slovenia. Mercator exceeded the Slovene average in almost every item measuring organisational climate, and also scored above the average for the trading companies group. The only exception was satisfaction with the work environment. The company's score for "Employees find the working hours suitable" was low, and that brought their total evaluation in this category to below the average. Accordingly, Mercator regards this issue as a serious challenge. It is fair to say, though, that the research was conducted only in those Mercator units that operate on Sundays.

The measurements of organisational climate indicate that there is still much to be done before Mercator can achieve the maximum score. The company has identified the following areas for possible improvement (percentage targets):

- management (31%);
- internal communicaton and information (31%);

- career development (33%);
- rewards (34%).

Mercator employees work in a positive organisational climate which, however, still offers scope for improvement. Being committed to excellence, the company is determined to identify the most appropriate ways to improve, for example by increasing employees' satisfaction with working hours. In spite of some deficiencies all the indicators score Mercator substantially higher than the national and trade averages.

CONCLUSIONS

Slovenia has quite a long tradition of professionalisation in the personnel and HR functions. By the late 1950s the first courses for personnel managers were already available. In the 1960s these courses were offered at post-secondary level (Kamušič, 1972). Today there are one bachelor-degree programme of 4 years' duration and one master's degree programme of 2 years' duration publicly accredited for the education and training of HR managers. They are run by the Faculty of Social Sciences at Ljubljana University. HRM is also taught as a component of other programmes, such as economics, business administration and organisational studies. In 2001, the Slovenian Human Resources Management Association celebrated its 25th anniversary. The Association provides a forum for professionals in the field, with different professional backgrounds, such as law, psychology, sociology, organisational studies, economics and business administration.

In Estonia personnel management did not exist during the Soviet occupation and represents a new field. After independence at the beginning of the 1990s, three entrepreneurial psychologists established an HRM association called PARE and started to provide a 1-year basic training in HRM. The first course started in 1993 and proved very popular. In the second half of the 1990s several universities and business schools began to offer diploma and degree programmes in HRM. In 2001 the Estonian Business School, in co-operation with PARE, started the Executive MBA programme in HRM for HR managers of Estonian companies.

Early and extensive professionalisation of HRM in Slovenia has contributed to its favourable status in the business world and also to its involvement in the preparation and implementation of HRM strategy. This involvement is far above the Estonian level and even above the EU average. In Slovenian organisations the person responsible for HR is involved in business strategy development from the outset in much more often than in Estonian ones.

The emphasis on HR professionals in Slovenia explains why they take more responsibility than line managers for recruitment and selection as well as for training and development. In Estonia the situation is the opposite. The result of HR professionalisation in Slovenia could also be more frequent monitoring of training effectiveness as well as more widespread use of attitude surveys and performance appraisal for all the main groups of employees than in Estonia. More Slovenian than Estonian organisations have introduced performance-related pay for all groups of employees.

Professionalisation of HR may have disadvantages also. It is very likely that early professionalisation of HRM in Slovenia contributed to its conservative orientation. The data could indicate that in Slovenian organisations it is traditional personnel management that prevails rather than modern HRM. The situation in Estonia could be interpreted as the opposite. The difference lies primarily in the role of professionals on one hand and the role of line managers on the other (Dessler, 1988). As already mentioned, responsibility for recruitment, selection and training and development in Estonian organisations is conferred on line managers rather than on the HR department. The responsibility of Estonian line managers has increased in the last 3 years more than the responsibility of their Slovenian counterparts in most management fields.

Other data support the thesis of the modern orientation of Estonian HRM. In more Estonian organisations a greater variety of recruitment and selection methods is used than in Slovenian ones. Performance in Estonian organisations is appraised not only by superiors but in many organisations by employees (43%), subordinates (12%) and peers (15%) as well. This is seldom the case in Slovenian organisations, where the respective percentages are 8, 2 and 5. It seems that Slovenian managers have not understood the importance of involving all "internal customers" in their business.

Performance appraisal in Estonian organisations is not used only for individual performance-related pay (62%) and promotion purposes (53%), as is most frequently the case in Slovenia, where the percentages are 77 and 61. It is also used more often than in Slovenian organisations for the analysis of individual (68%) and organisational (43%) training needs and for the improvement of the organisation of work (53%). The corresponding percentages for Slovenia are 34, 34 and 27.

One could conclude that HRM in Slovenia is more professionalised and influential, and enjoys a higher status in organisations, than in Estonia. However, it is also more personnel-function oriented. On the other hand, Estonian HRM is younger and weaker, with a lower status in organisations. People responsible for HR more often advise on, and implement, business strategy than contribute to its formulation. The situation in Slovenia is the reverse. However, Estonian HRM seems to be more innovative and more authentic in its transformation from personnel management to HRM.

One possible explanation of the differences between the two countries is the early formation and professionalisation of Slovenian personnel management, which represent an obstacle to any rapid adaptation to modern needs. This difficulty in Estonia was avoided because of the later development and professionalisation of HRM, which was due partly to the fact that only a few big organisations can afford specialist HRM departments. Another explanation might be that it is Slovenia's industrial relations structure, with its strong trade unions, which prevents the speedy development of HRM (Mayrhofer et al., 2000).

Estonia needed – and made – a more radical break with the past than Slovenia. In the same way more profound and quicker changes have been introduced in the HRM field also. Slovenia has taken time for consideration, with the result that change has been slower and perhaps better controlled. One sign of this difference is the change in forms of work over the last 3 years. In practically all the cases where the use of flexible forms

of work grew significantly, the increase was higher in Slovenia than in Estonia. The only important exceptions were tele-working and shorter working hours. Unlike Estonia, Slovenia has only gradually liberalised its labour market and has allowed for flexible forms of work and employment. Now it is trying to catch up with other countries. Even so, the increases in most of flexible forms of work in Slovenia were smaller than the EU average. Slovenia seems to be lagging behind, especially with more recently expanding forms of work, such as tele-working, home-based work and annual hours contracts. It can be observed also that in Estonia the use of some forms of flexibility, such as weekend work, shift work, overtime, annual hours contracts, part-time work, job sharing and temporary work has decreased. Experience with these novelties has perhaps not been as good as expected. In Slovenia only the use of annual hours contracts fell in more organisations than it increased in.

The differences in the changes in flexible working practices between Estonia and Slovenia could be explained also by other factors. Big rises in tele-working in Estonia could be partly explained by widespread computer networks and personal computer ownership. We can also observe that in Estonia the most common flexible form of work is part-time. The most frequently used flexible form of work in Slovenia is temporary work. The difference could be ascribed to the institutional arrangements. In Europe part-time is more frequently used in the north and west, while temporary work is widespread in countries with specific institutional arrangements, such as Spain, Belgium and Israel.

Part of the explanation for the differences in flexibility may lie in the smaller size, and greater service orientation, of organisations in Estonia, as well as in the fact that the Estonian population is concentrated in the cities.

Greater labour market flexibility in Estonia is indicated also by the use of various methods of recruitment and retention. In Estonian organisations especially recruitment from abroad, increased pay and benefits and marketing of the organisation's image are more frequently used than in Slovenian ones. Estonian organ-isations also spend significantly more on training than their Slovenian counterparts. The difference is somewhat smaller in case of re-training. All these differences exist in spite of higher unemployment in Estonia.

Clear differences between the two countries may be observed with respect to centralisation and management-focused HRM. In Slovenia basic pay for all groups of employees except management is determined on a national or industry-wide level for more than 70% of organisations. This happens in the case of management in one-third of organisations. In Estonia for no one group of employees is basic pay determined nationally or industry-wide in more than 17% of organisations. Managers are not an exception. For the rest of Slovenian organisations, about one-third, basic pay is determined at company or division level. The exceptions again are managers, whose pay in 62% of organisations is individually determined. This happens in the case of professionals and technicians only in 23% of organisations. In Estonia basic pay is determined in more than half of organisations for all groups of employees at company or division level. However, in many cases it is determined also at establishment or site level, which is seldom the case in Slovenia, or individually. It is interesting to note that individually determined basic pay is more often used in Estonia than in Slovenia. The exceptions are managers. In Estonia basic pay is determined individually more often for clerical and administrative workers (75%) than for managers (41%). This approach is often used also for professionals and technicians (34%) and manual workers (21%). The respective percentages for Slovenian organisations are 23 and 6 only.

One plausible explanation for these differences is that in Slovenia there are quite strong nationally organised unions. There is a centralised bargaining process resulting in nation-wide agreements including the payment system. Even if there is merit pay or variable pay based on performance appraisal it is based on the central regulations. Only managers are exempt from this arrangement. In Estonia the situation is very different. Because the unions are weaker, organisations are free to determine their own payment systems, including delegation of this responsibility to their subsidiaries. Nevertheless, it is worth remarking that management here is on an equal footing with the other groups of employees, which is not the case in Slovenia.

The use of performance appraisal in both countries underlines the main differences. In Slovenia it is predominantly a management responsibility, while in Estonia other groups of employees play a significant part. The practice of performance appraisal in Estonia may be close to the 360° model. In Slovenia performance appraisal is primarily used for payment and promotion purposes. In Estonia it is used more frequently for determining training needs than for payment. It is also more frequently used than in Slovenia also for the determining organisational training needs and for improving work organisation. These differences reflect the hierarchical nature of Slovenian organisations, where HRM is more management focused and less concerned with wider organisational issues.

This story could be continued indefinitely. In both countries management is consulted most frequently over organisational strategy, financial performance and the organisation of work. However, there are differences in roles played by professionals and particularly clerical workers, who are much more commonly consulted in Estonian than in Slovenian organisations. Slovenian organisations are less participatory than Estonian and do not use HRs at the same extent. In this respect Estonian organisations are much closer to those from the EU than Slovenia.

The flow of information from below to the top of organisations confirms this picture. In the last 3 years the flow of information to management in Slovenian organisations increased, particularly through trade union and works council representatives (34%) and through immediate superiors (27%), as well as directly (27%). In Estonian organisations the flow of information has increased primarily through team briefings (45%), and only next through immediate superiors (35%), but also through regular workforce meetings (27%). The percentages for Slovenian organisations are 22, 27 and 16. The importance of management hierarchy and indirect participation through trade unions in Slovenian organisations seems obvious, while in Estonian ones direct participation seems to be more significant.

These differences could be explained in various ways. One is the strength of trade unions in Slovenia and their weakness in Estonia. Slovenian trade unions are respected as a strong social partner not only at national level. Their influence extends down to the organisation, where it is respected by management. In the organisations a management–union coalition is acceptable to both partners. When trade unions control the employees, other forms of communication with them seem unnecessary to the management. Management has obviously not yet discovered the possibility of mobilising HRs by involving them directly in non-executive activities. Trade unions themselves are not interested in developing direct democracy either, because they fear losing their dominant representative function. This was clearly demonstrated during the debate over the new Labour Relations Law. Trade unions have refused other forms of workers' representation than their own. In the absence of trade unions, management in Estonia have had to develop other forms of communication with the employees. They appear to have adopted the HRs approach instead of the more traditional labour relations one.

Trade unions are by tradition rather hierarchical organisations. This explains the highly centralised decision-making on HR issues in Slovenia. It seems that the self-management system inherited by Slovenian organisations is regarded as applying to the past rather than the present. The self-management system, which was said to have promoted direct democracy in organisations, was in fact focused primarily on strategic issues. The main decision-making body was the workers' council, which represented various groups of employees. Direct involvement of employees in tackling workplace issues was in fact very limited. It could be said that the management structures bequeathed by history have been preserved. While workers' councils have been abolished or have become weak, trade unions have taken their place (Stanojević, 2000).

Part of the explanation for the less hierarchical, less management-focused, more participatory relations in Estonian organisations may perhaps lie in their profound restructuring and their small size. The Lutheran cultural background, as opposed to the Catholic one in Slovenia, could also have had an impact.

Overall, it seems that in Slovenia HRM is dominated by three parties: strong management and trade unions and rather traditionally oriented personnel management professionals. These players have been under less pressure from economic restructuring than their Estonian counterparts, or perhaps their coalition has proven a sufficient instrument for the maintenance of social peace and organisational effectiveness. Therefore they have been less inclined to innovation, especially decentralising HRM decision-making, greater involvement of employees in non-executive activities, employment flexibility and the new HRM practices. In Estonia trade unions are weaker or lacking. Therefore management, with the help of newly trained HRM professionals, is searching for new ways of communicating with employees and mobilising HRs. Estonian organisations are therefore more open to change and innovation in the HRM field.

Some of the differences between the two countries could be ascribed to the smaller size and more service-oriented stance of organisations in Estonia than in Slovenia. Their location in big cities in Estonia, as opposed to all over the country in Slovenia, and the cultural tradition of the two countries may also be factors.

Although different, the two countries seldom fall outside the range of the other European countries with respect to the observed HRM indicators recorded. Estonia comes closer to the north European countries with a Lutheran background and Slovenia to the central and south European countries with a Catholic background. Deviations from these groups of countries could be explained by the process of economic restructuring, which, to-date at least, seems to have had a greater effect on Estonia than on Slovenia.

TEACHING QUESTIONS

1. Describe personnel management in Slovenia and Estonia during the communist regime. Identify key similarities and differences?
2. Based on your reading, how would you say this historical heritage has influenced today's HRM in Slovenia and Estonia?
3. How has the different speed of change in the beginning of the 1990s influenced the HRM function in both countries?
4. In reviewing the Cranet data, how would you characterise the similarities between the countries?
5. How would you account for the differences in influence of trade unions in both countries?
6. How has the relative weakness of trade unions in Estonia influenced other aspects of HRM?

REFERENCES AND SOURCES

References

Atlas Slovenije (1996) *Atlas of Slovenia*. Mladinska knjiga: Ljubljana.

Bilten Banke Slovenije (2000) *Bulletin of The National Bank of Slovenia*. Ljubljana, December.

COST A13 Project; the group on unemployment; unpublished papers.

Dessler, G. (1988) *Personnel Management*. New Jersey: Prentice-Hall.

European Training Foundation (1998) *Vocational Education and Training in Central and Eastern Europe*. Key Indicators, Turin.

European Training Foundation (2000) *Employment and Labour Market in Slovenia*. Published by the National VET Observatory of Slovenia, Ljubljana.

Eurostat, Statistical Office of the European Communities (eds.) (1995, 1996) *Yearbooks and Labour Force Surveys*.

Investment Profile of Estonia (2001) EBRD Country Promotion Programme.

Kamušič, M. (1972) *Naloge vodilnih delavcev pri upravljanju kadrovske funkcije (The Tasks of Mangers in Personnel Management)*. Kranj: Moderna organiazacija, p. 605.

Mayrhofer, W., Brewster, C., Morley, M. and Gunnigle, P. (2000) Communication, consultation and the HRM debate. In: Brewster, C., Mayrhofer, W. and Morley, M. (eds.), *New Challenges for European Human Resource Management*. Basingstoke: Macmillan.

Stanojević, M. (2000) Slovenian Trade Unions – the birth of labour organizations in post-communism. In: Družboslovne razprave, *Journal of Social Science Studies*. University of Ljubljana and Slovenian Sociological Association, Vol. XVI, No. 32–33.

Stanojević, M. (2001) *Predstavljanje interesov zaposlenih in HRM: primerjave med Slovenijo, Veliko Britanijo, Nemčijo in Češko (Representation of Workers' Interests and HRM: comparisons between Slovenia, Great Britain, Germany and the Czech Republic)*. In: Kadrovski benchmarking (HRM benchmarking), Kadri (review of the Slovenian HRM Association).

Stanojević, M. and Vrhovec, P. (2001) *Industrial Conflict in Slovenia*. South-East European Review for Labour and Social Affairs, Vol. 4, No. 1.

Statistični letopis Republike Slovenije (Statistical Yearbook of the Republic of Slovenia). Ljubljana, 1992, 1993, 1994, 1995, 1996, 1997, 1998, 1999, 2000.

Statistični letopis Socialistične Republike Slovenije (Statistical Yearbook of the Socialist Republic of Slovenia). Ljubljana, 1986, 1987, 1988, 1989, 1990.

The Estonia page (WWW) http://www.einst.ee/, 4 May 2001.

Toomas Piliste, Research Fellow of Estonia (1999) *Working Life Barometer in the Baltic Countries*.

Zavod Republike Slovenije za zaposlovanje (2001) *Employment Service of Slovenia*. Letno poročilo 2000, Annual Report 2000, Ljubljana.

Sources for Slovenie Institutional Background

(1) Atlas Slovenije (1996) *Atlas of Slovenia*. Mladinska knjiga: Ljubljana.

(2) Bilten Banke Slovenije (2000) *Bulletin of The National Bank of Slovenia*. Ljubljana, December.

(3) COST A13 Project; the group on unemployment; unpublished papers.

(4) European Training Foundation (1998) *Vocational Education and Training in Central and Eastern Europe*. Key Indicators, Turin.

(5) European Training Foundation (2000) *Employment and Labour Market in Slovenia*. Published by the National VET Observatory of Slovenia, Ljubljana.

(6) Eurostat, Statistical Office of the European Communities (eds.) (1995, 1996). *Yearbooks and Labour Force Surveys*.

(7) Stanojević, M. (2000) Slovenian Trade Unions – the birth of labour organizations in post-communism. In: Družboslovne razprave, *Journal of Social Science Studies*. University of Ljubljana and Slovenian Sociological Association, Vol. XVI, No. 32–33.

(8) Stanojević, M. (2001) *Predstavljanje interesov zaposlenih in HRM: primerjave med Slovenijo, Veliko Britanijo, Nemčijo in Češko (Representation of Workers' Interests and HRM: comparisons between Slovenia, Great Britain, Germany and the Czech Republic)*. In: Kadrovski benchmarking (HRM benchmarking), Kadri (review of the Slovenian HRM Association).

(9) Stanojević, M. and Vrhovec, P. (2001) *Industrial Conflict in Slovenia*. South-East European Review for Labour and Social Affairs, Vol. 4, No. 1.

12

Turkey and Israel: HRM as a Reflection of Society

Amnon Caspi, Batia Ben-Hador, Jacob Weisberg, Cavide Uyargil, Gönen Dündar and V. Lale Tuzuner

INSTITUTIONAL BACKGROUND

TURKEY

Area	780,850 km^2
Population	65,293,000
Density	84 inhabitants per km^2
Capital and population	Ankara (3,690,000)
Other important cities and population	Istanbul (9,100,000) Izmir (3,115,000) Bursa (1,959,000)
Official language	Turkish
Business languages	Turkish and English
Religion	Muslim

Topography and climate

Turkey is bordered on the east by Georgia and Armenia, on the south by Iraq, Iran, Syria and the Mediterranean Sea, on the west by the Aegean Sea, Greece and Bulgaria and on the north by the Black Sea. It is divided into seven geographical regions: the Black Sea region, the Marmara region, the Aegean region, the Mediterranean region, Central Anatolia and the East and Southeast Anatolia regions. It is surrounded by sea on three sides, the Black Sea to the north, the Mediterranean to the south and the Aegean to the west. In the northwest of the country there is an internal sea, the Sea of Marmara, between the straits of the Dardanelles and the Bosphorus, which are important waterways connecting the Black

Figure 12.1 Istanbul Ortakoy Mosque

Table 12.1   Turkish population

Density	84 inhabitants per km^2
Life expectancy at birth (boys)	66.9 years
Life expectancy at birth (girls)	71.5 years
Employment rate (men)	75%
Employment rate (women)	27%
Unemployment rate	7%

Table 12.2   Population by age and sex (1995) (1000 people)

Age (years)	Men	Women
15–24	6012	6214
25–49	11,050	10,659
50–64	3130	3215
65+	1640	1900

Sea with the rest of the world. The coastline of Turkey (excluding islands) is 8333 km long.

Although Turkey is situated in a geographical location where climatic conditions are quite temperate, the diverse nature of the landscape and in particular the existence of the mountains that run parallel to the coasts, result in significant differences in climate from one region to the other. While the coastal regions enjoy milder climates, the inland Anatolia plateau experiences hot summers and cold winters with limited rainfall.

Principal characteristics

Table 12.1 shows the principal characteristics of Turkish population.

Special features

Turkey is located where the three continents making up the old world, Asia, Africa and Europe, are closest to each other and straddles the point where Europe and Asia meet. Because of its geographical location, the mainland, Anatolia, has witnessed the mass migration of diverse peoples, shaping the course of its history. The home to countless civilisations, Anatolia has developed a unique synthesis of cultures. The Anatolian hinterland gives glimpses of other ancient civilisations: the Hattis, the Hittites, the Phyrigians, the Urartians and the Lydians. As both an ancient land and a modern nation-state Turkey today is the inheritor and conservator of the common heritage of mankind.

People

Turkey's population is 65,293,000. The Turkish population has experienced a growth rate of almost 20% over the past 20 years. In 1990 the percentage of the population living in cities reached 59% (60% for women and 58% for men) and the weighted average age was

26.43. Table 12.2 shows the Turkish population by age and sex.

The average Turkish household comprises 4.8 persons. The divorce rate (1994) is 0.9%.

Economy

Turkey has been identified as one of the ten most promising emerging economies, and a recent World Bank study also declared Turkey as one of the ten countries most likely to enter the top tier of the world economy.

Historically, the agricultural sector has been Turkey's largest employer and a major contributor to the gross domestic product (GDP). However, as the country has developed, the relative importance of agriculture has declined, while the position of industry and the service sectors has strengthened.

In the early 1980s Turkey implemented a series of important economic reforms aimed at liberalising the Turkish economy and integrating it into the global economy. Turkey's entrance into international markets and the resulting increase in international competitiveness have further accelerated the industrialisation process. During this period, Turkey has developed a diversified industrial base producing a variety of products. From 1980 to 1999, the share of agricultural products in exports declined from 57 to 10%, while industrial exports rose from 36 to 88%, signalling a wholesale shift from an agrarian to an industrial economy.

In 1999, Turkey suffered two devastating earthquakes in its nine most developed provinces. The provinces affected account for 50% of Turkey's value-added manufacturing, 48% of all business establishments and 47% of all jobs.

The shares of sectors in the gross national product (GNP) are not equal: services 62%, industry 23% and agriculture 15%. The service sector in Turkey increased its share in the national income in parallel with developments in the world economy. Tables 12.3 and 12.4

Table 12.3 Gross national product

	1997	1998	1999
GNP at current prices (TL trillion)	29.393	53.518	78.282
GNP at constant prices 1987 (TL trillion)	114.874	119.303	112.044
GNP (US$ billion)	194.1	203.9	185.3
GNP growth rate (%)	8.3	3.9	−6.1

Table 12.4 Gross domestic product (at producers' price)

	1997	1998	1999
GDP (TL trillion)	28.720	53.522	82.925
GDP (US$ billion)	189.9	201.2	185.7
GDP growth rate (%)	7.5	3.1	−4.7

indicate Turkey's GNP and GDP as to years 1997, 1998 and 1999.

Legal and institutional environment/political system

The power to legislate is vested in the Turkish Grand National Assembly (TGNA), which performs this function on behalf of the Turkish nation. The TGNA was first empowered to exercise legislative power in Ankara on 23 April 1920 by Mustafa Kemal Atatürk. This assembly functioned under extraordinary circumstances and exercised legislative, executive and judicial powers according to the concept of the unity of these powers.

An important step was taken on 29 October 1923, when a Council of Ministers was established with more freedom of movement based on the idea that the form of the state should be ''Republic''. The President of the Republic was to be elected from among the members of the Assembly. According to the law, the President would select the Prime Minister from among the members of the Parliament. In turn the Prime Minister would select the other Ministers from among the members of Parliament and finally the President would submit the whole of the Council of Ministers for the approval of Parliament.

The 1924 Constitution was prepared on the principle of unification of power. In the 1961 Constitution the power to legislate was vested in the two chambers: the National Assembly and the Republican Senate.

Table 12.5 Persons in employment (million people)

	1980	1985	1990
Total	18.5	20.5	23.3
Male	11.7	13	14.9
Female	6.8	7.5	8.4

While the 1982 Constitution kept the basic structure of the 1961 Constitution, it nevertheless made significant changes in several areas. The Republican Senate was abolished in the 1982 Constitution.

According to the present Constitution, all citizens have the right to vote, to be elected, to engage in political activities independently or within a political party and to take part in referenda in conformity with the conditions specified by the law. All Turkish citizens over 18 years of age have the right to vote in elections and to take part in referenda. The formation, activities, supervision and dissolution of political parties are governed by the provisions of the 1982 Constitution and the Political Parties Law of 22 April 1983. All political parties must establish their headquarters in Ankara and formation requires the signatures of at least 30 Turkish citizens eligible for election to Parliament.

Labour market

Tables 12.5–12.7 show some important figures about the Turkish labour market. Nearly two out of three people employed are male. By age, there is a relatively constant labour participation rate between 25 and 45 of about 60%. The unemployment rate over the past years has been between 6 and 7%.

The foundations of industrial relations in Turkey in the modern sense were laid by the Constitution of 1961, which not only recognised the right to organise unions for both workers and employers but also the right of collective bargaining and the right to strike and lockout.

Unions Act No. 274 and the Collective Agreements, Strikes and Lockouts Act No. 275 were prepared and issued in 1963 following the guidelines of the Constitution of 1961 and instituted a system of democratic industrial relations. The Constitution of 1982 regulated the system of industrial relations in a more detailed manner than the former Constitution which puts particular emphasis on peaceful labour relations in its social and economic rights and obligations chapter. Today, trade unions and employer associations and their

Table 12.6   Labour force participation rate by age

Age (years)	15–19	20–24	25–29	30–34	35–39	40–44	45–49	50–54	55–59	60–64	65+
Per cent	32.8	50.0	60.4	60.7	60.8	60.2	51.0	43.4	37.0	29.7	20.1

Table 12.7   Unemployment rates

	1991	1992	1993	1994	1995	1996	1997	1998	1999	2000
Per cent	7.9	8.1	7.8	8.1	6.9	6.0	6.7	6.8	7.7	6.6

confederations are governed by the provisions of the Unions Act No. 2821 and the Collective Agreements, Strikes and Lockouts Act No. 2822 passed pursuant to this new Constitution.

In Turkey, employer associations in the real sense have been organised only after the Constitution of 1961.

In 2001 there are four labour unions confederations and 104 labour unions, 1 employers confederation with 49 employers' associations in Turkey. As of January 2002 the unionisation rate is 58.04.

Table 12.8   The current situation in education

Levels of education	Number of schools	Number of students	Number of teachers
Preschool	9882	251,596	15,690
Primary school	43,324	10,053,127	324,920
Secondary school	6168	2,444,407	143,460
General high school	2633	1,506,379	70,240
Vocational and technical high schools	3505	938,028	73,220

Educational system

In Turkey education is under the supervision and control of the state. Government programmes and development plans also place great emphasis on education because education is recognised as the most important component for Turkey's economic, technological and social development.

The Turkish National Educational System is composed of two main sections:

- formal education;
- non-formal education in accordance with Basic Law No. 1739 for National Education.

Formal education means the school system and comprises the institutions of preschool education, primary school education, secondary education and higher education (Table 12.8). Non-formal education includes all activities organised outside or alongside the school.

In Turkey, preschool education, which is optional, includes the education of children in the 3–5 years of age group. The duration of primary education in Turkey is 8 years and it includes the education/training of

children in the 6–14 years of age group. Primary education takes place in 8-year schools and a diploma of primary education is awarded to graduates. Secondary education includes all the general, vocational and technical institutions of education, following primary education, that provide at least 3 years' education and consists of high schools offering a variety of programmes.

The development of higher education appropriate to an increasingly globalised world, in terms of both quality and quantity, has been adopted as the primary goal. The relevant plans and programmes have always reflected this perception. Since the foundation of Republic until the present time, many important improvements have been made in both the quantity and the quality of higher education. This developments process, which started in 1933 when the Darülfünun, the Ottoman language term for the university of that time, was transformed into Istanbul University and gained momentum especially in recent years. As of 2000, the number of universities reached 71, 18 of which are private foundation universities and the rest are state universities.

ISRAEL

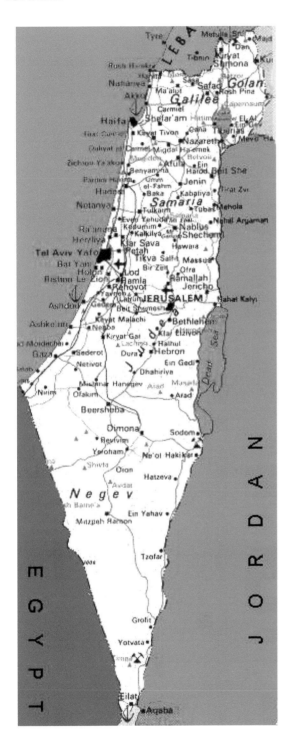

Area	20,770 km^2
Population	6,800,000
Density	297 inhabitants per km^2 (2001)
Capital and population	Jerusalem (646,000)
Other important cities and population	Tel Aviv-Yafo (349,000) Haifa (268,000)
Official languages	Hebrew and Arabic
Business languages	Hebrew, Arabic and English
Religions	81% Jews 15% Muslims 2% Christians 2% Others

Israel is located in the Middle East along the eastern end of the Mediterranean Sea. It is bordered by the Mediterranean Sea to the west, Lebanon to the north, Syria to the northeast, Jordan to the east and Egypt to the southwest.

History

Following World War II, the British withdrew from their mandate in Palestine, and the UN partitioned the area into Arab and Jewish states, an arrangement rejected by the Arabs, who started a war against Israel. Subsequently, the Israelis defeated the Arabs in a series of wars without ending the deep tensions between the two sides. On 25 April 1982 Israel withdrew from the Sinai pursuant to the 1979 Israel–Egypt Peace Treaty. Outstanding territorial and other disputes with Jordan were resolved by the 26 October 1994 Israel–Jordan Treaty of Peace. On 25 May 2000 Israel withdrew unilaterally from southern Lebanon, which it had occupied since 1982.

Topography and climate

Israel is divided into four topographical regions:

1. The coastal plain, which is a narrow strip of land along the Mediterranean Sea and contains 66% of the population.

2. The mountains, which consist of soft stone or dolomite ranges in the north, such as Mt Hermon, Upper Galilee, Lower Galilee and Mt Carmel, as well as the lofty granite peaks of Samaria and Judea in the south.
3. The valleys, which include the Hula, Capernaum, Jordan and Jezreel.
4. The deserts, which account for up to 66% of the land area and include the Negev and Judean. The main rivers are the Jordan, Yarkon, Na'aman, Kishon, Taninim, Alexander and Ga'aton.

Israel has a Mediterranean climate characterised by long, hot, dry summers and short, warm, wet winters. About 17% of the annual precipitation occurs between November and February in heavy storms, while further inland rainfall is heavier than the average annual precipitation of 550 mm and snow may occasionally fall in the mountains. Average temperatures in Jerusalem range from 5 to 13°C in January to 18–31°C in August.

People

About 79% of the population belong to the Semitic races, principally divided ethno-religiously. The chief division is between the immigrants from European and Anglo-Saxon countries (Ashkenazim) and the immigrants from Arab Muslim countries (Sephardim) who currently constitute the majority. Traditionally, the Ashkenazim were politically and economically dominant, but this trend is changing. In addition, there are two smaller Jewish sects in Israel, the Karaites and

the Samaritans. Other ethnic minorities include the Arabs, Druse, Bedouin and others, who account for 22% of the population (Table 12.9).

About 91% of Israel's inhabitants live in some 200 urban centres, some of which are located on ancient historical sites. About 5% are members of rural cooperative settlements – the kibbutz and the moshav.

Economy

History

For the first 25 years after its establishment in 1948 Israel's GDP grew at a very high average rate – up to 10% annually – while at the same time the country absorbed several waves of mass immigration, built a modern economy, fought four wars and maintained security (Table 12.10). Between 1973 and 1979 the growth rate fell as in most industrialised countries, partly due to the oil crises of 1973/1974 and 1979/1980, to a yearly average of 4% and in the 1980s it dwindled to 3%. In 1990–1996 the growth rate was 6%. In 1997 the total GDP grew by 2% to $98.5 billion ($16,950 per capita). Since 2000 there has been a decline in Israel's economic growth due to the world economic crisis and the prolonged armed struggle with the Palestinians.

Industry

Israel's industry concentrates on manufacturing products with a high-added value that are primarily based on

Table 12.9 Population in 2000

	1980	1990	Annual growth (%) (Av.) (1980–1990)	1999	Annual growth (%) (Av.) (1990–1999)
Population	3,921,700	4,821,700	2.29	6,209,100	3
Civilian labour force	1,318,100	1,649,900	1.25	2,345,100	2
Life expectancy					
Female	75.7	78.4	1.03	80.3	1
Male	72.1	75.7	1.04	76.1	1
Infant mortality (per 1000 live births)	15.6	9.9	−0.6	5.8	−0.6
School population	1,200,700	1,451,300	1.2	1,875,600	1
Percentage of the population with 13 years or more of formal schooling	21	28	1	40	1

Source: Statistical Abstract of Israel (no. 52) Central Bureau of Statistics, 2000.

technological innovation. These include medical electronics, agro-technology, telecommunications, computer hardware and software, solar energy, food processing and fine chemicals.

Agriculture

Israel's farmers have to contend with harsh conditions, including a scarcity of water and arable land. Today, agriculture represents some 3% of GDP and 3% of exports. Israel produces 93% of its own food requirements, supplemented by imports of grain, oil seeds, meat, coffee, cocoa and sugar, which are offset by a wide range of agricultural products for export.

Trade

Trade is conducted mostly with the USA, Germany, the UK, France, Belgium and Luxembourg. Some 56% of

imports and 36% of exports are with Europe, boosted by a free-trade agreement with the EU concluded in 1975. A similar agreement was signed with the US (1985), whose trade with Israel accounts for 20% of Israel's imports and 35% of its exports (Table 12.11).

The main exports are chemicals, fertilisers, finished diamonds, fruit and vegetables, machinery and textiles. The main imports are consumer goods for direct consumption, raw materials, uncut diamonds, petroleum and mineral fuel.

Legal and institutional environment/political system

Israel is a parliamentary democracy with legislative, executive and judicial authorities. The head of the state is the president, whose duties are mostly ceremonial and formal; the office symbolises the unity and sovereignty of the state.

The Knesset is the parliament of the State of Israel; its main function is to legislate. Its name and the number of 120 members is taken from the Jewish leadership convened in Jerusalem by Ezra and Nehemiah in the fifth century BC. The Knesset starts to function after general elections, which determine its composition.

Table 12.10 Gross domestic product, exports and imports

GDP	$100.8 billion ($16,470 per captia)
Exports, goods and services	$39.3 billion
Imports, goods and services	$47.5 billion

Source: Statistical Abstract of Israel (no. 52) Central Bureau of Statistics, 2000.

Table 12.11 Economic indicators

GDP (at 1995 prices – NIS millions)	1980	1990	Annual growth (%) (Av.) (1980–1990)	1999	Annual growth (%) (Av.) (1990–1999)
Total	138,975	197,644	1	302,206	2
Per capita	36,005	42,411	1	49,359	1
Net exports of goods (millions of dollars)	5291.9	11,603.1	2	23,554.7	2
Of which: industrial products (excluding diamonds)	3340.4	7696.8	2	16,424.8	2
Agricultural products	555.7	657.2	1	782.3	1
Net imports of goods (millions of dollars)	7845.7	15,107.1	2	30,629.7	2
Tourists arriving	1,065,800	1,131,700	1	2,312,300	2
Air passengers (annual)	2,847,000	3,720,000	1	8,734,000	3
Freight shipped by air (annual in tons)	105,800	194,160	2	297,080	2
Production of electricity (in millions of kilowatt/hours)	12,400	20,900	2	39,180	2
Private cars	410,000	803,000	2	1,317,000	2
Telephone subscribers	860,000	1,626,000	2	2,880,000	2

Source: Statistical Abstract of Israel (no. 52) Central Bureau of Statistics, 2000.

The government (cabinet of ministers) is the executive authority of the state, charged with administering internal and foreign affairs, including security. Its policy-making powers are very wide and it is authorised to take action on any issue not delegated by law to another authority. Like the Knesset, the government usually serves for 4 years, but its tenure may be shortened if the Prime Minister is unable to continue in office due to death, resignation or impeachment, when the government appoints one of its members (who is a Knesset member) as acting Prime Minister. In the case of a vote of no confidence, the government and the Prime Minister remain in post until a new government is formed.

The judiciary's absolute independence is guaranteed by law. Judges are appointed by the president, on the recommendation of a special nominations committee composed of supreme court judges, members of the bar and public figures. Judges' appointments are for life, with a mandatory retirement age of 70.

Magistrates and district courts exercise jurisdiction in civil and criminal cases, while juvenile, traffic, military, labour and municipal appeal courts each deal with matters coming under their competence. There is no trial by jury in Israel.

Labour market

Employment conditions for about 50% of the workers in the country's various economic sectors are governed by agreements negotiated between representatives of the employers and employees. Minimum requirements, however, are laid down by law and include a maximum 47-hour workweek, minimum wages, compensation for overtime, severance payments, paid vacation and sick leave.

Wages in the public sector are determined through negotiations conducted between the government (also the country's largest employer), whose wage scale affects all segments of the economy, and the Histadrut (General Federation of Labour). Wages in the private sector are determined through negotiations conducted between the organisation of private sector employers and the trade unions. The agreements reached constitute a framework of wage scales for the different sectors of the economy and, with occasional changes of detail, also provide for automatic payment of a cost-of-living allowance as compensation for inflation. Thus the wage situation is rather inflexible, especially at the lower end.

Waves of unemployment in Israel do not significantly reduce wages, although in times of labour shortages wages rise with greater elasticity in those sectors where the demand for workers is more acute. In the middle of 1999 the average monthly wage was NIS 6323 (about $1540) (Table 12.12).

Education

The educational system aims at preparing children to become responsible members of a democratic, pluralistic society in which people from different ethnic, religious, cultural and political backgrounds coexist. It is based on Jewish values, love of the land and the principles of liberty and tolerance. It seeks to impart a high level of knowledge, with an emphasis on the scientific and technological skills essential for the country's continued development.

The educational profile in 1999 of those aged 25 or over was as follows: 3% – no formal schooling, 25% – primary, 35% – secondary, 37% – higher (Table 12.13).

The Ministry of Education, in cooperation with schools of education at the country's universities, is engaged in bringing educational standards into line with modern pedagogic practices, including ensuring gender equality, upgrading teacher status, broadening humanities curricula and promoting scientific and technological studies. A key aspect of its policy is to provide equal opportunities in education for all children and to increase the number of pupils passing matriculation examinations.

Health

The National Health Insurance Law, in effect from January 1995, provides for a standardised "basket" of medical services, including hospitalisation, for all residents of Israel. All medical services continue to be supplied by the country's four health care organisations, Kupat holim Klalit, Maccabi, Leumit and Meohedet.

In 1999 life expectancy was 80.3 years for women and 76.1 years for men. The infant mortality rate was 5.8 per 1000 live births. The ratio of

Table 12.12　Employment and wages (in thousands)

	1980	1990	1996	2000	Annual growth (%) (Av.) (1996–2000)
Civilian labour force	1318.1	1649.9	2156.9	2345.1	2
Percent civilian labour force	49.5	51.5	53.7	53.8	2
Percent unemployed	4.8	9.6	6.7	8.9	3
Economic branches					
Agriculture	:	:	2.5	2.3	−2
Manufacturing	:	:	20.2	18.3	−2
Electricity and water	:	:	0.9	0.9	0
Construction (building and civil engineering)	:	:	7.5	5.6	−1
Trade and repair of vehicles	:	:	12.8	13.2	2
Accommodation services	:	:	3.8	4.2	2
Transport and communication	:	:	6.2	6.3	2
Banking, insurance and finance	:	:	3.4	3.4	0
Business activities	:	:	9.7	10.5	2
Public administration	:	:	5.4	5.4	0
Education	:	:	12.1	12.6	2
Health and welfare	:	:	9.0	9.9	2
Community, social, personal and other services	:	:	4.8	4.6	−2
Private households with domestic personnel	:	:	1.7	1.8	2
Average weekly work hours per employed	36.5	36.1	37.8	37.4	−2
Males	40.2	40.4	42.9		
Females	30.0	29.5	30.9		
Average monthly wage per employee post (NIS)	2.81	2299	4876	6323	2.5

Source: Statistical Abstract of Israel (no. 52) Central Bureau of Statistics, 2000. ":" Data not available.

Table 12.13　Education profile

	1980	Annual growth (%) (Av.) (1980–1985)	1985	Annual growth (%) (Av.) (1985–1990)	1990	Annual growth (%) (Av.) (1990–1995)	1995	Annual growth (%) (Av.) (1995–1996)	1996
Adult illiteracy rate (%) (age 15+)	:		7	−2%	6	−2%	5	−2	5

Source: Statistical Abstract of Israel (no. 52) Central Bureau of Statistics, 2000. ":" Data not available.

physicians to population and the number of specialists compare favourably with those in most developed countries.

Social welfare

The social service system is based on legislation which provides for workers' protection and a broad range of national and community services, including care of the elderly, assistance for single parents, programmes for children and youth, and adoption agencies, as well as prevention and treatment of alcoholism and drug abuse.

The National Insurance Institute provides all permanent residents (including non-citizens) with a broad range of benefits, including unemployment insurance, old-age pensions, survivors' benefits, maturity grants and allowances, child allowances and income support payments.

Culture

Thousands of years of history, the ingathering of Jews from over 70 countries, a society of multi-ethnic communities living side by side, and an unending flow of international input via satellite and cable have all contributed to the development of an Israeli culture which reflects worldwide elements while striving for an identity of its own. Cultural expression through the arts is as varied as the people themselves, with literature, theatre, concerts, radio and television programming, entertainment, museums and galleries catering for every interest and taste.

The official languages of the country are Hebrew and Arabic, but in the country's streets many other languages can be heard. Hebrew, the language of the Bible, long restricted to liturgy and literature, was revived a century ago, accompanying the renewal of Jewish life in the Land.

HRM IN TURKEY AND ISRAEL

INTRODUCTION

Turkey and Israel differ in demographics, size, culture, level of economic development and so on: while Israel is a small country with a population of about 6 million, the population of Turkey numbers about 65 million. On the other hand, the annual GDP per capita in Turkey is $3000, whereas in Israel it is $16,470. Yet despite these and numerous other differences, there are many similarities between the two countries in respect of HRs and its management practices.

In both Turkey and Israel, HR departments have successfully established themselves in their organisations, and most HR managers are strategic partners in the development of corporate strategy. Moreover, in both countries the role of young educated women in the HR field is growing, especially in global companies, although in the more traditional organisations men still tend to dominate.

The differences between HRM in Israel and Turkey stem from the particular culture of each country. While Turkish society is more cooperative, Israeli society is more competitive. This may explain why Turkish organisations invest more in appraisal systems and training, whereas the most common methods for retaining employees in Israel involve increased pay or benefits. Furthermore, most Turkish employment agreements are company based (even for managers and professionals), while, according to the Cranet findings, for the majority of Israeli workers base pay is determined through individual negotiation. The unionisation rate is 67% in Turkey and 42% in Israel (Cohen et al., 2001). In addition, it is easier to hire temporary

workers in Israel, as Turkish law limits recruitment on a temporary basis.

ANALYSIS*

Statistical analysis of the Israeli Cranet survey indicated that most of the businesses sampled (75%) employed more than 200 workers and 75% of them were private rather than public enterprises. The organisations had been in existence for an average of 35 years, and 42% could be defined as manufacturing or industrial.

Analysis of the Turkish survey indicated that all the businesses in the sample employed more than 200 workers, and 90% belonged to the private sector. They had been in existence for an average of 25 years, and 23% were manufacturing and industrial organisations (Table 12.14).

The Cranet sample in both countries in 1999 was close to 200 organisations. However, the private sector

Table 12.14 Number of organisations responding to the Cranet survey

	Turkey			Israel		
	1992	1995	1999/ 2000	1992	1995	1999/ 2000
N	123	131	195	No survey	No survey	194

*The statistics presented here should be viewed with caution, as the Cranet sample may not be truly representative of the labour market owing to its voluntary nature.

was over-represented in both countries: 75% in Israel and 90% in Turkey.

The role of HRM – marginal or core?

Representation of HR managers on board of directors

As Table 12.15 shows, in Turkey in 1999 in 46% of the companies in the survey the heads of personnel or HR sat on the firm's board of directors or belonged to the executive management team or its equivalent, while in the remaining 54% they did not. Although it is often emphasised in Turkey that HR directors are strategic partners of management, studies indicate that in many organisations the function in question is not yet actually fulfilling this role (Uyargil and Dündar, 2001).

The data show that the rate of representation of HR managers on the board or executive committee of Israeli companies is substantially higher (77%). However, a comparison of the Turkish figures for 1999 with those of 1992 reveals a slight increase (from 38 to 46%), indicating a positive trend.

The Cranet survey also sought to determine who was responsible for HR functions when personnel or HR managers did not sit on the company's board of directors or its equivalent. In such cases, in 69% of the firms in Turkey and 54% in Israel, the managing director or CEO of the organisation was found to bear responsibility for representing these issues at top management level.

HR major characteristics

HR managers – experience   Of the HR managers who completed the Cranet questionnaire, 63% in Turkey and 84% in Israel defined themselves as the senior personnel director or HR executive. In both countries, they had been working in the HR field for an average of approximately 11 years.

Table 12.15 Percentage of HR managers on board or members of executive management team

| | Turkey | | | Israel | | |
	1992	1995	1999/2000	1992	1995	1999/2000
Yes	38	42	46	No survey	No survey	77
No	62	58	54	No survey	No survey	23

HR managers – education   Some 92% of the Turkish HR managers and 80% of their Israeli counterparts held a university degree. The Turkish managers' degrees were primarily in business (35%), economics (21%) or engineering (16%), while the degrees of the Israeli managers were most often in economics (24%), business (12%) or other fields (36%). A significant difference was found in Israel between the genders with regard to field of study. For example, 12% of the male HR managers had studied engineering, whereas no female engineers whatsoever were working as HR managers. In addition, the Turkish HR managers were found to be better educated and to have a more technical background. Although in Turkey 28% from the population have more than 12 years of schooling, in Israel 37.4% from the population have more than 12 years of schooling.

The higher participation of HR managers at top management level in Israel, together with their lower level of education, can be explained in terms of historical context. In the past, higher education was not a job requirement for HR managers in Israel, as it is today. Furthermore, traditionally, participation in upper management results from the accumulation of years of experience, power and influence.

HR managers – gender   Of the Turkish HR managers, 32% were women, as compared to 36% in Israel. This ratio differs from that of managers in the Israeli labour market in general, where about 80% are men and 20% women.

A recent study (Uyargil and Ozcelik, 2001) of the characteristics of HR managers and professionals in Turkey indicates that their profiles vary greatly in accordance with their education, years of experience and sector. For instance, in the current survey, of the 63% of Turkish respondents who were senior HR executives, the majority (80%) was skilled and experienced in the field, while the others were young and inexperienced. In our opinion, such differences influence the representation of these functions on the board of directors, executive management team or their equivalent.

On the whole, then, it appears that both in Turkey and in Israel, the HR manager and HR department play an important role in the organisation. However, in Israel we find a higher rate of participation of HR managers at upper management level, while in Turkey HR managers display a higher level of education.

HRM strategy – its status and role

Existence of HR strategy   Data collected as part of this study reveal that almost all companies in Turkey and Israel with a corporate strategy also have an HR strategy. This is a sign that the management of these firms attaches importance to HRs and designs strategies for it in accordance with corporate needs. This is also indicated by the fact that a large number of organisations – 93% in Turkey and 90% in Israel – have separate HR departments. In addition, most senior HR managers (71% in Turkey and 85% in Israel) play an active role in strategic decision-making as it relates both to their departments and to their organisations.

Stage at which HR is involved in the development of corporate strategy   As can be seen from Table 12.16, in both countries the HR executives of about 60% of the companies are involved in the development of corporate strategies from the outset. Although the data for the two countries appear fairly similar, the consultation responsibilities of Turkish HR managers are fewer than those of their Israeli counterparts, while their involvement at the stage of implementation is 25 and 15% in Turkey and Israel respectively. These findings can be explained by the fact that Israeli HR managers are higher in the organisational hierarchy: more Israeli HR managers sit on the board of directors or are members of the upper management team and closer to the CEOs than their Turkish counterparts. However, consultation and implementation are not mutually exclusive.

HR department and line managers – decentralisation of responsibilities

A comparison between Israel and Turkey indicates that Israeli HR departments keep more responsibility to themselves. This finding might very well be related to the fact that 88% of the Turkish organisations have an HR strategy, which appears in writing in 59% of these cases, while only 70% of the Israeli organisations have an HR strategy and in a mere 25% of them is it written out. Thus a written HR strategy would seem to affect the decentralisation of HR functions. One explanation for the centralisation of Israeli HR departments might be the desire of company headquarters to ensure uniformity of HR policy in each of the organisation's units (Table 12.17).

Line managers in Turkey are most responsible for wages and benefits (34%) and the expansion/reduction of manpower (31%). The areas for which they are most responsible in consultation with their HR departments are recruitment and selection of personnel (32%) and expansion/reduction of manpower (37%). The HR department in consultation with line managers is most

Table 12.16   Stage at which HR is involved in the development of corporate strategy

	Turkey			Israel		
	1992	1995	1999/2000	1992	1995	1999/2000
From the outset	45	57	61	No survey	No survey	59
Through consultation	9	18	10	No survey	No survey	25
On implementation	33	21	25	No survey	No survey	15
Not involved	13	4	4	No survey	No survey	1

Table 12.17   Primary responsibility for major policy decisions regarding pay and benefits

	Turkey			Israel		
	1992	1995	1999/2000	1992	1995	1999/2000
Line management	33	39	34	No survey	No survey	16
Line management with HR department	21	23	26	No survey	No survey	18
HR department with line management	19	21	34	No survey	No survey	40
HR department	16	8	6	No survey	No survey	26

responsible for training and development activities (48%). About 48% of the companies surveyed reported that their HR departments hold primary responsibility for recruitment and selection policy decisions in consultation with line managers. The areas for which the Turkish HR department alone is most responsible are employer–employee relations (23%) and training and development (11%).

In Israel, nearly all the areas examined are the responsibility of the HR department in consultation with line managers: wages and benefits (39%), recruitment and selection of personnel (44%), training and development (50%) and expansion/reduction of manpower (36%). The only exception is employer–employee relations, which is generally the full responsibility of the Israeli HR department itself (46%).

The areas for which line managers in Israel are largely responsible are expansion/reduction of manpower (16%) and pay and benefits (16%). The fact that in both Turkey and Israel line managers typically bear responsibility for these two issues might be associated with the global decline in the power of trade unions. Traditionally, the trade unions had a dominant influence over pay and tenure. It is possible that, as the unions became weaker, line managers acquired greater responsibility for these tasks, probably because organisations believed that line managers would perform them more effectively than their HR departments, since they are in closer contact with the field and the workers.

Evaluation of HR department performance

In Turkey, 51% of the companies surveyed stated that the performance of their HR departments was systematically reviewed, and 40% of them conducted this review in accordance with "performance by objectives" criteria. Furthermore, they indicated that their companies apply internal measures of cost-effectiveness. In Israel, systematic performance evaluations of HR functions are carried out in only one-third of the organisations, and again most (38%) employ performance-by-objectives methods.

Retention, recruitment and selection

Retention

Companies use various mechanisms to retain employees and ensure that they meet their needs in terms of quality and quantity. In Turkey, 79% of the companies prefer the training/retraining method (training allows the employees to enhance their knowledge and skills, resulting in promotion), 48% increase wages and other material benefits, and 42% improve their corporate image. In Israel, the most common methods of retaining employees are increased pay/benefits (69%) and training (67%).

Recruitment methods

Table 12.18 indicates that the companies surveyed both in Turkey and in Israel recruit mainly by using existing employees to fill managerial vacancies (promotion from within) at all levels, especially middle and junior management. The second major resource in Turkey is recruitment companies, headhunters or consultancies, and the second major resource in Israel is newspaper advertisements, except in the case of senior managers, who are more commonly recruited through headhunters and consultancies. In both Israel and Turkey, primary responsibility for recruitment and selection remains with the HR department, in consultation with line managers.

Selection methods

Table 12.19 reveals that one-to-one interviews are used for every appointment by 43 and 79% of the companies in Turkey and Israel respectively. A review of the

Table 12.18   Recruitment methods: use of internal mechanisms for filling managerial vacancies

	Turkey			Israel		
	1992*	1995	1999/2000	1992	1995	1999/2000
Senior management		60	56	No survey	No survey	61
Middle management		74	77	No survey	No survey	82
Junior management		60	69	No survey	No survey	78
Total managerial only*	14	65	67	No survey	No survey	74

*The question in 1992 asked for "managerial positions" only.

Table 12.19 Selection methods: use of different methods for every/most or some appointments

	Turkey			Israel		
	1992*	1995	1999/2000	1992	1995	1999/2000
Interview panels						
Every appointment		17	20	No survey	No survey	15
Most appointments		17	17			14
Some appointments		26	31			26
Frequently used* (1992 only)	64.2					
One-to-one interviews						
Every appointment		52	43	No survey	No survey	79
Most appointments		24	31			12
Some appointments		11	13			3
Frequently used* (1992 only)	N/A**					
Application forms						
Every appointment		80	92	No survey	No survey	72
Most appointments		13	3			10
Some appointments		4	3			4
Frequently used* (1992 only)	95					
Psychometric testing						
Every appointment		13	20	No survey	No survey	12
Most appointments		11	11			13
Some appointments		23	16			29
Frequently used* (1992 only)	8					
Assessment centre						
Every appointment		4	13	No survey	No survey	1
Most appointments		9	6			4
Some appointments		9	10			25
Frequently used* (1992 only)	4					
Graphology						
Every appointment		19	18	No survey	No survey	5
Most appointments		15	11			7
Some appointments		19	10			17
Frequently used* (1992 only)	0					
References						
Every appointment		44	43	No survey	No survey	27
Most appointments		28	27			27
Some appointments		19	20			32
Frequently used* (1992 only)	69					

*The question in 1992 asked only for "frequently used".
**N/A: Question not asked.

selection methods employed in all the Cranet countries shows that the interview is the most popular tool for the employee selection process, and indeed it features as part of the process in 94% of the Israeli companies. However, the most popular selection method in Turkey is the application form, employed by as many as 92% of the organisations. Although this method is less common in Israel (72%), it is still very popular.

Since the number of Turkish companies providing recruitment consultancy has increased in recent years, psychometric tests are widely used for this purpose in the country. On the other hand, the cost of aptitude tests in Israel is quite high, so that most companies feel compelled to calculate the cost-effectiveness of these services. For similar reasons, assessment centres are used in Israel mainly for selecting senior managers.

Training and development

Training costs

In both Turkey and Israel, organisations are interested in investing in the training and development of their employees. In terms of monetary value, 24% of the

Table 12.20   Proportion of annual salaries and wages spent on training and development

(%)	Turkey			Israel		
	1992	1995	1999/2000	1992	1995	1999/2000
<1	30	46	9	No survey	No survey	15
1–1.9	25	18	24	No survey	No survey	28
2–2.9	13	7	24	No survey	No survey	31
3–4.9	7	12	14	No survey	No survey	7
5–9.9	12	13	18	No survey	No survey	12
>10	13	4	11	No survey	No survey	7

Table 12.21   Mean number of training days, by staff category

Mean	Turkey			Israel		
	1992	1995	1999/2000	1992	1995	1999/2000
Management	4	7	8	No survey	No survey	6
Professional/technical	6	8	10	No survey	No survey	6
Clerical	4	4	8	No survey	No survey	4
Manual labour	4	4	8	No survey	No survey	3

Turkish respondents spend from 1 to 3% of their annual outlay on salaries and wages on these activities, the average investment being 4%. As Table 12.20 shows, the data indicate an increase in the proportion of the annual cost of salaries and wages being spent on training since 1992. In fact, in 1999 as many as 18% of the Turkish companies devoted 5–10% of their annual salary and wage outlay to training programmes.

In Israel, the average investment in training and development is 4% of the total salary and wage outlay. Only 19% of the Israeli companies spend more than 5% of this figure on training, as compared to 29% in Turkey. Thus, Turkish organisations are investing more in training and development than their Israeli counterparts.

Training days

The average number of days of training offered to four staff categories, as shown in Table 12.21, increased steadily in Turkey from 1992 to 1999, with more training given to the technical staff than to the other three categories. Comparison of Turkish and Israeli data shows that the average number of training days is higher in Turkey, perhaps because numerous training and consulting companies have emerged in Turkey in recent years, and because the importance attributed to quality management in general has increased. In about half (48%) of the Israeli organisations in the sample, employees participated in internal and external training activities in the year before the survey. However, these programmes catered mainly for managers and professional/technical workers, who received an average of six training days, in contrast to clerical/administrative or manual workers, who received only 3–3.5 training days in the course of the year.

The differences between the two countries in respect of the training provided for each staff category might be explained in terms of the differences between the two societies. As noted earlier, Israeli society is more competitive. As training is seen as a benefit, senior employees naturally enjoy more of it. Thus in Israel, managers and professionals receive significantly more training days than lower-level workers, whereas in Turkey there is almost no difference between the number of training days given to the managers and to clerical or manual workers.

The differences between the two groups in Israel (managers/professionals and clerical/manual) are similar to those found across the Cranet countries in 1999/2000 where managers received 6 training days on average, professional/technical workers 7, and clerical/administrative and manual workers 4.5.

Of the companies offering training, 72% in Turkey and 57% in Israel determine their training needs systematically. As part of this study, those that had analysed their training needs were asked to describe the methods they had employed. According to the Turkish responses, most companies give priority to a review of their training programme, followed by suggestions from managers and the results of performance evaluations. Furthermore, they report using needs analysis methods always or most of the time. The fact that Turkish companies did not begin to consider training important until a short time ago (relatively later than most other European countries) seems to encourage them act in a more meticulous and diligent manner, and to determine their training needs accurately and carefully.

Training in Israel is usually designed to meet the organisation's immediate needs – i.e. it is offered in response to the demands of line managers (43%) or workers (30%) – rather than future needs such as the analysis of future business plans (16%).

Training effectiveness

An issue of equal significance to training needs evaluation is the measurement of training effectiveness. In Turkey, 75% of the companies conduct an assessment to measure the efficiency of their training activities. In contrast, only 49% of the Israeli companies conduct such an assessment. Most of the organisations in Israel which evaluate their training programmes do so immediately after completion, but hardly monitor their long-term ramifications. The effectiveness of training in Israel is measured mainly by employee feedback and evaluations (88%), and is less likely to be monitored by formal methods such as examinations (37%).

Changes in the responsibilities of line managers

A comparison of the responsibilities of Turkish line managers in 1999 with previous years revealed no change save for an increase in responsibility for training and development. The Israeli data for 1999 similarly indicate the increased responsibility of line managers for this field. This may result from a change in the attitude towards training, from general to job-focused, and may also explain the growth of internal training staff in 1999 to 75% of the companies in Israel and 49% of the organisations in Turkey.

Performance measurement and rewards

Incentive programmes

The incentive most widely used by Turkish companies is merit- or performance-related pay. It is applied across the board for management, professionals and clerical workers, although less so for manual workers because of the existence of labour unions for these employees. Table 12.22 indicates that the rate at which merit/performance-related pay is implemented in Turkey has not changed significantly over the years.

Merit/performance-related pay is also popular in Israel, although to a lesser extent. On the other hand, stock options are becoming a more common incentive, especially in the high-tech sector. In about 82% of the organisations responding to the survey in Israel, managers' base pay was determined through individual negotiation. Most collective negotiation applied to manual workers (35%). Throughout the public sector, working conditions and wages are determined by an established system of collective bargaining, whereas this is much less common in the private sector.

Performance appraisal methods

Some form of performance appraisal (PA) system is widely employed both in Turkey and in Israel. As can be seen from Table 12.23, 73% of the Turkish

Table 12.22   Merit/performance-related pay by staff category

	Turkey			Israel		
	1992	1995	1999/2000	1992	1995	1999
Management	52	50	56	No survey	No survey	33
Professional/technical	53	53	57	No survey	No survey	33
Clerical	48	43	52	No survey	No survey	26
Manual labour	18	27	26	No survey	No survey	23

companies evaluate the performance of their executives, 80% of their professionals, 79% of their clerical staff and 54% of their manual workers. The corresponding data for the Israeli companies indicate a similar trend, the levels most frequently appraised being professional/technical staff (70%) and clerical workers (69%). In both countries, as well as in other European companies, the evaluation of the performance of manual workers is less widespread, partly no doubt as a result of the negative attitude typically displayed by trade unions towards PA. However, as mentioned above, the power of the trade unions has been waning, and line managers have taken over many of their functions, including responsibility for pay and benefits. Consequently, they are now also responsible for the evaluation of manual workers, and, as Table 12.23 shows, more than half of the companies currently conduct PA for this group as well.

Appraisers   Another significant aspect of PA is the identity of those who formally contribute to the process. In Turkey, the contribution of direct supervisors is quite high (79%), followed by next-level superiors (54%). In approximately 42% of the companies, the employees rate themselves in the PA process. The system by which subordinates evaluate superiors is not popular in Turkey, where it is found in only 9% of the companies. The participation of peers and customers in the PA process is likewise not very popular in Turkey.

Much as in Turkey, most of the organisations in Israel use traditional methods for employee appraisal, such as evaluation by superiors (78%), by direct supervisors (44%), or by peers (35%). Although methods such as 360° feedbacks are fashionable and reliable, they are less popular because of their high cost (many people have to spend time appraising each employee). In 40% of the Israeli companies, at least two appraisers are involved, but in only 14% are there more than four appraisers.

PA goals   In Israel, 54% of the organisations that conduct PA do so in order to determine promotion potential, and 40% to identify individual training needs. The use of appraisals to determine individual performance-related pay is not common, despite the increasing international trend to relate performance with incentives.

In Turkey as well, the outcome of PA (60%) is used most often to determine promotion potential (60%), followed by the identification of individual training needs (53%), individual performance-related pay (51%), career development (48%) and work organisation (30%). Thus Turkey and Israel employ PA for similar purposes.

The role of trade unions and works councils

Trade union influence

A review of the influence of trade unions shows limited change over the last 3 years in Turkey, whereas in Israel their influence has declined (Table 12.24). Of the Turkish HR managers who completed the questionnaire, 50% believe that union influence had remained the same in the course of the last 3 years. In contrast, despite the strength of Israeli trade unions in the past, there has been a remarkable decline in their power in recent years, especially, but not only, in the private sector.

Table 12.24   Change in trade union influence

	Turkey		Israel		
	1995	1999/2000	1992	1995	1999/2000
Increased	6	6	No survey	No survey	3
Same	60	50	No survey	No survey	46
Decreased	34	12	No survey	No survey	29

Table 12.23   Appraisal system for staff categories

	Turkey			Israel		
	1992*	1995	1999/2000	1992	1995	1999/2000
Management		79	73	No survey	No survey	60
Professional/technical		84	80	No survey	No survey	70
Clerical		80	79	No survey	No survey	69
Manual labour		68	54	No survey	No survey	59

* Question not asked in 1992.

Of the Israeli HR managers responding to the questionnaire, 29% agreed that the influence of trade unions had decreased, while only 3% believed the opposite to be true.

A comparison of the sectors reveals that workers in the public sector in Israel tend to be more inclined to affiliate with trade unions than those in the private sector. Currently, no trade unions of any kind exist in 43% of the private sector organisations in Israel.

Determination of basic pay

The basic pay of management executives and professionals in Turkey is determined mainly at the establishment/site level (39%). Israeli companies prefer to determine the basic pay of management executives (82%), professionals (52%) and clerical staff (45%) at the individual level. Clerical staff and manual workers in Turkey lead the employee groups whose wages are determined by collective agreements. In Israel, only the wages of manual workers are determined mostly by collective agreements (35%).

Employee communication

Top-down communication

A review of the changes in the methods by which management's messages are communicated to employees in Turkey reveals a steady increase in the frequency of meetings over the course of the three surveys. These are conducted as regular workforce meetings (47%) or team briefings by managers to various groups of workers

(45%). This is a significant finding, as it indicates that individual work is being replaced by teamwork.

In Israel, the most significant change in the method of communicating major issues to employees over the last 3 years is the increased use individualised means of communication: by computers and e-mail (64%), written messages sent directly to employees (58%) and face-to-face verbal communications (57%).

Bottom-up communication

Turkish employees communicate their views and suggestions to management mainly in workforce meetings (47%) or directly to senior managers (37%). Israeli employees often communicate directly with their immediate supervisors (an increase of 41% during the last 3 years). This is in line with the Israeli mentality, which is open and informal. Israeli employees also tend to communicate their views directly to senior managers (an increase of 41%), and to participate in team briefings (an increase of 39%).

Briefing by staff category

Another significant issue is the degree of formal briefing of the workforce by management about corporate strategies, financial performance and work organisation. As Table 12.25 shows, in both Turkey and Israel managers are provided with the greatest amount of information about corporate strategies, followed by professionals, clerical staff and lastly manual workers, few of whom get information in either country. Information regarding

Table 12.25   Formal communication on business strategy and financial performance (percentage)

Staff categories	Turkey			Israel		
	1992	1995	1999/2000	1992	1995	1999/2000
Management briefed						
About strategy	82	83	87	No survey	No survey	77
About finance	72	68	80			73
Professionals briefed						
About strategy	43	56	53	No survey	No survey	16
About finance	28	27	35			27
Clerical staff briefed						
About strategy	17	29	28	No survey	No survey	12
About finance	12	11	14			22
Manual workers briefed						
About strategy	15	21	17	No survey	No survey	4
About finance	8	11	7			12

the financial performance of the company is supplied to these groups in the same sequence, but to lesser degrees. In Turkey, it is again the managers who are briefed to the highest degree (62%) about work organisation, but in Israel it is the professional/technical staff who are most thoroughly briefed on this subject (62%). An examination of the extent to which the workforce in Turkey is briefed by management in relation to number of years in business indicates that companies find it easier to communicate with their employees and tend to adopt a more open policy as the years go by.

Work organisation and flexible working

Flexible working arrangements can help companies to organise and adapt their workforce to the demands of the local and international market and therefore to be more competitive. The policy of flexible working hours is usually defined in a country's labour laws, and might be described as an approach employed by HR departments to improve the quality of work life.

The data in Tables 12.26–12.28 suggest that flexible working arrangements are not widespread in Turkey. The present labour law stipulates part-time employment as the sole acceptable flexible arrangement. Other flexible arrangements in which the parties institute changes that are in the interests of both the company and the workforce are subject to certain limitations. Although individual labour laws traditionally relate to such arrangements (particularly part-time employment), they are rarely applied in Turkey. However, the economic crises suffered by Turkey in recent years may well increase the use of flexible working arrangements.

Table 12.26   Proportion of workforce on non-standard contracts (part-time and temporary/casual)

	Turkey			Israel		
	1992*	1995	1999/2000	1992	1995	1999/2000
No part-timers employed	67	65	70	No survey	No survey	12
>10% part-timers	4	4	2	No survey	No survey	3
No temporary workers	60	72	79	No survey	No survey	7
>10% temporary workers	3	0	3	No survey	No survey	38

* 1992 figure for no "part-timers" is the missing value, since a "not used" option was not included.

Table 12.27   Change in use of flexible working arrangements (part-time) (%)

	Turkey			Israel		
	1992*	1995	1999/2000	1992	1995	1999/2000
Increase	0	9	9	No survey	No survey	16
Same	31	22	16	No survey	No survey	45
Decrease	2	1	2	No survey	No survey	21
Not used	66	68	72	No survey	No survey	17

* 1992 data included a "Don't know" category, which was selected out.

Table 12.28   Change in use of flexible working arrangements (temporary/casual) (%)

	Turkey			Israel		
	1992*	1995	1999/2000	1992	1995	1999/2000
Increase	15	14	2	No survey	No survey	47
Same	14	12	11	No survey	No survey	34
Decrease	10	5	5	No survey	No survey	8
Not used	61	70	82	No survey	No survey	11

* 1992 data included a "Don't know" category, which was selected out.

Indeed, companies may prefer to take advantage of this option as a means of lowering labour costs, rather than to lay off workers.

In Israel, flexible working arrangements are more common, especially temporary/casual work. In fact, this type of arrangement is so widespread in Israel that trade unions are pressing for laws that will reduce the number of temporary workers and improve their working conditions.

In 33% of the Israeli organisations, shift work increased from 1997 to 1999, and in 25% of the companies there was a greater use of flexi-time.

Nevertheless, despite the upward trend in flexible working arrangements, 84% of Israeli employees still adhere to a traditional working day and conditions.

SUMMARY

Overall, Turkey and Israel, both operating in and affected by the global economy, share considerable similarities in respect of HRM. The differences can largely be explained in terms of the social, legislative and cultural differences between the two countries.

HRM IN ACTION

TURKEY: QUALITY CONSCIOUS COMPANIES AND HRM

During the last decade the HR function experienced drastic changes in its role, status and influence. Many senior HR executives agree that "HR is moving away from the transactional, paper-pushing, hiring/firing support function and is becoming a bottom-line business decision-maker". (Phillips, 1996: p. 1) Indeed HR is becoming a strategic partner – which means understanding the business direction of the company, including what the product is, what it is capable of doing, who its typical customers are and how it is positioned in the market place. The Cranet-G survey has shown that measurement and evaluation of HRM through which HR departments can make their contributions to the organisational goals more visible are not applied on a wide scale in the Turkish companies. A new study was therefore designed which was limited to those companies that applied for the National Quality Award in Turkey. The assumption is that those companies will attach more importance to measuring and evaluating HRM.

The purpose of this study is to articulate different approaches and techniques for measuring and evaluating the HRM function. Evaluating the HR function and specific HR programmes involves more than developing performance measures and administering evaluation instruments. It is a results-based philosophy that the organisation must adopt at all levels. One of the most important aspects of measuring the HR contribution is to identify measures that accurately reflect overall HR performance. The findings show that the companies are aware of the importance of measuring and evaluating the HR function. However, the challenge is to implement these approaches in a way that increases the efficiency and effectiveness of HR function.

In this exploratory study questionnaires were administered to 41 companies applying various EFQM (European Foundation for Quality Management) Model criteria. The questionnaires were conducted using techniques of interview with people who are mostly HR managers or professionals. Companies from a variety of sectors were evaluated in terms of the differences in the effectiveness and efficiency of their HRM. Whether the companies measured the HR function at all and, if they did, what kinds of analysis they performed, were among the subjects covered by the research. Thirty per cent of the companies were industrial and 70% were from the service sector, and all had HR departments. The research findings can be examined in a number of different ways.

When the efficiency and effectiveness of the companies applying for the National Quality Award are analysed, it can be seen that they have very different profiles regarding HR functions. The staffing function, the beginning of the HR process, represents one of the important elements of a successful HR effort. Effective staffing practices can have a significant positive impact on the organisation; poorly designed and executed staffing practices will have both short- and long-term negative impacts. From this perspective, the companies that applied for the National Quality Award measure mostly "selection ratio" and "recruiter effectiveness". Service sector companies normally use these two measures. In particular they try to measure "satisfaction of internal customers who requested the new recruits" and "recruiter effectiveness".

Manufacturing companies, and companies with more than 500 employees tend to measure and evaluate the recruitment function in detail. This is an important criterion in determining HRM effectiveness. The reason manufacturing companies analyse effectiveness more thoroughly is that they recruit both white-collar and blue-collar workers. Thus they differentiate between recruitment sources.

The next question to be explored is whether companies have specific orientation programmes for their new recruits. The study showed that almost all companies have such programmes but none of the companies tries to calculate their long-term costs and results.

The companies studied use various methods to evaluate the effectiveness of the training they provide to their employees for increasing their competencies. Nearly all of them monitor their annual training programmes on the basis of numbers and participation. They also keep records of training days/hours per person for both blue- and white-collar employees. Since expenditure on training is determined by the company's budget, the training programmes and related costs are planned – and alternatives prepared – in accordance with the budget for the year.

Industrial sector companies value external customer satisfaction more than the service sector companies. Since it is easier for service companies to access the final customer, it is normal for them to evaluate customer satisfaction more as compared to industrial companies. The methods used by industrial companies (balanced scorecard, EVA, etc.) emphasise the evaluation of customer satisfaction. Industrial companies therefore evaluate customer satisfaction over different periods and compare the results.

As regards performance evaluation as a whole, companies usually have systems for providing feedback to their employees. Most of the companies included in the research analysed the results of their performance evaluation on the basis of departments; some used grades or scores as a basis and the remainder seniority. The companies do apply traditional approaches to performance evaluation but they are also finding room for new evaluation techniques. For example, some industrial companies have developed a number of "competencies" for their blue-collar employees and measure the difference between "actual" and "desired" performance in certain periods. Systems such as 360° feedback – although still not common – are becoming more widespread as the number of hierarchical levels decreases and teamworking begins to predominate.

Service and industrial sector companies vary in terms of their compensation systems. Job evaluation is mostly used by industrial companies, but newer methods are being applied for white-collar employees. Service sector companies prefer competency-based payments instead of job evaluation. Most of the companies in our research preferred the "Hay system". Both service and industrial sector companies pay their employees on the basis of performance. However, there are differences in compensation packages at top management level. In service sector companies, employee share ownership plans are not much favoured, and only a few of the industrial sector companies use such long-term programmes in Turkey. Wages, which are a strategic tool today, should provide external equity and should also satisfy various needs of the employees. The companies in our research state that they participate in various benchmarking groups and use the information obtained to achieve external and internal equity in their compensation systems.

One of the factors involved in evaluating HRM is the industrial safety (job safety and employee health) function. Industrial sector companies evaluate work accidents more, record and benchmark the percentage of strikes and measure the number of working days lost.

One surprising result of our research is that service sector companies mostly evaluate employee complaints. Complaints are more commonly evaluated in companies with fewer than five employees in the HR department. In small companies, the close relationship between HR departments and employees permits easier access to information about complaints and rapid reporting of problems to managers, as well as making it simpler to apply solutions. On the other hand, in large companies formal complaints systems were not improved and in any case, in line with the open-door policies pursued by line managers, problems are solved before reaching the HR department. In industrial companies, the different complaints procedures and the existence of trade unions mean that complaints are dealt with differently, and prevent a rigorous pursuit of complaints by HR departments.

Industrial sector companies are more seriously concerned about absenteeism, the costs of absenteeism and benchmarking absenteeism than service sector companies. In companies with more than 500 employees, companies that are part of a group and companies with a majority of blue-collar employees absenteeism is closely monitored, the reasons for it are examined and relevant measures are planned by the HR department. Research is carried out to ascertain the probable main causes of absenteeism and measures are introduced to reduce it.

Another issue as important as absenteeism is staff turnover. This issue, which is a factor in any study of employee satisfaction, receives attention in companies that are part of a group and companies with more than five employees in their HR department. Companies taking part in various benchmarking exercises monitor turnover rates but they do not calculate its cost. Voluntary resignations, which are one element of staff turnover, are monitored by the companies just mentioned. Exit interviews are conducted and the consequent feedback from employees is evaluated, but the costs involved are ignored.

As required by their work, some service companies, as well as industrial sector companies, monitor work accidents rigorously. In industrial companies, accidents and safety problems are measured and controlled on a factory basis. Companies applying for a National Quality Award measure the number and frequency of work accidents, and benchmark them to sector, country, MESS (Turkish Employers' Association of Metal Industries) and ILO averages.

As mentioned earlier, economic value added (EVA) and balanced scorecard are both used as a management development tool to measure the performance of employees. Many companies hesitate to use the new techniques for measuring performance because they do not see what advantages they offer compared with traditional methods. Thus they continue to use such methods as "performance scorecard".

To sum up, we can say that HRM in industrial and service companies differ in terms of measurement and evaluation and that industrial companies pay more attention than service companies to some HR activities. However, because of their structure, industrial sector companies conduct some HR activities in collaboration with line managers, and that their HR departments are not very effective, particularly in recruitment and selection. This reduces the effectiveness of the department.

The measurement and evaluation of HRM is a new concept and one that is not yet fully understood in our country. Our assertion in this study is that when HR activities are measurable, comparable and accountable, it will provide additional value to the company. Measuring and evaluating HRM is not easy. It requires the collection of data relating to HR, the integration of all the information obtained and its systematic assessment, in addition to the measurement and evaluation of the different functions involved. It is equally important to compare past records with current data and to benchmark wherever possible.

Finally, HR managers and professionals working on the measurement and evaluation of HRM should submit the information they have to top management and to others in the company in an effective way. Even indirectly, communication with employees and customers is also an important element in making this exercise successful. In addition, HR managers and specialists working in this field should develop new competencies. HR staff will in future be judged by their ability to focus on measurement and their skill in statistical issues and presentation. Their familiarity with the financial and management concepts will also be under scrutiny. In brief, in the near future a transition from traditional HRM to results-based HRM is inevitable. There is no "best" method of HRM and organisations will need to develop measurements appropriate for their own structure, culture and management style.

ISRAEL: ALPHA-GAMMA LTD., A PROTOTYPICAL EXAMPLE*

An interview with Ms Michal Levi, director of HR at Alpha-Gamma Ltd., an Israeli telecommunications company.

Background

Q: Shalom, Michal. Thank you for agreeing to be interviewed. Tell us a little about Alpha-Gamma Ltd.

A: Alpha-Gamma is a privately-owned company that specialises in the development of telephony products. The company has been in existence for 34 years.

It employs some 430 workers, of whom 63% are male, and is divided into three production line units. Most of the employees are technical workers – engineers and technicians. Administrative workers constitute about 25% of our entire staff and 15% of the employees are managers.

In 1990, we moved to a new facility in an information technology park near Tel-Aviv.

Overall, we are a profitable company. Our profit margins, however, fell considerably between 2001 and 2003 owing to a global slow-down in orders for communications equipment.

The company's CEO is in his fifth year on the job and is considered a success. He is a patient and liberal man, who are always open to ideas for developing HR.

HR function

Q: Please describe your organisation's HR department.

A: The HR function at Alpha-Gamma consists of six women: three are HR co-ordinators who represent the three production units, the training and development manager who also serves as my deputy, a secretary and myself. I am also partially responsible for the payroll accountant, but he is officially part of the finance department.

---

* This case study is fictitious. It is based upon several resources and was written for educational purposes.

We are a relatively independent department. Although I am not a vice-chairperson, I sit on the executive board. Senior management consults with me during the development of corporate strategy, and they obviously seek my advice regarding all decisions that pertain to HRM strategy.

Q: According to statistics from the Cranet survey, 64% of Israel's HR managers are men. You are an exception.

A: True, but the survey also points to the fact that the field is dominated by women – 70% of all HR staff are women. I also "grew up" in the field. In my opinion, the trend towards male managers will decrease over time.

Q: What is your professional background? Did you "grow up" at Alpha-Gamma?

A: I have already been with the firm for 3 years. Before my present job, I worked for 5 years as HR manager at Tinten – a small printing products firm. Alpha-Gamma's chairman made me an offer, which I accepted because it was a promotion for me. I felt a need for a new and more substantial professional challenge and I was offered a higher salary.

I have a BA in social sciences and a MA in business management with a specialisation in organisational behaviour.

Q: Let's return to the HR function. Do you use external providers (outsourcing)? In what areas?

A: Personnel agencies and headhunters help us recruit workers. Of course, our recruitment coordinators interview the agencies' candidates, and they are then interviewed by the line managers as well. In certain circumstances (such as the recruitment of senior or technical staff) we send candidates to assessment centres, which conduct skills and aptitude tests. We are also assisted by an organisational consultancy that intermittently runs workshops for, primarily, middle level and junior managers.

Q: Has a change taken place in the scope of external providers' (outsourcing) activities over the last 3 years?

A: If you had asked me at the start of the millennium, I would have told you that there was a significant increase in outsourcing, but today its use has decreased by about 40%. This is mostly due to the slow-down in the communications market, which has forced us to cut back.

Q: Does your organisation have a written policy covering strategic planning and HR issues?

A: The organisation has a written mission statement and an unwritten corporate strategy. We still lack a comprehensive HR strategy. This is a topic that I am working on – to develop an HRM strategy based on our corporate strategy.

Q: How are you going about it?

A: Let's take as an example the company's mission statement concerning quality – to produce the highest quality products possible. First of all, to fulfil this goal I am planning training courses on product quality. Every employee in the company will participate in at least one such course. Additionally, I am labouring over the development of a system for managing and storing information so that every minor problem with a product will be recognised and solved as quickly as possible. This will also prevent the problem from recurring. We already have an ISO certification.

Q: Does the organisation have written policies for the different aspects of HRM?

A: There is a written policy for wages, salaries and compensation because we do not have collective bargaining. There is also a written policy for training and development.

Q: Does the company conduct a review of the HR function?

A: Yes. This is a new guideline that we implemented 2 years ago. All the managers evaluate the HR department's performance once a year using a questionnaire with 10 questions, which is arranged according to criteria such as satisfaction with the HR activities, satisfaction with the filling of vacant positions, etc.

Staffing practices

Q: How do you recruit employees?

A: We prefer to recruit internally, and to promote from within, or, if we are looking for someone outside the company, by word of mouth – if a company worker has recommended a candidate who was accepted, we give him or her a suitable gift. But if we can't find an appropriate candidate from within the organisation, we usually turn to personnel agencies or to headhunters. We advertise in the papers only when we can't find enough candidates using the other approaches. The advertisements also help to "market" the organisation.

Q: Please describe your company's selection process.

A: It really depends on the particular position. All candidates fill out admission forms, and we interview everyone at least twice: an interview to determine the candidate's personality traits and his or her fit with the organisational culture is conducted by the HR coordinator, and an interview in which their professional skills are discussed is conducted by the line manager. Technicians and engineers also take a professional aptitude test that was developed internally.

In addition to the in-house interviews we also send managers and engineers to assessment centres, which administer a battery of tests. My predecessors attempted to establish an in-house assessment centre, but came to the conclusion that it is not cost-effective. Today, many Israeli companies send executive-level candidates to the assessment centres of companies that specialise in this line of work. These centres focus on both the candidates' personalities and their interpersonal skills, which are evaluated with the help of situational simulations.

Q: What steps are taken to reduce turnover?

A: At the moment, we are not taking any special course of action. Obviously, we offer substantial pay rises for outstanding workers, and do our utmost to invest in employee training and development. During the information technology boom, many employees left the organisation to join start-up companies. Consequently, we invested much more in employee welfare, trips, etc. Today, the budget for these activities has been significantly reduced.

Training and developing workers

Q: How much does Alpha-Gamma invest in training?

A: Training and development makes up 4.85% of our total salary bill, which is higher than the national rate of 3.56%. On average, every worker gets 6 days of training and senior managers get up to 2 weeks. We also contribute to the tuition fees of any manager who wishes to take an advanced university degree (usually a second degree) in a relevant field of study.

Q: What types of training programme exist in your organisation?

A: We offer an array of technologically oriented courses. Additionally, there are specialist courses such as business English or business negotiation for employees who require such skills. We also hold induction seminars for new employees on the organisation and its values.

The crown jewel of our training programme is the "high flier" schemes for managers, which at the moment consists of 22 junior managers who require comprehensive management qualification. This includes leadership development workshops, the monitoring of senior managers, and practical experience that they acquire through succession plans.

Q: Are the workers' training needs examined in a methodical fashion?

A: Once a year we conduct a training needs survey in which the entire staff participates. We also collect relevant information from the managers throughout the year, especially after the performance evaluation. Naturally, priority is given to filling the organisation's needs and obtaining the required skills.

Q: Are training efforts appraised? How is this done?

A: We try to evaluate all the training programmes, but there are types of activity that are less conducive to evaluation such as our dynamic workshops. These workshops are held twice a year for managers, and their goal is to strengthen the leadership and teamwork of the managerial staff.

After every training event, the trainees fill out a survey in which they express their degree of satisfaction. Two months later, the supervisors fill out a report that we use to determine if the trainees' performance has actually improved. The professional training sessions are easier to evaluate.

Q: Does the evaluation improve the level of training?

A: That is a difficult question to answer. We constantly strive to improve our training sessions based on the evaluations and the requests and suggestions of both workers and managers. Test results and performance evaluations are other indicators that we rely on. In all, it seems to me that the appraisal process improves the training sessions' relevance and effectiveness. In other words, it enables us to check whether the training programmes do in fact fulfil their pre-determined needs and enhance our employees' skills. Nevertheless, it is difficult to demonstrate the effectiveness of the training process, and when the board decided to reduce company expenditure, the first thing to be cut down was training.

Performance evaluation and compensation

Q: How are wages and salaries determined? Do cooperative agreements exist?

A: All Alpha-Gamma staff are employed on the basis of personal contracts. While it is true that Israel has historically made widespread use of cooperative agreements, in the information technology sector – which is a relatively new field – most of the workers are employed through personal contracts.

When a new position occurs, we check what the average salary is for this position even before the selection stage. This is accomplished using tools such as salary surveys and benchmarking, which is done by talking and comparing notes with my colleagues in the HRM field. That said, the final salary is primarily determined during negotiations with the candidates.

Q: What incentive arrangements does your organisation use? Have changes occurred in the last few years?

A: The managers and top-level employees, who make up about 30% of our entire workforce, receive share options on being accepted into the company. In addition, we provide a bonus that is based on a formula that takes into account the performance of the entire organisation, the specific team, and the worker's personal productivity. Between 1999 and 2000, the variable portion of total salary expenditure (bonuses and incentives) decreased by 10% because of a fall in revenue.

Q: Do you carry out PAs?
A: Yes. Once a year we conduct an organised series of employee reviews. All the workers in the organisation have an evaluation meeting with their immediate supervisor. There are briefings for both evaluators and those being evaluated. Every worker receives the review sheet in advance and can fill it out before the appraisal; this enables the employee to compare his or her expectations with their manager's opinion.

During the review sessions, the decision is made whether to award a rise and if so how much. The organisation of work and training needs are discussed as well. Naturally, this information is passed on to the HR department and we use it to plan training sessions, deal with any special problems, and more.

Q: Is your system characteristic of the Israeli workplace?
A: For the most part, such an organised appraisal is only characteristic of the public sector and information technology companies.

Q: And how do you rate the process? Is it effective?
A: There are many problems with the PA process. Sometimes I get the feeling that people think that the HR department steals valuable hours from workers and especially managers. They even accuse the department of seeking to gain power at the expense of missed deadlines. A handful of employees feel that the organisation is constantly looking over their shoulder. Another complaint being made is that managers are unwilling to give negative feedback, and consequently the reports we receive are inaccurate.

Nevertheless, we are attempting to overcome these problems with the help of extensive guidance for workers and primarily for the evaluators. Furthermore, our department does use the data we receive and the comprehensive review of evaluations that we conduct in preparing training programmes, in planning career paths and in improving corporate efficiency.

Q: Please describe the relationship between the HR department and the production (or line) managers?
A: We make HR decisions jointly with the line managers, and try to pass on more and more authority to them. I have no doubt that the true management authority lies with them.

Work relations and professional unions

Q: What is the percentage of professional union members in Alpha-Gamma's workforce? How has union influence changed over the last few years?
A: Since we are an information technology company, there are no union members on our staff. A couple of years ago, some of our workers were still members of the traditional workers' organisation [the Histadrut], which absorbed into its ranks anyone who was a member of Kupat Cholim [Israel's health care providers]. In the 1990s, the link between union membership and membership of Kupat Cholim [Israel's health care providers] was abolished by the National Health Law. Consequently, the workers'

organisation was considerably weakened. So despite the fact that Alpha-Gamma has been in existence for 34 years, there are no longer any union members on the payroll and all our workers are employed on the basis of personal contracts.

Q: Who is responsible for preventing sexual harassment in your organisation? How is this issue handled?

A: In Israel, legislation was passed to prevent sexual harassment. The law obliges organisations to appoint a worker who will be responsible for this issue, and with whom complaints can be lodged. My deputy, Hila, oversees this issue. Once a year, she gives a lecture on the topic. Any complaints she receives from employees are taken seriously. We even fired a manager for this reason (although there was also a lack of satisfaction with his performance in general).

Communication

Q: Does management conduct formal reviews for workers on strategy, financial performance and organisation of work?

A: Managers hold comprehensive reviews on strategy and financial performance once every 2 months. The CEO also gives a general survey for the company's entire staff once a year.

Every supervisor calls a staff meeting on the organisation of work whenever he or she feels it's necessary.

Q: How do employees communicate their opinions to management?

A: Israelis tend to be very straightforward. Workers are usually not embarrassed to talk directly to their supervisor or for that matter to senior managers. Recently, there has been an increase in requests made by e-mail.

The organisation of work: flexible working practices

Q: What arrangements exist in your organisation that allow you, as manager of HR, to hire workers in a flexible manner?

A: A considerable proportion of the administrative staff are part-time workers, who make up about 7% of the entire staff – most of them are women. Some 5% of the employees work through personnel agencies. Recently, a law was passed in Israel requiring companies to take on temporary employees after a period of 9 months, but the law was suspended. In any event, if we are satisfied with their work, we try to absorb temporary employees into the organisation after a year. If we are unsatisfied, we send them back to the personnel agency so that they can find another job.

Q: Do you have flexible arrangements such as working from home or the splitting of posts between two or more workers?

A: These methods were considered, but were found not to suit our company's needs.

Q: Do you feel that there has been a change in the use of flexible working practices?

A: At the moment, no. All these new methods like working at home and remote employment are fine in theory, but are not that appropriate for Alpha-Gamma.

We would like to thank Michal for granting us this interview.

LEARNING QUESTIONS

1. What led the authors to believe that Turkey is more cooperative while Israel is more competitive? Refer to factors like retention, evaluation, pay and benefits, etc.
2. What changes have occurred in recent years in the representation of HR managers on boards of directors in Turkey and Israel?
3. How does the presence of the head of personnel or HR on the firm's board of directors (or the executive management team or its equivalent) affect HRM strategy? Illustrate your answer with reference to Israel.
4. Discuss the role of the HR department in developing business strategy in Turkish companies.
5. In Israel we find two generations of HR managers. Indicate the differences between the two generations. Would you define the differences between those two generations as a gradual evolution or as a substantial generation gap?
6. Compare the responsibilities of HR departments and line managers in Turkish companies for policy decisions on HRM functions.
7. Discuss the changes that have taken place over time regarding formal communication with employees about business strategy and financial performance.
8. What are the main areas in which PA outcomes are used in Turkish companies?
9. How do selection methods in Israel take account of cost–benefit considerations?
10. How might Israeli HR managers improve their training planning?
11. What are the advantages and disadvantages of flexible working arrangements in Israel?
12. Compare the two case studies with the HRM statistics arising from the results of the Turkish and Israeli Cranet survey. What are the key learning points?

REFERENCES AND SOURCES

References

Cohen, Y., Haberfeld, Y., Moundlak, G. and Saporta, Y. (2001) *The Rate of Unionization in Israel*. The Workforce Planning Institute, Jerusalem, Israel.

Phillips, Jack. (1996) *Accountability in Human Resource Management*. Houston: Gulf Publishing Company.

Uyargil, Cavide and Dündar, Gönen. Research on determining the strategic qualifications of human resource functions in companies. *Cranfield Study on International Strategic Human Resources Management*. Report 1999–2000, Istanbul 2001.

Uyargil, Cavide and Ozcelik, Oya. Some characteristics of the Turkish HR managers/professionals and a comparative study with 3 European countries (United Kingdom, Germany, Spain). Paper presented at the *HR Global Management Conference*. Esade & Cranet, Barcelona, Spain 2001.

Sources for Turkey Institutional Background

1999 Yili Ekonomik Rapor, Ankara, T.C. Maliye Bakanliği, 1999.

Aylik Ekonomik Veriler, İstanbul, İstanbul Ticaret Odasi Istatistik Şubesi, 2000.

Sektör Bilançolari (1997–1999), Ankara, T.C. Merkez Bankasi İstatistik Genel Müdürlügü, 1999.

Turkish Economy 98, Istanbul, TÜSIAD, 1998.

http://www.calisma.gov.tr
http://www.die.gov.tr
http://www.dpt.gov.tr
http://www.imbk.gov.tr
http://www.mfa.gov.tr
http://www.imf.org
http://www.turizm.gov.tr
http://www.tursab.org.tr
http://www.turkey.com
http://www.treasury.gov.tr

Sources for Israel Institutional Background

(1) Israel Ministry of Foreign Affairs web site: http://www.mfa.gov.il
(2) The Central Bureau of Statistics (CBS): http://www.cbs.gov.il
(3) Atlapedia Online: http://www.atlapedia.com
(4) The world's fact bank: http://www.odci.gov/cia/publications/factbook/index.html

Part 3

13

Convergence, Stasis, or Divergence?

Wolfgang Mayrhofer, Michael Morley and Chris Brewster

INTRODUCTION

In the first chapter, three potential developments were adduced regarding the question of convergence, stasis or divergences in HRM in Europe. They were labelled as the market-forces convergence model, the institutional convergence model and the divergence model. Linked with these three models were broad fundamentally different propositions:

1. Market forces are generating a convergence in HRM practices among European firms towards a US-style model of HRM.
2. Pan European institutional forces are generating a convergence in HRM practices among European firms towards a common European model that is distinctly different from that of the US model of HRM.
3. Deep seated and fundamental differences between European countries means either continuing divergence or, at least, no convergence in HRM practices among European firms.

The data used in the previous chapters come from a variety of countries across Europe. The country comparisons, drawn by local specialists in HRM from each country, highlight in detail the current situation in the respective countries as well as how the situation has developed during the past decade. In each case they point out areas of similarity and areas of difference. Implicitly, the third proposition above – how HRM practices develop within each country in Europe – is the point of reference. However, out of isolated comparisons the "big picture" does not emerge automatically, although some first hints can be gained.

This chapter tries to paint a broader picture. Using prominent examples of common HR practices widely discussed in practitioner and scientific literature as best practice and important for "modern" HRM, it analyses whether HR practices in European companies have become similar, remained stable or are more diverse than ever. The work in this chapter is based on a project funded by the Anniversary Fund of the Oesterreichische Nationalbank (Nr. 7978) and earlier work resulting from this project (Mayrhofer et al., 2002; Müller et al., 2001).

ANALYSING CONVERGENCE AND DIVERGENCE OF HR PRACTICES IN EUROPE – SOME PROBLEMS

Three major issues arise in attempting to analyse converging or diverging developments of HR practices in Europe:

- Which areas of HRM are included?
- What is the chosen unit of analysis?
- How is convergence and divergence conceptualised?

Areas of HRM included

Attempts to compare the developments of HRM in different European countries very quickly raise the question of what to include. It is hard to imagine how one could compare "all of HRM". What, indeed, does the subject of HRM cover? In some European countries, HR specialists spend much of their time on, e.g. health and safety or environmental issues. In others, these are minor considerations or are the responsibility of other departments. But, even if we were to reach agreement about what is covered by HRM, it is impossible to encompass all elements in a single piece of work.

Therefore, all research programmes have to restrict the subject matter in order to be able to make comparisons. In other words, useful indicators have to be chosen where potential developments over time are reflected.[1]

The approach taken here is to search for areas where change is likely to occur because of a number of internal and external change drivers. In these areas where change is likely, developments towards convergence or divergence are comparatively easy to observe. As a starting point for identifying such areas, we have taken the discussion about new organisational forms.

New organisational forms seem to be one of the heralds of the "brave new world of work". Over the past decade, academic literature as well as practitioners' contributions have dealt with this phenomenon extensively. Macro change drivers like globalisation, technological change or shortening of product life cycles promote organisational innovations. These new organisational forms are characterised by labels like atomic (Ryf, 1993), flexible (Volberda, 1998), fractal (Warnecke, 1993), individualised (Ghoshal and Bartlett, 1998), cellular (Miles et al., 1997), network (Sydow and Windeler, 2000), post-modern (Clegg, 1990), post-bureaucratic (Heckscher and Donellon, 1994) or virtual (Davidow and Malone, 1993).

Although different in their details, these labels have one common theme: centralised, bureaucratic and hierarchical structures are replaced by more flexible, decentralised, project oriented, forms where information networks and the "cultural glue" are more important than formal rules and regulations (Zenger and Hesterly, 1997). These new organisational forms offer several ideas which are either new or which, in their extent, change the previous assumptions about organisations.

---

[1] We find that working with international comparisons sharpens our perception of how singularly ethnocentric are some of the choices of what constitutes HRM, particularly in the literature on the link between organisational performance and HRM, where compliance with legislation or managing relationships with trade unions or other representative bodies is notable by its absence (see Learning from Diversity: HRM is not Lycra, editorial: special edition of *International Journal of Human Resource Management*, Patrick Wright and Chris Brewster (2000, 14(8): 1299–1307); Mick Marchington and Irena Grugulis (2000), "Best practice" human resource management: perfect opportunity or dangerous illusion? *International Journal of Human Resource Management*, 11(6): 1104–1124).

First, companies retain only the core competencies within the firm while outsourcing most low value-added activities. Second, front-line managers are provided with greater autonomy. They are allowed "to design their own jobs, fix their own processes, and do whatever it takes to satisfy a customer" (Hamel and Prahalad, 1994: p. 290). Hence, these new organisational forms question the degree to which responsibility between line and staff functions is shared (Mayrhofer, 1999; Larsen and Brewster, 2003). Third, there is much less emphasis on hierarchies, which generally become much flatter. Advocates of the new organisational forms suggest that hierarchies have become too expensive and have impeded information flows. Instead, they advocate more flexible, project-based forms of organisation (Whittington et al., 1999). Fourth, formal and informal information networks bind the autonomous units together (Chakravarthy and Gargiulo, 1998: p. 438). These changes increase demands on information technology (IT) and members of these new organisations have to exhibit higher degrees of co-operation, co-ordination, organisation and self-control (Drumm, 1996: p. 11). They need to have skills such as "strong interpersonal, communication and listening skills; an ability to persuade; a readiness to trade and to engage in reciprocal rather than manipulative behaviour; an ability to construct long-term relationships; … tolerance of high levels of ambiguity and uncertainty; … a good strategic sense, vision and ideas; … a capacity to learn quickly and to adapt in new situations" (Ferlie and Pettigrew, 1998: pp. 219–220).

The development of these new organisational forms is linked with new challenges for the management of organisations. This is no surprise, since such radical changes of organisational structures and processes necessarily do influence the way organisations are managed. Among the most important issues are new ways of co-ordination and control in order to support the integrative element in a "fluid" and diverse organisation (Drumm, 1996), the significance of creating and managing knowledge as a primary resource and competitive advantage of the organisation (Nonaka, 1991), and the increasing importance of resource flows across organisational and national borders (Bartlett and Goshal, 1991; see also Fink and Mayrhofer, 2001 for an international perspective). In addition to these issues the devolvement of responsibilities for decision making and the devolution of operative action from central,

Table 13.1   Main areas of HRM/chapter topics and HR practices analysed

Main areas of HRM/country chapter topics	HR practices analysed	Broad issues
The role of the HRM function and HRM strategy	Level of determination of HR policy	Decentralisation
	Devolvement responsibility from central HR specialists to line management	Decentralisation
	Size of the HR department	Flexibility/cutting slack
Training and development	Investment in T&D	Involvement of people
Performance measurements and rewards	Performance related compensation	Flexibility/cutting slack
Employee communications and the role of trade unions and works councils	Information to employees on strategic and financial matters	Involvement of people
Organisation of work: flexible patterns of work	Flexible work arrangements	Flexibility/cutting slack

specialised units with expert knowledge to line management or even the employee "down the line" are also important. Advocates of new organisational forms argue that decisions about the allocation of all resources should be assigned to front-line managers (Hamel and Prahalad, 1994).

While we might question the take-up of these approaches and argue about the extent to which these new organisational forms reflect reality for the "mucky average" of organisations, there is no doubt that both the rhetoric and the practice of HRM is influenced by these developments (see e.g. Scholz, 1995; Brewster et al., 2000). In their pure form, these new approaches pose a number of HRM questions hitherto rarely discussed in the literature. For example, when virtuality becomes an important element of an organisation, leadership processes and styles have to adapt to the fact that there is less personal contact between the members of a work team. Likewise, if a substantial proportion of the HRs needed for reaching the organisational goals is not on the payroll of the organisation, then many of the "traditional" tools of HRM are of only limited use (Brewster, 1998; Mayne et al., 2000; Brewster and Tregaskis, 2003). However, HRM faces a number of demanding challenges and changes not only in such pure versions of new organisational forms. Even in the case of "traditional" organisations moving some steps towards such a way of organising this has consequences for the management of HR. For example, if organisations are moving away from large, centralised (staff) units and assign more responsibility and resources to "local" or "front line" managers, this has a direct effect on the HR department: it has to think about new ways of supplying the necessary services, performing its functions and equipping line managers with the necessary skills

and competencies to handle the new HR tasks that they are confronted with. In a similar way, HR departments are challenged when they are included in the requirement for each organisational units to document their contribution to the overall organisational success. Under such circumstances, the evaluation of the contribution of the HR department becomes a crucial issue.

At least three broad issues emerge from the discussion about new organisational forms as well as new developments in HRM in general: flexibility/cutting organisational slack, decentralisation and people involvement. Our colleagues have examined a number of aspects of HRM in the previous chapters some of which are linked to the emerging issues to a greater or lesser extent. We have chosen eight of the most significant practices that have been covered in the previous chapters and are related to flexibility/cutting organisational slack, decentralisation and people involvement (see Table 13.1).

These HR practices were analysed as follows.

Level of policy decision making – decentralisation

The Cranet-E questionnaire asks about the decision making level of pay and benefits, recruitment and selection, training and development, industrial relations, and workforce expansion or reduction. Answers could be chosen from four options: the national or the international headquarters, the subsidiary or site/establishment. According to the respondents' choice the score for one single company could range between 0, indicating that all decisions are taken by the central unit, and 5, meaning that the subsidiaries or sites/establishments decide in all areas.

Devolvement of responsibility

Survey respondents were asked to identify practices of their own organisation on the same five issues as before: pay and benefits, recruitment and selection, training and development, industrial relations, and workforce expansion or reduction. In each case organisations were rated according to whether primary responsibility for major policy decisions rested with line management, line management with personnel or HR function support, the personnel or HR function with line management support, or with the personnel or HR department alone. We calculated an index ranging from 5 points, meaning that the HR department alone decided in all five cases, to 20 points, indicating that in all five cases solely the line managers were the decision makers.

Size of the HR department

The Cranet-E survey contains data concerning the number of employees within the HR department as well as the overall number of employees of the company. This enables us to calculate the ratio of the size of the HR department in relation to the overall number of employees.

Investment in human capital

The proportion of the annual salaries and wages bill currently spent on training is regarded as an indicator of the organisations' willingness to invest into their human capital.

Variable and performance related elements of compensations systems

The survey contains a section concerning compensation and benefits. Within this section respondents have to answer a question about different incentive schemes (employee share options, profit sharing, group bonus, merit/performance related pay). Furthermore, there is a differentiation between four employee categories: management, technical and professional, clerical and manual. This enables us to calculate another index ranging from 0 where none of the employee categories is offered any of the incentive schemes, to 16, indicating that all four of the incentive schemes are offered to all four employee categories.

Communication with employees

The Cranet-E survey asked which of the same four employee categories are formally briefed about the strategy and the financial performance of the company. We calculated an index ranging from 0, indicating that none of the employee categories is briefed regularly, to 8, meaning that all employee categories are informed of both of the topics.

Flexible working practices

Respondents were asked about several different working arrangements. In view of practices used within new organisational forms we looked at annual hours contracts, fixed-term contracts, home-based work and subcontracting/outsourcing, and calculated an index ranging from 0 to 4, indicating that none or all of these were used.

Unit of analysis

The second issue concerns the unit of analysis. In line with the approach taken in this book, we are interested in developments across European countries.[2] Therefore, those countries where sufficient data over the last decade were available are included in the analysis. Table 13.2 gives on overview of the countries included. The Methodology Appendix, as well as the individual chapters, show that we have more data than we use here, but unless there are at least 2 years data, we fall into the trap of numbers of previous writers who have confused identification of similarity or difference at one point in time with evidence of movement across time (convergence or divergence).

Conceptualisation of convergence and divergence

The third issue concerns what we mean by convergence or divergence. From a theoretical as well as an

---

[2] This is not to deny the significant contribution made by those who prefer to identify differences within firms, within regions or within countries, nor to underestimate the value of cross-sector comparisons, or indeed any of the numerous other ways that HRM can be studied. We believe that debates about which of these forms of analysis are most explanatory are wrong-headed (Brewster, 2001). The added value that we can bring arises from our cross-national data.

Table 13.2   Countries included and year of survey

	1990	1991	1992	1995	1999
France	•	•	•	•	•
Germany – East			•	•	•
Germany – West	•	•	•	•	•
Great Britain	•	•	•	•	•
Spain	•	•	•	•	•
Sweden	•	•	•	•	•
Denmark		•	•	•	•
Netherlands		•	•	•	•
Norway		•	•	•	•
Switzerland		•		•	•
Austria			•		•
Czech Republic			•		•
Finland			•	•	•
Greece			•		•
Ireland			•	•	•
Portugal			•		•
Turkey			•	•	•
Belgium				•	•

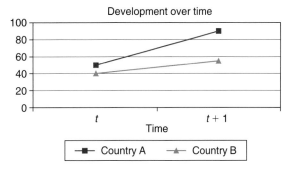

Figure 13.1   Directional convergence (Type I)

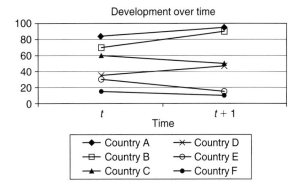

Figure 13.2   Final convergence (Type II)

empirical point of view, it is by no means clear what is meant by convergence.[3] Although the general meaning, intuitively, is clear, it becomes more complex at a closer look. In this chapter we differentiate between two different forms of convergence: directional convergence (Type I) and final convergence (Type II).[4]

---

[3] Obviously, *mutatis mutandis* the same is true for divergence. In the following, we will speak of convergence only, always including divergence in this sense.

[4] A third type of convergence – majority convergence – occurs if organisations in a country become more homogeneous or heterogeneous, respectively, in the use of a certain management concept or tool. For example, if 50% of the organisations in a country use a specific management tool and 50% do not, one can assume maximum divergence within a country since there is a clear "split" in the concrete use of this tool. However, if this value changes to 75% of the organisations using this tool, majority convergence has occurred. Note that this cannot simply be equated with an increase since one would also speak of an increase in majority convergence if the value dropped to 25%. In this case, there would have been an increased understanding by the companies not to use this tool. In more general terms: the closer a value in a country has moved to the 50% level, the greater the majority divergence has become. Vice versa, the more the value approaches the 100% or 0% level, the greater the majority convergence has become. However, since within country comparisons are not the focus of this chapter we ignore this form of convergence here (see Mayrhofer et al., 2002).

Type I – directional convergence

When comparing developments between various countries we will speak of directional convergence if the development tendency goes into the same direction. Regardless of a starting level in each country, if the variable analysed changes in the same direction in each country there is a convergence in direction at least. Figure 13.1 shows the basic idea. There, both in countries A and B the developments point in the same direction, e.g. the use of a certain management tool in each country increases. Nevertheless, the frequency of use in the two countries is at a different level.

Type II – final convergence

Final convergence exists if the developments of a variable in different countries point towards a common end point. In other words, the differences between countries decrease. This development is independent of directional convergence (Type I) as different developments in terms of, e.g. frequency of use of a certain management tool, can still result in final convergence. Figure 13.2 shows three country pairs as examples of final convergence. This is, perhaps, the meaning of convergence that is most commonly assumed in the literature, even if rarely stated and sometimes confused with the other forms.

SOME SPECULATIONS ABOUT HOW THE USE OF HR PRACTICES IN EUROPE DEVELOPED

Within the framework outlined above, and given popular notions about what might constitute "new organisational forms" as they relate to HRM noted in our discussion of change above, we might anticipate the following developments related to the HR practices chosen.

Directional convergence

Regarding directional convergence, i.e. the increasing or decreasing use of various HR practices in European countries, we start our investigation with the following assumptions.

1. The role of the HRM function and HRM strategy
   Hypothesis 1.1: The percentage of European companies determining their HR policy at the subsidiary or site level has increased throughout the past decade.

   Decentralisation of decision making and responsibility is one of the core characteristics of new organisational forms. In HRM, too, this might be regarded as one of the essentials of a "modern" version of managing HR.
   Hypothesis 1.2: The percentage of European companies devolving HRM responsibility away from specialists towards line management has increased throughout the past decade.

   In line with a general decentralisation of HRM one can expect that parts of the responsibility as well as operative tasks will no longer be assigned to the technical specialists in the HR department. Instead, line management will increasingly take over these tasks.
   Hypothesis 1.3: The relative size of HR departments in European companies has decreased throughout the past decade.

   Handing over responsibilities and operative tasks to line management, as well as an increasing cost pressure on overhead costs, will most likely lead to a reduction of central staff. Therefore, the size of HR departments – relative to the number of employees – should decrease.

2. Training and development
   Hypothesis 2: The proportion of the annual salaries and wages bill spent on training in European companies has increased throughout the past decade.

   New organisational forms not only require new structures and processes, but also demand a greater variety of new and/or different skills of employees. Therefore, investment in human capital becomes more important.

3. Performance measurements and rewards
   Hypothesis 3: The proportion of employees in European companies whose compensation package includes employee share options, profit sharing, group bonus or merit/performance related pay has increased throughout the past decade.

   Becoming more "entrepreneurial" at all levels of the company is one of the key characteristics of new organisational forms. As a consequence, proponents of that view would argue that the compensation of employees of all levels will increasingly include variable and/or performance related elements.

4. Employee communications and the role of trade unions and works councils
   Hypothesis 4: The proportion of employees in European companies that are informed about company strategy and financial performance has increased throughout the past decade.

   In new organisational forms, hierarchical and structural elements of co-ordination and control are, at least partly, substituted by other forms of communication. In addition, information for employees about crucial company indicators and issues contributes, it is argued, to a high level of involvement.

5. Organisation of work: flexible patterns of work
   Hypothesis 5: The proportion of European companies using flexible work practices like annual hours contracts, fixed-term contracts, home-based work or outsourcing/subcontracting has increased throughout the past decade.

   Replacing rigid structures by more flexible work arrangements is one of the key characteristics

of new organisational forms. These flexible work arrangements include different areas. A major issue is a more flexible approach in the area of contracting personnel (the largest element of operating costs for most organisations). To be able to adapt quickly to changing market demand organisations may try to contain their fixed obligations in the area of personnel. Therefore, work practices like annual hours contracts, fixed-term contracts, home-based work or outsourcing/subcontracting become more popular.

Final convergence

For final convergence (Type II) the common hypothesis for HR practices analysed is that over the analysed time span the differences between countries will decrease. This decrease is indicated by a reduced standard deviation of the mean values of each country variable by the end of the analysed time span.

METHODOLOGY

For directional convergence (Type I) a regression model for each country is estimated for the response variables. Estimates of the yearly changes in the response variable are obtained, and their significance is assessed by calculating their t-ratios. Size, sector and the status of being a subsidiary of a multinational company (MNC) were used as control variables.

For final convergence (Type II) the regression models for each country constitute the basis of the analysis. In addition to the actual time span covered by survey rounds (1990–1999) this procedure allows us to make a prognosis, in our case for the development 5 years beyond the measurement time range (until 2005). Thus, the regression equation for each country led to an assumed value for each quarter of a year between 1990 and 2005. This resulted in individual country values for 60 points in time. For each of these 60 points in time the mean and the standard deviation of all the countries included was calculated. In this way, we were able to determine the "bandwidth" of country values for each of these points in time. This "bandwidth" is constituted at the upper end by the mean value of all countries plus one standard deviation and at the lower end by the mean value of all countries minus one standard deviation for each point in time. The point of maximum convergence

was calculated by determining the point in time with the minimal difference between the mean value of all countries plus one standard deviation and the mean value of all countries minus one standard deviation.

FINDINGS ABOUT DEVELOPMENTS IN EUROPE

Directional convergence

The overall results can be found in Table 13.3.

The general picture concerning our hypotheses about convergent or divergent developments in Europe seems to be quite clear. There are three different types of outcome.

First, there is a group of hypotheses where the evidence is quite strong and all the available data supports our hypotheses: the change in the average developments over all countries is statistically significant, all statistically significant changes at the country level point in the same direction and are compatible with the average development, the majority of the non-significant changes at the country level are in the same direction as the significant changes overall and at the country level and all these changes are in line with the underlying hypothesis. This pattern of results applies to our hypotheses about the decreasing relative size of HR departments, the increasing investment in training and development, the increased information to employees about company strategy and financial performance and the more frequent use of performance related compensations systems.

Second, for the hypothesis about the increased use of flexible work arrangements all of the criteria above apply with the exception of the average development over all countries: this is still pointing in the hypothesised direction, but is not statistically significant. In this case, we would still argue that given the statistical evidence and the literature support allowing for theoretical generalisation the interpretation is on firm ground.

Third, for two hypotheses the empirical evidence is mixed and does not allow strong interpretation. In the case of the level at which the HR policy is determined, there is one country in which the observable developments are in the hypothesised direction and statistically significant. However, the average developments over all countries as well as the vast majority of country results point in the opposite direction, although no

Table 13.3a   Directional convergence (yearly change): the role of the HRM function and HRM strategy

	Level of policy determination	Distribution of responsibility between HR department and line management	Relative size of HR department
Range and explanation of scales	Scale range: 0–5 0 The policy in all five major HR areas is determined by (international) headquarter 5 The policy in all five major HR areas is determined at the subsidiary/site level	Scale range: 5–20 5 HR department is primarily responsible for crucial decisions in all five major HR areas 20 Line management is primarily responsible for crucial decisions in all five major HR areas	Percentage
Average value, all countries and points in time	Scale value: 2.6	Scale value: 12.6	1.5% (15 HR specialists for every 1000 employees)

Developments between 1990 and 1999
(values indicate average yearly change)

Hypotheses about developments	*HR policy determined at the subsidiary/site level*	*HR responsibility shifts from HR departments to line management*	*Relative size of HR department decreases*
Austria (2)[†]	−0.139	+0.045	+0.017
Belgium (2)	−0.028	−0.096	+0.044
Czech Republic (2)	−0.077	−0.089	+0.039
Denmark (4)	−0.037	−0.015	−0.012
Finland (3)	−0.060	+0.003	+0.014
France (5)	−0.062	−0.151	−0.024
East Germany (3)	−0.034	+0.038	+0.065*
West Germany (5)	−0.147	−0.027	+0.004
Great Britain (5)	−0.045	−0.039	+0.010
Greece (2)	−0.142	−0.150	+0.095
Ireland (3)	0.000	+0.130*	+0.018
Netherlands (4)	−0.035	+0.029	+0.021
Norway (4)	−0.041	+0.199*	+0.064*
Portugal (2)	−0.032	−0.077	+0.044*
Spain (5)	+0.011	−0.175	+0.038*
Sweden (5)	−0.087	+0.064*	+0.004
Switzerland (3)	−0.019	+0.034	+0.015
Turkey (3)	+0.142*	+0.005	+0.022
Average of developments, all countries	−0.046	−0.015	+0.026*
Proportion of countries with developments/statistically significant developments according to hypotheses (%)	11	50	89

Table 13.3b   Directional convergence (yearly change): training and development, communication with employees, compensation system and flexible work

	Proportion of annual salaries and wages bill spent on training	Information of employees about company strategy and financial performance	Compensation system includes variable/ performance related elements	Use of flexible work arrangements
Range and explanation of scales	Percentage	Scale range: 0–8 0 None of the four groups of employees is informed 8 All of the four groups of employees are informed	Scale range: 0–16 0 None of the four groups of employees has variable/ performance related compensation elements 16 All of the four groups of employees have variable/ performance related compensation elements	Scale range: 0–4 0 None of four flexible work arrangements is used 4 All of four flexible work arrangements are used
Average value, all countries and points in time	3.1% (3.1% of the annual salaries and wages bill is spent on training)	Scale value: 4.8	Scale value: 3.9	Scale value: 2.1

Developments between 1990 and 1999
(values indicate average yearly change)

Hypotheses about developments	*Increasing investment into training and development*	*More information of employees about company strategy and financial performance*	*More use of compensation systems including variable/ performance elements*	*More use of flexible working arrangements*
Austria (2)[†]	+0.061	+0.142*	+0.086	+0.010
Belgium (2)	+0.209*	−0.111	+0.012	+0.054*
Czech Republic (2)	+0.060	+0.026	−0.204	−0.045
Denmark (4)	−0.005	+0.027	+0.032	+0.127*
Finland (3)	+0.067	+0.044	+0.218*	+0.026*
France (5)	+0.069*	+0.062*	+0.540*	+0.044*
East Germany (3)	−0.044	+0.061*	+0.167*	+0.090*
West Germany (5)	+0.028	+0.091*	+0.103*	+0.059*
Great Britain (5)	+0.005	+0.079*	−0.026	−0.004
Greece (2)	+0.195	+0.053	+0.220*	−0.061
Ireland (3)	+0.101	−0.050	+0.040	−0.016
Netherlands (4)	+0.192*	+0.082*	+0.214*	+0.063*
Norway (4)	+0.182*	−0.062	+0.055	+0.045*
Portugal (2)	+0.214*	+0.046	−0.128	+0.054*
Spain (5)	+0.043	+0.132*	+0.063*	−0.103
Sweden (5)	+0.023	+0.127*	+0.010	+0.016
Switzerland (3)	+0.190*	+0.146*	+0.117*	+0.070*
Turkey (3)	+0.072	+0.052	+0.065*	−0.082
Average of develop- ments, all countries	+0.092*	+0.053*	+0.088*	+0.019*
Proportion of countries with developments/ statistically significant developments according to hypotheses (%)	89	83	83	67

[†] The values in brackets indicate the number of measurement points in time.
* Significant regression coefficient at the 0.05 level, one-tailed test of hypotheses.

statistical significance can be observed. In the case of the responsibility shift from HR departments to line managers, the evidence is even more mixed. Although in three countries the developments are in line with the hypothesis and statistically significant, the average results over all countries point in the opposite direction, statistically are not significant, and there is an even split between countries following or going against the hypothesis. For both hypotheses, the empirical evidence does not support our assumptions. However, the statistical basis for any interpretation is weak. Therefore, we have to be cautious in drawing inferences.

Given these general considerations and overall results, we now discuss the hypotheses in more detail, working through the three groups of results just highlighted.

Strong evidence

(1) The Role of the HRM function and HRM strategy – size of HR department   Hypothesis 1.3 assuming the declining size of HR departments is supported by the evidence: there is a clear tendency to reduce the proportion of employees in the HR department. The mean value of all countries within the 10-year frame is at 1.5% of the employees, indicating that companies tend to have 15 employees in the HR department for an overall number of 1000 employees. The overall reduction in the comparative size of the HR department is small but statistically significant and amounts to an average change of 0.26 points over the last 10 years.

At the country level, too, the results are in line with this trend. With the statistically not significant exception of France and Denmark, all the other countries report a decrease in the relative size of HR departments. To be sure, our measure of changes in the relative size of the HR department do not say anything about the absolute figures of the HR–staff ratio in these two countries. Take the example of those two countries going against the trend. Denmark, in that respect typical of Scandinavian countries, has a relatively decentralised way of managing HR. Nevertheless, in terms of HR–staff ratio in 1999, it belongs to the top third of the countries analysed here. France, on the other hand, being rather centralised in this respect, comes in the bottom third of countries in terms of HR–staff ratio in 1999. Thus, this seems to go against the common wisdom of centralised HR being also very personnel intensive. One explanation for that could be that economies

of scale can be reached by centralising specific tasks whereas a very decentralised way of managing HR requires also more people coordinating, training line managers for HR tasks, etc. This result is in itself an interesting case of debate, e.g. to what extent this reflects a varying degree of importance of HR in these two countries or what the scope of HR is in various countries. For the analysis of change in the relative size it is just background data.

The overall results indicating a small but significant reduction in size go in line with other empirical studies (IRS, 1996) as well as case study evidence (e.g. Gennard and Kelly, 1997). Another examination using Cranet-E data at two different points of time (1992 and 1995) has taken into consideration that the size of HR departments varies by sector and size of organisations. Therefore, particular sectors and only one size of organisations were examined and they also found an average reduction from 4.47 to 3.99 HR people within the 3-year frame (Mayrhofer and Mattl, 1997). Another study using the same Cranet-E data attempts to uncover the antecedents of the relative size of the HR department in Europe (Brewster et al., forthcoming).

(2) Training and development – investment in human capital   Hypothesis 2 presumes that the emphasis put on training and development will increase because a good training background is the basis for developments towards new organisational forms. The proportion of the annual salaries and wages bill currently spent on training is regarded as an indicator for the organisations' willingness to invest in its human capital.

The results support the hypothesis. The percentage of the annual salaries and wages bill spent on development and training has increased in nearly all of the countries in our study and currently stands, on average, at 3%. One-third of the countries show statistically significant results (see Figure 13.1). Within the 10-year frame the European average increases by 0.9 points.

Weber and Kabst, (2000: p. 247ff) examine the explanatory value of country-and-company-specific antecedents. They use the conceptual framework of Brewster and Bournois, (1991) to analyse 1995 data from Cranet-E. Weber and Kabst (2000) find that the explanatory value depends on the subject in question. Furthermore, they could show that country-specific influences are not as strong in HR training and development as they are, e.g. in recruitment and selection or equal opportunities (Weber and Kabst, 2000: p. 262).

An interpretation of the results of this hypothesis should therefore focus less on national variables than on company-specific elements.

Two groups of countries stand out as having made the most change in this respect. One possible explanation for the rather strong positions of Norway, the Netherlands and Switzerland may be that these countries are increasingly investing in high-flyer programmes and management development, both of which can be very cost-intensive. Another examination of management development shows these countries to be among those most likely to be introducing high-flyer policies (Larsen, 2000).

Apart from these three countries there are the Southern European countries, Greece and Portugal, among the countries with the biggest change in terms of increasing investment in training and development. One important reason may be that these countries started from a lower position, needing therefore bigger investments over the past few years than, e.g. most of the Northern European countries (Brewster and Larsen, 2000a).

(3) Employee communications and the role of trade unions and works councils – degree of communication with employees Communication of the financial performance as well as of corporate strategies can play an important role in all organisations including particularly, perhaps, the new organisational forms discussed above. Therefore, hypothesis 4 states that communicating these issues to all levels of employees should increase.

Again the results support the hypothesis. They show an increase in managements communicating these issues to employees in nearly all of the countries. The European average amounts to 0.5 points within the 10-year frame. Of course, what senior HR executives believe is being communicated and what is actually being received further down the organisation may not be the same thing. However, it is interesting to note that statistically significant numbers of these senior HR executives believe, at least, that more is being done now than it was a decade ago. The variety of "slopes" in these figures has been noted elsewhere (Mayrhofer et al., 2000; Morley et al., 2000). The slopes show that in some countries the information tends to be concentrated on senior levels with a steep decline when it gets to the numbers sharing that information with lower paid employees, while in others the slopes are more shallow as information is shared more generally.

Germany, Austria, Switzerland, Sweden and Spain show the most significant and positive development. From a cultural point of view this is a very mixed cluster consisting of Southern, Northern and Central European countries indicating that culture-specific variables may not be the most influential ones to explain this outcome. Furthermore, these countries have a very different structure of company sizes. These countries also include those with long established consultation rules in their legislation and those with more recently developed laws. More in depth analysis as well as case studies are therefore needed to give further explanations of that specific result.

(4) Performance measurements and rewards – variable and performance related elements of compensations systems Hypothesis 3 looks at performance related and variable elements of compensation systems and predicts an increased use of these elements during the development of new organisational forms. This hypothesis is again supported by the results. Half of the countries show statistically significant results. The mean value of yearly change of all countries amounts to 0.088. This implies that over the 10-year period from 1990 to 1999 the index for this variable increased by 0.88 units. Furthermore, this trend can be confirmed by other studies (see e.g. Müller, 2000).

The countries which show significant positive change on this aspect again exhibit a mixture of Southern, Northern and Central European countries. This seems to indicate that the cultural explanation is not very helpful here. However, the study by Weber and Kabst, (2000: p. 256) found that it is not only corporate strategy that has a very high explanatory value for the existence of a policy concerning pay and benefits. Country-specific context factors exert an important influence, too. To discover whether the institutional explanation is more valuable, one has to examine the legal and corporate framework within the different countries in depth to be able to find out which factors may be responsible for these results.

According to Weber and Kabst (2000), the Netherlands, France and Ireland have a rather high probability of formulating explicit policies on pay and benefits as compared to other countries like the UK or Germany. With the exception of Ireland, this is in line with our results.

Concerning the forms of flexible pay systems, it can be shown that Germany and France are more likely to use methods such as profit sharing whereas the UK and Ireland make more use of employee share options (Brewster and Larsen, 2000b: p. 139; Pendleton et al., 2002, 2003).

Considerable evidence

(5) Organisation of work and flexible patterns of work – flexible working practices   This hypothesis – hypothesis 5 from above – deals with the question of whether flexible working practices are increasingly used within Europe or not. In the Cranet-E survey respondents are asked about several different working arrangements.

The extent of increases in flexibility during the 1990s turned out to be very mixed. Seven of the countries (Belgium, Denmark, Germany, Finland, France, the Netherlands, Norway, Portugal and Switzerland) show statistically significant results going in line with our hypothesis. Other work on this data, using a more restricted group of countries, has shown that there are cases of sharp increases and that the host country effect over-rides that of indigenous or international ownership (Brewster and Tregaskis, 2003). Nevertheless, one-third of the countries we examined make less use of such flexible working practices over the period analysed. Most of them are situated in the south of Europe and we know from other studies that the development of flexibility shows a tendency to be driven by the north. Papalexandris (2000: p. 134) observes as a general trend that in countries where workers are more highly paid there is more room for part-time work whereas in countries with lower wages employees have difficulties accepting part-time pay. This observation is also confirmed by this study and given the significant role that part-time work holds among these non-standard work practices this may explain some of the variety of results. There is evidence from studies restricted to fewer countries that there is little sign of convergence in terms of flexible working practices (Tregaskis and Brewster, forthcoming) but more work on the convergence of flexible working patterns is clearly needed.

Weak evidence

(6) The role of the HRM function and HRM strategy – level of policy decision making   The first hypothesis 1.1 assumed that policy decisions in the HR field are taken less centrally and are increasingly being delegated to local or decentralised divisions such as subsidiaries.

Taking the mean value of all countries during the last 10 years as indicators, the results show an overall picture of increased centralisation. With the statistically significant exception of Turkey and, statistically not significant, Spain, there is no indication that HR activities are increasingly decided "locally". This is in contrast to expectations. Our data relates to HR policy decisions, but perhaps other important decisions like the overall strategy of a company or decisions concerning future investments are also decided more centrally. This is what Ruigrok et al. found in European companies: a high decentralisation of day-to-day decisions but only a very small tendency towards decentralisation concerning the overall strategy of the company (Ruigrok et al., 1999).

As already mentioned Turkey seems to be on a significantly different track – towards decentralisation. To be able to interpret this result we have to take a closer look at the different starting levels of the examined countries. Turkey started from a far lower level than the average of the other countries. If, furthermore, we take into consideration macro-level variables such as the inflow of direct foreign investments, Turkey experienced strong economic development during the decade. As compared to the other countries in our study the inflow of direct foreign investments into Turkey rose sharply from 1980 to 1999, especially investment coming from Germany, USA, Great Britain, France and the Netherlands (Erten, 1999). We can also observe a rising proportion of subsidiaries of foreign multinationals in Turkey. This increase in foreign influence might have had an effect on the countries' business practices as reflected in this result of a decentralisation of decision making. From a cultural point of view this seems to be a striking outcome. According to other studies (e.g. Hofstede, 1980; Trompenaars, 1994) Turkey is high on power distance. This normally means that all sorts of decisions from not so important things up to the highest strategic level decisions are all taken by the most important bodies of a company. The Turkish example therefore shows very well that it is important to combine the cultural view with data on behaviours to get a more complete picture of the actual situation and recent developments.

(7) The role of the HRM function and HRM strategy – decentralisation of responsibility   The second hypothesis 1.2 deals with the question of a possible allocation of HR responsibilities to line managers.

The mean value of all countries together does not support our hypothesis assuming a decentralisation tendency. On the contrary, we can see a slight centralisation of 0.15 points (see Table 13.3) from 1990 to 1999. This overall trend of centralisation is not in line with our hypothesis. It is supported by oral reports of head-hunters and consultants in the HR field. According to this group of practitioners the overall growing importance of HR, and their perception as "human capital" and the competitive advantage of organisations strengthens the positions of central HR specialists. Previously many companies placed less importance on the HR function. Smaller companies very often did not even have a formal personnel department. Those companies which have been successful in the new economy grew rapidly and often had no time to deal with questions of formal organised HR functions. Things had to happen and often they have been handled at the level of line managers because they knew best about actual needs. Now, as these companies have reached a certain size where, e.g. economic fluctuations in the IT sector become a problem, they are forced to pay attention to HR activities. They need specialists dealing in depth with these kind of problems and this strengthens the existing HR departments or fosters the establishments of central personnel functions.

Further explanations are possible at the country level where the results of our second hypothesis show Ireland, Norway and Sweden significantly on the way to decentralisation whereas approximately half of the other countries show the reverse trend. From a cultural point of view we can identify a Northern European cluster, showing a tendency to a decentralisation of HRM activities to line managers. This goes in line with Brewster and Larsen (2000a: p. 29) who identify Ireland, the UK, the Netherlands, Sweden, Denmark and Finland as countries of Northern Europe where "the commonalities between the approaches to HRM ... are, in comparison to other parts of Europe and the world, greater than the differences". There is Cranet-E survey evidence (cf. Brewster and Söderström, 1994; Brewster et al., 1997; Brewster and Larsen, 2000b) confirming the leading position in the decentralisation of HRM activities of the Northern European countries at different points of time. There is one exception, Denmark, holding a even more leading position within the Northern European cluster of other studies whereas in our study Denmark does not show such a development. But as the Danish result in our study is statistically not significant, there may be other influences responsible for this outcome. Furthermore, it is important to state again that the different countries are not starting from the same position.

Nevertheless, the question remains why Northern Europe seems to be more on a track to decentralisation. Although, of course, this does not imply any uniformity, there are some commonalities among the cited Northern European countries. Spyropoulos (1996) contrasts these countries, where freedom of association and collective bargaining rights are effectively ensured by legislation, with several Southern European countries, where such rights have been (and may be still are to a degree) absent or less effectively protected. This is connected with a significant legislative involvement in employment matters and the importance of equal opportunities (see also Brewster and Larsen, 2000a). Considering the five issues examined in our study (pay and benefits, recruitment and selection, training and development, industrial relations, and expansion and reduction of the workforce) we can see that in some way they are all open to such regulation.

This raises issues of the extent of regulation and the degree of enforcement. One argument may be that where there are a lot of rules the HR department, as experts on compliance, tend to have a greater role; the other that where rules are more likely to be enforced, line managers have clearer standards to follow and it is more possible to allow them greater autonomy. Very similar ideas concerning the characteristics of the Northern European countries might be assumed from Hofstede's cultural dimension of femininity (Hofstede, 1980). According to this study Northern European countries are high on the femininity index. Hofstede also stresses the lower power distance positions of the Northern countries which indicate a more "democratic" way of thinking and acting within organisations. Institutionally, characteristic features of the Northern European cluster are a substantial state-owned sector, the central role of the government in setting standards for wages and working conditions, rather high levels with trade union membership, and strong educational backgrounds.

Final convergence

Figures 13.3–13.9 present the final convergence (Type II) results for the HR practices analysed. Each second figure is based on analyses regression for all 18 countries. This provides a graphical display for longitudinal changes as well as the level at which this happens. The first figure for each variable gives a summary view. The straight line reflects the averaged values of the regression equations for each country for each quarter of a year, thus showing the overall trend (rise/horizontal/decline) as well as the absolute level for each variable. Thus, increases or decreases over the 10-year period can be visualised. Furthermore, the displays give an indication for the point of maximum convergence. Through calculating the bandwidth of country values for each point in time, a band can be drawn. Where the differences between the countries are smallest, the "waist" of the band indicating this development is smallest. These final convergence developments for the various HR practices analysed are worth more commentary.

Looking at where HR policy decisions are made (Figure 13.3), the point of maximum convergence is at the end of 1994, in the first half of the time span analysed. However, there is not too much change in the bandwidth, thus indicating a comparatively stable degree of diversity between European countries.

It is in the relative share of responsibility between personnel and line managers, or the devolvement of responsibility to line management, that European firms showed the least divergence in the early 1990s (Figure 13.4). Despite continuing recommendations and prescriptions for a devolvement of HR responsibility to line management during the 1990s, there was no coherent pattern of movement and developments across the European countries diverged during the 1990s.

The opposite can be claimed for the HR–staff ratio (Figure 13.5). The fact that maximum convergence is towards the end of the 10-year span of the analysis suggests that prescriptions for a reduction in the relative size of the HR department have been taken up. If we compare this and the previous results with the

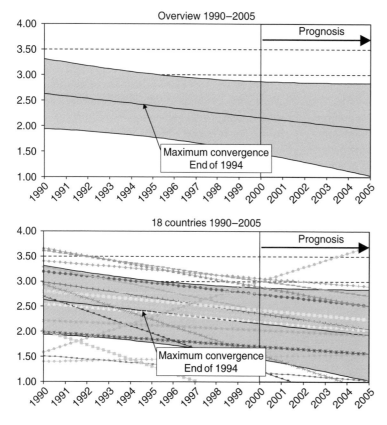

Figure 13.3   Final convergence – level of policy decision making

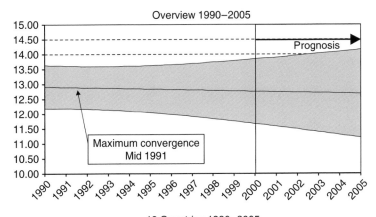

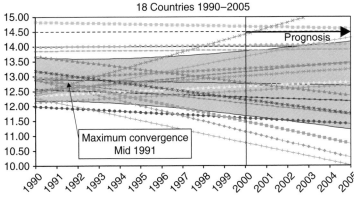

Figure 13.4 Final convergence – devolvement of responsibility from HR specialists to line management

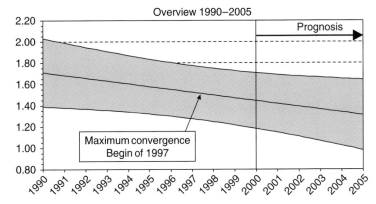

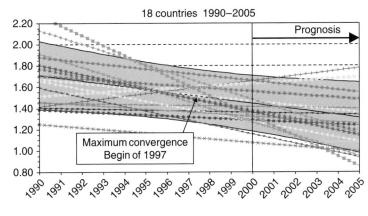

Figure 13.5 Final convergence – size of HR department (HR–staff ratio)

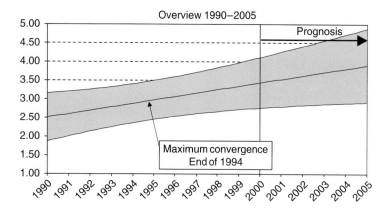

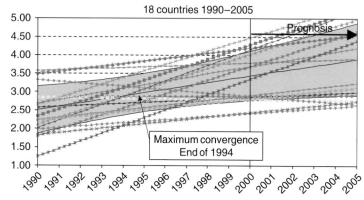

Figure 13.6 Final convergence – investment in human capital

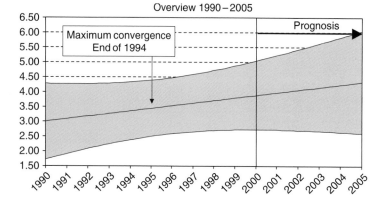

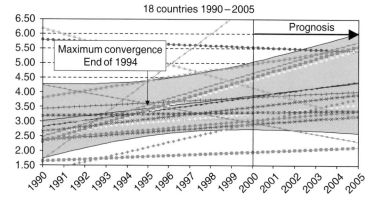

Figure 13.7 Final convergence – variable and performance related elements of compensations systems

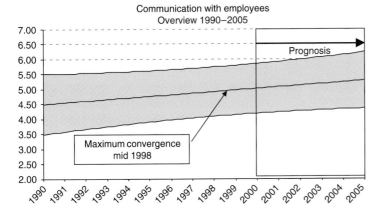

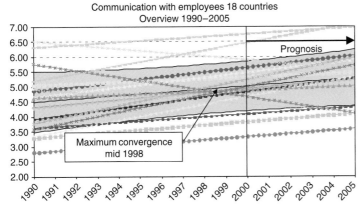

Figure 13.8 Final convergence – communication with employees

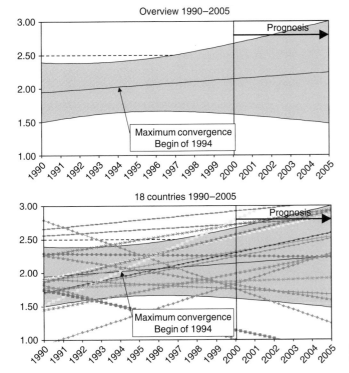

Figure 13.9 Final convergence – use of flexible working practices

directional convergence data for the same variables we can see that the results coincide.

With regard to investment in human capital (training spends), compared to the other HR practices analysed, the degree of differences as reflected in the width of the band is rather small (Figure 13.6). Here too, the point of maximum convergence is reached at the end of 1994. Again, this means that we cannot speak of a continuous trend towards final convergence.

Looking at variable and performance related elements of compensations systems, the width of the band is rather broad (Figure 13.7). Maximum convergence occurs at the end of 1994 from a clearly greater divergence at the beginning of the time span analysed. However, after the point of maximum convergence, developments become more heterogenous.

Communication with employees also shows a point of maximum convergence at the end of 1994 (Figure 13.8). From there on, developments start to get more diverse.

The point of maximum final convergence for flexible work is in the middle of the survey period (Figure 13.9). The bandwidth is rather large, indicating highly diverse approaches in different European countries towards flexible working practices over the period. This sheds new light on the directional analysis of this variable. It may well be that this did not show a clear trend, as there may have been a convergence until early 1994 and a divergence since then.

Overall, the evidence is clear that there is no unequivocal trend towards final convergence. On the contrary, developments across European countries diverged during the 1990s, having a maximum point of convergence in the middle of the decade rather than at the end.

DISCUSSION

Overall, how then are we to understand the evidence in the light of the discussion of convergence and divergence in this and the opening chapter? From a directional convergence point of view, there seems to be a positive indication of convergence. However, when one looks at the question from a final convergence point of view, the answer is no longer a clear positive. None of the HR practices converge at the end of the decade. Rather, the maximum point of convergence is reached in the middle of the decade with signs of divergence after that. An exception is the reduction in the comparative size of the HR department where we

have that point in 1997, close to the end of the analysed span. However, even there, after that point in time developments become more divergent again.

It seems clear that we need a more nuanced picture of convergence in HRM policies and practices. There are differences between the groups of countries that are chosen for analysis, there are differences between the elements of HRM that are considered and there are differences according to which time period is taken. Things appear to change slowly in HRM and perhaps the decade-long data presented here examines too short a period. In particular we have shown that there are differences in whether the focus is on directional convergence or on final convergence. We have not examined here a third potential form of convergence: majority convergence (see Footnote 4). Had we done so we would also have noted the range of practices within each country – sometimes minimal, sometimes extensive – and the degree to which they might in themselves be becoming more consistent.

Overall, a broad conclusion might be drawn that while there are some signs of convergence between countries in Europe in the direction of trends, there remain very substantial differences, perhaps even continuing further divergence, in terms of final convergence.

Having identified the drives towards convergent directional trends, and the absence of final convergence in HR practices across Europe, it is perhaps time to turn our research interests towards testing the various explanations of these developments. We encourage the readers of this text to start on the next steps in our journey of understanding.

REFERENCES

Bartlett, C. and Goshal, S. (1991) *Managing Across Borders: The Transnational Solution*. London: London Business School.

Brewster, C. (1998) Flexible working in Europe: extent, growth and challenge for HRM. In: Sparrow, P. and Marchington, M. (eds.), *HRM the New Agenda*. London: Pitmans.

Brewster, C. (2001) HRM: the comparative dimension. In: Storey, J. (ed.), *Human Resource Management: A Critical Text*, 2nd edn. London: Thomson Learning, pp. 255–271.

Brewster, C. and Bournois, F. (1991) Human resource management: a European perspective. *Personnel Review*, 20(6): 4–13.

Brewster, C. and Larsen, H.H. (2000a) The northern European dimension. A distinctive environment for HRM. In: Brewster, C. and Larsen, H.H. (eds.), *Human Resource Management in Northern Europe*. Oxford: Blackwell, pp. 24–38.

Brewster, C. and Larsen, H.H. (2000b) Flexibility in HRM. Contradictions in organizational survival. In: Brewster, C. and Larsen, H.H. (eds.), *Human Resource Management in Northern Europe*. Oxford: Blackwell, pp. 125–146.

Brewster, C. and Söderström, M. (1994) Human resources and line management. In: Brewster, C. and Hegewisch, A. (eds.), *Policy and Practice in European Human Resource Management*. London: Routledge, pp. 51–67.

Brewster, C. and Tregaskis, O. (2003) Convergence or divergence of contingent employment practices? Evidence of the role of MNCs in Europe. In: Cooke, W.M. (ed.), *Multinational Companies and Global Human Resource Strategies*. Ill: Quorum Books (Greenwood).

Brewster, C., Larsen, H.H. and Mayrhofer, W. (1997) Integration and assignment: a paradox in human resource management. *Journal of International Management*, 3(1): 1–23.

Brewster, C., Mayrhofer, W. and Morley, M. (eds.) (2000) *New Challenges in European Human Resource Management*. London: Macmillan.

Brewster, C., Wood, Brookes, M. and van Ommeren, J. (forthcoming) The determinants of HR staff in organisations: evidence from Europe.

Chakravarthy, B. and Gargiulo, M. (1998) Maintaining leadership legitimacy in the transition to new organizational forms. *Journal of Management Studies*, 35(4): 437–456.

Clegg, S.R. (1990) *Modern Organizations: Organizational Studies in the Post Modern World*. London: Sage.

Davidow, W.H. and Malone, M.S. (1993) *Das virtuelle Unternehmen. Der Kunde als Co-Produzent*. Frankfurt a. M.

Drumm, H.-J. (1996) Das Paradigma der Neuen Dezentralisation. *Die Betriebswirtschaft*, 56(1): 7–20.

Erten, C. (1999) *Die Türkei als Investitionsland – Chancen und Risiken*. Diploma Thesis. Vienna: WU Wien.

Ferlie, E. and Pettigrew, A. (eds.) (1998) Managing through Networks. In: *Strategic Human Resource Management* (Mabey, C., Salaman, G. and Storey, J. eds) London: Sage.

Fink, G. and Mayrhofer, W. (2001) Intercultural issues in management and business: the interdisciplinary challenge. In: Cooper, C.L., Cartwright, S. and Early, P.C. (eds.), *Handbook of Organizational Culture and Climate*. Chichester: Wiley, pp. 471–486.

Gennard, J. and Kelly, J. (1997) The unimportance of labels: the diffusion of the personnel/HRM function. *Industrial Relations Journal*, 28(1): 27–42.

Ghoshal, S. and Bartlett, C.A. (1998) *The Individualised Coorporation*. London: Heinemann.

Hamel, G. and Prahalad, C.K. (1994) *Competing for the Future*. Boston: Harvard Business Press.

Heckscher, C. and Donellon, A. (eds.) (1994) *The Post-Bureaucratic Organization: New Perspectives on Organizational Change*. Thousand Oaks, CA: Sage.

Hofstede, G. (1980) *Culture's Consequences*. Beverly Hills, CA: Sage.

Larsen, H.H. and Brewster, C. (2003) Line management responsibility for HRM: what's happening in Europe? *Employee Relations*, 25(3): 228–244.

IRS (1996) The changing world of personnel. *IRS Employment Trends* (604): 4–11.

Larsen, H.H. (2000) In search of management development in Europe – from self-fulfilling prophecies to organizational competence. In: Brewster, C., Mayrhofer, W. and Morley, M. (eds.), *New Challenges for European Human Resource Management*. London: Macmillan, pp. 168–196.

Mayne, L., Tregaskis, O. and Brewster, C. (2000) A comparative analysis of the link between flexibility and HRM strategy. In: Brewster, C.J., Mayrhofer, W. and Morley, M. (eds.), *New Challenges for European Human Resource Management*. London: Macmillan.

Mayrhofer, W. (1999) Personalpolitiken und -strategien im internationalen Vergleich. In: Elsik, W. and Mayrhofer, W. (eds.), *Strategische Personalpolitik*. München, Mering: Hampp, pp. 27–46.

Mayrhofer, W. and Mattl, C. (1997) HR professionals – endangered species or crucial actors? Paper presented at the *European Conference on HRM*, Athens.

Mayrhofer, W., Brewster, C. and Morley, M. (2000) Communication, consultation and the HRM debate. In: Brewster, C.J., Mayrhofer, W. and Morley, M. (eds.), *New Challenges for European Human Resource Management*. London: Macmillan.

Miles, R.E., Snow, C.C., Mathews, J.A. and Coleman, H.J. (1997) Organizing in the knowledge age: anticipating the cellular form. *Academy of Management Executive*, 11(4): 7–20.

Morley, M., Mayrhofer, M. and Brewster, C. (2000) Communication in Organisations. In: Brewster, C. and Larsen H.H. (eds.), *Human Resource Management in Northern Europe*. Oxford: Blackwell.

Nonaka, I. (1991) Managing globalization as a self-renewing process: experiences of Japanese MNCs. In: Bartlett, C.A., Doz, Y. and Hedlund, G. (eds.), *Managing the Global Firm*, 2. Aufl. ed. London, New York: Routledge, pp. S.69–94.

Papalexandris, N. (2000) Flexible working patterns. Towards reconciliation of family and work. In: Brewster, C., Mayrhofer, W. and Morley, M. (eds.), *New Challenges for European Human Resource Management*. London: Macmillan, pp. 124–140.

Pendleton, A., Poutsma, E., Brewster, C. and van Ommeren, J. (2002) Employee share ownership and profit sharing in the European Union: incidence, company characteristics and union representation. *Transfer*, 8(1): 47–62.

Pendleton, A., Poutsma, E., van Ommeren, J., and Brewster, C. (2003) The incidence and determinants of employee share ownership and profit sharing in Europe. In: Kato, T. and Pliskin, J. (eds.), *The Determinants of the Incidence and Effects of Participatory Organizations. Advances in the Economic Analysis of Participatory and Labor Management*, Vol. 7. Greenwich, CT: JAI Press.

Ruigrok, W., Pettigrew, A., Peck, S.I. and Whittington, R. (1999) Corporate restructuring and new forms of organizing: evidence from Europe. *Management International Review*, Special Issue (2): 41–64.

Ryf, B. (1993) *Die atomisierte Organisation: Ein Konzept zur Ausschöpfung von Humanpotential*. Wiesbaden: Gabler.

Scholz, C. (1995) Die virtuelle Personalabteilung: Ein Denkmodell für das Jahr 2000? *Personalführung*, (5): 398–403.

Spyropoulos, G. (1996) Regulation of direct participation in Europe. *European Participation Monitor*, EFILWC(12).

Sydow, J. and Windeler, A. (2000) Steuerung von und in Netzwerken – Perspektiven, Konzepte, vor allem aber offene Fragen. In: Sydow, J. and Windeler, A. (eds.), *Steuerung von Netzwerken*. Opladen, Wiesbaden: Westdeutscher Verlag.

Tregaskis, O. and Brewster, C. (forthcoming) Converging or diverging? A longitudinal comparative analysis of contingent employment practice in Europe. *Journal of International Business Studies*.

Trompenaars, F. (1994) *Riding the Waves of Culture. Understanding Diversity in Global Business*. Chicago, Ill: Irwin.

Volberda, H.W. (1998) *Building the Flexible Firm*. Oxford: Oxford University Press.

Warnecke, H.J. (1993) *Revolution der Unternehmenskultur. Das Fraktale Unternehmen*. Berlin.

Weber, W. and Kabst, R. (2000) Human resource policies in European organisations: an analysis of country and company-specific antecedents. In: Brewster, C., Mayrhofer, W. and Morley, M. (eds.), *New Challenges for European Human Resource Management*. London: Macmillan, pp. 247–266.

Whittington, R., Pettigrew, A., Peck, S., Fenton, E. and Conyon, M. (1999) Change and complementarities in the new competitive landscape: a European panel study. *Organization Science*, 10(5): 583–600.

Zenger, T.R. and Hesterly, W.S. (1997) The disaggregation of corporations: selective intervention, high-powered incentives, and molecular units. *Organization Science*, 8(3): 209–222.

Appendix 1 – International Survey Methodology: Experiences from the Cranfield Network

Olga Tregaskis, Caroline Mahoney and Sarah Atterbury

INTRODUCTION

In the past 10 years the number of studies on international human resource management (HRM) has steadily increased and we have seen a proliferation of journals and books disseminating the latest thinking and research findings. This is an area of study that has been incorporated into most relevant undergraduate programmes and is taking an ever-greater role in postgraduate management education. Non-US, in particular European, researchers have made a significant contribution to both the theoretical and methodological debates, and the empirical work underpinning this relatively embryonic field of study (e.g. Pieper, 1990; Poole, 1990; Bean, 1994; Boxall, 1995; Brewster, 1995; 1995; Brewster et al., 1996; Gooderham et al., 1999; Mayrhofer et al., 2000). As a consequence researchers are becoming more sophisticated in defining the parameters for international HRM investigation, selecting appropriate methodologies and recognising the universalist and contextual paradigm preferences of American and European studies, respectively (Mayrhofer et al., 2000).

The Cranfield Network project (Cranet) has contributed to the advances in this field by virtue of both its achievements and the recognition of the dilemmas and compromises made along the way. The Cranet project is not a perfect international research study, but it is a "live" one. The discussion that follows provides the reader with a route map of the conceptual and methodological questions facing international research teams and some insight into how these were addressed in the case of the Cranet survey on international HRM. The chapter begins by reviewing the aims and objectives of the project from its conception to now. Following this, some of the dilemmas faced by international researchers generally and the Cranet team specifically are reviewed. Then the methodology of the project is considered in detail, drawing on examples of the issues faced and the solutions and compromises these led to. Finally, a summary of the survey sample over the past 10 years is sketched, and the data profile for the 1999 survey is presented. The chapter concludes by considering the contribution of this survey to the wider debates in the field.

THE CRANET PROJECT IN CONTEXT

It was always an ambitious project to collect comparable data on the HRM practices of organisations in very diverse socio-economic and cultural contexts. The management of people in diverse national contexts has become increasingly important for organisations, policy makers and employee representative bodies in recent years. The rise of the multinational organisation, international labour markets and the Single European Market are but a few of the forces creating a greater demand for understanding the areas of convergence and divergence in management practice and the implications for the labour market stakeholders. However, comparative empirical data in the field, although increasing, remains limited. Available data from organisations such as the European Commission (EC), International Labour Organisation (ILO) or the Organisation for Economic

Co-operation and Development (OECD) focuses on the macro labour market perspective. It reflects the primary interest of these policy stakeholders. Evidence on management practice allowing similar large-scale comparisons across sectors, countries and a range of medium to large organisations is limited. It was this gap that the Cranet project was primarily interested in filling.

The consultancy arm of what was then Price Waterhouse, in the UK, initially sponsored the survey in its entirety. The central research question posed by the investigation was concerned with establishing the nature of HRM practice by organisations in Europe through identifying and explaining areas of convergence or divergence in practice. The study began modestly with

five countries in 1990 and was originally sponsored to run for 3 years. However, since then, although that sponsor has withdrawn from most countries, the number of countries participating has grown to over 30, expanding beyond Europe (see Table A.1.1) with each country finding its own sponsorship. This growth in the number of participating countries over time, and expansion beyond Europe, is indicative of the evolutionary nature of the project. Given the embryonic state of the field this approach has proven valuable on three counts. First, for early participants it has been a useful vehicle for mapping practice over time, e.g. in France, Germany, Spain, Sweden and the UK. Second, for newer members it acts as a starting point providing data on countries

Table A.1.1   Cranfield network on international HRM – Partner institutes

Australia	Macquarie University, Dr Robin Kramar
Austria	Vienna University of Economics and Business Administration, Prof. Wolfgang Mayrhofer
Belgium	Vlerick Leuven Gent Management School, Prof. Dirk Buyens
Bulgaria	International Business School, Dr Elizabeth Vatchkova
Cyprus (South)	Cyprus University, Prof. Eleni Stavrou-Costea/Cyprus Productivity Centre, Maria Mikellides
Cyprus (North)	Eastern Mediterranean University, Cem Tanova
Czech Republic	Katedra Personalistiky, Prof. Ing. Josef Koubek CSc
Denmark	Copenhagen Business School, Prof. Henrik Holt Larsen
Estonia	Estonian Business School, Prof. Ruth Alas
Finland	Helsinki School of Economics, Prof. Sinikka Vanhala
France	EM Lyon, Prof. Francoise Dany
Germany	University of Paderborn, Prof. Dr Wolfgang Weber
Greece	Athens University of Economics and Business, Prof. Nancy Papalexandris
Hungary	Institute for Political Science of the Hungarian Academy of Sciences, Dr András Tóth
Iceland	Reykjavik University, Dr Asta Bjarnadóttir, Dr Finnur Oddsson
India	International Management Institute (New Delhi), Prof. Venkata Ratnam
Ireland	University of Limerick, Prof. Patrick Gunnigle, Dr. Michael Morley
Israel	Bar Ilan University, Prof. Amnon Caspi
Italy	Università degli Studi di Milano-Bicocca, Dr Francesco Paoletti
Japan	Osaka-Sangyo University, Prof. T. Yamanouchi
The Netherlands	Erasmus Universiteit, Dr Jacob Hoogendoorn
New Zealand	The University of Auckland, Dr Erling Rasmussen
Norway	Norwegian School of Economics and Business Administration, Prof. Odd Nordhaug
Poland	Technical University of Lódz, Prof. Dr Czeslaw Szmidt
Portugal	Universidade Nova de Lisboa, Dr Rita Campos e Cunha
Slovenia	University of Ljubljana, Prof. Ivan Svetlik
South Africa	University of South Africa, Prof Pieter A Grobler
Spain	ESADE, Prof. Ceferí Soler
Sweden	The IPF Institute, Dr Bo Manson
Switzerland	University of St Gallen, Prof. Dr Martin Hilb
Taiwan	National Central University, Dr Tung-Chun Huang
Tunisia	University of Sfax, Prof. Riadh Zghal
Turkey	I.U. Isletme Fakültesi, Doç Dr Ayse Can Baysal
UK	Cranfield University, Prof. Shaun Tyson/Dr Richard Croucher

where little is available about HRM practice either on a national or an international level, e.g. Estonia, Slovenia and Cyprus. Third, the inclusion of countries beyond Europe (e.g. Australia, India, Japan, Taiwan and USA) enables comparisons on issues, such as convergence/divergence in Europe to other HRM models, previously hindered by a lack of data.

The objectives today remain anchored in those at the time of inception. However, as the field and the research team have developed, the level of analysis and the convergence/divergence questions posed on the data have become more sophisticated (e.g. Gooderham et al., 1999; Brewster and Larsen, 2000; Brewster and Tregaskis, 2002; Tregaskis et al., 2002; Cunha et al., 2003). In addition the questionnaire content, while having a core of comparable questions over time, has also evolved. These changes reflect issue-based developments in the field, but also monitoring by the international researchers for either ill-defined or highly culturally sensitive questions which can lead to misinterpretation of the data or non-comparability. The discussion in this chapter is confined to the countries participating in this book, for reasons of relevance, rather than the full composite of 34.

Before moving on to examine the research process involved in the Cranet project, some of the general issues facing comparative international researchers are considered.

DILEMMAS FACING THE INTERNATIONAL RESEARCHER

The term international HRM is in a sense misleading as it implies one body of knowledge, yet it encapsulates many (Boxall, 1995). For example, research can be classified in terms of its focus on the expatriate manager, HRM in the multinational organisation or, as in the case of this study, HRM practice in divergent national contexts. The conceptual issues facing researchers across these bodies of knowledge are relatively constant. Critical areas relate to questions over the use of the etic and emic perspectives, cognitive referential system, and issues of conceptual and methodological equivalence across national contexts.

Contextualisation is critical in international research for making sense of the data. Contextualisation is most usually linked with phenomenological approaches to research (Boxall, 1995; Chikudate, 1997). However,

contextualisation plays an equally important role, if somewhat different in nature, in comparative survey research. In this case understanding the context of the phenomena under investigation is important in the design and development of research instruments and in providing some degree of depth and understanding to the broad survey data. Context can be viewed from two perspectives. There is the emic perspective or "insider" viewpoint where "sense-making is dependent on inside communities" of knowledge (Chikudate, 1997: p. 172). The corollorary of this is the etic or "outsider" perspective where "sense-making is dependent on outside of the focal communities" (Chikudate, 1997: p. 172). The extent to which the research team adopts each perspective and the mechanisms adopted to tap into each perspective can have profound effects on the research process and interpretation of findings. For example, does the international research team include representatives from each country of interest? What are the consequences of excluding such sense-makers?

Turati et al. (1998: p. 191) discuss at length the importance of a cognitive referential system in shaping the actions of international research teams and therefore the level of co-ordination needed within teams. They define the cognitive referential system as "a wide concept that synthesises different levels of individuals' referential systems: institutional belonging, disciplinary belonging, paradigmatic belonging, cultural belonging, social networking, etc.". In essence they argue that members of an international research team each have their own cognitive referential system that is influenced by institutional, professional and intellectual environments. This can give rise to very divergent ways of thinking and creates an ambiguous information management and exchange environment. The sharing of a common theoretical framework or methodological perspective can help reduce this ambiguity and provide a common technical language for dialogue. Equally, the more ambiguous the environment, the greater the need for co-ordination across the international research team as a means of managing miscommunications and an exchange of meaning, and commitment to the research through a consensus of its direction (Teagarden et al., 1995; Turati et al., 1998). This raises issues for how this form of ambiguity is addressed in the organisation and management of international research teams. Importantly, co-ordination can, though for scientific understanding purposes it should not, imply a cultural dominance or ethnocentrism. Rather such co-ordination is of greatest value when it is a mechanism for managing the diversity that is inherent in international research teams.

Issues of equivalence prevail at every level of the research process (Sekaran, 1983; Cavusgil and Das, 1997). Some of the issues evolving around unmasking conceptual equivalence in terms of the theoretical frame of reference have been discussed above. Equivalence of method is also a concern. Comparative research is concerned with attempting to compare like with like. In international settings this is not an easy task. The labels used to describe practices are not always the same in different contexts. This raises issues around how legitimate is it to move away from exact or literal translations in survey instruments and still achieve comparability. Economic conditions and professional norms can make some management practices more relevant in some countries than others. Will a focus on only those common HRM practices ignore the central issues and ultimately misrepresent management practice in some countries, or lead to an extremely banal investigation? When it comes to the collection of data, the expectations of organisations, the research tradition, or the cultural norms for organisational access, are likely to vary, thereby making the same data collection mechanisms ineffective in certain contexts. How far can researchers deviate in their research method to accommodate local sensitivities without jeopardising standardisation principles? Thus throughout the whole of the research process investigators are faced with the dilemma of delineating the boundaries of equivalence and finding practical mechanisms for achieving equivalence.

The discussion that follows revisits some of these generic dilemmas in terms of the Cranet project and explains how they were addressed.

THE CRANET APPROACH

This section considers the survey method as an appropriate international research tool. The survey is frequently used in single country studies to provide standardised information that enables comparisons to be drawn on the basis of a range of independent variables, e.g. size and sector. Integral to the credibility of the survey as a scientific research tool are the notions of validity and reliability. In the case of the former the concern is with ensuring the questions have correctly operationalised theoretically and empirically the concepts of interest, i.e. they measure what we expect them to measure. In the case of the latter the concern is with ensuring whether the measuring instruments will elicit a similar response if used on multiple occasions, providing the underlying phenomenon remains constant. Validity and reliability concerns are approached from the premise of standardisation. However, in an international setting issues of standardisation are superseded by concerns for equivalence in terms of both the substantive content and the process. These and associated practices are discussed in detail below.

Survey method

Two dominant methods adopted by international researchers include the case study and the comparative survey. Each reflects strengths and weaknesses that equate to trade-offs and compromises. There is also a wide variety of ways both methods are applied, in part linked to debates on polycentric, ethnocentric and comparative approaches to international research as outlined by Adler (1984).

The case study's strength lies in its flexibility to adapt to the diverse national contexts, to explore the meaning of complex concepts, and specific features of the embeddedness of the phenomenon. The case study does not always demand strong theoretical or conceptual clarity prior to the primary data collection, allowing the research process to contribute to this refinement. Case studies on international HRM, however, vary substantially in the degree to which research frameworks and processes are predefined and the research teams co-ordinated. A highly ethnocentric approach to case research tends to be typified by a single country team that conduct case research in other country contexts that are novel to them, and largely go unrecognised by the team members. Their unfamiliarity with the cultural context or attention to the meaning and salience of the research phenomena in host country contexts can raise questions of the validity of the findings. In many instances the researcher(s) may not speak the language of the country being studied, using instead an interpreter, raising issues of whose interpretation is being reported. Fortunately, such research has declined over the past 10 years due to methodological developments in the field. The polycentric case study approach is concerned primarily with embedding the case within its institutional and/or cultural context.

The value of such work lies in its in-depth examination of meaning and process, and the identification of forces of institutional and cultural convergence–divergence. However, the degree of control adopted either through the co-ordination of the research process or the pre-specification of a generic or common research framework can determine if the study makes a useful international research contribution or ends up as a collection of loosely related single country studies. (For some examples of the former see Lane (1989); Ferner and Varul (2000); Ferner and Quintanilla (2001)). The comparative case by contrast is designed with much tighter controls and concerns for commonality both within the research process and the operationalisation of the phenomena being investigated (Muller, 2000). However, unlike the comparative survey, its primary interest is with the qualitative nature of the phenomena of interest. The distinction between the polycentric and the comparative case in practice can be a matter of subjective interpretation. However, in each of the case study approaches, the limited sample size and qualitative approach make questions of the generalisability to the wider population and identification of organisational trends redundant (Miles and Huberman, 1994).

The international survey method has been the subject of much criticism. As with criticism of national surveys some of these stem from its inability to do what the case study does. However, more useful are those criticisms that address the application of the survey method. Building on Adler's (1984) commentary, the survey can be applied in an ethnocentric fashion with disastrous consequences. As with the case study, this occurs when the inception and operationalisation of the phenomena is conducted by a research team in one country and then transplanted to other country contexts with no reference to endemic diversity issues. A polycentric survey has most value as one of multiple research methods adopted within an eclectic overall approach to the research. Its contribution is therefore best understood from a holistic discussion of the case, as survey data may not be collected in each country. Alternatively, an interview-based survey may be conducted which allows the meaning to be unravelled. However, this can be extremely time intensive and problems of limited resources, and the complexities of quantifying the qualitative outcomes, are extensive. Therefore the most widespread form of survey adopted in international research is the comparative. The aim of the comparative survey is to quantify the phenomena of interest. This was the approach adopted by the Cranet project.

Quantification, by necessity, shapes the types of questions that can be asked and the type of data that is of interest. The presence and absence, level and relative change in HRM practices and structures lend themselves more readily to quantification than HRM process and as such these became the primary interest of the Cranet survey on Strategic International HRM. The core themes included within the survey were: HR departments and HR strategy; recruitment policies; pay and benefits; training and evaluation; contract and working hours flexibility; industrial relations and employee communication. However, for each survey round changes within these areas would occur or sections would be added or deleted to reflect the concerns at the time of survey. For example, in 1991 a section on the introduction of the Single European Market was included and in 1995 the subject of older workers was expanded to reflect the EC's concerns with equality, particularly ageism. Revisions for the next survey include topics such as knowledge management, diversity and Internet mechanisms which are increasingly integral to HRM practices.

However, even within these limits national differences exist and must be recognised. When investigating HRM issues across countries there are many factors which can lead to the collection and analysis of erroneous data. For example, different levels and emphasis in employment legislation has implications for the wording or inclusion of some questions in all countries (e.g. Whitfield et al., 1994). In the case of the Cranet survey there were long debates about whether it was relevant to ask if "trade unions are recognised" as this is a legal requirement in many European countries. Similarly, some countries prohibited private recruitment agencies. As such questions were altered or excluded on a country-by-country basis as one mechanism to ensure that the results would *mean* the same thing.

A critical resource in international comparative survey work is the research team/partners. To address problems of ethnocentrism, research partners were integral to the identification and specification of the research phenomena (discussed in more detail below). They also played a critical role in the interpretation of the data. As such the assumption of the international research team was that sensible and comparative, although not perfect, data could be gathered and analysed by using the international researchers as cultural and institutional navigators and sense-makers.

The role of the research partners

The research partners play a vital role in international comparative survey research (Turati et al., 1998). They help guard against cultural bias and provide depth and understanding to the analysis of the survey data that is collected. These outcomes are influenced and achieved, to varying levels of success, by a range of factors. First, the collaborative working relationship of the research partners is vital. Different projects employ different strategies to achieve this. In the case of the Cranet project the partners from the original five countries had some knowledge of each other from past work. Previous working relations became one of the informal criteria for recommending new partners. This helped alleviate some of the miscommunications that Turati et al. discuss arising from the geographical and intellectual distance of research team members (see Mayrhofer, 1998).

Second, the cultural knowledge, expertise and assumptions of the researcher are critical. This gives the researcher easier access to understanding his/her own society. It enables an understanding of the intricacies of the systems being compared and their impact on practice (Sanders, 1994). In other words the national partner provides the insider "emic" perspective (Chikudate, 1997). As such the Cranet project consisted of partners from each of the countries included in the survey. However, this cultural knowledge is not problem-free. Being part of the system can hinder interpretation (Hofstede, 1983). It can lead inevitably to researcher bias in the selection of variables for investigation and interpretation of the data (Rosenzweig, 1994); multiple viewpoints help compensate (Cavusgil and Das, 1997). The Cranet experience demonstrated that good working relations helped ease the negotiation process between partner countries. This cultural knowledge also proved vital in tracking the "live" issues affecting HRM in each country and in particular helped guard against cultural dominance. For example, in the UK the issue of health and safety still tends to be a narrow, manufacturing related, issue and at the moment is not at the forefront of HR development. In Sweden, by contrast, the employer's responsibility for health and safety, in law, includes the psychosocial

welfare of employees and this, understood as a general reference to the working environment and employee development, is seen as one of the major challenges for personnel management in the next 10 years. Insider knowledge also helped alert the researchers to potentially sensitive questions. For example, equal opportunity issues have been an important area of study in the Netherlands tied into addressing discrimination against women, ethnic minorities and people with disabilities. However, in France this is a sensitive area where questions may be perceived as infringing civil liberties (Brewster and Hegewisch, 1994). Also linked to this issue of cultural sensitivity, it is unrealistic to assume that one individual can be cognisant of all the cultural variations and nuances that exist within the borders of a single country. As a consequence each researcher had strengths and weaknesses in their expertise and this on occasion influenced the interpretation of the data. This, of course, is an issue that affects every research team.

Third, the intellectual style of the research team can have profound effects on the research process through the intellectual exchange in terms of defining the research framework, methods and data interpretation (Teagarden et al., 1995). In many single country studies research teams are often, although not exclusively, formed on the basis of commonality in the theoretical frameworks, epistemological and ontological assumptions. However, international research makes this commonality more difficult and to some extent less desirable because of the integral nature of research traditions and the culture in which they are embedded. As a consequence it is often difficult to separate the two. For example, the scientific tradition in some of the continental European countries is founded on less positivistic thinking when compared with the UK or the USA. The difficulties these differences can create are multiplied, as the assumptions are usually implicit, rather than explicit. As such they frame the questions posed and the interpretation of the data (Smith and Meiskins, 1995). The commonality in the research method, i.e. the survey, enforced some degree of buy-in at the epistemological and ontological levels by those choosing to become active partners. However, inevitably this was an issue that the Cranet partners faced which on the most part led to compromises, for example the inclusion of country-specific questions. Only in one instance did this lead to a change in a national partner.

Fourth, the subject expertise of the partners has implications. For example, national research teams frequently have a range of subject experts that complement each other and together can cover a wide array of issues involved in the investigation of HRM/IR research. This was achieved across the international research partners; however, inevitably on a country-by-country basis the expert knowledge of the local partner was restricted. The Cranet project managed this deficiency by using the subject expertise from across the network with the culturally rooted knowledge of each local expert. This approach also gave rise to writing clusters where country partners worked together to interpret data on the themes they were most interested in and had most knowledge of. This analysis strategy has been adopted for this book.

The role of each partner was therefore multiple, namely, that of subject, cultural and academic expert. At this point it is perhaps appropriate to raise the issue of co-ordination of activities. The organisational processes involved in mounting an international survey on HRM across what is now 34 countries is no mean feat. To assist the process Cranfield School of Management has a design team working on supporting a range of activities for the research partners. The role of the Cranfield team has been central to the expansion of the project. Their role is in part historical as they were the institute initially approached by the survey sponsors in 1989. Since then they have assumed an important co-ordinating function on behalf of the research partners. Twice yearly meetings hosted by one of the partners further reinforces communications and facilities a range of Cranet activities (e.g. conferences, collaboration on funding proposals and dissemination opportunities).

The benefits of international research teams for comparative studies are many, and indeed the experience of the Cranet project would suggest they are a necessity rather than an option. However, they also raise important questions in terms of how partners are included and the basis of their expertise – issues that are not uncommon to single country research teams. However, the project structure acknowledges the significance of the collective strengths, in terms of intelligence, skills and resources, of the international research team. The Cranet research partners used the collective international "outsider" perspective combined with the local "insider" perspective to their advantage by using the resources they had across the network to support local expertise and to guard against ethnocentrism.

Sampling frames

The sample frame adopted for survey research has important implications for the representativeness of the data gathered and the extrapolation of the finding beyond the sample. However, this is an area fraught with difficulties. Ideally the sampling frame should be both consistent with the research aims and tap into similar samples across national boundaries (Collett, 1998). In practice establishing comparable databases across countries is not easy. Available international databases have many gaps (e.g. typically, public sector organisations). This leads many researchers to look into national databases: although these are also not without their problems. The Cranet project was interested in organisational level HRM practice as reported by the HRM director or equivalent. This meant the sample frame needed to list the organisational address and personal contact, to enable a postal survey. The international partners found that many of the commercial mailing lists available were not as comprehensive as they at first appeared. Alternatively, where lists existed they lacked the necessary information (e.g. size and sector details) to draw representative samples. In some instances public sector organisations were not included. The cost of commercial and government lists often made them prohibitive. One alternative was to create your own list, although this is an extremely time- and resource-expensive exercise. It is an area of activity that can be difficult to find funding for and was therefore not an option for many of the Cranet partners. However, where suitable databases already existed within the academic institution, these were sometimes integrated with other lists to give a more representative sample (e.g. Belgium). An alternative option was to use the best available list for each country and to understand its weaknesses. This meant that in some countries databases from national professional associations were used (e.g. Greece and Israel), in others commercial databases were used (e.g. UK, Germany, France and Norway) and in some either government lists (e.g. Sweden, Slovenia and Finland) or a combination of the above three sources (e.g. Portugal, Estonia and Turkey) were used. The formal nature of the questions presupposed the existence of an

HR/personnel function. Therefore a decision needed to be made regarding the appropriate cut-off for the size of organisation approached. Research by Semlinger and Mendius (1989) provided some guidance suggesting that formal HRM functions were more likely in organisations with 200 or more employees. This was therefore set as the standard on which comparisons across the countries would be made. However, in the case of some countries, such as Spain, Denmark and the Netherlands, this cut-off would have excluded at least half of the working population. Therefore it was important to acknowledge these national variations and lower the threshold to 100 or more employees in some countries. In practice, our survey findings showed that the Semlinger and Mendius data was limited, and that many organisations with less than 200 employees have formal HR departments. As the project has expanded with more partnering countries the 100-employee threshold has been adopted, allowing some degree of international comparisons at this level. However, the 200-employee threshold remains the dominant threshold and the one adopted for the country comparisons in this book.

Constructing the questionnaire

The comparative approach adopted by the Cranet team (discussed above) made the conflict between international comparability and local sensitivity less of a bi-polar dilemma. In addition the partnership approach, albeit with administration provided by Cranfield, enabled the project to strive for comparability while being vigilant to national sensitivities.

The questionnaire therefore consisted largely of the same questions for all countries. Some of the questions or categories were altered where national conditions demanded this. For example, most of the countries opted to use a four-fold staff classification system, i.e. management, professional/technical, clerical and manual. However this was inappropriate in some countries. For example, in France it is common to use three staff categories: "cadre" referring to management and some professional employees, "ETAM" (employés, techniciens et agents de maîtrise) who are administrative, technical and supervisory staff; and "operatives". In addition to being customary terms they are also defined in law. Therefore it made little sense to compromise local logic for international comparability. In Germany

and Austria, the category for manual workers was split between skilled and semi/unskilled to enable more specific national analysis, though these were combined for cross-country analysis. Issues of relevance and cultural sensitivity have also become more pronounced with the expansion of Cranet into other non-European countries. For example, in Tunisia where HR managers deal predominantly with the more traditional administrative issues, some questions such as those about evaluation, training needs and communication were not understood or answered by many respondents.

The process of questionnaire development is often a lengthy negotiation process. For example, the discussions about redrawing the 1999/2000 questionnaire went on over several bi-annual meetings and included working parties on different aspects of the questionnaire. It is critical in long running surveys to ensure that the questions are relevant to the debates at any particular time period and in all of the countries under consideration. However, it is also important not to jeopardise comparisons over time. As a result the partners, on this occasion, felt only modest changes would be needed. The process of negotiation to delete, insert or change questions then begins. Here Cranfield plays a critical role in co-ordinating all the responses. However, the decisions regarding changes lie ultimately with a working party made up of a sub-group of the partners, who nominate themselves onto the working party. Input is requested from all partners at the early stages of the process, which forms the basis of the discussions of the working party. Feedback on progress and suggested revisions from the working group are reported back to all partners at the regular 6 monthly Cranet meetings. At this stage, the meetings are therefore an important forum for ensuring national and cultural relevance of the suggested changes for each partner. The final survey is always agreed during one of the regular meetings. This inclusive process is critical to developing a shared and "consensual vision" for the research activity (Teagarden et al., 1995; Turati et al., 1998: p. 194).

The language of the participating country is adopted for the questionnaire. This required the English language copy to be translated. However, to ensure comparability the translation process is not straightforward. There are two approaches that may be adopted, namely literal translation (Elder, 1976) or equivalent translation (Lincoln and Kalleberg, 1990). The former is often insufficient as the meaning can be distorted giving rise to misleading results. It is vital that the conceptual equivalence of questions is retained which may mean using different words. For example, the term "school leaver" proved quite difficult when asking about the recruitment policy of companies in relation to this labour market sub-group. Problems arose because of the divergence in educational systems across countries making the concept of the "school leaver" different throughout Europe. This problem was overcome by adopting equivalent terms in each country or adding a supplementary explanation clarifying the parameters of the term. The other technique that was adopted to cope with and identify problems with conceptual equivalence was re-translation (Brislin et al., 1973; Brislin, 1976). Each questionnaire was translated from English to the designated language, usually by a native speaker and someone familiar with the HRM field. Using those for whom the designated language was their first language ensures the translation adopted the local linguistics as opposed to textbook linguistics. Having a translator familiar with the HRM field was found to be critical as the words often reflected a technical language that was unfamiliar to those outside of the profession. These translations were then re-translated into English by a second translator. The re-translation was compared, by the Cranfield team and the local partner, to the original version and any discrepancies were discussed with the relevant research partner. This helped address misinterpretations such as the translation of "fixed term" employment as "permanent employment". In addition, some countries such as Switzerland and Belgium used multiple languages (Swiss German/Swiss French and Flemish/French) to reflect the respondent's expectations and ensure a representative sample and strong response rate. The final stage involved the piloting of the translated questionnaires with personnel managers in each country. This provided a further check that the meaning has been translated and appropriate technical terms used.

Clearly the translation process is more than a technical process. It reflects and highlights the social and cultural embeddedness of language.

Data collection and processing

The project adopted a postal-survey approach. The postal survey has the advantage of being a cost-effective mechanism for large sample sizes compared with face-to-face visits. And as the aim of the project is to tap into general trends, the large-scale survey approach was more appropriate. However, this, as with every other aspects of the research process, needed to be sensitive to local issues. For example, in Greece, the research partner felt very strongly that a postal survey would simply be ignored by companies and therefore was a waste of resources. In this case companies were contacted by phone and questionnaires were delivered to and collected by research students from those respondents agreeing to participate. A similar procedure was used in Bulgaria.

In all countries the questionnaires went to a named individual, i.e. the HRM director. The limited resource made it impossible to collect data from more than one respondent per organisation. Experts in the field have pointed out that, when attempting to gain a view of the structure and behaviour of social phenomena such as HR, it is important, though not unproblematic, to obtain a "role-holder who can reasonably speak for the social unit concerned, reliably reporting its structure and behaviour" (Millward and Hawes, 1995: p.72). Given the objectives of this survey the HR director was considered the most appropriate role-holder.

The role of the Cranfield team came again to the fore in the processing and preparation of the international data. The rationale for centralising this phase of the research process was to ensure that the partners ultimately all had access to exactly the same comparable data. As questions varied across countries, for the reasons discussed above, it was important to ensure the international data set compared the same sets of questions. In addition, any anomalies with the country data identified by the research partners would then be corrected centrally and the clean and most current copy of the international data set distributed to all. For some countries, the centralisation of this process also provided a resource in terms of the people and the technology that would have otherwise excluded them from such research activities. For example, in the Czech Republic the financial resources to fund data processing would have been very difficult to find. The technological advances over the past 10 years have made the centralised processing and international distribution of this data even more flexible and speedy.

A number of researchers espouse the value of multivariate statistics for achieving a more sophisticated and accurate reflection of practice (England and Harpaz, 1983; Sekaran, 1983; Cavusgil and Das, 1997). Multivariate procedures, in the absence of longitudinal data, enable cause-and-effect relations to be explored via associations in the data. They allow complex relations to be examined by considering the joint effects of several variables on HRM practice. At the same time statistical controls can be used to guard against the influence of extraneous factors. They thus enable the complexity of international relations to be explicated more fully. However, they are also very demanding of the data in terms of the numbers and the distribution of the responses. While some of these problems can be overcome through data transformation techniques, e.g. weighting, de-skewing, in some instances this is not feasible. In the case of the Cranet project, multivariate procedures have been adopted to explore certain research questions (Tregaskis, 1997; Gooderham et al., 1999; Brewster and Tregaskis, 2002). However, in other cases, particularly where the state of our knowledge is scant, descriptive and exploratory statistics have proved equally useful (Morley et al., 1996; Brewster et al., 1997; Brewster and Larsen, 2000).

The value of muddling through

An old, though recently reprinted, and brilliant article by Lindstrom (1996) discussed management as "the art of muddling through" and has always been one of the more realistic articles which reflected the full flavour of the management process. While we are very proud of what we have done with the network and the visibility it has achieved, we should not leave this discussion of the Cranet process with readers having any misconceptions that this occurred because the team involved was especially brilliant or carefully planned the project from inception to its current state. There was a lot of "learning-by-doing"; there was a great deal of serendipity, particularly in the choice of country partners; there was much taking advantage of situations and funding that became available. And there remains much that we are conscious could be improved and extensive quantities of data that remain under-explored. It would seem that getting together an enthusiastic, knowledgeable and flexible team interested in exploring the international and intercultural issues we have outlined here, and those covered in the rest of the book, is the key to success.

1999/2000 SURVEY DETAILS

This section reviews the sample profile for the 1999/2000 survey, the data from which is at the core of this book. The data collection period lasted from September 1999 to the Spring of 2000 depending on the time schedules adopted by each country. For reasons of simplicity it will be referred to here as the 1999/2000 dataset. As mentioned previously the survey in 1999/2000 included 34 countries, although this book focuses on a subset of these. Table A.1.2 below illustrates the expansion of the countries participating in the research over the last 10 years and details the countries conducting the survey in 1999/2000.

In 1999/2000 a total of 5335 questionnaires covering organisations with more than 200 employees were returned from the 23 countries included in the book. This gave a 17% response rate (see Table A.1.3). There was, as in past years, some variation in response rates across countries (see Figure A.1.1). This may in part be due to differences in attitudes to surveys and the disclosure of organisational details across countries. There were also variations in data collection strategies for the reasons discussed previously. For example, all Bulgarian and some Greek organisations were first approached for their agreement to participate before receiving a questionnaire; others were interviewed face to face.

Sector categories are based on the NACE (*Nomenclature générale des activitiés économiques dans les Communautés européennes*) system of industrial classification. This is the classification of economic activities introduced by the EC in an attempt to collate statistical information on the labour market across countries. While the classification system used in the Cranet survey covers 15 divisions, for analysis purposes these divisions are collapsed into five broad sectors: manufacturing, other industry (which includes agriculture, energy and water, chemical processing and construction); business services (which includes banking, finance and insurance), other services (which includes transport, wholesale and retail, hotels and catering, personal and other services) and the public sector (which includes public health services, higher education, local and central government). The distribution of industry sectors is depicted in Figure A.1.2. It is clear that the sample is dominated by private sector organisations (67%), in particular manufacturing industries, which

Table A.1.2   Countries Surveyed

1989	1991	1992	1993	1995/1996	1999/2000
France	France	France		France	France
Germany (W)	Germany (W)	Germany (W)		Germany (W)	Germany*
Spain	Spain	Spain		Spain	Spain
Sweden	Sweden	Sweden		Sweden	Sweden
UK	UK	UK		UK	UK
	Denmark	Denmark		Denmark	Denmark
	Italy			Italy	Italy
	The Netherlands	The Netherlands		The Netherlands	The Netherlands
	Norway	Norway		Norway	Norway
	Switzerland			Switzerland	Switzerland
		Finland		Finland	Finland
		Germany (E)	Germany (E)	Germany (E)	Germany (E)*
		Ireland		Ireland	Ireland
		Portugal			Portugal
		Turkey		Turkey	Turkey
			Austria		Austria
			Czech Republic	Czech Republic	Czech Republic
			Greece	Greece	Greece
				Australia	Australia
				Belgium	Belgium
				Bulgaria	Bulgaria
				Cyprus	Cyprus
				Hungary	
				New Zealand	
				Poland	
					Estonia
					India
					Israel
					Japan
					Slovenia
					South Africa
					Taiwan
					Tunisia
					USA

* From 1999/2000, German data combined (covering east and west).

Table A.1.3   Response rates for countries included in book

Year	Sample	Returns	Response rate (%)	Returns for 200+ employees
1989	25,200	5682	22	5098
1991	32,200	5511	17	5449
1992*	37,360	6426	17	5316
1995/6	29,706	6342	21	4876
1999/2000	53,631	8216	15	6184

* 1993 data also included in these 1992 calculations.

make up 33% of the total sample. Importantly, the method of data collection has remained the same during all rounds, so the sampled distribution of organisations by industry sector has not, or has only marginally, changed since the start of the survey in 1989.

The size distribution breakdowns indicate that the sample is heavily represented by organisations employing more than 200 people (see Figure A.1.3). Approximately one-third of the sample employs between 200 and 499, two in ten employ 500–999 and three in ten

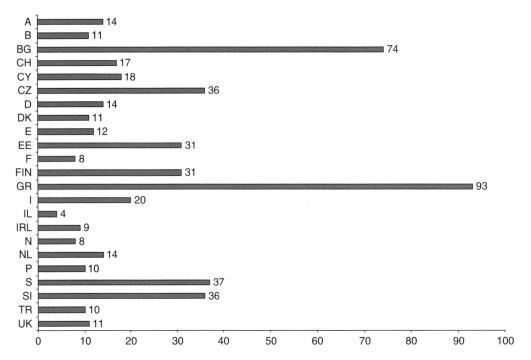

Note: Reponse rates for Bulgaria (BG) and Greece (GR) are relatively high due to variations in data collection (see text). The response rate in Italy (I) is unconfirmed.

A:	Austria	D:	Germany	FIN:	Finland	NL:	The Netherlands
B:	Belgium	DK:	Denmark	GR:	Greece	P:	Portugal
BG:	Bulgaria	E:	Spain	I:	Italy	S:	Sweden
CH:	Switzerland	EE:	Estonia	IL:	Israel	SI:	Slovenia
CY:	Cyprus	F:	France	IRE:	Ireland	TR:	Turkey
CZ:	Czech Republic	N:	Norway	UK:	United Kingdom		

Figure A.1.1   Response rates across countries for 1999/2000

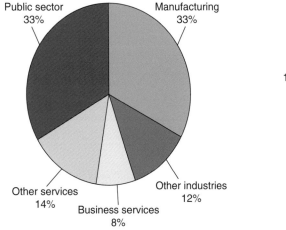

Figure A.1.2   Sample distribution by sector

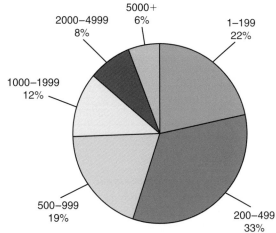

Figure A.1.3   Survey size distribution

organisations have more than 1000 employees. Since the survey began the size distribution has remained relatively constant.

CONCLUSION

The stock of knowledge on international HRM is increasing. The weight of empirical evidence underlines the importance of the institutional context in explaining the diversity of management practice across national borders. Equally, advances in globalisation have contributed to the sharing of common management approaches. Understanding the subtleties and duality of converging and diverging management practice is one of the theoretical challenges facing the field for the future. Equally, methodological demands are altering. The past 20–30 years have been concerned with the application of single methods and adapting the process to the complexities of international environments. The methodological issues involved are now much more widely understood. The strengths and weaknesses associated with the array of methods available now enable greater innovation. For example, the combination of methods borne from linguistic and phenomenological approaches (Chikudate, 1997), the use of historical case analysis (Quintanilla, 1998) or paradigm boundary-spanning approaches combining methods from the contextual and universalist camps (Mayrhofer et al., 2001). Greater methodological innovation is necessary to enable theoretical development within the field. It is also necessary to gain a fuller understanding of the meaning of concepts, HRM/IR systems and processes as understood by stakeholders in divergent and dynamic contextual environments.

REFERENCES

Adler, N. (1984) Understanding the ways of understanding: cross-cultural management methodology reviewed. *Advances in International Comparative Management*, 1: 31–67.

Bean, R. (1994) *Comparative Industrial Relations: An Introduction to Cross-National Perspectives*, 2nd edn. London: Routledge.

Boxall, P. (1995). Building the theory of comparative HRM. *Human Resource Management Journal*, 5(5): 5–17.

Brewster, C. (1995) Towards a European model of human resource management. *Journal of International Business Studies*, 26(1): 1–21.

Brewster, C. and Hegewisch, A. (1994) (eds.). *Policy and Practice in European Human Resource Management Practice*. London: Routledge.

Brewster, C. and Larsen, H.H. (2000). *Human Resource Management in Northern Europe*. Blackwells, Oxford.

Brewster, C., Larsen, H.H. and Mayrhofer, W. (1997) Integration and assignment: a paradox in human resource management. *Journal of International Management*, 3(1): 1–23.

Brewster, C. and Tregaskis, O. (2002) Convergence or divergence of contingent employment practices? In Cooke, W. (ed.) *Multinational Companies and Transnational Work Issues*.

Brewster, C., Tregaskis, O., Hegewisch, A. and Mayne, L. (1996). Comparative research in human resource management: A review and an example. *International Journal of Human Resource Management*, 7(3), 585–604.

Brislin, R.W. (1976) (ed.) *Translation Applications and Research*. New York: Goulder Press.

Brislin, R.W., Lonner, W.J. and Thorndike, R.M. (1973) *Cross-Cultural Research Methods*. London: Wiley-Interscience.

Cavusgil, S.T. and Das, A. (1997) Methodological issues in empirical cross-cultural research: a survey of the management literature and a framework. *Management International Review*, 37(1), 71–96.

Chikudate, N. (1997) Exploring the life-world of organizations by linguistic orientated phenomenology in sub-cultural analysis of organizations: a comparison between Japanese and U.S. banks. *Management International Review*, 37(2): 169–183.

Collett, P. (1998) Contrasting styles in international management research. *Journal of Managerial Psychology*, 13(3): 214–224.

Cunha, R.C., Cunha, M.P., Morgado, A. and Brewster, C. (2003) Market impacts on strategy, HRM practices and organizational performance: toward a European model. *Journal of Management Research*, 1(1): 79–91

Elder, J. (1976) Comparative cross-national methodology. *Annual Review of Sociology*, 2: 529–530.

England, G.W. and Harpaz, I. (1983) Some methodological and analytic considerations in cross-national research. *Journal of International Business Studies*, Fall, 49–59.

Ferner, A. and Varul, M. (2000) "Vanguard" subsidiaries and the diffusion of new practices: a case study of German multinationals. *British Journal of Industrial Relations*, 38(1): 115–140.

Ferner, A. and Quintanilla, J. (2001) Country-of-origin, host country effects and the management of HR in multi-nationals. *Journal of World Business*, 36(2): 107–127.

Gooderham, P.N., Nordhaug, O. and Ringdal, K. (1999) Institutional and rational determinants or organisational practices: human resource management in European firms. *Administrative Science Quarterly*, 44: 507–531.

Hofstede, G. (1983) The cultural relativity of organisational practices and theories. *Journal of International Business Studies*, 14(2): 75–89.

Lane, C. (1989) *Management and Labour in Europe: The Industrial Enterprise in Germany, Britain and France*. Worcester, UK: Billing & Sons.

Lincoln, J.R. and Kalleberg, A.L. (1990) *Culture, Control, and Commitment: A Study of Work Organisation and Work Attitudes in the United States and Japan*. Cambridge, Cambridge University Press.

Lindblom, C.E. (1996) The science of "muddling through". In: Campbell, S. and Fainstain, S.S. (eds.) *Readings in Planning Theory*. Oxford: Blackwells, pp. 288–304.

Mayrhofer, W. (1998) Between market, bureaucracy, and clan – coordination and control mechanisms in the Cranfield network on European human resource management (Cranet-E). *Journal of Managerial Psychology*, 13(3/4): 241–258.

Mayrhofer, W., Brewster, C. and Morley, M. (2000) The concept of strategic human resource management. In: Brewster, C., Mayhofer, W. and Morley, M. (eds.) *New Challenges for European Human Resource Management*. MacMillan: London.

Mayrhofer, W. and Fink, G. (2001) Intercultural issues in management and business: The Interdisciplinary Challenge. In Cooper, C.C., Cartwright, S. and Early, P.C. (Eds.) *Handbook of Organizational Culture and Climate*. Chichester et al: 471–486.

Miles, M.B. and Huberman, A.M. (1994) *Qualitative Data Analysis – An Expanded Sourcebook*, 2nd edn. London: Sage.

Millward, N. and Hawes, W.R. (1995) Hats, cattle and IR research: a comment on McCarthy. *Industrial Relations Journal*, 26(1): 69–73.

Muller, M. (2000) Employee representation and pay in Austria, Germany, and Sweden. *International Studies of Management and Organisation*, 29(4): 66–82.

Morley, M., Brewster, C., Gunnigle, P. and Mayrhofer, W. (1996) Evaluating change in European industrial relations: research evidence on trends at organisational level. *International Journal of Human Resource Management*, 7(3): 640–656.

Pieper, R. (ed.) (1990) *Human Resource Management: An International Comparison*. Berlin: Walter de Gruyter.

Poole, M. (1990) Human resource management in an international perspective. *International Journal of Human Resource Management*, 1(1): 1–15.

Quintanilla, J. (1998) The configuration of human resources management policies and practices in multinational subsidiaries: the case of European retail banks in Spain. PhD thesis, University of Warwick, England.

Rosenzweig, P.M. (1994) Influences of human resource management practices in multinational firms. *Journal of International Business Studies*, 20(2): 229–252.

Sanders, D. (1994) Methodological considerations in comparative cross-national research. ISS, 142, UNESCO, pp. 513–521.

Semlinger, K. and Mendius, H.G. (1989) Personalplanung und Personalentwicklung in der gewerblichen Wirtschaft, RKW, unpublished.

Sekaran, U. (1983). Methodological and theoretical issues and advancements in cross-cultural research. *Journal of International Business Studies*, Fall, 61–73.

Smith, C. and Meiskins, P. (1995) System, society and dominance effects in cross-national organisational analysis. *Work, Employment and Society*, 4(3): 451–470.

Teagarden, M.B. et al. (1995) Towards a theory of comparative management research: an idiographic case study of the best international human resources management projects. *Academy of Management Journal*, 38(5): 1261–1287.

Tregaskis, O. (1997) The role of national context and HR strategy in shaping training and development practice in French and UK organisations. *Organization Studies*, 18(5): 857–875.

Tregaskis, O., Heraty, N. and Morley, M. (2001) HRD in multinationals: the global/local mix. *Human Resource Management Journal*, 11(2): 34–56.

Turati, C., Usai, A. and Ravagnani, R. (1998) Antecedents of co-ordination in academic international project research. *Journal of Managerial Psychology*, 13(3/4): 188–198.

Whitfield, K., Marginson, P. and Brown, W. (1994) Workplace industrial relations under different regulatory systems: a survey-based comparison of Australia and Britain. *British Journal of Industrial Relations*, 32(3): 319–338.

Appendix 2 – Cranet Questionnaire

HOW TO COMPLETE THIS QUESTIONNAIRE

This questionnaire is designed to make completion as easy and fast as possible. Most questions can be answered by simply ticking boxes. Very little information will need to be looked up.

Wherever it says "you" in the questionnaire please answer from the point of view of your organisation.

"*Organisation*" means your firm, subsidiary or, if you are in a head office, the group in which you work. For the public sector it refers to the specific local or health authority, government department, etc.

"*Part of a larger group*" refers to subsidiaries or the parent company of a group. For central government departments the "larger group" is the civil service as a whole.

The questionnaire has been adapted for simultaneous use by private and public sector employers in 22 countries; some questions may therefore be phrased in a slightly unfamiliar way.

Thank you for your help

SECTION I: PERSONNEL/HUMAN RESOURCES FUNCTION

1. **Does your organisation have a personnel or human resource department/manager?**
   1 ❑ Yes   2 ❑ No

2. **Approximately how many people are employed by your organisation in the personnel/human resources function (including wage administration and training)?**
   a. ❑ In total: _____   ❑ Male _____   ❑ Female _____   1 ❑ Don't know
   b. Do you use external providers in any of the following areas?
      A. Pay and benefits   ❑ 1
      B. Recruitment and selection   ❑ 1
      C. Training and development   ❑ 1
      D. Workforce outplacement/reduction   ❑ 1
      E. No external providers used in personnel function   ❑ 1
   c. How has the use of external providers changed during the last 3 years?
      1 ❑ Increased   2 ❑ Same   3 ❑ Decreased

3. **Does the head of the personnel/human resources function have a place on the main Board of Directors or the equivalent?**
   1 ❑ Yes (If Yes, go to question 5)   2 ❑ No

4. **If No, who on the main Board of Directors has responsibility for personnel issues?**
   A. Chief executive/managing director   ❑ 1
   B. Administrative director   ❑ 2

C. Finance director   ❑ 3
D. Company secretary   ❑ 4
E. Production director   ❑ 5
F. Others, please specify _____

5. From where was the most senior personnel or human resources manager recruited?
A. From within the personnel department   ❑ 1
B. From non-personnel specialists in your organisation   ❑ 2
C. From personnel specialists outside of the organisation   ❑ 3
D. From non-personnel specialists outside of the organisation   ❑ 4
E. Other, please specify _____

Strategy and corporate policies

6. Does your organisation have a policy for the following personnel/human resource management areas:

	Yes, written	Yes, unwritten	No	Don't know
A. Pay and benefits	❑ 1	❑ 2	❑ 3	❑ 4
B. Recruitment and selection	❑ 1	❑ 2	❑ 3	❑ 4
C. Training and development	❑ 1	❑ 2	❑ 3	❑ 4
D. Employee communication	❑ 1	❑ 2	❑ 3	❑ 4
E. Equal opportunity/diversity	❑ 1	❑ 2	❑ 3	❑ 4
F. Flexible working practices	❑ 1	❑ 2	❑ 3	❑ 4
G. Management development	❑ 1	❑ 2	❑ 3	❑ 4

7. Does your organisation have a:

	Yes, written	Yes, unwritten	No	Don't know
A. Mission statement	❑ 1	❑ 2	❑ 3	❑ 4
B. Corporate strategy	❑ 1	❑ 2	❑ 3	❑ 4
C. Personnel/HR management strategy	❑ 1	❑ 2	❑ 3	❑ 4

8. If you have a corporate strategy, at what stage is the person responsible for personnel/human resources involved in its development?
A. From the outset   ❑ 1
B. Through consultation   ❑ 2
C. On implementation   ❑ 3
D. Not consulted   ❑ 4

9. Is the performance of the personnel/human resources function/department systematically evaluated?
1 ❑ Yes   2 ❑ No   3 ❑ Don't know
(If Yes, go to next question, otherwise go to question 12)

10. Whose views are considered in evaluating the performance?
A. Top management   ❑ 1
B. Line management   ❑ 1
C. Employees   ❑ 1
D. Personnel/HR function/department itself   ❑ 1
E. Other, please specify _____

11. What criteria are used for evaluation?

A. Internal measures of cost effectiveness   ❏ 1
B. External benchmarking of cost   ❏ 1
C. Performance against objectives   ❏ 1
D. Other, please specify _____

12. If your organisation is part of a larger group of companies/divisions, etc. please indicate where policies on the following issues are mainly determined.

	International HQ	National HQ	Subsidiary	Site/establishment
Private sector:		Headquarters	Service	Local offices
Public sector:			department/division	
A. Pay and benefits	❏ 1	❏ 2	❏ 3	❏ 4
B. Recruitment and selection	❏ 1	❏ 2	❏ 3	❏ 4
C. Training and development	❏ 1	❏ 2	❏ 3	❏ 4
D. Industrial relations	❏ 1	❏ 2	❏ 3	❏ 4
E. Workforce expansion/reduction	❏ 1	❏ 2	❏ 3	❏ 4
F. Management development	❏ 1	❏ 2	❏ 3	❏ 4

13. With whom does the primary responsibility lie for major policy decisions on the following issues?

	Line management	Line management in consultation with HR department	HR department in consultation with line management	HR department
A. Pay and benefits	❏ 1	❏ 2	❏ 3	❏ 4
B. Recruitment and selection	❏ 1	❏ 2	❏ 3	❏ 4
C. Training and development	❏ 1	❏ 2	❏ 3	❏ 4
D. Industrial relations	❏ 1	❏ 2	❏ 3	❏ 4
E. Workforce expansion/reduction	❏ 1	❏ 2	❏ 3	❏ 4

14. Has the responsibility of line management changed over the last 3 years for any of the following issues?

	Increased	Same	Decreased
A. Pay and benefits	❏ 1	❏ 2	❏ 3
B. Recruitment and selection	❏ 1	❏ 2	❏ 3
C. Training and development	❏ 1	❏ 2	❏ 3
D. Industrial relations	❏ 1	❏ 2	❏ 3
E. Workforce expansion/reduction	❏ 1	❏ 2	❏ 3

15. What do you consider to be the major challenge for personnel/human resource management in your organisation over the next 3 years?

_____

_____

SECTION II: STAFFING PRACTICES

1a. Has the total number of your employees increased or decreased in excess of 5% in the last 3 years?

1 ❏ Increased   2 ❏ Same   3 ❏ Decreased   4 ❏ Don't know

1b. Please provide approximate percentage change: _____%

2. Is it difficult to recruit/retain employees in the following categories?

A. Management   ❏ 1
B1. Professional/technical: Information Technology   ❏ 1

B2. Professional/technical: Others   ❑ 1
C. Clerical   ❑ 1
D. Manual   ❑ 1

3. Have you introduced any of the following in relation to recruitment or retention?
A. Recruiting abroad   ❑ 1
B. Retraining existing employees   ❑ 1
C. Increased pay/benefits   ❑ 1
D. Relocation of the company   ❑ 1
E. Marketing the organisation's image   ❑ 1
F. Others, please specify _____

4. Have any of the following methods been used to reduce the number of employees?
A. Recruitment freeze   ❑ 1
B. Early retirement   ❑ 1
C. Voluntary redundancies   ❑ 1
D. Compulsory redundancies   ❑ 1
E. Redeployment   ❑ 1
F. Outplacement   ❑ 1
G. No renewal of fixed-term/temporary contracts ❑ 1
H. Outsourcing   ❑ 1
I. Others, please specify _____

5. How are managerial vacancies generally filled? (Please tick as many as applicable for each management level).

	Senior management	Middle management	Junior management
A. Internally	❑ 1	❑ 1	❑ 1
B. Recruitment/head hunters/consultancies	❑ 1	❑ 1	❑ 1
C. Advertise in newspapers	❑ 1	❑ 1	❑ 1
D. Word of mouth	❑ 1	❑ 1	❑ 1
E. Others, please specify _____			

6. Please indicate how regularly any of the following selection methods are used.

	For every appointment	For most appointments	For some appointments	For few appointments	Not used
A. Interview panel	❑ 1	❑ 2	❑ 3	❑ 4	❑ 5
B. One-to-one interviews	❑ 1	❑ 2	❑ 3	❑ 4	❑ 5
C. Application forms	❑ 1	❑ 2	❑ 3	❑ 4	❑ 5
D. Psychometric test	❑ 1	❑ 2	❑ 3	❑ 4	❑ 5
E. Assessment centre	❑ 1	❑ 2	❑ 3	❑ 4	❑ 5
F. Graphology	❑ 1	❑ 2	❑ 3	❑ 4	❑ 5
G. References	❑ 1	❑ 2	❑ 3	❑ 4	❑ 5
H. Others, please specify _____					

7. Do you monitor the proportion of the following in your workforce with regard to recruitment, training and/or promotion?

	Recruitment	Training	Promotion	Don't know
A. People with disabilities	❑ 1	❑ 1	❑ 1	❑ 1

B. Women	❑ 1	❑ 1	❑ 1	❑ 1
C. People from ethnic minorities	❑ 1	❑ 1	❑ 1	❑ 1

8. Have you specifically targeted any of the following in your recruitment process?

- A. Long-term unemployed ❑ 1
- B. Older people (over 50 years of age) ❑ 1
- C. People with disabilities ❑ 1
- D. People from ethnic minorities ❑ 1
- E. Women ❑ 1
- F. School leavers ❑ 1
- G. University graduates ❑ 1
- H. Women returners ❑ 1

Flexible working practices

9. Has there been a change in the use of the following working arrangements over the last 3 years?

	Increased	Same	Decreased	Not used
A. Weekend work	❑ 1	❑ 2	❑ 3	❑ 4
B. Shift work	❑ 1	❑ 2	❑ 3	❑ 4
C. Overtime	❑ 1	❑ 2	❑ 3	❑ 4
D. Annual hours contract	❑ 1	❑ 2	❑ 3	❑ 4
E. Part-time work	❑ 1	❑ 2	❑ 3	❑ 4
F. Job sharing	❑ 1	❑ 2	❑ 3	❑ 4
G. Flexi-time	❑ 1	❑ 2	❑ 3	❑ 4
H. Temporary/casual	❑ 1	❑ 2	❑ 3	❑ 4
I. Fixed-term contracts	❑ 1	❑ 2	❑ 3	❑ 4
J. Home-based work	❑ 1	❑ 2	❑ 3	❑ 4
K. Tele-working	❑ 1	❑ 2	❑ 3	❑ 4
L. Subcontracting/outsourcing	❑ 1	❑ 2	❑ 3	❑ 4

10. Please indicate the approximate proportion of your workforce who are on the following working arrangements.

	Not used	Less than 1%	1–5%	6–10%	11–20%	More than 20%
A. Part-time	❑ 1	❑ 2	❑ 3	❑ 4	❑ 5	❑ 6
B. Temporary/casual	❑ 1	❑ 2	❑ 3	❑ 4	❑ 5	❑ 6
C. Fixed-term	❑ 1	❑ 2	❑ 3	❑ 4	❑ 5	❑ 6
D. Home-based work	❑ 1	❑ 2	❑ 3	❑ 4	❑ 5	❑ 6
E. Tele-working	❑ 1	❑ 2	❑ 3	❑ 4	❑ 5	❑ 6
F. Shift working	❑ 1	❑ 2	❑ 3	❑ 4	❑ 5	❑ 6
G. Annual hours contract	❑ 1	❑ 2	❑ 3	❑ 4	❑ 5	❑ 6

11. Has there been a major change in the specification of jobs over the last 3 years? (Please tick as many as are applicable for each job category).

	Management	Professional/technical	Clerical	Manual
A. Jobs made more specific	❑ 1	❑ 1	❑ 1	❑ 1
B. No major change	❑ 1	❑ 1	❑ 1	❑ 1
C. Jobs made wider/more flexible	❑ 1	❑ 1	❑ 1	❑ 1
D. Don't know	❑ 1	❑ 1	❑ 1	❑ 1

SECTION III: EMPLOYEE DEVELOPMENT

1a. Approximately what proportion of the annual salaries and wages bill is currently spent on training?

_____ %   1 ❏ don't know

1b. Approximately what proportion of employees have been on internal or external training activities within the last year?

_____ %   1 ❏ don't know

2. How many days' training per year does each employee in each staff category below receive on average?

		Don't know
A. Management	_____ days per year per employee	❏ 1
B. Professional/technical	_____ days per year per employee	❏ 1
C. Clerical	_____ days per year per employee	❏ 1
D. Manual	_____ days per year per employee	❏ 1

3. Do you systematically analyse employee training needs?

1 ❏ Yes   2 ❏ No   3 ❏ Don't know

(If No or Don't know go to question 5)

4. If you systematically analyse employee training needs, how often are the following methods used?

	Always	Often	Sometimes	Never
A. Analysis of projected business/service plans	❏ 1	❏ 2	❏ 3	❏ 4
B. Training audits	❏ 1	❏ 2	❏ 3	❏ 4
C. Line management requests	❏ 1	❏ 2	❏ 3	❏ 4
D. Performance appraisal	❏ 1	❏ 2	❏ 3	❏ 4
E. Employee requests	❏ 1	❏ 2	❏ 3	❏ 4

F. Others, please specify _____

5. Do you monitor the effectiveness of your training?

1 ❏ Yes   2 ❏ No   3 ❏ Don't know

(If No or Don't know, go to question 8)

6. If Yes, how often is formal evaluation used?

	Always	Often	Sometimes	Never
A. Immediately after training	❏ 1	❏ 2	❏ 3	❏ 4
B. Some months after training	❏ 1	❏ 2	❏ 3	❏ 4

7. Do you systematically evaluate training on the basis of:

	Yes	No	Don't know
A. Learning (usually assessed by a test)	❏ 1	❏ 2	❏ 3
B. Behaviour (changes in job performance)	❏ 1	❏ 2	❏ 3
C. Results (changes in organisational performance)	❏ 1	❏ 2	❏ 3
D. Reaction/evaluation (e.g. satisfaction expressed by employees)	❏ 1	❏ 2	❏ 3

8. Do you regularly use any of the following?

	Yes	No
A. Formal career plans	❏ 1	❏ 2
B. Assessment centres	❏ 1	❏ 2
C. Succession plans	❏ 1	❏ 2
D. Planned job rotation	❏ 1	❏ 2
E. "High flier" schemes for managers	❏ 1	❏ 2
F. International experience schemes for managers	❏ 1	❏ 2

9. Has there been a change in the use of any of the following to deliver training over the last 3 years?

	Increased	Same	Decreased	Not used
A. Internal training staff	❑ 1	❑ 2	❑ 3	❑ 4
B. Line managers	❑ 1	❑ 2	❑ 3	❑ 4
C. External training providers	❑ 1	❑ 2	❑ 3	❑ 4
D. On-the-job training	❑ 1	❑ 2	❑ 3	❑ 4
E. Coaching/mentoring	❑ 1	❑ 2	❑ 3	❑ 4
F. Computer-based packages	❑ 1	❑ 2	❑ 3	❑ 4

10. How important do you think the following training areas will be to your organisation over the next 3 years?

	Very	Quite	Average	Not very	Not at all
A. People management and supervision	❑ 1	❑ 2	❑ 3	❑ 4	❑ 5
B. Computers and new technology	❑ 1	❑ 2	❑ 3	❑ 4	❑ 5
C. Business administration	❑ 1	❑ 2	❑ 3	❑ 4	❑ 5
D. Strategy formulation	❑ 1	❑ 2	❑ 3	❑ 4	❑ 5
E. Marketing and sales	❑ 1	❑ 2	❑ 3	❑ 4	❑ 5
F. Health, safety and work environment	❑ 1	❑ 2	❑ 3	❑ 4	❑ 5
G. Customer service skills	❑ 1	❑ 2	❑ 3	❑ 4	❑ 5
H. Management of change	❑ 1	❑ 2	❑ 3	❑ 4	❑ 5
I. Quality management	❑ 1	❑ 2	❑ 3	❑ 4	❑ 5

Appraisal

11. Do you have an appraisal system in operation for any of the following staff categories?

	Yes	No
A. Management	❑ 1	❑ 2
B. Professional/technical	❑ 1	❑ 2
C. Clerical	❑ 1	❑ 2
D. Manual	❑ 1	❑ 2

12. If you have an appraisal system, do any of the following formally contribute to the appraisal process?

A. Immediate superior   ❑ 1
B. Next level superior   ❑ 1
C. The employee   ❑ 1
D. Subordinates   ❑ 1
E. Peers   ❑ 1
F. Customers   ❑ 1
G. Others, please specify _____

13. Is the appraisal system used to determine any of the following? (Please tick as many as applicable).

A. Individual training needs   ❑ 1
B. Organisational training needs   ❑ 1
C. Promotion potential   ❑ 1
D. Career development   ❑ 1
E. Individual performance-related pay ❑ 1
F. Organisation of work   ❑ 1

SECTION IV: COMPENSATION AND BENEFITS

1. At what level(s) is basic pay determined? (Please tick as many as applicable for each category of staff).

	Management	Professional/ technical	Clerical/ administrative	Manual
A. National/industry-wide collective bargaining	❏ 1	❏ 1	❏ 1	❏ 1
B. Regional collective bargaining	❏ 1	❏ 1	❏ 1	❏ 1
C. Company/division, etc.	❏ 1	❏ 1	❏ 1	❏ 1
D. Establishment/site	❏ 1	❏ 1	❏ 1	❏ 1
E. Individual	❏ 1	❏ 1	❏ 1	❏ 1
F. Others, please specify _____				

2. Has there been a change in the share of the following in the total reward package in the last 3 years?

	Increased	Decreased	Same	Not used
A. Variable pay	❏ 1	❏ 2	❏ 3	❏ 4
B. Non-money benefits	❏ 1	❏ 2	❏ 3	❏ 4

3. Do you offer any of the following incentive schemes? (Please tick as many as are applicable for each category of staff).

	Management	Professional/ technical	Clerical/ administrative	Manual
A. Employee share options	❏ 1	❏ 1	❏ 1	❏ 1
B. Profit sharing	❏ 1	❏ 1	❏ 1	❏ 1
C. Group bonus	❏ 1	❏ 1	❏ 1	❏ 1
D. Merit/performance-related pay	❏ 1	❏ 1	❏ 1	❏ 1

4. Do you offer any of the following schemes?

A. Workplace childcare ❏ 1
B. Childcare allowances ❏ 1
C. Career break scheme ❏ 1
D. Maternity leave (in excess of statutory requirements) ❏ 1
E. Paternity leave (in excess of statutory requirements) ❏ 1
F. Pension scheme ❏ 1
G. Education/training break ❏ 1

SECTION V: EMPLOYEE RELATIONS AND COMMUNICATION

1. What proportion of the total number of employees in your organisation are members of a trade union?

1 ❏ 0%   2 ❏ 1–10%   3 ❏ 11–25%   4 ❏ 26–50%
5 ❏ 51–75%   6 ❏ 76–100%   7 ❏ Don't know

2. Has the influence of trade unions on your organisation changed during the last 3 years?

1 ❏ Increased   2 ❏ Same   3 ❏ Decreased   4 ❏ No influence

3. Do you have a joint consultative committee or works council?

1 ❏ Yes   2 ❏ No

4. Has there been a change in how you communicate major issues to your employees during the last 3 years?

	Increased	Same	Decreased	Not used
A. Through representative staff bodies (e.g. trade unions)	❏ 1	❏ 2	❏ 3	❏ 4
B. Verbally, direct to employees	❏ 1	❏ 2	❏ 3	❏ 4
C. Written, direct to employees	❏ 1	❏ 2	❏ 3	❏ 4
D. Computer/electronic mail systems	❏ 1	❏ 2	❏ 3	❏ 4
E. Team briefings	❏ 1	❏ 2	❏ 3	❏ 4
F. Others, please specify _____				

5. Which employee categories are formally briefed about the following issues? (Please tick as many as applicable).

	Strategy	Financial performance	Organisation of work
A. Management	❏ 1	❏ 1	❏ 1
B. Professional/technical	❏ 1	❏ 1	❏ 1
C Clerical	❏ 1	❏ 1	❏ 1
D. Manual	❏ 1	❏ 1	❏ 1

6. Has there been a change in the way employees communicate their views to management in the past 3 years?

	Increased	Same	Decreased	Not used
A. Direct to senior managers	❏ 1	❏ 2	❏ 3	❏ 4
B. Through immediate superior	❏ 1	❏ 2	❏ 3	❏ 4
C. Through trade unions/works council	❏ 1	❏ 2	❏ 3	❏ 4
D. Through regular workforce meetings	❏ 1	❏ 2	❏ 3	❏ 4
E. Team briefings	❏ 1	❏ 2	❏ 3	❏ 4
F. Suggestion schemes	❏ 1	❏ 2	❏ 3	❏ 4
G. Attitude survey	❏ 1	❏ 2	❏ 3	❏ 4

SECTION VI: ORGANISATIONAL DETAILS

1. Please indicate the main sector of industry or services in which you operate?

A. Agriculture, hunting, forestry, fishing	❏ 1
B. Energy and water	❏ 2
C. Chemical products; extraction and processing of non-energy minerals	❏ 3
D. Metal manufacturing; mechanical, electrical and instrument engineering; office and data processing machinery	❏ 4
E. Other manufacturing, (e.g. food, drink and tobacco; textiles; clothing; paper, printing and publishing; processing of rubber and plastics, etc.)	❏ 5
F. Building and civil engineering	❏ 6
G. Retail and distribution; hotels; catering; repairs	❏ 7
H. Transport and communication (e.g. rail, postal services, telecoms, etc.)	❏ 8
I. Banking; finance; insurance; business services (e.g. consultancies, PR and advertising, Law firms, etc.)	❏ 9
J. Personal, domestic, recreational services	❏ 10
K. Health services	❏ 11
L. Other services (e.g. television and radio, R&D, charities, etc.)	❏ 12
M. Education (including universities and further education)	❏ 13
N. Local government	❏ 14
O. Central government	❏ 15
P. Others, please specify _____	

2. Approximately how many people are employed by your organisation?

   A. In total _____   Male _____   Female _____

   B. Part-time _____   Male _____   Female _____

3. Please provide the following information about your workforce:

A. Annual staff turnover	_____% turnover per year	❑ 1 don't know
B. Age structure	_____% of employees under 25 years	❑ 1 don't know
	_____% of employees over 45 years	❑ 1 don't know
C. Absenteeism	_____average days per year	❑ 1 don't know
D. Education structure	_____% of graduates	❑ 1 don't know
	_____% of post graduates	

4. Please provide the following information:

A. Manual employees	_____% of workforce	❑ 1 don't know
B. Clerical employees	_____% of workforce	❑ 1 don't know
C. Professional/technical employees	_____% of workforce	❑ 1 don't know
D. Managers	_____% of workforce	❑ 1 don't know

5. If your organisation is part of a larger group of companies/divisions, etc., approximately how many people are employed by the whole group?

   A. In the UK   _____   1 ❑ don't know

   B. World-wide, including UK   _____   1 ❑ don't know

6. What percentage of the operating costs was accounted for by labour costs?

_____ % of operating costs   1 ❑ don't know

7. If you are a private organisation, would you say the gross revenue over the past 3 years has been:

A. Well in excess of costs	❑ 1
B. Sufficient to make a small profit	❑ 2
C. Enough to break even	❑ 3
D. Insufficient to cover costs	❑ 4
E. So low as to produce large losses	❑ 5

8. Thinking of competitive success, how important are the following features of the main products and/or services of your organisation?

	Very important	Somewhat important	Not important	Not applicable
A. Price	❑ 1	❑ 2	❑ 3	❑ 4
B. Quality	❑ 1	❑ 2	❑ 3	❑ 4
C. Variety (customising products services)	❑ 1	❑ 2	❑ 3	❑ 4
D. Service (availability, speed of delivery)	❑ 1	❑ 2	❑ 3	❑ 4
E. Innovation	❑ 1	❑ 2	❑ 3	❑ 4

9. Compared to other organisations in your sector, where would you rate the performance of your organisation in relation to the following?

	Top 10%	Upper half	Lower half	Not applicable
A. Service quality	❑ 1	❑ 2	❑ 3	❑ 4
B. Level of productivity	❑ 1	❑ 2	❑ 3	❑ 4
C. Profitability	❑ 1	❑ 2	❑ 3	❑ 4
D. Product to market time	❑ 1	❑ 2	❑ 3	❑ 4
E. Rate of innovation	❑ 1	❑ 2	❑ 3	❑ 4
F. Stock market performance	❑ 1	❑ 2	❑ 3	❑ 4

10. **How would you describe the market(s) for your organisation's products or services?**
    A. Local   ❏ 1
    B. Regional   ❏ 2
    C. National   ❏ 3
    D. European   ❏ 4
    E. World-wide   ❏ 5

11. **Is your organisation a member of an employers association?**
    1 ❏ Yes   2 ❏ No

12. **Is the market you sell into:**
    1 ❏ Growing   2 ❏ Same   3 ❏ Declining

13. **Has your organisation been involved in any of the following changes in the last 3 years?**
    A. Acquisition of another organisation   ❏ 1
    B. Takeover by another organisation   ❏ 1
    C. Merger   ❏ 1
    D. Relocation   ❏ 1

14. **Is your organisation:**
    1 ❏ Private   2 ❏ State owned   3 ❏ Part-state owned
    4 Others, please specify _____

15. **Where are the corporate headquarters of your organisation based? (Please refer to ultimate parent company if your organisation is part of a larger group).**

Denmark	❏ 1	Norway	❏ 11	Poland	❏ 21
France	❏ 2	Sweden	❏ 12	Other Europe	❏ 22
Germany	❏ 3	Finland	❏ 13	New Zealand	❏ 23
Italy	❏ 4	Czech Republic	❏ 14	Australia	❏ 24
The Netherlands	❏ 5	Switzerland	❏ 15	Japan	❏ 25
Portugal	❏ 6	Belgium	❏ 16	Other Asia/Pacific	❏ 26
Austria	❏ 7	Greece	❏ 17	USA	❏ 27
Republic of Ireland	❏ 8	Turkey	❏ 18	Canada	❏ 28
Spain	❏ 9	Bulgaria	❏ 19	Cyprus	❏ 29
UK	❏ 10	Hungary	❏ 20	Tunisia	❏ 30

Other, please specify _____

16. **Is your organisation:**
    A. Corporate headquarters of an International group   ❏ 1
    B. Corporate headquarters of a National group   ❏ 2
    C. Subsidiary/division of an International group   ❏ 3
    D. Subsidiary/division of a National group   ❏ 4
    E. Independent company with more than one site   ❏ 5
    F. Independent single site organisation   ❏ 6
    G. Others, please specify _____

17. **If you are based in the UK, please tick your region:**

London	❏ 1	Rest of South East	❏ 2	East Anglia	❏ 3
South West	❏ 4	West Midlands	❏ 5	East Midlands	❏ 6
Yorkshire	❏ 7	North West	❏ 8	North East & Humberside	❏ 9
Scotland	❏ 10	Wales	❏ 11	Northern Ireland	❏ 12

18. **If you are based in the Republic of Ireland please tick.**   ❑ 1

19. **What year was your organisation established?**
     _____ 1 ❑ don't know/not applicable

Personal details

20a. **Are you the most senior personnel or human resources manager?**
     1 ❑ Yes   2 ❑ No

20b. **If No, please give your title:**
     1 ❑ Personnel/HR Manager/Director
     2 ❑ Specialist (training, pay, etc.)
     3 ❑ Chief executive, company, secretary, senior manager
     4 ❑ Others, please specify _____

21. **Are you:**
     1 ❑ Male   2 ❑ Female

22. **How long have you been working for the organisation?**
     _____ years   1 ❑ Not applicable

23. **If you are a personnel/human resource management specialist, how long have you been working in a specialist personnel/human resources or training job?**
     _____ years   1 ❑ Not applicable

24. **Do you have a university degree?**
     1 ❑ Yes   2 ❑ No

     If Yes, in what academic field did you study? (tick main one only).
     A. Business studies   ❑ 1
     B. Economics   ❑ 2
     C. Social or behavioural sciences   ❑ 3
     D. Humanities/Art/Languages   ❑ 4
     E. Law   ❑ 5
     F. Engineering   ❑ 6
     G. Natural sciences   ❑ 7
     H. Others, please specify _____

INTERNATIONAL TRAVEL QUESTIONS

This year we would like you to answer two additional questions on issues which have not previously been dealt with in the questionnaire. If they are relevant to your organisation we would appreciate your response.

1a. **Approximately how many people in your organisation travel to other countries frequently (more than once per month on average)?**
     _____ People   1 ❑ None

1b. **What are the major HRM problems you face with this group?**
     _____
     _____

2. **How many people in your organisation are expatriates (based outside their home country for more than 12 months)?**

_____ People   1 ❑ None

To ensure that you receive your copy of the Executive Report please complete the details below.

Name and Title   ....

Job Title   ....

Organisation   ....

Address   ....

....

....

....

Postcode   ....

Thank you for taking the time to complete this questionnaire.

Bibliography

The selection of publications below includes only those by members of the Network which present new data from the Cranet surveys. It does not include conference papers, or other publications by these authors, nor does it include the many citations by other authors. Students should be able to find these texts in good libraries.

Alas, R. (2001) Personalijuhtimine. Kylim.

Aparicio-Valverde, M., Kabst, R., Brewster, C. and Mayne, L. (1997) The flexibility paradox. *Employee Relations*, 19(6): 596–608.

Atterbury, S. (2001) Skills shortages. *Personnel Today*, October.

Atterbury, S. (2001) Flexibility in profile. *Flexible Working Briefing*, Croner Publications, Issue No.88, 24 July.

Atterbury, S. and Mahoney, C. (2000) Looking outside for HR solutions. *Flexible Working Briefing*, Croner Publications, November.

Atterbury, S. and Mahoney, C. (2000) Job sharing: Cranet data. *Flexible Working Briefing*, Croner Publications.

Atterbury, S. and Mahoney, C. (2001) Gender of HR directors. *Personnel Today*, July.

Atterbury, S., Croucher, R. and Farndale, E. (2001) Being flexible in Europe. *"t" Magazine*, November: 23–26.

Bournois, F. (1991) Gestion des RH en Europe: données comparées. *Revue Française de Gestion*, March–May: 68–83.

Bournois, F. (1992) Human resource management in France. In: Brewster, C. et al. (eds.), *The European Human Resource Management Guide*. London: Academic Press.

Bournois, F. and Brewster, C. (1993) The need for international comparisons. *P+: Journal of European Foundation for the Improvement of Living and Working Conditions*, Dublin.

Bournois, F. and Roussillon, S. (1994) The changing aspects of HR/line relationships in France. In: *The Changing Relationship between Personnel and Line Management: The European Dimension*. Report for the Institute of Personnel Management, Cranfield/UK, May.

Bournois, F. and Roussillon, S. (1995) Quid novi pour la gestion et le management des cadres en Europe? *Revue Personnel*, mars 1995.

Bournois, F. and Rousillon, S. (1996) Internationalisation et quête de flexibilité. *Revue Personnel*, 373, octobre.

Bournois, F. and Rousillon, S. (1996) Observatoire international de gestion des ressources humaines: rapport détaillé 1996. S*ynthèse réservée au répondant de l'enquête 1995*, Groupe ESC Lyon, 14 p.

Bournois, F. and Roussillon, S. (1996) Observatoire international de la GRH: internationalisation, flexibilité et convergence des pratiques en Europe. *Revue Personnel*, 370, juin.

Bournois, F. and Roussillon, S. (1996) Pratiques flexibles de GRH, emploi et internationalisation de l'entreprise: comparaisons internationales. *Les enjeux de l'emploi: société, entreprises et individus*. Collection: Les Chemins de la Découverte, Ed. CNRS.

Bournois, F., Roussillon, S. and Combes, J.E. (1993) La fonction ressources humaines en Europe: les nouveaux points de repère. *Revue Personnel*, 345, octobre.

Bournois, F., Chauchat, J.-H. and Rousillon, S. (1994) Training and management development in Europe. In: Brewster, C. and Hegewisch, A. (eds.), *Policy and Practices in European Human Resource Management*. Routledge, pp. 122–138.

Brewster, C. (1990) Corporate strategy: a no-go area for personnel? *Personnel Management*, 22(7): 36–40.

Brewster, C. (1992) The case against decentralised pay. *Human Resources*, Spring: 19–21.

Brewster, C. (1993) Developing a "European" model of human resource management. *International Journal of Human Resource Management*, 4(4): 765–784.

Brewster, C. (1994) Human resource management in Europe: reflection of, or challenge to, the American concept? In: Kirkbride, P. (ed.), *Human Resource Management in the New Europe of the 1990s*. London: Routledge, pp. 56–89.

Brewster, C. (1995) Different styles of human resource management in Europe. *Personalführung* 2/95: 126–131.

Brewster, C. (1995) Towards a "European" model of human resource management. *Journal of International Business Studies*, 26(1): 1–21.

Brewster, C. (1995) HRM: the European dimension. In: Storey, J. (ed.), *Human Resource Management: A Critical Text*. London: Routledge.

Brewster, C. (1995) IR and HRM: a subversive European model. *Industrielle Beziehungen*, 2(4): 395–413.

Brewster, C. (1996) Flexible employment in Britain. *Flexible Working*, 1(2): 15–17.

Brewster, C. (1996) Human resource management in Europe. In: Poole, M. (ed.), *The International Encyclopedia of Business and Management*. London: Routledge.

Brewster, C. (1996) Naar een Europees HRM? *Personeelsbeleid in Belgie*, HR Magazine Yearbook, Ghent.

Brewster, C. (1997) Nieuwe grenzen en modelijkheden voor de personeelsfunctie. *Human Resources Magazine*, November: 52–55.

Brewster, C. (1997) Flexsibelt arbeid oker sterkt I Europa. *Personal*, Norges eneste personaltidsskrift, Nr 2.

Brewster, C. (1998) HR management looking to the future. *Benefits and Compensation International*, London, 28(5): 28–29.

Brewster, C. (1998) Flexible working in Europe: extent, growth and challenge for HRM. In: Sparrow, P., McGoldrick, A. and Marchington, M. (eds.), *HRM: The New Agenda*. London: Pitmans.

Brewster, C. (1999) Major management styles and practices in Europe. In: Tayeb, M. (ed.), *International Business*. London: FT/Prentice Hall.

Brewster, C. (1999) Developing a European model of human resource management. In: Poole, M. (ed.), *Human Resource Management: Critical Perspectives on Business and Management*. London: Routledge.

Brewster, C. (1999) European human resource management. In: *International Encyclopaedia of Business and Management: Management in Europe*. London: Thomson.

Brewster, C. (1999) Different paradigms in strategic HRM: questions raised by comparative research. In: Wright, P., Dyer, L., Boudreau, J. and Milkovich, G. (eds.), *Research in Personnel and HRM*. Greenwich, CT: JAI Press Inc.

Brewster, C. (2000) Strategic human resource management: the value of different paradigms. In: Schuler, R. and Jackson, S. (eds.), *Strategic Human Resource Management: Linking People to the Firm*. London: Blackwell.

Brewster, C. (2001) HRM: the comparative dimension. In: Storey, J. (ed.), *Human Resource Management: A Critical Text*, 2nd edn. London: Thomson Learning.

Brewster, C. (2002) The HR function in local and overseas firms: evidence from the Price Waterhouse Coopers-Cranfield HR project. *Asia Pacific Journal of HR*, 40(2): 205–227.

Brewster, C. and Bournois, F. (1991) A European perspective on human resource management. *Personnel Review*, 20(6): 1, 4–13.

Brewster, C. and Bournois, F. (1991) Human resource management: a European perspective. *Personnel Review*, 20(6): 4–13.

Brewster, C. and Croucher, R. (1998) Flexible working practices and the trade unions. *Employee Relations*, 20(5): 443–452.

Brewster, C. and Hegewisch, A. (1993) Employee communication and participation. *P+: Journal of European Foundation for the Improvement of Living and Working Conditions*, Dublin.

Brewster, C. and Hegewisch, A. (1993) Methodology of the Price Waterhouse/Cranfield project on European human resource management. *P+: Journal of European Foundation for the Improvement of Living and Working Conditions*, Dublin.

Brewster, C. and Hegewisch, A. (1993) A continent of diversity: personnel management in Europe. *Personnel Management*, January: 36–40.

Brewster, C. and Hegewisch, A. (eds.) (1994) *Policy and Practice in European Human Resource Management: The Price Waterhouse Cranfield Survey*. London: Routledge.

Brewster, C. and Hoogendoorn, J. (1992) Human resource aspects of decentralisation and devolution. *Personnel Review*, 21(1): 4–11.

Brewster, C. and Kabst, R. (2000) Personalpraktiken national und international tätiger Unternehmen. In: Gutmann, J. and Kabst, R. (eds.), *Internationalisierung im Mittelstand: Chancen, Risiken, Erfolgsfaktoren*. Wiesbaden, S. 289–314.

Brewster, C. and Kabst, R. (2003) International vergleichendes Personal management. In: Gaugler, E., Oechsler, W.A. and Weber, W. (eds.), *Handwoerterbuch des Personalwesens* (HWP), 3rd edn. Stuttgart: Schaeffer-Poeschel.

Brewster, C. and Larsen, H.H. (1992) Human resource management in Europe: evidence from ten countries. *International Journal of Human Resource Management*, 3(3): 409–434.

Brewster, C. and Larsen, H.H. (1993) Human resource management in Europe: evidence from ten countries. In: Hegewisch, A. and Brewster, C. (eds.), *European Developments in Human Resource Management*. London: Kogan Page. (Reprint from International Journal of Human Resource Management, se A23.)

Brewster, C. and Larsen, H.H. (1997) Integration and assignment: a paradox in human resource management. *Journal of International Management*, 3(1): 1–23.

Brewster, C. and Larsen, H.H. (eds.) (2000) Human resource management in Northern Europe. *Trends, Dilemmas and Strategy*. London: Blackwell.

Brewster, C. and Lockhart, T. (1990) Employee involvement – which road to follow. *Single Market Monitor*, 2, 6, March.

Brewster, C. and Mayne, L. (1996) Flexible employment in Europe. *Journal of Professional HRM*, Issue No. 5, October: 3–8.

Brewster, C. and Mayne, L. (1997) Differences in HRM priorities across Europe. *Journal of Professional HRM*, Issue No. 6, January.

Brewster, C. and Tregaskis, O. (1996) International comparisons of overtime and annualised hours. *Flexible Working*, 1(4): 9–11.

Brewster, C. and Tregaskis, O. (1997) The non-permanent workforce. *Flexible Working*, 2(2).

Brewster, C., Tregaskis, O. and Mayne, L. (1997) Flexible working in Europe: a review of the evidence. *Management International Review*, 37, Special Issue 1/97: 1–19.

Brewster, C. and Tregaskis, O. (2001) Adaptive, reactive and inclusive organisational approaches to workforce flexibility in Europe. *Comportamento Organizacional e Gestão*, (2): 209–232.

Brewster, C. and Tregaskis, O. (2003) Convergence or divergence of contingent employment practices? Evidence of the role of MNCs in Europe. In: Cooke, W.M. (ed.), *Multinational Companies and Transnational Workplace Issues*. New York: Praeger.

Brewster, C., Hegewisch, A. and Lockhart, T. (1991) Researching human resource management: methodology of the Price Waterhouse Cranfield project on European trends. *Personnel Review*, 20(6): 36–40.

Brewster, C., Gunnigle, P. and Morley, M. (1993) Reports of death exaggerated: trade unions in Europe in the 1990s. *Management Consultancy*.

Brewster, C., Gunnigle, P. and Morley, M. (1993) Trade union representation: the UK and Ireland in a European context. *Management Research*, 16(5/6): 30–37.

Brewster, C., Gunnigle P. and Morley, M. (1994) Continuity and change in European industrial relations: evidence from a 14 country survey. *Personnel Review*, 23(3): 4–20.

Brewster, C., Hegewisch, A. and Mayne, L. (1994) Trends in HRM in Western Europe. In: Kirkbride, P. (ed.), *Human Resource Management in the New Europe of the 1990s*, London: Routledge, pp. 114–132.

Brewster, C., Hegewisch, A., Mayne, L. and Tregaskis, O. (1994) Employee communication and participation. In: Brewster, C. and Hegewisch, A. (eds.), *Policy and Practice in European Human Resource Management*. London: Routledge.

Brewster, C., Hegewisch, A., Mayne, L. and Tregaskis, O. (1994) European comparative survey: methodology. In: Brewster, C. and Hegewisch, A. (eds.), *Policy and Practice in European Human Resource Management*. London: Routledge.

Brewster, C., Hegewisch, A., Tregaskis, O. and Mayne, L. (1994) Flexible working practices: the controversy and the evidence. In: Brewster, C. and Hegewisch, A. (eds.), *Policy and Practice in European Human Resource Management*. London: Routledge.

Brewster, C., Morley, M. and Gunnigle, P. (1994) Trade union representation at organisational level: the UK and the Republic of Ireland in the European context. *Review of Employment Topics*, 2(1): 152–171.

Brewster, C., Tregaskis, O., Hegewisch, A. and Mayne, L. (1996) Comparative research in human resource management: a review and an example. *International Journal of Human Resource Management*, 7(3): 585–604.

Brewster, C., Mayne, L., Aparicio-Valverde, M. and Kabst, R. (1997) Flexibility in European labour markets? The evidence renewed. *Employee Relations*, 19(6): 509–518.

Brewster, C., Mayne, L. and Tregaskis, O. (1997) Flexible working in Europe. *Journal of World Business*, 32(2): 133–151.

Brewster, C., Tregaskis, O., Hegewisch, A. and Mayne, L. (1999) Comparative research in human resource management: a review and an example. In: Poole, M. (ed.), *Human Resource Management: Critical Perspectives on Business and Management*. London: Routledge.

Brewster, C., Vatchkova, E. and Petrov, B. (1999) Flexible staffing practices in Bulgaria, The Czech Republic and Poland – the difficult way of change. *Human Resources for Development: People and Performance Conference*, Manchester.

Brewster, C., Dowling, P., Grobler P., Holland, P. and Warnich, S. (2000) *Contemporary Issues in Human Resource Management: Gaining a Competitive Advantage*. Cape Town, South Africa: Oxford University Press.

Brewster, C., Mayrhofer, W. and Morley, M. (2000). The concept of strategic European human resource management. In: Brewster, C.J., Mayrhofer, W. and Morley, M. (eds.), *New Challenges for European Human Resource Management*. London: Macmillan, pp. 3–33.

Brewster, C., Mayrhofer, W. and Morley, M. (2000) The concept of strategic European human resource management: introduction. In: *New Challenges for European Human Resource Management*. London: Macmillan.

Brewster, C., Mayrhofer, W. and Morley, M. (eds.) (2000) *New Challenges for European Human Resource Management*. Basingstoke: Macmillan.

Brewster, C., Tregaskis, O., Hegewisch, A. and Mayne, L. (2000) Comparative research in human resource management: a review and an example. In: *New Challenges for European Human Resource Management*. London: Macmillan.

Brewster, C., Communal, C., Farndale, E., Hegewisch, A., Johnson, G. and van Ommeren, J. (2001) HR healthcheck: benchmarking HRM practice across the UK and Europe. In: *Management Research in Practice Series*. Prentice Hall, London: Financial Times.

Bruegel, I. and Hegewisch, A. (1994) Flexibilisation and part-time work in Europe. In: Brown, P. and Crompton, R. (eds.), *A New Europe? Economic Restructuring and Social Exclusion*. London: UCL Press.

Caspi, A. and Ben Hador, B. (2002) A comparison between managers in Israel to their colleagues in Europe. *Nihul – Israel Managers Magazine*, 144.

Caspi, A., Weisberg, Y. and Ben Hador, B. (2000) An analysis: Cranet – Israel survey 1999–2000, part one. *Nihul – Israel Managers Magazine*, 138.

Caspi, A., Weisberg, Y. and Ben Hador, B. (2000) An analysis: Cranet – Israel survey 1999–2000, part two. *Nihul – Israel Managers Magazine*, 139.

Caspi, A., Weisberg, Y. and Ben Hador, B. (2000) An analysis: Cranet – Israel survey 1999–2000, part three. *Nihul – Israel Managers Magazine*, 140.

Cleveland, J.N., Gunnigle, P., Heraty, N., Morley, M. and Murphy, K. (2000) Human resource management practices of U.S.-owned multinational corporations in Europe: accommodation or imposition? *Irish Business and Administrative Research*, 21(1): 9–27.

Clifford, N., Crowley, M., Morley, M. and Gunnigle, P. (1997) Flexible working practices. In: Gunnigle, P., Morley, M., Clifford, N. and Turner, T. (eds.), *Human Resource Management in Irish Organisations: Practice in Perspective*. Dublin: Oak Tree Press.

Clifford, N., Morley, M. and Gunnigle, P. (1997) Part-time work in Europe. *Employee Relations*, 19(6): 555–567.

Clifford, N., Turner, T., Gunnigle, P. and Morley, M. (1997) Human resource management in Ireland: an overview. In: Gunnigle, P., Morley, M., Clifford, N. and Turner, T. (eds.), *Human Resource Management in Irish Organisations: Practice in Perspective*. Dublin: Oak Tree Press.

Communal, C. and Brewster, C. (2002) European human resource management. In: Anne-Wil Harzing, A.-W. and Van Ruysseveldt, J.V. (eds.), *International HRM*, 2nd edn. London: Sage.

Communal, C. (2001) 360-Degree feedback. *Personnel Today*, June.

Croucher, R. (2001) Unions/social partnership. *Personnel Today*, July.

Croucher, R. and Atterbury, S. (2001) Over 50 and out. *Personnel Today*, September.

Croucher, R. and Druker, J. (2001) Decision-taking on human resource issues: practices in building and civil engineering companies in Europe and their industrial relations consequences. *Employee Relations*, 23(1): 55–74.

Croucher, R. and Kabst, R. (in print). Das Cranfield-Netzwerk: personal management im internationalen Vergleich am Beispiel Weiterbildung. *Journal Arbeit*.

Cunha, R.C., Cunha, M.P., Morgado, A. and Brewster, C. (2002). Market impacts on strategy, HRM practices and organizational performance: toward a European model. *Management Research*, 1(1): 79–91.

Cunha, R.C., Cunha, M.P., Morgado, A. and Brewster, C. (2003) Market forces, strategic management, HRM practices and organizational performance, a model based in a European sample. *Management Research*, 1(1): 79–91.

Dany, F. (2000) Observatoire international des ressources humaines. *Rapport E.M.LYON/Adecco*.

Dany, F. and Torchy, V. (1994) Recruitment and selection in Europe: policies, practices and methods. In: Brewster, C. and Hegewitsch, A. (eds.), *Policy and Practices in European Human Resource Management*. London: Routledge, pp. 68–88.

Druker, J. and Croucher, R. (2000) National collective bargaining and employment flexibility in the European building and civil construction industries. *Construction Management and Economics*, 18: 699–709.

Druker, J., White, G., Hegewisch, A. and Mayne, L. (1996) Between hard and soft: human resource management in the construction industry. *Construction Management and Economics Journal*, 14.

Dunkel, M. (1995) Betriebliche Weiterbildung in den neuen Bundesländern (Personnel development in the New Federal States (East-Germany). In: Schwuchow, K.-H. (ed.), *Jahrbuch Weiterbildung 1995 (Yearbook of Training and Development 1995)*. Düsseldorf: Verlagsgruppe Handelsblatt, 1995, pp. 204–208.

Dunkel, M. (1996) Personalentwicklung in den neuen Bundesländern (Training and development in the New Federal States (East-Germany). In: *Wissenschaftliche Zeitschrift der TU Dresden*. Dresden University of Technology. 45, 4/1996, pp. 16–20.

Erten-Buch, C. and Mayrhofer, W. (1998) Human resource management and national culture – two birds that flock together? Empirical evidence from 13 European countries. In: *Proceedings of the 24th Annual EIBA-Conference, International Business Strategies and Middle East Regional Cooperation*, Jerusalem, 13–15, 12, 1998.

Erten-Buch, C., Mayrhofer, W. and Strunk, G. (1999) The Cranfield Project on European Human Resource Management CRANET-E. Research Report Österreich, Wirtschaftsuniversität Wien.

Erten-Buch, E., Mayrhofer, W. and Strunk, G. (1999) The Cranfield Project on European Human Resource Management CRANET-E. Research Report Österreich – Detailauswertung Privat-Öffentlich 1999; Wirtschaftsuniversität Wien.

Erten-Buch, E., Mayrhofer, W. and Strunk, G. (2000) Exportorientierung und Personal management im europäischen Vergleich (Export orientation and personnel management – a European comparison), Research Report Fachhochschulstudiengänge des bfi Wien.

Farndale, E. (1999) A decade of flexible pay and benefits. *Flexible Working Briefing*, Croner Publications.

Farndale, E. (1999) Caring employment. *Flexible Working Briefing*, Croner Publications, Issue No. 42, 8 June.

Farndale, E. (2001) Background of HR directors. *Personnel Today*, September.

Farndale, E. (2001) E-mail. *Personnel Today*, May.

Farndale, E. (2001) Power to line managers. *Personnel Today*, October.

Festing, M., Groening, Y., Kabst, R. and Weber, W. (1999) Financial participation in Europe: determinants and outcomes. *Economic and Industrial Democracy*, 20(2): 295–329.

Foley, K. and Gunnigle, P. (1994) The personnel/human resource function and employee relations. In: Gunnigle, P., Flood, P., Morley, M. and Turner, T. (eds.), *Continuity and Change in Irish Employee Relations*. Dublin: Oak Tree Press.

Foley, K. and Gunnigle, P. (1995) The personnel function: change or continuity? In: Turner, T. and Morley, M. (eds.), *Industrial Relations and the New Order*. Dublin: Oak Tree Press.

Foley, K., Gunnigle, P. and Morley, M. (1996) Personnel management in Ireland: a new Epoch? *International Journal of Employment Studies*, 4(2): 1–24.

Foley, K., Gunnigle, P. and Morley, M. (1998) Personnel management in Ireland: a new Epoch? In: Mortimer, D., Leece, P. and Morris, R. (eds.), *Readings in Contemporary Employment Relations*. Sydney: Harcourt Brace.

Friedrich, A., Kabst, R. and Weber, W. (1998) Job rotation: common practice in organisations? *Flexible Working Practices*, 23: 8–9.

Friedrich, A., Kabst, R., Weber, W. and Rodehuth, M. (1998) Functional flexibility: merely reacting or acting strategically. *Employee Relations*, 20(5): 504–523.

Friedrich, A., Kabst, R., Rodehuth, M. and Weber, W. (2000) Job rotation: an empirical analysis on the utilization and strategic integration in European companies. In: Brewster, C., Mayrhofer, W. and Morley, M. (eds.), *New Challenges for European Human Resource Management*. Houndmills/ Basingstoke: Macmillan Press, pp. 56–71.

Gooderham, P. and Brewster, C. (2003) Convergence, stasis or divergence? The case of personnel management in Europe. *Beta* 17(1): 6–18.

Gunnigle, P. (1992) Human resource management in Ireland. In: Brewster, C., Hegewisch, A., Holden, L. and Lockhart, T. (eds.), *The European Human Resource Management Guide*. London: Academic Press.

Gunnigle, P. (1992). Human resource management in Ireland. *Employee Relations*, 14(5): 5–22.

Gunnigle, P. (1993) Changing management approaches to employee relations in Ireland. In: Hegewich, A. and Brewster, C. (eds.). *European Developments in Human Resource Management*. London: Kogan Page.

Gunnigle, P. (1993) Evaluating change in the management of employee relations: Ireland in the 1980s. *Arena: Journal of the Irish Institute of Training and Development*, October.

Gunnigle, P. (1993) The Republic of Ireland: employment law, pay and benefits and current issues in human resource management. *Multinational Employer*, 10(4).

Gunnigle, P. (1998) Human resource management and the personnel function. In: Roche, W., Monks, K. and Walsh, J. (eds.), *Human Resource Management Strategies: Policy and Practice in Ireland*. Dublin: Oak Tree Press.

Gunnigle, P. and Clifford, N. (1997) The personnel/human resource function. In: Gunnigle, P., Morley, M., Clifford, N. and Turner, T. (eds.), *Human Resource Management in Irish Organisations: Practice in Perspective*. Dublin: Oak Tree Press.

Gunnigle, P. and Morley, M. (2000) Continuity and change in Irish industrial relations. *Employee Relations Review*, 13.

Gunnigle, P., Morley, M. and Brewster, C. (1992) Changing patterns in industrial relations. *Participation+: European Participation Monitor*, 7.

Gunnigle, P., Brewster, C. and Morley, M. (1993) Changing patterns in industrial relations. *P+: Journal of European Foundation for the Improvement of Living and Working Conditions*, Dublin.

Gunnigle, P., Brewster, C. and Morley, M. (1994) Continuity and change in European industrial relations: evidence from a 14 country study. *Personnel Review*, 23(3): 4–20.

Gunnigle, P., Brewster, C. and Morley, M. (1994) European industrial relations: change and continuity. In: Brewster, C. and Hegewisch, A. (eds.), *Policy and Practice in European Human Resource Management*. London: Routledge.

Gunnigle, P., Flood, P., Morley, M. and Turner, T. (1994) *Continuity and Change in Irish Employee Relations*. Dublin: Oak Tree Press.

Gunnigle, P., Foley, K. and Morley, M. (1994) A review of organisational reward practices. In: Gunnigle, P., Flood, P., Morley, M. and Turner, T. (eds.), *Continuity and Change in Irish Employee Relations*. Dublin: Oak Tree Press.

Gunnigle, P., Heraty, N. and Crowley, G. (1994) Trends and developments in recruitment and selection: an analysis of practices in the Republic of Ireland. *Recruitment, Selection and Retention*, 3(4): 19–26.

Gunnigle, P., Morley, P. and Foley, K. (1994) Financial rewards and company ownership: an examination of reward practices in the Republic of Ireland. *Thunderbird International Business Review*, 36(5): 575–597.

Gunnigle, P., Morley, M. and Turner, T. (1994) Employee relations and human resource management: some recent developments. In: Gunnigle, P., Flood, P., Morley, M. and Turner, T. (eds.), *Continuity and Change in Irish Employee Relations*. Dublin: Oak Tree Press.

Gunnigle, P., Morley, M. and Turner, T. (1994) Employee relations in Ireland: an organisational level perspective. In: Gunnigle, P., Flood, P., Morley, M. and Turner, T.

(eds.), *Continuity and Change in Irish Employee Relations*. Dublin: Oak Tree Press.

Gunnigle, P., Morley, M. and Brewster, C. (1995) Changing patterns in European industrial relations. In: Syrrett, M. (ed.), *International Management Yearbook*. Geneva: World Management Council.

Gunnigle, P., Morley, P. and Foley, K. (1995) Human resource management in Ireland. In: Brunstein, I. (ed.), *Human Resource Management in Western Europe*. Berlin and New York: De Gruyter.

Gunnigle, P., Clifford, N. and Morley, M. (1997) Employee relations. In: Gunnigle, P., Morley, M., Clifford, N. and Turner, T. (eds.), *Human Resource Management in Irish Organisations: Practice in Perspective*. Dublin: Oak Tree Press.

Gunnigle, P., Morley, M., Clifford, N. and Turner, T. (1997) *Human Resource Management in Irish Organisations: Practice in Perspective*. Dublin: Oak Tree Press.

Gunnigle, P., Morley, M., Clifford, N. and Turner, T. (1997) Human resource management in Ireland: an overview. In: Gunnigle, P., Morley, M., Clifford, N. and Turner, T. (eds.), *Human Resource Management in Irish Organisations: Practice in Perspective*. Dublin: Oak Tree Press.

Gunnigle, P., Turner, T. and Morley (1998) Employment flexibility and industrial arrangements at organisation level: a comparison of five European countries. *Employee Relations*, 20(5): 430–442.

Gunnigle, P., MacCurtain, S. and Morley, M. (2001). Dismantling pluralism: industrial relations in Irish Greenfield sites. *Personnel Review*, 30(3): 263–279.

Gunnigle, P., Morley, M. and Kelly, J. (2002) Human resource management, employee relations and the labour market. *Employee Relations: The International Journal*, 24(4): 371–460.

Gunnigle, P., Morley, M. and Kelly, J. (2002) The impact of contemporary labour market developments on employee relations and HRM. *Employee Relations: The International Journal*, 24(4): 371–377.

Gunnigle, P., Murphy, K.R., Cleveland, J.N., Heraty, N. and Morley, M. (2002) Localization in human resource management: comparing American and European multinational corporations. *Advances in International Management*, 14: 259–284.

Gunnigle, P., O'Sullivan, M. and Kinsella, M. (2002) Organised labour in the new economy: trade unions and public policy in the Republic of Ireland. In: D'Art, D. and Turner, T. (eds.), *Irish Employment Relations in the New Economy*. Dublin: Blackhall Press.

Hanel, U. and Hegewitsch, A. (1996) Institutionelle Aspekte der Personalarbeit in den neuen Bundesländern. Eine empirische Längsschnittanalyse 1990–1995 (Institutional aspects of human resource management in the New Federal States East-Germany). An empirical analysis 1990–1995. In: Becker, M., Lang, R. and Wagner, D. (eds.), *Sechs Jahre danach: Personalarbeit in den neuen Bundesländern (Six years after – Personnel management in the New Federal States (East-Germany))*. München, Mering.

Hanel, U., Hegewisch, A. and Mayrhofer, M. (eds.) (1997) *Personalarbeit in Wandel: Entwicklungen in den neuen Bundesländern und Europa*. Munich, Mehring: Rainer Hampp Verlag (*The Changing Face of Personnel Management: Developments in East Germany and Europe*).

Hanel, U., Kabst, R., Mayrhofer, W. and Weber, W. (1999) Personal management in Europa – Ein Vergleich auf der Basis empirischer Daten. *Personal*, 51(1): 32–36.

Hansen, A.E., Andersen, S.S., Kiel, O. and Larsen, H.H. (red.) (1996) *HRM 96. Human Resource Management i europΦisk perspektiv. Dansk Management Forum og Handelshpjskolen i Kφbenhavn*, Kφbenhavn.

Hansson, B., Johanson, U. and Leitner, K.-H. (forthcoming) The impact of human capital and human capital investments on firm performance: evidence from the literature and European survey results. In: Descy, P. and Tessaring, M. (eds.), *Training in Europe: Third Research Report on Vocational Training Research in Europe: Background Report*, Cedefop, Thessaloniki, Greece.

Hegewisch, A. (1991) The decentralisation of pay bargaining: European comparisons. *Personnel Review*, 20(6).

Hegewisch, A. (1992) European comparisons in reward policies: the findings of the first Price Waterhouse Cranfield Survey. In: Trinder, C. (ed.), *Public Sector Pay*. London: PFF.

Hegewisch, A. (1993) Betriebliche Gleichstellungspolitik – Entwicklungen im Personal management in Europa. In: *Frauenerwerbstätigkeit: Forschungen zu Geschichte und Gegenwart*. Munich: Rainer Hampp Verlag.

Hegewisch, A. (1996) Job-sharing. *Flexible Working Briefing*, Croner Publications, Issue No. 6, October.

Hegewisch, A. (1997) Labour market flexibility in central and eastern Europe. *Flexible Working Briefing*, Croner Publications, Issue No. 15, July.

Hegewisch, A. (2001) Getting to the top in HR. *Personnel Today*, April.

Hegewisch, A. (2001) HR on the board. *Personnel Today*, May.

Hegewisch, A. (2001) Psychometric testing. *Personnel Today*, March.

Hegewisch, A. and Brewster, C. (eds.) (1993) *European Developments in Human Resource Management*. Management Research Series, London: Kogan Page.

Hegewisch, A. and Larsen, H.H. (1994) European developments in public sector human resource management. *SWP 10/94*. Cranfield: Cranfield School of Management (OgsΔ udgivet som Papers in Organization, nr. 19, se R 26).

Hegewisch, A. and Mayne, L. (1994) Equal opportunities policies in Europe. In: Brewster, C. and Hegewisch, A. (eds.), *Policy and Practice in European Human Resource Management*. London: Routledge.

Hegewisch, A. and Larsen, H.H. (eds.) (1996) International Executive Report 1995. *Cranfield Network on European Human Resource Management*, Cranfield.

Hegewisch, A. and Larsen, H.H. (1996) European developments in public sector human resource management. *Papers in Organization*, nr. 19, Institute of Organization and Industrial Sociology, (OgsΔ udgivet som Working Paper, Cranfield School of Management, se R23).

Hegewisch, A. and Larsen, H.H. (1996) Performance management, decentralization and management development: local government in Europe. *The Journal of Management Development*, 15(2): 6–23.

Hegewisch, A. and Mayne, L. (1996) Comparing part-time work in Europe. *Flexible Working Briefing*, Croner Publications, Issue No. 3, July.

Hegewisch, A. and Mayne, L. (1996) Part-time working in Europe. *Flexible Working*, 1(3): 14–16.

Hegewisch, A., Brewster, C. and Koubek, J. (1996) Different roads: changes in industrial and employee relations in the Czech Republic and East Germany since 1989. *Industrial Relations Journal*, 27(1): 50–65.

Hegewisch, A., Tregaskis, O. and Morley, M. (1997) The management of labour in Europe: is human resource management challenging industrial relations? *Journal of Irish Business and Administrative Research*, 18(1): 1–16.

Hegewisch, A., Tregaskis, O. and Morley, M. (1997) The management of labour in Europe: is HRM challenging IR? *Journal of Irish Business and Administrative Research*, 18(1): 1–15.

Hegewisch, A., Hanel, U. and Mayrhofer, W. (date) Institutionelle Aspekte der Personalarbeit in den neuen Bundesländern 1992–1995: eine empirische Längsschnittbetrachtung. In: Becker, M., Lang, R. and Wagner, D. (eds.), *Personalarbeit in den neuen Bundesländern*, Munich, Mehring: Rainer Hampp Verlag.

Heraty, N. and Morley, M. (1994) Human resource development in Ireland: position, practices and power. *Administration*, 42(3): 299–320.

Heraty, N. and Morley, M. (Guest eds.) (1998) Of paradigms, policies and practices: the changing contours of training and development in five European economies. *Special Edition of Journal of European Industrial Training*, 22(4 and 5): 154–228.

Heraty, N. and Morley, M. (1998) Recruitment and selection practices in Ireland. In: Roche, W., Monks, K. and Walsh, J. (eds.), *Human Resource Management Strategies: Policy and Practice*. Dublin: Oak Tree Press, 109–145.

Heraty, N. and Morley, M. (2003) Management development in Ireland: the new organisational wealth? *Journal of Management Development*, 22 (Forthcoming).

Heraty, N., Gunnigle, P. and Clifford, N. (1997) Recruitment and selection in Ireland. In: Gunnigle, P., Morley, M., Clifford, N. and Turner, T. (eds.), *Human Resource Management in Irish Organisations: Practice in Perspective*. Dublin: Oak Tree Press.

Hilb, M. (2003) *Integriertes Personal-Management*, 11th edn. Berlin: Luchterhand.

Holden, L. (1991) European trends in training and development. *International Journal of Human Resource Management*, 2(2).

Johnson, G. (2001) High flyer schemes. *Personnel Today*, August.

Kaarelson, T. (2000) Personalijuhtimise olukord Eesti avalikus sektoris. *Avaliku teenistuse aastaraamat 2000*. Tallinn: Riigikantselei, pp. 33–36.

Kaarelson, T. and Alas, R. (2002) Estonia – from personnel management to human resource management. *Human Resource Management*, 1A, Institute of Labor and Social Studies, pp. 25–50.

Kabst, R. (2001) Kurzlebige Moden oder dominierende Arbeitsgebiete? Personalpraktiken zwischen Wiedervereinigung und Jahrtausendwechsel. In: Bellmann, L., Minssen, H. and P. Wagner (eds.), *Personalwirtschaft und Organisationskonzepte moderner Betriebe, Beiträge zur Arbeitsmarkt- und Berufsforschung 252*. Nürnberg, pp. 1–14.

Kabst, R. and Brewster, C. (in print) International komparatives Personalmanagement. In: Gaugler, E., Oechsler, W.A. and Weber, W. (eds.), *Handwörterbuch des Personalwesens*. 3. Auflage, Stuttgart.

Kabst, W., Larsen, H.H. and Bramming, P. (1996) How do lean management organizations behave regarding training and development? *The International Journal of Human Resource Management*, 7(3): 618–639.

Koubek, J. (2000) *ABC praktické personalistiky (ABC of Personnel Management for Organizational Practice)*. Praha, Linde.

Koubek, J. (2002) *Rízení lidsk˝ch zdroju. Základy moderní personalistiky (Human Resource Management. Principles of Modern People Management)*, 3rd edn. Praha: Management Press.

Koubek, J. et al. (2000) The Cranfield project on European human resource management. *Acta Oeconomica Pragensia*, 8(4): 7–213 (A comparative analysis of results 1995–1996 and 1998–1999) Czech source of Cranet data.

Larsen, H.H. (red.) (1991) HRM 91. Human resources management i danske virksomheder. *Institut for Organisation og Arbejdssociologi, IP Dansk Institut for PersonalerΔdgivning samt Price Waterhouse/IKO*, Kφbenhavn.

Larsen, H.H. (red.) (1992) HRM 92. Human resources management i danske virksomheder. *Institut for Organisation og Arbejdssociologi, IP Dansk Institut for PersonalerΔdgivning samt Price Waterhouse/IKO,* København.

Larsen, H.H. (red.) (1992) Human resource management in Denmark. In: Brewster, C. et al. (eds.), *The European Human Resource Management Guide.* London: Academic Press, pp. 80–112.

Larsen, H.H. (1993) Strategic human resource management in Denmark. *"P+" European Participation Monitor,* Issue No. 7: 44–47.

Larsen, H.H. (1994) Key issues in training and development. In: Brewster, C. and Hegewisch, A. (eds.), *Policy and Practice in European HRM: The Findings of the Price Waterhouse Cranfield Survey.* London: Routledge.

Larsen, H.H. (1996) Har HRM-begrebet en fremtid? In: Hansen, A.E., Andersen, S.S., Kiel, O. and Larsen, H.H. (red.), *HRM 96. Human Resource Management i europΦisk perspektiv,* København: Dansk Management Forum og Handelshøjskolen i København, pp. 194–201.

Larsen, H.H. (1996) Human resource management – et sceneskift i forstΔelsen af arbejdslivets mennesker? In: Hansen, A.E., Andersen, S.S., Kiel, O. and Larsen, H.H. (red.), *HRM 96. Human Resource Management i europΦisk perspektiv,* København: Dansk Management Forum og Handelshøjskolen i København, pp. 4–21.

Larsen, H.H. (1997) In search of management development in Europe: from self-fulfilling prophecies to organizational competence. *Papers in Organizations, No. 22,* Institute of Organization and Industrial Sociology.

Larsen, H.H. (1997) In search of management development in Europe – from self-fulfilling prophecies to organizational competence. In: Hanel, U., Hegewisch, A. and Mayrhofer, W. (eds.), *Personalarbeit in Wandel. Entwicklingen in den neuen Bundesl ≅ ndern und Europa.* Mηchen: Rainer Hampp Verlag, pp. 136–159.

Larsen, H.H. (1998) Lidské zdaoje a odpov dnost liniov˝ch mana eru (Human resources and line management responsibility). *Personál,* 7/8: 24–27.

Larsen, H.H. (2000) In search of management development in Europe: from self-fulfilling prophecies to organizational competence. In: Brewster, C., Mayrhofer, W. and Morley, M. (eds.), *New Challenges For European Human Resource Management.* London: Macmillan, pp. 168–196.

Larsen, H.H. (red.) (2001) Human resource management i modlys – spydspidser og dilemmaer. Dansk Management Forum og Handelshøjskolen i København.

Larsen, H.H. (2002) Úvahy o rizeni lidsk˝ch zdroju: trendy a dilemata PMPP: Personální A Mzdov˝. 1: 114–127.

Larsen, H.H. *Towards the Disappearance of Middle Managers.* In: Livian, Y.-F. and Burgoyne, J.G. (ed.).

Larsen, H.H. (red.) Menneskelige ressourcer – den mindre virksomheds konkurrencekraft.

Larsen, H.H. Human resource management i modlys – spydspidser og dilemmaer. København: Institut for Organisation og Arbejdssociologi, Handelshøjskolen i København, 16 s (engelsk udgave: Human resource management – trends and dilemmas). København: Institut for Organisation og Arbejdssociologi, Handelshøjskolen i København, 16 s.

Larsen, H.H. and Bang, S. (1993) Development dialogues – an alternative to performance appraisal systems. In: Shaw, B., Kirkbride, P.S. and Rowland, K.M. (eds.), *Research in Personnel and Human Resources Management,* Suppl. 3. Greenwich: CT: JAI Press, pp. 171–188.

Larsen, H.H. and Thisted, L.N. (red.) (1997) Karriereudvikling. *Handelshøjskolen i København og Dansk Management Forum,* København.

Larsen H.H. and Brewster, C. (2003) Line management responsibility for HRM: what's happening in Europe? *Employee Relations,* 25(3): 228–244.

Lockhart, T. (1990) Preparing for 1992: a survey of human resource strategies. *Single Market Monitor.*

Mahoney, C.J. and Atterbury, S. (2000) Shared experience – Cranet's job sharing survey. *Flexible Working,* IRS, May.

Mahoney, C. and Atterbury, S. (2001) Employee-led flexibility – UK v Europe. *Flexible Working Briefing,* Croner Publications, Issue No. 78, 20 February.

Mahoney, C. and Brewster, C. (2002) Outsourcing the HR function in Europe. *Journal of Professional HRM,* 27: 23–28.

Matiaske, W. and Kabst, R. (2002) Outsourcing und Professionalisierung in der Personalarbeit: eine transaktionskostentheoretisch orientierte Studie. *Zeitschrift für Personalforschung,* Sonderband "Neue Formen der Beschäftigung und Personalpolitik". pp. 247–271.

Mayne, L. (1996) Subcontracting in Europe. *Flexible Working Briefing,* Croner Publications, Issue No 5, September.

Mayne, L. (1997). Flexibility in France. *Flexible Working Briefing,* Croner Publications, Issue No. 13, May.

Mayne, L. and Allen, M. (1996) Shiftwork in Europe. *Flexible Working,* October.

Mayne, L. and Atterbury, S. (1996) Overtime – out-of-date? *Flexible Working Briefing,* Croner Publications, Issue No 8, December.

Mayne, L. and Tregaskis, O. (1996) Flexible working patterns in Europe. *International Human Resources Journal,* 4(1): 31–36.

Mayne, L. and Barrow, C. (1997) Small is … beautiful or inflexible? *Flexible Working Briefing.* Croner Publications, Issue No. 10, February.

Mayne, L., Tregaskis, O. and Brewster, C. (1996) A comparative analysis of the link between flexibility and HRM strategy. *Employee Relations,* 18(3): 7–26.

Mayne, L., Tregaskis, O. and Brewster, C. (2000) A comparative analysis of the link between flexibility and HRM strategy. In: *New Challenges for European Human Resource Management.* London: Macmillan.

Mayrhofer, W. (1995) Human resource management in Austria. *Employee Relations,* 17(7/1995): 8–30.

Mayrhofer, W. (1997) Rahmenbedingungen der Personalarbeit in den neuen Bundesländern (Framework for human resource management in the new federal states). In: Hanel, U., Hegewisch, A. and Mayrhofer, W. (eds.), *Personalarbeit im Wandel.* München, Mering: Hampp, pp. 5–26.

Mayrhofer, W. (1998) Between market, bureaucracy, and clan – coordination and control mechanisms in the cranfield network on European human resource management (Cranet-E). *Journal of Managerial Psychology,* 13(3/4): 241–258.

Mayrhofer, W. (1998) Integration und Differenz – Personalarbeit zwischen Stabsabteilung und Linienmanagement in internationaler Perspektive (Integration and difference – HRM between staff unit and line management – an international perspective). In: Kutschker, M. (ed.), *Integration in der internationalen Unternehmung.* Wiesbaden: Gabler, pp. 297–324.

Mayrhofer, W. (1999) Personalpolitiken und strategien im internationalen Vergleich (Personnel policies and strategies – an international comparison). In: Elsik, W. and Mayrhofer, W. (eds.), *Strategische Personalpolitik.* München, Mering: Hampp, pp. 27–46.

Mayrhofer, W. (1999) Personalentwicklung und Weiterbildung im internationalen Kontext (Personnel training and developement – an international view). In: Martin, A., Mayrhofer, W. and Nienhüser, W. (eds.), *Die Bildungsgesellschaft im Unternehmen?* München, pp. 221–242.

Mayrhofer, W. (1999) Personalarbeit im Handel: eine europäische Perspektive (Human resource management in the trade sector: a European perspective). In: Beisheim, O. (ed.), *Distribution im Aufbruch.* München: Vahlen, pp. 641–652.

Mayrhofer, W. (1999) Personalarbeit im dezentralen Modell (Human resource management in a decentralised model). In: Scholz, C. (ed.), *Innovative Personalorganisation.* Neuwied: Luchterhand, pp. 178–188.

Mayrhofer, W., Hanel, U. and Hegewisch, A. (eds.) (1997) Personalarbeit im Wandel. Entwicklungen in den neuen Bundesländern und in Europa (Changes in human resource management in the New Federal States (East-Germany) – a European comparison). München, Mering: Hampp.

Mayrhofer, W., Brewster, C. and Morley, M (2000) Communication, consultation and the HRM debate. In: Brewster, C.J., Mayrhofer, W. and Morley, M. (eds.), *New Challenges for European Human Resource Management.* London: Macmillan, pp. 222–245.

Mayrhofer, W., Müller-Camen, M., Ledolter, J., Strunk, G. and Erten, C. (2002) The diffusion of management concepts in Europe – conceptual considerations and longitudinal analysis. *Journal of Cross-Cultural Competence and Management,* 3: 315–349.

Morley, M. and Gunnigle, P. (1994) Trends in flexible working patterns in Ireland. In: Gunnigle, P., Flood, P., Morley, M. and Turner, T. (eds.), *Continuity and Change in Irish Employee Relations.* Dublin: Oak Tree Press.

Morley, M., Gunnigle, P. and Heraty, N. (1994) The flexibilisation of working practices in Ireland: gradual incrementalism or radical path breaking developments? *Administration,* 42(1): 92–111.

Morley, M., Gunnigle, P. and Heraty, N. (1995) Developments in flexible working practices in the Republic of Ireland: research evidence considered. *International Journal of Manpower,* 16(8): 38–58.

Morley, M. and Heraty, N. (1995) Line managers and human resource development. *Journal of European Industrial Training,* 19(10): 30–42.

Morley, M. and Gunnigle, P. (1997) Compensation and benefits. In: Gunnigle, P., Morley, M., Clifford, N. and Turner, T. (eds.), *Human Resource Management in Irish Organisations: Practice in Perspective.* Dublin: Oak Tree Press.

Morley, M., Brewster, C., Gunnigle, P. and Mayrhofer, W. (1996) Evaluating change in European industrial relations: research evidence on trends at organisational level. *International Journal of Human Resource Management,* 7(3): 640–656.

Morley, M., Gunnigle, P. and Heraty, N. (1999) Constructing the reward package: the extent and composition of change in wage and non wage increases in Ireland. *International Journal of Employment Studies,* 7(2): 121–150.

Morley, M., Brewster, C., Gunnigle, P. and Mayrhofer, W. (2000) Evaluating change in European industrial relations: research evidence on trends at organizational level. In: *New Challenges for European Human Resource Management.* London: Macmillan, pp. 199–221.

Morley, M., Brewster, C., Gunnigle, P. and Mayrhofer, W. (2000) Evaluating change in European industrial relations: research evidence on trends at organisational level. In: Brewster, C., Mayrhofer, W. and Morley, M. (eds.), *New Challenges for European Human Resource Management.* Basingstoke, Hampshire: Macmillan.

Morley, M., Mayrhofer, W. and Brewster, C. (2000) Communication in organizations: dialogue and impact. In: Brewster, C. and Larsen, H.H. (eds.), *Human Resource Management in Northern Europe: Trends, Dilemmas and Strategy.* Oxford: Blackwell, pp. 147–170.

Müller, M., Mayrhofer, W., Ledolter, J., Erten, C. and Strunk, G. (2001) Neue Formen der Arbeitsorganisation in Europa – eine empirische Studie. *Journal für Betriebswirtschaft*, 51(5–6): 265–277.

Morley, M.J., Gunnigle, P. and Mayrhofer, W. (2003) Labour market developments and the flexibilisation of working practices: guest editor's introduction. *International Journal of Manpower*, 24(3) (in press).

Müller-Camen, M., Mayrhofer, W., Ledolter, J., Strunk, G. and Erten, C. (in print). Human resource management and new organisational forms in Europe. *Jahrbuch Universität Bruchsal*.

Müller-Camen, M., Mayrhofer, W., Ledolter, J., Strunk, G. and Erten-Buch, C. (in print). Pure Rhetorik? Populäre personalwirtschaftliche Handlungsempfehlungen der 1990er Jahre und ihre Umsetzung – eine international vergleichende empirische Analyse. *Zeitschrift für Personalforschung*.

Müller-Camen, M., Mayrhofer, W., Ledolter, J., Strunk, G. and Erten, C. (2003) Unternehmenserfolg und Personalmanagement – Eine international vergleichende empirische Analyse (Company performance and human resource management – an international comparative analysis). In: Schwaiger, M. and Harhoff, D. (eds.), *Empirie und Betriebswirtschaft – Entwicklungen und Perspektiven (Empirical Work and Business Administration – Developments and Perspectives)*. Stuttgart: Schäffer-Poeschel, pp. 331–349.

Nitsche, Sabine: *Human Resource Management of Multinational Organisations Operating in Europe*, Doctoral Thesis, University of St. Gallen 2003.

Papalexandris, N. (1994) Human resource management in Greece. In: Brewster, C. and Hegewisch, A. (eds.), *European Developments in Human Resource Management*, Kogan Page.

Papalexandris, N. (2000) Flexible working patterns. In: Brewster, C., Mayrhofer, W. and Morley, M. (eds.), *New Challenges for European Human Resource Management*. Macmillan Press.

Papalexandris, N. and Kramar, R. (1997) Flexible working patterns: towards reconciliation of family & work. *Employee Relations*, 19(6).

Papalexandris, N. and Chalikias, J. (2002) Changes in training, performance management and communication issues among Greek firms in the 1990s: intercountry and intracountry comparisons. *European Industrial Training*, 26(7): 342–352.

Papalexandris, N. and Panayotopoulou, L. (2000) Exploring the strategic vs. administrative role of HRM within the Greek context. *Conference of the Cranfield Network on European HRM*, Varna.

Pendleton, A., Poutsma, E., Brewster, C. and van Ommeren, J. (2002) Employee share ownership and profit sharing in the European union: incidence, company characteristics and union representation. *Transfer*, 8(1): 47–62.

Pendleton, A., Poutsma, E., van Ommeren, J. and Brewster, C. (2003) The incidence and determinants of employee share ownership and profit sharing in Europe. In: Kato, T. and Pliskin, J. (eds.), *The Determinants of the Incidence and Effects of Participatory Organization Advances in the Economic Analysis of Participatory and Labor Management*, Greenwich, CT: JAI Press.

Raghuram, S. and Larsen, H.H. Human resource practices for telework: the European experience.

Raghuram, S., London, M. and Larsen, H.H. Effects of organizational characteristics and change on flexible work practices in European organizations. Under review for publication in *Personnel Psychology*.

Raghuram, S., London, M. and Larsen, H.H. (2001) Flexible employment practices in Europe: countries versus culture. *International Journal of Human Resource Management*, 12(5): 738–753 (Tidligere udkommet som Papers in Organization, No. 37).

Raghuram, S., London, M. and Larsen, H.H. (2001) Links between organizational characteristics and change and flexible employment practices in european organizations. *Papers in Organization*, No. 41, Institute of Organization and Industrial Sociology.

Rogaczewska, A.P., Larsen, H.H. and Skovbro, C. (1999) Cranet-E undersøgelsen 1999. HRM i danske virksomheder på tærsklen til et nyt årtusinde: *Dansk Management Forum & Handelshøjskolen i København*. København.

Roussillon, S. and Torchy, V. (1993) GRH, un portrait européen. *Revue Stratégies Ressources Humaines*, Automne numéro 71.

Singe, I. (2001) Teleworking. *Personnel Today*, August.

Stanojevic, M. (2001) Uspesna nedozorelost: primerjava industrisjkih odnosov v Sloveniji in Madzarski (Successful immatureness: a comparison of industrial relations in Slovenia and Hungary). In: Stanojevic, M. (ed.), *Successful Immatureness: Social Institutions and Production of High Quality in Slovenia*. Faculty of Social Sciences, Ljubljana.

Stanojevic, M. (2002) EU enlargement and employee participation: new functions of an inhereted pattern within Slovenian organisations. In: Biagi, M. (ed.), *Quality of work and Employee Involvement in Europe*. Kluwer Law International, pp. 279–293.

Stanojevic, M. Predstavljanje interesov zaposlenih in HRM: primerjava med Slovenijo, Veliko Britanijo, Nemcijo in Cesko (Representation of employees' interests: a comparison between Slovenia, UK, Germany and Czech Republic). *Kadri*, 7(7): Slovenian HRM Association, pp. 40–50.

Stavrou-Costea, E. (2002) The role of human resource management in today's organisations: The case of cyprus in comparison with the European union. *Journal of European Industrial Training*, 25(6–7): 261–269.

Svetlik, I. (2001) The role of HRM in the transfer of knowledge and skills: new dimensions in human resource management: conference proceedings. Nicosia: University of Cyprus, pp. 111–126; also published in *Integration of work and learning: project documents: an ETF project in Hungary and Slovenia*. Torino, ETF.

Svetlik, I. (ed.) (2001) Upravljanje cloveskih virov – mednarodna primerjalna studija (HRM – International comparative study). *Bulletin of the Organisations and HR Research Centre*. Ljubljana, Faculty of Social Sciences, p. 187.

Svetlik, I. (2002) Slovenski kadrovski management v evropskem prostoru (Slovenian personnel management in the European space). In: Mozina, S. (ed.), *Management kadrovskih virov (HRM)*. Faculty of Social Sciences, pp. 379–401.

Thisted, L.N. and Jensen, K. (1997) Politikker, planer og programmer I praksis – en analyse af resultaterne fra Cranfield undersøgelsen. In: Larsen, H.H. and Thisted, L.N. (eds.), *KarriereUdvikling*, Dansk Management Forum, Handelshøjskolen I Køøbenhavn.

Tregaskis, O. (1995) The link between HR strategy and training: an examination of French and UK organisations. In: Whitfield, K. and Poole, M. (eds.), *Organising Employment for High Performance*, Hull: Barmick Publications.

Tregaskis, O. (1997) The non-permanent reality. *Employee Relations*, 19(6): 535–554.

Tregaskis, O. (1997) An alternative employment option: subcontracting. *Flexible Working*, March.

Tregaskis, O. and Brewster, C. (1998) Getting the answers: what is really involved in undertaking worthwhile research. *Journal of Professional Human Resource Management*, Issue No. 12, July, 9–15.

Tregaskis, O. and Brewster, C. (1998) Training and development in the UK context: an emerging polarisation? *Journal of European Industrial Training*, 22(4/5): 180–189.

Tregaskis, O. and Daniels, K. (1996) Teleworking in Europe. *Flexible Working Briefing*, Croner Publications, Issue No. 4, August.

Tregaskis, O. and Dany, F. (1996) A comparison of HRD in France and UK. *Journal of European Industrial Training*, 20(1): 20–31.

Tregaskis, O., Brewster, C., Mayne, L. and Hegewisch, A. (1998) Flexible working in Europe: the evidence and the implications. *European Journal of Work and Organisational Psychology*, 7(1): 61–78.

Tregaskis, O. and Mayne, L. (1996) The cost of flexible working. In: Brewster, C. (ed.), *Flexible Working Briefing*, Croner Publications, Issue No. 7, November.

Tregaskis, O., Heraty, N. and Morley, M. (2001) HRD in multinationals: the global/local mix. *Human Resource Management Journal*, 11(2): 34–56.

Turner, T., D'Art, D. and Gunnigle, P. (1997) Pluralism in retreat: a comparison of Irish and multinational manufacturing companies. *International Journal of Human Resource Management*, 8(6): 825–840.

Turner, T., D'Art, D. and Gunnigle, P. (1997) US multinationals: changing the framework of Irish industrial relations? *Industrial Relations Journal*, 28(2): 92–102.

Turner, T., Morley, M. and Gunnigle, P. (1994) Developments in industrial relations and human resource management in the Republic of Ireland. *Irish Business and Administrative Research*, 15(1): 76–92.

Uyargil, C. and Dundar, G. (1999–2000) Determining the strategic qualifications of human resource functions in companies (2001). *Cranfield Study On International Strategic Human Resources Management*. Report, Istanbul.

van Ommeren, J.N. (1998) From a distance: the future of teleworking. *"t" Magazine: Linking Training, Education and Employment*, May: 27–29.

van Ommeren, J. and Atterbury, S. (1998) Labour flexibility revisited. *Employee Relations*, Special Issue 20(5): 426–429.

Vatchkova, E. (1997) Human resource management in Bulgaria during the transition to market economy, European conference. *Human Resource Management in Europe: Trends and Challenges*, Athens.

Vatchkova, E. (1998) Human resource management: European comparative researches. *Stopanstvo*. Sofia: University Press.

Vatchkova, E. (1999) Application of the systematic approach – a decisive condition for the effectiveness of the corporate training. *Banks, Investments, Markets*, 5, Sofia.

Vatchkova, E. (1999) Necessary changes in human resource management in Bulgaria in the transitional period to market economy. *Personal*, Praha.

Vatchkova, E. (2000) Development of the HRM practice in Bulgaria during the transition to market economy. In: *XXI Century and the Challenges Before the Management*. Varna: University Press.

Vatchkova, E. (2000) Human resource management in Bulgaria – hot problems of the transition to market economy. In: Brewster, C., Mayrhofer, W. and Morley, M. (eds.), *New Challenges for European Human Resource Management*. UK: Macmillan Press Ltd.

Vatchkova, E. (2000) Human resource management. *A Practical Guide for Students*. IBS Transbusiness-E, Sofia.

Vatchkova, E. (2001) Bulgaria's participation in the globalization of labour markets. *Scientific conference Organized Markets in the Context of Management and Sustainable Development*. Jundola, Bulgaria, 09-11.03.

Vatchkova, E. (2001) Social responsibility in human resource management – fashion, pretension or necessity? *Second International Conference: Challenges before Human Resource Management in Bulgaria in the New Millennium*, Varna, 01-02.06.

Vatchkova, E. (2001) The speed of changes – the Bulgarian way to the integrated European HRM. 5th Chemnitz East Forum: Human Resource Management in Transition. In: *Personal Management im Transformations Process.* Chemnitz University of Technology, Rainer Hampp Verlag Munchen; Mering, Hampp.

Vatchkova, E. and Gaidarov, M. (2001) Human resource management in the global society. *Banks, Investments, Money*, 1: Sofia.

Weber, W. and Kabst, R. (1997) Personalwirtschaftliche Strategien im europäischen Vergleich – Eine Analyse organisations- und landesspezifischer Prädiktoren. In: Klimecki, R. and Remer, A. (eds.), *Personal als Strategie* (Neuwied et al.), pp. 20–45.

Weber, W. and Kabst, R. (1999) Die Bedeutung betrieblicher Informationskanäle: Eine Analyse vor dem Hintergrund aktueller personalwirtschaftlicher Entwicklungen. In: Breisig, T. (eds.), *Mitbestimmung: Gesellschaftlicher Auftrag und ökonomische Ressource*. München, Mering, pp. 407–425.

Weber, W. and Kabst, R. (2000) Personalpraktiken in europäischen Unternehmen: Gemeinsamkeiten und Unterschiede. In: Regnet, E. and Hofmann, L.M. (eds.), *Personalmanagement in Europa*. Göttingen, Bern, Toronto, pp. 320–332.

Weber, W. and Kabst, R. (2002) Internationale Vergleichsuntersuchung schreckt auf: Deutsches Personalmanagement offenbar nicht immer Spitze. *Zeitschrift für Personalführung Heft*, 10: 40–49.

Weber, W., Habich, J. and Kabst, R. (2000) Perspektiven personalwirtschaftlicher Forschung. In: Schwuchow, K. and Gutmann, J. (eds.), *Jahrbuch Personalentwicklung und Weiterbildung 2000/2001*. Neuwied/Kriftel.

Weber, W., Kabst, R. and Gramley, C. (2000) Human resource policies in European organizations: Country vs. Company-Specific Antecedents. In: Brewster, C., Mayrhofer, W. and Morley, M. (eds.), *New Challenges for European Human Resource Management*, Houndmills/Basingstoke: Macmillan Press, pp. 247–266.

Wiltz, S. and Koppert, W. (1990) Personnel management in international comparison. *Personal Europa-Report*, 12–16.

Index

(Page numbers in *italics* refer to information in Figures and Tables)